*Hope in the Age of Anxiety*

# Hope in the Age of Anxiety

ANTHONY SCIOLI, PhD
HENRY B. BILLER, PhD

OXFORD
UNIVERSITY PRESS

2009

# OXFORD
UNIVERSITY PRESS

Oxford University Press, Inc., publishes works that further
Oxford University's objective of excellence
in research, scholarship, and education.

Oxford    New York
Auckland   Cape Town   Dar es Salaam   Hong Kong   Karachi
Kuala Lumpur   Madrid   Melbourne   Mexico City   Nairobi
New Delhi   Shanghai   Taipei   Toronto

With offices in
Argentina   Austria   Brazil   Chile   Czech Republic   France   Greece
Guatemala   Hungary   Italy   Japan   Poland   Portugal   Singapore
South Korea   Switzerland   Thailand   Turkey   Ukraine   Vietnam

Published by Oxford University Press, Inc.
198 Madison Avenue, New York, New York 10016

www.oup.com

Oxford is a registered trademark of Oxford University Press

Library of Congress Cataloging-in-Publication Data
Scioli, Anthony.
  Hope in the age of anxiety / Anthony Scioli, Henry B. Biller.
    p.   cm.
Includes bibliographical references and index.
ISBN 978-0-19-538035-4
1. Positive psychology.   2. Hope.   3. Optimism.   I. Biller, Henry B.
II. Title.
BF204.6.S25 2009
149 '.5—dc22

                                                        2008055735


1   3   5   7   9   8   6   4   2

Printed in the United States of America
on acid-free paper

*To my parents, Felice and Filomena Scioli, first-generation Italian Americans, who have personified hope with their love of family, mastery of rich traditions, and enduring resoluteness.*
—Anthony Scioli


*To my inspirational soul-mate Suzette River, who with her "PhD in Life Experience" and daughter Soleil, has taught me the true meaning of wisdom, resilience, and love.*
—Henry B. Biller

# Acknowledgments

We would like to acknowledge the many individuals who directly or indirectly helped make this book a reality.

A. S. had the good fortune to be mentored by several eminent psychologists. At the University of Massachusetts–Amherst, his first advisor, Dr. George Levinger taught him the importance of research and was the first to instill in him the hope of becoming a professional psychologist. From Dr. James Averill, his honors thesis advisor, he acquired a lifelong interest in the study of emotions, a dedication to conceptual clarification, and a commitment to interdisciplinary scholarship. As a research assistant for the late Dr. Shula Sommers, he developed a better understanding of the link between emotions and moral commitments. At Harvard University, the late Dr. David McClelland, his fellowship advisor, demonstrated the importance of going beyond conscious self-reports of emotions and motives, and the importance of intellectual courage. Through his wife and soul-mate, Dr. Erica Scioli, he has experienced a deeper understanding of hope, one born of integrity, love, and unflinching resilience.

H. B. was fortunate to have had the opportunity to attend Brown University as an undergraduate and to do his graduate work at Duke University. At both institutions he encountered outstanding role models from a variety of academic disciplines. Now a professor for more than four decades, he continues to be stimulated by scores of colleagues and students. Along the way, he has also learned a great deal about individual differences and life's challenges from the development of his children (Jonathan, Kenneth, Cameron, Michael, and Benjamin) and his grandchildren (Connor, Emily, John, Sophia-Rose, Sammy, and Danny). His close relationship with Suzette River, and her daughter Soleil, has been especially important in furthering his life-long pursuit of greater self-understanding and everlasting hopefulness.

A number of individuals played a vital role in securing research participants, discussing various nuances of hope, and collaborating on empirical investigations. They include Drs. Arnie, Friederika, and Tom Aceto, Dr. Phil Friedman, Dr. Erica Scioli, and Dr. Homer Stavely. Bonnie Powers helped with the construction of a professional Web site. Others whose comments were helpful include Liz Alexander, Richard Amaral,

Julio Apicerone, Alan Berman, Bruce Berman, Benjamin Biller, Hope Biller, Kara Biller, Patricia Biller, Sheldon Cashdan, George Carbone, Charles Collyer, Anthony Davids, Daniel DeNoon, Robert Emmons, Antoinette Favazza, Euda Fellman, Leonard Ferrara, Rosemary Gianno, Mike Giles, Marvin Gordon, Allan Gregory, Fr. Benedict Groeschel, Ken Hamilton, Fr. John Halloran, Lisa Harlow, John Harney, Galen Johnson, Lou Lipsitt, Susan MacNeil, Ralph Madonna, Peter Merenda, Trish Morokoff, Natalie Comstock Murphy, Peter Olssom, Louise Danielle Palmer, James Prochaska, Suzette River, Joseph Rossi, Carol Susan Roth, Ed Sammartino, Bernie Siegel, Al Silverstein, Tony Stavely, John Stevenson, Susan Theberge, Jamie Toth, Dom Valentino, and Judy Van Wyk.

Our students have also been a great help, from undertaking honors theses on the topic of hope to data entry and bibliographic work. These include Carla Beckmann, Kaitlyn Christopher, Christine Chamberlin, Courtney Dillon, Christopher Friar, Alicia Lambert, Tiffany Noel, Thanh Nguyen, Mike Ricci, Jessica Smith, Scott Thomas, and Krystal Sullivan. Phil Scioli assisted in the early phases of developing the hope questionnaire mentioned in this book. He also was instrumental in helping with the notes section and tracking down references.

At Oxford University Press, we would like to thank Lori Handelman, who unwaveringly supported this project from the start, and editorial assistant Jenna Hocut for her efficient yet warm administration of the many details involved in a project of this scope. Marion Osmun did a brilliant job of editing and was an enormous help in the final preparation of the manuscript. Karen Harmon, Preethy Micheal, Leslie Anglin, and Woody Gilmartin were instrumental in the production and marketing phases.

Finally, we would like again to thank our families and friends for their many years of emotional support, nuggets of wisdom, and tireless reassurance.

# Contents

*Hope in the Age of Anxiety*

# INTRODUCTION

In *A Tale of Two Cities*, Charles Dickens artfully recreated the chaos that was London and Paris at the end of the eighteenth century. On the verge of entering a new era of violent uncertainty, the masses found themselves pitching back and forth between the zenith of hope and the nadir of despair.

> It was the best of times [and] the worst of times . . . it was the season of Light, it was the season of Darkness . . . we had everything before us, we had nothing before us.

Today we live in a world that is equally volatile. Indeed, if you look at the front page of any newspaper or tune in to any newscast, you would be justified in feeling that we live in the worst of times: rampant crime, disenfranchised masses, abject poverty, plunging stock markets, endless wars, devastating natural disasters—all these and much more confront us regularly with their messages of doom and misery. We may weep over or curse the state of our unfriendly, unstable, damaged world, but we otherwise seem powerless to do much about improving it or the state of our lives. We seem to have few opportunities for securing the sense of belonging, prosperity, peace, and security that makes life worth living. In this darkest of seasons, a true sense of community is hard to find, governments and other institutions appear increasingly impotent, and faith, be it in the future or in human endeavor or in a higher power, has seriously eroded. Even in the most industrialized countries, many have achieved great affluence without deriving any clear sense of purpose in life. Instant messages are sent around the globe, yet countless individuals feel lonely and isolated. Occasional scientific and political advances provide glimmers of potential transcendence, only to be soon eclipsed by ominous reports of resistant and deadly microbes and increasingly brazen acts of global terrorism.

More than ever, the world needs hope. This was clearly evident during the 2008 United States presidential race. Barack Obama, author of *Dreams from My Father* and *The Audacity of Hope,* won a clear mandate. It was hardly a coincidence that his campaign revolved around the themes of "hope and change". Particularly striking was a poster of Obama looking skyward and the word "hope" emblazed in big, bold letters along the bottom. According to one source, this depiction became so "iconic" that not only did it become "synonymous with the 2008 Obama presidential campaign", but after Obama won the election, the image was acquired by the Smithsonian Institution for its National Portrait Gallery.

"True hope," Shakespeare wrote, "flies with swallows wings." Catholic spiritual leader Solanus Casey exhorted his followers to hope not for "tasks equal to your powers [but] for powers equal to your task." Rumi called the mystic's flight a "portal of hope," while St. Paul noted that "Love always hopes." Hope yields a kind of inner peace that Ralph Waldo Emerson may have imagined when he wrote, "The wise man in the storm prays to God; not for safety from danger, but for deliverance from fear." Hope is also, according to the eighteenth-century writer Samuel Johnson, "Itself a species of happiness, and, perhaps, the chief happiness which this world affords."

Above all, hope implies faith. In Hebrews 11:1, St. Paul wrote "Faith is the assurance of things hoped for, a belief in things unseen." To paraphrase scientist and philosopher Blaise Pascal:

All [seek faith] . . . princes and subjects, noblemen and commoners, old and young, strong and weak, learned and ignorant, healthy and sick, of all countries, all time, all ages, and all conditions.

Hope is, in short, an essential element of our spiritual lifeblood. And it is the best medicine for overcoming feelings of helplessness, alienation, and fear. Individuals who are hopeful reap more than a mental strategy for grasping at goals, solving problems, or managing crises. They achieve a different way of being in the world.

How did we come to write a book about hope? On a personal level, we both share a lifelong passion for hope, derived from our own experiences in overcoming significant personal challenges. For both of us, these included multiples losses and relationship disruptions beginning in early childhood, rather humble family origins, and more than one encounter with significant trauma. On a professional level, we are both college professors and clinical psychologists who approach the study of human behavior from an interdisciplinary perspective. One of us (A. S.) is a clinical-health psychologist with an interest in emotions, coping, and health, while the other (H. B.) is a clinical-life-span psychologist with a special focus on fitness, parenting, and the role of the father. This book grew out of our increasing dissatisfaction with both current scientific and popular approaches to the study of hope.

Books written by psychologists or other healthcare professionals are usually field dependent, meaning they rarely incorporate insights about hope from other disciplines. Psychological researchers have primarily focused on goal expectations. Medically oriented investigators have filled their professional journals with coping-oriented accounts of hope and speculations about its potential role in health and healing. Philosophers and theologians have tended to highlight the interpersonal and spiritual aspects of hope. Meanwhile, professional writers and self-help gurus are more likely to include passages on hope from literature, scripture, and everyday life, but they typically do not anchor their insights in any sort of overarching philosophical or scientific understanding. Some self-help books only feature specific formulas or strategies for building hope in one's life, while others are limited to case studies that seek to model the hopeful life. Surely, we thought, there must be a way to integrate and organize these different perspectives and approaches. Moreover, there must also be a way to include the rich hope legacy left to us by the great literary figures and other artists throughout history.

We have sought to provide a very different book than is currently available on the topic of hope—part psychological study, part philosophical inquiry, and part personal guide. We have also done our best to write a book that will inspire you and increase your understanding of our most important emotion. The many case studies and examples you will find in this book are embedded within a larger theory of hope that we have developed over several decades. To enliven and deepen your appreciation of the breadth and depth of hope, we have blended scientific discoveries with insights from art, literature, and classic wisdom. In short, this is not your typical pop psychology book. It is instead a book about *understanding and using hope.*

According to Hodding Carter, the American journalist, "Two of the greatest gifts we can ever give our children are *roots and wings*." In truth, human beings require roots and wings throughout their lives, or they will wither and perish, if not literally then in an emotional and spiritual sense. And because hope may very well be *the* primary vehicle for realizing the roots and wings of the soul, we believe Carter's metaphor may well serve as the overarching theme for this book.

Thus, the chapters in Part One explore the roots of hope—its various biological, psychological, and cultural origins and underpinnings. To deepen your understanding of this material, we have included brief reflections ("Meditations") at the end of the first eight chapters. Chapter 1 provides a broad overview of the experience of hope— what it is, what it is not, and how it factors into people's lives in various ways. In Chapter 2, we review various perspectives from the science of hope and then introduce a new, integrative approach to hope, combining classic insights with our own ideas and latest research findings. Within this broad context, we further define the vital motives of mastery, attachment, and survival, which together form the very foundation of hope.

The remaining chapters in Part One elaborate further on the substantive elements of this foundation, from its development over the course of human evolution, to its different cultural expressions, to its expression in the world's major religions. We also examine the nature of faith, that cornerstone of hope, and its place in the human condition, explore spiritual development across the human life span, and describe various centers of value, or sources of faith. In Chapter 8 you will find strategies for developing your spiritual intelligence as determined by your own unique spiritual type; a spiritual type assessment is also included to help you identify your spiritual disposition and particular faith needs.

The practical orientation that emerges toward the end of Part One becomes the dominant thrust in Part Two, when we shift focus to the wings of hope. There we explore the practical benefits of a hope-centered way of life, including the promise of stronger relationships, the promise of genuine empowerment, and the promise of protection and liberation. We identify the skills needed to be a hope provider and offer an assessment tool to help you determine your own potential in this regard. Equally important, you will discover how to cultivate a spiritual life that can foster health and healing in the present while assuring a hope strong enough to inoculate you from the despair that engulfs many individuals. The last three chapters of the book focus on hope for children, for healing, and for general health and well-being.

We believe that hope is not merely a process by which you arrive at some desired destination. It is also, as we noted earlier, a way of being in the world. Ultimately, the chapters that follow aim to provide a deep and comprehensive understanding of hope that can help you fully realize and gain greater possession of what is already inside you—those vital motives of mastery, attachment, and survival—so that your own "being" in the world is more empowered, connected, and secure. Along the way, we address a number of practical concerns:

- What is the nature of hope?
- How do you build and sustain hope in this age of anxiety?
- How can hope improve your relationships with others?
- How can hope increase your sense of mastery?
- How can hope buffer your anxiety and bring peace of mind?
- How does hope relate to your faith and spiritual beliefs?
- How can hope aid your recovery from illness or trauma?
- How can hope increase your chances for a lifetime of good health?

In a letter to his brother, the artist Vincent Van Gogh reflected that when you understand one thing in great detail, the light of that knowledge can illuminate many areas of your life. This is certainly true of hope. In gaining a greater understanding of hope, you will be able to address countless other life concerns. You will undoubtedly look at relationships in a new way. You will think differently about issues of religion and spirituality. Your approach to stress and coping may be dramatically altered. Perhaps you will find it easier to get inspired or make progress toward some important goal. We can provide a road map, but the journey is yours.

# Part One

THE ROOTS OF HOPE:

*UNDERSTANDING YOUR HOPE LEGACY*

# One

## REKINDLING HOPE: HONORING THE FIRE WITHIN

Before starting my school I had three significant dreams—you see I still believe in dreams.

I was standing on the bank of a river and had to cross but seemingly there was no way for me to get over. . . . I looked back of me and there was a great army of young people, all coming towards me . . . someone came up to me and said, "You are planning to cross this river, but before you cross it you must take this book . . . and register the names of all those young people that you see [behind] in the distance."

I was again on the bank of the same river and was making another attempt to cross . . . Dr. Satterfield was on one side and my mother and father were on the other side. They started out with me, wading out into the deep currents. They held on and went as far as they could go and mother turned and said to me—"My child, we have brought you as far as we can go, but now we must leave you and you must make it for yourself."

I was standing on the banks of another river praying for help . . . I saw a man galloping down the street on a beautiful horse. He said, "I am Booker T. Washington", and he pulled out a parcel that had evidently been used for mopping off perspiration—and out of this handkerchief he gave me a large diamond . . . I felt that this diamond represented confidence, will power . . . friends . . . wisdom.

—Mary McLeod Bethune

Within the Judeo-Christian tradition, hope has long been recognized for its special powers. Saint Paul placed it alongside faith and love. "For now we see [the future] in a mirror darkly, but then face to face . . . So faith, hope, love, abide, these three." If you were to read the Bible from cover to cover, you would find that the word "hope" appears over 180 times or approximately once every seven pages. Christians and Jews, however, are not the only ones sustained by hope. Buddhists, Hindus, Muslims, the African Ifa, Native Americans, and the Australian Aborigines all draw their spiritual light from hope-oriented belief systems.

Many prominent scientists have also lined up in support of hope. Karl Menninger, one of the great psychiatrists of the twentieth century, believed that hope was an essential component of the healing process. Puzzled and frustrated by the lack of pertinent research attention it received within his profession, he bemoaned, "Our shelves are bare. The journals are silent." Hope was the topic of Menninger's 1959 presidential address to the American Psychiatric Association. He exhorted his audience to nurture this indispensable "flame" and "divine fire."

A decade later, psychiatrist Jerome Frank published an exhaustive review of 25 years of research on the effectiveness of psychotherapy. Frank noted the successful track record of many different types of therapy and speculated that each might be linked to a single underlying factor, "the instillation of hope." His findings contributed to a dramatic shift in therapeutic interventions during the final decades of the twentieth century, culminating in a new healing paradigm that acknowledged the power of positive beliefs, emotions, and attitudes. By the end of the 1970s, practitioners could boast a variety of wellness programs designed to buffer the cardiovascular and endocrine systems against the wear and tear of stressful encounters. Throughout the 1980s and 1990s, scientific understanding of the mind–body connection grew by leaps and bounds as investigators and clinicians shed new light on the health implications inherent in the interconnections involving the nervous system, the heart, glands, and other internal organs, as well as various elements of the immune system.

Foremost among the early promoters of the power of a positive attitude was Norman Vincent Peale, dubbed the "voice of hope" by *Newsday*. Peale attracted a huge following through his advocacy of a program for wellness that combined a hopeful mindset with unfailing trust in a higher power. He displayed a genius for crafting pithy one-liners, such as "Change your thoughts and you change your world," "Do not build up obstacles to your imagination," and "Throw your heart over the fence and the rest will follow." His *Power of Positive Thinking* has sold over 5 million copies and remains one of the best-selling inspirational books ever published.

Lending credibility to Peale's promises, researchers have found that hope can play an important role in enhancing wellness. It can, for example, promote quicker recovery following surgery and boost resilience among patients battling life-threatening disease. In a survey of oncologists, over 90% rated hope as the most important psychological factor associated with increased survival rates among cancer patients. And since 1986, with the publication of *Love, Medicine and Miracles*, Dr. Bernie Siegel has been offering hope and assurance to the sick and dying with his tales of heroic cancer patients. According to Seigel, "Hope is a wonderful resource for the physician. Even when things seem hopeless, to give a family hope is never wrong. I am not talking about lying, but about hope." At one point he encouraged a cancer survivor, Fay Finkelstein, to pass on her gift of hope by writing an encouraging letter to another one of his patients with the same disease. Fay wrote, "I understand that you have liver cancer. I was told over a year ago that I would probably die within six weeks. I didn't die. I don't plan to die for a long time."

Contrast this hopeful resolve with its counterpart, hopelessness, and the picture can look quite different. Evidence suggests, for example, that hopelessness may be the underlying cause of escalating youth violence, as in the 1999 shootings at Columbine High School. In the aftermath of that incident, a number of experts unearthed signs of alienation and despair that may have contributed to the massacre of 13 people and the subsequent suicides of the two teenage gunmen.

## Hope, Not Denial

The quest for hope is not limited to the sick or troubled but applies to every man, woman, and child who seeks a brighter tomorrow. The relatively few who have abandoned hope appear more confused than liberated in their decision making. Some of them presume that hope is synonymous with denial of the painful or difficult realities of life. Some view hope as a passive mindset designed to delay gratification of their desires. And others simply harbor a fear of hope. They prefer to brace themselves for the worst and cannot imagine anything better coming their way; they have already suffered too much and would rather settle for a predictable routine than open themselves up to a myriad of future possibilities.

There have been doubters of hope since the time of the ancient Greeks. In Sophocles' *Antigone*, one of the characters exclaimed: "We are the tribe that hates your filthy hope, your docile, female hope, your whore." The philosopher Friedrich Nietzsche, deeply ambivalent about hope, once called it "the worst of evils for it prolongs the torment of man," ostensibly referring to those instances when false hope might promote wishful thinking in the face of certain inevitable realities. Psychiatrist David Viscott, author of several popular self-help books, has written, "Hope has destroyed more lives than any other emotion . . . Hope is a reflection of powerlessness . . . When you have hope, you really are in denial."

These critics have confused false hope for the real thing. True hope is active rather than passive. It offers a real alternative to surrender borne of pain, suffering, or loss. It does not derive from blind optimism, or thwarted desire, or deluded fantasy. Rather, it arises from the most basic longings of humanity—among them our needs for mastery and protection, for social and cultural attachments, for the love and care required to achieve our potential as human beings. It derives from our capacity to envision the future and create a better life for ourselves and our loved ones. When blended into a "full hope," these underlying motives result in a lifelong quest for love, mastery, and future well-being. In this sense, hope represents the most profound expression of the "roots and wings" of the soul.

*Active hope* is the kind that sustained Motts Tonelli through nearly four harrowing years of confinement and abuse as a prisoner of war during World War II. His most challenging ordeal was the infamous Bataan Death March in the Philippines, a brutal 65-mile trek in which the Japanese military herded over 70,000 captured American and Filipino soldiers from the Bataan Peninsula to prison camps. The march can only be described as a moving concentration camp. For days at a time, Tonelli's Japanese captors would not allow him and the other POWs any access to fresh water or food. Those who resisted were beaten, bayoneted, or shot. In some instances, prisoners were actually forced to dig their own graves and thrown into them while still alive.

Tonelli refused to quit. His hopeful spirit had been fostered in childhood by a very determined father. When Motts was just 6 years old, his legs were badly burned in a fire and doctors declared he would never walk again. His father rejected this hopeless prognosis, instead devising a rigorous program of rehabilitation for Motts. He even fashioned a makeshift "cart," attaching wheels to an old door and insisting that his son push his way around until he regained full use of his legs. Motts subsequently attended Notre Dame and joined the football team, securing a measure of fame for his exploits on the gridiron. His greatest moment occurred in 1937 when he scored a 70-yard fourth-quarter touchdown to keep his team's hopes alive for a national championship. Five years later, in the sweltering jungles of the Philippines, his Notre Dame class ring became a "source of comfort and hope" for him, serving as a constant reminder that he had not only survived adversity before but had triumphed over it. That ring became the secret weapon that helped him survive his wartime ordeal by keeping him connected to his past achievements.

A sense of *connected hope* is inspiringly captured by the relationship between Helen Keller, blind and deaf since late infancy, and her teacher, Anne Sullivan. Beginning when Anne was 21 and Helen 7, the pair lived and worked together for nearly 50 years. At public lectures, Anne read Helen's speeches aloud word for word. Helen wrote a best-selling book about their collaboration entitled *Teacher*. Eventually their experiences would be dramatized in a Broadway play and an Oscar-winning film.

Anyone who has seen *The Miracle Worker* or read about Helen and Anne knows of the events that took place on April 5, 1887. Desperate to teach young Helen the meaning of words, Anne poured water over her student's hand while tracing w-a-t-e-r on the palm of the other. Helen later recalled, "Suddenly I felt a misty consciousness as of something forgotten, a thrill of returning thought." In June of 1960, nearly 25 years after Anne's death, a fountain was dedicated to her at Radcliff College. When it was Helen's turn to address the crowd during the dedication ceremony, she offered but one word, "water." Working together, Helen Keller and Anne Sullivan demonstrated the power of relationships to create hope while bringing out the best in the human spirit.

The experience of Christine King offers an especially poignant example of a *courageous hope* that transcends adversity and fear. In her early thirties, Christine became a breast cancer survivor. Although the disease was in remission, doctors warned her that there was a greater than 50% chance it would recur. Nevertheless, she was determined to live a life of meaning and purpose. She even organized a large fundraising event, *Art for Hope,* to increase public awareness about breast cancer. Upon her wrist she had engraved a tiny tattoo comprised of four letters, h-o-p-e.

The saga of the late actor Christopher Reeve presents yet another dramatic example of the healing power of hope. Paralyzed from the neck down in a horseback riding accident in 1995, Reeve could no longer move his arms or legs or breathe without a respirator, but in the spring of 2002, after years of dedicated rehabilitation, he announced that he had regained some movement and sensation in his extremities. For the first time since his accident, he was able to endure brief spells without a respirator and to respond to touch. Calling the Reeve case "unprecedented," neuroscientist Naomi Kleitman suggested that it might provide the impetus to revisit the notion of "seemingly hopeless spinal injuries." Sadly, Reeve died in 2004, but the spirit of his resolve, now embodied in the advocacy work of the Christopher and Dana Reeve Foundation, remains a sustaining beacon of hope for countless others struggling with spinal cord injuries.

Is hope really a reflection of powerlessness as David Viscott suggested? Tell that to Motts Tonelli and the others who had to face daunting, sometimes horrific realities. They did not deny those realities—they couldn't if they tried—but rather they confronted and embraced them with a hope born of courage and will to surmount the odds. Win or lose, their efforts were hardly a reflection of powerlessness. Indeed their examples reflected the very essence of the life force.

## A Virtue for All Seasons

Six months after the attacks of September 11, 2001, the city of New York staged a "tribute in light." Two high-powered searchlights, equaling the wattage of 2 million bulbs and representing the now-destroyed twin towers of the World Trade Center, sent mile-high beams of light into the night sky. Architect Gustavo Bonevardi, one of the designers of the project, stated, "The idea of light is almost like the souls of those who died rising up to heaven . . . It is a memorial . . . it's also [meant to reflect] light as life, light as hope, light as renewal."

Whenever the economy starts to dip, economists and politicians are quick to monitor the state of "consumer confidence." They are keenly aware of hope's role in sustaining the local economy as well as the heartbeat of international commerce. Without a positive view of the future, how many consumers will buy a new car, purchase a home, or make some other long-term investment? In 2002, after the stock markets in Germany, Tokyo, and China simultaneously plummeted, more than one economist blamed it on an epidemic of "public hopelessness." In 1929, when the world of finance imploded on Black Thursday, it precipitated the Great Depression. Fortunately, it was then that a "crooked-legged racehorse" named Seabiscuit entered the scene:

> Times were hard, there was little to cheer about . . . Seabiscuit had short legs, asymmetrical knees . . . a crouching stance, an odd, inefficient "eggbeater" gait. . . . Nevertheless, he gave people hope. Hope that they too could come from behind and win in life . . . . By the end of 1938, Seabiscuit had won 33 races and set 16 track records. With war looming, America now had something that gave them hope . . . (David Cole, *The Long Shot that Captured America's Heart*)

Indeed, the passion that surrounds all sports, the so-called thrill of victory and agony of defeat, is fundamentally about hope. Take baseball, for example—that American national pastime played by "the boys of summer." The late Bart Giamatti, former commissioner of baseball, observed:

> The game begins in the spring when everything else begins again and it blossoms in summer, filling the afternoons and evenings . . . . You count on it. Rely on it to buffer the passage of time, to keep the memory of sunshine and high skies alive.

In the Oscar-winning film *Field of Dreams*, Terrence Mann (James Earl Jones) tells Ray (Kevin Costner):

> The one constant through all the years, Ray, has been baseball . . . it has marked the time. This field, this game, is a part of our past, Ray. It reminds us of all that once was good, and that could be again.

In many other countries the national pastime is soccer. Millions of fans have been flocking to soccer stadiums in South America and Europe for nearly a century. More recently, Africa and Asia have witnessed a soccer surge. Every 4 years, when the World Cup is staged, billions of fans huddle around television sets and radios, rooting for their national team. Onlookers marvel at the extent to which soccer fans identify with their football club. The reason is simple: soccer offers its fans, especially the poor and disenfranchised, a sense of collective hope.

No continent may be more hope challenged than Africa. Three hundred million of its inhabitants live in total poverty. More than 26 million are infected with the HIV/AIDS virus, and more than 12 million children have lost their parents to the disease. Nevertheless, these youngsters are resilient. For example, in Rwanda many of the older orphans, HIV positive themselves, manage to care for their younger siblings while working in the fields. They look toward soccer to provide them with some hope. A photo taken in one AIDS devastated village shows a young girl, also HIV positive, smiling and clutching a soccer ball made of rags.

Liberia, a country of 3 million people, has been ravaged by more than a decade of civil war. Over 50,000 have been killed and countless others have been tortured or maimed. On a wall, the misspelled graffiti of a desperate child says it all, "We one peecee" (we want peace)." Meanwhile, corruption and infighting among rival warlords have eroded trust in the country's political leaders and institutions (failed attachment). The educational system is in shambles, and only 20% of the population is able to read and write (failed mastery). Firefighters are without trucks, and wheelbarrows serve as makeshift ambulances (failed survival). Large sections of the country have been without electricity or running water for decades. One foreign observer called it the "world's most stark example of a failed state."

But there is at least one ray of hope in Liberia, and that's soccer sensation George Weah. As a child, Weah roamed barefoot through the capitol city of Monrovia, dividing his time between playing soccer and picking through the trash for scraps of redeemable salvage. Alerted to his athletic potential, the government arranged for Weah to train in South America and Europe where he could learn from the game's elite.

Weah confirmed their hopes, becoming an international superstar. In 1995, the International Soccer Federation rated him the world's top performer. Three years later he was named the African player of the century. When Liberia's national team was nearly disbanded due to a lack of funds, Weah donated his own money to pay the players' salaries, purchase uniforms, and transport them to matches. Nelson Mandela called him the "African Pride." A Liberian official put it even more bluntly, "George Weah and soccer are the only things we can hold onto."

Sportswriter S. L. Price made a pilgrimage to Liberia in 2001 to observe firsthand the "holy positions" maintained by George Weah and the game of soccer. When interviewed, a teammate suggested that Weah's emergence "had been designated by God." Price also noted that whenever Weah attends a youth soccer clinic or visits a hospital, the locals begin to murmur, "He is coming. Jesus is coming." On the day Liberia was scheduled to play a pivotal match against Sierra Leone, the scene was very much like a religious procession. Throngs of adoring fans formed a caravan around the team bus, cheering and singing to the players. "Church services stopped in mid-sentence. People smiled for the first time in a month . . . A man with no legs tried to crawl after the bus as it passed." Weah understood the enormous responsibility that had been placed on his shoulders. "Soccer is a game of hope, and in this country . . . there is very little [hope]."

It is hope that stirs the soul and moves the masses. Its symbols are universally present, from the Christian's statue of St. Jude to the green light that beckoned *The Great Gatsby*. Vaclav Havel, the first president of the Czech Republic, signed his documents with a green pen to accentuate his "hopes for humanity and the planet earth." The bright yellow daffodil, one of the first flowers of spring, is the official hope symbol of the American and Canadian Cancer Societies. *Daffodils Days*, held every March in both the United States and Canada, generate millions of dollars for cancer research. Shakespeare paid homage to daffodils in his *Winter's Tale*, noting that they "come before the swallows dare, and take the winds of March with beauty." The ancient Romans believed the daffodil, long revered as a symbol of hope and renewal, could heal wounds.

Two of the most enduring myths of antiquity deal with the restorative nature of hope. In one myth, Prometheus cures Zeus, Lord of the Gods, of a terrible headache by hitting him on the head with a rock; the blow releases Athena (goddess of perseverance) into the world. Later, Prometheus ventures to earth with his brother Epimetheus and they fashion figures of clay. The waiting Athena breathes life into them. Epimetheus's figures turn into hopeless beasts while Prometheus's become humankind. Defying Zeus, Prometheus plots to bring fire to his mortal progeny and, with Athena's help, reaches the sun where he lights his divine torch. Aware that Zeus will try to extinguish his flame to keep humanity shrouded in darkness, Prometheus prepares glowing embers and sneaks them back to earth.

The second myth is a continuation of the first. Furious that Prometheus dared to share heat and light with humanity, Zeus orders his gods to create Pandora, the first mortal woman, and deploys her as a naive accomplice in his plan to saddle mortals with every known evil. The gods endow Pandora with every possible charm and present her as an irresistible gift to the impetuous Epimetheus, who marries her despite Prometheus's warnings against doing so. The gods also give Pandora a beautiful box but tell her never to open it. After a period of blissful tranquility as the wife of Epimetheus, the curious Pandora can no longer resist and she takes a peek inside the box. Out rush *Old Age, Sickness, Death, Famine, Pestilence, Vice, Greed*, and *Lies*. However, at the very bottom, almost unnoticed, one spirit remains inside the box—the "gift of hope," there to console and assist humanity in confronting the upheavals unleashed upon the world.

Whenever disaster strikes, we all look for hope. Whether in a tribute of light following unspeakable horror, in a winning racehorse during the depths of the Depression, in a game played by the boys of summer, in a soccer star from a ravaged country, or in ancient myths designed to explain to us our blighted world and give meaning to our place in it, we look for hope to sustain us, whenever and wherever we can.

You can, however, only learn so much from case histories and ancient myths. Every individual has a unique personality and each life situation is different. Thus, in the following chapters, we introduce and elaborate on a basic philosophy of hope that is intended ultimately to help you achieve a greater sense of attachment, mastery, survival, and spirituality in your own life.

*First Hope Meditation*

Take a moment to reflect on your most memorable encounters with hope. Imagine before you a billboard with the word "hope" printed in giant letters. What was your most significant experience with this emotion? Perhaps it involved you or a close friend. Maybe it was a particularly inspiring story about an act of love, a heroic deed, or a tale of survival. Perhaps it dealt with hope in the aftermath of September 11 or some other calamity. What kinds of thoughts, feelings, and images come to mind? Give yourself as much time as you need. Close your eyes and think about a few situations in which you strongly hoped for something. Were these hopes realized? Why or why not? Which of these hopes have you abandoned and which do you still harbor?

# *Two*

## THE FAR-FLASHING BEAM: PERSPECTIVES

## ON HOPE

Prejudice is a burden that confuses the past, threatens the future and renders
the present inaccessible.

—Maya Angelou

The great pragmatist philosopher and psychologist William James once noted that our
passion for life is apt to be wasted unless it is joined with the "far-flashing beam" of a
philosophical perspective. The same holds true for hope: our desire to secure it, in bad
times and in good, should not outstrip our intellectual need to understand its complexities. A broader perspective is called for—a "hope perspective" that is both scientifically
grounded and practically useful in enhancing both your knowledge about this complex
emotion and your own personal well-being. Ultimately, as the myth of Prometheus
suggests, we need both light and heat to make our way in the world. Having both with
respect to hope will, simply put, help you chart your way to a better quality of life.

So far, we have introduced you to only a sampling of hope themes, whether those
recorded or exemplified by others or those we have conceived ourselves. Now let us go
into a bit more depth and look at the different ways that hope has been described by
psychologists, psychiatrists, philosophers, and theologians in the past century.
Interpretations of hope have of course been given to us by artists, philosophers, and
scientists since the time of the ancient Greeks, and we will look at those in the next
chapter as well as refer to them periodically throughout this book. But it is the actual
science of hope, a relatively young field, that we want to examine in this chapter.

Broadly speaking, the science of hope comprises two divergent traditions: one that has focused on hope within the individual, and another that highlights external sources of hope. The first generally includes research psychologists showing a preference for a goal-related understanding of hope and clinicians wanting to know more about its role in coping. The second is represented by philosophers, theologians, and some psychologists who have contributed greatly to our understanding of hope's social and spiritual dimensions. These traditions are not mutually exclusive: theorists in the second group, for example, do factor in the individual in their social or spiritual formulations about hope. Still, collectively, each tradition has succeeded in grasping only part, but not all, of what we call "hope," and so after summarizing each one's contribution briefly, we will introduce our own integrative approach to hope. Together, this background will establish the conceptual foundation upon which later chapters are based.

## Hope Within the Individual

### Hope in Goal Attainment

O. Hobart Mowrer, a renowned learning theorist, believed that hope springs from simple conditioning. An object or event generates hope when it is associated with another object or event that once satisfied a biological need. For example, the bell engendered hope in the Pavlovian trained dog because it signaled the arrival of food in the very near future. In contrast, Mowrer found that his laboratory rats stopped moving when they "lost hope" of eliciting a food reward:

> The rats learn that most of the time there is no point in moving . . . during this period they are, relatively speaking, "hopeless" and "depressed" whereas, when the situation changes, thus giving promise of food, the subjects become hopeful and active.

Mowrer reasoned that fear was the opposite of hope. He assumed his inactive laboratory animals were frightened as well as depressed and hopeless, although he had no direct evidence to support this conclusion. In fact, "freezing" can result from a variety of emotional and physical states. Animals stop moving when they are too tired, too hot or too cold, too full or too hungry, fully content or very scared. But they can also fly into an agitated panic, sometimes to the point of heart failure, when frightened.

Human hope is *sometimes* sustained by simple associations. We may pin our hopes on signs and symbols that we link to a positive outcome. Physician and author Larry Dossey, for example, shared the story of a man whose immune system functioning would alternatively rise and fall in synchrony with positive and negative media reports of an experimental drug.

But humans, unlike rats, can also maintain hope with little or no positive reinforcement. In the Nazi concentration camps, old women swapped recipes and made cookbooks from scraps of paper, and children carved butterflies on the walls of their cells. On a fragment of a building destroyed by bombing in Cologne during Word War II, someone had written, "I believe in the sun even when it is not shining. I believe in love even when I do not feel it. I believe in God even when he is silent."

In 1969 psychologist Ezra Stotland published his influential book, *The Psychology of Hope*. According to him, hope is critical for goal attainment because it is a key component of motivation. Stotland understood hope as a joint function of the perceived probability and the perceived importance of attaining particular goals. The more likely one is to reach a significant goal, the more one's hopefulness increases. Unlike Mowrer, who equated the absence of hope with fear, Stotland suggested that the opposite of hope was anxiety.

### A Hopeful Mindset

Stotland's approach also included a simplified notion of schemas or mindsets. Individuals with *hopeful mindsets* are confident that they will reach their goals, whereas those who think they have little chance of success possess a "hopelessness schema." However, Stotland did not believe these mindsets had to be recharged by ongoing experiences of reinforcement. He suggested they could be sustained indefinitely by *persistence schemas* or hoped-for images created from past experiences.

Stotland's work on schemas anticipated the next phase of hope research, which emerged in the 1980s and 1990s and was strongly influenced by the cognitive psychology movement then sweeping the field. A cognitive psychologist would argue that positive emotions derive from healthy or adaptive thoughts. In contrast, negative feelings such as depression are presumed to arise from irrational and maladaptive beliefs. This is an old idea. The ancient stoic philosopher Epictetus declared, "What disturbs men's mind is not events but their judgments on events." In poet John Milton's *Paradise Lost*, when the fallen angel Beelzebub is banished to hell, he defiantly suggests, "The mind is its own place and can make a hell out of heaven or a heaven out of hell."

Nor is Stotland's idea of a hope schema, or what many contemporary cognitive psychologists would call a hopeful outlook or "frame of mind," especially original. The concept of hope as an intellectual or thought-based "passion"—a quiet and private experience lacking the fury of rage or the widened eyes and raised hair of fear—has long been appreciated. Both the seventeenth-century philosopher René Descartes and, much later, William James created a special category for hope and other similarly "gentle," more "thought-full" emotions. But then the work of psychiatrist Louis Gottschalk and of psychologists Lyn Abramson and C. R. Snyder elevated the concept of a "mindset" to another level, broadening the hope framework beyond just "memories of persistence."

Louis Gottschalk described hope as "the belief that a favorable outcome is likely to occur." He attempted to gauge how much hope a person has by analyzing his or her response to a simple open-ended question: "Can you speak for five minutes into this tape recorder about any interesting or dramatic personal life experiences you have ever had?" These speech samples were analyzed for the presence of themes that suggest either hopefulness or hopelessness. What distinguished Gottschalk's perspective from Stotland's approach is that he included each person's expectation of outside help, as revealed in the tapes, as part of the hope equation.

Lyn Abramson expanded the concept of a hopeful mindset to include expectations about ends and means. In essence, hopeful individuals expect good things to happen (positive outcome expectancies) and feel that they have the necessary resources to achieve their goals (positive resource expectancies). C. R. Snyder further elaborated on the concept by identifying hope as a product of two expectancies: adequate *agency* or willpower, and the perception of available *pathways* or options for goal attainment. From his perspective, individuals with increased willpower gain a sense that they have more options for achieving their goals and are strengthened in their resolve by finding ways around the obstacles to those goals.

## Hope as Coping

Health service providers are especially interested in hope as a mechanism for coping with serious illnesses, loss, and other highly stressful events. This is why most of the coping theories of hope have come from fields such as nursing, medicine, clinical psychology, or psychiatry. For example, in the late 1960s, psychologists Beatrice Wright and Franklin Shontz interviewed severely disabled children, their parents, and therapists for insights about sustaining hope in the presence of a chronic illness. The children, ranging in age from 5 to 19, were afflicted with extremely debilitating medical conditions, such as cerebral palsy, spina bifida, and achondroplasia.

An undifferentiated positive emotional state was found in all of the children who demonstrated hope. But whereas younger boys and girls expressed their hope through present concerns, the older ones relied more on their positive expectations for the future. Among the adults (parents), the most important component of the hoping process involved scanning and monitoring aspects of reality for evidence to support their hopes. Labeled "reality surveillance" by the authors, this behavior consisted of such efforts as collecting anecdotes of related success stories, talking to doctors about "best-case" scenarios, and taking stock of the smallest signs of progress or improvement in their children. However, "reality surveillance" was just one of four hope-related behaviors that these parents exhibited. The others involved seeking encouragement, managing anxiety, and coping with loss.

For psychologist Ija Korner, the primary function of hope is to activate an individual's motivational system to ward off despair. Its secondary function is to help the individual bypass negative emotions that surface in times of stress. In both aspects, hope becomes a stress buffer, a kind of "psychic balm." Korner viewed hope in terms of two components, an emotional side similar to "faith" or to a heartfelt assurance that one's troubles will resolve, and an intellectual component (the reasons for hope) that he labeled the "rationalizing chain."

## Hope Metaphors

Shlomo Breznitz, an Israeli stress researcher, probed the language of hope to better understand its role in helping people cope with stress and serious illnesses. He began by analyzing the "work of hope"—the ways in which people with cancer and other daunting life circumstances labor to sustain themselves in the face of difficult odds. He then explored their "hope metaphors"—the various language they used to characterize and cope with their experience. Another metaphor hunter, psychologist James Averill, searched the literature for famous hope quotes and asked volunteers to jot down their ideas about how they imagined hope. From Averill and Breznitz, as well as other sources, we have identified five categories of hope metaphors (summarized in Table 2.1).

The first category, *hope as a protected area*, refers to positive experiences that an individual retains and revisits while hoping. Breznitz cites a definition of hope in the *Oxford English Dictionary* as "a piece of enclosed land, in the middle of marshes and wasteland." Along these lines, the writer Ruth O' Lill described the harrowing wartime experiences of a 14-year-old girl named Irene. While escaping Russian tanks during World War II, Irene was forced to lay face down in shallow ditches for many hours. She also recalled crossing the frozen Elbe River on a ferry as it was bombarded by enemy planes. Nevertheless, "She felt totally safe, protected, and in spite of everything that was going on in her war-torn world—she felt hope."

The notion of *hope as a bridge*, the second type of metaphor, highlights its role in helping individuals to work themselves out of trouble, transporting them from danger to safety. Psychiatrist Arnold Hutschnecker, who wrote extensively on hope and the will to live, shared a critical insight from one of his clients, a woman named Ariel. After a year of treatment for severe depression, she told him, "I have crossed the bridge. I did not fall. I did not drown. I did not go insane. I came out of the panic to safety."

In *How to Live between Office Visits*, Bernie Siegel recalled the experiences of a recovered patient who had been told he would die within 6 months. After being given his death sentence in the underground chamber of a tumor institute, he was transported up an incline back to the main hospital. "The ride became a visual and physical metaphor for my recovery . . . I glanced ahead and realized I was facing an upward climb. It was a small thing at the time, but it was the spark of hope and inspiration I needed."

The third type of metaphor, *hope as a vital principle*, implies that it is an essential part of our humanity, an energizing core. As we will see in clearer detail shortly, we can

TABLE 2.1. *Metaphors of Hope*

| Hope Metaphors | Coping Aspects | Selected Quotes and Common Phrases |
|---|---|---|
| *A protected area* | A safe place or retreat; A psychological "bunker" | I'm secure in my hope; I cling to Hope; I harbor the hope |
| *A bridge* | A way of imagining or of psychologically transporting oneself to a better time and place | Hope is the dream of those awake; Hope will carry you through |
| *A vital principle* | A life-sustaining force | The patient's hopes are the physician's secret weapon; Hope springs eternal in the human breast |
| *A skill* | A quality of character and resiliency | Hope is a second soul; Great hopes make great individuals; Hope is the best possession |
| *An end in itself* | A goal; a preferred end state; What is most desired | Where there's hope, there's life; Keep hope alive; Give the gift of hope |

trace this dimension of hope all the way back to the motives for mastery, attachment, and survival.

Breznitz's fourth metaphor characterizes hope as a *problem-solving feat*, a skill requiring certain capacities such as planning and the use of imagery. In this sense, hope is an art form or act of adaptation that some people seem to carry off with particular grace and skill.

The fifth type of metaphor implies that hope may be the goal rather than a means to an end. Sometimes all a person seeks is *hope itself*. Bernie Siegel provided a simultaneously amusing and wise tale of an exceptional cancer patient named Stephanie. "After the diagnosis of cancer, her doctor outlined the rest of her life, as predicted by statistics, right to an early grave. She asked what she could do, and he told her, 'All you've got is a hope and a prayer.' She snapped back, 'How do I hope and pray?' "

## Hope from Others

What is the origin of hope? Is it a private resource or a product of family, friends, and culture? Are religious or spiritual beliefs necessary for the establishment of hope? What, in short, are the external factors in the development of hope?

### The Family and Culture of Hope

Psychologist Erik Erikson saw hope as the most fundamental human virtue, the bedrock on which the other human virtues might be established. "Hope is a very basic human strength without which we couldn't stay alive," he asserted, thus conceptualizing basic hope, like other human virtues, as a strength, power, or capacity. It is "the enduring belief in the attainability of fervent wishes, in spite of the dark urges and rages which mark the beginning of existence." He believed that favorable early family experiences can impart in a child a sense of hope that "pervades surface and depth, consciousness and the unconscious." But he also emphasized the importance of cultural influences in the development of hope, noting that at every stage in the human life cycle, there is an interdependent relationship between individual human needs and particular cultural institutions. He emphasized how children come into the world dependent, ready to receive and ready to trust. While adults are programmed to care for the receptive child, they also need their own trust reawakened and consolidated. They receive a hope booster shot from the experience of mutuality that characterizes the infant caretaking process. The cultural institutions that humans have created further reinforce this need to trust and hope.

Adding support to Erikson's cultural perspective, psychologist James Averill and his colleagues compared the hope-related beliefs of American and Korean students. They found that Americans were more concerned about the odds of realizing their hopes and were more apt to act on them. Koreans expressed more caution about doing so: viewing hope as an enduring and controllable aspect of one's character, they believed that its potential for bringing personal happiness should be carefully weighed against its social costs.

Much of psychologist Gina O'Connell Higgins' provocative book *Resilient Adults* dealt with the development and maintenance of hope. She conducted detailed interviews with 40 adults who were relatively well adjusted despite having had terrible childhood experiences. Many had experienced extreme poverty, serious illness, or multiple forms of abandonment. Virtually all of them had suffered physical and/or sexual abuse. "Despite these backgrounds, all subjects were deemed by various measures to be mature and healthy."

Among these individuals was Dan, who grew up with a physically abusive, alcoholic father and a mother who, when not in a psychiatric hospital, subjected him to bizarre sexually intrusive enemas. Both parents routinely dumped him and his screaming siblings into a tub of boiling-hot water. Amazingly, Dan was able to maintain an unflinching and deep resoluteness. He reflected, "If a tornado went through my town and destroyed my house, I wouldn't stand there devastated, saying 'This is the end of all I know . . . I can't go on' . . . I'd look at the house, and I'd say, 'well let's see, this wall's still standing . . . I guess we can start with that. Let's rebuild the rest of it', and we'd go on." When asked who gave him reason to hope in the midst of his childhood chaos, Dan replied, "There were so many men who were kind and good people at boarding-school, they didn't shout at you . . . They didn't beat you. It was such a revelation."

To Higgins, Dan's ability to extract hope from disastrous experiences exemplified a major factor in the development of resilient individuals. Understanding hope as a "resource," Higgins repeatedly alluded to a "light," "safe harbor," or "safe haven" that such individuals had been able to gravitate toward as children. Unlike Erikson, who suggested that hope depends on experiences in the very first years of life, Higgins' research points to circumstances that can promote a hopeful attitude in later phases of childhood and adolescence. Her views also differ from Erikson in that she presumed that early hope resources and surrogate providers could be found outside of the parent–child relationship.

Both Higgins and the psychiatrist George Vaillant stressed the importance of a redemptive hope that comes from experiences of care and connectedness. In *Wisdom of the Ego*, Vaillant traced the odyssey of playwright Eugene O' Neill from a childhood of neglect through one early-life disaster after another. O'Neill's misspent youth included problems with alcohol, addiction to morphine, living among prostitutes, and frequent homelessness. At the age of 24, he contracted tuberculosis, then spent the next 6 months in a sanatorium finding "hope and harmony" in the presence of a dedicated and caring staff. He would later write, "Human hope is the greatest power in life and the only thing that defeats death." Finding his voice, Eugene O'Neill would eventually write two of the most celebrated plays of the twentieth century, *Long Days Journey into Night* and *The Iceman Cometh*.

### Philosophies of Hope

In contrast to most social scientists, philosophers and theologians have tended to highlight the role of attachments and spiritual beliefs in their study of hope, emphasizing trust and community as well as imagination and spiritual transformation. The contributions of Christian existentialist Gabriel Marcel are particularly noteworthy. Illuminating the inner experience of hope with the most sublime reflections on the importance of trust, values, and time perception, his writings are especially applicable to dire situations that involve an inevitable loss, for example, a prisoner facing certain execution or an individual dealing with a terminal illness.

Marcel's oft-quoted phrase, "I hope in thee for us," refers to a creative effort whereby individuals cease to focus exclusively on their own salvation or release. Instead they reflect on an experience of communion with some other person, group, or entity that shares similar ultimate concerns, a common purpose or a belief in a higher power. Hope is invested in a more transcendent aim that encompasses both self *and* other. The following quotation from psychologist David McClelland hints at this "larger purpose."

> My wife died of cancer a few years ago. . . . We had been very much in love,
> happily married for 42 years . . . Yet when she died I did not feel the amount of
> pain that [psychological theories] would require that I should feel . . . We had felt
> that we were part of something which was much bigger than ourselves—which had
> nurtured and supported us . . . and which continued to support me after her death.

Marcel's insights are particularly relevant in today's world. Humanity continues to be challenged by many forms of evil that can lead to feelings of entrapment and chronic despair. There is hunger and poverty, diseases that resist our best medical technology, and the constant threat of local violence and international terrorism. A hope focused only on individual wellness may be dwarfed by these larger evils. In contrast, Marcel's "communal hope" offers a viable alternative to "spiritual helplessness."

Marcel's interest in the inner experience of hope also led him to consider the ways that having or not having hope can alter the experience of time. When one is hopeless, the future seems to fade away, leaving behind only the sense of an insufferable present. But when one is blessed with hope, the future seems full of possibility, providing the sense that there is ample time to fulfill dreams, develop intimacy, and achieve liberation. Marcel realized that looking forward with hope involves having patience, "biding one's time," and waiting for the right opportunities to come along. But this waiting, Marcel emphasized, is not passive; rather, it is an active, hope-based effort balanced with patience. He also distinguished between hoping and refusing to accept reality. Whereas ignoring the facts of life can lead to "psychic stiffening," patient hoping is associated with an enlarged perspective and mental flexibility. Unlike despair, a "ready" hope does not lead to capitulation or giving into one's predicament.

Patrick Shade is a contemporary philosopher who has also explored the process of hoping. Echoing Stotland and other pragmatists of the past, he is especially interested in the role of hope as a means of goal attainment. His primary contribution has been to outline a number of key behaviors—"habits of hope," such as persistence, resourceful-ness, and courage—that may increase the probability of securing a hoped-for end.

Strongly influenced by Marcel, psychologist Paul Pruyser emphasized both social and spiritual forces in the evolution of hope. He explored whether hope can be "given" or "taken away." His answer was that true hope is a state of "being" rather than a form of "having." It is based on a philosophical or spiritual belief system that persists in the face of adversity. It cannot be torn away for it runs through the core of one's being.

Pruyser distinguished hope from selfish wishing and mere optimism. According to him, bona fide hoping, unlike these "unworthy contenders," is based on a spiritual contract with a higher power. For example, religious followers who adopt an apocalyptic view of revenge, seeking retribution and restitution, are really wishing rather than hoping. In contrast, those who trust in a "greater intelligence" and retain a broader concern for humankind show a more "open and restful" hope.

Philosopher Joseph Godfrey focused on *basic* and *directed hope*. Basic hope does not aim at a particular object or outcome but is rather a character trait that involves a general orientation toward the future. A foundation rather than an action plan, it is rooted in an attitude of openness to new experiences, a spirit of availability to whatever the future holds. It also requires a sense of possibility as well as adequate willpower and self-esteem. Directed hope, on the other hand, is pointed at a specific outcome, such as

"I hope the sun will shine today" or "I hope my leg heals." Godfrey identified a variety of *directed hopes* in the philosophical literature, including hoping for the "highest good" within oneself, hoping to inhabit the kingdom of God, and hoping for perpetual peace. Immanuel Kant fell into this category of "hope philosophers" (hoping for heaven and peace) as did Ernst Bloch (hoping for social/cultural evolution), and more recently, the theologian Jurgen Moltmann (hoping for a redemptive resurrection).

According to Godfrey, there are two ways that trust can foster the development of hope; one is *goal related,* while the other is *relationship based.* From a goal-oriented perspective, individuals must trust that a particular outcome can occur. In addition, they must trust that they have the necessary resources to achieve the desired goal by themselves or with the help of others. This kind of trust in the service of hope is cultivated through experimentation, observation, and calculation. The highest good that can be hoped for is effective mastery and adequate resources.

From a relationship perspective, individuals must trust in the availability and continued presence of a significant other, whether another individual, a group, humanity in general, or a perceived spiritual presence. This form of trust-related hope is derived through openness and intimacy. The highest good is a sense of union and an in-depth appreciation of the other.

In *Images of Hope*, theologian William Lynch argued that a healthy individual needs goals and plans. Agreeing with Pruyser, he wanted to keep hope separate from egotistical or mean-spirited wishes. Differing somewhat from Pruyser, he believed that wishing can indeed be a source of true hope as long as it is not pathological in nature and is instead grounded in affirmation and acceptance. In Lynch's view, one cannot fully understand hope without focusing on the imaginative process, the "sum total of all the forces and faculties in man that are brought to bear upon our concrete world from proper imaging of it." And yet hope also relies on reality as much as on imaginative fantasy: "The further it would soar," he wrote, "the deeper it must plunge into facts."

Lynch emphasized that "the wholly interior hope is a romantic fiction." Hope may be considered an interior resource, but it is also derived in large part from external provisions such as "liberating relationships" and "collaborative mutuality." Lynch lamented that Western culture appears to have lost touch with these social roots of hope, embracing instead a narrow and decontextualized view of the individual and an impoverished notion of human willpower.

## An Integrative Theory

As valuable as the contributions just surveyed are in shedding light on various aspects of hope, none captures the entire breadth, depth, and richness of the hope experience. A full account of hope must address the multiple levels which permeate the human experience, from the "sense of hope" that "pervades surface and depth, consciousness and the unconscious," to the varieties of "hope expressions" that are evident across individuals, cultures, and spiritual belief systems. What follows, then, is our own integrative theory, a new paradigm of hope.

First, we suggest that *hope is an emotion*. Like any emotion, it can be hard to control, it has a feeling tone, and it may motivate behavior. When the average man or woman is asked to rate lists of words to gauge whether they refer to an emotion, hope always emerges as a bona fide exemplar. To the ancient and medieval philosophers, hope was routinely listed among the "passions."

But what exactly is an emotion? We will spare readers the details of a tortured debate that occurred throughout most of the twentieth century on this topic. Suffice it to say that there are two main approaches to the topic of emotions. Some experts espouse a "core" view, while others endorse a "construction" view. Core theorists presume that regions or centers in the brain house individual emotions. For example, some attempt to isolate rage within the amygdala, a tiny, walnut-shaped structure deep in the center of the brain. In contrast, construction theorists assume that emotions are more like systems or networks that draw on multiple areas in the mind and body to form patterned responses. As our understanding of both mind and body becomes increasingly sophisticated, fewer and fewer emotions are being viewed as "cores."

*We define hope as a future-directed, four-channel emotion network, constructed from biological, psychological, and social resources. The four channels are the mastery, attachment, survival, and spiritual subsystems. The hope network is designed to regulate these subsystems via both feed-forward (expansion) and feedback (maintenance) mechanisms, resulting in a greater perceived probability of power and presence as well as protection and liberation.*

By definition a network is simply a complex system of interrelated parts. What is particularly appealing about designating hope as a network is that it makes available associated metaphors that further clarify the regulatory functions of hope. For example, the promise of power can be likened to a control network, the promise of presence to a social network, and the promise of protection/liberation to a safety network. Extending the safety network further, consider the network of silken strands that a spider sometimes uses as a shield to remain safely in one place (self-regulation) and other times deploys as a set of pulleys to scurry away from intruders (liberation).

The four hope channels have developed in a semiautonomous fashion, meaning they sometimes operate alone and sometimes work together. When they work together, one channel may, like a television network, feed two or more other channels. For example, an individual with a strong spiritual foundation may have his or her mastery, attachment, and survival responses heavily influenced by spiritual beliefs. Conversely, two or three channels may feed one channel, much like your television set might receive input from a receiver, DVD player, and a set of speakers. For example, an individual's attachment, mastery, and survival channels can influence his or her spiritual development.

The hope network is a "deep structure." Picture a three-dimensional grid rather than a flat series of lines on a piece of paper. Spanning across the top of the grid (network) are the four interlinked channels of mastery, attachment, survival, and spirituality. Running vertically from top to bottom are the developmental roots of each channel and its interactions with the other channels. The vertical span is akin to a five-level foundation, ranging from biological motives and genetic endowments to social and spiritual elements. These levels are presented in Table 2.2 in descending order to indicate

TABLE 2.2. *Levels of the Hope Network*

| | | | |
|---|---|---|---|
| 5<sup>th</sup> Level: *Beliefs and Behaviors* | | | |
|   Daily hope beliefs<br>  Daily hope feelings<br>  Daily hope actions | Help is near<br>Empowered<br>Collaboration | The universe is kind<br>Connected<br>Openness | Protection is available<br>Safe<br>Self-regulation |
| 4<sup>th</sup> Level: *The Faith System*<br>  Elements of faith | Centers of value | | |
| 3<sup>rd</sup> Level: *The Hopeful Core*<br><br>  Mastery-oriented traits | Goal-oriented trust<br>Mediated (collaborative) control<br>Sanctioned commitments | | |
|   Attachment-oriented traits | | Relational-trust<br>Connectedness<br>Openness | |
|   Survival-oriented traits | | Survival-oriented trust and care recruitment<br>Terror management and liberation beliefs<br>Resiliency and self-regulation<br>Spiritual integrity and symbolic immortality | |
| 2<sup>nd</sup> Level: *Nature and Nurture*<br>  Psychological endowments<br>  Social and cultural endowments<br>  Spiritual endowments | Talent, goal-directness<br><br>Support and guidance<br><br>Purpose | Trust and openness<br><br>Care and love<br><br>Presence | Resiliency, coping skills and ego defenses<br>Cultural terror management<br>Salvation |
| 1<sup>st</sup> Level: *Hope Blueprints*<br>  Biological motives | Mastery motive | Attachment motive | Survival motive |

that, like any foundational structure, the strength of the upper levels depends on the firmness of the lower levels. For example, an adequate attachment system (level 1) facilitates basic or primary trust (level 2), which spawns greater secondary trust (level 3), leading to stronger faith development (level 4), which translates into adaptive daily hope responses (level 5). We will elaborate on the various parts of the hope network in upcoming chapters, but let us briefly examine each of its levels here, beginning with the most fundamental.

### Level 1: Hope Blueprints

The deepest level of the hope network consists of biologically based motives relating to mastery, attachment, and survival. These might be considered the genetic *blueprints for hope.* Indeed, there is overwhelming evidence that certain brain structures and pathways are primarily associated with these motives, whose very hardware and software dominate the anatomical and physiological makeup of the human organism.

For example, the frontal lobes of the brain account for nearly 40% of the total human cortex, allowing for mastery-associated initiative and planning. Damage to the frontal lobes, most strikingly seen in lobotomies, can produce apathy and indifference.

Moreover, research has isolated three important brain components associated with the biology of attachment: parts of the right hemisphere; the hormone oxytocin; and the amygdala, the walnut-shaped structure within the temporal lobe. The right hemisphere is involved in the recognition of emotions expressed in the spoken word or in facial expressions. Oxytocin, the so-called cuddle chemical, cements bonds by rewarding intimate encounters with feelings of warmth, closeness, and safety. The amygdala helps both humans and other animals to distinguish between appropriate and inappropriate social displays and between safe and unsafe social encounters.

Our survival is further assisted by our immune system as well as by a complex set of reflexes and the stress-related "fight or flight response." The immune system includes the skin and specialized cells for destroying foreign invaders such as bacteria, viruses, and cancer cells. Examples of self-protective reflexes include the startle response to sudden noise, the reaction of the pupil to light, and the patellar or "knee-jerk" reflex. The human stress response consists of both a short-term crisis reaction and a long-term adaptation process. At the first sign of danger, adrenaline is released, increasing heart rate, respiration, and the concentration of glucose in the blood. If the stress is ongoing, the endocrine system comes into play, resulting in the discharge of various stress hormones.

### Level 2: Nature and Nurture

The second level of the hope network consists of natural endowments and early nurturing experiences. Very early in life, individuals by nature demonstrate varying degrees of mastery and attachment motivation and different levels of stress tolerance.

Nevertheless, it is also true that human beings are among the most pliable of creatures, profoundly affected by early environmental influences. In short, the quantity and quality of social and spiritual nurturing that an individual receives will greatly affect that person's development of higher levels of the hope network.

A talent for mastery includes a sense of *goal directedness*. Psychologists refer to this in terms of greater or lesser amounts of "achievement motivation" while more poetically inclined observers wonder about an individual's depth of "vision" or "sense of purpose." Novelist Erica Jong opined, "everyone has talent" but not everyone has the ability to "follow the talent . . . where it leads."

Talent can be wasted in those who languish without direction, but if supported and guided, it can become the basis for the felt sense of purpose from which true mastery derives. In the Western world the need for formal apprenticeships does not receive enough attention. All too often, young people are inadequately mentored through high school and college only to encounter, when they graduate, confusion and existential angst about how best to make use of their talents as they move into the next phase of their lives. In contrast, the Ifa of Africa invoke an elaborate set of puberty rites to provide adolescents with the opportunity to participate in a symbolic bonding with, and separation from, their parents. This ritual is followed by a test of courage, then instruction by tribal elders, and finally initiation into the ways of securing the aid of various forces of nature. Many Hindu followers, on the other hand, seek direction from a personal guru to ensure their success in both the material and spiritual realms; in fact, *guru* in Sanskrit means both "teacher" and "heavy," the latter connotation referring to the weight that Hindus put on the advice they receive from their spiritual guides.

Sometimes goal directedness is present but lies dormant in the subconscious, ready to surface in the right medium or only apparent after the fact. Arthur Schopenhauer, the great mystical philosopher of the nineteenth century, suggested that destiny is often revealed in the wake of one's past events and actions. It is as if our hidden dreams have blazed a path and kept this secret from our conscious minds. His contemporary, Soren Kierkegaard put it more plainly when he wrote that life "must be lived forward" but can only be "understood backwards."

Trust and openness, the products of positive attachments to others, are indispensable in the formation of hope. These twin engines of emotional growth feed off of one another. Without openness, trust is stymied. Without trust, openness is shut down. In Marcel's view, openness "allows hope to spread," yielding the "fruits and pledges" of trust and continued openness. Personality researchers have found that openness is one of the most basic dimensions of personality. Genetic predispositions certainly play a role in personality development, but the quality of care and attention received early in life is also a factor.

Care and love as well as the experience of a spiritual presence, all of which are also connected to attachment, help to create the second level of the hope network. Erikson and others have described the childrearing process as a *dance of hope*. The new child, heralding promise and possibility, comes into the world equipped with ways of eliciting love and tender care. Parents, energized by this symbol of renewal, experience a way of reinvesting in themselves, their loved ones, and the world as a whole. And that investment may in turn nurture a spiritual sense in the child. Some of us come to speak of "blessings." Others come to explain the inexplicable—a narrowly averted tragedy, for example, or a chance encounter with a future mate or benefactor, or a golden opportunity that materialized without rhyme or reason—as a positive twist of fate. Still others may gain an intimate sense of an abiding presence in the form of a God or higher power.

Humans are exquisitely programmed for survival, for handling the strains and perils of life. These include the evils symbolized in the myth of Pandora, in the biblical tale of the Four Horsemen of the Apocalypse, and in the Buddha's reflections on pain, disease, and impermanence. On a psychological level, individuals are equipped with both coping skills, which are often learned, and defense mechanisms, which are usually rooted unconsciously in one's personality. Both can be summoned to defend oneself against harm.

Additional layers of protection are found in attachments and group memberships. As the saying goes, "there is strength in numbers"—be they birds that fly in tight formation, schools of fish, prides of lions, or packs of wolves. Human groups go further and devise sovereign nations with "departments of defense" and "border patrols." If pressed, a country may erect a "Great Wall" to protect itself from outside enemies or create a "Department of Homeland Security" to preempt the next terrorist attack.

Humanity has also sought assurance in the great religious and spiritual systems of the world. Although enormously diverse, all of them, from Buddhism to Catholicism, offer some form of salvation. Perhaps it is a heavenly reunion with God and loved ones who have died. Perhaps it is manifested through a belief in reincarnation or in a final release from want and suffering. Indeed, some scholars have even argued that the *main* function of these religious and spiritual beliefs is to provide the basic hope that one can transcend one's fears about life and death.

### Level 3: The Hopeful Core

The middle level of the hope network consists of three kinds of personality dispositions or traits. The first set is forged from the mastery and attachment motives in level 1 and yields an empowered mastery comprised in part of *goal-related trust* in oneself and others. The ongoing investments and perceived support of secular and sacred others inspire sanctioned commitments and higher aims.

*Mediated control* is a key component of facilitated mastery. At times, individuals may believe they are completely responsible for certain outcomes. In other circumstances, they may see themselves as the beneficiary or victim of outside forces, whether human, divine, or both. In the scientific literature, these two ends of the perceived control spectrum are called "internal control" and "external control." But hope frequently stems from a psychological middle ground, an experience of control that emerges from a felt association with a larger force or presence. The locus of control resides neither completely within nor completely outside of the self but is mediated through a valued relationship. This sense of shared power is the backbone of a healthy physician–patient relationship, a good bond between a psychotherapist and a client, or a positive student–teacher alliance. In the words of Pruyser, when hope is present, "the ego is not felt as a center of action." Instead, the process of hoping involves a powerful feeling of support by some benevolent force. Hope is a shared burden, a team effort.

The idea of empowered mastery has persisted for several millennia. Sophocles wrote, "Heaven helps not the men who will not act." St. Paul likewise declared, "I can do all things through Christ which strengtheneth me." The elegant sayings of the Tibetan monks have long included the following insight: "Men . . . by depending upon the Great, may prosper; a drop of water is a little thing, but when will it dry away if united to a lake?" A Qur'an prayer implores, "Add to my strength through him and make him share my task." William James discussed the "more" in religious experiences, the sense of union with a power that is simultaneously beyond us and at the same time felt as part of our core.

The second category of hope traits emanates from the attachment motive and includes *relational trust* based on openness and disclosure as well as intimacy and appreciation. Hopeful individuals trust in the availability of a valued person or transcendent presence. They maintain *openness* towards the object of trust, striving for increasingly deeper levels of intimacy. Their reward is a constant ally, such as a Christian "shepherd," Hindu "inner god," or Native American "guiding spirit." Hope is about connection.

Hope is also about *self–other bonds*. The development of these bonds begins in a forgotten infancy, in a psychic fusion of self and caregiver that attachment theorists call the "self-object." By unconsciously joining with an ever-present caregiver, the infant's emerging self is buttressed. In some form, this process endures throughout life. As individuals join with significant others, they can forge a sense of self that is transformed by an ongoing sense of presence and unity.

The third set of hope traits in level 3 springs from attachment and survival-based experiences. Together, they provide a way of addressing the major challenges of the human condition: fear, pain, loss, and death. *Survival-oriented trust* is a general sense of assurance that your welfare matters to some other person, group, or higher power. When you need help, care and protection can be found; you will not be abandoned.

A capacity for *terror management* helps the individual to remain resilient and centered in the midst of a crisis (i.e., self-regulated). One is neither overaroused nor paralyzed by the crisis, nor does one deny or have false hopes about its significance. On the contrary, true hope flows from an enhanced perspective that incorporates one's sense of vulnerability and finiteness within a resilient frame of mind capable of facing the crisis resolutely. In a hopeful person, fear may be replaced by tranquility and the comfort that a benign higher reality exists, that there is always a chance for liberation. The German poet Johann Goethe listed, among his "nine prerequisites for a good life," "hope enough to remove all anxious fears."

Sustaining hope in the midst of pain and suffering also requires mindfulness—a full understanding of the nature and meaning of any potential threat of harm or loss and an awareness of any and all opportunities for growth, transcendence, and spiritual transformation. A mindful approach can give rise to a profound sense of *spiritual integrity,* a feeling of wholeness and continuity across space and time that physical insult and loss cannot easily violate. Old age, disease, or serious injury may threaten anyone's sense of integrity, but in the hopeful individual, a deeper spiritual core exists, relatively untouched by declining physical strength or sudden disfigurement.

*Symbolic immortality*—the legacy one hopes to leave behind after death—is acquired by investing one's life and self in a continuum of more enduring aspects of reality—in loved ones, for example, or in long-term projects or cherished institutions. Death is transcended by sharing one's wealth—love, talent, and so on—with others during life, by releasing all that lies trapped in one's "mortal coil." Christian philosophers such as Marcel as well as atheistic scientists like Erik Erikson agreed on this point. So did Rabbi Mordecai Kaplan, who viewed "God" and "religion" as "living energy" residing in people and groups; to him, "God" was both a process and a means for delivering hope through creativity, integration, love, and justice.

### Level 4: The Faith System

Faith is the fruit that grows from the seeds of trust, mediated control, and self–other bonds. When tested, faith discloses whether a person has adopted a mindful approach to pain and suffering. Faith is a barometer of an individual's terror management capacities, and it reveals the presence or absence of spiritual integrity and symbolic immortality. Faith is the bedrock of hope. Kahlil Gibran called it "an oasis in the heart." "Without it," wrote Mary McLeod Bethune, a daughter of former slaves who became a prominent educator and political activist, "nothing is possible. With it, nothing is impossible."

In later chapters, we explore the many types of faith ("centers of values") that can enter into the development of hope. Here we note simply that faith is the only hope-building block that spans all three of the motive systems in level 1: that is, it can be developed through mastery, attachment, or survival experiences. However, faith cannot thrive in a climate of denial. Moreover, if an individual is completely devoid of faith, he or she will likely be plagued by a chronic sense of hopelessness. True faith (like hope) calls for a willingness to remain fully engaged in the task of living. Psychologist Ann Kaiser Stearns recounted the experience of Steven and Naomi Shelton, a young couple whose faith was severely tested when their first child was stillborn. After a year of mourning, they found renewed hope in genetic counseling and were then able to take an even greater leap of faith, soon conceiving another child.

## Level 5: Beliefs and Behaviors

The building blocks and traits we have outlined give rise to beliefs, feelings, and actions that are the manifestations or exterior signs of hope. They are its "lights and outward flourishes," the visible signs of hope that spring from the various levels of the hope network.

From a strong foundation of mastery and its building blocks, we develop the belief that we are empowered. It is a belief instilled by faith, trust, and guidance, and it is accessed through a felt inner strength. To Reverend August Gold, that strength is spiritual in nature:

> It is only when we believe we are separate from Spirit that we remain ill, ill-at-ease, frightened, weak, powerless, tied to the past, resentful, stuck, hopeless. It is the belief that we are separate from Spirit that leaves us unable to release the powerful healing life-force in us and through us.

Mastery-related hope involves a sense of being "raised" or "lifted up" as, for example, when a positive event occurs or an encouraging word is given that supports and advances our higher goals. Erikson believed that this notion of an "elevated" hope was attributable in part to the upward gazes of tiny infants lying on their backs, looking at a seemingly all-powerful provider. Other experiences undoubtedly add to a sense of supportive hope as well. Every brush with a concerned person, group, or perceived spiritual presence elevates the spirit further, engendering high hopes.

From a strong foundation of attachment and its building blocks, we can develop a belief that we are part of something larger than ourselves, that "somewhere in the universe there is a benign force." To retain that feeling of connectedness, hopeful individuals demonstrate their openness by actively seeking or recruiting signs and symbols of hope. For example, Lila Jane Givens, a breast cancer survivor, found a symbol of hope in her grandmother, who despite two mastectomies, lived past the age of 100. Majorie Mowlam, when she was Britain's Secretary of State to embattled Northern Ireland, discovered hope in a bunch of flowers left outside the famed Hillsborough Castle. They had been placed there after a bomb had ripped through an apartment, horribly burning three boys.

From a strong foundation of survival and its building blocks, we develop a belief that protection is possible and indeed available when needed. We believe in the continuance of all that is good in the world. We feel safe. In times of calamity, a hopeful individual can remain centered on tasks and priorities without being cast physically, emotionally, or spiritually adrift. In contrast, hopeless individuals are often stuck in their tracks, frozen with dread. In *Hidden Spring*, Sandy Boucher chronicled her confrontation with cancer. Expressing her Buddhist beliefs, she wrote, "When I received the news of cancer, I understood that what is required of me now is that I be fully present to each new experience as it comes and that I engage with it as completely as I can."

---

*Second Hope Meditation*

As you have learned, there are many different ways of imagining hope. Some thinkers have favored a more goal-oriented hope, while others have focused primarily on attachment or survival concerns. How do these varied ways of explaining hope align with your own experiences? Specifically, which approach is the closest fit with your sense of hope? Write down the name of the theorist or approach you liked the best, then indicate your second- and third-place finishers. You may also want to revisit the most significant hopes you recollected in the meditation in Chapter 1. Can you match up each of your hope experiences with one or more of the perspectives described in this chapter? What are you learning about the ways in which you hope? Are you primarily oriented toward mastery? Are attachment concerns more pressing? Is survival the dominant issue in your life? Or are your hopes oriented around two or more of these motives?

# Three

## PILLARS OF HUMANITY: HOPE ACROSS TIME

> First came famine, and then toil, disease, strife, wounds, and ghastly
> death . . . then the Titans brought shafts of frost and fire, sending the
> shelterless, pale tribes to mountain caves . . . Prometheus saw, and waked the
> *legioned hopes* which sleep within folded Elysian flowers . . . That they might
> hide with thin and rainbow wings the shape of death . . . love he sent to bind
> the disunited tendrils of . . . the human heart . . . he tamed fire . . . and
> tortured to his will iron and gold, the slaves and signs of power.
>
> —Percy Shelley, *Prometheus Unbound*

Arguably, the greatest sources of human joy and suffering are rooted in the three motives that underlie hope: mastery, attachment, and survival. More time and energy goes into understanding, controlling, satisfying, sustaining, repairing, and honoring these *motivational vital signs* than any others. Indeed, we have a natural inclination to gravitate toward moving accounts of these very forces.

Five of the top-rated films of all time, for example, are *Citizen Kane, The Godfather, Lawrence of Arabia, Casablanca,* and *Gone with the Wind,* each in their own way a compelling story of one or more of the vital motives, whether thwarted or triumphant. Consider *Citizen Kane*: Beneath the obvious power imagery is a story of frustrated attachment and longing. In one scene an old man reflects on a beautiful girl he glimpsed only fleetingly as a youth, realizing he has thought of her every day for more than 50 years. The most often cited scene in the film is also dominated by a sense of loss and lament. Charles Foster Kane, the great publishing magnate, is shown lying in bed, drawing his last breath and pining for his "Rosebud," the simple wooden sled he cherished as a little boy.

But fictional treatments of our abiding hope motives are nothing compared to what can happen in real life. Did you read about the temporary reunion of families that was permitted by the governments of North and South Korea in 2002? Can you imagine a sadder scene? Parents and children as well as brothers and sisters who had been forcibly separated for five decades were allowed only a 72-hour visit. This brief experience of intimacy proved too excruciating for many of the family members. Soon after returning to their respective sides of the border, many became deeply depressed.

There are few things more gripping than a dramatic tale of survival. In one such story, also in 2002, 89-year-old Edwin Holba was riding a farm tractor when his foot slipped off the clutch. The tractor rolled backward, pinning his wife, Florence, underneath. To make matters worse Edwin fell while getting off the vehicle, further damaging his already feeble legs. Unable to walk, he crawled on the ground for 23 hours to get help.

George Orwell, the author of *1984*, also wrote one of the most profound reflections on the will to live. As a policeman in India during the 1930s, he was obligated to witness a public execution, which he then documented in an essay titled simply *The Hanging*. He quoted a boy who had been present when the prisoner learned that his appeal had been denied. The boy told Orwell, "He pissed on the floor of his cell." Later, Orwell followed the doomed man to the scaffold, studying his hair, the muscles on his back, his Hindu profile. He remembered a dog jumping in the middle of the procession, trying to lick the prisoner's face. The death march continued. Suddenly, "in spite of the men who gripped him by each shoulder," the doomed man "stepped slightly aside to avoid a puddle." Wrote Orwell, "When I saw the prisoner step aside to avoid the puddle, I saw the mystery, the unspeakable wrongness, of cutting a life short when it is in full tide."

In this chapter, we explore in greater depth the origins of hope as well as humanity's profound investment in sustaining a constant supply of attachment, mastery, and survival lessons. Consciously or unconsciously, individually or as a collective, humans seek to perpetuate symbols of hope. The ancient writer, Pliny the elder, went further, suggesting that hope is "the pillar that upholds the world." Many centuries later Martin Luther agreed, declaring that "everything that is done in the world is done by hope." And in his Nobel Prize acceptance speech (1950), the novelist William Faulkner commented in particular on the artist's cultural obligations to share the gift of hope and exhorted the aspiring writer to focus on "the old verities and truths of the heart. . . . Until he does so, he writes not of love but of lust, of defeats in which nobody loses anything of value, and victories without hope . . . His griefs grieve on no universal bones." According to Faulkner, it is the artist's "privilege to help man endure by lifting his heart, by reminding him of courage and honor and hope and pride and compassion and pity and sacrifice which have been the glory of his past." For Faulkner, the "poet's voice" was not merely "a record of humankind" but "one of the props . . . the pillars to help humankind endure and prevail."

From prehistoric times to the dawn of civilization and on to the present day, ordinary men and women as well as famous artists, philosophers, and scientists have each contributed in their own ways to the higher goal of "keeping hope alive." This chapter examines some of these contributions against a broad evolutionary context, ultimately focusing on selections from the written record on hope from the past 4,000 years. We then look at the darker side of the hope saga, a different sort of literature, to shed light on the tragic consequences that have occurred in recent history when the underpinnings of hope were disrupted and humanity failed in its "hope mission."

## Evolution of Hope

The word which God has written on the brow of every man is hope.
—Victor Hugo

Hope is a universal emotion. Goethe called it a "second soul." Hope is a mainstay of Chinese farmers planting their seedlings of rice in the murky waters of Shanghai. Hope "centers" the dedicated Hindu meditating by the Ganges. Hope is summoned by Native Americans as they practice their ritual offerings to nature and is recruited by African shaman imploring the assistance of their spiritual benefactors. We trust in the poet's insight, as suggested by Goethe and Shelley, that hope is part of human nature, and that it literally, as well as figuratively, springs eternal in the human breast.

However, not everyone shares this primordial view. In *The Gift of the Jews*, Thomas Cahill suggested that 3,000 years ago a new worldview, one envisioning that humanity could play a role in shaping the future, paved the way for an entirely different form of hope. According to him, ancient Jewish culture, by transforming our conceptions of time, history, and future from cyclical to linear, was responsible for bequeathing a new, "progressive hope."

Cahill's "hope thesis" is debatable. First, many cultures that are identified as having a cyclical worldview embrace the deeper notion of a "spiral" of progression that will presumably manifest over a longer time frame. For example, in most of Asia, the dominant Theraveda and Mahayana Buddhist traditions emphasize the notion of progression to higher levels of spiritual being via successive reincarnations. Second, hope appears to be a virtually universal experience. In Africa, the Swahili speak of "matumaini," while in Asia the Japanese refer to "kibo." Hope is found throughout the Middle East and Europe; the Turks call it "umit," the Persians "omid," the Poles "nadzieja," the Italians "esperanza," and the Germans "hoffnung."

Third, there is compelling support for the primacy of hope in the context of human evolution. For example, the anthropologist Lionel Tiger related the emergence of hope-related thought processes to geographical changes. He believed that two prehistoric shifts in the physical environment were responsible for important alterations in the human capacity to experience particular emotions. In the first, the transition from forests to the grasslands several million years ago marked the start of the hunter-gatherer phase of human evolution. From his perspective, this change necessitated the development of brain structures for planning and forethought. The second shift occurred with the advent of an agricultural existence, approximately 10,000 years ago. Tiger speculated that this new way of life required more than just planning ability. The act of sowing seeds, waiting for a harvest, and remaining in the same locale for the next planting season could only occur if there was now a human propensity toward viewing the future as benign. Tiger suggested that this new way of experiencing the future might be due to a second major expansion of the frontal lobes.

Nevertheless, we believe that Tiger, like Cahill, may have underestimated the hopefulness of our earlier ancestors and that the origins of hope are much older than either of them envisioned. Drawing on the latest developments in evolutionary biology, cultural anthropology, neuroscience, and philosophy, we have put together a plausible evolution of hope, as shown in Table 3.1. The time frames are gross approximations, calculated by averaging the different time estimates that experts across various disciplines have given for each era.

To focus on the main highlights of this timeline: The chimpanzees that appeared on earth 6 million years ago were the first species to possess all of the hope pre-adaptations. Then and now, they exhibit traces of foresight in the mastery domain (preparing tools in advance of gathering food). They were the first species to cluster in permanent social groups and are subject to grief-like reactions following separation and loss. They express fear when threatened. But does the chimpanzee have the actual ability to hope? We are not aware of any specific attempts to answer this question via experimentation. We hypothesize that chimpanzees can anticipate the continuation of a well-established pattern or make simple preparations for the immediate future (a few hours or so), but we would not otherwise attribute hope to this species.

The next significant step in the development of hope occurred approximately 1 million years ago with the advent of *Homo erectus*. In this species we see major advances in both the mastery and attachment domains. They created advanced tools and engaged in long-distance hunting. The utterances of their predecessor, *Homo habilis*, now gave way to rudimentary forms of speech. Kin obligations and community taboos made for a more complex social life.

Approximately 150,000 years ago, the Neanderthal species appeared. The brains of Neanderthal were a little bigger than *Homo erectus*, and they are credited with the controlled use of fire. To this day, experts argue over the spiritual capacities of

TABLE 3.1. *Hypothesized Evolution of Hope*

| Species/Years. Ago | Brain Changes | Mastery | Attachment | Survival | Hope |
|---|---|---|---|---|---|
| Pan Troglodyte (Chimpanzee) 6,000,000 | Significant expansion of cerebral cortex | Foresight; tool-making | Close mother–infant bonds; permanent social groups | Grief-like reactions; fear when threatened | First species with all hope "pre-adaptations" |
| *Homo habilis* 2,000,000 | 30% increase in overall size of brain | Stone tools; simple weapons | Utterances; division of labor | Grief; fear of present dangers | |
| *Homo erectus* 1,500,000 | More parietal, occipital, and temporal area | Distance hunting; better tools | Speech; kin obligations; social taboos | Fear of imminent dangers | Emergence of a goal and attachment-based hope |
| Neanderthal 150,000 | Modestly larger frontal lobes | Imaginative capacities; use of fire | Care of elders and the injured; ritual burials | Grief; fear of imagined dangers | |
| 60,000 40,000–50,000 | Dating of possible "spiritual burial" in Shanidar, Iraq<br>Evolution of self-consciousness (e.g., jewelry, body ornaments) | | | | Externalized memory systems (art and symbols) |
| Cro-Magnon 40,000 | Vastly larger frontal lobes and cerebellum | Long-term plans; deeper sense of time | Ancestors preserved via art and tombs | Terror management requirements | Dawn of a full hope experience |
| 25,000–40,000 5,000 2,500 | Cave art of Lascaux; undisputed spiritual burial at Sungir, Russia<br>Great Pyramids of Giza; Stonehenge site prepared<br>Major religious, spiritual, and philosophical systems appear | | | | Social investment in, and construction of, hope |

this primitive human. For example, the discovery of flower pollens in a Neanderthal grave at Shanidar, Iraq, initially led many to presume that religious or spiritual beliefs were present. But scholars have debated the meaning of the pollens: some believe they were part of a planned ritual; others believe they indicate a coincidental comingling of nature. We would in any case not hypothesize a major hope transition from *Homo erectus* to Neanderthal. Rather, the evidence suggests the emergence and gradual evolution of a mastery and attachment-based form of hope starting approximately 1 million years ago and continuing through the evolution of the Neanderthal species.

Departing from Tiger's estimations, a number of prominent anthropologists now believe that significant changes in the Cro-Magnon brain occurred not 10,000 years ago but more like 25,000 to 40,000 years ago. In addition, the latest evidence suggests that the "agricultural evolution" occurred sometime during the second half of the Cro-Magnon era. Anatomically, the Neanderthal and Cro-Magnon brains were approximately the same overall size. However, the prefrontal area of the Cro-Magnon brain was much larger, suggesting a huge increase in higher-level cognitive functions such as planning, developing goals, and choosing among alternatives. In addition, the Cro-Magnon cerebellum was significantly bigger than the Neanderthal version, indicating a greater capacity for time perception.

In the era of Cro-Magnon, we see the dawn of a full experience of hope, rooted in attachment, mastery, and survival needs. In short, Tiger was correct in attributing a new level of emotional intelligence to this species. But we believe that this and other hope-related developments associated with Cro-Magnon occurred much earlier. Many scholars now believe that symbolic capacities, so critical to the generation of hope, originated before but progressed rapidly during this time period. These capacities were *external memory systems*, that is, visual symbols and written records.

More compellingly, Cro-Magnon's terror-management needs, the final piece of the motivational puzzle, were in full force by this time. Consider that the best evidence we now have for a spiritual burial is a 23,000-year-old Cro-Magnon grave found at Sungir, on the outskirts of Moscow. Two children are laid head to head in a line, dressed in ivory jewelry and armed with weapons of mammoth bone. This may be as close as we will come to marking the dawn of a consciousness capable of understanding the finitude of existence and the need for a full experience of hope.

Tiger and others have assumed that the evolution of human intelligence and consciousness ended with Cro-Magnon. Some scholars, for example, have correctly noted that there is little evidence of significant brain alterations or genetic transformations from the Cro-Magnon period to today. Nevertheless, we believe that subtle but important evolutionary changes since the time of Cro-Magnon have prompted corresponding shifts in degrees of consciousness, levels of self-awareness, and complexity of emotional experience.

Drawing on the theories of physiologist Jared Diamond, psychologist Merlin Donald, and others, we believe that cultural shifts as well as physical changes in the landscape can trigger a host of behavioral changes and that the notion of *symmetrical co-evolution* is possible—that is, the idea that depth of changes in brain anatomy and physiology parallel the degree of shift in ecological pressures. The more punctuated and dramatic brain transformations, such as those found in Cro-Magnon, were likely the result of profound climatic changes. Since the time of Cro-Magnon, however, the environmental changes have been more technological and cultural and the corresponding brain changes have thus been more graduated, probably in the organization of the left and right hemispheres and in the reordering of neural circuits dealing with problem solving, imagination, speech, and memory.

The first subtle change that probably affected hope occurred about 10,000 years ago when a hunter-gatherer existence was replaced by permanent agricultural settlements. More than likely, the attachment system was most affected by this development, as evidenced by fossils and artifacts of this period that suggest an increasing concern for the welfare of elders and disabled members of the community.

Approximately 5,000 years ago, the first mummies were prepared and burials took place in stone tombs rather than simple holes that were dug in the sand, dirt, and rock. The pyramids of Giza appeared, along with the first signs of construction at Stonehenge. What was taking place in the human mind? These developments suggest a small but potentially important change in the self-protective system, perhaps involving another refinement of the cerebellum and time perception. Such changes may well have been triggered by what Merlin Donald refers to as a second phase in the progression of external memory systems. Specifically, when the interplay between genetic changes and environmental challenges led to written records, an even greater demand was placed on the brain's capacity to remember both place and time. A side effect of this heightened awareness of past, present, and future may have been the need for stronger terror-management skills.

The final chapter in the evolution of hope began roughly 2,000–4,000 years ago. This time frame coincides with the period that psychologist Julian Jaynes associated with the "breakdown of the bicameral mind," a controversial theory based on his interpretation of ancient Greek epics such as Homer's *Iliad* and *Odyssey*. Jaynes proposed that the omnipresent gods of Greek myth were the product of utterances recorded by the brain's left hemisphere, emanating from an independently functioning right hemisphere. According to Jaynes, Homer's lament over the gods' apparent abandonment of humanity reflects the disappearance of those utterances from the human mind: the gods "disappeared," in other words, when the hemispheres united, the speech center was preserved on the left side, and the right side was effectively silenced.

We take a different view. A less dramatic form of brain reorganization probably did occur around this time, affecting primarily the mastery system. The triggers were probably several, including the increased complexity of social systems in terms of stratification into economic levels, the greater contact between cultures and their competition for resources, and the emergence of new technologies, such as the first successful smelting of iron, immortalized in Shelley's *Prometheus Unbound*. In Merlin Donald's theory, this era marked the third phase in the development of the external memory system, the production of theories. These are represented in the grand religious, spiritual, and philosophical systems of the ancient Greeks, of Buddhism and Confucianism, of Ifa and Judaism, and so on.

The formal emergence of these belief systems raises some interesting questions about the evolved capacity of the human brain during this period to experience hope in all its various guises. Was the hope blueprint of mastery, attachment, and survival now so deeply etched within the structure of our DNA as to allow, at the highest level of the hope experience, for feelings of empowerment, connection, and salvation? Are we hardwired to encounter those powerful and yet seemingly ineffable feelings of awe and reassurance that we call the "numinous"?

Certainly, a small group of scientists, working in the field of "*neurotheology*," have suggested that the basis for believing in a higher power may reside in the very architecture of the human brain. For example, Eugene d'Aquili, a psychiatrist and anthropologist, developed a theory in the 1970s that the brain may be hardwired to believe in God. He suggested that a unique activation of brain processes underlies transcendent experiences across time, cultures, and varieties of faith. D'Aquili sought an anatomical and physiological explanation that would embrace the Buddhist's "Nirvana," the Catholic's "state of grace," the Native American's communion with "the great spirit," and the Ifa's encounters with "Olorun." Using the latest available imaging techniques, he teamed up with radiologist Andrew Newberg to capture brain activity during moments of spiritual contemplation. Brain scans of Tibetan Buddhists and Franciscan nuns involved in deep meditation and prayer revealed a similar "symphony of neuronal activation."

Newberg cites additional evidence that, when a transcendent experience reaches its zenith, changes occur in three key brain sites involved in the activation of mastery, attachment, and survival behaviors: the frontal areas, the parietal lobes, and the limbic system. Such changes in the frontal areas, usually associated with planning and making life choices, can contribute to a sense of peace and acceptance. Lessened activity in the parietal lobes, which are responsible for the distinction between "self" and the world, has been linked to the temporary dissolution of ego boundaries, allowing for a powerful sense of connection with nature and the divine. And a quieting of certain structures in the limbic system, the brain's "emotion center," has been implicated in the diminishment of fears and an increased sense of well-being.

Neuroscientist Michael Persinger has insisted that his research proves religion is simply "a property of the brain, only the brain, and has little to do with what's out there." Some popular writers on the topic have coined such phrases as "your brain on religion" or "your brain on God." Needless to say, these assertions infuriate many devout believers, who view the idea that "God" is a biochemical illusion as nothing more than an attempt to reduce religious experience to nature's version of a "spiritual trip."

In their defense, believers could cite theologians and religious scholars such as James Fowler and Huston Smith, who unwaveringly posited a transcendent plane of reality that is equal or superior to our material world. Or they could cite William James, who insisted that scientific explanations of the personal or subjective aspects of religious life did not rule out the possibility of objective religious experience. Consistent with this point of view, Andrew Newberg stated, "There is no way to determine whether the neurological changes...mean that the brain is causing those experiences." Science writer Sharon Begley agreed, concluding her provocative *Newsweek* article on the topic with a similar challenge:

> For all the tentative successes that scientists are scoring in their search for the biological bases of religious, spiritual and mystical experience, one mystery will surely lie forever beyond their grasp. They may trace a sense of transcendence to this bulge in our gray matter ... a feeling of the divine to [other neural tissues]. But it is likely that they will never resolve the greatest question of all—namely, whether our brain-wiring creates God, or whether God created our brain-wiring.

Our conceptualization of hope suggests a different way of looking at these mind–spirit interactions. Fundamentally, we do not believe that spiritual experiences are merely the random and purposeless side effect of human brain wiring. Instead, we believe that the activation of neuronal circuits occurs in the context of groups invested in jump-starting the motives underlying hope. As Table 3.2 suggests, the rites and ceremonies of the world's spiritual belief systems can be thought of as means for eliciting *spiritualized hope experiences*.

## From the Archives of Hope

With the emergence of external memory systems, the written or otherwise symbolically rendered record of human experience began and subsequently evolved into a prodigious body of work. That work, of course, encompasses an extensive historical archive on hope, including various writings we cite throughout this book to illustrate specific points about the hope experience. Now, to round out our survey of the evolution of hope and to explore its latest chapter, we examine highlights from that archive—that is, some of the lessons in hope that the best art, philosophy, and science have given us over the past 4,000 years. Presented roughly according to their emphases on specific motives in the hope blueprint, these lessons come from three eras: the period from antiquity through the

TABLE 3.2. *Neurotheology of Spiritual Hope Experiences*

| Underlying Motives | Cultural Rituals and Practices | Brain Areas and Processes | Hope Concepts and *Feelings* |
|---|---|---|---|
| Mastery | Deep contemplation | Prefrontal changes | Mediated control |
| | Purposeful chanting | Frontal lobe alterations | A higher purpose |
| | Acts of supplication | Temporal lobe shifts | *Uplifted* |
| | Controlled postures | Increased alpha | *Supported* |
| | Totem offerings | Amplified theta | *Empowered* |
| Attachment | Group prayers | Parietal dampening | Trust |
| | Communion exercises | Right brain access | Openness |
| | Pipe ceremonies | Brain wave synchrony | *Loved* |
| | Drum circles | Choreography of bodies | *Touched* |
| | Hallucinogen usage | Emotional contagion | *Unified* |
| Survival | Banishing evil spirits | Amygdala quieting | Terror management |
| | Amulets or talismans | Increased GABA | Self-regulation |
| | Healing ceremonies | Elevated serotonin | *Calm* |
| | Cleansing rituals | Heightened delta | *Safe* |
| | Entraining to rhythms | Rising theta | *Protected* |

Middle Ages, the post-Renaissance period, and the twentieth century. Our discussion of this last period, which heralded the arrival of psychology as a formal discipline, dovetails somewhat with our review of the science of hope in the previous chapter.

## From Antiquity through the Middle Ages: 1600 B.C.–1250 A.D.
### Survival

Some of the earliest writings on record address the survival motive. In Egypt, at the start of the eighteenth dynasty (1600 B.C.), the *Egyptian Book of the Dead* was assembled by three unknown scribes. For centuries, it would serve as an indispensable manual for negotiating the afterlife, providing spells, formulas, and maps of the spirit world. Scribes and priests offered simple versions for the lower class and ornate, lavishly illustrated copies for important officials and members of the ruling family.

A similar tradition of literary terror-management arose in the remote mountains of Tibet. The widely cited *Tibetan Book of the Dead* originated in the eighth century A.D. It provides instructions on what to expect at the moment of death and during the 49 days of "Bardo," the intermediate resting time for the soul before its next rebirth. It also attempts, in contrast to the earlier Egyptian writings, to facilitate multiple levels of "soul transformations," including various forms of spiritual renewal as well as transcendence of physical death. For spiritual growth, it promoted a higher level of psychic awareness through integration of the conscious with the unconscious. Because of its strong emphasis on a never-ending hope, some Tibetan scholars have renamed this text, *The Tibetan Book for Living and Dying.*

Classical Greek writers also took into account the instinct for self-preservation. In *Antigone* (440 B.C.), Sophocles celebrated humanity's "undying hopeful spirit." He eloquently captured the endless adaptations that mortals have made in negotiating the harshest of environments, including their ability to "flee the arrows of the frost, when 'tis hard lodging under the clear sky, and the arrows of the rushing rain." The stoics wrote extensively about "terror" and other adaptive and maladaptive emotions. According to Chrysippus, "fear" and its derivatives—"apprehension," "hesitation," "shame," "perplexity," "trepidation," and "anxiety"—were irrational and should be eliminated. However, "caution" was viewed as a rational and adaptive disposition that should be retained in the face of "legitimate threats."

### Attachment

Attachment was very much on the minds of the ancient Chinese and Greeks. By 450 B.C. Confucius had codified the principle of "jen," the ideal or prototype for relating to others. "Jen" was the linchpin of a philosophical system designed to inspire a "community of hope." It encompassed "benevolence," "humanity," and "moral goodness." Although rooted in the attachment drive, it depended on the cultivation of numerous social skills. These included ways of comporting oneself in the presence of benefactors and political officials as well as showing proper respect to grieving or handicapped members of one's society.

Plato's *Symposium* (380 B.C.) was dedicated to the topic of love. Twelve men are gathered at a banquet in honor of a prominent Athenian. One of the guests, a physician, suggested that they exchange thoughts on the nature of love. In the course of their discussion, they dealt with a number of enduring issues, including the link between human and divine love, the potential healing power of relationships, and the existence of "soul-mates."

When the political philosophers of this era drafted their plans for erecting "cities of hope," they invariably highlighted the need to preserve and protect human attachments. In the fourth century B.C., Aristotle assumed that kinship bonds surpassed even the needs for wealth and power: "No one would choose the whole world on condition of being alone . . . man is a political creature and one whose nature is to live with others." Elsewhere, Aristotle questioned the humanity of anyone who could live apart from others: "He who is unable to live in society, or who has no need because he is sufficient for himself, must be either a beast or a god."

In *The Enneads* (250 A.D.), Plotinus found a way to ground his Christian hope by affirming the value of friendship and sexual bonds. He argued that such relationships are right and just if rooted in natural inclinations. Friendship should be based on a desire to be "knit in the closest union with beauty," while sexual desire ought to be reserved for the evolutionary purpose of species and self-perpetuation. For Plotinus, "as long as they are led by these motives, both [friendship and sexual relations] are on the right path."

Attachment concerns rose to prominence in the Middle Ages with the Sufi sect in the Middle East. Alghazzali (1058–1111), the philosopher-mathematician, rejected all secular approaches to hope in favor of a mystical reunion with God. Following in this early romantic tradition is the great Sufi master and poet of love, Mevlana Jalaluddin Rumi (1207–1273). In his words, "Everything other than love for the most beautiful God is agony of the spirit . . . an advance toward death without seizing hold of the water of life."

## Mastery

The golden era of mastery occurred between 400 and 200 B.C. Plato fashioned his tripartite soul to include emotion, desire, and reason. The feeling part was entirely mastery oriented, consisting of ambition and courage. Desire referred to an attachment-based sexual appetite as well as other basic affiliation needs. And reason assured some control over these impulses, serving much like a charioteer harnessing a team of wild stallions.

One of Plato's most famous *Dialogues* (380 B.C.) dealt with the nature of courage, an often ignored component of hope-centered mastery. His ideas were presented in the form of a debate between his mentor Socrates and a student Laches. Put in modern psychological terms, Socrates aimed to challenge the adequacy of Laches' courage schema. At one point, Laches suggested that "courage is a sort of endurance of the soul," to which Socrates responded that "not every form of endurance is to be deemed courage."

In all of the ancient literature, it is hard to find a more poetic expression of "hope-driven mastery" than the following passage in Sophocles' *Antigone*:

> Wonders are many, and none is more wonderful than man; the power that crosses the white sea, making a path under surges that threaten to engulf him . . . [He rules] the Earth, the eldest of the gods by turning the soil with the offspring of horses, as the ploughs go to and fro from year to year . . . man excellent in wit . . . masters the beast whose lair is in the wilds . . . he tames the horse of shaggy mane, he puts the yoke upon its neck, he tames the tireless mountain bull . . . speech, wind-swift thought, and all the moods that mould a state, hath he taught himself . . . yea, he hath resource for all.

Two of the most influential writings on "empowered hope" appeared in China between 500 and 200 B.C. Lao Tzu's *The Way and Its Power* challenged the orthodox recipes for mastery and offered a means of indirectly achieving one's aims through nonviolence, working with nature, and self-discipline. Zung Tzu's military masterpiece, *The Art of War*, dating from around 200 B.C., continues to fascinate generals and politicians, as well as business leaders, coaches, and athletes.

Another millennium would pass before the next great treatise on power would emerge. The lessons would come from the Middle East, in the writings of Al-Farabi (870–950 A.D.). An early Muslim philosopher, he described the ideal city-state and the qualities of an effective "hope provider." Rejecting Plato's notion of a philosopher-king, Al-Farabi insisted that an effective ruler must derive power from the higher intellect of God.

The fifth-century Christian philosopher St. Augustine was tormented for years with spiritual uncertainty. On one hand, he had an intellectual desire to believe in God. On the other, he had insufficient faith to forge a genuine commitment. His persistence in "mastering" his ambivalence was ultimately rewarded by a powerful mystical experience. He found himself "lost" in a "spiritual merger" with God. In his *Confessions*, he argued that willpower is one of the few traits of the soul that cannot be denied and that must be cultivated if humanity desires to realize the "hope for spiritual oneness."

In the Middle Ages, the dominant European intellectual figure was St. Thomas Aquinas. In *Summa Theologica* (1274), he argued that the feeling aspects of the soul could be divided into simple perceptions and primary emotions. The various human affections, including "hope," were further sorted in terms of a person's relationship to the object of his or her passion, whether it was something desired or feared, and in terms of the difficulty or ease in obtaining or avoiding that passion. More than any other premodern thinker, Aquinas anticipated the need to include multiple dimensions of goal attainment when trying to explain hope-based mastery.

## Post-Renaissance: 1650–1900

While it resulted in stunning transformations in art and culture, the Renaissance did not initially yield major advances in psychological theory. The first significant contributions came in the middle of the 1600s with the philosophical writings of René Descartes and Thomas Hobbes. The great minds of this period still referred to the "soul," but they were beginning to explore emotions and motives in increasingly greater detail, incorporating many of the anatomical and physiological findings generated by their contemporaries in medicine and science. In *Passions of the Soul* (1650), for example, Descartes gave a detailed presentation of how the mind and body act upon one another. Discussing the influences of the emotions on the intellect, he suggested that "the passions in man . . . incite and dispose the mind to will the things to which they prepare the body, so that the sentiment of fear incites it to will to fly; that of courage, to will to fight; and so of the rest."

## Mastery

In eighteenth-century China, an early self-help book offered hope by stressing self-disciplined mastery. Chang Nai Zhou was a classics scholar and martial arts master who descended from rulers of the Ming Dynasty. In *Chang Family Boxing*, Nai Zhou focused primarily on the development of techniques for hand-to-hand combat, but he also incorporated the wisdom of the *I Ching* as well as other available Chinese philosophical and medical texts.

In the West, interest in human mastery peaked in the nineteenth century. The best known writings are those of Alexander Bain, whose two volumes, *The Senses and the Intellect* (1855) and *The Emotions and the Will* (1859), served as the primary psychology references for more than three decades. Bain's second volume included chapters on the emotions of wonder, power, and pursuit. Wonder, like courage, is another forgotten element of the hope experience. A moment of wonder, to paraphrase Rumi, can serve as a "spiritual portal" for those on the brink of a transcendent hope experience. In his description of wonder, Bain observed how "respiration is stimulated . . . the arms and hands are acted on in the way of being spread or extended . . . [there is a] rounding and protrusion of the mouth . . . the voice sends out a sudden cry."

Among Bain's contemporaries, the most passionate advocates of a power-oriented approach to mastery were the German philosophers Arthur Schopenhauer and Friedrich Nietzsche. Rejecting the eighteenth-century emphasis on rationality, Schopenhauer argued that philosophy, logic, reason, and character were ultimately products of the human will. As a young man in Frankfurt, Nietzsche was heading off to war when he came across the spectacle of an imposing military procession. He would later write, "I felt for the first time that the strongest and highest will to life does not find expression in a miserable struggle for existence, but in a will to war, a will to power, a will to overpower!"

## Survival

Thomas Hobbes asserted in the seventeenth century that the need for self-preservation was "a right of nature," so vital to humanity it resulted in "neither the power nor wish to do otherwise." Seeing death as the most evil of the "natural threats," he believed that humans were born with an innate tendency to fight this "evil" with a force as natural as that "whereby a stone moves downward."

Self-preservation also preoccupied eighteenth- and nineteenth-century thinkers. In 1755, philosopher David Hume published his heretofore-secret manuscript, *On Suicide*. Challenging church doctrine, he argued that suicide does not necessarily violate the individual's duties to God, self, or community. Rather, viewing suicide as an interruption of God's will assumed that humans possessed a power greater than the "Almighty" himself. Moreover, if an individual's life has become filled with pain, illness, and sorrow, it is his or her personal right to end such a troubled existence. Or if one is entrusted with national secrets, and is threatened with torture to divulge them to enemies of the state, one's suicide may benefit rather than harm the community. Hume's analysis not only highlighted the occasional predominance of mastery over survival needs but also paved the way for a broader consideration of spiritually oriented "hope commitments."

Written in the East, *The Dream of the Red Chamber* (1791) is considered a masterpiece of literary tragedy. Critics have compared it to the epics of Homer, Dante, Goethe, and James Joyce. Although early sections are attributed to Cao Xuequin, a poor Chinese painter, no one is sure who completed the later chapters. Superficially, the plot concerned the demise of two once powerful families and the anguish of two young lovers. At a deeper level, the author dealt with the limits of a hope exclusively grounded in mastery and the inevitability of human suffering. All foreseeable threats to human welfare are examined, including the ravages of age and illness, uncontrollable and destructive passions, and historical, political, and geographical obstacles.

In the West, by the middle of the nineteenth century, leaders of the emerging social sciences were beginning to explain the survival of the species in terms of naturally selected emotions and motives. In *Positive Polity* (1853), August Comte assembled an influential chart of basic sentiments that includes those relating to nutritional sustenance, maternal care, and the desire to reproduce. In *The Emotions and the Will*, Bain provided a vivid description of terror, the "emotional flip-side" of hopeful serenity.

The known aspect of terror is made up of a relaxation of parts commonly tense, and the ension of other parts beyond the ordinary degree . . . The tension is seen in the stare of the eyes, elevation of the eyebrows, and inflation of the nostril—in the hair standing on end . . . The relaxation is seen in the dropping of the jaw, in the enfeebled expiration, in the loosening of the sphincters . . .

A particularly moving nineteenth century reference to "hope for survival" can be found in Dostoevsky's (1866) classic, *Crime and Punishment*. After being jailed for murder, Raskolnikov is obsessed with his desire to remain alive:

Where did I read about a certain condemned man, who, an hour before his death, says or thinks that if he should ever have to live somewhere on a height, on a crag, on a little square so narrow that only two feet can be put on it—and all around would yawn the abyss, ocean, eternal darkness, eternal isolation and eternal storm—and he would have to remain there like that, standing on a yard of space, a whole lifetime, a thousand years, an eternity, it would be better to live like that than to die right away! Just to live, live, and live!

## Attachment

The great minds of the Dark and Middle Ages espoused "mystical" rather than "worldly" hopes. The Catholic Church reinforced this view with its policy of celibacy. In the eighteenth century, one of the few who offered a challenge to this restricted view of human affiliation was an Ethopian, Zera Yacob. A progressive thinker, he believed that many of the principles of Judaism, Christianity, and Islam were inconsistent with the notion of a benevolent and omniscient creator. Moreover, he found many religious principles at odds with the order of nature, particularly in the sphere of attachment. Yacob stressed the importance of sexual intimacy as well as family commitments. His views resound with those of Plato and Aristotle, who also founded their hopes in nurturing relationships within the here and now.

A century later, Comte's *Brain Chart* included inherited social emotions such as attachment, veneration, and goodness. The English philosopher Herbert Spencer linked these and other "primary emotions" to evolution, discussing in *Principles of Psychology* (1855) the inheritance of "gregariousness" and other "altruistic sentiments."

French philosopher Charles Fourier developed a detailed theory of group attachment. In *Passions of the Human Soul* (1851), he distinguished among four types of human bonding: friendships, group-based affiliations, love, and familial attachments. An idealist, he proposed that a utopian society could be fashioned by creating "phalanxes," or economic clusters of 1,600 people united by similar needs and interests.

In *Descent of Man* (1871), Charles Darwin offered some of the most profound insights regarding attachment motivation. For example, he noted that all social animals demonstrate some degree of parental and filial desire, expressing both "pleasure" and "a certain amount of sympathy" in the presence of their kin. He also chronicled the impact of separation and loss, vividly describing the pained, grief-like reactions found in many species.

At the close of the nineteenth century, the Indian spiritual leader Vivekandanda challenged Westerners to reexamine their utilitarian social ethic, with its presumptions that right conduct is that which is most useful in bringing "the greatest good to the greatest number." Speaking at the World's Parliament of Religions, Vivekandanda called for a "morality of hope" that was not based entirely on a logical analysis of costs and benefits. Instead, he argued that only a belief in the unity of all things could establish a basis for sympathy and altruism. He reasoned that people should be good to one another because they are part of a greater whole: "I do good to others because they are myself."

## The Twentieth Century: 1900–Present

During the twentieth century, psychologists contributed greatly to our understanding of human motivation, providing an even clearer scientific foundation for understanding the roots of hope. Through the 1950s many of them focused primarily on the needs for power, control, or personal effectiveness. Nevertheless, beginning in the 1960s, an increasing number of psychologists and other social scientists turned to the other two great human imperatives, attachment and self-defense.

## Mastery

Most twentieth-century conceptions of human personality include a mastery compo-nent. In *Psycho-analysis and Social Psychology* (1936), William McDougall listed the human "propensities" for "self-assertion," "curiosity," and "acquisitiveness." In *The Achieving Society* (1961), David McClelland went so far as to examine the role of achieve-ment motivation in fostering the "hopes of nations." His scope was broad, encompassing ancient Greece and modern India as well as the Protestant Ethic and various Communist reform movements. McClelland presented data indicating that an underlying need for achievement was a major force in promoting cultural and economic progress.

A closer look at Erikson's conception of the life span reveals that three of his four initial stages involve the development of self-assertion, with only the first focusing on attachment. The second stage deals with the emergence of *will power* via experiences of autonomy, the third with the development of *initiative* and the generation of purpose, and the fourth with achieving a sense of *competence* through industriousness. Harvard psychologist Robert White, in *Motivation Reconsidered* (1959), emphasized that humans and other primates have "an innate desire to play, explore and master their world." In this perspective, he joined others of the period who challenged the then-prevailing models of a passive humanity that adherents of the psychoanalytic perspective of Sigmund Freud and followers of behaviorist B. F. Skinner embraced. In the 1990s, Richard Ryan and Edward Deci expanded on White's thesis with a "self-determination theory," stressing the "the inherent tendency to seek out novelty and challenges, to extend and exercise one's capacities, to explore."

## Survival

During the first half of the twentieth century, a number of behavioral scientists sought to bring Darwin and evolution into their models of human nature. McDougall's list of instincts included a "fear propensity," elicited in the presence of threatening stimuli. Five of the basic needs put forth by Henry Murray and his colleagues in *Explorations in Personality* (1938) also dealt with self-protection. His list of motives included an inclination to avoid fear, criticism, danger, humiliation, and rejection.

Early Freudian-based theories focused on ways in which the ego defended itself against sexual and aggressive impulses. However, later psychoanalytic thinkers would propose a wider range of self-protective strategies designed to offset feelings of hopelessness resulting from other threats and fears. Karen Horney believed that struggles to lower anxiety might be achieved by trying to move toward, away from, or against others. Harry Stack Sullivan suggested that the need to control anxiety was the first motive underlying the infant's "self system."

Psychiatrist George Valliant developed a model of ego development that contrasted primitive with mature defenses. In *Wisdom of the Ego* (1993), he probed the coping strategies of men and women living ordinary lives as well as of those who had achieved extraordinary success such as Sylvia Plath, Eugene O' Neill, Beethoven, and Mother Teresa. His analysis produced a hierarchy of 18 defense mechanisms, organized in four levels: psychotic, immature, neurotic, and mature. In his view, wisdom can be achieved by those willing to take a creative approach in dealing with their particular life circumstances.

Humanistically oriented social scientists have also acknowledged the significance of self-protective needs in crafting a "hopeful inner life." Carl Rogers (1951) viewed "unconditional positive regard" as an antidote to the daily fears threatening an individual's sense of self-worth. Abraham Maslow (1968) championed the pursuit of self-actualization but acknowledged more basic needs, including those relating to security and safety. Erik Fromm's faith in human potential was clearly expressed in *The Art of Loving* (1956), but in *Escape from Freedom* (1941) he had focused on social aggression and linked many acts of human destructiveness to irrational and unchecked fears.

In the latter half of the twentieth century, existentially oriented writers traced psychological distress back to life's "ultimate concerns," including the struggle for meaning and personal responsibility and the fears of isolation and death. Rollo May (1950) pointed out that for many individuals much of the "life force" is inevitably directed toward the hope of warding off "annihilation." In his Pulitzer Prize–winning book, *The Denial of Death* (1973), Ernest Becker explored the endless distractions and strategies humans have devised, individually and collectively, to obscure the reality of their mortality.

## Attachment

Terms referring to the "sociability" of an individual have long appeared in the list of basic traits generated by psychologists who study the makeup of personality. For example, in the 1920s and 1930s, McDougall included a "gregariousness" propensity and Murray listed several varieties of "affiliative needs." Three of the "big five" building blocks of personality proposed by Robert McCrae and Paul Costa dealt with an individual's desire and ability to connect with others (openness, agreeableness, and extroversion). David Buss provided evidence of strong "biological-based hopes" that may fuel mate selection, including the imagined "resource potential" of males and the anticipated "reproductive capacity" of females. However, the strongest evidence that being able to relate to others is a basic component of human personality may come from the work of psychologists Gordon Allport and Henry Odbert. Using *Webster's International Dictionary*, they identified more than 18,000 words that could be used to describe a person's character. The largest category consisted of social adjectives such as "amiable," "agreeable," "difficult," or "withdrawn." Their findings indicated that the bulk of the "personality lexicon" focused on how well an individual can relate to other human beings.

It was not until the second half of the twentieth century that scientists would begin to carve out a full-fledged science of human relationships and delve more deeply into such issues as "romantic love," "attachment disorders," and "social intelligence." Ironically, it was a series of animal studies that prompted behavioral scientists to take a more careful look at the human attachment process. Ethologist Konrad Lorenz demonstrated the imprinting phenomenon in geese while psychologist Harry Harlow and his colleagues studied the effects of maternal separation in rhesus monkeys. In Harlow's research, he found that infant monkeys preferred a cloth-covered inanimate mother surrogate over a wire-mesh alternative that was equipped with a milk bottle. (The cuddly "mother" did not have a milk bottle.) Such findings led investigators to more fully appreciate that the role of the mother–infant bond was more complex than traditional psychoanalysts had envisioned and that it encompassed more than the infant's simple nutritional or oral needs.

The writings of psychiatrist John Bowlby also challenged the traditional psycho-analytic understanding of the infant–mother relationship by demonstrating how poor attachments can undermine the hopeful countenance of the most resilient infant or child. While Freud and his immediate followers focused almost exclusively on the mother–infant feeding dynamic and a narrower set of potential drive-related "fixations," Bowlby sought to document all of the potential social and emotional "fallout" resulting from attachment disruptions or disturbances.

In the 1970s, Bowlby's collaborator, child psychologist Mary Ainsworth, introduced the "strange situation," a research strategy that provided an "ethical laboratory" for classifying children as "secure," "anxious," or "insecure." Children were sequentially observed (1) with their mother, (2) with their mother and a stranger, (3) with the stranger as their mother leaves the room, (4) with the stranger and their mother when she returns, (5) alone when both adults leave, (6) with the returning stranger, and (7) with the returning mother as the stranger leaves. The children's reactions to each of these situations enabled Ainsworth to identify different patterns of childhood attachment. Later research would show that anxious or insecure children were destined to struggle with both the attachment and mastery aspects of hope.

Although steeped in the psychoanalytical tradition, Heinz Kohut viewed the attachment process as a far more complex meeting of "hearts and minds." In particular, he hypothesized that the healthy internalization of the caregiver's presence was critical in helping infants to establish an inner foundation for the development of hope. For him and most of his contemporaries, the caregiver was usually the mother, but in the 1960s and 1970s a small handful of investigators, including one of us (H. B.), began to incorporate the role of paternal factors in attachment formation.

## From the Annals of Hopelessness

One might deduce from the discussion in this chapter so far that we believe the trajectory of human life on this planet has been seamlessly "hopeward" bound, evolving happily unchecked over time in its capacity to create, honor, and ultimately record ever more complex and life-affirming manifestations of the vital motives of mastery, attachment, and survival. If only this were so! Unfortunately, history does not support this cheerful notion. Rather, it is littered throughout with events of the most grotesque inhumanity, each of them signaling a disruption of hope, even a perversion of it. On the world stage, the annals of hopelessness are particularly bloody: in the past century alone, there were two world wars, innumerable regional and civil conflicts, and countless atrocities resulting from them. The causes of such events are many, and it is beyond the scope of this book to address them all. We can and should, however, focus on one of them, a phenomenon that in recent years seems to have resurfaced with an especially shocking malignancy.

When the economic, social, and political conditions of a nation disintegrate, many of its people may experience a chronic sense of powerlessness, alienation, fear, and entrapment. In essence, their hope motives have been undermined. As we will discuss in Chapter 13 with respect to hopelessness in individuals, powerlessness reflects a thwarting of the mastery drive; alienation disrupts the attachment motive; and fear and entrapment subvert the instinct for survival. When examined in the context of an entire nation, these disruptions signal a failed "hope mission"—an inability or unwillingness to attend fully to the hope needs of its people. The level of despair that these conditions spawn may in fact become so intense that it breeds extremes of belief and behavior, including fanaticism and terrorism.

Fanaticism gives rise to false hopes that, through a single, rigidly held, often outraged worldview, one will find salvation. Not all fanatics resort to extremes of behavior that harm others, but for those who do, the results are tragic. Consider the suicide bombers in the Middle East, killing everyone in their path as they blow themselves up. The September 11 attacks were a stunning variation of that terrorist tactic. What causes people to bring such destruction?

The anthropologist Margaret Mead viewed fanaticism as a belief system that one adopts in an attempt to counter a sense of hopelessness in one's life and a growing realization of one's likely failure to thrive as a result.

German economist Wilhelm Kasch attributed terrorism to a chronic sense of despair that culminates in an urge to destroy oneself and others. Psychologist Ervin Staub described such acts of violence and brutality as frantic efforts to "regain hope." Indeed, shortly after the September 11 attacks, a *USA Today* editorial suggested that Osama Bin Laden maintained a loyal following by "dispensing hope to the hopeless."

Followers of fanatical and terrorist groups are typically emboldened by a charismatic leader who refuels the power motive, creates a sense of belonging to a group with common values, and offers a blueprint for salvation. Groups that address all three of these needs are likely to be especially compelling because they offer a broad but perverted strain of hope.

Whether Fidel Castro's ascendancy in Cuba can be considered a terroristic development, his revolutionary movement occurred at a time when Cubans felt weakened, alienated, and trapped by a failed Batista Regime. They were ripe for a "hope revolution." Castro sought to inspire a country struggling with political oppression, inadequate housing, unemployment, illiteracy, and poor health care. He promised liberation from a "sick" and "captive" justice system. In a landmark (1953) speech, he declared that his efforts were on behalf of the people who yearn for "great and wise changes," those whose "future is dismal . . . who die working on land that is not theirs, looking at it with sadness as Moses did the promised land." He also addressed the "young professionals . . . anxious to work and full of hope, only to find themselves at a dead-end with all doors closed."

But providing hope is not the main concern of every terrorist. Some experts identify three types of terrorists—the insane, the criminal, and the ideological crusader—with most terrorist leaders demonstrating qualities representative of two or three of these categories. Highly unstable terrorists can sometimes bring about the most extensive and prolonged acts of inhumanity. The 1850 Taiping Rebellion, started by a "holy man" who declared himself the younger brother of Jesus, led to the slaughter of some 20 million people. Among criminal or insane terrorists, the level of despair is so profound that they no longer seek hope via empowerment, connections, or salvation, but instead merely crave some form of apocalyptic revenge. Crusading or "idealistic" terrorist groups are, however, primarily *engines of hope*. They offer a collective sense of power, a sense of belonging, and an escape from tyranny, oppression, or poverty. While most groups attempt to satisfy several of these basic needs, some of them only capitalize on frustrations in one particular hope domain, such as a thwarted sense of power or a perceived total absence of freedom.

Explanations of terrorism invariably refer to *"perverted dreams of power."* Staub included a "desire for a feeling of efficacy, control and power" in his list of causes underlying the mistreatment of others, whether by individuals or groups. Dutch scholar Alex Schmid listed a variety of power-related themes in his analysis of terrorist groups, including intimidation, enforcement of obedience, psychological isolation, and projection of strength.

Psychoanalyst Alice Miller suggested that "Nazi terrorism" was ignited by the unconscious defense mechanism of "projection." According to her, a method of harsh and punitive child-rearing combined with a series of catastrophic events, including humiliation in World War I, produced a generation of Germans for whom all feelings of tenderness and vulnerability were "verboten." In Miller's view, because the German people harbored such a profound, collective sense of impotence, they were compelled to unload or "project" their feelings of inferiority onto the Jews and other minority groups that they considered inferior to themselves.

*Disrupted attachment needs* have also been considered among the root causes of terrorism. Staub noted the need to "protect and elevate social identity," Schmid cited "cohesion building," and Wilhelm Kasch wrote of the pining for a lost sense of "community." When profoundly alienated individuals find their way into a group with deeply shared grievances and common values, the experience can be a powerful, if pathological, antidote for their misery.

Those devoid of any meaningful social ties are especially at risk for seduction by cult leaders. In *Child Maltreatment and Paternal Deprivation*, one of us (H. B.) reviewed a large number of studies that linked inadequate fathering to poor developmental outcomes in children. Such paternal deprivation seems to play an especially important role in the individual's later susceptibility to maltreatment and exploitation by strangers.

Early paternal absence or abuse has been consistently implicated as a contributing factor in the development of destructive radicalism and other forms of antisocial behavior. For example, psychologist Klaus Wasmund analyzed the backgrounds of members of the Red Army Faction, a West German terrorist group, finding a common theme of disturbed parent–child relations, particularly those involving the father. Wasmund observed how participation in radical groups can be particularly compelling for alienated individuals who "find their strong desire for community, personal contact, and human relations satisfied" and their "lack of self-confidence compensated for by a 'we-feeling' of common strength." An ex-member of the Red Army Faction explained, "I . . . was treated there like a comrade among comrades . . . and felt . . . the pride of being acknowledged and accepted as one of many."

Terrorists also promise to bring "hope" to those who feel *their survival or liberation needs have been seriously compromised.* Indeed, the stated agenda of many of these groups is to rally people against political systems that have produced a feeling of entrapment or cultivated widespread fear. Hence, one finds the "Black Liberation Army," "Irish National Liberation Army," "Jewish Defense League," and "Uganda Freedom Fighters" among the ranks of so-called radical elements. Whether some may be sympathetic to such organizations while others condemn them, the point is that they all seem to latch on to the "hope game."

Along these lines, English philosopher Jonathan Glover offered an *immobility thesis* to describe state-sponsored "cold violence," a policy of inhibitory politics limiting individual freedom through intimidation and the establishment of arbitrary moral boundaries. Agreeing with Glover, Italian sociologist Franco Ferrarotti argued that "immobility" is a particularly lethal prescription for social rebellion. In a similar vein, political scientist Luigi Bonanate insisted that "a society that knows terrorism is a 'blocked society' . . . A situation seems blocked when there seems to be no innovation capable of bringing about a new situation." To Volker Kasch, these are "static societies" in which the "spirit of possibility" is replaced by *methodological atheism*. Edward Hyams, the English novelist and student of anarchy, found "no single case in which recourse to terrorism was not forced on an organization by denial of all other means of fighting against social injustice."

Perhaps it was Camus who provided the clearest profile of the "hopeless terrorist":

These [rebels] forget the present for the future, the fate of humanity for the delusion of power . . . They despair of personal freedom . . . reject solitary death and give the name of immortality to a vast collective agony . . . despair at being a man . . . have finally driven them to inhuman excesses.

---

*Third Hope Meditation*

As we have shown in this chapter, the motives underlying hope are fundamental to human life. As you reflect on events at home and abroad, does the information in this chapter shed any more light on the role of hope in addressing our present challenges, from international conflict and terrorist threats to energy concerns and global warming?

How much time are you putting into *your* mastery, attachment, and survival needs? List three things that you might do to achieve greater balance. Be as specific as possible. You are most likely to succeed if you stick to behaviors with at least an 80% chance of completion.

# four

## CULTURES OF HOPE: ABSORBING THE VIRTUES

## OF A COMMUNITY

Customs create the spirit of the whole . . . By absorbing the virtues of a community, one becomes an able human being . . . For only culture can guide humanity through something universal. Such virtues are acquired by education but in the end they become second nature . . . They are experienced as part of the individual's being . . . creating firmness, assurance and freedom.

—Confucius

In this chapter and the next, we focus on the profound ways that culture and religion can affect an individual's "private" experience of hope. Although it may seem strange, the feeling of hope shared by most Americans is not exactly the same experience as that felt by Israelis living in a Kibbutz. Muslim hope is somewhat different from that of Native Americans. Buddhist hopes can be distinguished from those of the Hindus. Within each culture, there are certain motives that tend to be pushed to the foreground while others are relegated to the background. Cultural influences also affect *the manner in which members of a group express their attachment, mastery, and survival impulses.* By permeating the marrow of hope in these fundamental ways, cultural norms profoundly alter hope's perceived origins and potential beneficiaries as well as its foreseeable destinations.

## Biosocial Foundations

William James once wrote that he would rather study the rocks on the New England coast than read another huge, boring text about "animal spirits" or struggle with the myriad and conflicting views about emotion and motivation that plague the social sciences. Professional debates that dragged on throughout the twentieth century often tied emotion and motivation to the larger issue of nature versus nurture. In the 1960s, for example, one biologically oriented theorist attributed grief to the single-celled amoeba. At the nurture end of the spectrum, anthropologist Catherine Lutz suggested that emotions were not "essences" inside the physical boundaries of the person but rather "cultural inventions."

Our view is more intermediate, emphasizing that both biology and culture must be factored into the hope equation. Because an emotion has a foundation in biological processes, this does not mean that it is free from cultural and historical influences. In fact, the relative degree of biological, as opposed to social or psychological input, varies depending on the particular emotion. Fear is an example of an emotion derived from the self-protective system that is primarily hardwired. By comparison, love and mourning are two human experiences that tend to be profoundly influenced by cultural factors.

The infrastructure of hope may lie in the fibers of the frontal lobes and other central nervous system pathways, but these biological functions do not operate in a vacuum. Biological and cultural evolution are codependent processes, which means that emotions and motives should be construed as *biosocial* systems that develop from the dialectic between nature and nurture. With respect to the motives underlying hope, it is impossible to ignore the accumulated effects of thousands of years of social programming, including the evolution of daily customs, spiritual beliefs, childrearing practices, and patterns of social interaction.

Hope is a particularly clear example of biological systems and social forces working together. We have already discussed some of the biological underpinnings of hope. Cultural factors are equally fundamental, from establishing the social value of hope to affecting the expression of the attachment, mastery, and survival motives. Although we emphasize these cultural influences in the rest of this chapter (see Table 4.1), we are not suggesting that hope is entirely a social construction. Moreover, in discussing the role of spiritual beliefs, we realize that faith can come in many forms, including varieties that are independent of formal belief systems or even recourse to a higher power. In later chapters, we examine the psychological development of the attachment, mastery, and self-protective motives and their implications for individual differences with respect to hope.

### The Attachment System

Newborns have certain recruiting capacities, including physical features and responses that elicit caregiving behaviors and gestures, contributing to an exquisite synchrony that

TABLE 4.1. *Cultural Influences on Hope*

| Dominant Cultural Ethos | Ultimate Source(s) of Hope | Attachment Who Benefits from Hope | Mastery Where Hope Leads | Survival Form of Salvation |
|---|---|---|---|---|
| *Individualist* | | | | |
| Catholicism | God, then Self | The self | Forward | Heavenly reunion |
| Protestantism | Self, then God | The self | Forward | Heavenly reunion |
| *Collectivist* | | | | |
| Aust. Aborigines | Tribe and spirits | Tribe and spirits | Back and forth | Dreamtime bond |
| Buddhism | Self and Buddha | The self | A spiral | Liberated release |
| Hinduism | The God within | The self | A spiral | A higher rebirth |
| Ifa (West Africa) | Tribe and spirits | Tribe and spirits | A cycle | Join spirit world |
| Islamic | God and group | Group and self | Forward | Heavenly reunion |
| Judaism | God and group | Group and self | Forward | A final gathering |
| Native American | Tribe and spirits | Tribe and spirits | A cycle | Join spirit world |

can develop between them and their caregivers. Our integrative approach to hope underscores the importance of these early attachment experiences in the development of hope, but it goes beyond them in several important ways. Previously, we suggested that the influence of the attachment motive can be observed in an individual's level of trust in and openness to others. However, we can also illustrate how the perceived origins and potential destinations of hope (where it may lead or take you in life) is profoundly affected by the social and cultural context.

## Hope Origins
In their widely cited review of cultural orientations, social scientists Florence Kluckhohn and Fred Strodtbeck distinguished between "human–nature" relationships and "human–human" relationships. The first dimension captures those cultures that espouse an ethic of subjugation to nature and a higher power. For many Latino Catholics in the American Southwest, hope is found in Jesus, God (the ultimate cause), and their "Lady of Guadalupe." Veronica Alvarado, a devout worshipper from San Antonio explained, "She is our mother, a star, a sun, a hope, love, faith, everything." Mary Esther Bernal, a parish leader agreed, "She is love, but first and foremost she is hope." In contrast, the Chinese, Japanese, and the Navajo seek harmony with natural as well as supernatural forces. On the other hand, most Americans and many Western Europeans tend to share a worldview promoting mastery over nature with the assumption of only minimal supernatural interference.

With regards to *human–human relationships*, some cultures are more collectivist in orientation while others promote an ethic of individualism. For monks in

Thailand, the meaning of hope derives from the collective, the strength of human bonds. While participating in solemn graduation ceremonies, they will pray in a large circle while holding one long string that symbolically binds them into a spiritual community.

Before the intrusion of the white man in North America, the Apaches maintained an ancient system of clans known as the *gota*. These groups ranged in size from about a dozen to as many as 40 individuals. Their collectivism was rooted in a "matrilineal" and "matrilocal" tradition, meaning that all of the members of the clan except for the men who married into the group would be related by a maternal bloodline. In addition, every effort was made to live as close as possible to the original land of the maternal bloodline. It is interesting to consider this custom in light of Erikson's notions about hope and basic trust. Not surprisingly, the meaning of hope ("ndahondii") in Apache suggests "trust" rather than potential goal attainment or survival expectations.

The Apaches and Navajo share similar social constructions of hope. The Navajo feel "they are glued together with respect." Their cosmology has the creator enlisting the help of the "holy people" to create a natural world characterized by "hozjo" or "balance." In Navajo the word "sih" means to hope but also to "take mercy upon" or "to take pity." The emphasis on connections and a positive relationship with nature is also symbolized in the Navajo flag, which displays their land under the protective umbrella of a rainbow surrounded by four sacred mountains.

The clan is also the major source of Navajo identity. Before asking strangers any personal questions, they inquire about their clan of origin. For them, the source of hope is neither inside nor outside the self but lies in their relationships with kin and nature. This is vividly expressed in their prayer to the sun: "Father give me the light of your mind, that my mind may be strong. Give me some of your strength, that my arm may be strong."

Compare this communal hope with the privatized Anglo-Saxon version. In *Das Prinzip Hoffnung*, one of philosopher Ernst Bloch's primary goals was to show that hope could be achieved without recourse to God and the angels or saints. Nietzsche similarly declared God dead, insisting that "super-earthly" hopes were "poisonous" and that there will "cometh a time when man will no longer launch the arrow of his longing beyond man."

Bloch and Nietzsche were intellectual heirs of the Protestant Reformation, that seismic shift in Christian faith that Martin Luther helped to usher in during the sixteenth century, freeing the individual from the hold of the Catholic Church and paving the way for increasingly potent strains of individualism. This promethean zeitgeist, with its emphasis on personal strivings and subjective truths, was furthered by John Calvin, Immanuel Kant, Johann Goethe, and the Romanticists. In this sense, it can be said that the Reformation played a major role in shifting the locus of hope within the Western world.

Among the beneficiaries of this zeitgeist was Ralph Waldo Emerson, whose *Self-Reliance* (1841) is still regarded as one of the grandest expressions of American individualism. Convinced that inspiration, direction, and hope must come from inside the person, he wrote that human beings

> should learn to detect and watch that gleam of light that flashes across [their minds], more than the lustre of the firmament of gods and sages . . . and accept in the highest mind the same transcendent destiny . . . [Human beings can be] guides, redeemers and benefactors obeying the almighty effort, advancing on chaos and the dark . . . [otherwise] there is no genius . . . no muse . . . no hope.

*Self Reliance* begins with two quotes: The first is attributed to the ancient satirist, Persius, "Ne te quaesiveris extra" ('seek nothing outside yourself'), while the second is from Beaumont and Fletcher's, *The Honest Man's Fortune* (1647): "Man is his own star . . . nothing to him falls too early or too late. Our acts [serve as] our angels, [reaping] good will or ill."

Ayn Rand, one of the foremost symbols of the capitalist spirit in the early part of the twentieth century, was also a rugged individualist. In *The Fountainhead* (1943), she argued that a man's "vision, strength, and courage came from his own spirit . . . There is no such thing as a collective brain. There is no such thing as a collective thought . . . The creator faces nature alone."

Within societies that promote individuality, the experience of hope derives from a greater emphasis on personal goals than on relationships. In collectivist cultures, however, both the source and aim of hope are found in attachment concerns benefiting not the individual but a group, whose members may range from the nuclear family to the whole population.

## Hope Beneficiaries

A clear example of a kind of hope aimed at benefiting both the self and others is provided by the followers of Islam. Muslims traditionally give away one fortieth of their annual income to the poor, reflecting their deep concern for those less fortunate than themselves. The thirty-ninth Surah of the Qur'an is a meditation on "companions." Here it is suggested that the faithful are entitled to hope for a reunion with their family and Allah. "He who is obedient . . . takes care of the hereafter and hopes for the mercy of his lord . . . Those who are careful of their duty to the Lord shall be convened to the garden in companies."

Both the Navajo and the Hindus engage in rituals of hope for the protection of their homes and families. For example, one Navaho prayer reads, "This home, my home, shall be surrounded . . . This fire shall be for the good of the family." Hindus construct altars within their homes to contemplate their various deities. Among the most important figures is "Gruhadevata," the family godhead who is invoked to provide protection for all members of the household.

For many Christians, the ultimate hoped-for benefit is a reunion with God. After confession, Catholics may participate in communion. This ritual is considered a temporary fusion with the body of Christ, a way of sampling heaven and an eternal connection with God. In Paul's second letter to the Corinthians, he described life on earth as a deposit, an earthly gift that must suffice until we can be brought under the "heavenly tent."

The collectivist view stands in sharp contrast to the more individualized hope characteristic of American society and many Northern European cultures. Near the close of *Atlas Shrugged*, Rand made a powerful appeal for the solitary hero in pursuit of individual dreams:

> All life is a purposeful struggle and your only choice is the choice of a goal . . . check on your virtues and on the nature of the enemies you are serving . . . leave them to the death they worship . . . Do not let your fire go out . . . in the hopeless swamps . . . the world you desired can be won, it exists, it is real, it is possible, it's yours . . . I swear-by my life and my love of it—that I will never live for the sake of another man, nor ask another man to live for mine.

## The Mastery System

Hope is influenced by the capacities that individuals have for active engagement with their environment. Most of the major theoretical approaches to the development of motivational systems also assume that environmental opportunities and constraints play a large role in the expression of goal-related behaviors. Harvard psychologist Jerome Bruner emphasized that effective parents have a way of remaining just a few steps ahead of their children to foster assertiveness and mastery. Similarly, the influential Russian psychologist Lev Vygotsky challenged educators to build on the child's "zone of proximal development," that is, on both the child's actual ability and the ability that he or she can achieve under the guidance of an instructor. Adult sensitivity to a child's capacities is, in fact, one of the best predictors of the child's achievement and mastery-related motivation. It is also possible to identify how different cultures further shape the mastery drive, thereby influencing the ultimate destinations of their members' hopes.

## Hope Destinations

The ancients were spellbound by the repetitive phases of the moon, the recurrent changing of seasons, and the endless encounters with life and death. Their many drawings and engravings of spirals, zigzags, and lozenges were designed to represent the heavenly drama of the gods and the destiny of earth-bound mortals. This cyclical perspective was eloquently expressed by the French historian Henri-Charles Puech in *Gnosis and Time*. "No event is unique, nothing is enacted but once . . . every event will be enacted perpetually; the same individuals had appeared, appear, and will appear at every turn of the circle."

In *The Gift of the Jews*, mentioned in the previous chapter, Thomas Cahill wrote that the tradition of Abraham and Moses forever altered humanity's conception of life, substituting a forward-moving journey for the never-ending cycle. Cahill argued that this change was the foundation for a new kind of hope based on the idea of a future that humanity could actively shape. His assumption that cultures can be neatly divided into "progressive" or "cyclical" is questionable. Nevertheless, most religious and philoso-phical worldviews can be characterized as *primarily sequential or circular* in their eschatology, and when combined with other cultural and historical factors, give rise to different conceptions of "where" and "how far" a group or individual may go, in effect setting the mastery-related "bounds of hopeful imagination." More circular cosmologies, such as those found in many parts of Asia, offer an experience of hope that differs from the Christian version. Followers of Theraveda Buddhism hope to be reborn into a more favorable realm somewhere "within the thirty-one planes of exis-tence." In their spiritual guidebook, *Vinyana Pitaka*, believers are instructed to meditate on both their past and future lives:

> I directed my mind to the knowledge and recollection of former habituations.
> I remembered a variety of former habituations, thus; one birth, two births . . . or
> fifty or a hundred or a thousand or a hundred thousand births; or many an aeon
> of integration, disintegration, integration-disintegration.

In contrast to the cyclical course of Buddhism, the Judeo-Christian tradition is grounded in a more linear view of life, beginning with the epic biblical migrations. One of the great Old Testament stories concerns the exile and return of the Jews to their homeland, following the defeat of Babylon by the Persians. According to religious scholar Marcus Borg, the dominant biblical themes of exodus, exile, and return may be based on historical facts but also serve a larger symbolic function. Their purpose is to offer a perspective on the human condition. The notion of an exile speaks to a deeply felt sense of dislocation in the human psyche, while the "return to a promised land" reflects a desire for reunion and repossession of a safe place in the universe.

Conveying a similar spirit of hope, The New Testament offers John's visions from Patmos, a harsh, island territory used by the Romans to banish prisoners. The 22 chapters of *Revelations*, the New Testament's final book, contain his predicted succes-sion of events leading to salvation. The reader is confronted with a plethora of startling images, including locusts with golden crowns and human faces, the four horsemen of the apocalypse, and the waters of the river of life. Nevertheless, the final chapters portray "a new heaven and a new earth." With the triumph of good over evil comes the removal of every barrier to human fulfillment. A new paradise is created to house the resurrected Christian soul and to guarantee the hope of an eternal reunion with God and loved ones.

### The Survival System

Psychologist Rick Snyder noted that hope may serve as a form of "reality negotiation," buffering individuals from painful life experiences. This process is complex, involving spiritual factors as well as other aspects of the self-protective and attachment systems. To some extent reality negotiation is an individualized process. It is partly derived from personal modes of coping that are influenced by the level of an individual's emotional development. However, there are also culture-specific modes of escape and transcendence that can be accessed to offset personal threats and universal challenges.

*Terror Management Theory* (TMT) is the most extensively researched model of cultural defense. It was inspired by the Pulitzer Prize–winning anthropologist Ernest Becker, who emphasized the role that death anxiety plays in human development. According to him, individuals are motivated to maintain faith in a particular worldview because of their underlying desire for self-preservation. Although every species of animal shares the instinct for survival, humans are especially vulnerable to the experience of terror. The developers of TMT, psychologists Jeff Greenberg and his colleagues, stressed that a capacity for self-consciousness and an ability to project oneself into the future, produce the added threats of "death awareness" and "annihilation anxiety." To control their terror, human beings immerse themselves in a cultural worldview that gives life meaning while also promising safety and a sense of symbolic immortality. Implicit in TMT is the idea that individuals are motivated to preserve their self-esteem. Their wish is to remain valued in a universe capable of saving its prized members from annihilation.

Going beyond TMT, cultural and religious factors play an important role in the establishment of a hope-based defense system. For example, the forms of salvation offered by Buddhism and Christianity are profoundly different. For the followers of Theraveda Buddhism, the ultimate authority is the *Pali Canon*, consisting of three sections or "baskets of wisdom." Each of these three baskets is further divided into two to six subsections, which in turn may contain hundreds of individual discourses. In one subjection of the second basket (the Sutta pitaka), a particularly illustrative discourse deals with emptiness and recommends a process of meditation for those seeking spiritual advancement and favorable rebirth, through "the thirty-one planes of existence" to "saga" or heaven. In short, the hope of the good Buddhist is for escape from an endless cycle of transmigration through a kind of dissolution of mind, body, and spirit, which brings complete release from all connections, spiritual and worldly. This spiritual progression, associated with greater and greater withdrawal and isolation, is rendered in a positive light. For example, upon reaching the twenty-eighth plane of "infinite space," the [Buddhist] "mind takes pleasure, finds satisfaction, settles and indulges in its perception of the sphere of nothingness."

In contrast, Christian salvation is a fusion of two promises, escape from suffering and a connection with God. It is this great difference between Christianity and "religions of renunciations" that Pope John Paul II highlighted in his *Crossing the Threshold of Hope*. The Revelations of St. John, for example, conclude with the unambiguous hope of a final reunion with God: "I heard a loud voice from the throne saying, 'behold, the dwelling of God is with men. He will dwell with them, and they shall be his people, and God himself will be with them.'"

Hope is thus grounded in a worldview that promises a *new and better experience*. This is the guarantee of the Christian faith. Although there is hope within Buddhism, it is cast differently. Most strains of Buddhism offer an end to suffering by promising a *termination of awareness*. In essence, by altering the meaning of salvation, different religious systems produce varied types of hope structures.

The private experience of hope is also affected by spiritual beliefs. The Buddhist meditating on the infinitude of space is experiencing something that is quite different from the Christian praying for a reunion with God. Buddhists and Hindus sit with their heads forward, eyes closed or fixed on a flickering candle, focusing on oneness, the elimination of all distractions, and hope for a calmed state of total emptiness. Christians kneel with hands clasped and raised to the chest, gazing upward toward the heavens, and their prayers focus on passion, communion, and intimacy.

## Cultural Influences

We have mentioned previously the study by psychologist James Averill and his colleagues suggesting that American college students are far more likely than their Korean counterparts to infuse hope with a transcendent, spiritual dimension. Koreans associate hope with ambition, success, earthly desires, specifically the pursuit of material possessions. Averill suggested that an adherence to Confucianism may underlie this negative perception of a "materialistic hope" among Koreans. Confucianism engenders an enormous pressure to conform for the greater good, to exercise self-control, and to live modestly. Since in Korea, hope is viewed primarily as a means for achieving individualistic, pedestrian goals, it is relegated to a baser quality rather than a prized virtue.

Psychologists Shula Sommers and Corinne Kosmitzki discovered that cultural factors may also help to explain why Germans seem to put more emphasis on hope than do Americans. When adults were asked a number of questions about their preferred emotions, *Germans ranked hope second* in the category of the most useful emotions while *Americans ranked it seventh*. The researchers hypothesized that hope is viewed more favorably by Germans because they see it primarily as a tool for "mastery," a motive that sustains rather than undermines the larger cultural emphasis on striving and individual effort. In support of this notion, the authors cited the angels in Goethe's *Faust* who proclaimed, "Whoever strives in ceaseless toil, him we grant redemption."

In Japan, where Buddhism is the dominant religion, the emphasis is on escape from suffering. One of the four noble truths of Buddhism is that suffering is created by desire while peace is achieved through a renunciation of world pursuits. In Japanese, the word for hope ("kibo") refers to a "wish" or a potential "trick" that lies waiting in the future. Not surprisingly, the Japanese appear wary, if not downright fearful, of hope. Why? Because from a Buddhist perspective, an emotion grounded in selfish and uncertain pursuits will clearly eventuate in great suffering.

Ultimately, the cultural significance of hope is to be found in the relationship that exists between the particular social formation of this emotion and the broader world-view that defines a culture. When the construction of hope is at odds with the values of a group, it will be deemphasized. This is somewhat the case in the United States, and even more so in Japan and South Korea. In contrast, both the Germans and the Israeli Jews place a greater value on hope. Although these cultures are quite different, their concep-tions of hope support rather than undermine cherished values.

## Cultural Clocks

Gabriel Marcel wrote about the painful sense of timelessness that occurs when an individual feels hopeless, but very little else appears in the philosophical literature regarding the time–hope connection. A more thorough exploration of this issue from a cultural perspective, however, demonstrates how multiple aspects of time perception can affect the experience of hope.

According to anthropologist Hoyt Alverson, time can be experienced as a "cause," a "substance," a "medium in motion," or a "direction" in physical space. Each of these dimensions of time can have an effect on the inner experience of hope (see Table 4.2). For example, the sense of time as a "cause" relates to that aspect of hope that arises from faith in the future, from the confident belief that time can yield something positive. The experience of time as a "substance" permits the feeling of hope that results from having enough time to succeed, find love, or secure healing. This particular dimension of time is greatly affected by an individual's age, health status, work style and other daily commitments, and spiritual beliefs. As for the "medium of time," when individuals are hopeful and content, life seems to move quickly, perhaps even to the point of

TABLE 4.2. *Time and Hope*

| Dimensions of Time | Hope-Related Concerns | Spiritual and Cultural Influences on Time and Hope |
|---|---|---|
| *Time as a cause* | | |
| Time can cause or allow things to happen as well as prevent them from occurring | Is time on my side? Is time my friend or foe? Will time enslave or free me? | Buddhist: Release from suffering Hindu: Chance for a better rebirth Judeo/Christian: Salvation or damnation Shaman: Self/group reparations |
| *Time as a substance* | | |
| Time is a resource or commodity that can be used for growth, change, or healing | How much time do I have? Can I buy more time? What will the future bring? | Buddhist: Infinite time to gain release Hindu: Infinite trials of finite rebirths Judeo/Christian: Limited time for salvation Shaman: Limited access to the infinite |
| *Time as a medium* | | |
| Time is a vehicle that carries individuals along at varying rates of perceived speed | When will tomorrow arrive? Can I get into the flow? Is time passing me by? | Buddhist: Slowed pace Hindu: Moderate pace Judeo/Christian: Quickened pace Shaman: Multiple time experiences |
| *Time as a direction* | | |
| Time is experienced as a straight line, a neverending cycle, or a two-way street | Is there life still ahead of me? Am I stuck in a vicious cycle? Can I revisit my past? | Buddhist: Cycles with a possible spiral Hindu: Upward or downward spiral Judeo/Christian: Linear progression Shaman: Bidirectional time |

resembling a continuous "flow state." However, when the future looks bleak, the movement of time appears to grind to a halt.

The pace of life within a culture can also transform the perceived flow of time. For example, in a number of southern European countries, trains rarely arrive at their scheduled hour, and shops close and reopen throughout the day to accommodate family meals and restorative naps. Time appears to move more slowly. In contrast, because time is marked more carefully in many northern European countries, it appears to move at a more rapid pace. Germans, for example, are renowned for their punctuality and are more likely to be insulted by late arrivals for business or personal engagements. A similar difference is found when comparing the more time-oriented North American continent with the predominately event-oriented South American countries.

Cultural clocks inevitably affect the way in which individuals approach mastery, attachment, and survival issues. In other words, there are discernible hope-related timetables that vary across cultures. For example, in the mastery domain, psychologists have found that Russians and Americans perform equally well on the *untimed intelligence tasks* that comprise a standard [American] IQ test. However, Russians tend to score lower on the *timed tasks* because they live in a culture that has traditionally valued accuracy and precision rather than speed. With respect to attachment and survival, there are striking cultural differences in terms of how long and how much the living should invest in a deceased loved one. In the United States, there is a much shorter mourning timetable, highlighted by the emphasis on "grief work" (see also Chapter 12). But in Chinese ancestor rituals, according to religious scholar Dennis Klass, "the dead remain part of the family, defining the values by which the family lives and creating the shared identity of the living members of the family."

Time also raises a number of spiritual questions. Should time be viewed as an evil menace that inevitably destroys all that humanity has achieved, nurtured, or tried to protect? Or is it possible to envision time as a creative force that can facilitate human achievement, love, and healing? Among Buddhists, those who follow the Theraveda tradition ("the way of the elders") believe that while the present can only yield suffering and pain, the future may bring release. Theraveda Buddhists hope for a spiral of evermore favorable rebirths, and ultimately Nirvana, a complete escape into nothingness. Adherents of the Pure Land sect of Mahayana Buddhism, however, hope to be reborn within a paradise surrounded by seven tiers of railings, seven layers of netting, seven rows of trees, pools of jewels, and golden sands. While most Christians believe that time may usher in the "grace of God," many Protestants anticipate a more palpable or earthly reward.

The substance of time is apt to be handled very differently by followers of varied spiritual systems. Buddhists may use their time to perfect longer and longer periods of quiet detachment. Protestants might busy themselves in accomplishing the good works deemed necessary for *their* salvation. Hindus and Australian Aborigines have more than one temporal substance to consider. A Hindu must address ethical shortcomings in the moment to generate a karma deserving of a more elevated existence at a future time (via reincarnation).

Meanwhile, Australian Aborigines are likely to be preparing themselves for a dream-time ceremony that will allow them to access the past and make the necessary community reparations to assure a more benign present and future.

Spiritual life also affects the perceived movement of time. For example, the scriptures of a particular faith can affect the perceived passage of time through recollections and prophecies. In the Christian Bible there are many allusions to a last day. Witness the countless millennium groups that convene in preparation of doomsday and the many publications that seek to decipher the time of the Apocalypse. In St. Paul's letter to the

Romans, it is written: " . . . you know what hour it is, how it is full time now for you to wake from sleep. For salvation is nearer to us now than when we first believed; the night is far gone, the day is at hand."

For Buddhists who contemplate 31 planes of existence and numerous rebirths, there is a different sense of time, a different level of urgency, a different experience of hoping. In one passage from the second basket of wisdom, known as the Anapanasati Sutta, the "blessed one" instructs a group of monks on how to employ mindful breathing to reach a level of dispassion about worldly matters. In another passage from the same Pali basket, it is written:

> He trains himself to breathe in focusing on inconstancy, and to breathe out
> focusing on inconstancy. He trains himself to breathe in focusing on dispassion,
> and to breathe out focusing on dispassion. He trains himself to breathe in focusing
> on cessation, and to breathe out focusing on cessation. He trains himself to breathe
> in focusing on relinquishment, and to breathe out focusing on relinquishment.

Time can also be expressed in linear or circular terms. Linguistically, linear time can be expressed as "long" or "short," as "here" or "there." Circular time may be couched in terms of "the round of life," "a circle," or "a wheel of fortune." Such descriptions of time were among those listed by Alverson in his final category, *time as a course* or *direction*. This dimension of time also relates to Cahill's distinction between *cyclical* and *progressive cultures*. How do cyclical and linear worldviews of time differentially affect the experience of hope? In our view, these aspects of time may influence hope by altering the perceived "bounds and limits of imagined possibilities." Where can one go? How far can one go? What is possible and what is impossible?

Most of the major religions espouse either an escape from cycles of suffering (Orthodox Buddhism), a linear progression toward paradise (Christians and followers of Islam), or a combination of these two forms of salvations (The Pure Land Buddhists). However, much of Asia has turned away from Theraveda (Orthodox) Buddhism to the "greater vehicle" of Mahayana Buddhism. The "salvation" possibilities of Mahayana Buddhism go beyond a solitary, postdeath release from suffering, to include an "awakened mind" in the present, nested within a spiritual collective. What this suggests is that human nature may require a form of faith that incorporates the experience of a reachable and communal "good" and not simply the abolishment of "evil." In short, some might argue that we are in the midst of a sociocultural evolution in hope. With this in mind, the philosopher Ernst Bloch speculated that all religions would eventually evolve into faith systems that conceptualize the "good" as both something "above" and "in front" of humanity, implying that religion's ultimate "hope responsibility" would be to sustain a sense of future time as a "directed cause towards goodness and light."

*Fourth Hope Meditation*

Where does your hope come from? Does it come from within? Do you find hope in a higher power? Does your hope derive from Nature? Who do you hope for? Do you reserve your greatest hopes for your children or loved ones? What is your ultimate hope? Is it to achieve release from pain and suffering? Is it geared toward a permanent "reunion" with loved ones or a higher power? Is it focused on achieving a sense of peace and tranquility?

Do you experience time as a friend or foe? Does your life appear to be progressing along a straight line, or is it more reflective of a circle or a spiral?

# Five

## RELIGIONS OF HOPE: ALLIES IN THE SKY

The greatest gains need no tally. To glimpse what belonging means to a Chinese; to sense with a Burmese grandmother what passes in life and what endures; to understand how a Hindu can regard his personality as only a mask overlaying and obscuring the infinite beneath . . . to swing such things into view . . . is to have another world to live in.
—Huston Smith, *The World's Religions*

Philosopher Huston Smith relied on the language of the performing arts to introduce his classic text on world religions. Borrowing from Nietzsche, he encouraged readers to become "cosmic dancers," able to "leap beyond" a singular view of the universe. Smith fervently believed that there was much to gain by sampling the faith of others. He added that the different belief systems could be viewed collectively as a part of a "mysterious harmony" or treated individually as essential contributors to a "solid chorus." In this chapter, the pluralism that Smith espoused is presented as a "motivational tapestry" of alternative faith sources and "hope constructions."

### Hopes of the World's Religions

The religions of the world represent different ways of thinking about and experiencing hope. In large part, this spiritual diversity is attributable to varying levels of investment in the mastery, attachment, or survival motives. Presumably these hope patterns arose as a result of unique historical, geographic, and sociopolitical conditions. For example, some cultures may have fostered a strong mastery-focused religious system as a result of having an abundance of natural resources, a pattern of successful explorations beyond existing borders, conquests of other lands and cultures, or a favorable geographical position. Attachment-oriented cultures and religions might be traced back to a nomadic past or prolonged national fragmentation as well as constant political instability, resulting in a strong emphasis on the tribe, clan, or family. In contrast, some cultures and their resulting faith systems may place a premium on survival due to a hostile climate, frequent or large-scale natural disasters, repeated invasions from foreigners, or few natural resources. As a consequence, some religions, as shown in Table 5.1, tend to be more "mastery-oriented," while others tend toward "attachment-centered" or "survival-based" emphases; most, however, do incorporate at least some aspects of each motive system.

To identify the key motive system(s) operating within each major religion, we used two different types of content analysis. First, we recorded *all references to hope* in the sacred texts of ten major belief systems, including those of the African Ifa, Australian Aborigines, Buddhists, Christians, Hindus, Jews, Muslims, and three Native American groups (Alaskan and Arctic dwellers, Lakota, and Navajo). Five of these had a recognized sacred text that we could search. However, for the Australian Aborigines, Ifa, and three Native American groups, we had to consult a collection of classic legends and folktales.

Whenever hope was cited in a given text, we noted whether it applied to mastery, attachment, or survival issues. Although there was variability in the size of the selected texts, they were comparable, especially when the percentage, rather than the absolute number, of relevant citations were taken into account. To substantiate the findings derived from this initial sorting process, we then conducted a *second cross-check* of each sacred text or story collection, this time to search for the *number of attachment, mastery, or survival references, irrespective of whether they directly dealt with hope.*

TABLE 5.1. *Varieties of Hope Expressed in Different Religions*

| Varieties of Hope | Religious Systems |
|---|---|
| Attachment based | Australian (Aboriginal) |
| Salvation based | Buddhist |
| Mastery and attachment based | Hindu |
| Attachment and survival based | |
|   Religious subvariety (human bonds) | Judaic |
|   Spiritual subvariety (nature bonds) | Ifa (Western Africa) |
|   Spiritual/religious subvariety (nature and human) | Native American |
| Attachment and survival, with limited mastery basis | Islam |
| Attachment and survival, with moderate mastery basis | Catholic and Greek Orthodox |
| Mastery, attachment, and survival basis | Protestant (most denominations) |

We found striking parallels between hope types (first analysis) and the overall emphasis on attachment, mastery, or survival within a particular belief system (second analysis). Interestingly, the connection between hope types and motive patterns seemed as clear for those texts that contained only a few references to hope as for those that had many hope-related passages. In essence, the emphasis on attachment, mastery, and survival within a religion appears to be a very good spiritual barometer, predictive of the way hope is expressed and experienced within that faith (see Table 5.2).

For example, the majority of Buddhist hope references were about salvation, mirroring the greater number of survival themes found in the Pali Canon. Aboriginal references to hope were strongly rooted in attachment, with 90% of the "Dreamtime" stories dealing with the preservation of ties to humanity or the natural world.

Hope is most explicitly recognized within the Christian faith, but this does not mean that it is only important for Catholics and Protestants. For instance, hope is the underlying theme in the great epic tales of the Lakota and Navajo. Moreover, *there were striking similarities among Christians, Jews, and Muslims;* with some subtle differences, all three of these faiths place a premium on attachment and survival in their construction of hope. This is particularly intriguing given the ongoing conflict in the Middle East and rifts involving the West and segments of the Arab world.

### Buddhist Pali Canon

Analyzing the scripture of Buddhism presented the most difficult challenge. Anyone interested in a serious review of this literature must contend with its sheer immensity (the most condensed edition runs 40 volumes) and the fact that some of the Pali text has not been translated into English. We began our search with the "Tipitaka Online," a website offering an extensive and representative sample of the Pali Canon, the most important text in Theraveda Buddhism. We discovered only four references to hope, three dealing with survival and one involving attachment.

A construction of hope based on survival rather than attachment or mastery concerns might have been predicted for Buddhism, traditionally viewed as the great salvation religion. Classic or Theraveda Buddhism is marked by a renunciation of futile worldly pursuits and a diminished emphasis on the need for attachments of any kind. In contrast, the increasing popularity of the offshoot Mahayana school might be due to its promise of a better afterlife, including a heavenly encounter with a savior saint ("Bodhisattva").

The two initial references to hope in the Tipitaka come from the first "basket of wisdom," the Vinaya Pitaka. This includes the story of Prince Digvaruh and the behaviors expected of a dutiful adherent. The first account deals with the wisdom of reconciliation in wartime to ensure mutual survival, while the second describes ways to endure various natural disasters. The third mention of hope, from the Sutta Pitaka (second "basket of wisdom"), offers guidelines designed to assure the continued success

TABLE 5.2. *Hope- and Motive-Related Passages in Spiritual Writings*

| Spiritual Belief Systems | Sacred Texts, Myths, or Folktales | Motives Associated with Hope-Related Passages | | | Hope-Related Motives throughout Text/Collection | | |
|---|---|---|---|---|---|---|---|
| | | Mastery | Attach | Survival | Mastery | Attach | Survival |
| Australian Aborigine | Dreamtime stories | 0 | 1 | 0 | 0 | 9 | 1 |
| Buddhism | Pali Canon | 0 | 1 | 3 | 1 | 0 | 36 |
| Christianity | New Testament | 9 | 29 | 29 | 223 | 294 | 272 |
| Hinduism | Rig Veda | 11 | 12 | 3 | 1,652 | 961 | 272 |
| Ifa | Ijo Orunmila | 0 | 1 | 0 | 4 | 14 | 11 |
| Islam | Qur'an | 2 | 9 | 9 | 191 | 208 | 321 |
| Judaism | Torah | 0 | 4 | 5 | 46 | 121 | 83 |
| Native American | Collected stories | 1 | 7 | 6 | 4 | 34 | 15 |

of one's family in both the social and spiritual domains. In the fourth hope passage, it is suggested that earthly pursuits are a feeble response to the human condition, with real salvation coming only through an unwavering spiritual devotion.

To validate these findings, we searched throughout the Pali Canon for all references to the hope motives. The emphasis on survival was quite compelling. Whereas 97% of the citations dealt with ways of limiting suffering, there was but one allusion to mastery and not a single reference to attachment. Many of the survival references were found in the famed *Book of Protection,* which provides advice on eluding death and on methods for coping with grief, sorrow, and loss.

### Christian Bible

The New Testament contains 67 hope references, with most linked to either attachment (43%) or survival (43%). The strong emphasis on community and safety is rooted in the very origins of Christianity, which flourished in the chaos of a disintegrating and danger-filled Roman Empire. Those who confronted the demise of a world order that had stood for a thousand years were undoubtedly beset with profound alienation and tremendous fear. The traditions of the past could no longer be trusted. The present was filled with terror. There was internal mayhem even as barbarians chipped away at the empire's borders. The future looked bleak. Against this backdrop, early Christianity held out the promise of a lasting connection with Jesus and the Lord, as well as the opportunity for salvation in the heaven of God's kingdom.

But despite the emphasis on attachment and survival, the salience of hope-related mastery is also apparent in the New Testament. Approximately one seventh of its references to hope are linked to mastery pursuits. Furthermore, all references to major motives revealed an even more balanced distribution, with mastery accounting for 28%, attachment for 37%, and survival for 35%.

Sociologist Malcolm Hamilton touched on two historical factors that might explain the incorporation of goal-related elements into Christian hope. He pointed out first that prior to the advent of Christianity, the dream of many Jews was to overthrow the leadership of Rome. Some of these sects, wrote Hamilton, "retained and promoted the idea of the ultimate deliverance of Israel by a superhuman hero and military leader, the Messiah, who would overthrow all enemies." And second, historical records show that many of the early Christians, including Paul, aggressively labored to extend their influence throughout the Italian Peninsula, Greece, and the Middle East.

Within the various Protestant denominations, the role of mastery motivation is even more prominent. In contrast to Catholicism, with its greater emphasis on spiritual gains, the Calvinist tradition vigorously supports the pursuit of material rewards. In fact, this so-called Protestant ethic has been implicated in the development of virtually every aspect of social, economic, and cultural progress in the West. Moreover, the history of hope within the Judeo-Christian tradition is a tale of increasing mastery influences and decreasing attachment concerns. From an ancient "gift of the Jews" to a Christian virtue and then a part of the Protestant ethic, conceptions of hope have become progressively more goal oriented.

An interesting recent phenomenon attests to this Protestant focus on a "goal-centered" hope. Based on a short, five-line prayer buried in the middle of the Book of Chronicles in the Old Testament, Bruce Wilkinson's 2001 bestseller, *The Prayer of Jabez*, sold over 4 million copies in several months. On its back cover, one reads, "Do you want to be extravagantly blessed by God?" In addition, prospective buyers are guaranteed the "keys to a life of extraordinary favor with God" as well as "miracles on a regular basis." Meanwhile, the actual prayer seems to be less focused on material gains and more on spiritual blessings:

> Oh that thou wouldst bless me and enlarge my border [mastery], and that the hand might be with me [attachment], and that thou wouldst keep me from harm so that it might not hurt me [survival].

In asking God for his own territory to explore and master, as well as an ongoing connection with the almighty and a sense of safety, Jabez is asking for hope. Thus, what should draw Christians to the *Prayer of Jabez* is not the promise of riches but the fact that it provides a brilliant encapsulation of the most important human needs. In essence, it is a *perfect hope prayer*. Perhaps its phenomenal success is due to its simultaneously addressing, on a conscious level, the Western concern for mastery and, on a deeper level, the need for a fuller experience of hope.

Nonetheless, we searched the scientific literature, as reflected in contemporary psychological research, to assess the extent to which Western hope continues to move in the direction of "goals" and "mastery." Between 1887 and 2002 there were 391 publications originating from Europe and the United States that dealt with the subject of hope. Using virtually the same criteria that we applied in analyzing sacred texts, we broke down the number of times that hope in these references was associated with attachment, mastery, or survival themes. Mastery-related references (94) appeared twice as often as attachment themes (41) and approximately 20% more often than survival-related concepts (see Table 5.3).

### Ijo Orunmila (West African Ifa)

Ifa originated more than 8,000 years ago in Western Africa. Similar to Kongo worshippers, the other popular faith in this region, members of Ifa share beliefs and practices designed to "preserve harmony with nature and the Creator." The Ijo Orunmila contains the Ifa's cherished prayers and parables. While there is only a single meditation on hope, it is the dominant theme in one of the longest and most important Ifa tales. The story clearly implies that hope flows from attachments rather than mastery or survival

TABLE 5.3. *Shifts in Western Hope in Terms of Motives*

| | | Hope References | | |
| | | Mastery based | Attachment based | Survival based |
| Faith System | Text Searched | | | |
| --- | --- | --- | --- | --- |
| Judaism | Torah (1300 B.C.) | 0% | 45% | 55% |
| Christianity | New Testament (150 A.D.) | 14% | 43% | 43% |
| Scientific psychology | Online database (1887–2002) | 50% | 22% | 28% |

efforts. The narrative is about wayward ancestors who have attempted to strike out on their own without community assistance or spiritual guidance. Lacking support or guidance, they aimlessly wander into isolation, suffering, and despair. Hope is finally restored when the lost souls reestablish their bonds with loved ones.

> There was a time long ago when all was in harmony . . . We started to do things counter to the law . . . We lost the path . . . After a century of parched dreams . . . The people were refreshed with the hope of faith . . . They found the truth by returning to the arms of those they left behind.

When searching the remaining 29 tales and prayers in the Ijo Orunmila for references to attachment, mastery, or survival concerns, we found that almost half (14) dealt exclusively with ways of repairing or enhancing valued relationships. This was to be expected, given the multitude of special bonds that constitute the Ifa way of life. In addition to Olorun, their "Creator," the Ifa devote themselves to countless lesser spirits, deified ancestors, and departed loved ones. Only 4 stories focused on mastery, and while 11 dealt with survival, 8 of these also incorporated attachment themes.

### Qur'an

Most of the 20 references to hope in the Qur'an relate to attachment or survival, with only 2 associated with mastery. One of the mastery-related stories refers to the conquest of enemies while the other concerns the desire for personal or collective gain. Given only a single reference to a "conquest-driven hope," one wonders if the Western stereotype of an Islamic warrior heritage has been overdrawn. On the other hand, the more numerous references to an "attachment-driven hope" support the notion that the initial spread of Islam was greatly fueled by the "binding power" of socially and economically interdependent clans.

Nearly half of the hope terms in the Qur'an are associated with attachment. Followers are seeking "access to Allah" or expressing hope that important relationships will continue to flourish. Another 45% of the hope-related references are linked to survival.

They are embedded in requests for mercy and forgiveness from Allah, who can be harsh in his judgment: "He shows you the lightning causing fear and hope."

When we examined the Qur'an for all motive references, survival emerged as the most salient concern, followed by attachment and then mastery. Overall, Islamic hope is primarily survival and attachment based, with a more limited incorporation of the mastery motive.

### Torah

Despite its shared roots with Christianity, Jewish hope is different. Devoid of any reference to power or mastery pursuits as in the New Testament, the hopes expressed in the Torah focus exclusively on attachment and survival, themes that dominate four of the first five books. Of the nine references to hope, four involved attachment and the other five dealt with survival issues. In Genesis, Abraham and Sarah are consumed with their hope for offspring while Jacob pines for one more chance to see Joseph, his favorite son. After the promise of Genesis, Exodus is filled with stories of entrapment, suffering, and social fragmentation—of sacrifice and strict religious observances, years of desert wandering, and ongoing intergroup conflict. Indeed, when hope is not associated with preserving and nurturing relationships, the focus in the Torah turns to survival, particularly dreams of "lost tranquility." In Leviticus, reassurance along the weary path to the "promised land" is withheld from those who forsake God ("[They] shall be shamed . . . [and] buried in the earth"), whereas those who stay close to God are permitted to exclaim, "Heal me . . . and I shall be healed . . . Save me and I shall be saved." In *Numbers*, God promises vineyards and a valley to "a door of hope" that will restore Israel to the glory it had known prior to Egyptian domination.

When we searched the Torah for references to motives, the primacy of attachment and survival was again quite evident. Compared to mastery, we found nearly twice as many references to survival and nearly three times as many to attachment. It is noteworthy that more than a third of the 250 motive-related citations involved either family welfare or concerns about death. The overall findings suggest that Judaic hope is essentially a two-fold construction, fashioned from attachment and survival concerns. Recalling Cahill's thesis, it thus might be more accurate to suggest that the new kind of hope the Jewish culture inspired was one that binds together the collective and assures them of care and protection.

### Rig Veda (Hindu)

The references to hope in the Rig Veda are concentrated in those passages that deal directly with the qualities of Agni, the fire god who rules over the earth and is the "adorable friend of man . . . found everywhere, including the vast offspring of the firmament that are the seven eternal and ever-youthful rivers . . . Agni . . . [is] their common embryo." Of the 26 references to hope in Agni, only 3 dealt with survival.

The basis of Hindu hope appears to be a combination of attachment (46%) and mastery (42%), with considerably less emphasis on self-preservation. The Hindu focus on relationships is not surprising in light of India's caste system, which influences every dimension of life, including marital choices and friendships as well as business opportunities and even available forms of rebirth. (The sociologist Émile Durkheim suggested that the Hindu castes flourished because they constituted forms of refuge within a chronically fractured India).

Because many assume that Eastern religions espouse renunciation and asceticism, the Hindu emphasis on mastery might come as a surprise. Nevertheless, there is empirical support for a mastery-related view of Hinduism. Psychologist David McClelland analyzed the goal-related imagery in children's stories from 21 nations and found that India ranked third in need for achievement, ahead of such countries as Germany and Japan, while trailing only Turkey and the United States.

Our search for references to attachment, mastery, and survival in the Rig Veda confirmed that self-preservation is not a pressing concern among Hindus. Less than one tenth of the motive references concerned self-preservation. Attachment related themes such as love and friendship account for three times as many references as those involving death, fear, and related topics of survival. Moreover, mastery-related references such as those pertaining to power and strength appeared six times as often as themes of self-preservation.

In the West there is a tendency to equate "mastery" with acts of aggressive control of the external environment, but Hinduism acknowledges various levels of human strivings, including mastery in the service of material goals such as pleasure, success, or social status, and mastery for the sake of more spiritual or transcendent goals. The achievement of spiritual transcendence may take several different paths. Enlightenment can be found through knowledge, love, work, or meditation. True spiritual success demands a great deal of effort and training, and Hindu spiritual exercises can be very physically demanding. For example, the well-known lotus position is extremely difficult to assume, and especially painful for a novice to maintain. It places enormous strain on the bones, muscles, and tendons. When practiced in the correct manner, it results in a temporary numbing of the lower limbs, leading to a disembodied state and creating a rarefied form of pure sensory awareness. The goal of this and other forms of Hindu yoga and meditation is two-fold: cultivation of strength via self-discipline and union with the powerful resources of an inner God or "Atman."

To achieve spiritual transcendence, Hindus must also follow the laws of Karma and Samsara. These beliefs deal with the spiritual implications of everyday actions and the transmigration of the soul. Together, they further highlight the influence of the attachment and mastery drives in the construction of Hindu hope. While the cultivation of good karma is important, achieving a more favorable rebirth without the support of your caste is considered difficult, if not impossible. Samsara or reincarnation is also closely tied to membership within a caste: With support from his or her particular social group, a Hindu will have greater hope of ascending to a higher rung on the eternal ladder of spiritual rebirths. (In this sense of moving up, reincarnation may be more of a mastery and attachment-oriented hope than a pure survival issue.)

Consistent with our finding that there is little emphasis on survival and terror management within Hinduism, the religious scholar Huston Smith noted that tragedy is the only form of art that India has failed to produce on a world-class level. The Hindu conception of both death and the afterlife is undoubtedly a factor. Hindus conceive of "Hell" as a temporary resting place for wayward souls rather than a spiritual dead end.

## Native American Spirituality

The belief systems of Native Americans are considered to be more spiritual than religious. Their sacred spaces encompass both the material and the immaterial. Divinity is found in the abundance of the immediate flora and fauna and in a vast pantheon of distant gods and spirits. While this nature-based spirituality binds together the "people of the first nations," there is a great deal of diversity among various tribes, including scores of languages and striking contrasts in ceremonies, dress, and diet. Even so, Native Americans are unified in their devotion to kinship ties and respect for nature. They also find a common bond in surviving both the perils of the physical environment and the dangers presented by hostile outsiders.

By design, our discussion of Native Americans is rather detailed, reflecting their diversity as well as their prominent role in shaping contemporary views of spirituality. We begin with an examination of the beliefs of the Yupik and other indigenous tribes of Canada and the Arctic regions. Like their neighbors to the south, they are deeply committed to living in harmony and balance with nature and one another. Phyllis Morrow, who chronicled the life of the Alaskan Yupik, highlighted their belief in the interrelatedness of all things living and dead:

> Naming is a basic means of perpetuating relationships among the living and between the living and the dead, for those who share the same name may share a spiritual essence . . . The dead person "enters" the new namesake, who acts just like the one after whom he or she is named . . . The living namesake is called by the kin term appropriate to the deceased and often treated as if he or she were that person . . . In this way naming relationships collapse generations and multiply layer kinship ties, creating a dense social network among the living and the dead.

Survival is the other great theme among these "people of the north," understandable for a culture that must grapple with some of the coldest temperatures on earth, an inconsistent food supply, and many months without sunlight. Many of their songs and myths suggest that the weather itself, as well as human hunger and seasonal darkness, must be understood as necessary elements in the balance of nature. Their tales focus on the awesome powers that lie behind the blanketing snow, the crackling thunder, and the ubiquitous mountains of unyielding ice.

The Yupik have many conceptions of death and several modes of depicting the fate of the soul in the hereafter. For a better understanding of their multilayered view of death and the afterlife, it is necessary to take into account the Yupik's daily encounters with pain and peril. Clearly, from a terror management perspective, it is highly adaptive in such an unforgiving environment to sanction a wide array of salvation possibilities.

One of the most comprehensive sources of Native American literature is *Coming to Light*, edited by Brian Swann. Approximately half of the tales are drawn from the Yupik and other tribes of the Artic and subarctic regions. Five of these are hope-related stories, with four dealing with attachment, the other survival. In one tale, "Speech for the Removal of Grief," a Tlingit community gathers to help one of its grief-stricken members cope with the death of a family member. Each participant takes a turn paying homage to the deceased, offering hope in the form of cherished memories and promises of a lasting legacy.

In "The Wolverine," a classic Innu survival tale, the title character must enlist the help of other animals in establishing a safe haven. Against the backdrop of an ensuing flood and perched on a few remaining stones, the wolverine implores his fellow creatures to search for soil. One by one, they dive to the ocean depths, until finally the muskrat surfaces with a plentitude of earth to save the day. Two excellent examples of attachment fused with survival concerns are "The Boy and the Killer Whale" (Dena'ina) and the "The Girl Who Married the Bear" (Tlingit).

A further analysis of *Coming to Light* was done to record the presence of mastery, attachment, and survival themes across the entire collection of Native American tales. Attachment was the primary focus in 23 of the stories, 9 emphasized survival, and only 2 dealt with mastery. This dual focus on attachment and survival parallels our findings from the five hope-centered arctic region stories and foreshadows the hope of the Lakota and Navajo.

For the Lakota, the most powerful symbols of hope are the White Buffalo Calf and the peace pipe. The first reported citing of the rare white buffalo took place in the sacred Black Hills of South Dakota more than 2,000 years ago. According to legend, two hungry warriors searching for food noticed an albino calf descending from the sky. However, as the calf drew closer, it was miraculously transformed into a beautiful Indian maiden who stayed but 4 days yet bequeathed to them a precious gift, the sacred peace pipe. The Lakota believe the peace pipe is a "spiritual conduit," a "vehicle of hope" for securing protection for themselves and their tribe while also granting a more intimate audience with the "Creator." By smoking the pipe while praying, they can directly ascend to Tackushkanshkan, "the prime mover." Indeed the Lakota "pipe carriers" may be viewed as the "hope bearers" for the tribe and the entire Indian nation.

The birth in 1994 of an albino calf in a small Wisconsin town prompted Lakota tribal leaders to herald the dawning of a more peaceful and spiritually minded era, and a cosmic shift in human consciousness. The widely publicized account by storyteller "Night Sky" concluded with the following passage: "along with these calves was born a new tenet of hope. I pray that hope will prevail."

Julian Rice, an authority on the Lakota, described their culture as being much more concerned about "community" than mastery pursuits. According to him, "The first priority of Lakota culture has always been the preservation of its spiritual identity." The Lakota hero has typically been depicted as someone who succeeds in preserving tight kinship ties and other cherished family and tribal traditions. To substantiate Rice's view, we did a cross-check of the five Lakota tales contained in *Coming to Light*. Three of these dealt exclusively or primarily with relationships among family members or with the preservation of bonds between nature and humanity.

However, it is also clear that survival concerns play a significant role in the spiritual life of the Lakota, with two of the five tales focusing on issues of protection and safety. In "Wilderness Mentors," an anxious man finds that he is traveling with ghosts that cannot be shaken, no matter how fast he runs. Realizing that he is "haunted by fear," the man finds salvation by acknowledging his inner demons and then accepting the help of a coyote who brings him into the fold of a nurturing village. In this and other Lakota tales, the legendary coyote serves as a symbol of both communal hope (attachment) and primal fear (survival).

The Navajo of the American Southwest have lived for centuries in matrilineal clans. For the Navajo, leaving one's territory is synonymous with forsaking one's identity. In fact, within their culture there is no word for "relocation." The Navajo also cultivate a close relationship with nature, finding "godliness" in a vast array of flora and fauna and in the soil, air, and water. The world is their altar, with "father sky" above, "mother earth" below, and four sacred mountains to the north, south, east, and west. In the words of a Navajo elder, "we the five-fingered beings are related to the four-legged, the winged beings, the spirits . . . We are all relatives."

Many Navajo myths are designed to teach lessons in morality. A common protagonist is the coyote, [here] a trickster who showcases many of the social evils that the Navajo rail against, including selfishness, mistreatment of elders, and disrespect for tribal ancestors. Invariably, the coyote is killed or ostracized in some dramatic fashion, highlighting the fate of those who violate community standards while reinforcing the Navajo belief that survival and attachment are deeply intertwined.

We analyzed 18 Navajo myths, 6 from *Coming to Light* and 12 from *The Pollen Path*, a collection of Native American tales edited by poet Margaret Schevill Link. Eight references to hope were found, three relating primarily to attachment, four emphasizing survival, and only one dealing with mastery. "The River of Separation" is one of the clearest examples of the Navajo tendency to link attachment and survival. In this story, the inability of men and women to live in harmony leads to both individual suffering and community disintegration. Another passage, from "The Changing Coyote," offers a striking metaphor for an attachment-based hope. This tale depicts a selfish coyote threatening a clan's effort to build a better community just as "people were tying to get more light into the world." An attachment- and survival-based hope is also reflected in the "Blessingway." This two-day devotional ritual to peace and harmony is designed to solidify tribal members' bonds with the protective forces of nature as well as with their family and the rest of the community. Part of this spiritual centerpiece pays homage to "God and the Sun... the Dawn and the Afterglow... the Turquoise Boy and the Corn Kernel Girl." Interestingly, more than one Native American writer has explicitly interpreted the "Blessingway" as an appeal for "good hope."

An examination of the motivational content in Navajo myths indicated that attachment themes were predominant in approximately two thirds of the stories. Although survival themes accounted for only one fifth of all the motive references, they appeared twice as often as mastery concerns.

### Australian Dreamtime

The aboriginal population of Australia is an ancient and diverse mosaic, representing scores of different languages and a multitude of customs. Similar to Native Americans, they value kinship ties and treasure the sacredness of the natural world. There is a strong emphasis on totems, which represent each family and tribe as distinguished by a special relationship with a particular species of plant or animal. Despite variations in customs and dialects, the Aborigines are united by a complex religious tradition known as the "Dreamtime."

The "Dreaming" is a multilayered spiritual ritual that should not be confused with the simpler Western notion of a nighttime reverie. Participants join in elaborate dances punctuated by frequent foot stomping, interwoven with repetitive, hypnotic verses, chronicling the lives of valued ancestors. The playing of a flute-like instrument, the "Didgerirdoo," provides a mesmerizing musical background that is experienced as a veritable echo of the "soul of mother earth."

The "dreaming" allows Aborigines to penetrate multiple dimensions of time and reality. Once there, they can make contact with spiritual protectors, celestial guides, and powerful totems. Most importantly, by reaching into eternity, they can reconnect with long departed ancestors and make reparations for their various sins. Similar to the Hindus who attend to karma, Aborigines are deeply wary of the eternal consequences of past and present transgressions. In short, the "Dreamtime" is a beautiful example of an attachment-based hope, offering future well-being in exchange for strengthening one's emotional and spiritual connections with the interpersonal and material worlds as well as with the plane of the sacred.

The insights of the existentialist philosopher, John Paul Sartre, can be used to provide an even deeper understanding of the Aborigine's "Dreamtime hopes." *Sartre argued that every emotion is an attempt to either restore or change the world in which we live.* When we become angry, it is because we are trying to reestablish a "just-world" that should treat us fairly. When we are proud, we "create an audience" of admirers that holds us in high esteem for a valued accomplishment. On a group level, the "Dreamtime" appears to be following the same emotional blueprint.

According to anthropologist Michael Winkelman, rituals such as the "dreaming" and other totem ceremonies are carefully orchestrated attempts to thrust the individual and the group into a more transcendent reality. In the course of cultural evolution, groups have found that they can create or restore a desired world via chanting, drumming, foot stomping, and the use of music. These practices create a "neurological symphony" that brings serenity and a sense of mystical connection. Winkelman noted that such experiences are frequently described in the new age literature as "soul journeys," "flying," "out of body experiences," or even "astral projections." Participants have the experience of being delivered from the clutches of evil and delving into a mystical union with benign forces of nature and the spirit world.

The single aboriginal hope reference appears in the legend of "Baiame," "the maker and bountiful provider." This attachment-centered myth describes the hopes of the world in terms of peace, harmony, and a life managed in cooperative balance with the rest of creation. According to this legend, in the beginning "all was well in the world." However, when human beings violated their covenant with Baiame, they caused a "rupture of hope" that brought suffering and death. In his mercy, Baiame offered humanity another chance by establishing for them a safe harbor in the heavens. To this day, the Aborigines believe that "the bright Southern Cross . . . is a place for them in the limitless regions of space, the home of the All-father Himself."

We did our second (motive) search of 14 popular dreamtime stories for references to attachment, mastery, and survival. Only a single myth dealt with survival, featuring a black duck totem who warns the community of encroaching dangers. In contrast, nine centered on relationship issues, again paralleling the dominant attachment thrust of the Baiame tale.

## Hope as the Essence of Religion

According to anthropologist Desmond Morris, religion springs from three human urges: the need for an omnipotent leader; the need for a super-parent; and the need to be protected from the threat of death. His insights are consistent with our integrative framework, emphasizing that hope, as well as religion, is rooted in mastery, attachment, and survival needs. In fact, throughout most of recorded history, hope has been discussed primarily within a religious context. Philosophers and theologians have been drawn to the concept of hope while attempting to sort through the purpose of human existence, the pain of existential alienation, and the longing for ultimate salvation.

Ernst Bloch found several common themes that cut across the world's religions, including the promise of deliverance by something "above" and a strong focus on a "future good." Similarly, Erik Erikson noted that hope is typically presumed to occupy an "elevated space" and to be future directed. Most religions are oriented around a trusted deity (attachment) who offers an ultimate form of empowerment (mastery). Moreover, as noted previously, many individuals find themselves gravitating toward religion for hope in times of crisis (survival).

Viewing hope in terms of the "vital motives" permits a deeper consideration of the ways in which it is linked to faith, religion, and spirituality. Systems of faith are fundamentally about growth and renewal, reintegration and salvation. Likewise, from a motive perspective, hope is the emotion that embodies goal strivings, sacred connections, and terror management. Hope in one guise or another is at the core of every major religious or spiritual belief system and shares with each a common ground (see Table 5.4).

### Atheism and Hope

But is religion a prerequisite for hope? Or is hope a virtue that is within the reach of an agnostic or atheist?

The philosopher and scientist Bertrand Russell was probably the most well-known atheist of the twentieth century. In *Ideas That Have Harmed Mankind*, he openly derided any form of religious belief, and in *Why I Am Not a Christian*, he dismissed classic arguments for the existence of God. Going further, Russell asserted that terror is the underlying source of all religious beliefs, "Fear is the basis of the whole thing—fear of the mysterious, fear of defeat, fear of death."

Russell's response to the human condition was to invest in a different kind of terror management, one based on the scientific method and human potential.

TABLE 5.4. *Religion and Hope: The Common Ground*

| Needs Underlying Religious and Spiritual Beliefs | Motives Underlying Hope | Psychological Building Blocks of Hope |
| --- | --- | --- |
| Renewal | Mastery | Goals, dreams, mediated control beliefs, a legacy, collective vision |
| Reintegration | Attachment | Trust, openness, internalized others, presence |
| Salvation | Survival | Coping and defense mechanisms, terror-management skills |

Science can teach us, and I think our hearts can teach us, no longer to look around for imaginary supports, no longer to invent allies in the sky, but rather to look to our own efforts.... A good world needs knowledge ... it does not need ... words uttered long ago by ignorant men ... it needs hope for the future, not looking back ...

How successful was Russell in cultivating an atheistic hope? We are given a partial answer in his eloquent autobiography. Not surprisingly, he alluded to three great quests that preoccupied him throughout his life:

I have sought love [attachment] ... because it brings ecstasy ... it relieves loneliness, that terrible loneliness in which one shivering consciousness looks over the rim of the world into the cold unfathomable lifeless abyss ... I have sought knowledge [mastery] ... to understand the hearts of men ... why the stars shine ... to apprehend the Pythagorean power by which number holds sway above the flux ... Love and knowledge ... led upwards towards the heavens. But [survival issues] pity always brought me back down to earth ... children in famine ... victims tortured ... helpless old people ... and the whole world of loneliness, poverty, and pain.

Russell emphasized that he "found [life] worth living" and "would gladly live it again if the chance were offered." Nevertheless, he acknowledged it had been a difficult journey, and that his "passions," like "great winds," had blown him "hither and thither, in a wayward course, over a deep ocean of anguish, reaching to the very verge of despair." As a consequence of witnessing tragedies great and small, he confessed that "echoes of pain reverberate in my heart." Russell found that seemingly unavoidable dimensions of the human condition "make a mockery of what ... life should be." He went on to lament, "I long to alleviate the suffering, but I cannot and I too suffer."

We will never know if a religiously grounded faith would have made Russell's odyssey less painful. The larger question is whether any humanist or atheist can derive adequate hope from a purely secular worldview. When Nietzsche declared "God is dead," he pictured a cosmic void that could only be filled in a far-off time by a highly evolved "superman." In contrast, Russell shared with Hegel, Feuerbach, and several other noted philosophers the idea that science and humanism could substitute for a belief in God.

Some degree of hope that is based on progress and goals would appear within reach through science and technology. Science provides a powerful means of exercising the drive for exploration, mastery, and control over the environment. Humans have commanded space ships among the stars, plumbed the ocean depths, climbed Everest, and traversed both the North and South poles. Nevertheless, hope is based on more than mastery. A full experience of hope also requires trust and a loving presence as well as potential solutions to the existential realities of human vulnerability and mortality.

Through studies of human development, scientists have arrived at a better under-standing of the attachment process. Practitioners have developed various techniques for repairing parent–child and romantic relationships, improving communication skills, and building intimacy. Nevertheless, some attachment disruptions and disturbances appear resistant to traditional psychological interventions, and even the well adjusted are subject to a variety of losses in the course of a lifetime.

Does science offer viable solutions for addressing the pain of loss and the fear of death? Can a humanistic worldview rooted in science overcome death anxiety or what the existentialists refer to as "ego chill"? Is there enough salvation in the here and now to deal with these universal challenges? Alternatively, must humanity reach for a more transcendent reality, a higher plane of hope, if it wishes to effect more enduring bonds and realize some semblance of immortality?

From our perspective, there must be enough degrees of freedom in our under-standing of hope and faith to accommodate believers and nonbelievers, professionals and lay persons, traditionalists and New Age disciples. While the need for hope is nonnegotiable, not everyone can or wants to believe in a higher power. Likewise, there are countless others who reject the notion that "God" may be found in the laboratory. To paraphrase the philosopher Daniel Dennett, it is important to carve out enough elbow room in establishing faith possibilities, lest we underestimate the human capacity for creativity in the pursuit of hope.

---

*Fifth Hope Meditation*

After learning more about the hope content of the various religions of the world, have your opinions about these belief systems shifted in any way? Were you surprised by anything that you read? Do you feel comfortable with your present religious or spiritual beliefs? One way to think about this is to ask yourself, does your present belief system—religious, spiritual, agnostic, or atheist—meet your deepest mastery, attachment, and survival needs? If not, are you drawn to a particular faith system discussed in this chapter? Do you think it would be possible to integrate or complement your present beliefs with one of the other views presented in this chapter? Alternatively, do you believe that you might have to consider a new faith?

# Six

## FAITH: THE ASSURANCE OF THINGS
## HOPED FOR

If all of us could read the different faiths from the standpoint of the followers
of these faiths, we should find that they were at bottom all one.

—Gandhi

In this chapter we explore the diverse ways that human beings have expressed their
deepest beliefs and highest values. We identify some of the biases about faith and show
how true faith differs from blind devotion and can be distinguished from unhealthy
forms of impoverished spirituality.

### Hope's Underpinning

"Faith," according to the New Testament, "is the assurance of things hoped for, a belief
in things unseen." Without faith in karma, what hope sustains the Hindu? If Buddhists
abandon faith in the eight-fold path, what will guarantee their hoped-for release from
suffering? Without faith in the dreamtime, what hope is there for the aborigine of
Western Australia?

In daily conversations, "faith" and "hope" are used interchangeably, as if they were
one and the same thing. In private prayer or public pronouncement, they are often

uttered in a single breath. Recall the Reverend Billy Graham's post-September 11 sermon, a spiritual tapestry woven from alternating threads of faith and hope:

> I cling to that hope that I started with many years ago.
>
> There is hope for the future because of God's promise.
>
> As a Christian, I have hope.
>
> That's the hope of us who have our faith in God.

Similarly, when Czech freedom fighter Vaclav Havel accepted an honorary doctorate from the University of Michigan, he implored the graduating class to "remain faithful [in] the hope" that they could make the world a better place. He himself has traveled the world as an "ambassador of hope," appealing for a more hopeful attitude in addressing international conflicts.

Think for a moment about the words used to describe someone's faith. There is an allusion to a *foundation*: someone is a person of "deep faith" or has an "unshakable faith." Now reflect on the language of hope: you can "pin your hopes on science," or "place your hope in God," or feel that your hopes "rest" on a particular leader or hero. The implication is that hope is a *derived virtue*, that something is presumed to lie "under" or "beneath" it.

Faith, in short, underpins hope; it serves as an essential foundation and a critical ingredient in hope's development. This is especially true of *basic hope*, which is a generalized sense of trust in oneself, the world, and the future, as opposed to *directed hope*, which points toward a particular goal or outcome. Basic hope is the capacity that Erikson identified in trusting infants with healthy attachments, and it is the "spiritual virtue" that Havel so admired and strove to cultivate. It is also a major factor in determining one's response to life's greatest challenges.

When confronted by disaster, war, genocide, or any other form of evil, some see a world that has turned dark, and imagining that all is lost, they slip into despair. But others refuse, even in an earthly "hell," to abandon all hope. For those who are spiritually minded, the only adequate response to human evil is unwavering faith and hope.

A classic literary example can be found in Dostoevsky's masterpiece, *The Brothers Karamazov*. The devout Alyosha refuses to relinquish his faith in God. The young priest-in-training steadfastly maintains that a higher power will counter any brand of human evil. In contrast, his elder brother Ivan is plunged into despair for he is unable to imagine any conceivably adequate response to certain acts of human cruelty. He [Ivan] asked, for example, how it could ever be possible for anyone to atone for the evil perpetrated on innocent children. He is convinced "it is quite beyond my grasp" and wonders what harmony there can be if this cosmic debt cannot be repaid. Increasingly frustrated, he explodes:

> Tell me yourself . . . let's assume you that you were called upon to build the edifice of human destiny so that men would finally be happy and would find peace and tranquility. If you knew that, in order to attain this, you would have to torture just one single creature, let's say the little girl in the outhouse, and that on her unavenged tears you could build that edifice, would you agree to do it?

Undaunted, Alyosha replied that his faith is unshaken:

> No, I wouldn't consent . . . But there is a Being and He can forgive everything, all and for all, because He gave His innocent blood for all and everything. You have forgotten Him, and on Him is built the edifice, and it is to Him they cry aloud, 'Thou art just, O Lord, for Thy ways are revealed!'

## Hope in Times of Darkness

In a span of just a few years, beginning on April 24, 1915, an estimated 1.5 million Armenians were deported, raped, or murdered in towns and villages throughout the Turkish Empire. In a systematic program of genocide, Armenian men were tricked into turning in their hunting weapons for a draft they were never intended to serve. Deceived and helpless, they were immediately killed or systematically worked to death. The women, children, and elderly were told to abandon their settlements as part of a phony relocation plan that in reality amounted to a death march into the scorched Arabian Desert. According to an eyewitness:

> The most typical scene was that of the goon squads—bare-chested, wearing their loose trousers, accompanied by a police officer—attacking the Armenians. The latter fell on their knees, extending their hands hopefully to heaven.

On June 5, 1944, a similar spirit of prayer came over the United States. It was the day before the Word War II invasion of Normandy:

> The whole country knew that . . . something dire, something that might fail, was taking place . . . in a Brooklyn shipyard, welders knelt on the docks . . . and recited the Lord's prayer . . . the New York Stock Exchange observed two minutes of silent prayer . . . In Columbus, Ohio at 7:30 in the evening, all traffic stopped for five minutes while people prayed in the streets.

One year later, in Japan, on August 6, 1945 at precisely 8:15 in the morning, the clear blue sky over Hiroshima suddenly became incandescently white. Over 100,000 people met a new kind of death, a nuclear fate punctuated with a ghastly mushroom trail evoking archetypal images of Dante's *Inferno*. Those who were not killed by the blast had their clothes and skin blown off, then lingered in agony for days while helpless relatives tried to pull maggots out of their wounds. Taeko Teramae, a teenager when the bomb fell, was knocked down and covered with debris. Days later, she found a piece of glass large enough to see her seriously disfigured face. Years later, she spoke of a higher purpose:

> My hope is to have a comprehensive meeting of survivors . . . I hope to do
> something to support always [these] lonely people . . . We must testify in the hope
> that our experience will help to keep mankind from perishing.

Beginning in the late 1960s, the Khmer Rouge slaughtered 200,000 of their brothers and sisters in the "killing fields" of Cambodia, targeting just about anyone who was not poor, illiterate, or a part of their fringe organization. Their brutal practices precipitated mass starvation and disease, ultimately resulting in the death of one seventh of the country's total population. One survivor was Mardi Seng, only 10 years old when the carnage began. He and his family were imprisoned, chained, beaten, starved, and forced to watch helplessly as loved ones were maimed or randomly shot without warning or provocation. According to his essay, entitled *Hope*,

> We lived in the prison camp . . . we witnessed and experienced inhumane
> events . . . a few tried to escape but were gunned down and left to rot . . . even in the
> midst of these trials, we still hoped; hoped for supernatural events to take place.

A few days following the September 11 attack on the World Trade Center, Adam Goldman of Chicago spoke about the fate of his best friend, James Gartenberg, who had been trapped on the 86th floor of the north tower. A reporter prefaced Goldman's remarks with the following: "At 10:28 Gartenberg's building collapsed . . . It should have been the end of hope . . . But Goldman refused to give up hope."

> I hold out hope that he made it down, that elevators might have been
> working . . . Others might not want to build up their hopes and see them
> dashed . . . I just don't want to slip into the other camp and believe anything else.

## Acts of Faith

What is an act of faith? Is it an unwavering religious conviction in the midst of a great calamity? Is it when you put your trust in a complete stranger? Can you have a true and enduring faith in yourself? From our perspective, the answer to each of these questions is yes. We believe there are many different ways of experiencing and expressing faith. The following are some classic examples.

## Lourdes

The grotto of Lourdes in southern France, where Bernadette Soubirous experienced a vision of the Holy Mother in 1858, is the ultimate pilgrimage for a Christian. Upwards of 4 to 6 million people visit the shrine each year, including thousands seeking healing of one form or another. To enter the shrine, visitors must symbolically pass over the bridge of St. Michael to find a sacred garden decorated with immense statues, inspiring basilicas, and gilded crypts. To the left of the main walkway are the "Stations of the Cross," consisting of life-sized statues depicting Christ's tortured path to his crucifixion. At the far end lies the basilica of Bernadette atop a grotto where her vision of Mary was reported to have occurred.

Decades after returning from the shrine, many are still moved to tears as they recall images of sick children and adults on crutches, wheelchairs, or even stretchers. According to English novelist and Catholic priest Robert Hugh Benson, who visited Lourdes in 1907:

> A young [blind] man . . . touched me more than I can say. He was standing by the head of the bath, holding a basin in one hand and a little image of our Lady in the other, and was splashing water . . . into his eyes; these were horribly inflamed . . . I cannot describe the passion with which he did this . . . seeming to stare all the while towards the image he held, and whispering prayers in a quick undertone—hoping, no doubt, that his first sight would be the image of [Mary].

Despite thousands of healing testimonials, as of 2006, only 66 "miracles" had been recognized by the Medical Bureau of Lourdes as "certain, definitive and medically inexplicable." One such documented "miracle" involved Jean-Pierre Bely, who arrived at Lourdes severely crippled by multiple sclerosis.

> In June 1987, I underwent medical tests and a commission of several doctors declared me 100 percent disabled . . . Arriving at Lourdes I feel like I am elsewhere . . . a sensation of cold came over me . . . . Then, slowly it is replaced by a warm sensation of heat goes through all my body, starting at my feet and climbing up the spinal column . . . An idea came into my mind like an order, an invitation: Get up and walk!

## God's Natural Health Plan

> "You have cancer. You're going to die!" The doctors told me. But they were wrong!
>
> —Lorraine Day, M.D.

A best-selling author and former orthopedic trauma surgeon, Lorraine Day toured the country, speaking about her amazing recovery from invasive breast cancer. Her appearances have included *Sixty Minutes*, *Nightline*, *CNN*, *Oprah*, and *Larry King Live*. Upon visiting her Web site (http://www.drday.com/), you can view photos of her grapefruit-sized tumor and learn how she was wasting away before taking matters into her own hands.

> I refused mutilating surgery, chemotherapy and radiation, the treatment methods all physicians are taught, and got well by using God's natural remedies instead.

From Day's perspective, there are inherent flaws in traditional medical interventions for cancer. For example, she believed that the recommendation to remove her breast was ludicrous: The problem was "cancer," not "excess breast tissue." She felt it was equally senseless to have her cells blasted with harmful radiation in an effort to make them healthy. Likewise, she believed it was counterproductive to submit to powerful chemicals that would only further weaken her immune system. What was Day's preferred treatment?

> In order to get well, the body must be given huge amounts of nutrition in the form of carrot and green leafy vegetable juices, lots of water, lots of rest in order to repair diseased tissues and organs, freedom from stress, and plenty of time for prayer and Bible study, since God is the actual healer! He just does it through His natural health plan.

### Miracle Drug

An especially poignant example of an individual who placed all his faith in medical science was provided by psychologist Bruno Klopfer:

> Mr. Wright had far advanced lymphosarcoma. All known treatments had become ineffective. Tumors the size of oranges littered his neck, armpits, groin, chest and abdomen. His spleen and liver were enormously enlarged . . . one to two quarts of milky liquid had to be drained from his chest each day. He had to have oxygen to breathe, and his only medicine was a sedative to help him on his way . . . Despite his state, he still had hope.

Then Mr. Wright learned of an experimental cancer drug known as Krebiozen. Doctors were at first reluctant to administer the drug to Wright, but they gave in to his relentless begging and administered a single dose. Klopfer was stunned at what happened next:

> I had left him febrile, gasping for air, completely bedridden. Now, here he was, walking around the ward, chatting happily with the nurses, and spreading his message of good cheer to anyone who would listen . . . The tumors had melted like snowballs on a hot stove . . . Within less than two weeks, he was fully active, breathing normally and ready to be discharged.

Unfortunately, Mr. Wright soon learned from media reports that Krebiozen was a "total bust" with a failure rate of 100%. He "began to lose faith in his last hope . . . after two months of practically perfect health, he relapsed . . . becoming very gloomy and miserable." Klopfer decided to try his own experiment with Mr. Wright, telling him that the drug was as good as originally advertised. He suggested that the cause of the failed clinical trials was probably due to the drug's "sensitive chemical composition," meaning the test patients never received an "effective" dosage.

> Mr. Wright became his optimistic self again, eager to start over . . . his faith was very strong . . . I administered the first injection . . . consisting of fresh water and nothing more . . . Recovery from the second near-terminal state was even more dramatic . . . Tumor masses melted, chest fluid vanished . . . He was the picture of health.

### Mother Earth

A marine biologist and tireless environmentalist, Rachel Carson devoted her life to educating the public about the dangers of pesticides and other pollutants. Her research was attacked by members of the chemical industry but upheld by numerous scientific groups. Eventually her writings would play a central role in launching the environmentalist movement and in the banning of DDT. Her masterpiece, *Silent Spring* (1962), is considered one of the most important books published in the twentieth century. Undergoing treatment for breast cancer at the time of its publication, she died in 1964 and did not live to see Earth Day, the recycling movement, and other signs of rising environmentalism that she helped to inspire.

In 1954, addressing an audience in Columbus, Ohio, Carson spoke passionately about her love for nature and the spiritual power inherent in our ties to the earth.

> I believe natural beauty has a necessary place in the spiritual development of any individual . . . There is symbolic as well as actual beauty in the migration of birds,

in the ebb and flow of the tides, in the folded bud ready for the spring. There is something infinitely healing in these repeated refrains of nature—the assurance that dawn comes after night, and spring after winter.

Six years after Carson's death, another provocative environmental hypothesis was introduced, suggesting the earth itself is a living organism. Named after the Greek goddess of earth (Ge), the Gaia hypothesis presumes that our planet is a giant super-organism. From this perspective, all the earth's elements, including humans, have been organized by a powerful life force, a living "mega-cell" that orchestrates both the "terrestrial and atmospheric dance." Vaclav Havel, the former president of the Czech Republic, recognized the spiritual implications of the Gaia hypothesis. For him, not only did it imply that humans are all one but that there were even deeper forces joining the organic and inorganic. He surmised that, "the only real hope of people today is probably a renewal of certainty that we are rooted in the earth."

The African Ifa, the Australian "Dreamtimers," and various Native American tribes also share a spiritual perspective regarding the natural world. Among the Ifa, for example, individuals seek guidance from the powers of nature associated with their particular trade, craft, or role in society. Carvers and blacksmiths turn to the "spirit of iron"; healers offer respect to the "spirit of medicine and plants"; farmers praise the "spirits of the wind, rain and soil."

## A Candle in the Dark

> Science may be hard to understand . . . but it delivers the goods.
>
> —Carl Sagan

Carl Sagan is remembered as the brilliant astronomer who brought the mysteries of the universe to the general public through his popular television series, *Cosmos*. He was also a staunch atheist who, in one of his last books, *The Demon-Haunted World*, characterized science as "a candle in the dark." To him, "The cosmos is all there is, all there ever was, and all that will be." For many scientifically inclined atheists, his views have become their version of Genesis.

> Science is not only compatible with spirituality; it is a profound source of spirituality. When we recognize our place in an immensity of light years and in the passage of ages, when we grasp the intricacy, beauty, and subtlety of life . . . that soaring feeling, that sense of elation and humility combined . . . that is surely spiritual.

Sagan insisted that there is only one true source of faith, only one legitimate form of assurance:

> You can go to the witch doctor to lift the spell that causes your pernicious anemia, or you can take vitamin B12. If you want to save your child from polio, you can pray or you can innoculate...has there ever been a religion with the prophetic accuracy and reliability of science?...No other human institution comes close.

### "The Greatest Hitter Who Ever Lived"

Ted Williams was a Hall of Fame baseball player whose 1941 season marked the last time in the twentieth century that anyone finished with a batting average of .400 or better. He served in both World War II and Korea. With his excellent vision and superb coordination, he even set a gunnery record during pilot training. Williams had supreme faith in his ability, on or off the field.

> I *lived* a book on pitchers....[my first coach] used to say that in seven years on the playground I never broke a bat hitting a ball incorrectly, that all my bats had the bruises in the same spot, like they were hammered there by a careful carpenter, right on the thick of the hitting surface.

Immediately after Williams died in 2002, his son, John Henry, sent his father's body to a cryogenics laboratory to be frozen. While some of the media devoted considerable time to psychoanalyzing John Henry's motives, others suggested a different scenario. Pointing out that Ted Williams was an atheist, historian Jim Hijiya wrote that:

> Looking forward to no afterlife...some atheists retain a desire for some kind of immortality...He called hitting a science but made it a religion...his .406 average became a sacred number...In an inversion of conventional religion, the spirit might perish but the body would live forever. Maybe Williams' DNA would be passed on to somebody else....Maybe someday the Splendid Splinter himself would be thawed out and brought back to life.

### Friends for Life

In the spring of 1944, while imprisoned at the Budzyn concentration camp, Max Edelman was severely beaten by a group of guards. "I was left to die a bloody mess," he said. "My brother and my friends gathered around me to offer words of hope." Permanently blinded, he was rendered unfit for most forms of prison labor. If word spread of his condition, he might be shot on the spot. Risking their own lives, other prisoners did everything in their power to assure his safety. Surprisingly, one of his German captors also protected him.

> Without the help of Eric . . . I would not be here to tell you about it . . . He lied to the guards about my whereabouts at every morning's head count, and kept me out of their sight. He warned the inmates in our barrack not to do me harm or steal my food.

One morning all the prisoners were all abruptly gathered together and marched out of the camp. Edelman wondered if they were being led to a crematorium or an execution site. Fortunately, he was able to stay in formation, accompanied by his brother on one arm and a friend on the other. But his feet were throbbing from ill-fitted shoes. He was hungry, tired, and blind. At one point, he faltered during the march and expressed his desire to give up. His brother and other marching companion reminded him that it was April 20, Hitler's birthday, and that he could not choose that day to give away his life. "Not if we can help it," they declared.

## The Great Leap Forward

Mao Tsetung placed his faith in the oppressed masses of China. As a child, Mao had chafed under the tight control of his domineering father and dreamed of a life outside the bounds of a simple peasant routine. Nicknamed "the scholar" by friends and family, he immersed himself in historical and philosophical writings. Becoming increasingly interested in politics, he cofounded the Chinese Communist Party in 1921. For the next three decades, he struggled to gather enough support to overthrow the ruling majority. This effort proved to be extremely bloody, with both sides engaging in torture, mass executions, and guerilla warfare. In 1949 the communists came to power, with Mao as the chairman of the People's Republic of China.

The China that Mao took over was on the verge of collapse. The country of 700 million was languishing under the control of a feudal political system and a badly outdated agricultural economy. Mao's greatest act of faith was the implementation of a 5-year economic plan known as "The Great Leap Forward." The plan was based on a massive steel production drive as well as the formation of semi-independent communes. "Everywhere, small backyard furnaces were built . . . there were around-the-clock shifts. . . . cooking pots were smashed, door handles were melted down." As a prelude to this massive social experiment, Mao offered the following words of encouragement to his people:

> We must have faith in [ourselves] . . . there is great hope for this program. China can be changed, ignorance can be changed into knowledge, and lethargy into vitality . . . I say this country of ours is full of hope. The Rightists say it is hopeless, they are utterly wrong . . . We are brimming over with confidence.

## Faith Myths

Prior to the twentieth century, faith was considered a virtue. Individuals were proud to show their faith in words and deeds, in good times and bad, in the company of friends as well as strangers. Now, however, many express ambivalence about faith. Some find it hard to believe in a higher power or the reality of a heaven or hell. Others wonder if modern science has made faith obsolete. Although most individuals still make some room for faith when facing a major life crisis, far fewer consider it the centerpiece of their daily life. Why? What are their concerns about faith?

### Faith Is Blind

There are countless anecdotes about individuals who appeared to have encountered pain and suffering as a direct result of their unwavering and unquestioning religious faith. One middle-aged woman, for example, claimed that her close friend had shown "too much faith." Having suffered a series of terrible strokes, with increasing dependence on life-support devices, breathing tubes, feeding devices, and incontinence bags, her friend "stubbornly" clung to his faith in God rather than going "gently into the night."

However, unwarranted faith can also be placed in secular powers, including modern medicine. One example involves a young woman with a broken arm and a badly bruised chest who was referred to one of the best orthopedic specialists in New York. After treating her arm, he asked her to return for several follow-up visits. Compliant and showing absolute trust in him, she adhered to his every suggestion. She continued to remind him of the deep bruising surrounding her breast, but he repeatedly assured her that such injuries take a long time to heal. Finally, after 9 months, her growing anxiety led her to seek a second opinion. Unfortunately, she was then diagnosed with metastasized breast cancer that proved to be fatal within a year.

### Faith Is Immature

The unabashed atheist Henry Louis Mencken charged that faith had retarded the progress of Western civilization by a full millennium:

> It was a fixed moral code and a fixed theology which robbed the human race of a thousand years by wasting them upon alchemy, heretic-burning, witchcraft and belief in spiritual intermediaries.

Mencken presumed that only young children or naive adults can be nourished by faith, asserting that the rest of humanity should put aside such primitive illusions. Nietzsche wrote that it is the child who says, "I am body and soul," but the enlightened adult who believes, "I am body entirely and nothing else." In *Chicken Soup for the Christian Soul,*

Laverne Hall paid tribute to youthful innocence and the purity of unfettered belief.

> The fields were parched from lack of rain . . . the crops lay wilting from thirst . . . .The ministers called for an hour of prayer on the town square . . . the townspeople showed up with Bibles, crosses, and rosaries . . . a soft rain began to fall . . . [However] From the middle of the crowd, one faith symbol seemed to overshadow all the others: A small 9-year-old child had brought an umbrella.

### Faith Is Lazy

Some scientists and philosophers liken acts of faith to escapist fantasies born of suspended critical faculties. On a popular New Age Web site, visitors were told that, "when [faith] comes in, brains go out."

> Seek instead the Truth . . . found by search, examination, and inquiry . . . This will require discipline . . . Never accept any thing on faith . . . Get out and do some research . . . Don't accept ignorance. Faith is the great cop-out, the great excuse to evade the need to think and evaluate evidence.

Mencken, with his penchant for sarcastic barbs, wrote, "A man full of faith is simply one who has lost (or never had) the capacity for clear and realistic thought." The Harvard biologist E. O. Wilson drew the wrath of religious scholars when he suggested that individuals prefer religion to empiricism because it is "easier." The popular science fiction writer Robert Heinlein stated that "faith strikes me as intellectual laziness."

### Faith Is Religious

For many people, the word "faith" implies religious conviction. It conjures up images of crosses and incense or turbans and flowing veils. Some imagine desperate men, women, and children seated in wheelchairs or lying atop stretchers before the shrine of Lourdes. Others cringe at the memory of a Buddhist monk, expressing his faith in an act of self-immolation.

If you surf the Web, looking for "faith," roughly 80% of your hits will involve religious topics. And if you click on the *Columbia Encyclopedia's* "faith links," the first 20 examples relate to some aspect of religion. You will find references to creeds and icons, faith healing and religious revivals, Lutherans and Quakers, as well as mosques and churches of God.

## The Human Condition

Try to put aside any biases that you might have about faith. Instead, reflect for a moment on your current state of well-being. On a scale of 1 (terrible) to 10 (excellent), how would you rate the quality of your physical, emotional, and spiritual life right at this particular moment? Do you feel fit? Are you happy? Do you enjoy peace of mind?

On any given day, you might find yourself feeling better about one particular aspect of your life over another. On Monday it might be satisfying for you to reflect on your job, while on Wednesday it could be thoughts of your friends and family that give you a feeling of comfort. On Friday, it could be your love life that brings a smile. Nevertheless, it is very hard for most people to sustain a sense of wellness in every sphere of life. Even if you diligently pursue a relatively well-balanced existence, such factors as aging and unexpected illness as well as family and work responsibilities will invariably upset your hard-won equilibrium. So can that troubling world outside: global warming, rising crime rates, the seemingly never-ending threat of terrorist acts, war, famine—the list goes on and on. How can one sustain a balance in the face of all of that?

Beyond the grind of personal stressors and distant threats loom perennial existential challenges such as the search for meaning, the quest for an abiding sense of connectedness, and the desire for a lasting legacy. These fervent needs define the human condition, taxing serious thinkers from all walks of life. More than 2,000 years ago Ecclesiastes halted his search for worldly pleasure, lamenting in frustration that "there is nothing new under the sun." In his remarkably modern sounding message, he attacked the futility of riches or fame or beauty while emphasizing the need for a deeper, more lasting spiritual foundation.

Centuries later, philosophers Camus and Sartre warned that humanity was heading toward a catastrophic existential crisis. The dramatic and progressive decline in humanity's belief in a higher power, or in ultimate destinations such as heaven or hell, had left stranded and unmet the human need for order and purpose. Gone was the Elizabethan notion of a "chain of being." If matters of life and death could no longer be attributed to the will of God, or the work of a higher power, where could meaning be found?

Aging and death have always been with us, and it is human to try to defy them. The ancient Egyptians devoted staggering amounts of time and manpower to develop a sophisticated process of mummification. In modern times, people search for a fountain of youth in the form of anti-wrinkle creams, human growth hormone, and Botox injections. The shipping of Ted Williams' body to a cryogenics lab after he died is an especially poignant example of death defiance.

Putting aside moral and philosophical considerations, perhaps someday there will be the technological tools to significantly extend the human life span beyond the current outer limits of approximately 120 years. Will this assure an improved human condition? No. Such "progress" may actually make things worse by perhaps doubling the time spent worrying about an elusive sense of meaning, lost attachments, or the inevitability of death. Technology, by itself, can do little to address these larger psychological and spiritual issues.

Ultimately, you must have some kind of faith to get along in life. Many individuals will settle on a set of core beliefs derived from a culturally shared worldview. Others will derive meaning and purpose from more private, personal beliefs that they have cultivated as a result of life experience. In contrast, individuals who are totally lacking faith in anything or anyone are likely to feel lost, isolated, and vulnerable. As Ecclesiastes put it, they risk the "the vanity of chasing the wind."

Voltaire compared humanity's dependence on sentiments such as faith to "the winds which fill the sails of the vessel . . . without them it would be impossible to make way." In *Auguries of Innocence*, the poet William Blake also suggested that life is apt to be especially challenging for those who dismiss faith.

> He who mocks the infant's faith
>
> Shall be mocked in age and death
>
> He who shall teach the child to doubt
>
> The rotting grave shall never get out
>
> He who respects the infant's faith
>
> Triumphs over hell and death

## Science and Spirituality

Both Bertrand Russell and Carl Sagan put their faith in science alone. Indeed, science in the past century has given rise to at least a few of the biases about faith in other spheres that we identified previously. Although it was common for the great scientist-philosophers of centuries ago to devote themselves to both scholarship *and* God, scientists of the modern period have tended to espouse a total abandonment of any form of religious belief or to advocate the development of a dogma-free spirituality. Unlike William James, who functioned primarily as a philosopher in his later years, many psychologists in particular have been hostile toward organized religion. John Watson and B. F. Skinner, two of the best-known behaviorists, saw little need for traditional religious faith and instead erected an altar to "the sacred laws of conditioning." A 1984 survey of academicians revealed that psychologists were among the least religious, with "fully 50% responding that they had no current religious preference, compared with only 10% of the general public." A 1990 survey of therapy providers revealed that clinical psychologists were the least religious, with "only 33% of them describing religious faith as an important influence in their lives."

Some scholars have suggested that the tension between psychology and religion may reflect an underlying turf battle rather than a genuine difference in principle. Both psychology and religion vie for the hearts of humankind. Both are in the business of finding "the truth" while advising people on how to conduct their daily lives. Psychologist Stanton Jones pointed out that "Science has goals that transcend the mundane description of discrete empirical reality, and religion often has aspirations of saying something about the empirical aspects of human reality."

And yet many more people seek advice on personal and family matters from members of the clergy rather than from mental health professionals. A growing number of clergy even provide formal pastoral counseling and publish self-help books. On the other hand, therapists have often found themselves assisting individuals struggling with moral and spiritual questions. What is the nature of that assistance? While acknowledging that spirituality is important to the individual, they still insist that it must be cleansed of any form of institutional dogma. Both Abraham Maslow and John Dewey promoted such a humanistic spirituality. Maslow asserted that spirituality was an inherent human capacity that did not depend on revelations or external guidance from church authorities.

> I want to demonstrate that spiritual values have naturalistic meaning, that they are
> not the exclusive possession of organized churches, that they do not need
> supernatural concepts to validate them, that they are well within the jurisdiction
> of a suitably enlarged science, and that, therefore they are the general
> responsibility of all mankind.

On the surface, a less rigid, no-strings-attached spirituality may seem to be an intriguing existential solution. But what disadvantages are inherent in adopting such a belief system? What are the implications of a demythologized brand of spirituality with respect to understanding hope?

Most adults do tend to form representations of God or a higher power that are both "religious" *and* "spiritual" in nature. Only one quarter of those in a recent survey considered themselves "spiritual" but not "religious." Typically this subgroup indicated that their faith had failed them in some fashion early in life or that they had a negative experience with organized religion. Along these lines, a penetrating analysis of Freud's life uncovered evidence of family and personal experiences contributing to his hostile atheism.

We do not reject the possibility that some individuals may develop a positive spirituality that is free of religious influence, but some may find it difficult to develop a full experience of hope if they are strongly anti-religious. Hope derives in part from attachment experiences, which in turn influence religious and spiritual experiences. A search for metaphysical support beyond culturally sanctioned beliefs may, in some cases, mask a deeper sense of abandonment and alienation coupled with a basic distrust of institutions. A spirituality based on disconnection, low trust, and diminished solidarity may not provide adequate grounding for the full development of hope. We are not saying that all potential types of spirituality will inevitably lead to an impoverished hope. Nor are we denying the possibility of repairing the attachment system through healing relationships, or of transcending early trauma by forging creative and meaningful internalizations. In the service of these goals, humanistic therapies can and do play a valuable role. Rather, our view is that certain forms of spirituality can sometimes reflect an entrenched island of unresolved hurt instead of a transcendent bridge to a better tomorrow. Humanistic therapies can heal that hurt, but the bridge they offer can take an individual only so far.

## Faith and Reality

An adaptive faith that can sustain hope is not blind, immature, lazy, or necessarily based on religious dogma. In fact, some of the most astute observers of the human condition have argued that faith can be a positive and vital life force. Leo Tolstoy, for example, contrasted an "informed faith" with the "hypnotism" of slavish devotion. Likewise, he discounted the desperate beliefs of those who passively wish to be transported out of poverty, misfortune, or other conditions of misery. He declared "this is not really faith, for instead of throwing light on man's position in the world, it only darkens it."

Among theologians and religious scholars, Paul Tillich characterized faith as a "companion to truth seeking." In his estimation, only a deep faith can give you the spiritual stamina to honestly examine the meaning and purpose of your life. Similarly, James Fowler presented a view of a "maturing faith" that is increasingly engaged with the universe rather than disconnected or ego centered. And Huston Smith has emphasized that faith is a way of "seeing" rather than thinking, suggesting that it allows believers to access the light of a transcendent reality that is veiled off to those without conviction. Smith went on to invoke the following words of the poet William Blake: "If the doors of perception were cleansed, we would see everything as it is: Infinite."

Humans are unlikely to outgrow a need for some sort of faith. To completely do away with faith would require the elimination of all mysteries, from the deepest secrets of the mind to the most profound questions about the universe. Until we can predict, with absolute confidence, the behavior of people and nations as well as every atom of matter, there will always be a need for trust and faith. Religious or spiritual convictions, the most maligned forms of faith, will also be difficult to abandon. According to Smith, our knowledge of the universe will never be sufficient to provide adequate answers to the ultimate questions of meaning and purpose. From this perspective, modern science cannot provide us with a big-picture answer, having nothing to say about why we are here and what we should do with our lives.

Fowler has coined the term "vertical pluralism" to refer to the different kinds of faith that emerge during the course of human development. A number of spiritual guides, including Mark in the New Testament, have put it more simply, contrasting *childish* with *child-like* faith. As they see it, the former suggests true immaturity, rooted in narcissism and materialism, directed only toward personal safety or gain. A "child-like" innocence, however, translates into an ongoing curiosity and openness toward the world and other people.

Keeping the faith is not always easy. It may be tested, shattered, or destroyed. Sometimes a leap of faith is required. Recall Augustine's great personal struggle to develop a sincere faith in God. Imagine the discipline needed to maintain the demanding postures of the Hindus or the level of belief that lies beyond the rigorous adherence of Buddhist monks to their many rules of private and public conduct.

To E. O. Wilson's remark that religious faith is preferred over science because it is "easier," Smith responded, "When you, Mr. Wilson, have undergone any one of the following trials, it will be time to talk about the ease of religion":

An eight-day Buddhist meditation, sitting cross-legged daily for 12 hours. The crucifixion of Jesus on Golgotha. Jewish prisoners retaining dignity and faith in a Nazi concentration camp. Mother Theresa's care of lepers and the poor.

But faith is not always about religion. In fact, four of the five definitions of faith in *Webster's Dictionary* have nothing to do with God or religion. They involve nonspecific references to beliefs, confidence, trust, or loyalty. Similarly, Fowler saw faith as a generic activity that is not at all dependent on religious content. According to his view, faith involves a process of developing valued interests, spiritual or otherwise.

Faith can be invested in science as well as in religion. Scientists themselves acknowledge that belief in either evolution or creationism is ultimately a matter of faith. Higher mathematics and theoretical physics, the "edges of hard science," are ultimately based on trust and belief in the human intellect. Consider the views of Albert Einstein:

As far as the laws of mathematics refer to reality, they are not certain; and as far as they are certain, they do not refer to reality.

Quantum mechanics is very impressive. But an inner voice tells me that it is not yet the real thing.

I have deep faith that the principle of the universe will be beautiful and simple.

The role of faith and hope in economic matters is greatly underappreciated. In 2002, the Dow Jones Industrial Average went into a free fall, dropping nearly 30% in less than a year. Experts pointed to the corrosive effects of corporate greed and fraud, which had diminished investor confidence and consumer trust. *America Online* ran a feature article entitled "Is There Any Hope?" In 2008, a mounting mortgage crisis on

Wall Street sent the United States and other world markets into a similar tailspin. Banks and other lenders tightened their purse strings, which left those on Main Street with little hope of securing future credit. Desperate for a solution, 11 of the largest mortgage servicers created a partnership called HOPE NOW in an effort to keep more Americans in their homes.

### Multiple Realities

Critics argue that faith may be an illusion without factual basis—that it is not based on reality. But what is real? Is there only one type of reality? Can there be more than one truth? Are there multiple realities? Voltaire, who often lampooned religious beliefs, noted that "there has never been a dispute as to whether there is daylight at noon." This perspective suggests there is but one scientifically grounded truth that disallows the possibility of an opposing faith-based reality. But in fact our human nature brings us into contact with at least two kinds of reality, *physical and psychological truths.* Blaise Pascal captured the essence of this two-fold view with his famous dictum, "The heart has its reasons which reason does not understand." Along these lines, psychologists have repeatedly found that an individual's *subjective well-being* frequently shows little correlation with his or her *objective reality.*

Many of the world's religions also presuppose multiple realities. The Australian Aborigines routinely shuttle back and forth between the natural world and the "dream-time." Buddhists entertain 31 planes of heaven. Hindus recognize six realms, including the moral world of Karma, the provisional land of Maya, and the cosmic theater of Lila. In the West, many Jews, Christians, and Muslims conceive of various levels of heaven and hell.

Taking such religious diversity into account, Huston Smith proposed a four-fold division of reality. From his perspective, "this-world" is separable into "visible matter" and "invisible human experiences." In addition, there is also the "other-world," which in turn can be broken down into a "knowable God" and an "ineffable Godhead."

From our point of view, a singular approach to reality is hard to justify. First, reality can be both constructed and discovered. We are all familiar with the saying, "beauty is in the eye of the beholder." Second, there is the subjective truth that lies within you (Pascal's "heart") as well as the interpersonal truth that you and a loved one share. In addition, there is the cultural truth created by your group or national affiliations.

Within each of these realms, one can even envision additional layers of reality and truth. This suggests a great variety of potential faith constructions. Your faith can be primarily based on beliefs about yourself. Alternatively, it can be secured from your relationships or stem from shared cultural and religious beliefs. Most often, it will derive from some combination of these varied sources of life experience.

What lessons are contained in this chapter? You need faith to build hope. Having faith should not be a source of shame or something to hide from the world. You can have an enlightened faith that is mature, strong, and invested in various ways. Moreover, your experience of truth and reality is partly discovered and partly created, partly private and partly shared. Rather than a cause for concern, these varied doors of perception can provide you with added ways of sustaining a more positive and productive spiritual life.

---

*Sixth Hope Meditation*

What is your single most important source of faith? Is it a higher power, your family or friends, yourself, the government or science? Have you ever questioned or examined your faith? Has your faith increased or decreased over the years? How would you rank the eight different "acts of faith" described in this chapter (Lourdes, Lorraine Day, and so on)?

# $\int$even

## SPIRITUAL GROWTH: THE LIFE CYCLE OF HOPE

> If you would understand anything, observe its beginning and its development.
>
> —Aristotle

In this chapter we trace the development of spiritual beliefs across the life span, utilizing a comprehensive, four-stage model in which we combine our integrative framework with concepts from developmental and clinical psychology, psychiatry, and theology. This in-depth analysis is designed to help you to better understand the importance of the attachment, mastery, and survival motives at different points in the life span. In addition, you should come away with a deeper appreciation of the hope–spirituality connection, including both the transpersonal and personal experiences that can affect the development of various forms of faith and spirituality.

Clearly, hope and spirituality converge in important ways. It is a convergence that begins early in life through the attachment drive and then develops through personally and socially derived modes of self-protection to shape one's spiritual beliefs. At the heart of those beliefs for most individuals is a God or higher power representation inherited from the religion of their culture. Indeed, all of the world's major religions appear to recognize some form of supreme transcendent being (see Table 7.1). Even the polytheistic systems of the Native American Indian tribes have a concept of a higher power that reigns above all others.

Sigmund Freud attempted to reduce such beliefs to a private, "subjective delusion," suggesting that images of God were nothing more than residues of early parent–child interactions. In contrast, some religious scholars have sought historical data to substantiate their beliefs in the objective reality of a higher power. Psychiatrist Donald

TABLE 7.1. *Supreme Beings of Various Belief Systems*

| Spiritual Belief System | Supreme Being |
| --- | --- |
| *Africa and the Caribbean* | |
| Ifa of Western Africa | Olorun, "The Remote and Unknowable" |
| Kongo of Central Africa | Nzambi, "The Supreme Creator" |
| Vodun of Haiti and the Dominican Republic | Bon Dieu, "The High God" |
| *Australia's Eastern Aboriginal Tribes* | |
| Kabi | Dhakan, "The Rainbow God" |
| Kamilaroi | Baiame, "The Maker" |
| Wurunjerri | Bunjil, "Our Father" |
| *Global Faiths* | |
| Buddhism | Ma Itrey, "The Second Buddha" |
| Christianity | Jesus of Nazareth |
| Hinduism | Another Avatar of Visnu |
| Islam | A Hidden Iman |
| Judaism | The Messiah |
| *Mexico, Central and South America* | |
| Aztecs | Ometecuhti, "Divine Creator of Life" |
| Incas | Viracocha, "God of the Sun" |
| Mayans | Itzamna, "Lord of the Hearth" |
| *North America and the Arctic Regions* | |
| *Inuit (Eskimo)* | Anguta, "Father" and "Gatherer of the Dead" |
| *Lakota* | Takushkanshkan, "Prime Mover" |
| *Navajo* | Atse Hastin, "The First Man" |

Winnicott took a third approach and hypothesized an intermediate area of human experience that was neither wholly subjective nor entirely objective. He believed that early interactions between the mother and child produced a unique psychological "space" or "interpersonal reality," but as the child's capacity for symbolic representation expands, he or she relies on transitional objects (such as a blanket or a favorite toy) to evoke feelings of maternal comfort. In his view, religious symbols and objects, including visions of God or a higher power, later emerge as "transitional objects" to bridge the separation from the primary caregiver.

Although Winnicott provided a framework for viewing religious beliefs from an attachment perspective, he did not elaborate on how individual differences in the quality of the mother–infant bond might influence the child's spiritual development. Psychoanalyst Ana-Maria Rizzuto took a broader perspective, realizing that children receive a religious education through parental rites of worship, such as church attendance and community observances, and through references to God in the media. Her case studies of children's early attachments highlighted the following developmental factors: the child's inflated parental representations, personal grandiosity, a need for love and affection, fears of separation, and classic "oedipal urges." In her view, these needs were fueled by three even more fundamental factors: a child's primitive notion of causality, a natural desire for answers to the larger questions of life, and an existing template of "powerful others," particularly parents and possibly other role models. According to Rizzuto, it is this mix of influences that fosters a child's anthropomorphic understanding of a benign, omniscient, and omnipotent being.

Psychologist William Meissner, heavily influenced by Winnicott and the notion of "transitional phenomena," believed that Freud was wrong in his dismissal of religion as a mere subjective fantasy stemming from infantile fears. He conceptualized faith, beliefs in a higher power, and even prayer as "transitional" in nature. For him, this means that religious life cannot be located in either subjective or objective reality but only within a dialectic of mutually sustaining internal experiences and external phenomena.

Meissner's work overlaps with that of psychologists and sociologists who believe that reality is constructed as well as discovered. However, most of these scholars have concentrated on epistemology or the nature of reality. Meissner, Rizzuto, and Winnicott are making a different claim, one about the nature of humanity. They have focused on the emotional impulses that underlie spiritual beliefs, including the desire to address questions such as: Who are we?, Why are we here?, and Where are we headed? According to Meissner, religion helps to "reveal our personal history and the transitional space each of us has created between his objects and himself to find a 'resting place' to live in."

While sympathetic to a psychodynamic view of religious experience, psychologist Michael St. Clair argued that Freud and his followers failed to grasp important differences between human and religious representations, thus ignoring "transcendent realities" and a "sense of the holy." Incorporating concepts from Rizzuto, Meissner, and other scholars, his perspective encompasses the primitive fusion between mother and child as well as the more complex and expanded God images of adulthood. In his view, what begins as an initial aggrandized sense of self-importance evolves by later childhood into an increasingly differentiated personal God. In the most mature adults, spirituality is ultimately transformed into a cosmic feeling of love and concern emanating from the sense of a more abstract universal force.

Drawing on the work of some of these and other scholars, we turn now for the remainder of this chapter to our four-stage model of spiritual growth throughout the life span, summarized as follows: In phase one, early childhood needs and parental interactions come together to form an initial representation of a supreme being. Rizzuto has referred to this as the "first birth of God." This private God undergoes further development in middle childhood with exposure to sacred rites and rituals. During this period a critical layer of institutionalization is added to the self-protective system. A third important spiritual transformation occurs in adolescence when profound

TABLE 7.2. *The Life Cycle of Religion, Spirituality, and Hope*

| Phase | Motive Priorities | Hope Building Blocks | Spiritual Gains |
|---|---|---|---|
| 1. 0–5 years | First: attachment (bonding) Second: survival (assisted regulation) Third: mastery (autonomy) | Basic trust Stable introjects | Empowered hope |
| 2. 6–puberty | First: mastery (competence) Second: attachment (support) Third: survival (coping) | Valued goals Community support Cultural terror management | Institutionalized hope |
| 3. Adolescent– young adult | First: survival (viability) Second: mastery (purpose) Third: attachment (intimacy) | Self-regulation Long-term goals Commitment to love | Individuated hope |
| 4. Mid–late adulthood | First: mastery and attachment (sharing) Second: attachment and survival (caring) | Personal legacy Collective vision | Transcendent hope |

cognitive advances lead to new levels of individualization as well as a growing capacity to envision future possibilities. However, these adolescent gains come at a price, for they also permit greater reflection on losses, some past and others yet to come. During adulthood spiritually motivated individuals deepen their investment in a set of trans-cendent values that foster a widening concern for all present and future life. This far-reaching moral infrastructure is the linchpin of a hopeful psyche in the fourth and final stage of spiritual life. As depicted in Table 7.2, our model also incorporates concepts from the integrative theory of hope outlined in Chapter 2.

## The "First Birth of God"

> Each person's religious story is a story of relationships
>
> —Andrew Greeley

From a psychological perspective, the initial development of religious feelings can be explained in terms of relationship-focused object relations theory. According to this view, initial attachments are the basis for all later relationships. Religious behavior is also fundamentally relational in nature. Erik Erikson's ideas regarding the mother–infant bond, basic trust, and later religious experience assume a transformation of "internal representations" of significant others.

The research of psychologist Lee Kirkpatrick with adults indicated that religious behavior, like attachment, is describable in terms of degrees of intimacy, a form of intense love, and dependency with respect to an omnipotent caregiver. He found that both self and parental representations contribute to personal experiences of God. For example, those securely attached adults reporting more satisfactory bonds with their mothers were more likely to view God as available and responsive and to imagine themselves as worthy of love and protection. However, those who felt undeserving of love were more likely to perceive God as controlling and wrathful.

Kirkpatrick also pointed out that mystical religious experiences, particularly conversions, have been described in terms of an intense bonding process, in words and images characteristic of falling in love. Israeli psychologist Chana Ullman noted this phenomenon as well when describing her landmark study of religious converts: "What I initially considered primarily a change of ideology turned out to be more akin to a falling in love . . . a sudden attachment . . . which occurs on a background of great emotional turmoil." Mystical experiences are not a rare phenomenon restricted to a few extraordinary individuals. Numerous surveys have indicated that more than a third of the population have had moments when they "felt very close to a powerful, spiritual force that seemed to lift you out of yourself." A Gallup poll revealed that more than half of American adults acknowledged "a moment of sudden religious awakening or insight."

Among the many psychodynamic constructs that can be used to advance our understanding of mystical experiences, the concepts of psychoanalyst Heinz Kohut are uniquely compelling. His idea of "self objects" refers to key figures in one's early life who have become a part of the self. "Idealizing self objects," however, are a special category of significant others, models of perfection and power, and purveyors of comfort that, once internalized, create a sense of personal strength and safety. They parallel the characteristics typically attributed to God or a higher power. An important source of idealizing self objects are parents, who through their promptings and praise encourage the child to merge with their superior capacities. Kohut's approach shifts the domain of the hallowed and powerful, Erikson's "numinous," from a purely external resource to a force that is both internal and external, akin to the "more" in William James' description of the sense of union with a power that is both beyond and part of us. Along these lines, consider the following quote from Plotinus, the great Christian mystic of the Dark Ages.

> We are not separated from the One, not distant from it, even though bodily nature has closed about us and drawn us to itself. It is because of the One that we breathe and have our being: it does not bestow its gifts at one moment only to leave us again; its giving is without cessation so long as it remains what it is. As we turn towards the One, we exist to a higher degree, while to withdraw from it is to fall (Plotinus, *The Enneads*).

Much of the early research on infancy and child development focused on the role of maternal attachments, but as we noted previously, a few investigators, including one of us (H. B.), began in the 1960s to document the impact of fathers. The children of fathers who are positively involved with them develop more secure attachments to both parents and, in fact, show a clear "two-parent advantage," revealing better relationships with others (attachment), greater academic and work skill development (mastery), and superior coping abilities (survival). In essence, fathers have as much potential to be "hope providers" to their children as do mothers. On the other hand, paternal deprivation has been associated with childhood despair and hopelessness.

To summarize, the notion of a higher power that lies at the core of religious and spiritual belief systems is strongly influenced by attachment and childrearing processes. Nevertheless, as scientists we must be careful not to overestimate the impact of any single caregiver. Since the seventeenth century, it has been common in the West to ascribe a level of importance to maternal love that rivals the power attributed in other cultures to God, magic, or various supernatural forces.

A preoccupation with the "motherhood mystique" has led many to ignore the role of other influences, from fathers and peers to the larger community. For example, psychologist Judith Rich Harris challenged this myopic focus on the mother by detailing the crucial impact of peers in her provocative book, *The Nurture Assumption*. Similarly, many religious scholars have neglected to take into account paternal childrearing factors. This is unfortunate given the predominance of father prototypes in the construction of supreme beings around the world.

## The "Second Birth of God"

Middle childhood, beginning at age 6 and ending roughly at the age of 12 or with the onset of puberty, is a time when many societies introduce children to sacred and secular institutions beyond the family. During this period, children rapidly acquire symbolic capacities that permit new feats of imagination and communication and a fuller incorporation of cultural beliefs. They develop stronger mastery and interpersonal skills and gain a more mature understanding of death as universal, inevitable, and irreversible. In short, the beginnings of a more "social self" emerge as cultural and institutional layers of mastery, attachment, and survival support are added.

Freud was not the only one recognizing that parent–child interactions remain critical beyond the preschool period. Developmental psychologists have also emphasized the child's need to be valued by caretakers during middle childhood. Psychologist Jerome Kagan made a distinction between the unqualified caregiver love provided in infancy and the growing need of 5- to 7-year-olds to satisfy parental and community standards. Paternal love and involvement may play an especially valuable role during this time. Involved fathers, prone to emphasizing mastery-related achievements and active coping strategies, can be particularly instrumental in developing in their children healthy mediated control beliefs and adequate terror management skills.

Religious and spiritual development in middle childhood is profoundly shaped by various experiences. Psychologist David Elkind wrote about the "relational needs" that underlie the spiritual development of young children while psychoanalyst Helmut Reich emphasized the "empathic religious socializing" that occurs as children begin to reach out to compare and contrast their personal and family religious experiences with those of other children and institutions. Research has indicated that a child's faith, or lack thereof, in a particular belief system is not solely dependent on the depth of parental beliefs. A more powerful mediator of religious belief is parental warmth. Children who are raised by religious yet cold parents may be as unlikely to adopt the faith of their family as their counterparts who grow up in warm but nonreligious families. Conversely, cold or rejecting parents who are nonbelievers may precipitate a strong need for religiosity in their disaffected offspring.

In middle childhood, performance pressures can radically alter a child's perception of control. In the face of unrealistic demands or excessive domination, especially from parents, the child may develop a completely "externalized locus of control." On the other hand, in the absence of adequate parental direction, children may form an internalized locus of control at an early age that can lead them to expect too much of themselves in terms of self-reliance. Psychoanalyst Alice Miller has discussed the burden of "narcissistic obligation" that plagues children forced into a premature caretaking role by overwhelmed or incompetent parents.

By the end of middle childhood, flirtations with increased autonomy and responsibility are likely to lead to at least occasional experiences of failure, helplessness, loneliness, and separation. Kagan noted that it is common in most societies for 8- to 12-year-olds to experience some of the harsher and bittersweet "dialectics of existence," including those involving freedom vs. responsibility, autonomy vs. self-reliance, and opportunity vs. danger. To complicate matters, the school-age child is typically exposed to a host of new social challenges (e.g., organized sports, music lessons, recreational and academic camps). In this context, consistent parental support lessens the chance that a child will emerge from this stage feeling "hopelessly incompetent." Children who are fortunate to have two involved parents, or at least strong adult role models, are especially likely to thrive in the face of increasing social competition and to maintain a hopeful attitude.

In many cultures, children nearing or at the age of puberty also undergo certain rites of passage, some of which are geared toward imparting institutionalized terror management skills. In the Catholic faith, 8-year-olds may become altar boys or girls, and during adolescence they are eligible for confirmation. The Jewish Bar Mitzvah allows 13-year-olds to publicly affirm the truths of the Torah while donning sacred vestments. The Ojobway tribes of the American Midwest required all those approaching puberty to fast and pray as a part of a "dream-seeking" venture meant to bring them into contact with a "personal spirit" capable of granting them a lifetime of guidance and protection. In a well-known Lakota tale, a boy is given animal hairs and feathers, "which makes it possible for him to move into an uncertain future with tangible proofs of protection." The Ifa of Western Africa have a tradition in which older men provide attachment and mastery skills to youths. The men offer spiritual assistance, including advice on how to create a "sacred space" and bond with the spiritual forces known as Orisa. But perhaps the most explicit example of imparting terror management strategies is found among Hindus. At puberty, boys participate in the Upanayana, the *Ceremony of the Sacred Thread*. Each receives a girdle to symbolize three encircling "vedas" that will keep them safe and secure.

## Adolescent Spirituality

The challenge for adolescents is to fashion an identity that is both unique and yet interwoven within a larger social fabric. Erikson wrote of the "tension" between personal and psychosocial identity formation. In his view, the optimal adolescent outcome was fidelity to the self *and* an emerging worldview. Without a sense of personal uniqueness, the adolescent may experience "identity confusion," but without faith in others, he or she may have insufficient means to comprehend broader, cosmic questions (e.g., about the meaning of life). However, for some adolescents, a feeling of connectedness to an organized group or religious system can facilitate their acceptance of the social order.

In contrast, Elkind emphasized the impact of the adolescent's development of formal operational thought, "the new mental system that enables the adolescent to accomplish feats of thought that far surpass those of the younger child." This enlarged capacity allows for a logical reflection upon different courses of action and upon alternative systems of values. He or she can ponder the meaning of God, the concepts of good and evil, and creatively experiment with prayer and meditation.

The philosophical inquiries that mark the adolescent stage have been portrayed in both film and literature. For readers of the classics, there is the fateful encounter between Ivan and Aloysha in Fyodor Dostoevsky's *The Brother's Karamazov*. Ivan, the faithless intellectual, insists on debating the existence of God with his younger brother, the mystical-religious Aloysha who is studying for the priesthood. Ivan's anecdotes about the sufferings of little children are heart wrenching in their detail and culminate in his tormented visions of a spiritually frustrating "final age" that reunites victims with their abusers. His exploration of possible heavens and hells serves as a perfect illustration of the cognitive dexterity that is the hallmark of formal operational thought.

We callow youth, we first of all have to settle the eternal verities that worry
us . . . Imagine the little [girl] . . . beating her sore little chest, weeping hot, meek

tears . . . and begging "gentle Jesus" to help her. Do you understand the purpose of that absurdity? Who needs it and why it was created?

Religious scholar James Fowler took a more balanced position, viewing the development of adolescent faith as both a cognitive *and* a social achievement. He was particularly interested in the adolescent's social and ethical growth rather than in his or her individual pursuits for self-understanding or cosmic meaning. Fowler's *synthetic-conventional stage* underscored the emergence of new cognitive abilities in the adolescent and their role in developing multiple perspectives. According to him, adolescent faith is primarily characterized by a commitment to values that simultaneously strengthen identity and support the community through "emotional solidarity."

Psychoanalyst Helmut Reich viewed adolescent religious development in an even more social light. He believed that family climate, peer groups, and church organizations all can play a pivotal role as forums for addressing an adolescent's fundamental religious questions. Adolescents may rely on such social contexts to help them further construct their theories about the meaning of life, the nature of God, and the possibility of an afterlife.

The term "adolescence" covers a lot of developmental territory, encompassing a sea of complex changes ushering the child into early adulthood. A more fine-grained analysis of this period suggests there are additional and equally important developments that are superimposed upon the general quest for individuation and integration. Such developments include shifts in motivational priorities from early to middle adolescence and then from middle to late adolescence. The youngster entering adolescence, struggling with separation from parents and family, may mourn the comforts and security of childhood. The high school student, preparing for college or involved in vocational training, is intensely preoccupied with achievement. However, by the end of adolescence, the attachment motive is again likely to take precedence.

Researchers examining conceptions of death have also found support for a three-phase model of adolescent spiritual development. Psychologists Illene and Lloyd Noppe administered a survey to middle-school, high-school, and college students. The responses of the middle-school children revealed that most of their fears about death revolved around the loss of important attachments. For example, one young teen wondered if "death means you are not able to be with your family." In contrast, high-school students were more likely to report concerns about unrealized accomplishments, with one teen musing about "not being able to do everything I wanted to before I die." On the other hand, college students were more apt to reflect on the severing of emotional bonds through death, tending to focus on the disruption of intimacy rather than on the loss of protective caregivers.

## Adult Spiritual Development

For Freud and Erikson, the mature adult is able to both "love and work," but the balance of this imperative may vary between men and women. Most cultures still promote a traditional division of labor in which men are the breadwinners and women the caretakers. Even in industrialized societies many men limit their "attachment investments" until they have established a solid footing in their careers, whereas many women begin or resume careers only when they complete a long stint of childrearing. The work of scholars such as Mary Belenky and Carol Gilligan has given credence to these shifting motivational priorities between the genders at various phases of the life span, with men showing tendencies toward mastery and then attachment, and women showing tendencies toward attachment and then mastery.

But self-help writers Mindy Bingham and Sandy Stryker have produced an interesting synthesis of the gender and mastery literature, offering a five-stage model that offers a somewhat different view of female development. According to them, females confront the following developmental tasks: acquiring a hardy personality (0–8 years), becoming an achiever (9–12 years), building self-esteem (13–16 years), cultivating self-sufficiency (17–22 years), and finding satisfaction in work and love (adulthood). Their views overlap a great deal with Erikson's stages of life span development, but there are significant points of divergence. Although both perspectives acknowledge the importance of mastery in the early years, Bingham and Stryker placed less emphasis than Erikson does on female attachment needs. Moreover, when discussing the kinds of relationships that women cultivate in adulthood, they presumed that these connections were interwoven with mastery concerns.

The notion of shifting needs over the course of the life span has been preserved in classic works of art and literature. Engravings from the fifteenth and sixteenth century depict the "seven ages of man." They begin with the swaddled infant, a curious toddler, and a youngster absorbed in revelry. Emphasizing a traditional male emphasis on the mastery motive, the adult representations highlighted bold explorers and enterprising merchants, thrifty clerks and ambitious lawyers.

Perhaps the most famous reflection on the seasons of a man's life is found in Shakespeare's As You Like It, where Jacques observed how each man "plays many parts... His acts being seven ages." The early scenes feature "the infant mewling and puking" and "the whining school-boy." The adult stages of attachment and mastery introduce "the lover, sighing like a furnace... Then a soldier full of strange oaths, sudden and quick in quarrel... [followed by] the justice... with eyes severe... full of wise saws and modern instances."

Erikson wrote that generativity (i.e., creatively fulfilling one's responsibilities to the next generation) was required in the "seventh passage of life," or middle age. He understood that healthy adult development necessitated an investment in something beyond the limited reaches of the self. A recurring theme that emerges from the findings of life span research is the quest for a healthy melding of attachment and mastery concerns into a generative commitment. In *Seasons of a Man's Life*, psychologist Daniel Levinson presented interviews with middle-aged men that unearthed a conflict between established habits of self-absorption and the need to engage in original acts of generativity to promote a greater good.

For the mature male or female, a primary source of hope revolves around a *personal or social legacy*, broadly conceived in terms of creative acts flowing from a deep emotional investment. By "creative" we mean authentic expressions whereby a valued part of the self is imparted to an object of commitment. Along these lines, Erikson viewed every manifestation of adult generativity as a mode of self-extension. Through a caring attitude and support of shared values and social causes, individuals achieve a kind of immortality. They are bequeathing a part of themselves to an enduring spiritual and existential reality.

For many individuals, their greatest legacy is children and grandchildren who embody their hopes for the future. Those who remain childless may nevertheless manifest their creative needs via career and artistic or social pursuits. For Erikson, creativity in the broadest sense is the capstone event of middle adulthood, building upon previous developmental gains. In *Childhood and Society*, he wrote, "Only in him ... [who has been] the originator of others or the generator of products and ideas—only in him may gradually ripen the fruit of these seven stages."

Adults must also learn to love on a grander, cosmic scale. A higher level interfacing with the social order can be considered a prerequisite to full maturity. Psychologist Heinz Werner wrote of the integration of the "person-in-the-world." Developmental psychologist Robert Kegan proposed a mature adult stage where ideas and values are no longer viewed as exclusive possessions of the self. In this phase of development, relationships take on a more dialectical quality to create new levels of connection and harmony, with social interaction becoming an end in itself rather than merely a means to an end. Psychologist Nancy Popp expanded Kegan's "mental growth model," adding a stage of spiritual development in which one flexibly modulates the degree of openness between "self and the universe."

Theories of spiritual and religious development also presume a greater openness in maturing adults toward the world and others. Reich believed that spiritual development in middle-aged adults should involve "enlarging religious horizons" and an "unconditional" faith, permitting a degree of connectedness that can be relied upon in hard times. Fowler also discussed "multiple interpretations of reality," "oneness with the power of being," and "an in-breaking commonwealth of love and justice." These ideas are also compatible with Gabriel Marcel's and Joseph Godfrey's examinations of the role of "trust" and "participation" in a community of spiritually linked others in the full development of hope.

In midlife, individuals may feel pressure to put their past and hoped-for achievements into some kind of perspective. For many, the mastery motive loses its hold as the needs for attachment and self-preservation return to prominence. Levinson's interviews revealed that one of the four seminal challenges of later adult development is abandoning one's sense of "youth" while accepting being "old." In fact, psychologist Elliot Jaques, who coined the term "middle-life crisis," argued that *the* major task of adulthood is coming to terms with one's own mortality. The specter of a finite existence and an approaching horizon inevitably prompts questions about meaning and purpose as well as sobering reflections on past life decisions. For example, despite his worldwide fame, Leo Tolstoy became obsessed in middle age with death, the meaning of life, and the failure of success to soothe his anxious soul. "I said to myself, All right, you will be more famous than Gogol, Pushkin, Shakespeare, Moliere, and all the writers in the world—what of it?"

The older adult often dwells on a variety of past and potential losses. For many, the fear is not of death itself but of the potential consequences of aging, such as irreversible physical disabilities, loss of mental acuity, death of loved ones, and the inability to live independently. As one elderly man put it, "At my age I don't dream of winning a million dollars or dating a movie star. I just don't want to lose the things I have."

Erikson implied that death can be confronted with calm assurance, integrity retained, and hope preserved if earlier life tasks have been successfully resolved. He offered a possible solution to the existential challenge of mortality without advocating any belief in a tangible higher power. Underlying his faith in social participation, he assumed that "psyche and society" can be mutually sustaining, with the latter serving as a "reified proxy for a metaphysical God." In short, Erikson suggested that an individual can maintain a deep and meaningful involvement in various social rituals without a belief in God. As *the* proponent of a psychosocial approach to human development, perhaps Erikson was demonstrating his own "faith" in a collective investment in the "god" of social institutions.

What might narrow the gulf between a purely materialistic worldview, such as Erikson's, that reifies society, and traditional metaphysical forms of spirituality that downplay social or psychological factors? The unifying concept that might integrate these two perspectives is that of a *transcendent collective vision,* a worldview that simultaneously embeds the individual within a daily sustaining social context and fosters a shared investment in "legacy building." By adopting this dialectical process of "gathering and sowing" within a spiritual community, one can realize meaning in life whether or not it is religiously based. The development of a collective vision depends on a transcendent hope, grounded in one's capacity for trust and social engagement as well as in flexible ego boundaries and a genuine concern for future generations.

*Seventh Hope Meditation*

What do you remember about your childhood religious or spiritual education? Were these positive or negative experiences for you? If you never received any spiritual direction as a child, do you have any regrets? Can you relate to the Dostoevsky passage that deals with the impassioned spiritual questioning of an adolescent or young adult? (Can you recall having a similar discussion with your friends or family?) What were your thoughts and feelings after reading the passage in which Tolstoy wonders if life has any meaning or "point"? Which of your spiritual building blocks needs further development (e.g., trust, higher goals, a personal legacy)? What can you do to make this happen?

# Eight

## SPIRITUAL INTELLIGENCE: DEVELOPING A

## SMART SOUL

> In the Middle Ages, a favorite image is the wheel of fortune . . . if you are attached to the rim of the wheel of fortune, you will be either above, going down, or at the bottom, coming up. But if you are at the hub, you are in the same place all the time . . . centered.
>
> —Joseph Campbell, *The Power of Myth*

In Chapter 6 we described some classic expressions of faith. In this chapter, we examine faith choices in greater detail. Putting aside the beliefs of others for a moment, where should you put *your* faith? Should *you* turn to religion or put *your* trust in science or technology or invest in something else of value? What are your faith needs? What are the long-term consequences of investing your faith in a certain way of life?

You will find eight faith alternatives in this chapter. To choose wisely from them requires your trust, openness, and spiritual honesty in arriving at a true assessment of your faith needs. Such needs vary from individual to individual, depending on each person's disposition and life experience. Reflecting the varied ways of "being in the world," they are also akin to "spiritual types." Which type are you? At the end of this chapter, you will find several types to consider, as well as the faith possibilities for each type. You will also find an assessment tool designed to help you clarify or discover your own spiritual disposition.

## Centers of Value

Faith revolves around something that cannot be directly observed or easily put into words. "Articles of faith" are deemed intrinsically "valuable" for they are presumed to reflect transcendent elements of an enduring "spiritual plane." Faith provides meaning and direction in life. It is not an easily quantifiable substance but rather more of a qualitative aspect of human experience.

It has been argued that science and faith mix about as well as oil and vinegar—that their domains are irreconcilable. We have created Table 8.1 to capture this apparent split. Is it possible to forge a bridge between these seemingly disparate worlds? Although the traditional scientific method penetrates certain aspects of reality better than others, philosopher and theologian Huston Smith noted that scientists are ill prepared to deal with "values," "meaning in life," "final causes," "ineffable truths," "issues of quality," and "higher realities." *Nevertheless, it is within these realms of human experience that we are most likely to grasp the essence of faith.*

TABLE 8.1. *Classic Faith and Traditional Science*

| Higher Domains | Language of Science | Language of Faith |
|---|---|---|
| Values | "There are no creeds in mathematics. " —Peter Drucker | "I do not pray for success, I ask for faithfulness." —Mother Teresa |
| Meaning | "Science . . . has no concern whether a behavior is good or bad, is purposeful or not." —Warren Weaver | "All effort is, in the last analysis, sustained by the faith that it is worth making." —Ordway Tead |
| Final causes | "Exclude purpose, and nature will reveal its causes." —Mason Cooley | "The only limit to our realization of tomorrow will be our doubts of today." —Franklin D. Roosevelt |
| Ineffable truths | "Science is what you know; Philosophy is what you don't know." —Bertrand Russell | "Faith is an oasis in the heart which will never be reached by the caravan of thinking." —Kahlil Gibran |
| Issues of quality | "Science is facts." —Henri Poincare | "Faith in the soul . . . changes all things and fills their inconstancy with light." —James Joyce |
| A higher reality | "The cosmos is all that is or ever was or ever will be." —Carl Sagan | "A little faith will bring your soul to heaven; a great faith will bring heaven to your soul." —C. Spurgeon |

And what about other divides? Can we bridge the religious faith of traditional believers—be they Buddhists, Muslims, Hindus, Jews, Christians, or adherents of native faiths—and the zeal of committed atheists? Simply put, is it possible to create a model of faith that embraces the vast panorama of human spiritual experience?

Faith is about values. The nature of these values is not limited to religious objects and ideals, and it may even include the assumptions and methods of traditional science. Note how easily the word "values" can be substituted for "faith." You can speak of "valuing" yourself or another person, science or technology, nature, or a higher power.

Indeed, theologian James Fowler suggested that the basis of faith consists of one or more *centers of value.* There is nothing in his perspective that specifies whether a center of value is secular or sacred, object or idea, visible or invisible, quantitative or qualitative, grounded in the past or situated in the present or future. Summarized in Table 8.2, these various centers encompass religious as well as nonreligious sources of faith. Individuals may invest all of their faith in one center of value or cultivate a personal belief system comprised of two or more "domains of worship." These faith possibilities are rightly called "centers" for they tend to operate as hubs or primary points of reference that ground thoughts, feelings, and behaviors. In essence, they lie at the center of human experience. In our opinion, it is this centrality that confers upon each of these faith sources a spiritual dimension, regardless of their "religious" bearing. They have sprung from the most basic interactions involving human beings and their inner and outer worlds.

To Carl Jung, these interactions have been preserved in the "collective unconscious" as "archetypes" and have been retained as a blueprint in every individual mind. When an individual "revisits" these events (e.g., takes a walk in the

TABLE 8.2. *The Eight Centers of Value*

| Centers of Value | Expressions |
| --- | --- |
| A higher power | God-centered religions |
| Nature | Earth-centered religions; environmentalism; natural health and healing |
| Social customs | Confucianism; Hindu castes; other social groups |
| Economics | Smith's "invisible hand"; Keynes' active governing; other economic models |
| Diversity and equality | Social reform; political activism; communism; socialism; postmodernism |
| Science | The scientific enterprise; technology; faith in experts |
| The self | Athleticism; conquests of nature; problem solving; creativity |
| Others | Family; friends; lovers; teammates; comrades |

woods, or encounters a snake in the grass), these "inner templates" of "potential energy" are activated, giving rise to powerful emotions. Whether one believes in inherited archetypes or prefers to think in terms of "instincts" or "conditioned internal representations," it is obvious that human beings show immediate and powerful reactions to a wide array of objects and symbols.

In ancient times, humanity's faith sources were restricted to members of one's community, a higher power, or the forces of nature. The Renaissance added faith in astronomy and mathematics. By the middle of the eighteenth century, the Enlightenment had brought into focus the need for "faith in social reform." During the nineteenth and twentieth centuries, two more centers of value appeared: "faith in a planned economy" and "faith in diversity and equality." In the modern era, the self has been promoted as a worthy object of faith.

Pause and reflect for a moment on your own faith. You are free to place your faith in a multiplicity of things, including yourself, family, friends, political leaders, or one or more spiritual powers. If you are an avid sports fan, your faith might also be in a particular team or an individual player. If pressed, you may be able to order your faith sources into some kind of hierarchy, but this does not necessarily imply a singular or unified center of value. Nonetheless, faith is a very personal matter, and people may choose any number of things to believe, worship, or deify. Now we will examine the faith possibilities in greater detail.

### Faith in a Higher Power

The demise of "faith in a supreme being" has been greatly exaggerated by many critics of traditional religion. Statistics from the late 1990s suggest that less than 5% of the world's population is atheistic. Europe and Asia claim the most nonbelievers, between 5% and 6%. In Africa, Australia, and Latin America, only about one half of 1% of the population appear to deny the existence of a higher power. A 2002 survey conducted by the Pew Research Council indicated that only 1% of Americans considered themselves atheists. A 2003 Gallup Poll suggested that 90% of Americans prayed on a regular basis while 82% were "conscious of the presence of God." Across the American landscape you will find numerous references to God in public rituals and patriotic songs: "One nation, under God"; "So help me, God"; God Bless America; and so on.

"In God We Trust" appears on U.S. currency. Just to the right of this inscription on the one-dollar bill can be found "the eye of providence" and the Latin phrase "annuit coeptis" (God has favored our undertakings). The United States is not alone in including religious iconography on its currency. Before the issue of the euro, you could find angels on a 50-franc note and a representation of St. Jacques Church on the 500-franc bill. In Egypt, a 10-pound note is decorated with a mosque. India's currency reflects both its religious and spiritual roots. A 20-rupee banknote shows the Buddhist wheel while a 100-rupee bill displays Gandhi and the sacred Himalayas.

What kind of God is presumed to exist by most people? Do you believe in a supreme personality who evokes images of a father, king, or judge? Do you believe, as Einstein did, in a transpersonal divine intelligence such as Pascal described in his *Penses*? ("If there is a God, He is infinitely incomprehensible, having neither parts nor limits.")

According to spiritual writer Deepak Chopra, an individual's experience of God is a product of his or her current emotional needs and spiritual development. Early in life, one tends to project human-like qualities onto God. As an individual's spiritual development progresses, he or she is increasingly able to grasp a more transcendent "higher power." According to Chopra, one's progression of knowing God evolves in seven stages: God the Protector, God the Almighty, God of Peace, God the Redeemer, God the Creator, God of Miracles, and God of Pure Being.

Huston Smith took a different approach. He argued that since the human mind is unable to fully comprehend an infinite and eternal reality, there is a need for a knowable God to supplement our sense of an "ineffable spirit"—for a personal God who demonstrates human-like qualities. While human beings can sense an even greater presence beyond these personal expressions of God, they must rely on more concrete representations for emotional assurance and communion.

From a hope perspective, Chopra's rank ordering of god experiences seems unwarranted. We are more comfortable positing individual differences in faith needs, and by extension, different preferred ways of knowing God. Some desperately want to be strengthened or empowered while others may be seeking a mystical union or deliverance from fear and anxiety. These different spiritual preferences may require different ways of knowing God. In short, if seekers aspire to a fuller realization of hope, we would recommend that they broaden rather than narrow their faith investments to encompass a god who is simultaneously powerful, protective, and present.

Smith's distinction between the knowable god and an "ineffable spirit" can be related to our previous discussion of how childhood events can influence an individual's perception of god. Among those inclined to put their faith in a higher power, some will struggle to reconcile with the "knowable" God of their family, community, or nation. For them, it might be wise to reexamine the nature and quality of their secular bonds before abandoning their quest for "an ally in the sky."

### Faith in Nature

The nature-based belief systems of the Australian Aborigines as well as those of their counterparts, the African Ifa and Native Americans, can be classified as "spiritual." These cultures share a deep faith and find hope in the wind, fire, rain, and other aspects of the natural world. The ultimate source of power and salvation is to be found in the interconnectedness of nature.

There are, however, subtle but important differences among these cultures with respect to their spiritual beliefs. The Ifa are slightly more earth centered than the others; followers of "Ifa" (translated as "wisdom of nature") presume that all things possess consciousness and that one must cultivate empathy for every facet of nature. In contrast, Native Americans and the Australian Aborigines place greater faith in human bonds. The Apaches, for example, invest in matrilineal and matrilocal traditions, while the Navajo believe that they are "glued together with respect." Likewise, the "dreamtime ceremony" among the Australian Aborigines is geared primarily toward reconnecting with ancestors.

What prompted these differences? One important factor is the physical landscape. The Ifa tradition developed in a rain forest habitat. Its members were surrounded and shaded by a complex flora. Intruders were rare or nonexistent. But Native Americans and Australian Aborigines occupied harsher terrain, including plains and tundra as well as bushy patches among parched desserts. They had open vistas and more contact with other tribes.

Beyond these native cultures, many parts of the industrialized world have, beginning in the early 1970s, seen a resurgence of faith in and respect for nature. Especially noteworthy were the introductions of Earth Day and the formation of Greenpeace and other environmental organizations, along with the first systematic attempts at recycling waste. Awareness of the fragility of the entire ecosystem has since grown significantly, as has our realization that the fate of humanity is tied to the survival of the planet. The threat of global warming is now front-page news on a routine basis.

In addition, increasing awareness of the dangers of pollutants and the origins of different illnesses has given rise to environmental protection, both at the public level (e.g., large-scale efforts to clean up toxic waste sites to reduce the risk of cancer in the general population) and the private (e.g., individuals purchasing home water filters or bottled water). The movement toward natural health and healing has also taken shape in recent decades. Distrustful of any goods that contained artificial ingredients, more and more consumers began to seek out products devoid of additives, dyes, or fillers, and traditional food stores started to stock soy products, whole grains, and organic produce to meet the growing demand for natural foods. Whether seeking to protect themselves from a toxic world, or hoping to treat existing health problems, more and more people turned to natural immune enhancers or organic cell protectors. In the United States, sales of such products soared from less than 2 billion dollars in 1980 to more than 45 billion in 2003. There now seems to be as much faith in naturopathy or nature's way as in the practice of traditional medicine.

While some individuals who place their faith in nature also retain a deep trust in a higher power, others do not. For every "God grateful" Lorraine Day, there is a Lance Armstrong. The latter made a miraculous recovery from advanced testicular cancer to win the Tour de France. Armstrong has frequently touted the benefits of various natural healing strategies. When asked if a belief in God played any part in his healing,

Armstrong expressed doubt. Viewing himself as "spiritual but not religious," he explained, "I hoped hard but I did not pray."

### Faith in Tradition

Individuals may place their greatest trust in time-honored social customs or traditions. A compelling example of a fully socialized faith can be found in the works of Confucius. The great sage of China developed his codes of conduct in the fourth century B.C. He put his trust in adherence to tradition and the virtue of living in communal harmony. Among his most important concepts are *Li*, the ethic of "right manners," and *Jen,* an attitude of "humanness" that combines altruism with self-respect. His most famous treatise on these topics is *The Five Relationships*, a guide for maintaining "honorable relations" between friends, young and old, parents and children, husbands and wives, and rulers and subjects.

A few decades later, Plato and Aristotle would come along to offer their own utopian formulas, placing their faith in government reform by "philosopher-kings." And some four centuries later, millions would put their faith in the Roman Empire, which at its height provided much of the known world with an enormous sense of hope. Being "a citizen of Rome" meant that you were part of the strongest political and military force ever assembled. You enjoyed the protection of "Pax Romana," a guarantee of peace, prosperity, and safe travel across the empire. You were bound to other members of the empire by virtue of a common language and set of laws as well as an intricate system of aqueducts and roadways. Your "prophet of hope" was Virgil. In the *Aeneid* and other writings, he bolstered your spirits with phrases like "mind moves matter," "they can because they think they can," and "look with favor upon bold beginnings." No wonder Virgil appears in Dante's *Inferno* as the guide who will lead the author through the very circles of hell.

In the Middle Ages and the Renaissance, much of Europe was anchored by the notion of a "great chain of being." Perhaps you have seen classic depictions of this cosmic hierarchy in a book or museum, with God at the top and a processional of angels following him. Humans are next, led by a king or queen who is followed in order by nobles, wealthy landowners, farmers, peasants, and finally the animal kingdom. As long as you maintained your place in this preordained chain, everything would be fine. But if you tried to challenge "heaven's mandate," you would bring chaos and misfortune upon yourself and others.

In the modern era, most tradition-grounded faiths are highly localized, confined to isolated and dwindling tribes, remotely situated clans, or other small pockets of society. A striking exception is the caste system in India. Like Confucianism, Pax Romana, or the great chain of being, the caste system transcends the normal bounds of religious beliefs, encompassing every aspect of living and dying. Caste membership determines your place of residence, marital choices, and employment opportunities. Moreover, if you wish to be reincarnated into a higher rung of this social ladder, you must follow the dictates of your current caste.

A need for socially cohesive traditions and rituals is no less important in other parts of the world, but many individuals are sorely lacking a sense of place. The increased incidence in clinical depression since World War II may in part be due to this diminished sense of community. Interestingly, studies of close-knit groups such as the Amish in Pennsylvania or the Kiluli in New Guinea reveal a consistently lower incidence of depression than in the general population.

However, one need not travel to Pennsylvania or New Guinea to find social connection. Individuals seeking local customs and traditions to ground their faith can readily find them in their own communities—in, say, civic-minded organizations such as the Rotary Club, Shriners, or Masons, or ethnic organizations, scouting associations, special-interest clubs (e.g., book groups), sports leagues, veterans' groups, or workers' unions.

### Faith in the Economy

The writings of economists such as Adam Smith and John Maynard Keynes reflect a deeply held faith in a particular economic system. Smith was certain that whenever individuals operated out of self-interest, an "invisible hand" would ultimately steer their actions toward the betterment of the "commonwealth." In contrast, Keynes was convinced that governments should play a more active role in controlling the economy by varying spending and taxation. Like Smith, Keynes also demonstrated a quasi-religious fervor, invoking the notion of the economist as a "savior." The disciples of these economic traditions have continued to debate the relative merits of their respective faiths. Those on the conservative side of the political spectrum remain faithful to Smith's "invisible hand," while those with more liberal leanings put their trust in Keynes' plan to rescue the downtrodden by more aggressive government interventions.

Of all the economic visionaries, Karl Marx expressed the greatest "faith in a planned economy." Accounts of his early life point to a fascinating confluence of issues that spawned a passion for political revolt and a fierce hatred of institutionalized religion. Fearing that anti-Semitic forces might erode his economic gains, Marx's father, a cold and overly pragmatic man, converted from Judaism to Christianity. Permanently estranged from his religious roots, the younger Marx attacked all religion as the "opiate of the masses," and in so doing he not only joined his father in dismissing the general importance of Jewish traditions but also rejected the elder Marx's capitalist-motivated conversion to Christianity.

Marx's faith was a form of sociopolitical atheism. He envisioned not a struggle involving "God and the devil" but a battle between "economic good and evil" that pitted the frustrated needs of the working class against the selfish priorities of the wealthy bourgeoisie. Marx popularized the notion of dialectical materialism, a philosophy that asserts the primacy of matter over thought or spirit and emphasizes that human progress follows from confrontations between and syntheses of opposing economic and political systems (the "dialectics"). This philosophy served as the catalyst for a "contemporary faith" in communism and socialism.

### Faith in Equality

During the eighteenth century, philosopher Jean Jacques Rousseau was Europe's leading proponent for equal rights. He famously declared, "Man is born free, but everywhere he is in chains." In the nineteenth century, sociologist Auguste Comte offered a "religion of humanity" to replace the "childish illusion" of Christianity. He chose the study of norms over doctrine, love of others over devotion to God, and faith in the social order over belief in a divine chain of being. At one point, he even proposed a new humanistic calendar that paid homage to great individuals. The days of the week were to be named after such luminaries as Homer, Aristotle, and Shakespeare instead of the mythical gods, Thor, Freya, etc.

Among the many sharing a faith in social reform were those who saw an opportunity to meld it with Marxist principles. Thus were born communism and socialism. In theory, these "reform movements" were based on the idea of transferring all (communism) or most (socialism) of the material resources to the general populace, giving them control over the means and ends of economic production.

Helen Keller was an avid supporter of the first American Socialist Party. Battling controversy and ridicule, she passionately voiced her support for the "alienated and disenfranchised." In New York, on December 31, 1920, her words eloquently spoke to a crowd of marchers prepared to celebrate the Russian Revolution.

> Let us join the world's procession marching toward a glad tomorrow. Strong of hope and brave in heart . . . All along the road beside us throng the people sad and broken, weeping women, children hungry, homeless like little birds cast out of their nest . . . With their hearts aflame, untamed, glorying in martyrdom they hail us passing quickly. Halt not, O comrades, yonder glimmers the star of our hope.

Other prominent activists in the 1930s and 1940s joined the crusade for equality. Bertrand Russell promoted "a liberal philosophy rooted in logic." B. F. Skinner presented his blueprint for a utopian society that was based entirely on principles of behavioral conditioning. Gandhi's faith in civil disobedience helped him secure the freedom of an entire nation. In the 1960s, Martin Luther King punctuated *his* struggle for equal rights with one of the great speeches of the twentieth century:

> I have a dream that one day on the red hills of Georgia, sons of former slaves and sons of former slave-owners will be able to sit down together at the table of

brotherhood . . . I have a dream that my four little children will one day live in a nation where they will not be judged by the color of their skin but the content of their character . . . *This is our hope.*

In the late twentieth century, the postmodernist movement surfaced as another expression of faith in equality and diversity. Postmodernists maintain that art, philosophy, and science are ultimately based on nothing more than subjective opinions and cultural conventions. Not surprisingly, their political agenda is to challenge the status quo. Dismissing traditional sources of authority or the counsel of "experts," they place their faith in a multicultural, pluralistic mosaic of "opinions" and "points of view." Some postmodernists argue that their perspective represents the ultimate statement against a unified belief system. Others, however, believe it *is* a worldview, consisting of "faith in relativism" or the belief in the equality of divergent ways of constructing reality.

### Faith in Science

Centuries ago, many of the greatest scientists and philosophers were also religious leaders. For example, Augustine was considered one of the greatest minds of the early Christian period, and Thomas Aquinas was known as the towering intellect of the Middle Ages. During the seventeenth century, "The Reasonableness of Christianity" was among John Locke's essays, and Benedict de Spinoza wrote passionately about the "mind of God," "the sum of all customs and laws . . . and all the mentality that is scattered over space and time."

The life of Blaise Pascal vividly demonstrates an interweaving of scientific genius with religious passion. Pascal was a child prodigy who made enormous contributions to the fields of mathematics and philosophy. On November 23, 1654, he experienced a 2-hour "ecstatic vision". Joining a monastery at age 28, he devoted his remaining years to "meditate on the glory of God," and for the rest of his life, he carried in the lining of his coat pocket a written account of his "religious awakening."

Whenever the existence of God comes up in philosophical discussions, someone is bound to mention *Pascal's wager*. Given what is at stake, namely, the possibility of salvation or eternal damnation, there are four discernible possibilities to consider.

If I wager *for* and God *is*—infinite gain;

If I wager *for* and God *is not*—no loss;

If I wager *against* and God *is*—infinite loss;

If I wager *against* and God *is not*—neither loss nor gain.

We have already discussed at length scientific atheism and the conflict between science and faith in contemporary times. We wish only to note here that faith *in* science offers an especially powerful means of addressing mastery needs, but that there are important differences in the *faith focus* of different scientific disciplines. For example, those who place their faith in physics believe that it can provide both mastery and survival solutions, including answers about the origins of life and the fate of the universe. For similar reasons, many biologists put their faith in understanding living organisms, in the hope of uncovering their biochemical secrets, while many medical scientists put their faith in medicine, hoping to diminish suffering and extend the lives of the seriously ill. Social scientists put their faith in ideas designed to improve the quality of human relationships and assure the viability of essential cultural institutions.

## Faith in the Self

For Carl Jung, the supreme archetype was the hero. From Ulysses to Luke Skywalker, in a story line that was etched centuries ago, the hero is the one chosen to undertake a sacred quest of dire import to him (and the hero in these tales usually is a him) and his society. The hero's path is arduous, fraught with peril. He suffers serious wounds, but with the help of a benign sage or great protector, he emerges transformed. In the words of mythologist Joseph Campbell, the hero is now prepared to "bring a boon to society that restores a valued way of life."

Despite having a timeless and universal substrate, the hero myths of various cultures reflect variations on a theme. For example, there are striking differences between Ulysses, Thor, and King Arthur in the West and the "high gods" of India in the East: Shiva, Vishnu, and Brahma. Each script represents the "hope profile" of a particular nation or people, a unique pattern of investment in attachment, mastery, or survival.

The Western tales describe feats of extraordinary personal mastery, and the heroes are "valiant warriors" and "shrewd tacticians." Their Indian counterparts reflect a greater focus on attachment concerns. The "beneficent" Shiva "clutches the whole world to himself" while the "benevolent" Vishnu is portrayed as the radiant "friend of humankind." Brahma is the personification of the universal godliness that permeates all matter and is inherent in every human being.

Whether viewed as an archetypal, mythic, or a spiritually inspired lesson, the hero's tale is compelling because it reflects the hope of self-actualization. Personal growth is a journey of discovery involving differentiation from others as well as an integration of talents and life experiences. It demands courage and entails risks. The process is difficult, if not impossible, without spiritual guidance. However, in the final analysis, it is the individual who must assume the greatest responsibility for his or her self-development. In Herman Hesse's *Steppenwolf*, the fainthearted protagonist enters a dream world where a "supreme grandmaster" compares the process of personal growth to a game of chess.

This is the art of life . . . You may as an artist develop the game of your life and lend it animation. You may complicate and enrich it as you please. It lies in your hands.

The hero archetype is especially relevant for those who have experienced great adversity or received little in the way of emotional support. This includes neglected children who surmise that they must fend for themselves as well as victims of abusive relationships or a life-threatening illness. The hope of these faith-deprived individuals often derives from an attitude of self-sufficiency or from assuming the role of a battle-toughened survivor. Nevertheless, without a guiding myth or inspiring role model, it can be extremely difficult for individuals to craft a heroic vision for themselves. Thus, it is common for the dispossessed to strongly identify with the hero's wounds and impulse toward transformation.

Heroic inspiration comes in many forms. Some draw inspiration from spiritual heroes such as Buddha, Jesus, and Mohammed, and others from war heroes or political leaders. Celebrities and sports figures may also activate the hero within. Even nonmythic fictional characters can sometimes serve as role models to further a kind of heroic self-development. Many readers will undoubtedly recall a heroic comic book figure or television character who inspired them as children.

The hero myth can be viewed as a lesson in balanced personal growth. It suggests that where you finish is more important than where you began. It underscores the struggles and sacrifices that accompany character development while acknowledging the need for a guide or mentor. It affirms the worth of the individual but at the same time suggests that the greatest gains transcend even the self.

Crafting a heroic vision for your "self" is not to be confused with hero worship. Some individuals who put all of their faith in perceived "super humans" view themselves as incapable of dealing with the vicissitudes of life. Their very sense of self may be largely derived from the success or failure of a particular entertainer, athlete, or politician. The media contribute to this problem of idle "hero awe" through slick marketing campaigns that generate unrealistic, idealized celebrity profiles. The point is to live and not merely to observe a heroic existence. For example, even within the most earth-centered or attachment-based faiths, there is the clear implication that the individual must "bring the power of the exterior into the interior."

In *Little Girl Lost*, Leisha Joseph shared her inspiring story of courage and faith. Leisha's father died when she was very young. She was later sexually abused by several of her mother's boyfriends. Her mother attempted to burn their house down and went after Leisha with a knife. Nevertheless, Leisha persevered, became an honor roll student, and reached the finals of the Miss Teen USA pageant. A short time later, she was attacked by a serial rapist. Rather than live in fear, she chose to confront him in the courtroom. Leisha's faith is a great example of "guided heroism," a spiritual meld of "inspiration from above" and "fierce self-reliance." Not surprisingly, she noted that "all of my Bible heroes are survivors."

### Faith in Others

One of the most basic centers of value is derived from faith in other people, including family and close friends. Faith in others is also the emotional glue that underlies team chemistry on the ball field and *esprit de corps* on the battlefield.

Regarding friendships, Cicero declared that "nothing better has been given to human beings by the immortal gods." Ralph Waldo Emerson called friendships "nature's masterpiece" and "a possession for all time." One of the most comprehensive studies on friendship involved over 40,000 *Psychology Today* readers. More than half replied that they would seek out a good friend in a time of crisis before doing anything else. Nearly three-quarters responded that they would also risk their life for their best friend.

In the sports world, some analysts insist that teamwork or team chemistry is an overrated cliché. Nevertheless, a poll of former professional athletes indicated that the majority believed it was an important factor, especially with respect to being "accountable to" and "having faith" in other members of the squad. Vince Lombardi, "crusader of the gridiron," elevated teamwork to a spiritual quest and engendered a champion's faith in a group of perennial losers, the Green Bay Packers. One of his former players confessed, "We'd go through fire for him."

In 2002, the once lowly Anaheim Angels shocked the baseball world by winning the World Series. As one writer put it, the team was largely composed of "guys who shouldn't have been there." A noted baseball official observed, "I don't think many people gave them much of a chance. This shows what can happen when you have good team chemistry and all twenty-five guys contribute." A player from another team said of the Angel's success, "It absolutely gives us hope."

In *The Art of War*, Sun Tzu praised the power of a closely banded fighting unit: "He will win whose army is animated by the same spirit throughout its ranks." In modern parlance, that spirit is called "unit cohesiveness," the military parallel to team chemistry. According to Lt. Colonel Richard Hooker, effective military action requires both *horizontal and vertical cohesion*. The former addresses trust within a company of soldiers, while the latter concerns their degree of faith in their unit leaders or higher-level commanders.

Hooker argued that modern battlefield conditions require that military leaders pay particular attention to unit cohesiveness. The use of high-tech weapons, including unmanned drones and GPS-guided smart bombs, means that ground troops tend to be deployed in smaller, widely scattered units. They are no longer united by physical proximity and do not enjoy the infusion of confidence that comes from marching in a vast caravan. Hooker's suggestions for creating "unbreakable units" (horizontal cohesion) included the rotation of small groups who have trained together rather than the constant exchange of individual soldiers. He also emphasized the need for establishing unwavering faith in leaders at every step in the chain of command.

Agreeing with Hooker, a number of historians have traced the success or failure of past military campaigns to varying levels of cohesiveness. For example, some American Civil War experts have commented on the Confederacy's mistake of allowing regiments to select leaders from within their own ranks. This practice drastically reduced the level of vertical cohesiveness or faith in the leadership because such individuals often turned out to be inexperienced soldiers.

In contrast, the army of the Roman Empire was a marvel of "planned horizontal cohesiveness." At the height of its power, the Roman army consisted of approximately 30 legions. Each legion was divided into cohorts that were further broken down into "centuries" of 100 men. Legions carried standards or flags emblazoned with references to the history and accomplishments of the group and with the initials SPQR, *senatus populusque Romanus:* "We represent the senate and people of Rome." To assure even greater unity, the cohorts and centuries were organized according to social class, age, and experience. Furthermore, a small percentage of each soldier's pay was dedicated to the legion to assure that every fallen soldier would have a proper burial.

## Faith Wisdom

An intelligent faith requires a dedication to spiritual growth. The specific ingredients for developing a smart soul are the following: depth, honesty, openness, trust, and spiritual chemistry. Do you recall philosopher William Lynch's suggestion that the further hope "would soar the deeper it must plunge into facts"? More than a poetic twist of language, Lynch's insight reflects a basic fact of nature. The botanist will tell you that the penetration of a root system into soil limits the height of a plant. The civil engineer will explain that the depth of a building's foundation determines the number of floors that can be erected above the ground. Thus, like a giant redwood or a tall skyscraper, a strong faith requires a well-established base.

*Spiritual depth* is achieved through a significant investment in one or more centers of value. On the other hand, a shallow faith is revealed in superficial engagements with a higher power, the forces of nature, family and friends, or other faith sources. Psychologist Gordon Allport contrasted *intrinsically religious* with *extrinsically religious* individuals. The latter limit their investment in religion to public displays and social gatherings, filling their prayers with laundry lists of personal requests. In contrast, the intrinsically religious tend to be more private in their devotion, expressing a strong desire to develop a more intimate relationship with a higher power.

Allport's religious typology can be extended to describe an individual's relationship with any center of value. Take, for example, faith in science. The extrinsically motivated scientist is primarily interested in fame and fortune, while the one who is intrinsically directed could be characterized as a dedicated truth-seeker. In Chapter 5 we noted how Bertrand Russell desperately longed to "apprehend the Pythagorean power by which number holds sway above the flux."

*Spiritual honesty* refers to your relationship with a particular center of value. Are you genuinely invested in a higher power? Are you truly devoted to social reform or equal opportunity? Is your investment in nature, science, or your own capacities based on an abiding respect for that faith center?

To what extent are you merely going through the motions of "faithing"? It is critical to make sure that your faith is grounded in spiritual honesty as opposed to political correctness, peer pressure, or attempts to escape the past. For example, writer Ken Wilber introduced the term "spiritual bypass" to describe the unconscious agendas of certain "new age" disciples who forge an inauthentic spiritual attachment as a way of skirting "secular demons" such as a history of abuse or unresolved losses.

Spiritual honesty is reflected in a passionate commitment. If you are emotionally drawn to a center of value for the right reasons, your faith development will be a joyous process and will not feel like a chore or sacrifice. The time spent in prayer, meditation, or service to your cause should be deeply engrossing. It should resemble the "flow experience" described by psychologist Mihaly Csikszentmihalyi: "We have all experienced times when, instead of being buffeted by anonymous forces . . . we feel a sense of exhilaration, a deep sense of enjoyment that is long cherished and that becomes a hallmark in memory of what life should be like."

The opposite of flow is resistance and turmoil. Recall Augustine's years of struggle to develop a deep-seated belief in God. Consider those who feel they ought to express more faith in their fellow human beings but lack strong affiliative impulses. In *The Brothers Karamazov*, Ivan, the faithless intellectual, implores his brother Aloysha, who is studying for the priesthood, to avoid the evil of "forced spirituality":

> I must make one confession . . . I could never understand how one can love one's neighbors . . . I once read somewhere of John the Merciful, a saint, [who upon meeting] a hungry, frozen beggar . . . took him into his bed, held him in his arms, and began breathing into his mouth, which was putrid and loathsome from some awful disease. I am convinced that he did that from "self-laceration," from the self-laceration of falsity, for the sake of the charity imposed by duty, as a penance laid on him.

*Openness to experience* is fundamental to faith development. According to Gabriel Marcel, "Openness allows the space for hope to spread." It helps the individual to fully engage centers of value, allowing the spiritual bounty of available resources to be more fully integrated into daily thoughts and actions.

There are two main forms of openness, external and internal. Both involve a permeability of consciousness based on biological, social, and psychological needs. Humans are genetically wired for openness toward others because they are social beings in need of love and support to reach their potential. Some anthropologists even believe that the evolution of the human brain may have been stimulated largely by a need to keep up with an increasingly complex social life.

Many of the world's faith systems include practices designed to foster external openness. For example, the Ifa of Western Africa dance in front of a mat used to symbolize the interweaving of the natural and divine worlds. Through this process, they are opening themselves to the possibility of spiritual guidance. Similarly, Hindus practice a form of yoga that is designed to open the various "chakras" or "energy systems" in the body. Jews in the holy city pray at the Western Wall, while Moslems orient themselves in the direction of Mecca when they kneel down to pray. Native Americans in the Southwest partake of peyote, the "holy medicine" that "opens the senses to the spirit world."

There is also a need for an inner openness to reclaim hidden parts of the self. Over the course of an individual's lifetime, memories and images are imprinted in various realms of the brain, including storage areas that can be hard to access using typical memory recall strategies. Such psychic dispersion calls for a reintegration of experience. Sometimes these significant traces of life appear in dreams, during meditation, or while listening to music. Being open to such experiences is crucial for achieving greater self-understanding and ultimately connecting with the wider self or what William James called "the more."

Multiple centers of value, whether experienced as an internal or external faith source, are already prewired in the human psyche. It does not matter whether we refer to these emotional response patterns in terms of archetypes or instincts. The important point is that you harbor a vast reservoir of potential energy for connecting with multiple faith sources. Mystics understand this notion very well because it underscores their belief that each individual is part of a greater whole. Moreover, this is why many religious and self-help groups encourage their members to look within for their "inner god" or "wise mind."

Faith arises from a satisfaction of the trust needs associated with the motives underlying hope. *Goal-oriented trust* engenders the belief that one is adequately empowered to achieve mastery. *Relational trust* fuels the expectation of continued involvement with a valued presence. *Safety-based trust* imparts a sense of security or the assurance of ultimate salvation.

The keys to developing trust in one or more centers of value are self-examination and patience. Begin with a spiritual inventory of your faith needs. Some individuals are primarily mastery oriented, while others seek greater intimacy or peace of mind. Perhaps your faith needs encompass more than one of the hope motives as well as multiple centers of value. Once you begin to understand your spiritual needs, adopt an attitude of active waiting, remaining patient but simultaneously mindful. Be ready for investment opportunities related to mastery, attachment, or survival.

Trust and openness are mutually reinforcing virtues. Without openness, you will be unable to engage with trustworthy others. Without trust, you will be unable to cultivate an attitude of openness. Summoning the courage to achieve greater trust and openness will create psychological space for you to engage one or more centers of value and will assure you what Marcel dubbed the "first fruits and pledges" of fundamental hope. The "fruits" include dependability (goal-oriented trust), intimacy (relational-trust), and security (survival-trust) as well as the "pledges" of continued success, ongoing presence, and future wellness.

*Spiritual chemistry* is the final ingredient for faith development. As an individual, you have a unique set of physical and emotional characteristics that influence your relationship with the outside world. You may be active and relish a brisk morning walk. Perhaps you are more sedentary and happiest when lounging before a fireplace. You may enjoy the outdoors and delight in the changing seasons or prefer a climate-controlled interior. You may be able to eat ice cream, cheese, and yogurt, or you may suffer from lactose intolerance.

Similarly, on a spiritual level, you may find yourself unable to digest certain religious beliefs, but may feel that others are more suited to your tastes. You may find spiritual sustenance in nature or a social cause or a scientific interest. Whatever your inclinations, *you need some type of faith to live fully in the world*. The key to finding a good enough faith lies in meeting the needs of your particular spiritual type.

## Six Spiritual Types

Our research suggests that there are six basic ways of being spiritual. Each represents a culmination of many factors, including temperament and critical life events as well as family and cultural experiences. In Table 8.3 we summarize these spiritual types and pair them with associated faith possibilities.

Looking at these options, which one do you think most suits your spiritual type at this time? Ultimately, you will want a faith system that addresses your needs for attachment, mastery, and survival, one that delivers a full sense of hope. But first, it is important that you focus on at least one clear-cut center of value. After achieving some spiritual depth, you will be in a better position to add breadth to your faith foundation.

Depending on your spiritual type, you will probably find yourself initially attracted to a particular center of value. For example, if you are a *follower*, you may need to believe in a higher power and seek the presence of that being or essence in your daily life. You desire external structure in the form of an ordered cosmos, spiritual doctrine, and rules for living. You might therefore gravitate toward Islam, Catholicism, or traditional Judaism.

TABLE 8.3.  *Faith Possibilities for Spiritual Types*

| Spiritual Types (and hope motives) | Options for Jumpstarting Faith |
| --- | --- |
| Follower (Attachment and survival) | Catholicism (e.g., Roman Catholic, Greek or Eastern Orthodox), Islam (e.g., Sunni or Shiite), Judaism (e.g., conservative or Orthodox), Confucianism |
| Collaborator (Mastery and attachment) | Protestant sects (e.g., Methodist, Presbyterian, Quaker), Hinduism, African Ifa, Native American (e.g. Apache, Inuit, Lakota), Reform Judaism |
| Independent (Mastery) | Emerson, Rand or Russell, science-based hobbies or careers, athletic pursuits, skills-oriented education and training, Unitarian Universalism |
| Mystic (Attachment) | Judeo-Christian (Martin Buber, Thomas Keating, Thomas Merton, Kabbalah), Sufism (Rumi), nature-based (Rachel Carson, Jane Goodall) |
| Reformer (Attachment and mastery) | Sociopolitical activism, union membership, writings of Gandhi, Martin Luther King, Rousseau, Thoreau, postmodernism (e.g., Foucault or Derrida) |
| Sufferer (Survival) | Buddhism, Dialectical Behavior Therapy, relaxation and meditation training, biofeedback, massage, polarity therapy, reflexology, yoga |

However, if you are *collaboratively oriented*, you prefer to develop alliances and cultivate support for spiritually acceptable ends rather than to adhere to a fixed code. In that case, you may prefer one of the various Protestant sects emphasizing a God who "helps those who help themselves." You may also feel drawn to the Hindu concept of an "inner Atman" or one of the nature-oriented faiths such as that of the African Ifa.

*Independents* strive to analyze and explain the world. They prefer to place their faith in reason and logic, and seeking to increase "faith in the self," they are particularly apt to draw strength from inspiring role models, such as the hero archetype. If this is your preferred way of being in the world, look for inspiration in the poetry of Emerson, the impassioned logic of Bertrand Russell, or the bold philosophy of Ayn Rand. Role models can be drawn from virtually any field of human endeavor, including the arts, science, business, politics, sports, or entertainment. A possible list of hope stalwarts might include Lance Armstrong, Carl Sagan, or Oprah Winfrey.

*Mystics* tend to be emotionally sensitive, intuitive, and primed to experience a union with a transcendent presence. They desire contact, merger, and oneness rather than enduring a separate sense of self. Do you seek a faith based on an emotional merger with a higher power or spiritual presence? If so, you may be a mystic. Christian mysticism dates back to Plotinus and St. John of the Cross. In its modern guises, it includes "the contemplative life" as described by Thomas Merton and the more recent "centering prayer" of Thomas Keating.

Jews who prefer a brand of "traditional mysticism" may resonate to the teachings of the Kabbalah, while those of a more secular persuasion might be more attracted to the writings of Martin Buber. Muslims who seek a deeper bond with Allah can turn to the offerings of the Sufi sect such as Rumi's inspired poetry of love. If you seek a "merger with nature," you might want to consider incorporating aspects of Native American spirituality or the faith beliefs of the African Ifa or Australian "dream-time" followers. (Note that "nature worship" can serve as a source of mysticism as well as collaborative spirituality. The determining factor is whether you are more invested in "empowerment-seeking" or experiencing a sense of "fusion and oneness.")

*Reformers* are acutely sensitized to acts of injustice or barriers to equal opportunity. They believe in changing the world, seeking a "pluralistic mosaic" or "spiritual cooperative." Most of them have personally experienced injustice, discrimination, or alienation of one kind or another. If this is true for you, your path to a stronger faith is likely to involve some form of activism. For example, you might want to consider helping underprivileged children or getting involved in local or national politics. Other faith-building exercises for the "reformer" include volunteering at a hospital, school, or community shelter.

Gina O'Connell Higgins described the "inner dynamics of activism" that can serve to positively motivate victims of past cruelty and abuse. In her interviews with resilient adults, she explored the process of "giving what one did not receive" and the gratification of fostering "symbolic corrections" to restore one's vision of a "just world." For example, one "survivor," badly abused as a child, became the head of large human-service agency. He described his work as a "crusade of joy."

*Sufferers* are acutely sensitized to the pain and dangers that characterize the human condition. They seek liberation from distress, frequently through changing themselves rather than struggling with unalterable constraints. They may find solace in Buddhist practices. Known as "the great salvation religion," Buddhism is the only major faith that highlights specific strategies for escaping the torment of pain, loss, and death. It promises a "tranquil mind" and a peaceful alternative to "futile cravings." Many psychotherapists have begun to incorporate Buddhist principles in treating trauma survivors and other chronic-stress sufferers.

It is important to have some awareness of the many faith options at your disposal. Moreover, do not feel that you must restrict yourself to just one spiritual possibility. The human mind is multilayered. Just imagine all the data stored in those folds of cortex encasing the even deeper structures of your brain! As you grow in spiritual wisdom and integrate more and more of your inner and outer worlds, certain spiritual alternatives will inevitably move to the foreground while others may recede into the background.

Remember that openness to experience is one of your greatest resources for building faith and hope.

---

## Spiritual Type Assessment

*Directions*: For each of the following questions, rate your agreement using the following scale. When you have finished, total your scores for each of the six spiritual types, placing your ratings next to each item in the spaces provided below. Your highest score is your *primary spiritual type*. Your second highest score is your *secondary spiritual type*.

0 I strongly disagree
I I mildly disagree
2 I mostly agree
3 I strongly agree

2 — I. My life is ultimately in the hands of God or a higher power.
0 — 2. Quite often I have been keenly aware of the presence of God or a higher power.
3 — 3. When I get what I want it is usually because I have worked hard for it.
1 — 4. To prosper, I must be in harmony with the will of God or a divine force.
2 — 5. I am often amazed at how tense and anxious I have become.
2 — 6. I frequently go out of my way to make sure a fair and just outcome will take place.
2 — 7. Without my faith in a higher power, I would feel lost and without direction.
0 — 8. I often pray or meditate to become closer to God or a higher power.
3 — 9. My life is primarily determined by my own actions.
1 — 10. I feel most satisfied when I'm working hand in hand with a spiritual presence.
2 — II. I have a difficult time relaxing my mind and body.
3 — 12. Everyone has unique gifts; we need to do our part to assure their potential is realized.
0 — 13. I often turn to scripture or spiritual leaders for guidance and support.
2 — 14. My faith is based on developing a closer connection to God or a higher power.
2 — 15. Few feelings in life are greater than pride in one's own accomplishments.

_____ *1* 16. In dealing with life, I manage what I can and leave the rest to Mother Nature.

_____ *3* 17. Compared to others, I have had a rather painful life.

_____ *1* 18. I feel that one of my life goals is to work for justice and equality.

*Scoring Your Type:*

Follower: 1 *2*  7 *2*  13 *3*  My Total = *7*

Collaborator: 4 *1*  10 *1*  16 *1*  My Total = *3*

Independent: 3 *3*  9 *3*  15 *2*  My Total = *8*

Mystic: 2 *0*  8 *0*  14 *2*  My Total = *2*

Reformer: 6 *2*  12 *3*  18 *1*  My Total = *6*

Sufferer: 5 *2*  11 *2*  17 *3*  My Total = *7*

(Highest Score)        Primary Spiritual Type _____

(Second Highest)    Secondary Spiritual Type _____

---

*Eighth Hope Meditation*

Are you surprised at your questionnaire results? Do they make sense to you? Does your spiritual type shed any further light on the meaning of critical events in your life? Can you relate your spiritual type to the kind of belief systems, philosophies, people you have been attracted to, or the kinds of work and career choices that you have made? Is your spiritual type consistent with your religious affiliation or spiritual belief system? Regardless of your answers, which of the faith possibilities listed on page 142 in Table 8.3 might you explore further?

# Part Two

THE WINGS OF HOPE:

*BEAMS OF POWER, PRESENCE, AND PROTECTION*

# Nine

## ATTACHMENT MATTERS: LOVE ALWAYS

## HOPES

> Above and below me hovers the beautiful . . . Talking God . . . With your feet I walk. I walk with your limbs. I carry forth your body . . . For me your mind thinks. Your voice speaks for me. I am surrounded by it. I am immersed in it . . . In my youth I am aware of it. And in old age I shall walk quietly the beautiful trail.
>
> —Native American prayer, author unknown

You have reached the halfway point in this hope journey. Chapters 1 through 8 dealt with your hope legacy, from the biological infrastructure for mastery, attachment, and survival to cultural factors and spiritual influences. We now shift to the wings of hope— to varied strategies for drawing upon the virtue of hope to unleash within you a greater a sense of purpose, connectedness, and capacity for terror management and healing. We begin with those strategies that are attachment related.

As social creatures we cannot live in isolation. Recall that Aristotle labeled as "beasts or gods" those who seemed content to live by themselves. The fifteenth-century poet John Donne echoed this sentiment when he wrote, "No man is an island." It is human bonds, said the Chinese sage Mengzi, "that fill the space between heaven and earth."

What are the bonds that fill your space? Is your primary relationship to a child, parent, another adult, a personal god, an ineffable spirit, or the forces of nature? A strong infant–caregiver bond spawns basic trust and provides the first taste of empowerment. Affiliations in the here and now offer intimacy, inspiration, and comfort. The promise of new relationships sustains a hopeful countenance of trust and openness while also framing a horizon of specific hoped-for encounters. Ultimately, to experience the fullness of hope, there must always be a perceived living "other" in your life that can give as well as receive, trust and be trusted.

## Profiles in Attachment

The three stories of hope you are about to encounter illustrate the power of attachments to people, places, and ideas. Moreover, these particular vignettes illustrate the frequent intertwining of the attachment motive with the drive toward mastery or the impulse for survival. To situate these examples in a broader context, we then explore what we call the attached core and examine psychoanalyst Erich Fromm's insights concerning "the powerful striving force" of love. Next, because "hope building" is a reciprocal process, we outline the qualities needed to be an effective hope provider, with specific suggestions for parents and caregivers as well as for lovers and friends. The chapter concludes with a set of strategies for creating hope-based spiritual connections.

### Arthur Ashe: Who Is Watching Me?

Growing up in the segregated south of the 1940s, Arthur Ashe was a skinny little boy who loved to read and listen to music with his mother. Despite humble roots, his talent on the tennis court and in the classroom earned him a scholarship to UCLA. In 1965 he won the NCAA tennis championship, and 4 years later he became the top-ranked tennis professional in the United States.

Ashe reached the finals of Wimbledon in 1975. His opponent was the fiery Jimmy Connors, known for his aggressive play and brash demeanor. Tennis experts predicted that Connors would rout the soft-spoken Ashe. Astounding everyone, Ashe dismantled Connors fairly easily, using his patented slices and low, short drives. A few days later the cover of *Sports Illustrated* would read: "Shocker at Wimbledon." Ashe finished the year ranked number one in the world.

You probably know the rest of the Ashe story. Due to heart trouble, he twice underwent surgery, in 1979 and 1983. In 1986, doctors discovered that he was infected with the AIDS virus, most likely the result of contaminated blood that he received during the second operation. His few remaining years were spent traveling around the world, serving as an outspoken advocate of civil rights causes and promoting AIDS awareness.

Shortly before his death in 1993, Ashe noted that if he were remembered only as a tennis player, his life would have been a failure. Instead, he wanted his legacy to include the causes for which he fought as well as the integrity that he maintained in the face of worldwide scrutiny and frequent intolerance. Ashe viewed the source of his strength and hope in terms of the enduring attachment that he maintained with his deceased parents.

Who is watching me? The living and the dead. My mother, Mattie, watches me. She died when I was not quite seven . . . My last sight of her alive: I was finishing breakfast and she is standing in the side doorway looking lovingly at me . . . And then I remember the last time I saw her, in a coffin at home . . . Every day since then I have thought about her . . . She is with me everyday, watching me in everything I do. My father is watching me, too. He is still a force in my life . . . [although] he died of a stroke in 1989.

## The Pennsylvania Miners

All mankind is of one author, and is one volume . . . therefore the bell that rings to a sermon calls not upon the preacher only, but upon the congregation to come . . . any man's death diminishes me, because I am involved in mankind; and therefore never send to know for whom the bell tolls; it tolls for thee.

—John Donne, *Meditation XVII*

One of the most memorable images of 2002 was the sight of nine miners as they were rescued from a collapsed shaft in rural Pennsylvania. They had endured 77 hours in a cold, dark hole that was nearly 250 feet below the earth's surface. In terms of hope, what is most interesting are the relationships that sustained them during their ordeal. They huddled together for warmth, shared bites of one dry sandwich, and related stories of their lives and families.

The men alternated between thoughts of rescue and concerns about abandoning their loved ones. Blaine Mayhugh agonized over the fact that he had forgotten to kiss his wife before going to work. Once rescued, he fought back tears, explaining it was "the only day in my life I didn't kiss my wife before I went to work . . . that had to be the day." A number of his fellow workers stated they would never mine again, emphasizing not their own mortality fears but also their reluctance to ever put their families or community through any future tribulations.

When they were trapped together, the miners quickly developed a profound sense of unity that soon encircled their families, the rescuers, and the entire nation. Randy Fogle recalled telling the others that they needed to put their faith in the rescuers: "I told them we have the resources of the whole world around us and they will have everything that we will need." When the miners were finally pulled to safety, the 150 rescuers danced and shouted the nicknames of each miner. Family and friends staying at a nearby firehouse erupted into celebration. Signs were erected at rest stops and gas stations, declaring "Nine alive!" and "Prayers answered." Looking back, Blaine Mayhugh noted that "We vowed to live or die as a group . . . My father-in-law tied us all together with a rope so we wouldn't float away from each other."

### Mystical Unions

> Come, come again, whoever you are, come! Heathen, fire worshipper or
> idolatrous, come! Ours is the portal of hope.
>
> —Rumi, *Discourses*

Sometimes a mystical experience is described as *corporal,* filled with perceptions of
images and objects such as a godlike figure, a pool of water, or a rainbow. Alternately, a
mystical state may consist entirely of an *inner experience.* One is aware of a presence or
feels engulfed by strong positive emotions. Mystical experiences can be delineated into
three categories:

*Theistic*: Sensing the presence of God or a higher power.
*Monistic*: Sensing the unity of all matter, time and space; everything may seem to
   collapse into a white hole of bright light or circle of radiance.
*Pantheistic*: Sensing a connection with nature and all of creation; experiencing a
   link to the animal kingdom, natural world, or some other aspect of the cosmos.

The anthropologist Jane Goodall provided one of the most far-ranging discussions of
spiritual awakening. In *Reason for Hope*, this world-renowned scientist recounted two
stirring mystical experiences, the first at Notre Dame Cathedral:

> I gazed in silent awe at the great Rose Window, glowing in the morning sun. All at
> once the cathedral was filled with a huge volume of sound . . . Bach's Tocata and
> Fugue in D Minor . . . it seemed to enter and possess my whole self . . . That
> moment, a suddenly captured moment of eternity, was perhaps the closest I have
> ever come to experiencing ecstasy.

And the second in an African jungle:

> Lost in the awe at the beauty around me, I must have slipped into a state of
> heightened awareness. It is hard—impossible, really—to put into words the
> moment of truth that suddenly came upon me then. . . . It seemed to me, as I
> struggled afterward to recall the experience, that self was utterly absent: I and the
> chimpanzees, the earth and trees and air, seemed to merge, to become one with
> the spirit power of life itself.

Reports of mystical experiences like Goodall's have come from all over the world.
Among Hindus, Zen Buddhists, and Islamic Sufists, transcendence and union *is* the
daily spiritual goal of each and every follower. Although not as common in the West,

vivid examples of mystical transformation are hardly rare. Among others, Shakespeare, Goethe, Longfellow, Emily Bronte, and Pope John Paul II all testified to their encounters with the "numinous." Albert Einstein referred to such mystical states as the "center of true religion," adding that anyone "who can no longer wonder and stand rapt in awe, is as good as dead." William James viewed them as unsolicited and ineffable streams of timeless illumination, while writer Annie Dillard preferred the imagery of light and fire to capture the mystical experience.

## The Attached Core

In later chapters, we will discuss the role of relationships in strengthening the mastery and survival aspects of hope, but here we focus only on the attachment system as a primary source of hope and as the basis for our most compelling desires. In particular, we examine the amalgam of components that form the *attached core*, an essential building block of the hope foundation.

Human beings rely on relationships with others to forge a stable, cohesive, and continuous sense of self. But such interactions create something far more profound than simply a self-concept, or in psychoanalyst Heinz Kohut's terms, a self-object. They also influence how we experience ourselves, the world, and the future. From a hope perspective, the emotions they engender can reverberate for a lifetime, impacting how connected, empowered, or safe we feel in the world. To Kohut, the critical interactions or bonds that occur early in life between parents and children include: A "mirroring transference," which takes place when parents confirm and admire a child's "strength and specialness," and an "idealizing transference," which occurs when parents encourage the older child to "merge with their own strength and power." The self-object, or the child's sense of self, emerges from both experiences and internalizes them, and it can be either positive or negative, depending on the qualities "transferred" from the parent. We prefer the term "hopeful imprints" to describe the positive aspects of these internalized experiences with a strong and caring presence. These imprints are a fundamental part of the attached core.

So, too, is trust of the sort we have described previously, particularly the *relational trust* that develops in part from the stable presence of a caregiver, friend, or lover. As opposed to *goal-related trust*, which is placed in someone (e.g., a teacher, coach, or manager) you believe can aid you in achieving a valued mastery-related outcome, or *survival-based trust*, which relates to your prospects for continued well-being (e.g., confidence in your doctor), relational trust is the assurance of a *continued presence*. You are confident that someone or something will stay by your side. The importance of having this feeling cannot be stressed enough. We all need a stable parental figure in childhood, a steadfast friend in adolescence, a committed lover in adulthood, and even a trusted spiritual presence support our quest for a permanent, incorruptible bond.

Also part of the attached core is openness, which as we emphasized earlier, is intertwined with trust. Present to some extent at birth, this basic trust will develop into a growing sense that the world is benign and receptive if an infant's caregiver provides a reliable presence. Encouraged by attentive caregivers, especially a positive maternal and paternal presence, infants will naturally reach out to make social contacts and to explore their surroundings. In time, they will develop an increased capacity for dealing with unfamiliar individuals as well as other novel and complex situations.

Indeed, that capacity enables the individual to become attuned to the presence of others and to interact meaningfully with them. William James noted, "the most important part of my world is my fellow-man . . . his attitude toward me unlocks most of my shames and indignations and fears." A simple word of kindness, delivered at the right time, can be thoroughly uplifting. An isolated verbal attack, delivered at the wrong time, can be incredibly demoralizing.

Nevertheless, words are just one mode of interaction. More than 75% of communication is nonverbal. People internalize silent deeds as well as a vast array of unspoken feelings. Psychiatrist Thomas Lewis and his colleagues dubbed this capacity for sharing deeper emotional states "limbic resonance." If parents, friends or mentors reverberate with love, strength, and safety, either verbally or nonverbally, it can engender a sense of connectedness, power, and security. Conversely, if an air of powerlessness, emotional distance, or anxiety is radiated, it is likely to create feelings of helplessness, alienation, and fear.

Whenever two or more people come together, an emotional force field is created. If the emotions between them are ones of empowerment, intimacy, or reassurance, that field becomes a hopeful refuge. The field metaphor, common in Greek and Roman myths, Celtic lore, and Egyptian sacred writings, is especially apt in the case of hope. Among the Greeks, for example, the Elysian Fields were a blessed paradise where the bravest and most virtuous mortals would enjoy everlasting life and happiness. While the Elysian Fields were always envisioned as long off and far away, their true locus may be in the here and now, between parents and their children, among friends and lovers, in secular as well as spiritual unions. Central to all of these attachments are psychic connection, love, and hope.

In *The Art of Loving*, Erich Fromm argued that the experience of being apart is the most painful aspect of the human condition. According to him, the disquieting feeling of being totally alone has preyed on the human consciousness throughout history.

The question is the same for primitive humans living in caves, for the nomadic herder taking care of his flock, for the peasant in Egypt, the Phoenician trader, the Roman soldier, the medieval monk, the Japanese Samurai, the modern clerk and the factory hand.

Fromm believed that humans had been "torn from nature" by virtue of their "self-awareness," making them the only species of "life aware of itself." No longer enveloped in an "Eden of oneness," they suffer the vulnerability of conscious self-reflection.

> This separate, disunited existence could be an unbearable prison . . . humanity would become insane if they could not liberate themselves from this prison and reach out, uniting itself in some form with others and the world outside . . . Humankind can only go forward, finding a new harmony to replace the pre-human harmony that has been lost forever.

A sense of separateness can breed overwhelming anxiety, triggering maladaptive attempts to dissolve the pain of isolation. Fromm alluded to the use of drugs and sex as powerful but transitory antidotes. He noted that conformity and group membership provide more lasting possibilities but these are too mild to allay intense feelings of isolation. For Fromm, the only adequate solution is to master "the art of loving." Love "is the most powerful striving force in humankind . . . it keeps the human race together."

It is hard to minimize the power of love and its essential place in human life. Christians may recall that in Genesis, the first human need addressed by the creator is Adam's loneliness: "And the Lord God said, it is not good that man should be alone . . . . For this reason a man will leave his father and mother and be united to his wife, and they will become one flesh."

Fromm's brilliant insights suggest an even deeper need than love. While mastering the art of loving may go a long way toward offsetting feelings of separateness, it alone may not quell the "soul's unrest." A more pressing need derives from the *hope for restored harmony and intimacy*. Being torn from nature, humans seek an enduring physical, emotional, and spiritual connection. They hope for continuing social contact and comfort. They hope for a common purpose as well as shared values and ideals.

One could devote an entire library to the various expressions of attachment-focused hopes. Moreover, these various hopes often cross-fertilize. The experience of greater physical or emotional intimacy may bring an individual closer to god, nature, or some other higher power. Alternatively, a transcendent or mystical encounter can sometimes spark a more intimate bond with one's community, family, or friends (see Figure 9.1).

## Hope Providers

A good hope provider offers *availability, presence, and contact*. If given in the right way, at the right time, and in the right amount, such gifts can inspire trust and openness. Moreover, availability, presence, and contact can lead to the development of hopeful imprints, or lasting images of positive and supportive relationships.

THE HUMAN CONDITION   ATTACHMENT NEEDS   ATTACHMENT HOPES

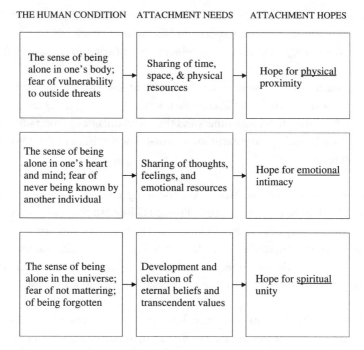

| The sense of being alone in one's body; fear of vulnerability to outside threats | Sharing of time, space, & physical resources | Hope for physical proximity |
| The sense of being alone in one's heart and mind; fear of never being known by another individual | Sharing of thoughts, feelings, and emotional resources | Hope for emotional intimacy |
| The sense of being alone in the universe; fear of not mattering; of being forgotten | Development and elevation of eternal beliefs and transcendent values | Hope for spiritual unity |

FIGURE 9.1.   The Basic Attachment-related Hopes

To be clear, it is not possible or even appropriate to be completely available, present, and involved with every member of your social network. As the saying goes, "You can't be all things to all people." Dispensing hope in an emotionally intelligent manner requires an awareness of your interpersonal skills and limits as well as of the actual hope needs of another.

### Availability and Trust

The "vail" in the word "availability" conveys that something of value has been placed within your reach. It is noteworthy that every major religion stresses the availability of spiritual blessings. In the New Testament, Matthew quoted Jesus, "Ask and it will be given you; seek, and you will find; knock and it will be open to you." In the Pali Canon, the Buddha listed the benefits of a contemplative life that are visible in the here and now, including "inner assurance," "tranquility," and "rapture."

In both sacred and scientific sources, there is agreement about the basic components of availability:

Access: A hope provider makes time for and shares space and remains flexible with others. In the Qur'an, Allah is situated "closer than the vein of thy neck." The Rig Veda assures all Hindus that Agni is "knower of all that lives" and "standeth in the presence of all beings." Surveys indicate that patients seek physicians and therapists who are interpersonally as well as technically skilled. A need for trust is repeatedly emphasized, along with "responsiveness," "availability for appointments," and "sufficient consultation time." (Research on effective mentoring in business and education highlights the importance of one-to-one time and the development of sufficient trust between mentor and protégé.)

*Reliability*: The hope provider remains dependably nearby. The Navajo legend of "The Dreamer" assures humanity that God can be heard in the crack of thunder, felt in a steady rain, and seen in the rising cornfields. Similarly, psychological studies indicate that regular family visits reduce the stress levels of patients following a myocardial infarction and speed the recovery of elderly patients undergoing major surgery.

*Anticipation*: The hope provider is able to anticipate the needs of others. In the Qur'an, it is written of Allah: "Thou needest not raise thy voice, for he knoweth the secret whisper, and what is yet more hidden." Humans are programmed to look for such signs of attunement. It has been found that infants constantly monitor the facial expressions of their caregivers. They show contentment when there is synchronicity between their actions and those of the care provider. Conversely, if the adult is disengaged or insensitive to emotional cues, the child becomes distressed. Moreover, if the caregiver is chronically depressed, the child is at risk for developing a more enduring sense of helplessness.

Thus, the first step in imparting hope is to be available. When you are accessible to, reliably consistent with, and sensitive to, the needs of another person, your behavior reinforces the notion that goodness is present and the universe can be trusted. When you are absent, unreliable, or indifferent, it stymies the development of hope. Along these lines, research indicates that adults with a history of unsatisfying relationships often acknowledge a sufficient number of social contacts but are stymied by a shortage of trustworthy allies.

### Presence and Openness

Presence literally means "to be in front of." If you wish to bring hope to others, they must be confronted by your presence. You must have the right kind of presence, open and full-bodied, not ghostlike or feigned. The components of a hopeful presence are listed here:

*Focus*: Hope providers weigh in with their full presence and are focused. Their attention to others is undivided. As a case in point, focus is undoubtedly one of the major factors accounting for the demonstrated effectiveness of quality time as a predictor of adaptive family functioning. What can you do on a daily basis to be more focused? First, practice self-care. If you are depleted, it will be far more difficult to give fully of yourself. Practice limit-setting with yourself. If you spread yourself too thin, there will be very little of you to go around. By avoiding overextensions, you can put a little more time into organization and preparation, which will also increase your ability to focus on the needs of another.

*Safeness*: The hope provider offers a safe haven and listens without judgment to the concerns of others. As trauma expert Judith Herman noted, the first and "central task" of the therapist is to provide a context in which clients feel safe enough to express their thoughts and feelings openly, without fear of condemnation. The same holds true for personal relationships, whether between parents and children, between lovers, or between friends. A Nigerian proverb sums it up this way, "One does not love if one does not accept."

*Authenticity*: Hope providers, to paraphrase the Moody Blues, must "mean what they say and say what they mean." They are genuine in their interactions with others. The humanistic psychologist Carl Rogers believed the best counselors were those who maintained a high level of congruity between their inner truth and outward demeanor. Likewise, the Buddhist eight-fold path encourages the use of "right speech" as a means of shedding all pretenses. Promoted as a means of assuring an honest self-transformation, this strategy can also be a powerful vehicle for sparking positive change in others.

Presenting an authentic presence requires a high degree of self-awareness born of courage and honesty. What can you handle? What makes you uncomfortable? Can you tolerate another's sadness or anger? Taking stock of these and other likely emotional challenges on a regular basis is a first step in knowing the bounds of your capacity for authentic relating.

### Contact: Leaving a Hopeful Imprint

How do you give a part of yourself to others? How do you help them to incorporate positive and sustaining images that can go to the core of their existence? We suggest that you can most effectively become a part of another's experience, a presence within them, through appropriate involvement, clarity, and repetition. When you make contact with others in this manner, you will more likely bestow a hopeful imprint.

*Involvement*: A hopeful imprint results from a potent presence that becomes deeply embedded in the thoughts, feelings, and actions of another, ultimately affecting his or her very sense of self (e.g., as a problem solver, as someone who matters to others, as a part of a caring and forgiving world). In the West, many individuals tend to live fractionated lives. Their impact on others is limited by a myriad of muted involvements or passing encounters. One unfortunate byproduct of such casual encounters is the transfer of diluted empowerment, a watered-down presence, or half-hearted compassion. In contrast, consider the total involvement of the Australian Aborigines who routinely devote an entire night to the "dreaming" ceremony. Similarly, Orthodox Jews engage in a complex series of spiritual rituals every weekend Sabbath, sanctifying cups of wine and eating special meals while prohibiting themselves from nearly 40 categories of weekly activities.

In *Making Contact*, Psychiatrist Leston Havens highlighted the role of verbal and nonverbal communication in "finding the other." He also stressed the importance of establishing the right "working distance." His suggestions can be applied to any form of interpersonal involvement. Do you make adequate eye contact? Is your body language inviting, receptive, and suggestive of care and interest? Can you switch gears and speak in the language of a child, a highly educated professional, or a blue-collar laborer? Can you discern whether the other requires more emotional space or, conversely, what Havens called greater "noninvasive closeness."

*Clarity*: Love comes in many forms. However, the most hope is transmitted by providing the right sentiment, in the right way, at the right time, in a way that can be absorbed by the other. This requires *clarity of perception* (What does the person need?), *clarity of intent* (What is appropriate to offer?), and *clarity of timing* (What is the person ready to "take in"?). Hindus who practice Bhakti Yoga recognize four ways of loving. Similarly, Rollo May identified care, lust, romantic love, and friendship. Confucius delineated nearly a dozen types of kin and community relationships. You build hope by responding to the real needs of others. You diminish hope by blurring emotional or physical boundaries, by offering the unwanted, the unneeded, or the undesired. You build hope by grasping where the other is coming from in terms of his or her life experiences, culture, gender, etc. You build hope by respecting what the other is willing and able to absorb at a particular moment in time. In the realm of counseling, it has long been recognized that therapists need to get their clients on the same page in terms of understanding an issue and should never run too far ahead of them. This lesson can be applied to any relationship. Strive to meet the other where he or she is at when you are trying to make contact.

*Repetition*: A hopeful imprint is more likely to take hold with your repeated involvement in another's life. The "internalization of hope" takes time and a depth of commitment akin to that reflected in religious ritual, as in the five times a day that Muslims kneel and pray or the hours that Buddhists and Hindus devote to meditation. A classic Russian Orthodox tale celebrates the redemption of a man who is saved after uttering the name of Jesus 12,000 times. Certainly, the imprint you leave can occur with far fewer utterances of faith in another person, but it does call for your repeated commitment in order make a meaningful impression.

On a more secular level, the adherence to simple rituals (always offering a cup of coffee or tea, beginning and ending your time together with the usual "pleasantries", or making reservations at the same restaurant) can go a long way in making a more lasting impression on the heart and mind of another.

## Parents

Parents are positioned to be the first hope providers. As the initial source of attachment for most children, they are also in a unique position to foster a sense of mastery and provide feelings of security. Adequate fathering and mothering can result in more hopeful offspring. In contrast, inadequate parenting has been associated with learned helplessness in children, as well as social withdrawal and poor stress tolerance.

Children require an available caregiver who is emotionally present and able to forge a positive connection with them. As a parent or caregiver you must do an honest self-assessment. Are you a hopeful person? Do you feel a sense of connection with others? How strong are your feelings of competence and effectiveness? Do you feel safe in the world? Are you willing to shore up those areas in which you are weak? Remember that your outlook on life will be transmitted to your child's emotional core.

If you can bolster your attachment, mastery, and survival skills, you will not only increase your personal resilience but also become a more effective hope provider. As we noted at the start of this chapter, hope building is a reciprocal process. As your hope levels rise, so will your child's. In imparting hope to your son or daughter, you will inevitably experience in yourself a renewed sense of empowerment, connection, and peace of mind. The basic principles we discuss in this section are applicable not only to parents but also to relatives, teachers, coaches, and others who are entrusted with the care of children.

### Parental Availability

Children need ready *access* to their caregivers. Lacking positive emotional input, infants and toddlers may slide into despair. Many never recover. Those who are otherwise well-fed and clothed may still suffer terribly in the absence of love. As we will see in Chapter 14, the work of researchers such as René Spitz, Anna Freud, and John Bowlby has told us much about the effect upon infants and children of prolonged separation from their parents: In these youngsters, the loss of hope was the greatest casualty, and they appeared to lose their zest for life, their abandoned cries giving way to empty gazes and silent resignation. In foundling homes that cared for large numbers of separated children, investigators also noted unusually high rates of infection and unexplained deaths.

Children also need consistent *reliability*. Erik Erikson theorized that infant trust was the single greatest factor in the development of hope. Moreover, like Freud, he believed that experiences related to feeding were central in the first year of life. In particular, Erikson wondered if there was a particular pattern of feeding that would result in higher levels of adult trust. For example, did it matter if parents fed their children on demand or on a regular schedule? What would you predict? Interestingly, Erikson observed that both approaches worked: parents who consistently fed their offspring either on demand or on a definite schedule seemed to raise trusting children "who knew what to expect from life."

The best caretakers *anticipate* the needs of children. They are aware of the child's communication style and emotional rhythm. (The psychoanalyst Alfred Adler was once described as virtually "psychic" in his ability to read children.) Research on attachment suggests that pleasant but out-of-synch mothers may run the risk of rearing children who are clingy and anxious. However, there is also ample research indicating important temperamental differences in the ability of children to attach themselves to parents. Some children are less socially responsive than others. Moreover, a parent and child may possess incompatible personality styles. Anticipating a child's needs under these circumstances can thus prove to be a particular challenge.

If you are finding it difficult to establish or maintain a positive relationship with your offspring, consider doing a simple "parent–child inventory" of emotional needs. Get out a piece of paper and draw two lines, forming a cross. In the top left quadrant, list your four or five most striking characteristic (e.g., achiever, persistent, loyal). In the top right quadrant, list your child's four or five most obvious characteristics. In the bottom left quadrant, under *your* traits, list four to five possible ways that others might misjudge your intentions as a result of your characteristics. For example, might someone mistakenly view you as overly competitive because you like to achieve, or see you as hard-headed instead of persistent? Do the same exercise on the bottom right quadrant, using your child's traits. Now reflect on how to address these potential sources of miscommunication involving you and your child. Consider ways of fine-tuning your interactions to better meet the needs of both of you.

## Parental Presence

Children can sense when you are emotionally adrift. For example, one of us (H. B.) found that fathers who are around the house a great deal but are constantly preoccupied or otherwise unpredictable in their emotional availability put their children at risk for feelings of inadequacy and poor social adjustment. Quality time is about being emotionally present and *focused*, and yet of the thousands of scientific publications on attachment, less than 5% mention this factor. Nevertheless, in those studies that do take a more holistic approach to family functioning, quality time often emerges as a key variable. Children with emotionally withdrawn parents typically fair no better than those whose parents spend little time with them.

Children require a *safe* presence. Cold, rejecting, or intrusive parents tend to raise avoidant children. Fearful of rejection or criticism, they cannot risk being open with their caregivers. The threat of physical or sexual abuse may also limit openness. (In contrast, the risk of later abuse is lessened if there is a caring and nurturing bond established in infancy. This is true for both biological and stepparents.)

Children have limited defense mechanisms. They are vulnerable to adult manipulations and find it hard to escape the clutches of twisted communications or so-called double binds. When parents say one thing but express another, they are leaving children few other options but to shut down and disengage or to act out in desperation. Fostering openness requires a sincere, *authentic* presence.

### Parental Contact

Parents must show the right kind of care. In the psychological literature, parents who are firm but flexible with their children are often described as "authoritative," whereas those who are harsh, punitive, and controlling are considered to be "authoritarian." Authoritative parenting has been associated with better social adjustment and higher levels of academic achievement in children.

The *involved* parent is attuned to a child's emotions. Along these lines, many researchers distinguish between *emotion-coaching* and *emotion-dismissing* parenting styles. Aware of their children's feelings and valuing their expression of hopes, dreams, fears, and protests, parents with an emotion-coaching style help their children understand and regulate their experiences. In contrast, emotion-dismissing parents seem either unaware of their child's feelings or disapprove of emotional displays, viewing them as something to be limited or controlled.

A hopeful inner life, or the *clarity* of a *hopeful imprint*, is also enhanced in children by *repeated* encounters with positive rituals. Ancient wisdom, as well as psychological science, intimate that children benefit greatly from revisiting the traditions that their parents honor. In addition to regular religious observances, these may include birthday parties, family outings, or visits with grandparents. These celebrations of faith transfer a sense of hopefulness to the next generation while also strengthening the prevailing hopes of their elders. (In Chapter 14 we provide many more suggestions for instilling hope in children.)

## Lovers and Friends

> There are places I'll remember all my life . . . some have gone and some
> remain. All these places have their moments, with lovers and friends I still can
> recall. Some are dead and some are living, in my life I've loved them all.
> —John Lennon and Paul McCartney

Who provides *you* with hope? For a moment, set aside any thoughts that you might have about potential spiritual connections. Who are your earthly hope providers? Do you derive hope from a mentor or teacher? Is your hope based on your interactions with peers or members of your family, such as your spouse, parents, siblings, or children? For many individuals, relationships with lovers and friends engender a tremendous amount of hope.

When it comes to love, we are not referring to those unhealthy relationships fueled by an unbridled ego, excessive dependency, or some other addictive weakness. In contrast to these desperate pairings, the deeper expressions of human love offer a true and lasting hope. Such a distinction appears in the scriptures, as in Paul's letter to the Corinthians, probably the most popular reading at Christian weddings: "Love is patient, love is kind . . . It always protects, always trusts, always hopes . . . ." And it appears in great art and literature. Consider for example, *East of Eden* (1952), John Steinbeck's favorite creation, the masterpiece he called his one "true book." A twentieth-century classic, it is a novel filled with sadness and heartache, repeated acts of pathological cruelty, unfulfilled longings, and unnecessary losses. Yet it is also a saga of transcendent hope.

Of the many hope lessons in *East of Eden*, four stand out. *The first lesson is that an especially gifted hope provider can stimulate all three of the hope motives: attachment, mastery, and survival.* Samuel, the patriarch of the Hamilton family, is the most powerful of the hope providers. He is a jack of all trades and a first-class inventor. He is supremely kind and intuitive, one of the very few characters in the novel who finds his way into the center of another's soul. His deep attunement to his friend Adam's suffering at the hands of Cathy offers the best antidote for a soul sickened by false hope, pining for the attentions of a woman incapable of love. After Samuel's death, Adam reflects on the life of his good friend, noting, "Somehow he made a man better than he was."

The second lesson tells us that *those who offer false hope perpetrate a great evil.* Cathy (a.k.a. Kate) is the clearest embodiment of counterfeit hope. Her mastery consists of egotistical pursuits. She never shares her power, and her achievements are always rooted in deception, manipulation, and lies. Her attachments are superficial. She is unable to see, hear, or feel love. She killed her parents, and she abandons her children. Even as a child, she used her body to lure young men into her evil snare. She allows Adam to fall in love with her but keeps him at a distance while sleeping with his brother. Her survival skills are also quite limited. She cannot control her rage. She trusts no one and never feels safe. She denies Adam the certainty of a legacy and mockingly insinuates that his brother may actually be the biological father of Adam's children. As her outer beauty fades, her inner chaos takes over. Her growing helplessness is symbolized by the arthritic condition of her hands. She is literally and figuratively "losing her grip." Shortly before she kills herself, she acknowledges her utter hopelessness.

*The third lesson is that repeated abuse can push an individual beyond fear and rage into a state of complete indifference about his or her fate.* As a child, Adam Trask tries his best to earn the love of his family. Toward his brother Charles, he is loyal, trusting, and kind. But Charles is cruel and takes every opportunity to torture Adam emotionally and physically. Cyrus, his father, is less vicious but his actions prove equally destructive. Insensitive to his son's needs, he forces him into the army, selfishly trading Adam's life for his own twisted agenda of gain and glory and effectively ending Adam's chance for a hopeful life.

Having lost his will to hope, Adam goes through the motions of being a soldier. Having forgotten his own dreams and desires, he keeps reenlisting, preferring extra duty to a fated and barren future. When he is finally cut loose from the army, Adam wanders about, lost and confused. He is arrested for vagrancy and assigned to a road gang where he learns firsthand what captivity and abuse can do to the soul.

> He learned how men can consider other men as beasts . . . a clean face, an open face, an eye raised to meet an eye . . . these drew attention and attention drawn brought punishment . . . the savage whippings for the least stir of will, for the smallest shred of dignity or resistance . . . Adam, like anyone in the world, feared what whipping would do to his body and his spirit . . . He drew a curtain around himself . . . He removed expression from his face, light from his eyes, and silenced his speech . . . It was much more horrible afterward than when it was happening . . . Adam reduced his personality to minus. He caused no stir, put out no vibration, became as invisible as it is possible to be.

*The fourth lesson is that an abiding sense of hope comes from believing in a future that is filled with possibility.* Some of the most hopeful words in the novel are uttered by Lee, Adam's Chinese servant. Lee adores the biblical account of Cain and Abel, especially the 16 magical lines that revolve around the Hebrew concept of "timshel." Translated as "thou shall" or "thou mayest," timshel suggests that humanity's fate is far from sealed. The intimation of possibility, openness, and renewal fills Lee with hope.

> This is a ladder to climb to the stars . . . You can never lose that. It cuts the feet from under weakness and cowardliness and laziness . . . I have a new love for that glittering instrument, the human soul. It is a lovely and unique thing in the universe. It is always attacked and never destroyed—because "thou mayest."

In the final pages of the book, Lee declares his faith in the future even more strongly:

> When Samuel Hamilton died the world went out like a candle . . . I re-lighted it to see his lovely creations, and I saw his children tossed and torn and destroyed as though some vengefulness was at work . . . I thought the good are destroyed while the evil survive and prosper . . . I thought that once an angry and disgusted God poured molten fire from the crucible to destroy or purify his little handiwork of mud . . . [But] Maybe you'll come to know that every man in every generation is re-fired . . . All impurities burned out and ready for a glorious flux, and for that more fire . . . Can you ever think that whatever made us—would stop trying?

Film is another art form in which the *love–hope connection* is prominent. In fact, the greatest love stories, the real masterpieces, such as *Casablanca* or *West Side Story* are filled with heartache and loss as they dramatize the most profound hopes that human beings can express within the context of an intimate relationship, culminating in a desire for the life of another to be transformed for the better.

Indeed, few other aspects of the human condition evoke as much passion as love and hope. They are blended in the dramas of Shakespeare, the poetry of Dante, the music of Mozart, and the lyrics of Lennon and McCartney. This is why the hope of a healing love excited Plato, Confucius, and Carl Jung. This is why the hope for love moved even the atheistic Bertrand Russell to place it first in his pantheon of dreams.

In truth, our investment in love is based on a myriad of great and small hopes. Psychologist Nathaniel Branden listed several types of romantic needs, which we prefer to conceptualize as expressions of converging hopes: hope to be nurtured and valued; hope for a companion with whom to share your joys and sorrows; hope to realize yourself sexually; hope to fully express your love; hope to be seen as you truly are; and hope to fulfill your true potential.

Considering all the hopes that go into a love relationship, it is no wonder that human beings invest so much time and energy "trying to get it right." The momentum of *hope* that is generated by giving and getting in romantic love is enormously powerful. The nineteenth-century French writer Stendhal wrote, "Love is the only passion which pays itself in a coin which it mints itself."

## Loving Availability

Love is about closeness (*access*). In *Too Good to Leave; Too Bad to Stay*, Mira Kirschenbaum highlighted the willingness of partners to make themselves available for one another. She viewed openness to the other as a vital regenerative property in healthy relationships. In contrast, an intimacy killer is "off-the-table-itis." This occurs when one or both partners block the other's attempt to discuss issues of importance to their relationship.

Love is built on *trust* and *reliability*. Kirshenbaum noted the fundamental need for trust in love relationships. You must be able to feel that promises and agreements will be kept and that commitments will be honored. She put it bluntly, "When you're married to a liar, your marriage is a lie."

Love is wise; it *anticipates* another's thoughts and feelings. Couples who are deeply in love refer to "being on the same wavelength." They easily read each other and have a strong sense of being in synch. In one study, Psychologist Dan McAams asked couples to write imaginative stories. The couples who were greatly in love more often used words such as "harmony" and "true understanding." Another psychologist, John Gottman, has spent his career studying the foundations of successful marriages, including both verbal and nonverbal communication patterns. From his perspective, partners should familiarize themselves with each others' facial expressions, voice inflections, and body language, as well as pay close attention to spoken words.

### Loving Presence

Love is fully present and *focused*. Relationship expert Harville Hendrix encouraged his clients to move toward a "conscious marriage," one in which partners act purposefully toward each other rather than react out of habit or on the basis of old attachment wounds. Hendrix also implored his clients to look below the surface, to seek the truth of their partner's inner life.

Love is *safe*. Saint Paul's love is patient. Shakespeare's love "is not love which alters when it alteration finds." Kirshenbaum, as well as the myth scholar Joseph Campbell, emphasized that your primary relationship should feel like a "home within a home."

Love is honest; it is *authentic*. According to Hendrix, a "conscious marriage" includes a couple's commitment to close all "relationship exits." These unstated forms of "invisible divorce" may range from rather subtle emotional manipulations to not-so-hidden affairs. "Both feet" must be in a love relationship to assure a hopeful connection based on emotional as well as physical presence.

### Loving Contact

Love is about "chemistry." Your unconscious can operate much like a gyroscope, pointing you in the direction of a particular person. That attraction has long roots. Hendrix, for example, wrote a great deal about the "imago" or love template that is derived from your early attachment experiences. Part of the healing power of love comes from confronting old attachment wounds.

Love is about *involvement*. According to Gottman, "People form much more positive emotional connections when they encourage one another's dreams and aspirations." He encouraged lovers to become "dream detectors," adding that the source of conflict within a relationship is often the failure to acknowledge the individualized hopes and dreams of each partner.

Love is about the *clarity* and *repetition* of shared meaning between people. Gottman believed that "rituals of emotional connection" are the secret to increasing this sense of shared meaning. These rituals can be as simple as sharing a weekend breakfast buffet, sitting down to watch a favorite television show, going to the movies on a regular basis, or arranging for a weekly card game. They might also involve sharing in religious, cultural, or sporting activities. The magic and meaning of rituals is complex, but from a hope perspective, a key factor is experiencing something together that is both positive and predictable.

## Friendships

Friends are a prime source of hope. They can nourish our lofty dreams while providing a secure base of earthly support. They also provide comfort and assurance in times of stress. Scientists have generated some interesting statistics about friendships, including mounds of demographic data on factors such as the respective age, gender, and income of friendship pairs. But what is the essence of a good friendship? What should you seek in a good friend? How can you be a true friend? There is little research on the inner workings of friendships, but fortunately, classic literature provides innumerable nuggets of wisdom on these questions.

A true friend, like a good parent or lover, will inspire trust, foster openness, and contribute to the formation of a hopeful inner life. Cicero observed that friendship "holds out good hope and does not permit souls to either fade or fall from view." Francis Bacon suggested that friends "double joy and cut grief in half" and "maketh daylight in the understanding out of darkness." Ralph Waldo Emerson declared that "In the company of friends there is no winter and no night." Kahlil Gibran unearthed the magic of friendship in shared rituals, noting how "In the dew of little things the heart finds it morning and is refreshed."

## Friendly Availability

Friends are *accessible* to one another. In *The Little Prince* by de Saint-Exupéry, the fox explained that a friend must "sit a little closer to me, every day." When asked who is a friend, the preschooler is apt to say, "Someone who will play with you." However, among adult friends, availability is less about face-to-face contact (which remains important) than about perceived intimacy.

Friends are *reliable* and dependable. Saint-Exupéry's fox told the little prince that his visits should "always be at the same hour." When adults are asked to complete the sentence, "A friend is _____," their most common response is "someone I can trust." In an oft-cited *Psychology Today* survey, it was found that "keeping confidences" and "loyalty" were most frequently selected as the key ingredients of a lasting friendship. Centuries ago, Epicurus wrote, "It is not so much our friends' help that helps us as the confident knowledge that they will help us."

Friends *anticipate* needs. According to Gibran, "Your friend is your needs answered." Lasting friendships endure between people who are attuned to each other's degree of desire for closeness, change, and personal growth. Aristotle believed that true friendship grew out of respect for the virtues embodied by the other. Stated differently, friends find our center and honor us by validating our dreams and values.

## Friendly Presence

Friends are fully present and *focused*. Emerson's standards for friendship included a level of invested spontaneity. In his words, a meeting of friends "should never fall into something usual and settled; but should be alert and inventive." A friend provides a full-bodied embrace rather than a half-hearted handshake. According to a Nigerian proverb, "A friend must be held with both hands."

Friends offer a *safe* haven. How often is it said of a good friend, "I can be myself; I can let my hair down; I can drop all my pretensions." Preschoolers say that friends "don't hit you." Emerson felt that in the company of a friend, "I can think aloud." An Arabian proverb states that "a friend is one to whom one may pour out all the contents of one's heart." Francis Bacon likened the safety of friends to a family doctor who knows which medicine is best suited to your particular constitution.

Friends are honest; they are *authentic* with each other. Feminist Letty Cotton Pogrebin found that "duplicity" was one of the few irreversible and fatal transgressions that could end a longstanding friendship. In a *Psychology Today* survey, "frankness" was ranked among the top five ingredients of true friendship. Cicero warned that "nothing at all artificial or simulated" may be tolerated among friends. Emerson declared, "Let me be alone to the end of the world rather than that my friend should overstep, by a word or deed, his real sympathy."

### Friendly Contact

Friends are *involved* but respect *clear* boundaries. Cicero wrote, "Great fallings-out arise when something is demanded from friends which is not honorable." He advised "would-be friends" to hold the reins loosely on the heart of another and not to burden them with shameful demands, lest they wish to incur "eternal hatred." According to him, the best friendships demonstrate a total absence of any power differential. Friends, he noted, are able to "give counsel as well as take it."

Friends have regular contact with each other (*repetition*). National surveys have revealed that more than half of all Americans call their best friend at least once a week. Sociologist Claude Fischer found that *frequency* of intimate exchanges, rather than type of communication, was the key to sustaining close friendships. Again, the key is intimacy, which *Psychology Today* readers rated as the most important component of a good friendship.

Preschoolers will tell you that a friend is "someone who shares toys." An increasingly broader range of similar interests and activities cements the lives of older children and adolescents. Among adults, the focus shifts to shared values and meanings. Adult friendships are sustained and enriched by a common history as well as by mutual joys and sorrows.

## Spiritual Bonds

The deepest romantic and platonic relationships can rise to the level of a true "spiritual connection." Two lovers may refer to each other as "soulmates" while a best friend might be called a "kindred spirit." But beyond love relationships and friendships lies the realization of hope through a more encompassing spiritual union. We are able to differentiate between at least two types of spiritual experiences. One is the secular "brotherly love" that appeals to scientists and humanists while the other involves the experience of a divine presence or higher power. Although varying in content and meaning, the basic requirements for connecting with these sources of hope are quite similar.

### A Shared Humanity

A broad sense of humanity underlies all of the major faiths. We are all mortal. We all share certain fears and anxieties as well as hopes and dreams. An appeal to these overarching existential realities is plainly evident in the New Testament gospels as well as the teachings of Buddha, Gandhi, and Confucius.

According to Erich Fromm, a sense of shared humanity is the most fundamental of all the experiences of love. This oceanic state encompasses feelings of care and respect along with the wish to enhance another's life. Above all, brotherly love requires knowledge of, and identification with, another person. This is the basis for compassion and the impetus for a full recognition of one's shared humanity.

The experience of a shared humanity can be overwhelming and life altering. It may develop over time or emerge suddenly. The trigger for one person might be observing a newborn child in the arms of a parent, while for another it could be encountering an elderly couple lovingly holding hands. For a third, the inspiration may come from reading a letter written by a soldier who is longing for his wife and children. For a fourth, the catalyst may involve taking part in a solemn funeral ceremony.

A feeling of a shared humanity can also stem from exposure to a great piece of literature, a fine play, or a film masterpiece. In fact, psychologist Michael Wallach proposed that the greatness of any work of art can be measured in terms of the extent to which it evokes certain universal emotions. A good example is Van Gogh's famous painting of *Fishing Boats on the Beach*, completed in the summer of 1888 during one of the more positive periods in his tumultuous life. It consists of a simple but reassuring array of four colorful boats sitting on the margins of a beach, nearly touching the sea. If you look closely, there is a rope tied to each bow that extends all the way to the left edge of the painting. Rather than held in place by an anchor or a dock post, the boats are attached to an inland moor. Subconsciously, this imagery evokes a powerful sense of an "attached hope," on the part of sailors in other boats floating in the nearby surf and their loved ones left on shore. They may be separated for months, or even years, by miles of ocean, but they are nevertheless bound by love and unfailing devotion.

Thornton Wilder's *Our Town* is another great work that evokes a powerful response of love and hope. A play with "little action, hardly any scenery, and dialogue based on philosophical ideas," it is ostensibly about daily life in a small New Hampshire town, Grover's Corner, around the turn of the twentieth century. But a good deal of the play's setting is in a cemetery, where Emily, a young woman who has died in childbirth, communes with other dead souls. At one point, the dead warn Emily not to revisit her life in Grover's Corner. They caution her that it will be too painful to watch as she and her loved ones fritter away precious moments with petty concerns. But this is exactly what Wilder intended, to have both Emily and the audience simultaneously straddle the domains of the living and the dead. Only in this difficult space does humanity realize the need for a transcendent hope, one that can override the limits of human finitude through love of life and love of all that is mortal.

## Nature and Divine

Jane Goodall's powerful mystical experience in a cathedral and an African jungle exemplifies the hope that many people find while communing with a higher power or nature. Countless others have reported feeling the presence of God, or an "ineffable spirit," while standing on a mountaintop, exploring a darkened cave, lying in a hospital bed, or sitting quietly by the ocean.

Some scientists believe that these states of emotional merger result from a "developmental backslide." From their perspective, some adults may temporarily revert to a mode of undifferentiated bonding reminiscent of their "infant years": when overwhelmed by stress or desire, They shed their normal ego boundaries, regressing back to a time when they experienced themselves and their parents as a single entity. According to these experts, merger experiences may be nothing more than a brief and disorienting confrontation with one's "infantile self-objects."

Other scientists, however, believe that "mature states of merger" are possible. They emphasize that healthy emotional fusions can and should be distinguished from the more primitive states of early life, or the psychotic experiences of disturbed individuals.

Is there a way to integrate these seemingly disparate views? Perhaps the secret of a healthy spiritual merger lies in the generalization of hopeful imprints, those internalized ways of connecting with significant and powerful others. Specifically, humans have the capacity to store memories of hopeful interactions with parents and significant others that date back even to infancy and early childhood. As individuals mature emotionally and spiritually, their ways of relating continue to evolve and expand. In essence, they develop more complex "internal models" of connecting with others.

At some point in the individual's development, these multiplying hopeful imprints may reach a critical spiritual mass. One or more of them may come to resemble the archaic, relatively immature self-objects, not in content but in terms of emotional resonance. These archaic self-objects are largely unconscious, involving more permeable self–other boundaries, meaning they may be evoked rapidly, outside of conscious awareness. In other words, the more evolved individuals become in a spiritual sense, the more likely they will experience, triggered within them, a profound and familiar sense of belonging. Perhaps this is why many of the great religious leaders have espoused an attitude of childlike innocence and acceptance.

### Spiritual Bonding Guidelines

There are several keys to achieving a sense of common humanity or a feeling of intimacy with a larger spiritual force. While the content may differ, both experiences derive from virtually the same set of psychological processes that occur in any emotional merger. The following guidelines are based on our integrative approach to hopeful encounters, including research on individuals who have reported recurring mystical encounters.

*Trust*: Both the humanistic and divine forms of spiritual connection begin with a trusting attitude. If you have been fortunate to have a positive early attachment experience, then you probably have sufficient basic trust to jumpstart the spiritual bonding process. On the other hand, if your early caregivers were unreliable or otherwise inadequate, you might find yourself prone to an anxious or avoidant attachment style that can greatly interfere with spiritual bonding. If so, it is important to come to grips with the extent of your anger, bitterness, and mistrust. It is also crucial for you to seek out "corrective emotional experiences" by surrounding yourself with relatively healthy and caring adults.

*Humility*: Spiritually prepared individuals are self-accepting but also aware of their shortcomings. They take pleasure in their talents while, at the same time, appreciating the need for external support and guidance. In contrast, those who have illusions that they are unusually special or exceptional will struggle to gain a sense of common ground. Moreover, they will find it difficult to enter into the midst of a higher power. If you yourself harbor such illusions of superiority, you may be trying to deny your weaknesses and may even be projecting them onto others.

*Focus*: Pay attention to those around you. Do not let your prejudices or stereotypes get in the way of seeing the inner person when you interact with others. Eric Fromm wrote that brotherly love is dependent upon connecting from the *center* of one's being to the *center* of another's being. How often do we succeed in spanning this spiritual bridge? If you are seeking the presence of a higher power, you may require even more focus and energy. For example, you might find it helpful to adjust your time of meditation to coincide with your personal rhythms. One woman reported an "infusion of spiritual presence" into her life *after* she decided to get out of bed an hour earlier each morning to engage in prayer.

*Openness*: Make an effort to put yourself in the company of others who appear to be quite different from you and open yourself up to new experiences. Travel to a new location. Visit a neighborhood whose ethnic roots differ from yours. Sample a new cuisine. Read a *National Geographic* article or watch the *Discovery Channel*. Spend some quiet time within a place of worship, by a waterfall, a babbling brook, or a canopied forest with sunlight filtering down on you. Experiences of divinity are more often reported in the context of such sacred spaces.

*Involvement*: You are more likely to feel the stir of a common humanity if you get to know different people at a variety of different levels. An ancient proverb suggests that faith must involve the "head, heart and hands." You cannot simply will experiences of oneness. Try to open your heart and consider participating in some form of spiritual routine. Those who report experiences of a higher power tend to read scripture, engage in regular prayer, chant, or meditate in some systematic fashion. They are apt to participate in retreats and bible studies or to make pilgrimages to revered sites.

*Repetition*: Repeated images and sounds can aid in the alteration of consciousness. Sustained exposure to drumbeats, music, or dance tends to suppress those parts of the brain that divide the self from the external world and to stimulate regions that contribute to a feeling of oneness. Perhaps this is one of the reasons why Muslims pray several times a day or why Hindus utter the name of God thousands of times in one sitting.

*Ritual*: Consider cultivating a ritual that is comforting and consistent with your beliefs and lifestyle. It can be an individual or group activity as long as it is deeply engrossing and performed on a regular basis. It can range from an established religious practice to daily exercise or playing a musical instrument. According to some researchers, you may derive the most benefit by including a spiritual component. For example, if you select exercise or music as your ritual, try to coordinate it with an accompanying focus on the principles, beliefs, and values that define your journey of hope.

---

*Hope Provider Assessment*

*Directions*: Rate each of the following statements as they relate to *your typical thoughts, feelings, and behaviors*. Use the scoring system that is provided below to quantify your rating.

Never True = 0; Rarely True = 1; Often True = 2; Always True = 3.

1. I let friends and loved ones know where and when they can reach me (time, place, etc.). _____
2. I stay focused when people tell me their stories. _____
3. I make time for one-on-one conversations. _____
4. I'm honest with others and myself about my willingness to be available. _____
5. I am a good listener. _____
6. I like to remind friends and loved ones of experiences we have shared together. _____
7. I make an effort to understand the needs of others. _____

8. When spending time with someone, I take into consideration their fears and worries. ———

9. In dealing with others, I try not to overstep their boundaries. ———

10. My first impressions about a person usually prove to be right on the mark. ———

11. I make an effort to help people feel comfortable in my presence. ———

12. I keep things from my friends and loved ones that might upset, hurt, or embarrass them. ———

13. I feel bad when I can't follow through on a commitment. ———

14. I do not hide my feelings from others. ———

15. I like to share rituals with friends and loved ones. ———

16. I will stop in the middle of a project to make sure that I meet someone on time. ———

17. I'm direct with others and can tell them what is really on my mind. ———

18. I make a strong effort to preserve family and cultural traditions. ———

## Computing Your Scores

Fill in your scores for each of the questions and add across the rows to compute your levels of availability, presence, and contact.

Availability: 1___ 4___ 7___ 10___ 13___ 16___ Total = ___
Presence: 2___ 5___ 8___ 11___ 14___ 17___ Total = ___
Contact: 3___ 6___ 9___ 12___ 15___ 18___ Total = ___

## Interpreting Your Scores

Low: = 0–6
Medium: = 7–11
High: = 12–18

If you scored in the low or medium range on one or more of the scales, consider reviewing the corresponding sections of this chapter. You may also want to examine more closely your scores on the specific components of availability, presence, or contact (access = 1, 4; anticipation = 7, 10; reliability = 13, 16; focus = 2, 5; safety = 8, 11; authenticity = 14, 17; involvement = 3, 6; clarity = 9, 12; repetition 15, 18).

# Ten

## MASTERY AND INSPIRATION: YOUR LIFE IS CALLING

True hope is swift, and flies with swallows wings.

—Shakespeare, *Richard III*

This chapter can help you to become more hopeful in your quest for mastery. This chapter is *not* about get-rich-quick schemes, ill-advised power plays, or stock formulas for immediate gratification. Instead, we hope to provide a more transcendent and enduring set of principles for directing your life with greater clarity and purpose.

To develop a true sense of mastery, an individual must have a will for hope, a feeling of mediated power, and one or more guiding aspirations. In our discussion of these and other mastery-related skills, we take into consideration some of the advice provided by self-help gurus as well as by the scientific literature on motivation and goal attainment. In addition, you will find a wealth of mastery-related insights culled from varied philosophical perspectives and spiritual belief systems. Combining these various sources of wisdom, we offer a *four-fold strategy* for hope-based mastery. But beyond strategy, you must also have a sense of purpose that is continuously guided and nurtured. Thus, in the second part of this chapter, we explore various ways of drawing inspiration from within yourself and from outside sources. We also discuss how to provide inspiration to others, to learn from previous successes or failures, and to find inspiration through dreams.

## Profiles in Mastery

Our discussion begins with profiles of three individuals who each possessed a determined will for hope as well as aspirations that were privately nurtured, yet widespread in their impact on humanity. While hope sustained them, they served as pillars of inspiration for future generations.

### Miguel Cervantes: Time and Character

Spain's greatest author was born in 1547. Miguel Cervantes' family was very poor, and it is doubtful whether he ever received much in the way of a formal education. He left Spain at the age of 24 and enlisted as a private soldier to battle the Turks. During his first campaign, he was seriously wounded, rendering his left hand permanently disabled. Captured more than once, he spent a total of 5 years as a prisoner of war. Devising one escape plan after another, he kept failing in his bid for freedom, but much like Don Quixote, the protagonist of his famed novel, Cervantes refused to quit.

When he was finally released, Cervantes was penniless. Crippled and nearing the age of 40, he realized he had little chance of having a productive military career. He tried to write plays but achieved little success. In one account, he expressed gratitude that, at least, no "cucumbers or missiles" were hurled during the staging of his plays. He found employment as a tax collector, but cunning merchants took advantage of him. Approaching the age of 60, Cervantes once again found himself in serious legal and financial trouble. He had only one good hand and was facing another possible stint in jail.

It was during this dark period that he began to write *Don Quixote*. In 7 years it would become the best selling novel in Europe. In time, only the New Testament would be translated into more languages. One nineteenth-century historian dubbed it "the bible of humanity." Cervantes taught millions to appreciate starry-eyed knights who chase after windmills and dare to dream "the impossible dream." Moreover, his personal odyssey emphasized the power of human resiliency, working over the course of time to forge the character necessary for hopeful mastery. On many occasions, Cervantes could have given up but instead he persevered, transforming his painful experiences into a masterpiece of world literature.

### Roger Bannister: Mediated Power

In the 1950s every middle distance runner was obsessed with one goal: to run a mile in less than 4 minutes. Many experts considered it an unbreakable barrier. Doctors warned that maintaining the necessary pace to break this barrier could be fatal even to the best-conditioned athlete. Some scientists even suggested that such a feat would constitute a violation of certain "immutable laws of nature."

It finally happened on May 6, 1954. Roger Bannister of England achieved "the impossible" at the Iffley Road Track in Oxford. Truth be told, two human pacesetters helped Bannister to achieve his goal. In a well-executed three-man assault on the record, Chris Brasher took the initial lead, maintaining a fast but controlled pace. After 3 minutes he tired and Chris Chataway took over, leading the group until the final 200 yards. At that point Bannister sprinted past him toward the tape, finishing in the heretofore unbelievable time of 3:59:4.

After the race Bannister made several very poignant comments. He felt as if he had been "propelled by some unknown force." He had found "a new unity with nature" and a "new source of power and beauty, a source I never dreamed existed." He reflected that such an achievement can only occur when there is "the ability to take more out of yourself than you've got." But would he have broken the record without the help of his two pace-setting friends, and their added supply of "legs, hearts and lungs"? From our perspective, his experiences of "power," "unity," and "beauty" were "mediated" by the collaboration with his two running mates. In addition to taking "more out of" himself than he had, he undoubtedly drew upon the power inherent in his alliance with Brasher and Chataway.

### Mary McLeod Bethune: Values and Self-Mastery

Mary McLeod Bethune, the "voice of black hope," was born in 1875, on the northern edge of South Carolina in the small country town of Maysville. She was the last child born to Patsy and Samuel McLeod, but the first in her family to be born free, the other children as well as her parents having entered the world in servitude. Mary spent her early childhood in the cotton fields, developing a "keen work ethic" and experiencing first hand the importance of stamina and physical labor. Raised in a time and place where educational opportunities for African Americans were scarce, Mary desperately wanted to learn to read and write "like the white kids." Many years later she would recall her first "great wound" occurred when she was six or seven and tried to look over a book while visiting a neighboring family. A little girl took the book away, telling her, "You can't read that – put that down."

Mary would ascend from her humble beginnings to become "the foremost woman of her race in the United States." By the time she was in her early 60s, she was president of Bethune-Cookman College, head of the National Association of Colored Women, and director for Negro affairs of the National Youth Administration, advising President Franklin D. Roosevelt on race relations. In her famous "last will and testimony," Mary wrote,

> I leave you hope. The Negro's growth will be great in the years to come. Yesterday, our ancestors endured the degradation of slavery, yet they retained their dignity. Today, we direct our economic and political strength toward winning a more abundant and secure life.

Although Mary would receive some critical help along the way, her innate curiosity, determination, and self-discipline played a critical role in her meteoritic rise from her humble roots. Indeed, it was this inner fire that inspired the sociologist Charles Johnson to confess to Mary, "Most persons who attain greatness can boast at least family status . . . a tradition of education . . . or the advantage of economic position, or class, or a [favored] race . . . you had none of these." Mary would later state, "Nothing comes without faith and prayer. And nothing in my life has ever come without sweat too."

One of Mary's fondest memories involved a visit to France where she observed a single black rose growing among the cluster of whites and reds. As the African American intellectuals Henry Louis Gates and Cornel West would later write, "She herself was a black rose in the midst of American racism—a beacon of hope in the darkness."

## Hopeful Mastery

There are three levels of hopefulness that can arise from the mastery motive. Individuals can feel hopeful because they believe it is possible for them to obtain certain goals, because they feel capable of handling particular tasks and challenges, or because they believe in their own potential for change and growth. The fortunate individual who has acquired all three of these mastery mindsets approaches life with a can-get, can-do, and can-be attitude.

### The Will for Hope
Developmentally, the first sense of hopefulness that derives from the mastery system is forged from the overlay of *will and purpose* upon basic trust. These two virtues, will-power and a sense of purpose, are both essential for any kind of human mastery. This is why scholars from many different fields take an active interest in them. Biologists and psychologists study the parts of the brain responsible for planning and decision making. Existential philosophers suggest that human volition may represent the only true form of sacredness left in the world. Humanistic writers champion the pursuit of a life filled with purpose and meaning.

Willpower derives from your frontal lobes. Without this infrastructure a human being is "as good as dead." You might recall the film, *One Flew over the Cuckoo's Nest*. McMurty, played by Jack Nicholson, brought an emboldened brand of hope to a ward of psychiatric patients who were more impotent than crazy. Unable to subdue his fighting spirit, the hospital administrators finally drugged him and then surgically deactivated his frontal lobes by performing a lobotomy. His Native American friend, "Chief," snuck into the recovery room to find his friend had been reduced to a "vegetable."

The Chief was aware that patients on the ward continued to draw inspiration from McMurty's example. While their once free-spirited friend lay in an eternal stupor, they still traded fantasies, speculating on the daring acts of resistance that McMurty might have engineered. To preserve hope for the other patients, the Chief decided that he must end McMurty's life. He smothered him, then hurled a heavy sink through a window and ran to freedom as his ward companions cheered him on. With these acts of affirmation, the formerly mute and passive Chief found the strength to speak and the will to live as a free agent.

Since the middle of the eighteenth century, there has been much speculation regarding the primacy of certain human motives. Nietzsche argued that the *will for power* was paramount. Freud suggested that humans were guided primarily by a *will for pleasure*. After enduring the Nazi death camps, psychiatrist Viktor Frankl deduced that the *will for meaning* is the primary motive of human existence. From our perspective, the central motive is, in fact, the *will for hope*.

The will for hope incorporates a number of ideas put forth by existential and humanistic psychologists. It encompasses Abraham Maslow's idea of "being motivation" and Erik Erikson's notions of "I am what I will" and "I am what I can imagine to be." It covers the "growth-centered attitude" emphasized by Carl Rogers and Anthony Sutich as well as Robert White's notion of "competence" and Eric Klinger's outline of a meaningful life in terms of "receptive engagement with the world." The will for hope also borrows from Gabriel Marcel's philosophy of hope-based "readiness," "openness," and "availability."

Having the will for hope means that you believe people and circumstances can change. It means that you believe there are hidden resources waiting to be found within you, the world, and the future. It also means that your circle of influence is enlarged and that you are empowered to make a lasting difference in this world. In Emerson's words, "we are taught by great actions that the universe is the property of every individual in it."

### Mediated Power

A sense of "hopeful effectiveness" is the next mastery virtue to unfold developmentally. We prefer to call it "mediated power" because of the important role that caregivers, supportive others, and cultural institutions play in facilitating and maintaining mastery strivings in children. The roots of mediated power lie in the early fusions of a child's self with more powerful parents or other caregivers. Individuals with mediated power feel that they have the resources necessary to meet the demands of life. To paraphrase the words of Saint Paul, "they can do all things through their experiences with other people who have helped to strengthen them." In contrast, hopeless individuals feel constantly stressed and overwhelmed, believing that external demands or internal needs exceed their available resources.

## *Hopeful Aspirations*

The things that people hope for can be distinguished from those things that they wish for, compete for, or lust for. Philosophers of hope such as Gabriel Marcel, William Lynch, and Joseph Godfrey were plainly aware of the role of values in hope strivings. In surveying young adults, psychologist James Averill and his colleagues found that "hopes" were reserved for important life goals, while "wishes" were aimed at more trivial, selfish objects and outcomes.

When addressing the goal expectations that fuel a hopeful mindset, it may be more fitting to speak of "aspirations" rather than "needs" for achievement, power, or control. Achievement-oriented individuals strive for productivity and accomplishments, while those who are power- and control-minded may seek domination and ownership. Contrast these aims with Lynch's descriptions of hope in terms of "collaborative mutuality" and "affirmation with acceptance," or Immanuel Kant's allusions to the pursuit of the "highest good." The word "aspiration" carries three meanings that link it with hope. In one sense it refers to cherished dreams, in another, it implies the pursuit of high ideals, and in a third rendering, it may refer to the act of inhaling or drawing in air. Like spirituality, this last definition suggests that an individual has been infused with a breath of something vital and powerful.

## *Hope Goals*

Many people have dreams of power, money, and influence, but some people are particularly keen to pursue those ends at all costs, usually at the expense of others. In the nineteenth century, get-rich-quick schemes were often limited to shady real estate deals, ill-conceived ventures in fur trading, or gold-rush manias. Since then, there has been the advent of pyramid marketing schemes, unethical insider trading practices, and endless infomercials touting "smart pills," "carb busters," and "ab blasters." Some of the self-help literature also promulgates this game of "smoke and mirror mastery." One author promises to "completely transform your life in five minutes" while another proclaims that in less than a week you can achieve personal, financial, health, and family success. In *The 48 Laws of Power*, Robert Greene noted how certain individuals prey on the human "need to believe in something" and achieve "a cult-like following" by using words that are "vague but full of promise."

For every guru preaching a simplistic formula for success, there is a countervailing message that warns of the bodily, emotional, and spiritual costs that may be associated with a narrow-minded pursuit of mastery. In fact, some psychologists have found that very early success among politicians, scientists, and world leaders tends to be associated with a shorter life span. They speculated that "the strains, challenges and obligations accompanying outstanding achievements may set in motion, or accelerate physical and perhaps mental declines."

There is a middle ground. Like Aristotle's "golden mean," hopeful aspirations derive from a personal balance of power and from a sense that achieving a true and lasting mastery requires time and perseverance. Truly hopeful individuals are not passive or resigned; their actions are neither forced nor strained. Quite the contrary, hopeful mastery imparts a flow state that may be compared to the peaceful mastery cultivated by followers of feng shui or of the principle-centered philosophy of author Stephen Covey.

Erikson referred to the dawn of hope as a unique state, in between the two extremes of complete trust and total mistrust. Further support for a centered approach to mastery comes from research on "fantasy realization theory." This research indicated that individuals who adopt either a totally positive or a totally negative attitude are very likely to abandon their hopes of achieving their goals. In contrast, those who focus on the positive consequences of obtaining their goals but who remain aware of the negative consequences of failure are more likely to achieve their life plans.

## Mastery Strategies

*The keys to successful mastery are four-fold.* They consist of *self-mastery, values, support, and time.* These are the same factors discussed by experts in human motivation as well as by various spiritual leaders and personal growth gurus, such as Napoleon Hill and Stephen Covey.

### Self-Mastery

If beauty lies in the eyes of the beholder, then true success must reside in the heart of the doer. How do *you* define success? Do you seek power and influence? Is love and connectedness your primary objective? Do you long for greater tranquility and peace of mind? Are you hoping to realize two or even three of these aspirations?

Perhaps you have heard "the riddle of the piano lessons." One child shows musical talent and her parents decide she must give up everything to cultivate this gift. The child becomes a successful concert pianist but resents her parents and regrets the loss of her childhood. Another child shows musical talent but his parents decide that he should have a normal and balanced childhood. He grows up resenting his parents, wondering how successful he might have been if they had more actively structured his life around music.

Knowing what path to choose is difficult. We live in an age that creates needs and desires, often blurring the line between necessary aspirations and harmful indulgences. Seeking to instill fear rather than hope, advertisers are constantly questioning our capacities for attachment, mastery, or survival. They suggest that perhaps we are not lovable enough, that our teeth could be whiter, that our bodies should be leaner, that we must substantially increase our bank accounts or life insurance policies.

Some self-help books are really no help at all. Promising gains without investments and ignoring basic laws of human development, they should be shelved under "fiction." If any one of these books had the answer, there would be no need for the hundreds of others published every year. True success begins with *self-mastery*. This is the most difficult form of mastery, but achieving it is the necessary first step toward building the foundation that underlies the other three major building blocks: values, support, and time. You should think of self-mastery in terms of creating a centered presence of *self-awareness* and *self-discipline*.

In the West, a great premium is placed on developing self-awareness, particularly in the domain of feelings. For several decades, mental health professionals and self-help gurus have emphasized the importance of "getting in touch with your feelings." However, there is now an increasing realization that self-regulation and emotional intelligence may be even more important than the mere ability to give vent to your feelings. In addition, there is a growing awareness of the need to be more mindful of negative, distracting, or otherwise self-defeating thoughts.

Unfortunately, another cornerstone of the insight puzzle, *awareness of actions*, has received relatively little attention in the West. But in the great earth-centered religions such as those of the Australian Aborigines, the Ifa, and various Native American tribes, individuals are taught to be perpetually cognizant of the potential impact of their actions upon the family, tribe, land, and spiritual world. And yet such self-awareness without self-discipline may lead to complete inaction.

Conversely, Eastern societies place a great premium on *self-discipline*. Buddhists are encouraged to follow "the eight-fold path." Hindus readily assume the "karmic con-sequences" of immoral actions, and Confucians honor the principles of "Jen," the rules of appropriate social conduct. Throughout the East, the practice of martial arts serves as a prototypical example of intense self-discipline in the pursuit of mastery. Nevertheless, self-discipline without self-awareness can lead to a life of superficial and meaningless ritual.

In short, to achieve full self-mastery, you should strive to develop self-awareness *merged* with self-discipline. The following suggestions, drawn from various traditions, may help you to cultivate this balance:

*Disciplined thinking*: Buddhist forms of meditation offer an excellent way of
focusing an easily distracted mind that tends to obsess without end. Buddha
observed, "As the craftsman whittles and makes straight his arrows, so the
master directs his straying thoughts."

*Disciplined feeling*: Confucianism and Taoism, though considered the two
opposite poles of Chinese philosophy, both provide a broad perspective for
dealing with emotions that are harmful to self or others. By focusing on
appropriate boundaries, Confucianism teaches the art of showing the right
emotion at the right time to the right person. Taoism encourages a calm and
less desperate reaction to the whims of the world and may be particularly
helpful to those plagued by intense worry, impatience, or hostile feelings.

*Disciplined action*: Hinduism is an excellent model for disciplined action because it highlights the vital role of a guiding belief system. While Hindus believe in karma, they equate destiny to a seed that cannot grow without the "soil of exertion" and the practice of "holy living." The words "discipline" and "disciple" both suggest a moral or philosophical aim as well as a practical agenda. You must preach what you practice and vice versa. This is true whether your commitment is to a religious faith, a career, or a particular program of exercise.

*Awareness of thoughts*: The Roman stoic philosophers argued that we are not troubled by events but by our perception of them. "The mind is its own place," wrote John Milton in *Paradise Lost*, "and can make a hell out of heaven or a heaven out of hell." Cognitive therapy offers one way out of that hell. It is about changing the destructive beliefs that can destroy your mind, body, and soul. It is based on the idea that negative thought patterns can be analyzed, challenged, and exchanged for healthier alternatives.

*Awareness of feelings*: In emphasizing the human need for unconditional positive regard, Carl Rogers realized that many adults pass on their "fear of feelings" to their children. Raised in such an atmosphere, individuals may find themselves in a no-win situation, whereby their emotional authenticity is pitted against their self-worth and social acceptance. If you have a problem expressing your emotions, draw on Rogers's simple but powerful formula for personal growth and seek out nonjudgmental and supportive individuals who are comfortable with their own feelings.

*Awareness of actions*: Reflect on the possible implications of your actions as well as on your full intentions. If necessary, seek feedback from a trusted friend or a supportive group. Many people with the right intentions fail to succeed because they fail to anticipate the results of their actions. Native Americans, as well as the Ifa and Australian Aborigines, seek harmony with nature because they realize the interconnectedness of all living things. Herman Melville wrote "a thousand fibers connect us with others . . . our actions run as causes and come back to us as effects." What goes around comes around, in other words. In addition, you should also cultivate a greater awareness of the various influences on your behavior: the limitations imposed on you by the time and place of your birth (cosmic destiny), your genetic makeup (genetic destiny), your ethnic and religious background (cultural destiny), and the reality of random accidents and coincidences (circumstantial destiny). As the humanist Rollo May noted, each individual's behavior is simultaneously "free" and yet "constrained."

By paying attention to your thoughts, feelings, and actions in a disciplined fashion, you can gain a full sense of yourself in the world. Confident thoughts are a true source of power, while self-defeating thoughts will undermine your potential for mastery. Feelings and actions can serve as windows into your life calling or higher purpose. (This idea is further examined later in this chapter, under "Hidden Dreams.") And while various factors may define the outer limits of what you can accomplish, your range of available options is, in fact, still quite extraordinary.

### Values and Principles

The most enduring self-help books have dealt with values. In fact, the greatest selling "self-help" books of all time are the sacred texts: the Bible, the Qur'an, the Torah, and the Pali Canon. And in the so-called secular self-help category, the two biggest blockbusters have been Napoleon Hill's *Think and Grow Rich* and Norman Vincent Peale's *The Power of Positive Thinking*, with both authors placing mastery within a larger ethical and religious framework. Hill's ten rules for success included an adherence to "the golden rule" and "sublimating one's energy to a major purpose." Peale emphasized "prayer power" and "moral strength."

Returning to the classics of the ancient world, *The Art of War* by Sun Tzu is probably the quintessential values-oriented mastery text. Tzu listed the various moral factors that a wise general should contemplate while preparing for battle, including the following "spiritual considerations": Is my side "imbued with moral law?" Do I "hold the advantages derived from heaven and earth?" Is my army "animated by the heavenly spirits?"

Attending to values is a primary factor for the success of Stephen Covey's book, *The Seven Habits of Highly Effective People*. Covey correctly identified resiliency as one of the key elements underlying a valued-centered approach to mastery. To be successful in any endeavor you must persevere, but as Covey notes, a values-based perspective can serve as a buffer against the inevitable obstacles and disappointments that will come your way.

Values can advance your mastery pursuits in two other important ways: they assure self-consistency and increase the amount of support that you are likely to receive. Be clear about your values, putting them at the center of your life. This will make it less likely that you will end up disoriented or disillusioned in your efforts. If others sense your commitment to a calling, they are more likely to offer their support.

In the mountains of Stowe, Vermont, *The Weekend of Hope* was started in 2001 by a few dedicated individuals as a simple weekend gathering for women affected by breast cancer. It has grown to become the largest 3-day event of its kind for cancer survivors and their families. More than 1,000 participants now gather each year from across the United States and Canada. The amount of support garnered for this weekend is truly inspiring. Cancer survivors and their families receive free housing in hundreds of hotel rooms donated by Stowe lodging owners. Leading scientists and practitioners donate their time to make presentations on the latest cancer research and treatments. Amtrak runs a free a "Train of Hope" that departs from Washington, D.C. and stops in 15 cities, including Philadelphia and New York, providing transportation for cancer survivors without other means of getting to Stowe. Other sponsors include the Susan G. Komen Foundation and the pharmaceutical giant Astra Zeneca.

### Social Support

"Let your friends help you." So spoke Bonnie Strickland, an engaging and influential faculty member who later became president of the American Psychological Association, to a class of undergraduates who aspired to be professional psychologists. In the course of her talk, Strickland related her own story of growing up poor in the South. She had been settling toward a safe but relatively low-paying job when a mentor took her aside and told her she could be more and dream more. The point of her story: be assertive, work hard, but also recruit help from those with the means and resources to support you on your journey.

Many great achievements are the result of a team of individuals working toward a common goal. Roger Bannister needed "three pairs of legs" to break the 4-minute mile. Gertrude Ederle, the first woman to swim the English Channel, was spurred on by a "floating fan club" of supporters who rowed alongside and by crowds of onlookers who built huge bonfires on shore to guide her home. The pyramids required some 20,000 workers. One account of the Great Wall of China suggested that more than 800,000 laborers were necessary to erect just the initial portion. Many of the Renaissance artists relied on a team of apprentices to prepare frescoes, outline figures, and paint the trunk of the bodies in each scene; the master would paint only the eyes, hands, and other delicate features. Here are some more recent examples:

- Hollywood filmmakers may promote one or two leading actors in a given year. Yet these individuals are typically surrounded by a half dozen other supporting actors, a sizable cast of extras, and more than 50 behind-the-scenes professionals, including producers, directors, and technicians. Writers put words in their mouths. Makeup artists mask their physical imperfections while enhancing their plainer features.
- An author gets the credit for writing a book, but its development, production, and distribution is typically a collaborative effort, requiring the resources of agents, editors, and scores of staff at a publishing company. At the beginning of his bestseller, *Awaken the Giant Within*, Anthony Robbins acknowledged the help of more than 40 individuals. Some self-help gurus merely dictate, or draft outlines of, their books, while ghostwriters do the actual writing. This is particularly ironic when the "author" advocates a simplistic "Do it yourself" approach to mastery and success.

- The President of the United States is the commander in chief. Yet he has access to 21 high-profile Cabinet-level members, including secretaries of agriculture, transportation, and labor. Behind the scenes, several thousand White House staff members are busy supporting the president's administration in various matters of state and politics.

These examples of "supported success" highlight the power of a shared effort in very concrete terms. With a team behind you, you can accomplish more because others are helping you. However, the consistent support or presence of others can run even deeper, affecting the very core of your sense of self.

In hope-based strivings, the marriage of collaborative power and perceived support can lead to experiences of *mediated success*. This is the realization of aspirations that have been made possible by an individual's hopeful inner core and aided by the emotional support of others. The ultimate outcome results from several mastery-related benefits that are bestowed on the hope-filled individual. These benefits include *flow experiences* as well as feelings of *interdependent mastery* and *spiritual justification*.

Psychologist Mihaly Csikszentmihalyi was the first to highlight flow experiences. These are states of undivided attention and total absorption in one's activities. Time seems to slow down as individuals experience their performance rising to peak levels. The person may feel as if nothing can go wrong. Athletes refer to these moments as "being in the zone." Flow states have been reported by successful individuals from all walks of life, including musicians, painters, dancers, rock climbers, and surgeons.

Researchers have found that youngsters who are challenged to perform at higher levels and are given sufficient emotional support experience more "flow." Such observations dovetail with findings linking early childrearing patterns with subsequent achievement strivings. Adults with strong achievement motivation were found to be more likely to have had parents who set high standards while also providing a warm and accepting environment.

Growing up in a context of challenge and acceptance can also foster an "interdependent spirit." Individuals who are best prepared for mastery pursuits are those who are neither limited by a rigid sense of individualism nor weakened by an extreme feeling of dependency. Given a hopeful core, an individual with high aspirations can balance autonomy with appropriate help-seeking. Stephen Covey believes that interdependence emerges after an individual moves from dependence to independence. From our perspective, however, a hopeful core is more likely to be built on a sense of "ingrained interdependence," beginning in infancy and continuing over the course of the life span.

When individuals feel that at least one other person supports their dreams, they can experience a sense of "integrated mastery." They do not feel alone in their pursuits. Their goals are nested within the larger aims of a dyad, family, community, world of values, or a perceived religious or spiritual presence. Finding their goals converging with some exterior presence, they have a sense of destiny or positive fate, a belief that "I am meant to do this."

Hank Aaron's pursuit of Babe Ruth's homerun record is a great example of *spiritual justification*. On April 14, 1974, he surpassed Ruth's previous record of 714 home runs. But leading up to that night, Aaron had to endure tremendous pressure from hoards of media who barraged him with questions. Far worse were the hateful and threatening letters sent by racists across the country, vowing to murder him or members of his family if he did not stop chasing the Babe's hallowed mark. One such letter:

> Dear Nigger Henry,
>     It has come to my attention that you are going to break Babe Ruth's record.
> I don't think you are going to break this record if I can help it . . . if you hit one
> more home run it will be your last. My gun is watching your every black move.
> This is no joke.

What allowed Aaron to persevere? When interviewed on this topic, he always began by citing the support of his wife Billye, several close friends, and his mother (who ran to his side that historic night after hearing the popping sounds of celebratory cannons and fearing that assassins were shooting at him). Aaron was also grateful for the thousands of encouraging letters he received from fans of all colors. Superimposed on these layers of support, he believed that there was an additional benefactor on his "team."

> I didn't feel like I had to deal with it alone. Whatever forces seemed to be working
> against me in my career—whether it was bigotry or neglect or whatever—I always
> felt that a higher power was working for me. I might not have known what my
> destiny was, but I knew I had one, and something was helping me to attain it.

Mediated success can also develop in whole teams. The story of the 2001 New England Patriots provides a great illustration. They had finished the previous season with 11 losses and only 5 wins. During the 2001 preseason, one of the assistant coaches died after a long battle with heart disease. On September 11, 2001, offensive lineman Joe Andruzzi nearly lost two of his brothers, New York City firefighters who narrowly escaped the collapsing towers of the World Trade Center. A week later, the Patriot's starting quarterback was sidelined with a serious injury. Despite all of these obstacles the team played well enough to make the playoffs and then to advance to the Super Bowl. No matter, each Patriot victory was dismissed as mere luck or attributed to fluke plays and opponent miscues. As center Damien Woody put it, "no one believed in us."

Indeed, few gave them any chance in the Super Bowl against the mighty St. Louis Rams, "the greatest show on turf." The Rams had cruised toward the championship game with relative ease. Everyone expected a rout, with the betting line favoring the Rams over the Patriots by 14 points. Five different computer game simulations showed the Rams winning big, perhaps by as many as 30 or 40 points. The Rams' roster was filled with highly paid stars. In 13 of the 18 individual statistical categories kept by the NFL, a Ram player was ranked above his counterpart on the Patriots.

During the pregame introductions, the Rams came out as individuals, while the Patriots chose to walk out as as a team. (Baseball's Joe Torre would later remark that it gave him "the chills" to witness such an inspiring display of team unity.) And incredibly, the Patriots not only won, but they dominated their opponent for most of the game. Despite a furious comeback by the Rams, the Patriots prevailed 20-17.

Several months later, the Patriots players received their championships rings during a red carpet ceremony. The Associated Press reported the event:

Players' names and numbers are raised along the left side, along with a Patriots helmet pictured over an American flag next to the team's 14-5 record. The word "TEAM" is engraved nearby. Patriots players often referred to their team chemistry as the key to their championship run.

To increase your own sense of mediated power, you might consider adopting these four strategies:

*Absorb the lessons of role models*: Some of the most successful people will tell you how they "picked the brain" of a mentor, coach, or highly valued colleague. Pay attention to every aspect of your role model's presence: how does he approach problems and situations? How does she feel about her craft? What they have learned from experience, and what they would do differently if they were starting over?

*Evaluate*: As successful as your mentors or colleagues may be, you are a unique individual. You may have similar but not identical interests as well as a different set of talents. As you absorb all that you can from others, run a parallel process of evaluating what is, or is not, relevant for you.

*Integrate*: As you absorb and evaluate the lessons from your role models, think about how you can modify their principles, specific behaviors, and strategies to fit your skills, interests, and values.

*Call forth*: Stay alert for opportunities to exercise your mediated power. This can help you to prepare for specific situations. As part of your mastery preparation, visualize what you have learned from your role models.

## Time Mastery

> Talent develops in quiet places. Character is formed in the full current of
> human life.
>
> —Goethe

The very concept of mastery suggests that an individual's behavior has changed or evolved in some meaningful way over the course of time. Indeed, time is a critical factor in achieving mastery, a fact that has not gone unnoticed by publishers: in 2005, for example, there were more than 2,000 books dealing with "time management" listed on Amazon.com.

But time management is only one part in the four-part temporal schema that we discussed in Chapter 4. As an approach based on a management philosophy of control, organization, and distribution of products, it treats time "as a substance," rather than as a cause, a medium, or a direction. We would argue, however, that this management dimension probably ranks *last* among the four elements of time that must be mastered for an individual to experience true success.

*Master "causal time."* Time understood as a cause has the power to create or destroy as well as to heal or harm. Viewed from this perspective, it can be seen as either a friend or foe. Unfortunately, we live in an era that has adopted a restrictive philosophy of time: that taking less time is superior to devoting more time, and moving faster is better than traveling more slowly. Part of the driving force behind this ethos of impatience is the rapidly increasing, split-second barrage of information that we receive from the Internet and other media and that we are expected to process just as instantaneously. In this context, it is difficult to experience time as anything but an enemy that must be controlled, limited, or managed as we race to accomplish whatever it is we think we need to do in our daily lives.

But confront a true masterpiece and you will experience the force of time in a very different manner. As you gaze at a classic portrait or at a marvel of architectural design, you can appreciate the creator's enormous time investment. Perhaps you feel a sense of timelessness when you read a great work of literature or listen to a transcendent symphony. You may also experience time differently as you slowly savor a finely aged wine or a 16-year-old, single-malt scotch.

Both the Great Pyramid of Giza and the Taj Mahal required more than 20 years to complete. Construction of China's Great Wall began in the fifth century B.C. and continued until the seventeenth century. On a more individual basis, Michelangelo spent a total of 10 years lying on his back, painting the Sistine Chapel, while Dante devoted 21 years to perfecting *The Divine Comedy*. Rod Laver, one of the greatest tennis players of the twentieth century, sometimes practiced for 6 hours *after* a tournament match.

How do you work with, rather than against, time? Try to adopt the mentality of a craftsperson. Think of time as an ally, helping you to hone your craft while allowing your creation to reach its full potential. Picture the two beakers of sand in an hourglass. The amount of time you invest is equal to the time it takes for the sand in one beaker to run out. The extent of your impact, measured in hours, days, or years, will be no more or less than your input, or than the time it takes to fill the other side of the hourglass.

Take pride in your experience and be assured that there are no shortcuts on the road to true mastery. Trust that time will bring you to your highest level of meaningful accomplishment. Do your part and have faith in the power of time to do the rest. Realize that even the most gifted may need a decade or more of dedicated practice to produce a world class performance in art, music, science, sports, or most other endeavors. Research by psychologist Dean Keith Simonton and others has also suggested that the age of peak performance varies greatly from field to field. Here are some examples:

Swimmers and gymnasts, ages 14–25
Musicians, ages 20–30
Marathon runners, ages 30–37
Mathematicians, ages 20–40
Social scientists, ages 40–50
Philosophers, ages 60–80

*Master "time as a medium."* Time can also conjure up the image of a conveyer belt that transports people and events at varying rates. This variable relates to time perception and has been the focus of numerous studies. Such investigations reveal a great deal of temporal diversity across geographical zones and sociocultural groups. *Perceived time also moves more quickly as an individual advances in age.* This is because we take stock of each passing year against the backdrop of all past life experiences. For 10-year-olds, 1 year represents 10% of their total existence. By comparison, 1 year in the life of 50-year olds accounts for only 2% of their past. Extrapolating further, it can be estimated that a man or woman who is now 40 will experience the amount of time that elapses from ages 40 to 60 as being roughly equivalent to that which elapsed between the ages of 20 and 30.

Mastering this dimension of perceived time requires paying attention to your "four clocks." Beyond the age factor, there are biological, social, and emotional factors to consider. Individuals vary greatly in terms of their metabolic rates and biological rhythms. For example, people idle at different rates at different times of the day, and some are early risers while others are night owls. Your social clock is the pace of life that you experience as a result of personality, geographical, cultural, religious, and spiritual factors. For example, a Buddhist meditating on the shores of the Ganges River experiences the passage of time in a different manner than does a Catholic in New York during rush hour. And your emotions, particularly mood and arousal levels, affect how you perceive the duration of events. Positive experiences seem to pass by more quickly when you are highly aroused. Perhaps you recall a spirited wedding or party that you attended years ago as just a blur. In contrast, accounts of terrifying accidents or assaults often include the agony of time unfolding in apparent slow motion.

If you are young, realize that there is not an infinite time to procrastinate in goal deferments. But even if your age classifies you as a senior citizen, realize that you still have time to enhance your sense of mastery. It only seems to you as if time is passing more quickly. Do not shy away from making an investment in mastery that may take 5 to 10 years. If you are prone to worrying or frequent bouts of agitation, opportunities for mastery may pass you by while you fret over the possibility of failure. To relax your body, engage in regular exercise or a favorite relaxation technique, preferably in pleasant surroundings. To soothe your mind and spirit, also consider meditation or yoga.

*Master the direction or "orbit of time."* Most Western cultures have constructed a linear view of time. In contrast, many Eastern cultures presume a circular view of time. There are advantages and disadvantages to each perspective. A linear view holds the promise of progress and "getting the past behind you." A circular approach promises greater opportunities for redemption and healing old wounds.

You can combine the concepts of linear and circular time, creating a *spiral of hope.* The concept of a forward moving or ascending spiral combines the promise of progress with the opportunity to rework the past. While you spiral toward greater levels of mastery, you can revisit the same territory without fear of stagnation, realizing that each iteration is bringing you closer to your ultimate destination.

Not only is the hope spiral a more encouraging metaphor for comprehending time, but it also rings true. Change is an undeniable fact or life. As Heraclites wrote, "One cannot stand in the same river twice." However, you can also bear witness to the seemingly endless cycles of nature while resonating to the words of Ecclesiastes, "For everything there is a season." If life teaches us anything it is that we *can* revisit the past and make repairs. This merger of past, present, and future was beautifully captured by the poet T. S. Eliot in *Four Quartets*: "Time present and time past are both perhaps present in time future, and time future contained in time past. . . . . What might have been and what has been point to one end, which is always present."

## Finding Inspiration

Hope and inspiration form a natural pair. They are the twin virtues sought by every individual who is facing a difficult life challenge. They are the spiritual currency of support groups and community organizations. Corporate leaders invest great amounts of money, time, and other resources to instill hope and inspiration in themselves and their employees. Booksellers also acknowledge the marriage of these two virtues, sometimes even establishing aisles labeled "hope and inspiration." An Internet search revealed more than 60,000 links related to these conjoined terms.

This pairing is not simply a poetic arrangement. An individual's hopes tend to be directed toward matters of deep importance, bearing on their values, higher principles, and enduring aspirations. Realizing such hopes may require all the resources an individual can muster, including every available form of inspiration.

## Sources of Inspiration

Without inspiration, musicians struggle to compose, writers are blocked, painters languish before an empty canvas, and actors cannot get inside their characters. Lacking a muse, politicians hesitate before crowds and corporate leaders flounder in the boardroom. Aware of the great need for inspiration, Emerson observed how creative individuals will pursue it at any cost, "by virtue or vice, by friend or by fiend, by prayer or by wine."

The word "inspiration" suggests that something has been "taken inside" the individual. Plato believed that inspiration was a piece of divinity that came bursting into the soul. Philosopher Ignacio Gotz called it "one of the most mysterious moments in anyone's life, the instant when things 'click' and fall neatly in place, or a new idea flashes in the dark."

> The mysterious instant goes by many names: inspiration, enlightenment, illumination, intuition, insight, vision, revelation, and discovery . . . Religious mystics speak of ecstasy and satori; poets, painters, musicians, dancers, and historians invoke their Muses; while scientists and mathematicians, parsimonious and prosaic, claim only hunches and intuitions.

The common element in each of these experiences is *discovery*. Sometimes this discovery happens after a deliberate search, but often it hits without warning. We may "seek and find inspiration" or it may "wash over us." However, as Plato suggested, inspiration is typically experienced as something that "finds us" rather than the other way around.

Hope can be viewed as a precondition for the experience of inspiration. The open and trusting attitude of hopeful individuals makes it more likely that they will be receptive to the voices of inspiration. In turn, inspiration can deepen hope. For example, psychologist Tobin Hart noted that inspiration can improve mood, increase self-worth, and enhance motivation. Translated into the language of our hope-centered perspective, inspiration strengthens the mastery motive.

Individuals find inspiration in many ways. For example, when psychologist Robert Ornstein tried to research this topic, he found there were nearly as many sources of inspiration as the people reporting them in his study. Australian health researchers Debbie Kralik and Kerry Telford asked individuals suffering from various chronic illnesses where they turned for inspiration. Their responses were similarly diverse, encompassing religion and nature, loving relationships and friends, as well as the inspiration from within that is derived from experiences of perseverance in the face of adversity. A number of them also emphasized the presence of an inspiring role model who had shown great courage in the context of similarly dire circumstances.

Turning to self-help books, popular magazines, or new age websites, you will find a confusing hodgepodge of inspirational sources. Some provide formulas, including, in some cases, a magic number of potential places or practices for deriving inspiration. However, beneath the apparent chaos, all sources of inspiration can be captured in two basic strategies. You can try an *inside-out approach* to discover inspiration from within yourself, or adopt an *outside-in technique* to draw inspiration from your external world.

If you seek inspiration from within, you could begin by using a simple but powerful technique recommended by many self-help gurus, including the late Dale Carnegie. Challenge yourself with empowering questions: for example, "I work hard. I have skills and talent. Why can't I be just as successful as my co-worker (or neighbor, etc.)?"

If you are interested in finding inspiration from your external world, read widely, make contact with nature, visit new places, or watch inspirational films. Researchers have found that music can be a powerful source of inspiration. You can select songs to fit your particular mastery needs. If you are looking for general inspiration as well as a boost in attention and concentration, some studies suggested that classical music may be especially effective in this regard, particularly the works of Bach or Mozart.

If you are facing a difficult challenge, try to reframe it as a growth opportunity, or part of a larger life lesson. Committing oneself to some form of action can unleash previously dormant, powerful inner forces. You may benefit from a combination of approaches. Many of those who have persevered, despite years of pain and adversity, have been able to combine a will to act with the belief that they are pursuing a higher calling.

Regardless of your chosen path toward inspiration, maintaining an attitude of trust and openness to new experiences will be critical. Abandon your need for complete control or perfect knowledge. You might begin by slowing down your mind and body at least once or twice a day with the help of meditation, a quiet walk, or some form of exercise that you enjoy. A more tranquil mind is a more receptive mind, one primed to receive inspiration from wherever it may come.

### Role Models

There is a wealth of evidence about the power of heroes and role models to transform lives. For example, consider the influence of the Siddhartha legend on millions of Buddhists, or imagine the empowerment felt by Native Americans at the mere mention of Sitting Bull. How many American children have gained inspiration from Abraham Lincoln while reciting his Gettysburg Address? How many Hindus were lifted out of despair by the vision of Gandhi defying the entire British Empire? The following description of the impact of another great hero was provided by a high school student competing for a college scholarship:

> When I see pictures of Dr. Martin Luther King . . . I dream of the privilege to be able to listen to such a great speaker . . . He must have given so many people hope . . . [I would have told him] . . . Please never give up . . . I love you and what you are doing for our people. You are truly an angel sent down from the heavens to preach your dreams. . .Many things that I am able to do today I attribute to the contributions of Dr. King (Felicia H, Fitch Senior High, Mystic, CT).

You may want to purchase or rent a DVD or CD of inspiring speeches. In 2004 Soundworks International released *The Greatest Speeches of All Time*, a DVD featuring selections from 15 renowned world leaders. In 1991 Rhino Records came out with a CD box set of the *Greatest Speeches of the Twentieth Century*, which included selections from political leaders and sports icons as well as aviation and science heroes. (You can find detailed descriptions of these and similar products at http://www.amazon.com.)

But a hero does not have to be a famous figure. Best friends, parents, and teachers have served as inspirational figures for many individuals. In fact, the heroism of the average person is often more compelling because it is more immediate and real. Earlier in this chapter, we suggested strategies for getting the most from the role models in your daily life, but you might also want to seek inspiration from the wider world of unsung heroes out there. At http://www.myhero.com you can find books, films, and thousands of stories of people who have made a difference in the life of a child or an adult.

If you seek to be inspired by celebrities, then do your homework. Get to know them a little better by reading books or feature articles about them. For the truly motivated, there are fan clubs and Web sites. You may even be able to submit questions or chat live with your particular hero. The Classic Sports Network, the E Channel, as well as MTV and the Arts and Entertainment Network have put together some great 1-hour biographies. In the realm of sports, one of the most inspiring book collections of hope profiles is entitled *More Than a Game*, edited by A. Lawrance Holmes and published by the MacMillan Company.

## Providing Inspiration

What does it takes for someone to be inspiring? Clearly, both words and deeds matter, but depending on the context, they may vary in their relative importance. For children, the examples set by parents or friends are often most crucial, whereas words of inspiration from teachers and mentors may carry more weight. Nevertheless, creating an inspiring presence usually depends on both words and deeds. For example, the coach who preaches dedication but shows up late for practice or fails to prepare a well-conceived game plan may not be much of an inspiration. In any endeavor, you may be able to take someone only as far as you have gone yourself.

Consider the example of Frank Leahy, legendary coach of the Notre Dame Football team. In twelve years (1941–1953), he led his teams to six undefeated seasons and five national championships. In the late 40s, his "fighting Irish" won 39 games in a row. Leahy was a relentless taskmaster who demanded perfection from both himself and his players. Famous for his interminably long, complex drill sessions, he also insisted on full-contact scrimmages that ran deep into the playing season. He was even harder on himself, often eating at his desk and sleeping on a nearby cot.

Inspiring words require certain key ingredients to have an impact on those you want to reach. First, you really have to know what you are talking about, inside and out. Secondly, you must be passionate about your subject matter. Ask yourself: Do you feel a sense of joy, curiosity, and zest for the ideas and principles that you present? Many charismatic speakers "work themselves up" prior to a presentation by engaging in positive self-talk and inspiring visualizations. Make sure to build this *emotional prep time* into your own approach.

The right delivery is also crucial. The best speakers have developed a feel for the tone, scope, and level of detail that is appropriate for their particular audience. They often use stories to begin, end, or embellish their talks. They speak the truth but avoid diluting their message with too many qualifications and exceptions. They frequently interject superlatives and pepper their speeches with dramatic references. For example, instead of referring to someone or something as merely "competent" or "among the best," they will insert a phrase such as "the greatest of all time" or "the best that money can buy." Like any great performer, they have developed a keen sense of pacing and timing, knowing when to go fast or slow, when to pause and when to stop.

## Hidden Dreams

The mastery guidelines provided in this chapter are broadly framed, applicable to just about any foreseeable endeavor. While these open blueprints presume that one has a specific goal or direction in mind, we recognize that many people will reevaluate and perhaps even revise their goals as they move through life. We are also aware that sometimes the greatest obstacles to mastery are discovering and clarifying the nature of one's dreams or desires.

Hope tends to beget hope. Sustained by trust and openness, individuals can confidently enter into the process of self-discovery with a sense of joy and wonder, eventually finding their voice or mission in life. Perhaps this is what Aristotle meant when he referred to hope as "a waking dream." Sometimes the process of self-discovery goes slowly. Individuals sense that something is not quite right in their lives and try to find themselves. They may switch jobs or careers, start a new relationship, or relocate to another city. Or they may have an epiphany, a sudden realization of a higher purpose.

A full commitment to self-discovery requires a courageous leap of faith. Any soul-searching journey is arduous. Both Homer's Odysseus and Virgil's Aeneas had to battle demons on foreign soil before they could come home with a sense of inner peace. Siddhartha wandered all over India searching for the meaning of life. After 44 years of tortuous asceticism, he finally learned that his truth actually lay within.

It is not really necessary, however, for you to travel far and wide to decipher your calling in life. Although there is no substitute for acquired wisdom or hard-won life experience, there *are* strategies that you can use to accelerate your self-understanding. For example, you might want to begin with a simple *values clarification exercise,* such as the one developed by psychologist Milton Rokeach. As shown in Table 10.1, his list of values included 18 terminal values (desired ends) and 18 instrumental values (desired means). Individuals are asked to rank the values from 1 to 18, from most important to least important. Try it for yourself. How you rank each set of values will shed considerable light on those most important to you.

## Learning from the Past

The philosopher Soren Kierkegaard believed, "Life can only be understood by looking backward, but it must be lived by looking forward." In *Four Quartets,* T. S. Eliot suggested, "In the end is my beginning" and "at the end of our exploring [we] arrive where we started and know the place for the first time."

The journey of self-discovery can mean delving into the past, for sometimes one's deeper needs and feelings as well as hidden talents can only be viewed in retrospect. Social pressures and personal defense mechanisms may obscure them from present consciousness. The more individuals are limited by injunctions and fears, the less they are able to embrace the present and to be fully alert to their potential. Secondly, even without the baggage of old scripts, it is difficult for anyone to fully experience the moment.

Your ability to learn from the past dictates how much you can profit from experience. Some quick learners only need a few weeks to settle into a new position while others take months, if not years, to feel comfortable. When the lessons extend to your life as a whole, the art of reflection becomes far more complex. Here are some suggestions for looking back:

*Success reviews*: What have you already mastered because it was a labor of love?

*Failure autopsies*: What have you failed because your heart wasn't in the task?

*Perceived effort*: What kinds of tasks or activities have come easy for you?

*Happy times*: What endeavors have brought you joy?

*Miserable times*: What tasks or activities have brought you misery?

*Pride experiences*: What have you accomplished that is a source of pride?

*Anger/resentment*: What activities have left you feeling angry or resentful?

TABLE 10.1. *Milton Rokeach's Values Clarification Exercise. Within each list, rank each value from 1 to 18, from most to least important. Note: Each list is organized alphabetically and adjacent values do not denote correspondence with each other*

| Terminal Values (Desired Ends) | Your Rank? | Instrumental Values (Desired Means) | Your Rank? |
|---|---|---|---|
| A comfortable life | | Ambitious | |
| Equality | | Broad-minded | |
| An exciting life | | Capable | |
| Family security | | Clean | |
| Freedom | | Courageous | |
| Health | | Forgiving | |
| Inner harmony | | Helpful | |
| Mature love | | Honest | |
| National security | | Imaginative | |
| Pleasure | | Independent | |
| Salvation | | Intellectual | |
| Self-respect | | Logical | |
| A sense of accomplishment | | Loving | |
| Social recognition | | Loyal | |
| True friendship | | Obedient | |
| Wisdom | | Polite | |
| World at peace | | Responsible | |
| A world of beauty | | Self-controlled | |

## Inspiring Dreams

The un-interpreted dream is like an unopened letter from God.

—The Talmud

We have so far discussed dreams in terms of the goals that individuals aspire to achieve. But the dreams we all experience during sleep are no less compelling and in fact have long been a source of inspiration. Some of the earliest bestsellers were dream books prepared by Egyptian scribes or Roman philosophers. In the Old Testament, Joseph won the favor of a foreign ruler through his uncanny knack for interpreting dreams. The grandmaster of the collective unconscious, Carl Jung, devoted his life to analyzing more than 80,000 dreams. Sigmund Freud considered *The Interpretation of Dreams* his single greatest contribution, declaring, "Such discoveries occur but once in a lifetime."

Analyzing your dreams is an excellent way to learn about your past. In fact, it has been found that only 5% of dreams typically deal with the future. By analyzing your dreams, you can gain insight into longstanding problems and receive ideas for more creative solutions than you have been able to devise in your waking life.

In a landmark study, psychologists Calvin Hall and Robert van de Castle collected dreams from 1,000 individuals. They separated the dreams into various categories that can be directly related to mastery. Using their data, we were able to extract dream probabilities for each of the four mastery elements (self-mastery, outside help, values, and time mastery). Table 10.2 can be used as a guide for tracking as few as 10 dreams or as many as 100. If this type of analysis interests you, keep a notebook next to your bed. Write down your dreams as precisely as you can, right after you wake up. Once you have collected at least 10 dreams, compare your percentages to those in the table.

For example, starting with self-mastery, Hall and van Castle's findings suggest that themes of success and failure appear in approximately 30% of dreams. Moreover, their results indicate that about half of these represent success, while the other 50% may

TABLE 10.2. *Hope-Based Dream Analysis (Extrapolated from Hall and van Castle, 1966)*

| Mastery Themes | Hall and van Castle Findings | | No. to Expect (per number of dreams) | | | |
|---|---|---|---|---|---|---|
| | | | 100 | 50 | 20 | 10 |
| *Self-mastery* | | | | | | |
| (~30% of dreams) | Success | 50% | 15 | 8 | 4 | 2 |
| | Failure | 50% | 15 | 8 | 4 | 2 |
| | Dreamer succeeds | 90% | 14 | 7 | 4 | 2 |
| | Another succeeds | 10% | 1 | 1 | 0 | 0 |
| *Outside help* | | | 100 | 50 | 20 | 10 |
| (~40% of dreams) | Providing assistance | 45% | 17 | 9 | 4 | 2 |
| | Getting help | 45% | 17 | 9 | 4 | 2 |
| | Collaborating | 10% | 4 | 2 | 1 | 0 |
| *Values* | | | 100 | 50 | 20 | 10 |
| (Every dream) | On familiar ground | 30% | 30 | 15 | 6 | 3 |
| | Distorted surroundings | 50% | 50 | 25 | 10 | 5 |
| | Unfamiliar territory | 20% | 20 | 10 | 4 | 2 |
| *Time and movement* | | | 100 | 50 | 20 | 10 |
| (~40% of dreams) | Situated in the past | 60% | 23 | 12 | 4 | 2 |
| | Situated in the present | 30% | 12 | 6 | 2 | 1 |
| | Situated in the future | 10% | 4 | 2 | 1 | 0 |
| | Dreamer moving | 60% | 24 | 12 | 4 | 2 |
| | Dreamer stationary | 40% | 16 | 8 | 2 | 1 |

symbolize a failure of some kind. If you decide to track 100 of your dreams, then about 15 should deal with success (50% of 30). However, if you are harboring feelings of ineffectiveness, you might very well experience a preponderance of failure dreams. Approximately 90% of your success dreams should feature you as the effective, achieving, or masterful protagonist. A much lower percentage suggests that you may not be taking ownership of a successful outcome, even when it does occur.

You may want to pay special attention to the third category in Table 10.2, pertaining to values. Dreams that take place on familiar ground suggest that you are following your bliss. Myth expert Joseph Campbell commented that individuals feel most at home when they are following their higher calling and honoring the values they cherish and hold dear. This moral basis for feeling at home or in a familiar space was beautifully captured by Henry David Thoreau who advised his readers to "dwell as near as possible to the channel in which your life flows."

Note that typically about 60% of dreams include some sense of physical movement. Movement in dreams and other imaginative exercises suggest a readiness or potential for change, an active coping style, and a strong level of motivation. Too little movement might indicate deep feelings of stagnation, emotional paralysis, or even depression.

A number of self-help writers have suggested that there may be certain universal dream symbols. In particular, Patricia Garfield has referred to the following mastery-related dream elements: "driving well" or "driving poorly," "falling down" or "flying high," "performing well" or "performing poorly," "missing the boat" or "traveling well." If you are comfortable with the idea of universal symbols, the following list of mastery-related objects and themes might be of interest to you. For greater depth of understanding, pay attention to the emotions or general moods that permeate your dreams.

Self-mastery: (decision time) exiting or entering a cave, standing at a crossroads or on a diving platform; (goal pursuits) running toward or chasing something; (competence and drive) planes, trains, automobiles, horses, eagles, hawks.

Environmental support: (general environment) living room, kitchen, dining room, garden; (social support) father, mother, teacher, mentor; (financial support) money, banks; (emotional support) milk, honey, hearts.

Values and principles: (moral standards) judge, jury, courtroom, lawyers; (things held sacred) church, temple, synagogue, mosque; (orienting or purpose-driving values) compass, roadmap, path in the woods.

Time: (time as causal) father time, primetime, downtime; (time as a medium) river, road, obstacle course; (time as a substance) changing shadow, sand in an hourglass, a ticking clock; (time as a direction) a one-way street, going around in circles, a spiral staircase.

*The Vision Quest*

Perhaps you have already tried some of the suggestions we have identified for finding inspiration, but you still feel mired in the hopeless grind of an uninspired life. In reviewing your past, was it hard to recall any true moments of flow or joyful engagement? In exploring your values, was it difficult for you to achieve any sense of clarity? Do you feel as if you have hit a wall in terms of mastery development? If this is the case, then consider a vision quest.

In ancient cultures, it was common for both young and old to leave the group and venture into the wilderness in search of guidance and wisdom. In fact, within many tribal societies, such vision quests were considered an essential component of the adolescent rite of passage. Today, this practice has become popular among individuals in industrialized countries as a means of achieving inner peace and a deeper clarity of purpose.

A vision quest is aimed at transforming the self through a three-step process of *separation, transition,* and *incorporation.* The *first goal* is to pull your "self" away from the forces and elements that are inhibiting your spiritual development. This can be achieved by venturing into a remote area such as an island, forest, or desert, where you can experience yourself freed from the usual constraints of daily life.

The *second goal* is to effect a transition from a world-centered focus to an inner-centered state. Fasting, going without sleep, or living off the land are some of the strategies that, in moderation, can be used to facilitate this shift. Certain indigenous groups also rely on special foods, herbs, or beverages. The more dramatic accounts of this spiritual migration liken it to a symbolic death of the old self.

The *final stage* is one of incorporation or rebirth. Very often, this phase is facilitated by a spiritual guide who helps to impart new beliefs and values. Additional support may be provided by a group of like-minded individuals who uphold a similar vision. In this manner, individuals can fashion a new image of themselves, the world, and the future.

*Circles of Air, Circles of Stone* is a Vermont-based organization that specializes in four-day vision quests. Journeys are conducted in Vermont as well as various parts of the American Southwest and Mexico. Several different forms of a vision quest are offered, including those rooted in the traditions of Native Americans, Mayans, and Australian Aborigines. For mastery development, we recommend the "Journey of the Soul" and "The Medicine Walk." Or for a more immediate primer, you may want to try psychologist John Suler's "mini-vision quest." The following guidelines are adapted from his posting at http://www.rider.edu/~suler/vquest.html:

For a period of at least four hours, leave your home and go out somewhere. Don't plan ahead. Just follow your instincts and go where your intuition leads you. Do this alone. If you encounter friends or acquaintances, limit your time with them to just a few minutes.

As you move about, reflect on some "big questions" that you would like to answer such as "Who am I?," "What is important to me?," and "What do I want from life?" Try to balance thinking and reflecting with moments of unfocused "drifting."

Frequently remind yourself that you are on a "quest," a "search mission." Expect to "find" something and trust that insights will occur. Stay open to any signs or symbols that may provide you with inspiration. It could be something that happens to you, or something you see or hear.

Bring a notebook and a pen. Every half hour or so sit down and write. Note your reactions, including your thoughts, feelings, and insights. If you're feeling anxious, frustrated, or bored, ask yourself why and write about this aspect of your experience. If nothing important has happened, you should reflect and write about this as well.

In summary, each individual marches to the beat of a certain drummer. Sometimes it is a universal tune that beckons, whereas in other cases it is reflective of a personal calling, a unique individual mission. In addressing mastery needs, an individual must look deep within, far ahead, and everywhere around. Only then will he or she be able to summon the discipline and inner truth, vision and time perspective, as well as support and inspiration needed to achieve meaningful success.

# Eleven

## SURVIVAL SKILLS: BECOMING A "KNIGHT OF FAITH"

Those who meditate on me and worship me . . . those I soon lift from the
ocean of death.

*The Bhagavad-Gita*

Hope lets you breathe a little easier. It gives you a chance to live a more peaceful life,
one that is defined by a deep sense of trust, a strong feeling of support, and
considerably less fear and worry. Hope can also help you to transform experiences
of loss and rise above the gloom and doom of a death that appears devoid of honor or
purpose. These might be considered valuable gifts in any era, but they are particularly
prized in our time, an age of anxiety fraught with war, disease, and a host of other
threats.

These threats have of course been a part of the human experience since the beginning
of recorded time. But things are different today. The weapons are more deadly, the
spread of disease more rapid, and our awareness of danger more thorough. Moreover,
these are only the more proximate or obvious sources of our unease. We are faced with
other, more covert problems as well, such as diminished community, disengaged
families, mistrust of institutions, and a sense of nihilism manifest in the widespread
lack of faith in God or a higher power. Given all these stresses and uncertainties, is it at
all surprising that anxiety disorders have become the world's most prevalent form of
psychopathology, affecting roughly one in every nine individuals?

You may be wondering how anxiety relates to fear. Traditionally, psychologists have used the term "fear" to describe an externally directed response to a specific threat. In contrast, the term "anxiety" has usually been reserved for an unfocused or "object-less" state that resides within the person. According to this view, fear is about something "out there," while anxiety is about something "in here."

But in reality, the distinction between the two states is not so clear cut. Many generalized fears are often treated as forms of anxiety. For example, while some social scientists refer to the "fear of death," others write about "death anxiety." In addition, chronic states of anxiety can result in the development of specific fears. To further complicate the picture, the current edition of the *Diagnostic and Statistical Manual of Mental Disorders*, the mental health providers' classification bible, combines both undifferentiated states of anxiety and specific fears under the heading of "Anxiety Disorders." These conditions include generalized anxiety disorder, post-traumatic stress disorder, panic attacks, phobias, and obsessive-compulsive disorder.

In this chapter, you will discover ways to strengthen your psychological and spiritual survival skills and to better manage both your fears *and* anxieties. You will learn about the building blocks of *the resilient self*, the part of your hopeful core that is critical for dealing with issues of survival. In Chapter 12, you will read about specific fears associated with one or more of the hope motives. To use a medical analogy, this chapter can help to boost your psychological and spiritual immunity, while Chapter 12 provides antidotes for more specific ailments related to attachment, mastery, and survival. Attending to all of these aspects of hope-based survival is akin to holistic medicine for the spirit and psyche. Later chapters (15 and 16) focus on issues relating to physical healing and health.

## The Gift and Burden of Fear

All living things are built for survival. Green plants bend toward the light. A single-celled amoeba is capable of adapting to a variety of physical conditions. Spiders collapse into a ball when they sense an intruder. In *Winter World*, biologist Berndt Heinrich detailed the amazing survival strategies employed by animals living in cold climates. Heinrich appeared to be particularly fascinated by tent caterpillars and kinglets. Caterpillars have the ability to create glycerol in their blood, a kind of natural antifreeze. Kinglets are tiny birds that must consume three times their body weight on a daily basis in order to generate enough energy to survive even the coldest nights. In the Kinglet, apparently his favorite creature, Heinrich sensed "a grand, boundless zest for life," a testament to [hope], and proof that "the fabulous is possible".

Another poignant example of animal survival was demonstrated on a scorching summer day when at the edge of a parking lot, a man found an injured squirrel. Every few minutes the poor creature would give out a pathetic cry. The blood oozing from the side of its mouth and its limp condition suggested it had been hit by a vehicle and had probably dragged itself to the side of the lot. The man called the local humane society and placed a bucket over the animal to offer it some protection and mark its location for the rescuers. But within a few seconds, the squirrel found a way to crawl out from under the container. This sequence was repeated three times until the man finally stopped trying to cover the squirrel, sensing that the animal knew what was best. It dawned on him that the squirrel found it to be too hot and airless under the bucket. Or perhaps, the man mused, this defiant little creature was simply resisting premature burial.

As human beings, we share a vastly more complicated survival system. Endowed with highly evolved frontal lobes, we can anticipate a host of possible threats. If trapped, our imaginative capacities can produce a plethora of alternatives. You may recall the story of Aron Ralson, the 27-year-old rock climber from Colorado, who nearly died when an 800 pound boulder shifted and rolled on top of his arm. Demonstrating a remarkable degree of hopeful resiliency, he immediately thought of several possible ways that he might get free, including hailing a passerby, chipping away at the rock, or fashioning a pulley system to lift the weight. If these strategies failed, Ralston was even prepared to cut off his own arm.

Ralston had enough water to survive for at least 3 days. Unfortunately, not a single other climber ever ventured his way. He tried valiantly but was unable to chip or dislodge the rock. On the fourth day, he started to cut off his arm with a pocketknife. After 2 more days of unimaginable pain, he was able to free himself. However, he still had to rappel one-armed down the side of the canyon, and then hike an additional 6 miles for help. Those closest to Aron noted that while his pocketknife may have severed his arm free from the rock, the true instrument of his liberation was his "hopeful countenance." According to Reverend Steve Miller, his pastor at Hope Methodist Church,

> [Ralston] is a very clear-thinking man of faith and not bashful about talking about the *presences* that were with him . . . He knew his friends were praying for him and actively searching for him. He felt in touch with his mother. He felt tuned in to the Spirit.

Some fear is necessary to assure an individual's survival. In *The Gift of Fear*, psychiatrist Gavin De Becker stressed that the key to staying out of harm's way is to follow your "hard-wired intuition." As he described it, "you have the gift of a brilliant internal guardian that stands ready to warn you of hazards and to guide you through risky situations." Unfortunately, an overabundance of fear can drive some individuals into a state of emotional paralysis or total withdrawal. They devote so much time and energy to the "work of worry" or "anxiety management" that they have few resources left for anything else. *Too much fear is not a gift but a burden.*

Some individuals are temperamentally more fearful than others. Families can also bequeath healthy or unhealthy ways of coping to their children. In some cases, an early encounter with trauma, illness, or loss instills a chronic state of generalized anxiety and a heightened sense of personal vulnerability. At the other end of the coping spectrum, there are children, as well as adults, who demonstrate an extraordinary degree of resiliency. Despite a myriad of encounters with the dark side of life, they seem relatively well adjusted and have moved beyond surviving into the realm of thriving.

*Some degree of fear and anxiety is necessary for personal growth.* As psychiatrist Rollo May and other existentialists have emphasized, "anxiety is essential to the human condition." It is the experience of anxiety that defines "the experience of being affirming itself against nonbeing." Putting it differently, if you are fully committed to realizing certain life goals, to defending a particular way of life, or to upholding a cherished institution, then any perceived attack on these centers of value may be experienced as an assault on your innermost self.

*In confronting any species of terror, you should aim high.* Strive for a deep-rooted hope that will empower you to address the endless vicissitudes of life. This does not mean that you should learn to ignore or deny the presence of danger. Aristotle noted that even courage can be "destroyed by excess." In his view, "the person who fears nothing" is not at all "courageous" but instead is foolish and "rash." A hopeful approach to life is not about denial, or attempting to evade the sober realities of life by retreating within a cocoon of blind optimism. True hopefulness is a "way of being," a manner of experiencing yourself, the world, and the future.

## Hopeful Resiliency

We have already described the traits and skills associated with two of the components that comprise the hopeful core. In Chapter 9 (Attachment Matters) the building blocks of the attached self were explored. Chapter 10 (Mastery and Inspiration) focused on the elements of the empowered self. Another dimension of the hopeful core is the resilient self.

According to the *Oxford English Dictionary*, "resiliency" implies "a tendency to rebound," "an ability to return to a natural physical state," and "the power of recovery." In a parallel fashion, hopeful resiliency refers to a capacity for sustaining hope in times of stress and uncertainty. An individual who is resilient has the ability to bounce back from a crisis and to maintain emotional equilibrium in the midst of chaos. To fully appreciate the nature of resiliency, however, it is necessary to understand the complexities underlying the human coping process.

There are many types of survival. *Physical survival* has been a preoccupation for most of human history. However, in this age of anxiety, you may be finding yourself far more focused on *emotional survival*. If you are older, have struggled with substance abuse, or battled a mental illness, you may be most concerned with sustaining a sound mind (*cognitive survival*). Perhaps you are especially worried about maintaining a particular lifestyle (*social or economic survival*). Alternatively, your priorities might be more transcendent, aiming toward a form of *ultimate survival*, involving a legacy or a spiritually assured afterlife. Understanding your particular needs is crucial.

Do your hopes revolve around changing your life? What are you trying to alter? Is it something internal or external? Are you hoping to modify some aspect of your personality? Do you want your loved ones to change in some fashion? Conversely, are you seeking greater stability in your life? Are you striving to remain emotionally grounded, or is your attention more focused on preserving some aspect of your environment?

Do you like to attack problems head on, or do you prefer indirect strategies, such as taking a different perspective of a given problem or going with the flow? Maybe your disposition is to focus on the positive aspects of a situation. Are you someone who attempts to address every issue on your own or do you feel more comfortable marshalling support from family and friends? How likely are you to rely on religious or spiritual beliefs when dealing with crises in your life?

Beyond varying individual needs and styles, significant coping differences result from cultural factors. In the West, there is a greater focus on direct problem solving or on what have been described as "primary control processes." In the East, there is a preference for "secondary control processes," which involve making subtle changes in behavior to indirectly affect the outcome of life events. For many individuals, spiritual beliefs play a major role in their daily confrontations with stressful events, but the focus of these beliefs may differ among individuals of different religious persuasions. Most protestants, for example, believe that grace from God is sufficient for salvation, whereas Catholics are more apt to believe that individuals can help to influence their salvation by partaking of the sacraments and undertaking good works.

An alternative style of coping is one that is not based on just the self or exclusively on a higher power. For example, psychologist Kenneth Pargament has written about the "collaborative coping" of many religious individuals. These believers see themselves as engaged in a joint effort. Although assisted by a higher power, they do not view themselves as passive souls needing explicit formulas to address life problems. They view their own strength and skill as important factors in coping with these problems. In Saint Paul's letter to the Philippians, he asserted, "I can do all things through Christ who gives me strength." The Hindu practice of activating the inner "Atman" (or divinity) is another example of a style of coping that lies somewhere in the middle of the control spectrum, halfway between purely internalized power and totally externalized dependence.

Against this summary of the psychology of coping, we can now explore the building blocks that underlie the resilient self, which include the following:

- Survival-based trust  *3*
- Care recruitment  *4*
- Personal terror management  *2*
- Spiritual terror management
- Liberation beliefs  *5*
- Spiritual integrity *;*

When threats surface, hopeful individuals draw on a *reservoir of trust* in others, including family, friends, and valued institutions. They have the capacity to *solicit care and support*. They are able to *manage their fears* in order to keep their minds at ease and bodies well regulated. In times of adversity, many hopeful individuals rely on *spiritual beliefs* to assure themselves of a benign universe and their ultimate liberation. And many are likely to demonstrate *spiritual integrity,* an impenetrable core linked to a deep sense of purpose and a steadfast commitment to establishing a legacy.

The growth of hopeful resiliency can be examined over different phases of the life cycle. For example, survival-based trust is usually developed during early childhood, while spiritual integrity typically arises during middle or late adulthood. However, the impact of individual differences, as well as extraordinary life circumstances, can shift the course of development, leading to either precocious hopefulness or the emergence of a resilient late bloomer.

In engineering, materials are rated in terms of their tensile strength and stress-strain ratios. These properties are the result of the constituent elements, the quality of the bond holding them together, and the curing process that hardens or sets the material in place. The same can be said for the factors determining individual resiliency. Nature, what we are born with, and nurture, how we are cared for, provide the raw materials for the resilient self. Life does the rest, during which we forge life skills in the presence of challenge and adversity. "Character," as Goethe observed, can only be developed in "the rush of the world." The individual with hopeful resiliency, like a strong metal, is held together by a "quality bond," matured by the fire of experience, and capable of handling the inevitable "strains of life." In *Farewell to Arms*, Ernest Hemingway put it well: "The world breaks everyone, and then some are strong in the broken places."

### Survival-Based Trust and Care Recruitment

Individuals who believe others can and will help them are more likely to solicit comfort and support. Conversely, those who lack trust are unlikely to reach out for help. *Survival-based trust* and *care recruitment* are thus intertwined elements of the resilient self, with the former construct greatly affecting the development of the latter. The first 5 or 6 years of life are critical for the development of survival-based trust, on which care recruitment is in a sense grafted. As trust builds, the ability to engage others increases throughout childhood. While the circle of trusted others is typically enlarged over the course of a lifetime, the biggest advances tend to occur prior to adolescence.

Human infants are truly among the most dependent offspring in nature, requiring more than a decade of care before they can survive on their own. They are nonetheless endowed with powerful survival skills and possess a robust immune system.  In 2002, Dr. Paul A. Offit, Chief of Infectious Diseases at The Children's Hospital of Philadelphia, reassured parents who worry about their children's health: "Babies emerge into a world teeming with bacteria, viruses and other microorganisms [but] their immune systems are designed to stand up to these challenges from the start."

The social responsiveness of children is part of their survival repertoire. Most children possess an inborn capacity for engaging the attention and care of others. Scientists who have studied infant–caregiver interactions confirm that even the newborn is an active participant in the social exchange. But when this capacity does not emerge or is thwarted, the effects can be devastating. *Reactive attachment disorder*, for example, is a condition that typically appears in children between the ages of 2 and 5. It seems to be associated with frequent changes in the primary caregiver and a disregard for the children's emotional needs. Children diagnosed with this condition show one of two patterns, both indicative of an inability to recruit or receive genuine care. Those who fall into the category of *inhibited attachment* manifest avoidance and hypervigilance in the presence of others. In the most extreme cases, they demonstrate an emotional paralysis, a kind of frozen watchfulness. In contrast, children who meet the criteria for *disinhibited attachment* manifest an appalling degree of indiscriminate sociability. They seem to have no sense of whom to trust or to distrust and therefore cannot discern appropriate care.

Fortunately, reactive attachment disorder is rare. It takes a profound degree of parental and community neglect to override the basic human tendency toward openness, trust, and care recruitment. The child's innate potential usually confers a kind of *psychological immunity* when parental involvement is less than adequate. As long as there is the consistent presence of some caring adult in the child's environment, he or she will typically emerge socially and emotionally intact.

Social resiliency has even been observed among infant monkeys isolated from their mothers since birth. Psychologist Harry Harlow and his colleagues found that "isolates" subsequently placed with a group of healthy juvenile monkeys were in time able to recruit and receive enough positive attention to develop into relatively healthy adults. At the human level, psychologist Judith Rich Harris has forcefully argued that peers can be just as important as parents in fostering the social development of children.

Psychiatrists Roberta Apfel and Bennett Simon focused on the particular resourcefulness of children thrown into the chaos of war. For example, they described how an orphaned 12-year-old Cambodian girl developed her acting talents in a refugee camp. This enhanced her possibilities for eliciting adult interest and eventually led to her adoption by an American woman. They also noted how Elie Wiesel, as a 13-year-old boy in Auschwitz, was able to obtain an extra bowl of soup from starving fellow prisoners for telling the best story of the day.

According to Apfel and Simon, children possess "the gift of being able to extract even very small amounts of human warmth, and loving-kindness in the most dire of circumstances." While using adults as polestars, they "promote a feeling of reciprocity" in their exchanges with others and participate in the establishment of "new emotional supplies." Foremost among these gains, in our view, is the spiritual capital of renewed hope.

### Personal Terror Management

An individual's ability to manage fear and stress—variously called self-soothing, self-assurance, or emotional self-regulation—is, in our terms, a capacity for *personal terror management*. It derives from two attachment processes, *empowerment* and *attunement*. As we discussed in Chapter 9, when adults lend their power to children for the purpose of reducing their fears and general distress, the resulting "self–object" bond imparts to the children an inner sense that they can survive in the world. Empathic caregivers who are attuned to their children's emotional and physical state also provide a calming presence in times of doubt or fear. Moreover, attuned or in-synch caregiving seems to affect the growth and refinement of a child's brain, specifically, the right hemisphere, which is sometimes referred to as the "emotional brain" because it is associated with many aspects of social intelligence (e.g., the ability to read facial expressions or to decode the emotional tone embedded in speech).

A child's need for attunement and self–other empowerment is most critical in the first 6 years of life. By 6 months of age, infants are capable of experiencing sadness, and by the end of the first year, they show signs of separation anxiety. At approximately 10 to 12 months, they begin to rely on *social referencing*, gauging their own responses to events by observing the emotional and physical reactions of their caretakers. By around age 2, they are better able to self-regulate. Now able to walk and to some extent use language, they can now exercise more control in approaching or avoiding particular people or situations while verbally expressing their fears and concerns. Nevertheless, young children still need to be close to a trusted caretaker. As their sense of self develops, so does their capacity for imagination and forethought, a precursor that ironically underpins both the development of more sophisticated fears and of the ability to comprehend hope.

In middle childhood, self-regulation is enhanced by several spurts in emotional intelligence. Children by this stage are more capable of coping with various fears, are beginning to understand how thoughts control emotions, and can comprehend the possibility of feeling one thing while expressing another. Most also have an expanding social network that includes peers and other adults, who may themselves offer lessons in alternative ways of coping with stress.

### Spiritual Terror Management

In our previous discussions, we noted how spiritual resources might be used in managing immediate fears and the distant terror of anticipated losses. For most individuals, the formative years for the development of *spiritual terror management* are those from early childhood through adolescence. However, it is not unusual to encounter spiritually transformed older adults who have found peace after decades of fear and anxiety. In short, no matter when it develops, spiritual resiliency reduces psychological distress. Psychologists Lee Kirkpatrick and Phillip Shaver found that individuals who felt securely attached to God, for example, reported much greater life satisfaction and less anxiety, depression, and physical illness than did those with an anxious attachment to a higher power. In another study, Kirkpatrick discovered that those who were "God-avoidant" tended to have a weakened sense of "symbolic immortality."

The first task of spiritual development is establishing a bond with a powerful other. As we discussed in Chapter 7, positive caregiver experiences can jumpstart a healthy spiritual life for a child. In middle childhood and continuing into adolescence, spiritual terror management evolves through exposure to the myths and rituals of particular religious or spiritual belief systems. Traditionally, this is when some children are formally admitted into a spiritual community via a Christian confirmation, a Jewish Bar Mitzvah, or other religious ceremony.

On the other hand, children with a negative or insecure attachment to a caregiver can develop a superficial spiritual veneer, if not a fervent antireligious stance. Or by the time they reach adolescence and young adulthood, their lack of spiritually based resources makes them so vulnerable to the vicissitudes of life that some turn to drugs for a quick dose of self-soothing, while others seek to insulate themselves within the fold of a street gang. Family dysfunction has something to do with these behaviors, and so do cultural influences. In particular, we suspect that the diminished emphasis in the West on spiritual development in young people may be one of the factors underlying the increased incidence of distressed and alienated youths.

### Liberation Beliefs

Hope is about options and possibilities. Hopeful individuals believe there is a way out of every difficulty. Those without hope tend to feel inescapably trapped by every difficulty and believe that there is no exit from their pain or suffering. Recall from Chapter 2 that one of the classic metaphors of hope is that of a bridge. Or recall psychologist C. R. Snyder's perspective on hope, emphasizing that it derives from both a sense of personal power and a dedication to seeking different routes to goal attainment. His approach paid homage to the old saying, "Where there is a will there is a way." Or consider the thoughts of Chinese novelist-philosopher Lin Yutang: "Hope is like a road in the country; there was never a road, but when many people walk on it, the road comes into existence." Writer Anne Lamott added, "Hope begins in the dark, the stubborn hope that if you just show up and try to do the right thing, the dawn will come."

Such liberation beliefs derive from the survival system and come into play when individuals feel trapped or endangered but resiliently believe that they can free themselves from their predicament. These beliefs are different from problem-solving strategies, which spring from the mastery system and are typically employed in achievement-related situations such as those involving school or work. In the course of human development, however, both of these survival and mastery elements may be fused together or further blended with aspects of attachment.

Liberation beliefs develop primarily during adolescence, when important shifts in reasoning ability occur with the onset of puberty. The defining feature of these cognitive advances—which developmental psychologists variously call "formal operational thought," "hypothetical reasoning," or "abstract problem solving"—is the ability to anticipate future problems while devising alternative solutions. A study conducted by one of us (A. S.) further established the link between this ability and the emergence during adolescence of liberation beliefs and hope.

In this research, the coping strategies of children and teens were compared with respect to age and degree of hopefulness. Each participant was told a story about a child lost in the woods. They were then asked, "How many ways of escaping or getting back home can you imagine?" On average, *children* were able to come up with *two solutions*, whereas the typical *adolescent* was able to think of *three alternatives*. When only the most hopeful participants were studied, an even more dramatic difference was noted, with adolescents averaging four solutions, and their younger counterparts averaging only two and a half solutions.

### Spiritual Integrity

As they age, individuals become increasingly aware of their personal limitations and of their mortality, the so-called portal of nothingness. In the resilient individual, this awareness goes a step further to encompass the notion of *spiritual integrity,* which is somewhat similar to Erik Erikson's concept of "ego integrity." Erikson was referring to a set of beliefs, values, and attitudes—for example, a sense of meaning and purpose in life, an absence of regret, and "a detached concern with life itself, in the face of death itself"—that could be found in those who successfully negotiated the final stages of the life span.

Our concept of spiritual integrity is not restricted to the final stage of the life cycle. As we will discuss shortly, spiritual integrity can emerge in the childhood years and may even reach a high level of maturity well before middle age. For most people, however, the qualities associated with basic integrity—moral strength and personal integration—do not develop until the second half of life. Granted, there are important changes in moral reasoning that begin in childhood and extend into young adulthood, but the establishment of true character requires a fully matured ethical system informed by a deep synthesis of life experiences. These personal qualities typically coalesce during middle and late adulthood.

Spiritual integrity, as one of the building blocks of hopeful resiliency, is at heart a life-affirming proposition. The formal qualities essential for its development are as follows:

- Meaning in life
- Purpose
- An "incorruptible core"
- Commitment to a legacy

Under "meaning in life" we include both *personal and cosmic meaning*. The former suggests that you believe your personal existence to be meaningful and that you have integrated your life experiences within a framework of values and principles. "Cosmic meaning" refers to belief in a larger plan, a vast design directed by a higher intelligence that is all encompassing. Such meaning is a prerequisite for *purpose in life and can become a guiding force in the worst of times.* Viktor Frankl, a psychiatrist who survived the horrors of Auschwitz, drew a measure of hope by recalling the words of Nietzsche, "He who has a why to live for can bear almost any how."

Many hopeful individuals believe that they have been endowed with special gifts. Furthermore, they presume their talents obligate them to play a role in upholding particularly cherished values, traditions, or institutions. An educational curriculum designed to foster this aspect of spiritual integrity can be found at the Center for Life Calling and Leadership at Indiana Wesleyan University. Their mission statement reads, "A life calling is larger than a job or occupation, deeper than a profession or life's work. It is the confidence of an overriding purpose for your life, based on who you are, carried out in a connection to the universal community around you."

In the process of creating a meaningful life, it is often necessary to *accept and forgive* others and yourself. Realize that people usually do the best they can, with the information available to them at the time. *This includes you.* Do not wallow in regret. Hindsight should be an ally in building hope for the future, not a foe. It should strengthen and inspire rather than debilitate and demoralize. Erikson put it succinctly when he suggested that healthy adults accept that the life they have lived is the one they were meant to live.

Hopeful individuals also understand that dealing with adversity is part of the process of affirming life. In the 1970s, psychologist Suzanne Kobasa conducted a large study of employees threatened by job loss or relocation. She found that some of the employees handled the stress better than others. This group of hardy individuals showed few, if any, signs of stress-related symptoms and saw change (e.g., potential unemployment) as a challenge that could engage their capacity for mastery and survival.

Rather than defining themselves in terms of a setback, a handicap, or a disease, hopeful individuals with spiritual integrity retain an *incorruptible core* of positive attitudes, feelings, and beliefs about themselves and life. By "incorruptible" we mean morally, as well as spiritually, resistant to inner deformation or ruin. Hopeful individuals refuse to allow their sense of self to be compromised by life circumstances or physical decline. Morrie Schwartz (of *Tuesdays with Morrie*) espoused this spirit of incorruptibility when he commented on his battle with Lou Gehrig disease:

> It was very important for me to make clear to myself that my body is only part of who I am. We are much greater than the sum of our physical parts. The way we look at the world is fashioned by our values and our thoughts about good and evil, things that go into making us who we are.

Persisting through their triumphs and travails, ever-hopeful individuals create a life story that can rise to the level of the heroic. The great nineteenth-century poet Lord Alfred Tennyson put it well:

> Come, my friends, 'tis not too late to seek a newer world. . . . It may be that the gulfs will wash us down: It may be we shall touch the Happy Isles, and see the great Achilles, whom we knew. Tho' much is taken, much abides; and tho' we are not now that strength which in old days moved earth and heaven; that which we are, we are.

Hopeful individuals also create a powerful *legacy of possibility* that serves as an example for peers, friends, and loved ones. What they bequeath is a kind of "hope script," a spiritual road map that can offer a unique approach to mastery, attachment, or survival. At the same time, these legacy makers are rewarded with a bounty of meaning, purpose, and hope. Their own joy comes from having helped to perpetuate a world and a way of life that is consistent with their values and sense of self. Erikson related this "grand generativity" to the sacred Hindu call for each of us to do our part for the "maintenance of the world."

## Precocious Integrity

Sometimes extraordinary circumstances accelerate the maturation of spiritual integrity. This precocity may occur in young adults, or even among children, who encounter tremendous adversity. Psychiatrist Robert Coles wrote a number of books about the experiences of poor and disenfranchised children. In *A Study of Courage and Fear,* he documented the struggles of African American children living in the South during the turbulent 1960s. Many of them, like 6-year-old Ruby, were thrust into a firestorm that erupted after the Supreme Court decided it was time to end school segregation.

> Ruby was six years old when it began. She came, by chance, to be the only Negro child entering one of the previously segregated schools in New Orleans. For weeks, angry whites mounted a boycott protesting her presence. Each day, accompanied to the door by her mother, Ruby walked past a threatening mob . . . She heard obscenities, insults, and from one white woman, the particularly fearful threat of death by poisoning. [Ruby told Coles] 'Maybe it'll have to be a race, and I hope we win . . . Some people think we won't . . . But I don't believe them for too long.'

Ryan White was another inspiring example of a child who developed spiritual integrity at an early age. He was 13 when he contracted HIV from a blood transfusion. When word spread of his illness, he was badly mistreated and initially barred from attending school. Journalist Taro Yamasaki wrote movingly of Ryan's plight:

> He would walk down a totally crowded hallway in the school and people would run and hug the opposite wall. He would have horrible things written on his locker. Kids would move their desks away from his . . . . He felt like he had been at the center of a freak show. On the other hand, he felt that it was important for people to start learning what AIDS was really about—how you got it and how you didn't.

Ryan White died of complications from AIDS on April 8, 1990. But his legacy has been enormous. Federal legislation has been passed in his name. Innumerable "Ryan White" HIV prevention and treatment programs have been created across the United States. Since 1993 there has been an annual Ryan White National Youth Conference. Teens from all over the country gather to help those diagnosed with HIV and to disseminate information to help prevent the further spread of the disease.

More than a decade after Ryan died, Yamasaki encountered a young teacher, working in Croatia. When she was a teenager in Connecticut, this woman had read Yamasaki's stories about Ryan. "She had cut them out [and] put them in a book. She framed one of those pictures of Ryan [and noted] that it was Ryan's story that had inspired her to give more of herself to other people."

It is important to make a further point about the resilient self. If individuals are deprived of basic survival-related resources, such as cultural traditions or spiritual beliefs, they may come to rely even more on mastery or attachment to achieve a sense of security. For example, there are many disadvantaged children who pin all their hopes on becoming professional athletes. In essence, they are banking on their physical mastery to help them escape the downward spiral of drugs, violence, and social oppression.

Perhaps you saw the documentary *Hoop Dreams*? The film covered 6 years in the lives of William Gates and Arthur Agee, poor kids from the streets of Chicago who shared the same unwavering dream of playing professional basketball. Because of their talent, they were recruited to attend St. Joseph's High School, a perennial basketball powerhouse. However, this meant getting up every day before dawn to commute 90 minutes to a school that had very few other African Americans. Gates and Agee, as well as their families, were willing to sacrifice everything for their common dream.

Film critic Roger Ebert was particularly impressed with *Hoop Dreams*. He believed that the film transcended the topic of basketball; that it was essentially about "much larger subjects," including "a determination and resiliency that is a cause for hope." Retired basketball star Charles Barkley was invited to write the introduction for the book version of *Hoop Dreams*. Barkley grew up in poverty, nurturing his own dreams of playing professional basketball. Despite being undersized for his position, he became an all-star power-forward who was selected as one of the 50 greatest NBA players of all time. Reflecting on the significance of *Hoop Dreams*, Barkley mused "N-B-A; those three letters spell hope, escape, and promise."

## Building Resiliency

Do you see yourself as lacking in hopeful resiliency? Perhaps you view your survival or coping skills as less than adequate. Maybe you felt abandoned or betrayed as a child and now find it difficult to trust others. Perhaps you were not blessed with a calm, easygoing temperament. Alternatively, you may have received little spiritual guidance as a child. Is it too late to shore up your resiliency? Is it possible to break free from the thoughts, feelings, and attitudes impressed upon you during the first 5 or 6 years of your life?

Sigmund Freud suggested that "the child is the father of the man." But using Gandhi as an example, Erikson suggested that great individuals can rise above their early circumstances to become "their own fathers." In a sense they find a way to be reparented, resocialized, and respiritualized. Gandhi himself demonstrated a remarkable degree of personal transformation. As a child, according to Erikson's account, "He was not a good student," was "very shy," and often "became tearful when doubted." However, by the time he was in his 20s Gandhi was leading nonviolent protests for civil rights in South Africa. Returning to India, he focused his attention on the liberation of his country and equal treatment for members of different castes, including the so-called untouchables. Having been a sensitive and somewhat alienated youth, Gandhi had a special place in his heart for those treated as outcasts.

Over the next half-century, Gandhi would suffer numerous beatings and imprisonments. On many occasions he would undertake long fasts that led him to the brink of death. He did this not only to inspire his people but also to win particular concessions from the British. In one instance, he even vowed to fast "unto death" unless "the untouchables" were given the same basic rights as those from the upper castes.

Another impressive model of transformed resiliency is self-help guru Lucinda Bassett, the author of *From Panic to Power*, a bestseller about coping with fear and anxiety, and the cofounder of the Midwest Center for the Treatment of Stress, Anxiety, and Depression. Afflicted since childhood with agoraphobia (a fear of open spaces), she suffered for decades from constant worry, panic attacks, and fears of dying. Nevertheless, she found the inner strength, as well as the external resources, to transform herself into a national expert on the treatment of anxiety.

Personal transformations such as those of Gandhi and Bassett are impressive but by no means rare. Glenn Cunningham, whose legs were so badly burned in a fire when he was a child that doctors considered amputating them, became an Olympic champion who set world records in both the 800 meters and the mile. Angelo Siciliano as a scrawny teenager was teased and bullied, but by the age of 24, he had transformed himself into "Charles Atlas," the "world's most perfectly developed man."

People can, in short, develop resiliency at virtually any point in their lives. They can transform themselves to rise above their personal travails. How? By drawing on a few strategies in survival, incorporating a few lessons in coping, and toward those ends, finding the courage to overcome their fears and to choose growth and hope over stagnation and hopelessness. Senator John McCain, who survived 6 years in a POW camp in Vietnam, pointed out that if we "exercise courage," it tends to grow much like a muscle undergoing repeated strength training. Moreover, a vulnerable psyche can actually spur some individuals to incredible acts of heroism. To quote an old English proverb, sometimes "fear lends wings."

### Lessons in Trust and Care Recruitment

If your resiliency is being hampered by trust issues, then keep these five Rs in mind:

- Respect
- Research
- Risk
- Receptiveness
- Repetition

First, *respect* your individuality and your individual needs. Some people are extroverts who are predisposed to be more outgoing and assertive than others. Others are introverts who are shy and reserved. Both types can profit from social support as long as it is tailored to their particular personality style. Ultimately, depending on your type, you will most likely build trust and find caring attachments in the company of people with whom you feel most at ease. If you are extroverted, you will likely feel comfortable in larger networks comprised of relationships that are moderate in terms of emotional intensity. If you are introverted, you will likely want to cultivate a smaller circle of friends with whom you can form an intense bond.

Those who have frequently been let down by others may cease to believe there is still goodness in the world. If you have had disappointing relationships, do a little social experiment. Consider it your job to *research* and find examples of what writer Ann Herbert called "random kindness and senseless acts of beauty." Watch a feel-good movie or read a heartwarming tale from a compilation such as the *Chicken Soup for the Soul*. A great collection of inspiring personalities can be found in *Hope Dies Last*, a book by Studs Terkel. If you have access to the Internet, visit the *Random Acts of Kindness Foundation* Web site (http://www.actsofkindness. org).

If you are religiously or spiritually inclined, consider doing some research on the lives of great saints, prophets, or humanists. An excellent example of selfless giving was demonstrated by Eric Liddell, whose athletic prowess was featured in the film *Chariots of Fire*. Liddell was a Scottish track and field star who won an Olympic gold medal. A devout Christian, he once refused to compete in a high-profile race because it was held on a Sunday. Foregoing the opportunity for further fame and fortune, Liddell became a missionary. He traveled to China and risked his life to serve the poor and care for the wounded during World War II. Only 43 when he died in a Japanese POW camp, he left a legacy of unwavering spiritual integrity that has continued to inspire generations of children in both Europe and Asia.

Some *risk* may be necessary to lead a hopeful life. The philosopher Gabriel Marcel wrote that "openness allows hope to spread." An effective degree of openness involves measured *receptiveness* and discretion as you take the risk to develop trust in others. Think of your task in terms of establishing reasonable boundaries, those invisible yet palpable emotional barriers that exist between individuals. A poor attachment history can engender boundaries that are either too rigid or too loose. Aim to define your boundaries according to concepts of "symmetry" and "degree of relatedness."

To assure symmetry, match your level of emotional disclosure and commitment to others' capacity for sharing and intimacy. Meet them halfway. If you travel less than halfway, they may experience you as distant, but if you overstep your bounds, they may view you as intrusive. Also consider the nature of your relationship with others. Are you trying to connect with a friend, lover, parent, or child? Recall the advice of Confucius who proposed guidelines for maintaining different kinds of relationships. Also consider the wisdom offered in Tolstoy's *War and Peace*, when Andrei tells his friend Pierre, "You can't everywhere and at all times say everything that is on your mind." An excellent contemporary resource for cultivating better boundaries is *Your Perfect Right* by Robert Alberti and Michael Emmons.

It is important to *repeat* the steps of research and risk. Do not give up if you are disappointed at the outset. Keep on trying and you will discover that there are kind and generous individuals in the world who are willing to listen and even provide you with direct assistance. Regaining trust takes time. We speak of building and earning trust for a reason. It does not happen overnight. Remember the infant monkeys that Harry Harlow resocialized after they had been isolated from their mothers since birth? The period of their resocialization equaled or exceeded the duration of their initial deprivation. Like them, you need patience and perseverance to build hope.

### Lessons in Terror Management

If you suffer from constant worry, consider an all-in-one treatment package for reducing distress. Two popular options are Lucinda Bassett's anxiety management program and *Dialectical Behavior Therapy*. Bassett's home-study course involves a blend of traditional cognitive and behavioral strategies. Such techniques have been found to be particularly effective in the treatment of mood disorders. For further information, you can visit Bassett's Web site (http://www.stresscenter.com).

University of Washington psychologist Marsha Linehan was the originator of dialectical behavior therapy (DBT), which combines cognitive and behavioral techniques with Buddhist principles such as mindfulness, detachment, and acceptance. It has been used primarily in the treatment of borderline personality disorder, a condition in which individuals find it very hard to control their reactions to daily stressors and are prone to severe bouts of anxiety, depression, and rage. But DBT offers hope for anyone struggling with destructive emotions. If you are interested in learning more about DBT, visit http://www.brtc.psych.washington.edu/. This Web site includes information on the DBT approach, ongoing research, clinical trials, and contact information for locating a trained professional in your area. In addition, you may want to read psychologist Scott Spradlin's book, *Don't Let Your Emotions Run Your Life: How Dialectical Behavior Therapy Can Put You in Control.*

As an alternative to DBT or Bassett's program, you might consider selecting from a menu of self-regulation techniques that target your particular issues. Do you need help with intrusive thoughts? Are you debilitated by beliefs that leave you feeling anxious or depressed? Are you tense? Do you feel constantly overaroused, or wired?

If you want to explore the full range of possibilities for dealing with such problems, take a look at the *Relaxation and Stress Reduction Workbook*. This resource is a compilation of techniques prepared by psychologist Martha Davis and her colleagues. Among techniques to use in a tailored self-help program, we recommend *meditation* to control obsessive thoughts and *cognitive restructuring* to reduce feelings of anxiety or depression. *Progressive muscle relaxation* can decrease tension and *biofeedback* will help to stabilize an overly active nervous system. (Further information on these resources and techniques can be found in the Notes section of this book.) Alternatively, you can seek out a professional to assist you in incorporating one or more of these techniques into your daily life. In either case, commit yourself to spending at least 30 minutes a day for a few months. Have faith in the process and do not despair if your desired results take some time to materialize.

*Regular exercise* offers an effective, if underrated, means of reducing tension and worry. In fact, research has indicated that it can be far more beneficial and healthier for most individuals than standard medications for anxiety or depression. A good workout can increase the availability of phenylethylamine (PEA), a kind of natural antidepressant. Another byproduct of exercise is the release of beta-endorphins. These are neurotransmitters that bind to the same receptors in the brain as morphine, resulting in lowered anxiety and increased pain tolerance.

Aerobic activities, such as running, swimming, or cycling, promote deep breathing, which helps to maintain a toned vagus nerve. This particular cranial nerve travels all the way from your brain stem to your abdomen and is a critical factor in determining how well your heart and autonomic nervous system react to stress. If you suffer from stress-related pain and muscular tension, also consider some weight training, yoga, or tai chi. (We comment further on the importance of consistent physical activity in Chapters 15 and 16.)

But techniques alone will not bring you inner peace. An element of faith is also required. Note that Marsha Linehan incorporated Buddhist principles in her DBT approach. Similarly, psychologist Jon Kabat Zinn, an expert in pain management, included Buddhist and Hindu teachings in his mind–body program. Even Herbert Benson of the Harvard Medical School, who spent decades promoting the benefits of a no frills "relaxation response," later modified his technique to incorporate a "faith factor."

Each of the major spiritual traditions offers a particular set of lessons in terror management. For example, Buddhism might help you to achieve a deep level of meditative detachment. This can be of enormous benefit in controlling obsessive thinking and managing the suffering that accompanies physical pain. Nevertheless, Buddhism may prove inadequate for more mastery or attachment-oriented individuals because of its emphasis on letting go and the renunciation of desire. Thus, a mastery-oriented individual who hopes to reduce stress levels may be more drawn to Hindu practices such as yoga. Attachment-oriented Christians might turn to the Book of Proverbs for guidance or draw comfort from the 23rd Psalm: "although I walk through the valley of the shadow of death, I will fear no evil; for thou art with me."

Regardless of whether it is religiously based, your belief system must provide you with enough faith-based hope to persevere in this age of anxiety. We cannot emphasize enough the limitations of a purely technique-driven approach to terror management.

It is one thing to borrow a meditative principle here, and an inspiring verse there, but it is quite another to craft an overarching philosophy of life. If this has eluded you, commit yourself to more fully incorporating the lessons in this section with those of Chapter 8 concerning spiritual intelligence. As a human being with particular faith needs, you will benefit most by fashioning a belief system that gives you "a hope for all seasons."

### Lessons in Liberation

To emphasize: Hope is about options and possibilities. A hopeful mindset is liberating because it includes the belief that you can find a way out of any difficult predicament. To be a genuinely hopeful person, you must be persistent and creative. To fully expand your degrees of freedom, you need to draw on all of your resources, psychological and physical as well as spiritual.

Within the psychological domain, the development of alternative solutions is called *divergent thinking*. According to educator Edward De Bono, divergent thinking can be enhanced by adopting multiple perspectives. Below we present a streamlined version of his "six hat" approach. While some have applied this methodology to mastery-related issues, we envision its greatest hope benefit in the context of survival and liberation in particular:

- The White Hat: Gather information, assemble facts and figures, and outline options
- The Red Hat: Draw on your feelings and intuition to enhance your possibilities
- The Black Hat: Critically evaluate the flaws or weaknesses inherent in each option
- The Yellow Hat: Evaluate the strengths and opportunities associated with each option
- The Green Hat: Assess the growth potential of each option
- The Blue Hat: Stand back, look at the big picture, and organize your options

Many mental health professionals rely on a short-term model of treatment called solution-focused therapy (SFT). This type of intervention bears some resemblance to De Bono's six hats in that it encourages the development of alternative strategies for dealing with the seemingly irresolvable quandaries of life. Sometimes referred to as an approach based on "hope and respect," SFT presumes that clients possess adequate resources for facing their difficulties. Its general principles can be readily applied to a wide range of life situations:

- Consider that existing "strategies" may be part of the problem; not the solution
- Learn something from every previous mistake or unsuccessful strategy

- Start with your desired hope or endpoint in mind and work backward
- Recall any past successes that may be related to your desired endpoint
- Envision the simplest sign of progress toward a large and complex goal
- Carefully track your progress on a daily or weekly basis

In your search for alternatives, do not neglect your body. You need to find ways to keep yourself calm and relaxed. Highly anxious individuals, regardless of their age, intelligence level, or educational background, do poorly on measures of creativity. In contrast, a limber body and a mind flowing with possibilities may be viewed as two sides of the same coin.

The Taoist approach to mind–body health revolves around the concept of "chi" or vital energy. To ensure the continued flow of chi throughout the body, millions of Chinese rely on tai chi or qigong. These "moving meditations" are designed to keep the body "operating like a hinge" and to cultivate such mental qualities as creativity, openness, and responsiveness. You can derive similar benefits from regular exercise that includes stretching and running or walking. Make sure to balance your workouts with adequate rest and an occasional warm bath or massage.

Stimulate the right hemisphere, the side of your brain that is involved in more creative and holistic approaches to problem solving. One effective way of doing this is to listen to some classical music. For example, there is evidence that just a few minutes of Mozart or Beethoven can suffice to activate *right brain activity*. By comparison, listening to acid or hard rock is more likely to stimulate the more analytic *left brain*.

For many, spirituality provides the ultimate grounding for liberation beliefs. Creativity researcher David Perkins contrasted "plans deep down" with "plans up front." The former refers to underlying beliefs and blueprints for action, while the latter involves conscious thoughts and plans for the future. A religious or spiritual belief system can be likened to a plan deep down, providing individuals with a set of hopeful blueprints for coping with feelings of anxiety and terror. Because spiritual liberation runs deep, accessing it may require solitude, prayer, or meditation.

Muslims can draw on the Qur'an to learn that Allah "does not lay a burden on any soul except to the extent of its ability." The Rig Veda encourages Hindus to "let noble thoughts come from everywhere!" Christians have their own liberation mantra: "When God closes one door he opens another." Buddhism, the ultimate "salvation religion," offers an eight-fold path to "open the eyes," "bestow understanding," and cultivate "peace of mind."

A fascinating example of spiritually based liberation is the Iroquois tradition of mask making. Iroquois healers or shamans constitute an informal medical society whose members wear special wooden masks. Each mask represents a particular spirit or force of nature, endowing the wearer with the ability to heal the sick and protect the clan. Historians have discovered that whenever foreign intruders or a dreaded disease invaded Iroquois territory, there was a subsequent proliferation of new masks. In this way, the "deep liberation plan" of the Iroquois assured an unending supply of threat-specific protective forces that could be invoked whenever necessary.

## Lessons in Spiritual Integrity

The key to building spiritual integrity is discovering your *mission in life*. This will assure a life of meaning and purpose while also establishing an "incorruptible core," thus providing an enduring legacy of hope. Pastor Rick Warren's book, *The Purpose-Driven Life*, is a testament to these building blocks of spiritual integrity. According to him:

> [Without a mission] life has no significance or hope . . . Hope is as essential to your life as air or water . . . If you have felt hopeless, hold on! Wonderful changes are going to happen in your life as you begin to live it on purpose.

Although many of Warren's suggestions presumed the existence of a Christian "God in heaven," most can be used by followers of other faiths as well as by humanistic atheists. In fact, his basic tenets were remarkably similar to Erikson's prescriptions for a successful negotiation of the adult stages of life. Both Erikson and Warren proposed that human beings must commit themselves to a larger cause. For Warren, this higher purpose was "God's will"; for Erikson, it involved a "faithful participation" in one or more cultural institutions such as religion, philosophy, politics, or economics. For Warren, the ultimate goal is glorifying God; for Erikson, it is perpetuating a valued way of life. It is in this broad, philosophical sense that Erikson saw a convergence between his call for a kind of "grand generativity" and the Hindu dedication to "maintaining the world."

Why, ultimately, is having an enduring life mission so crucial? Warren stated that "we are made to last forever" and invoked "God's plan for our eternal place in Heaven." Erikson alluded to the more basic need for humanity to "transcend its mortal confinement in time and space." Alternatively, an evolutionary biologist might suggest that the quest for immortality is a byproduct of the reproductive impulses embedded in our genes. Spiritual leaders may point to an underlying theme found in every major faith, suggesting that each human being is created in the image of a greater intelligence that seeks to manifest itself in the world.

We might also consider the thoughts of Hegel, the last great "philosopher of the spirit." According to Hegel, there exists an *Absolute Spirit*, a universal force that seeks its own self-development as well as the integration and unity of everything in nature. The *absolute* may be conceived of as a form of potential energy that is realized in the creation of each individual. Every person is therefore a "finite-infinite composite," incorporating a "unique mortal coil" along with the eternal elements of "a vast and infinite absolute." Inspired by a sense of the absolute, individuals are prompted to develop and maintain enduring values and institutions. In turn, these institutions function to push forward the spiritual development of each individual. Enlisted as "spiritual co-developers" in the service of the *absolute*, people and institutions can be viewed as mutually reinforcing parts of a forward-moving "cosmic chain of hope."

Even Ernest Becker, the skeptical humanist, concluded that there has to be a life force bridging the individual will to live and the increasing expansion of the universe. Becker insisted that we must honor this unifying impulse as "knights of faith":

> Man must reach out for support to a dream, a metaphysic of hope that sustains him and makes his life worthwhile... Who knows what form the forward momentum of life will take in the time ahead or what use it will make of our anguished searching?... We must fashion something, and drop it into the confusion, make an offering... to the life force... the person who prides himself in being a "hard-headed realist" and refrains from hopeful action is really abdicating the human task.

Both Erikson and Warren suggested that an individual's contribution to a larger purpose must include both unique and shared elements. The unique component consists of your particular talents and efforts. The shared aspect is your sense of fellowship and participation in a community of like-minded individuals. In turn, a life mission also unites the particular and the universal as well as the present and future. Erikson preached of literally "giving yourself to the future," while Warren noted the importance of "contributing to one's generation." He insisted, "There is no greater epitaph... [than to] do the eternal and timeless in a contemporary and timely way... this is what the purpose driven life is all about."

A "mission" will be evident when you grasp the nature of your unique gifts and discover something larger, a cause beyond yourself that is worthy of spiritual invest-ment. Your faith can be entrusted in one or more centers of value, but these need not be religiously grounded. As we discussed in Chapter 8, they can be rooted in science and technology, the forces of nature, or some other nonreligious center. The only perquisite for success is a lasting commitment to a center of value that reflects your passions and worldview. If you are still searching for your particular life mission, try answering the following questions:

- What are your core values and beliefs?
- What are your unique skills or talents?
- What is your spiritual type?
- Which particular faith options appeal to you (e.g., religion, politics, science, etc.)?
- How are you going to contribute to your chosen center(s) of value?

In closing this chapter, it is worth considering the complementary roles that Buddhism and Hinduism might play in helping you to become a more resilient human being. Pearls of wisdom can certainly be extracted from each of the various spiritual traditions, but you might want to at least think like a Buddhist when focusing on the development of terror-management skills. Also adopting a Hindu perspective may help you to craft a life mission by leading you toward greater appreciation for existing institutions and fostering a deeper understanding of your stake in their continued existence.

# Twelve

## FROM FEAR TO HOPE: PEACE IN TROUBLED WATERS

Awareness is the path of immortality.

—Buddha

Fear, like anxiety, can be overwhelming and draining. Some individuals are able to contain their fears. Although mindful of the dangers that exist in the world, they nevertheless manage to keep things in perspective. We might call them the "hope-buffered," those stout of heart who refuse to yield to their fears. Others are less fortunate; fear dominates their lives and exhausts their resources. In *The Fall of the House of Usher*, Edgar Allan Poe unveiled a character utterly consumed by the "work of worry."

> He could wear only garments of a certain texture; the odors of all flowers were oppressive; his eyes were tortured by even a faint light . . . there was little which did not inspire him with horror . . . I found him a bound slave. [He said to me] "I shall perish . . . I shall be lost. I dread the events of the future . . . I shudder at the thought of any, even the most trivial incident . . . the period will sooner or later arrive when I must abandon life and reason together, in some struggle with the grim phantasm of FEAR."

In the previous chapter, we mentioned the conditions that the *Diagnostic and Statistical Manual of Mental Disorders* labels as anxiety disorders. These various conditions are often comorbid, meaning that one or more types of anxiety disorder can occur in the same individual. Generalized anxiety, for example, is rarely an isolated condition. It tends to coexist with other problems such as panic attacks or posttraumatic stress disorder. When this happens, an insidious bundle of terror develops, held together by a vague sense that something awful is going to happen. Afraid of drowning in pools of emotional quicksand, individuals can no longer afford to hope and begin to divert all of their attention toward anxiety management.

Fears can also multiply. This is particularly likely when stressors fall upon the psyche too rapidly, like a set of cascading dominoes. Imagine the potential fears and losses that may envelop a young child after the death of a parent. The deceased may have been the family's primary wage earner. A reduced income might force the family to move to a poorer neighborhood. The child may lose contact with friends, neighbors, and other potential hope providers. The surviving parent may become mired in a severe and prolonged bout of depression. The child may overidentify with the distressed parent and develop a fear of the future.

In this chapter, we provide strategies for dealing with a variety of debilitating fears. The key to overcoming them does not lie in merely trying to reduce or eliminate them. If you truly want to be free of your greatest fears, think in terms of transformation rather than exorcism. The mind, like anything in nature, abhors a vacuum. A great fear must be supplanted by a great hope.

Think also in terms of confronting your fears piece by piece. In Sun Tzu's ancient classic, *The Art of War*, a military leader faced with a superior force is advised to take a "divide-and-conquer" strategy. Similarly, in higher mathematics, complex equations are dissembled into more manageable subsets using a "divide-and-conquer algorithm." Likewise, a bundle of terror can be reduced by dealing with fears one at a time. This philosophy of separation was exquisitely conveyed in an episode of the television drama, *Kung Fu*. Master Caine, the ever-wise Shaolin priest, drew on his Zen Buddhist roots to reassure a frightened acquaintance: "I too have many fears . . . small, fragmented, tiny terrors can be examined. They can be held in the hand, and broken. Only when all fears come together, will they become overwhelming."

In a divide-and-conquer fashion then, we will now examine each of the fears that tend to plague many people. Learning about the sources of these fears can help you to safely navigate through the dangers that lie around you. And greater *self-awareness* can help you to begin the process of repairing your *inner vulnerabilities* that give rise to one or more of these fears.

## Fear of Hope

According to Thomas Aquinas, "hope is contrary to fear" because the former involves an imagined "future good," while the latter is based on an envisioned "future evil." While fear does not always lie on the other side of hope, it happens enough to merit your attention. If you are a runner who hopes to win a particular race, it would be natural for you to fear losing or coming in last. Parents may bring a cancer-stricken child for chemotherapy, hoping for a cure, but they also may fear that the medication will not work or even make matters worse. In such situations, we would be hard-pressed to argue with Spinoza who claimed, "there is no hope unmingled with fear, and no fear unmingled with hope."

The element of fear that invades hope cannot be totally vanquished. There are no guarantees in striving, loving, or living. Some individuals cope with life's uncertainties by crafting an illusion of total optimism, but they are often unable to move forward when obstacles and calamities appear. Others are so afraid to take any kind of risk that they simply give up. They are defeated from the start. Neither blind optimists nor those paralyzed with fear demonstrate much hope. Indeed, they are afraid of it.

Hoping is based on faith as well as reason and openness. Hope requires trust as well as a form of courage that permits full awareness of our past, present, and future possibilities. To borrow a concept from psychologist Stephen Wolinksy, the truly hopeful person can exist free of self-induced "trances." As we see things, individuals may choose to live in one of three planes of existence, two of them appear to involve the kind of trance-like states that Wolinsky calls the "glue" that binds negative symptoms together. The most superficial level of existence is characterized by a haze of denial or naïve optimism; when that erodes many individuals slip down to a second-level trance defined by constant doubt and fear. Only at the third, deepest level of awareness does true hope emerge, fully engaged with the entire spectrum of life events and unencumbered by trances of false positivity or paralyzing fear.

The most crippling fears are those that threaten the motives underlying hope. As you will learn in the following discussion, fears associated with achieving success, being in the world, or dying may derive from mastery concerns and difficulties in attachment and terror management. Both the fear of harm and the fear of loss can involve disruptions in the needs for attachment and survival. No matter what their cause, however, these fears can be conquered and replaced with hope.

## Fears of Failure or Success

A first-year college student had battled with depression for most of his life. Despite a high IQ, he struggled to complete his schoolwork. Frustrated and confused, he made an appointment at the university counseling center. He described problems with time management and a "personality conflict" with a certain professor. He also revealed a very stormy relationship with his "controlling father."

This young man was simultaneously afraid of failure and *afraid of success*. He engaged in various forms of self-sabotage, including procrastinating in his schoolwork and battling with his professors. He unwittingly invited criticism and additional resistance from his father, who carried his own burden of abandoned dreams and lack of personal career fulfillment. The student's father once had aspirations of becoming an airline pilot but was forced to give up his plans when his own father fell sick. The son's difficulties in college pointed to a profound identification with his dad's thwarted aims.

The fears of failure or success tend to be submerged in the deep unconscious. It has long been observed that many individuals with great talent fail to realize their potential. Some are afraid to commit the time or energy necessary to develop their skills, while others shy away from any form of evaluation or competition. Some may be afraid that if they make their best effort, the results will be less than satisfactory, ending all doubt about their true lack of ability. They would prefer to preserve some glimmer of tainted hope for themselves and others that, if they had only tried harder, they would have succeeded.

There are a variety of factors that can underlie a fear of failure. A child may be subjected to an inordinate amount of criticism from parents, teachers, or coaches, quickly eroding any existing self-confidence. Sometimes demands are placed on individuals before they are emotionally or physically ready, leaving them feeling perpetually vulnerable to failure. Some may, by virtue of their temperament, find it difficult to withstand any form of public scrutiny. Some may feel overwhelmed by the pressure of representing their family, gender, or race, while others from humble origins may find themselves lost in uncharted waters, afraid to venture where no parent, sibling, or friend has ever gone.

As a matter of public consciousness, fear of success surfaced in the latter half of the twentieth century, during the struggle for equal rights by women and minorities. It was in this context that psychologist Matina Horner published her classic study, indicating that a significant number of college women remained ambivalent about succeeding in higher education. Horner suggested that such women might be unwilling to risk alienating power-sensitive males or their more traditional female counterparts. Moreover, according to Horner, these "conflicted achievers" might intentionally underperform and sometimes even engage in unwitting acts of self-sabotage. Later research indicated that other factors such as parental values, sex-role identification, and self-presentation strategies were often more important than fear of success in determining a woman's level of aspiration. Nevertheless, Horner's research had a profound impact, raising the consciousness of an entire generation of women.

Fear of success can also result from any set of restrictive racial or class-based norms that affect the motives underlying hope. For example, a young man from an economically impoverished neighborhood may deliberately underachieve if he believes that breaking new ground will lead to ostracism from his peer group (attachment) or to physical violence against him or his loved ones (survival).

Sometimes the fear of success derives from not wanting to replace a valued family member who has occupied a special niche. This can happen when a sibling dies, especially if he or she had a special talent or was somewhat precocious. In an unconscious effort to preserve the place of the deceased, surviving siblings may feel covert pressure to undermine their own mastery efforts.

### Hope for Fulfillment

The antidote for fear of success or failure is *hope for fulfillment*. By "fulfillment" we mean the actualization of your potential in whatever manner or direction is right for you. This is consistent with the values-oriented approach to mastery emphasized in Chapter 10. No one can or should define what "success" or "fulfillment" specifically means for you. Only you can decide that, and only you can transform your fears of success or failure into hope for fulfillment. This transformation is a multilayered process involving *improved self-awareness, detachment from inhibiting forces, finding supportive others,* and *lowering performance-related and other anxiety*.

Very often the fear of success or failure is associated with expectations and demands that have been imposed by parents or significant others. Try to separate what you really want from what others want *for* or *from you*. With respect to certain life choices, you may ultimately decide that some types of individual success are not worth the interpersonal cost. But first clarify, for yourself, who wants what and why. To realize your hope for fulfillment, find a supporting cast—family, friends, or others who understand and accept your goals and can support you in achieving them.

In addition, some individuals who fear success or failure are likely to suffer from high levels of double-anxiety: they are generally apprehensive and are particularly uncomfortable in performance-related contexts. Performance anxiety can arise when you have not clarified your fulfillment needs. Ask yourself: What will make you feel genuinely happy, complete, or at peace? Is your heart or sense of self at odds with the success scripts imposed by others? Perhaps you already know the answers to these questions, but generalized anxiety is making it difficult for you to pursue your bliss. Go back to the terror-management suggestions described in Chapter 11. Replace your work of worry with a calming and clearing routine that includes some aerobic exercise and meditative practice.

If you seek additional clarity of purpose and greater stillness of mind, consider incorporating Zen Buddhist principles into your daily routine. Particularly effective in helping those struggling with fears of success or failure, Zen principles have been applied to nearly every human endeavor from sports and martial arts to business and gardening. Proponents of this philosophy include Thich Nhat Hanh, the Vietnamese monk who helped spread the practice of mindfulness among Westerners, and NBA basketball coach Phil Jackson.

Individuals plagued by fears of success or failure are often divided against themselves as a result of trying to meet conflicting family, social, or gender expectations. Zen facilitates a fusion of mind, body, and spirit. In aiming toward "satori" or enlightenment, one encounters "kensho" or the "experience of seeing into one's true nature." Many Westerners are impatient and narrowly focused on results, a mindset that can seriously hamper the development of true mastery. In contrast, Zen is a philosophy of process and self-discipline. It uses a half dozen practice-related terms to capture a full spectrum of intentions and attitudes that may either facilitate or detract from an individual's quest for fulfillment. For example, it encourages a selfless approach, which can counter the constant flow of negative self-talk (inner-directed criticisms and doubts) that is associated with fears of success or failure. By removing the ego, one eliminates the object of distraction, freeing the mind and body to perform at a much higher level.

For inspiration, you might want to read *Zen in the Art of Archery* by German philosopher Eugen Herrigel. Considered a classic of spiritual literature, Herrigel wrote this book while spending 6 years in Japan under the tutelage of a master archer. At one point he confessed to his teacher, "When I have to draw the bow ... unless the shot comes at once I can't endure the tension ... So I must let loose whether I want to or not." The master replied, "The right shot at the right moment does not come because you do not let go of yourself. You must wait for fulfillment, not brace yourself for failure."

## Fear of Being

A man plagued by mysterious foot and hand problems was referred to a psychotherapist. As a result of his intolerable foot pain, he rarely left his house. His hand condition was making it impossible for him to succeed as an architect. The therapist outlined the various modalities offered at her clinic, including biofeedback, cognitive therapy, and hypnosis. As each treatment option was mentioned, the client sarcastically interjected: "Been there, done that."

When the therapist asked the man about his hopes for treatment, he angrily snapped back, "I don't believe in hope. I prefer the Buddhist approach to life. I don't think about hope." In essence, this man was *afraid of being*. His difficulty in leaving home was a metaphor for his inability to go forward in life. He lacked a sense of freedom and responsibility. He mistakenly sought refuge in Buddhism, believing (incorrectly) that it would eliminate the "burden" of hoping.

The fear of being is rooted in the avoidance of choices and responsibilities. Existential philosophers, as well as humanists such as Eric Fromm, have suggested that many individuals harbor a "fear of freedom." Endowed with an enormous capacity for planning and self-reflection, human beings are the only creatures that can actively participate in their own self-development. This is too frightening for some people who view freedom as a curse rather than a blessing. They cannot handle the responsibility that comes from committing themselves to a particular way of life, a mate, or a career. They cannot find it within themselves to make choices, to say yes to one possibility and no to another.

The fear of being is similar in many ways to the fears of success or failure. All three are associated with feelings of guilt and anxiety. Each can effectively undermine the development of an individual's potential. Each may be triggered by the fear that some form of rejection will follow if the individual moves forward in life. Each can lead to emotional paralysis unless one is prepared to rise above prescribed roles and responsibilities.

Despite their similarities, the fear of being is usually more insidious than fears associated with either success or failure. The fear of being represents a more thorough "straight-jacketing" of the mastery motive. The developmental disruption is more extensive, often involving disturbed attachment experiences, and the damage occurs earlier in childhood, usually before the age of 6. This is when virtues such as will and purpose, the prerequisites for truly being in the world, are acquired. By comparison, the fears of failure or of success are more likely to spring from problems in later childhood, when a sense of competence must be developed both within and outside the realm of family life.

### Hope for Autonomy

The antidote for a fear of being is the *hope for autonomy*. According to psychologist James Averill, "autonomy" is the capacity for "self-rule" as well as "the ability to make choices and pursue divergent goals." These conditions can be met if individuals act on the basis of their own chosen principles rather than those imposed by others. Such principles should be broad enough to guide various types of behavior, yet flexible enough to allow for growth and change.

As with "hoping for fulfillment," the road to autonomy begins with self-awareness. You need to carefully assess your values and priorities before you can arrive at a set of life principles. Are you really committed to autonomy? Are you ready to accept the responsibility for creating your own life? What will you have to give up in the process? Are you willing to absorb those losses? For more on this topic, refer back to the section on values and mastery in Chapter 10.

Some might argue that the task of establishing principles should be left solely to the individual. After all, the whole point of autonomy is to foster self-rule. However, for those who have tasted little freedom a bit of inspiration can go a long way. Role models who have blazed an innovative path can inspire others to consider new and more productive courses of action. If you follow Averill's advice and think in general terms, it will be easier for you to incorporate for your own purposes the strategies that others have developed.

Create a list of well-known people you admire. Try to identify the qualities they embody. Maybe you can find a book about them in your local library or get more information via the Internet. Descriptions of courageous historical figures can also be inspiring, especially if they chronicle the lives of individuals who displayed great integrity while challenging popular opinion. If you enjoy classic literature, read one of Emerson's essays such as "Self-reliance" or "Character." The latter begins with the boldest of pronouncements: "The sun set; but set not his hope: Stars rose; his faith was already up."

If you are religiously or spiritually oriented, you may want to consult the Christian *Book of Proverbs* or *The Sayings of Confucius*. Many of the "suras" found in the Qur'an offer counsel for dealing with doubters and hypocrites. The seventeenth sura, entitled "Night Journey," resembles a modern role-playing exercise, juxtaposing anticipated attacks on one's faith with carefully reasoned rebuttals. The forty-eighth sura is appropriately called "Victory." It promises that those who align with Allah will be like "seedlings" planted by a "great sower," growing "stout and straight" toward the achievement of a "mighty reward."

The Hindu *Upanishads* is another excellent source for developing character and inner strength. Known as the "wisdom of the gurus," this collection includes short books that deal specifically with the realization of one's *Atman* (or inner divinity). In particular, the Katha and Mundaka selections focus on the relationship between the false, or scripted self, and the "Atman," which is one's true source of power and autonomy. For example, in the Mundaka it is written: "Like two birds perched on the same tree, intimate friends, the ego and the Atman, dwell in the same body. The former [suffers] . . . the sour fruits of life, while the later looks on with detachment."

If you want to balance these sober renderings with a more lighthearted approach, obtain a copy of *All I Really Need to Know I Learned in Kindergarten* by Robert Fulghum. If your fear of being is especially deep rooted, you may want to invest in a more extended period of self-examination. Psychotherapy is also a possibility. If you enjoy process and assisted reflection, then seek out a therapist who offers a client-centered approach or stresses an existential perspective. On the other hand, if you are more skills oriented, seek out a cognitive-behavioral therapist or one who employs a solutions-focused approach. Both of these treatment options emphasize active coping and the development of specific behavioral strategies. (See Notes for more information.)

Ultimately, it is most important to feel fully involved in the process of choosing the principles that will guide your life. This truth is beautifully expressed in Kahlil Gibran's *The Prophet*. Asked to discuss the nature of good and evil, the great sage replied: "You are good when you are one with yourself . . . You are good when you are fully awake in your speech . . . You are good when you walk to your goal firmly . . . with bold steps."

## Fear of Harm

A survivor of sexual abuse told her therapist that she was grateful for two things, her 9-5 job and her computer. "If I didn't have these things in my life, I don't know what I would do." She confided, "My current job is beneath my skill level, but it gives me a secure income and a solid retirement plan." She loved "surfing the web." "Thank God I have unlimited Internet access. It lets me see what's going in the world from the comfort of my own home." Despite having some strengths, she complained of spiraling anxiety and chronic insomnia, adding "I never feel rested or at peace with myself."

This woman was *afraid of harm*. As an abuse survivor, she experienced the world as unsafe and had lost her faith in other people as well as the future. She settled for a job that was beneath her because it guaranteed safety and symbolized something she could "rest on." The Internet allowed her to connect with the world from a safe distance while distracting her from unsettling thoughts about the future. As psychiatrist Judith Herman pointed out, trauma survivors may continue to live under a constant "threat of annihilation," a cloud of vigilance that leads to a narrowed and diminished existence.

As noted in the last chapter, chronic anxiety is one of the most prevalent psychological disorders in the world, affecting tens of millions around the globe. The common denominator that cuts across a variety of anxiety-based conditions is a fear of future harm. Posttraumatic stress disorder (PTSD) is the most dramatic example of an anxiety-driven adaptation to harm-based fears. Situations that can precipitate PTSD include war experiences, natural disasters, kidnappings, robberies, and physical or sexual abuse. Other debilitating harm-based fears include *focused fears*, which encompass panic attacks, phobias, and various obsessions and compulsions "designed" to keep imagined threats under control. The underlying cause of focused fears is typically a combination of predisposing factors, including individual temperament, family coping style, and a history of early loss or serious illness. There may or may not be a history of trauma. *Unfocused fears* are the multiple fears and vague but pervasive sense of dread that characterize generalized anxiety. But across all forms of anxiety, the underlying experience is one of dread and foreboding.

In its most crippling and hopeless form, anxiety evolves into a fear of fear. This is often a continuing problem for trauma victims who would otherwise be able to secure their liberation. According to psychiatrist Lenore Terr, these individuals experience a profound sense of learned helplessness when repeated trauma exhausts their ability to regulate fear. Terr suggested, "The sensation of being reduced to nothing is such a hideous feeling that the victim seeks never to experience that sensation again. Fear of further fear . . . keeps victims from trying to escape even when their chances seem good."

### Hope for Peace

Those who fear harm are desperately in need of serenity. While they long to be free of worry and conflict, many have abandoned any hope for peace. Indeed they are always prepared for the worst when it comes to matters of loving, striving, or securing their long-term survival. For those living in countries besieged by war, or ravaged by disease, there are the added presumptions of oppression and an early death.

There is in fact hope for all those who suffer from some form of chronic anxiety. The most effective interventions for most nontraumatic (focused or unfocused) fears combine cognitive-behavioral therapy (CBT) with some limited use of medication. CBT involves retraining the way you think about yourself, the world, and the future. Moreover, it provides techniques for actively coping with anxiety-provoking situations. If you suffer from a phobia, generalized anxiety or panic attacks, seek out a mental health professional who can provide CBT. In some cases, a therapist may recommend a medication evaluation. If medication is suggested, you ought to think about it as a complement to CBT rather than as an alternative solution. By combining these two forms of intervention, you are more apt to effect long-term improvements as opposed to merely achieving a temporary state of relaxation. To boost your level of trait hope (hopefulness), you must do more than simply recharge your brain chemistry. You must develop new ways of thinking about, and responding to, the inevitable stresses of life.

There has also been tremendous progress in understanding and treating trauma. Drawing on the seminal work of psychiatrist Judith Herman, many trauma centers now employ a three-phase treatment program. *These phases can be construed as "sequential hope work," geared toward a systematic repair of the survival, attachment, and mastery systems.* During the first phase, the focus is on care recruitment and rebuilding survival-based trust. Herman described the relationship between the therapist and survivor as a "collaborative" process involving a "working alliance." As part of their "hope work," clients must reestablish or learn new methods of terror management and self-care.

In the second phase of treatment, survivors are encouraged to recall and repeat their story to a therapist or hope provider, who offers moral solidarity. They also share their experiences with a sympathetic group. This process allows the survivor to integrate and make sense of the trauma experience. Equally important, both the therapist and the group align themselves morally and spiritually with the survivor. By being available and fully present, they aim to establish a hopeful imprint upon the survivor's sense of self.

This second stage is often the longest and most difficult to negotiate. Struggling to assimilate and incorporate the full meaning of the trauma, some survivors experience a profound sense of helplessness and hopelessness. To restore hope, talk therapy may need to be supplemented by other techniques. Given the compelling evidence that highly traumatic memories may be stored differently in the brain than memories of normal life events, it may be necessary to include some form of mind–body therapy, such as calming hypnotic techniques, massage, exercise, or specially crafted breathing exercises.

In the third phase, the survivor must reengage with the world and establish bridges of intimacy. Similar to our hope-centered notion of shared or mediated control, this reengagement requires "a convergence of mutual support with individual autonomy." Survivors must learn to forgive and turn their attention to the future, including performing tasks of generativity that are directed toward the care and protection of others.

For survivors, a capstone experience often revolves around the realization of spiritual integrity within the framework of a life mission. For example, Herman quoted a survivor of domestic abuse who made the decision to become a district attorney. Describing her passion for prosecuting cases of domestic violence, she stated, "I want women to have some sense of hope, because I can remember how terrifying it was to not have any hope—the days I felt there was no way out. I feel very much like that's part of my mission."

## Fear of Loss

A woman in her early 40s was being treated for a longstanding hoarding problem. Never married, she occupied one floor of a large Victorian house owned by her sister and brother-in-law. Most of her rooms were filled with faded newspapers, old notebooks, and outdated grocery store circulars. An excellent student throughout her life, she had earned an MBA from an elite business school yet seemed unable to hold on to the most menial of jobs. Everything about her, from her slow gait and tired speech to her drooping eyelids, suggested a profound sense of despair. Nevertheless, she was highly resistant to making changes, fearing that "I might lose my true self." She wanted to stop bringing more "useless things" into her home, but she had no intention of discarding what was already there.

This woman was *afraid of loss*. A highly sensitive individual, she had internalized the wounds and sorrows of her entire family. At an unconscious level, she was striving to offset her fear of loss (and theirs) by holding on to as many material things as possible. Newspapers and old magazines were especially prized because they represented written records of the past. Grocery circulars highlighting comfort foods offered a semblance of the nurturance she sought but felt she had never received. Her fierce hold on the past was also reflected in her unwillingness to shed unhealthy aspects of her personality.

Losses are a painful but inevitable fact of life. There are *physical losses* such as the death of a loved one. There are *symbolic losses*, including losing one's reputation or role in society. In addition, there are *secondary losses* that might accompany a physical or symbolic loss. These include a financial setback after the death of a spouse or decreased social interaction following the loss of a job.

The fear of loss refers to the difficulties associated with *anticipatory grief* as well as the burden of coping that follows. If a loss is anticipated, such as the imminent death of a friend or loved one, individuals may find it hard to concentrate on anything else. They may experience nightmares, blame themselves, avoid others, and even begin to question their religious or spiritual beliefs. Following a loss, the grieving person may fear that the pain will never subside, that life will never again be meaningful, that the deceased will be permanently erased from memory.

Therese Rando, a clinical psychologist specializing in counseling the bereaved, noted that although death has always been a part of the human experience, individuals are less prepared to deal with it today: "A hundred years ago you would not have needed to read [a self-help book]... The typical American family had strong emotional ties... They had deep roots in their community... they observed how others coped with grief and mourning... there were strong religious beliefs that helped families cope... Rituals and ceremonies provided support and gave the family direction."

## Hope for Restoration

During the second half of the twentieth century, the dominant approach to bereavement counseling was based on the notion of "grief work." Central to its hypothesis is the task of letting go and moving on. Grieving individuals had to directly confront their loss. They needed to feel the pain, then emotionally detach themselves from the deceased, and finally move on to establish a new life for themselves. In contrast, those who experienced relatively little distress, or refused to let go, were thought to be in denial and at risk for long-term harm.

It was not until the early 1990's that some scientists and practitioners began to seriously challenge the grief work hypothesis. James Averill was one of the first psychologists to express concern that grief was being increasingly viewed as a disease rather than a natural human emotion. Danish investigator Margaret Stroebe noted that venting, detaching, and moving on were primarily a twentieth-century invention. Some lay people have also objected to the idea that letting go and moving on after a loss is a necessary step to healing. In *Give Sorrow Words: A Father's Passage Through Grief*, writer Tom Crider wrote about the loss of his only child in a fire. Gretchen was just 21 years old. According to Crider,

> What horrifies me is the suspicion that, like the uncaring world, I, too, might one day go on living as though nothing had happened... something very strong in me seems to not want to "recover" because as long as I stay aware of [her] absence, in a way I am keeping [her] alive in my inner being.

Denise, a young woman tortured by her own unresolved grief, was so moved by Crider's story that she wrote him a letter, which began with a Spanish proverb: "Traveler, there is no path. Paths are made by walking." Denise confessed to Crider that she had been unable to gain much solace from either traditional self-help books or her religious faith. Nevertheless, she was "open to that which may indeed put all this right some day... hopeful that some great and benevolent force that is beyond my comprehension will reveal itself upon my own death... maybe I do have a God after all... his name is HOPE."

Fortunately, there *are* some basic bereavement strategies in the here and now that offer real *hope for restoration*. They can help you to transform your relationship with the deceased, solidifying "a place of hope" within your heart and mind. They provide a means for restoring your connections with surviving loved ones and other members of your community. Equally important, these guidelines will help you to restore your emotional and physical equilibrium. Instead of thinking about the following suggestions as grief work, you might want to frame them as guidelines for hope work.

*Give yourself options.* Grieve in your own way. You are not obligated to go through prescribed stages of grief. You do not have to detach or move on. You are not even obligated to feel devastated. In fact, you may even discover a new source of hope and inspiration in the midst of your grief. Clearly, there are different meanings attached to various losses (e.g., the death of a spouse versus the loss of a child). Remember that hope is a bridge, capable of transporting one from a tunnel of darkness into a dawn of light. However, only you can fathom the kind of bridge that will restore your particular loss.

*Build two bridges.* The bridge work of bereavement is a psychological balancing act, involving an alternating investment in experiencing and coping. First, there is a definite need for some emotion-focused grief work, including dealing with the pain in whatever manner is best for you (e.g., crying, solitude, or venting your anger). If you are struggling with pent-up feelings, an excellent resource is Mary Jane Moffat's book, *In the Midst of Winter*. Designed to "serve as an axe for the frozen sea within," the book includes many of the greatest literary passages on grief, with selections from Shakespeare, Emily Dickinson, Pearl Buck, and Walt Whitman.

*Gradually try to reestablish your old routines.* However, it may also be necessary for you to develop some new skills. This is your second bridge to build. For example, the deceased may have been the one responsible for home repairs or managing the finances, and so you may now need to learn to handle those tasks yourself. For inspiration you might read the chapter on work in Kahlil Gibran's *The Prophet.* "To be idle is to become a stranger unto the seasons and to step out of life's procession."

*Create an inner presence.* Designate a certain time during the week, or a particular place in your home, to reflect on the meaning and impact of your relationship with the deceased. It might be comforting to invoke images of warm embraces, acts of expressed forgiveness, or moments of shared laughter. Maybe you will be able to more fully grasp what made your connection unique or special. It is natural, though, to experience moments of longing and regret in the midst of your reflections, especially in the first 6 months following a loss.

*Create an outer presence.* Organize and restore photographs of the deceased. Arrange for a plaque to be made, honoring his or her contributions and unique characteristics. Consider fashioning a memorial quilt for display or even to wrap around yourself. Many readers are probably aware of the AIDS memorial quilt, which by 2007 included more than 90,000 names and weighed more than 50 tons! For your own quilt, go on http:// www.originalquilts.com to get design ideas by reviewing dozens of pictures of handmade memorial quilts that individuals fashioned from clothing and photographs of their loved ones.

*Devise hope rituals.* If you are religiously oriented, consider having an annual memorial service. Light a candle in your place of worship. Provide flower arrangements for the altar. Marines honor fallen comrades during a dinner ceremony with designated place settings. A red rose is fixed on each plate, the glasses are turned upside down, and the chairs are tilted into the table.

Perhaps you will reconnect with your loved one by traveling to a favorite vacation spot or a restaurant that the two of you frequented on special occasions. Try to integrate these preservation efforts into your life in a manner that will also give you the opportunity to maintain a daily exchange of hope with family and friends. In other words, balance your vertical bridge work across time with lateral bridge-work across generations of the living.

*Make a public offering.* Consider supporting an organization devoted to preventing the illness that may have claimed the life of your loved one. You may even be able to gather community support for your efforts. For example, many individuals recruit sponsors to support their participation in such events as a statewide AIDS Walk, the Alzheimer's Association Memory Walk, or the Susan G. Komen Breast Cancer Foundation's "Race for a Cure." Former baseball player Mike Timlin, who lost his mother to Lou Gehrig disease, donated $500 to the ALS foundation every time he pitched. His team matched each contribution. In addition, you could offer support to any cause in the name of your loved one, regardless of whether its mission is related to the circumstances of his or her death. Whether planting a tree, giving funds to restore a community landmark, or establishing a scholarship fund, try to capture the spirit of the deceased.

*Pace yourself.* It is important to take regular breaks as you grieve. Psychologist Margaret Stroebe gathered some impressive data suggesting that individuals process a loss much better if they "oscillate." This refers to switching back and forth between grieving and focusing on the resumption of normal life activities. You need to interweave your mourning with breaks for work, socializing, and even play.

*Cut yourself some slack in reaching particular goals.* As with recovery from an operation or illness, it is normal to feel better one day and worse the next. You cannot rush the healing process. Keep in mind that there are typical risks associated with one's gender. Men frequently do not devote enough attention to the emotional side of grieving, whereas women are more apt to put off the tasks of daily living. For many people, however, the most intense phases of grieving pass relatively quickly. In his studies dealing with the temporal aspects of loss, psychologist James Pennebaker found that many individuals experience considerable relief after about 6 months, while for most, it takes another year or so to integrate the loss and shift from grieving to fond remembrance.

*Get support.* Sharing your grief with others can be extremely helpful. Because loss is one of the few truly universal experiences, it is very likely that someone will know firsthand a bit of valuable coping wisdom that he or she can pass on to you. You may even derive invaluable technical or financial advice for settling an estate or getting back on your feet. However, the most important benefit of having social support may be in facilitating your search for meaning and providing assurance of your loved one's continuing presence in the world. British sociologist Tony Walter wrote about the importance of reaching out to others in order to develop a stronger and fuller "sense of the deceased." He recommended sharing stories about your loved one with friends and family, as well as with other individuals who were well acquainted with the deceased, in order to enlarge your understanding of his or her place in the lives of others.

Recall from Chapter 5, the beautiful Native American funeral rite entitled *Speech for the Removal of Grief*. Each participant came forth to pay homage to the deceased by offering an anecdote that captured some vital aspect of his or her personality. By memorializing the impact of the deceased on various members of the community, the group affirmed that this individual truly made a difference in the world. It assured family and friends that the legacy of their loved one was safe and would continue to be felt in the presence of the group.

The funeral rites of the African Ifa rival those of Native Americans in terms of organized family and community involvement. To express their gratitude for being brought into *this world*, the offspring of the deceased help prepare the body for life in the *next world*. Family and friends provide cloth to wrap the body, the amount and quality of the material presumably linked to the degree of respect afforded to the deceased. After the burial, family and friends make contributions for several days of feasting and celebration. Musicians are hired to play throughout the village. The songs and instruments are carefully chosen to reflect the personality and tastes of the deceased.

If this kind of funerary support strikes a chord with you, make an effort to learn more about the practices of other attachment and survival cultures. For example, Jews sit shiva at home for seven days. During this period visitors come to pay their respects, share food, and often join in prayers. After a death, Quakers gather in their meeting house. They invite members as well as nonmembers to join in a spiritual retrospective, to rise and speak about the deceased individual when they are "moved by the spirit."

## Fear of Death

A 44-year-old salesman tried to convince himself that everything in his life was just fine. He constantly touted his career achievements and "wonderful" family life. In truth, his marriage was falling apart and he had become completely alienated from his children. He sought out a therapist when he found himself "unable to shake" increasingly intrusive and debilitating thoughts.

His obsessive preoccupations began on a business trip when he found himself fixated on signs that indicated a 45 mile per hour speed limit. For days he was unable to get the thought out of his mind that he might die at the age of 45. While driving over a bridge, he was struck by the fear that he might never again cross over that expanse. This man was *afraid of death*. Paradoxically, when he attempted to suppress the fear, it seeped into every corner of his life. As his thoughts grew darker, he even felt anxious in the presence of an evening sunset. His therapist asked him, "Do you hate sunsets because they represent the 'death of the day,' a reminder of your own mortality?"

What human beings fear most is death. They will do just about anything to keep it at bay. The ancient Egyptians developed an entire culture around their quest for immortality. They fashioned the great pyramids to serve as "resurrection machines" and oriented the Pharaoh's burial chamber to face a constellation of stars known as the "indestructibles." When the *Tibetan Book of the Dead* appeared in the eighth century, its tenets were already part of a well-established oral tradition.

Psychologist Sharon Farber described how the depiction of death was transformed by fourteenth-century European art and literature into a benign joker or seducer. This positive spin became a cultural necessity with the arrival of the Black Death, a continent-wide plague that claimed the lives of more than 25 million people. Over the next five centuries, death would eventually be forced into the margins of public consciousness. By the middle of the twentieth century, anthropologist Geoffrey Gorer was writing about the "pornography of death." He argued that death had become the new taboo, replacing Victorian sexual repression. Two decades later, Ernest Becker would be awarded a Pulitzer Prize for *The Denial of Death*, a brilliant synthesis of humanity's "flight from mortality." Becker summed it up best: "The idea of death, the fear of it, haunts the human animal like nothing else."

The United States remains a death-denying culture. More than 80% of Americans die without a will. Burial preparations are usually handled by funeral directors, one of the many cultural practices that sanitize death. Loved ones refer to the deceased as having "passed on" or "left this world" rather than as "dead." Psychologist Paul Wong has specifically commented on those individuals who "wage an all-out war against death," including extreme "calorie minimizers" who seek to lower their body metabolism in a desperate race to "slow the progress of life."

The extent of an individual's preoccupation with death is a function of many factors, including age and exposure to particular life events. The death of a loved one, news of a tragedy, or a serious illness can all bring about a more immediate sense of one's mortality. There are also periodic moments when each of us is so fully immersed in the realization of our finiteness that it produces a terrifying shock, what the existentialists call "ego chill."

As early as 1896, psychologist G. Stanley Hall found that more religiously oriented individuals reported less fear of death. Perhaps demonstrating their own death avoidance, few contemporary social scientists have followed up on Hall's findings. Though it is limited, the psychological literature on death-related fears does offer some guidance. Individuals with relatively low death anxiety are more likely to share the following characteristics:

- Purpose in life
- Quality relationships
- Spiritual beliefs
- Intrinsic faith

Psychological studies indicate that those who report having greater *purpose in life* produce imaginative stories about death and dying that are less negative and foreboding, suggesting a deep or well-anchored level of adjustment in this regard. *Quality relationships* can also provide one with a buffer against death anxiety, partly because they generate a sense that one has lived a meaningful life, and partly because they assure one of having touched others deeply, including members of future generations. *Religious beliefs* provide benign interpretations of death and the promise of an afterlife. On a more spiritual level, individuals who have a deep, *intrinsic faith,* whether religiously based or not, also tend to demonstrate fewer fears of death. In contrast, sheer frequency of engagement in religious or spiritual rituals, such as church attendance, meditation, or prayer, does not seem to be predictive of an individual's level of death anxiety.

Following up on such findings, one of us (A. S.) collected data to assess whether the spiritual and survival-related aspects of hope might reduce an individual's level of death-related distress. In one study, a "death depression" scale and a comprehensive hope scale were given to individuals. Those who were *higher* in survival-related and spiritually related hope reported *lower* amounts of death-related depression.

In a second study, young adults were shown a 10-minute segment from *Philadelphia*, starring Tom Hanks. The film is about a successful young lawyer who contracts AIDS. He deteriorates and ultimately dies. Prior to viewing the film, participants were given a multidimensional hope scale, a measure of self-esteem, and a spiritual transcendence questionnaire. These were the potential predictor variables. Before and after the film, participants completed a death anxiety scale. The outcome variable was a death anxiety difference score, computed by subtracting the pre-film score from the post-film score. A large positive score would have suggested a significant increase in death anxiety as a result of watching the film, whereas a zero or negative score would indicate either no change or a reduction in death anxiety during the viewing. The results were fascinating. Self-esteem was not a significant predictor of changes in death anxiety. However, higher scores on the spiritual dimensions of hope, as well as in the feeling of transcendent oneness with others, were associated with either a reduction or no change in death anxiety.

Fear of death can sometimes turn into denial of death, fostering false hopes that compromise the quest for genuine mastery, attachment, and survival. Psychiatrist Irving Yalom noted that high levels of death anxiety may lead to "work alcoholism" or "compulsive heroism" (false mastery). Intense death anxiety can also spawn obsessive dependence on "a powerful rescuer" or "rampant promiscuity" (false attachment). In addition, some individuals with high death anxiety may develop a deluded "sense of specialness," believing that the universal laws of life and death do not apply to them (false survival).

Consider the case of Howard Hughes, the brilliant but eccentric aviator. As a young man, he was a powerful and handsome athlete. Skilled as a pilot, he established world records for speed and distance, earning the title of the "world's greatest flyer." He was also a daring entrepreneur who produced major motion pictures, invested in posh hotels, and acquired control of several airlines. He amassed a multibillion dollar financial empire, while dating a bevy of Hollywood starlets that included Ava Gardner and Katherine Hepburn.

In his 50s, however, Hughes became a recluse, hiding from the world in his penthouse atop a Las Vegas Hotel. He became a severe hypochondriac with a multitude of phobias, afraid of life as well as death. He had his windows permanently sealed and covered with black cloth. He insisted that his staff follow strict "decontamination" procedures to assure that his food, water, and "life space" were totally germ free.

Hughes changed from a meticulously groomed individual to one with slovenly habits. His unkempt hair grew until it reached his lower back, and his fingernails became more than an inch long. He developed bizarre eating habits, at one point subsisting exclusively on small pieces of yellow cake, cut into perfect three-inch squares. The man who had once "chased the sun" suffered a miserable death. Although more than 6 feet tall, he had withered to a 90 pound husk. The medical examiner found it necessary to use a fingerprint analysis to identify his body.

Some biographers attributed Hughes' demise to a severe case of obsessive-compulsive disorder, others speculated that it was due to syphilis. However, numerous aspects of his life suggest that the primary cause may have been death anxiety. As a teenager, Hughes lost both of his parents in rapid succession. His daredevil exploits were certainly consistent with Yalom's notions of "compulsive heroism" and "deluded specialness." Moreover, his playboy lifestyle could be viewed as a form of "rampant promiscuity," a type of false attachment unconsciously designed to deny the passage of youth.

Awareness of one's mortality helps to define the human condition. However, in the case of Howard Hughes, the flight from death was associated with psychological deterioration. For most individuals, the impact is more muted, cushioned by a variety of hope sources. Chief among these terror-management buffers are the various religious and spiritual beliefs that offer hope for salvation.

Countless immortality formulas have been proposed in an effort to quell death anxiety. The *Egyptian Book of the Dead*, one of the oldest surviving texts, provided the ancients with a spiritual roadmap for the afterlife. Explicit guidelines for assuring the immortality of the soul can also be found in the Bible, the Qur'an, the Torah, and other sacred texts. In a "Sutta" (discourse) entitled *Fearless*, the Buddha outlined five "hopeful escapes" from the terror of death. Two focused on survival skills (cultivating deep faith or letting go of earthly cravings). Another two derived from attachment (showing goodwill toward others or offering peace to the distressed). The fifth required a commitment to mastery (dedication to "skillful" behavior).

In St. Paul's first letter to the Corinthians, he assured fellow Christians that "we will be changed in a flash; in the twinkling of an eye . . . The perishable will be clothed with the imperishable [and] the mortal with immortality." In "Death Be Not Proud," the poet-theologian John Donne created a salvation poem for the ages:

> Death be not proud, though some have called thee
> Mighty and dreadful, for, thou art not so,
> For, those, whom thou think'st, thou dost overthrow,
> Die not, poor death, nor yet canst thou kill me;
> . . . . . . . . . . . . . . . . . . . . . . . . . . . . . . . . . . . . . . . . . . . .
> Thou art slave to fate, chance, kings, and desperate men,
> And dost with poison, war, and sickness dwell,
> And poppy, or charms can make us sleep as well,
> And better than thy stroke; why swell'st thou then?
> One short sleep past, we wake eternally,
> And death shall be no more, Death, thou shalt die.

*What do people fear most about death?* In truth, it is not just one thing. What makes the prospect of death so overwhelming is its multifaceted nature. Death anxiety really encompasses a number of separate terrors rolled into one. Psychologist Ahmed Abdel-Khalek effectively summarized them as follows:

- Fear of pain and punishment
- Fear of religious or spiritual failings
- Fear of losing worldly involvements
- Fear of parting from loved ones

Abdel-Khalek's perspective coincides with our motive-based approach to hope. The fears of punishment and of spiritual failings concern *survival in the afterlife*. The fear of losing worldly involvements is about goal interruption or *loss of mastery*. The fear of parting from loved ones is a *crisis of attachment*. Abdel-Khalek's analysis can also be compared to psychiatrist Robert Jay Lifton's definition of "psychological death": severed connections (attachment), a lack of will (mastery), and real or perceived disintegration (survival).

Another perspective on death and dying that dovetails with our approach to hope can be found in the end-of-life literature. Members of this interdisciplinary specialty include scientists as well as practitioners who are dedicated to a better understanding of the dying process. The picture of a "good death" that emerges from their interviews with the dying consists of manageable levels of distress (survival), maintenance of social connections (attachment), and clarity of mind (mastery). In short, *death is humanity's greatest fear because it threatens the most basic foundations of hope.*

## Hope for Transcending Death
### The Double-Life Prescription

How should you cope with the fear of death? We believe that the best prescription calls for leading a double life. You must balance living in the here and now with a more long-range view that will provide an eternal perspective. Putting it another way, you should anchor your existence in the future as well as in the present, relying on strategies that encompass each of the hope motives.

*The wisdom of here and now.* Living in the present moment means temporarily letting go of the past and suspending any thoughts about the future. It represents a mindful or nonjudgmental approach to every aspect of life, from mundane tasks to rare encounters with the sublime. Mihaly Csikszentmihalyi's concept of "flow" is a vivid metaphor for this way of being in the world. According to him, it is the moments when you are "actively involved," as if "being carried away by a current," that confer the greatest amount of joy and life satisfaction.

Spiritual writer Eckart Tolle offered another rendition of this present-oriented philosophy in his book *The Power of Now*. He combined insights from a number of traditions, including Buddhist and existentialist. The following sums up his approach:

> Make it your practice to withdraw attention from past and future whenever they are not needed ... Things, people, or conditions ... for [assuring] your happiness now come to you with no struggle or effort on your part [so] you are free to enjoy and appreciate them—while they last ... Life flows with ease.

The idea of living in the moment dates back to the ancient Greeks. Epicurus wrote that "the art of living well and the art of dying well are one." Hafiz, a thirteenth-century

Persian poet, framed his message in verse: "Come, for the... [future] is built on sand: bring wine, for the fabric of life is as weak as the wind." In the nineteenth century, Ralph Waldo Emerson offered this sage reflection: "Our fear of death is like our fear that summer will be short, but when we have had our swing of pleasure, our fill of fruit, and our swelter of heat, we say we have had our day."

*The wisdom of "then and there."* Respecting the power of the present is a necessary ingredient for crafting a full life. However, it is not enough to quell death anxiety. A philosophy of the present must be combined with both hindsight and foresight, a balanced temporal existence that honors the *power of the past* along with the *power of the future.* This time-extended approach underlies many of the qualities that make us uniquely human, including religion and spirituality as well as love, honor, and other transcendent virtues.

Consider that a large percentage of the human brain is dedicated to either recalling the past or anticipating the future. The frontal lobes, responsible for planning, take up more than one third of the cerebral cortex. Memory storage is also pervasive, spanning the upper, middle, and lower regions of the brain. Moreover, as discussed in Chapter 3, there is evidence suggesting that humans are hard-wired for spiritual experiences that can dramatically transform their perceptions of time and space.

Rollo May argued that the dominant temporal orientation for humanity is toward the future rather than the past or present. According to him, humanity is primarily oriented toward "becoming" rather than simply "being." This does not imply escapism but an inherent human tendency toward growth and self-actualization. In fact, psychologist Herbert Rappaport found a connection between a future-oriented perspective and lower death anxiety. His research team surveyed a group of adults, asking them to report the number of significant thoughts and plans they associated with the past, present, or future. They found that a greater *focus on the present* was linked to *higher* scores on a measure of *death anxiety.* In contrast, a *stronger investment in the future* was related to having a greater purpose in life as well as *lower death anxiety.*

The wisdom of adopting an eternal perspective has its own ancient history. In the Book of Ecclesiastes, the "teacher" reflected on the futility of living exclusively in the present.

> Generations come and generations go but the earth remains forever... All streams flow into the sea yet the sea is never full... there is nothing new under the sun... I tried cheering myself with wine, and embracing folly [yet] my mind still guided me with wisdom. I wanted to see what was worthwhile for humans to do under heaven during the few days of their lives... Cast your bread upon the waters for after many days you will find it again... Sow your seed in the morning [so you may reap the harvest at day's end].

The German theologian Jurgen Moltmann went a step further. Grounding his ultimate hope in God and the prospect of a redemptive resurrection, Moltmann argued that the individual with faith did not have to choose between happiness in the present and a future satisfaction. According to Moltmann, "Does [such] hope cheat man of the happiness of the present? How could it do so! For it is itself the happiness of the present."

The call for a more eternal perspective is not limited to the Bible or even to those with a purely religious orientation. The great pragmatist William James opined that "the greatest use of a life is to spend it on something that will outlast it." Vaclav Havel, who has described his beliefs as more "spiritual" than "religious," had this to say about *hope and time*: "Hope is an orientation of the spirit, an orientation of the heart; it transcends the world that is immediately experienced, and is anchored somewhere beyond its horizons."

## Symbolic Immortality

*Death is not the last word*. Human beings can extend their hopes indefinitely through acts of symbolic immortality. Robert Jay Lifton developed this idea from his interviews with survivors of the Holocaust, Hiroshima, and the Vietnam War. Through his research, he was able to identify as many as five different ways of transcending death. You can achieve immortality through your progeny or by creating something of lasting value. You can follow the traditions of Native Americans or other earth-centered cultures that link the transient life of individuals to the eternal cycles of nature. You can seek salvation in religious or spiritual beliefs. You can also realize moments of immortality through meditative practices that temporarily suspend your awareness of time and space.

Psychologist Mario Mikulincer called attention to the role of close relationships in fostering a sense of symbolic immortality and reducing death anxiety. He noted that social bonds often serve as critical buffers across the life span, helping individuals of all ages to cope with their greatest fears. For example, infants and children seek out their caregivers when frightened. Similarly, adults look for the company of others when bracing themselves for a challenging or painful encounter.

A powerful example of securing peace in troubled waters can be found in Tom Brokaw's *The Greatest Generation*. Brokaw traveled around the United States, interviewing World War II veterans about their most harrowing combat experiences. He also joined a group of them in France for the fiftieth anniversary of D-Day. As they toured the beach at Normandy, an old solider recalled:

That hillside was loaded with mines . . . a unit of sappers had gone first, to find out where the mines were. A number of these guys were lying on the hillside, their legs shattered by the explosions. They'd shot themselves up with morphine and [now] they were telling us where it was safe to step . . . [then I knew] . . . I'd live another day.

Mikulincer argued that close relationships can also provide a shield against the deeper fear of losing one's social identity. He noted that all individuals fear that they will be forgotten. Having strong and lasting relationships instills a sense of having mattered to others and of having left a mark on humanity. "By forming and maintaining close relationships, people can feel more confident that their social identity will not be lost and their friends, spouse, and children will remember them after their death."

The greatest assurance of symbolic immortality often comes from having children. As a parent, you come face to face with your past, present, and future. In the company of your offspring, you literally see life before and after you. If you cast your imagination into the distant future, you can almost see infinity in the progress of coming generations. In the daily rituals of childcare, you can also wonder about the hopes and dreams that sustained your own parents when they embarked on the journey of raising a family.

Parenthood offers a concretized legacy. If you are a biological parent, half of your child's DNA comes from you. The child may inherit from you one or more distinct physical features such as the shape of his or her nose, mouth, or ears. Indeed there is a remarkable continuity in the chain of life. For example, a child's fingerprints, the most unique physical characteristic of the human body, are 98% inherited. For many other physical traits, the heritability quotients are also remarkably high (e.g., height, 87%; weight, 70%; and brain size, 94%).

*If you are an adoptive or stepparent, do not underestimate your influence.* Much of the child's inner core, including approaches to problem solving, attitudes about life, and ways of relating to others, can be profoundly affected by your positive involvement. For example, approximately 40% of the variation in IQ scores is attributable to environmental factors and not genetics.

The data on attitudes is even more reassuring. Psychologists James Olson and his colleagues studied more than 300 pairs of twins, including those reared together and those raised in different environments. They assessed a wide range of attitudes about specific issues, from abortion and the death penalty to reading books and playing sports. The findings indicated that approximately two thirds of the variability in social values and interests was due to environmental factors. Clearly, both genetics and life experiences interact in complex ways to shape human behavior. However, this does not diminish the fact that all parents, biological or not, can have a tremendous impact on the development of their children.

The unconscious also appears to be deeply affected by family experiences. Evidence for a "family unconscious" comes from the work of Carl Jung, who administered a word association test to 24 families, collecting over 22,000 responses. When he compared the responses of various family members, Jung was amazed at the degree of similarity. For example, when the word "law" was presented to a young woman, her association was "Moses." Her mother, although tested separately, replied, "God's commandments."To the word "strange," both women independently responded with "traveler."

We previously noted how the presence of effective and nurturing caretakers can facilitate the development of a hopeful core. Such emotional imprints also establish ways of relating to others, particularly in intimate relationships. Even the most casual observer of pop psychology is aware of the Freudian notion that individuals are destined to marry someone who reminds them of their mother or father. Psychologist Harville Hendrix's concept of an "imago" is a more recent expression of this notion, the idea that individuals harbor a kind of "prototype lover" in their unconscious as a result of early child–parent interactions.

In summary, whether you are a biological or adoptive parent, hope *can* be passed on to your children. As an involved caretaker you are helping to forge your child's capacity for attachment, mastery, and survival. Moreover, remember that in the process of serving as a hope provider, you are assuring your own symbolic immortality while increasing humanity's repository of spiritual capital.

Finally, try not to think of symbolic immortality as an inferior substitute for the real thing. While planning and imagining may burden us with death anxiety, these uniquely human qualities can also provide for our psychological salvation. Human beings inhabit two worlds, the physical and the symbolic. The latter consists of transcendent values and lasting memories as well as eternal hopes and dreams.

## Transcendent Hope

Likely your deepest wishes involve true mastery, fulfilling relationships, and a genuine sense of peace. You likely want a hope that is real, not false; one that will extend your creativity, love, and bliss into the future. Presuming this is the case, then your enemy is not death, but instead the total annihilation of hope.

To craft a transcendent hope, you must choose wisely when considering your options for achieving symbolic immortality. The strategies we have just outlined involve one or more of the motives underlying hope. The use of meditation to override the normal limits of time and space derives from the *survival motive*. Establishing a legacy of creative accomplishments brings forth the *mastery motive*. Both *attachment and survival* concerns are reflected in sustaining close relationships, identifying with nature, or becoming a parent. A religious or spiritually based belief system can involve one, two, or even all three of the hope motives.

To actualize a transcendent hope, you must keep two things in mind. First, it is important to address all three of these hope motives. For example, if you embrace many of the survival tenets of Buddhism, including regular meditation, consider also doing something to fulfill your mastery and attachment strivings. Secondly, you must commit fully to your faith choices. Hopeful assurance can only come from an intrinsic faith in one or more enduring centers of value. Invest in whatever is relevant for you as an individual. Think back to the guidelines and options presented in Chapters 6 and 8 dealing with faith and spiritual intelligence. What is your spiritual type? What are your particular faith needs?

Here are some further suggestions for navigating this part of your hope journey:

*Do your "blood work"* (attachment and survival). If you have children, be a consistently involved parent. Organize family reunions. Send photos and cards to loved ones. Create a calendar with pictures of family members, including birthdays and other important dates. Put together a scrapbook or produce your own family video. Do some research on your family tree. Write your memoirs and give a copy to younger family members.

*Be creative* (mastery and survival). You do not have to be an artist to create something of lasting value. Build a tool shed or a playhouse for your children. Grow a garden, showing your children how to prepare the soil and harvest a crop. Get involved in a neighborhood project to establish or improve a playground or ballpark. Spend a week with Habitat for Humanity, helping to provide housing for low-income families.

*Commune with nature* (attachment and survival). Go camping. Learn more about the inner workings of nature. Do some bird or whale watching. Spend a day walking in the woods or attend a science museum. Read about Jane Goodall's spiritual experiences in the wild or Rachel Carson's crusade against pesticides.

*Strengthen your spiritual beliefs* (attachment, mastery, and survival). Consider attending a spiritual retreat, joining a bible-study group, or obtaining an annotated version of your favorite sacred text. Teach a religious class for children. Devote a half-hour to prayer in the morning or evening. Take a continuing education class on world religions or alternative spiritual traditions. Contribute to a charity sponsored by your particular faith group.

*Meditate on a regular basis* (survival). There are many meditative traditions, including Japanese, Buddhist, Chinese Taoist, and classic Hindu. If you seek pure detachment, then try the Zen or Tibetan Buddhist varieties. If you desire a more active process that will relax your body as well as still your mind, try tai chi or some form of yoga. Regardless of which technique you choose, make it a priority and commit yourself to a daily ritual.

*Spread your love* (attachment and survival). Nurture your relationships. Look up old friends. Join Classmates.com or a similar Internet-based reunion network. Become a member of a community-based organization such as the Masons, the Chamber of Commerce, the Lions or Rotary Club. Heed Erikson's sage advice to include institutions as well as other people in your "circle of care." Donate your time to a local YMCA or a favored political party. Help the elderly. Sponsor a child from a third-world country or contribute some time to a youth sports league. Become a mentor to the younger generation, whether through teaching, coaching, or some other form of volunteering.

In considering these suggestions, choose the activities that are best suited to your spiritual type as well as your abilities and interests. Reflect on the possibilities and you will undoubtedly be able to generate additional options for yourself. You are free to fashion your own prescription for symbolic immortality. Just make sure to incorporate and balance all three of your hope motives: attachment, mastery, and survival.

# Thirteen

## OVERCOMING HOPELESSNESS: ESCAPE FROM DARKNESS

> My guide and I went into that hidden tunnel. And following its path through a round aperture, I saw appear some of the beautiful things that Heaven bears. There we came forth, and once more saw the stars.
>
> —Dante, *The Inferno*

Dante Alighieri spent the last 13 years of his life (1308–1321) in exile, banished from his beloved Florence. It was during this period that he crafted his epic masterpiece, *The Divine Comedy*. Hailed as "the greatest single poem ever written," it is a journey that spans Hell, Purgatory, and Paradise, an allegory representing "the soul's struggle to find God" after descending into the deepest regions of hell.

At the start of his journey, Dante found himself on a "deep and savage road." As he entered the "Inferno," "the city of woes," he gazed skyward, where over the portal of hell he saw inscribed the words, "Abandon all hope, you who enter here." But with the aid of his guide, the ever-confident Virgil, he found his way back to paradise.

Dante's "Inferno" provides an excellent backdrop for this chapter on hopelessness. His portrayal of hell featured nine "circles," spiritual "torture chambers" containing little air, yet plenty of fire and ice. Within each realm, the dead were subjected to unique and insidious forms of torment.

The sighs, groans and laments at first were so loud, resounding through starless air, I began to weep: Strange languages, horrible screams, words imbued with rage or despair. Cries as of troubled sleep or of a tortured shrillness rose in a coil of tumult, along with noises like the slap of beating hands, all fused in a ceaseless flail.

Chronic hopelessness has been similarly described as hell on earth. Moreover, like Dante's circles, the inferno of hopelessness is impossible to reduce to a single mode of suffering. Harriet Tubman, the Moses of her people, helped to liberate more than 300 African American slaves in the years leading up to the Civil War. Nevertheless, when she initially secured her own freedom, she felt cast adrift, like a "neglected weed" and a "stranger in a strange land." The novelist Virginia Woolf, plagued with debilitating mood swings most of her life, wrote in her diary, "It's like banging one's head against a wall at the end of a blind alley." Novelist William Styron, in *Darkness Visible*, described his own encounter with despair as a "toxic and un-nameable tide... most closely connected to drowning or suffocation."

This chapter focuses on various forms of hopelessness as well as on strategies for overcoming each type. But the treatments for hopelessness, to borrow a medical analogy, consist of more than a one-time inoculation. As in the case of many serious illnesses, booster shots are sometimes necessary to sustain an individual's resistance to breakdowns in mastery, attachment, or survival. Hence, in the following discussion, we provide periodic hope boosters by referring you back to previous chapters. Toward the end of this chapter, we also offer guidelines for dealing with depression and suicide, two of the most serious potential consequences of hopelessness, and address the phenomenon of hopeless rage.

## Varieties of Hopelessness

Fear, often considered the opposite of hope, is typically absent in the experience of hopelessness. In the Inferno, Dante asked Beatrice, his deceased true love, how she could live in hell without fear. She replied, "Fear befits things with power for injury, not things that lack such power." When you abandon all hope, there is nothing left to fear.

But if there is a single, unifying theme in the experience of hopelessness, it is a sense of entrapment—the sense that one cannot escape one's own hellish demons or free oneself from the bonds of a life gone awry. It is a feeling that has been captured in many folk traditions, where the devil comes bearing locks and chains. In Greek mythology those who upset the Gods were ensnared, bound, or otherwise immobilized. Angry Zeus chained Prometheus to the side of a mountain. Ulysses, caught "between a rock and a hard place," encountered a six-headed monster to his right (Scylla) and a deadly whirlpool on his left (Charybdis). Anyone who looked directly into the eyes of the snake-haired Medusa was petrified, literally turned to stone.

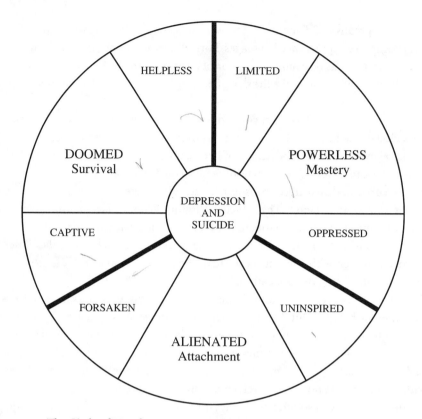

FIGURE 13.1.   The Circle of Hopelessness

Void of fear, trapped in hell, hopelessness comes in many forms. In keeping with Dante's nine circles of hell, we delineate *nine types of hopelessness,* arranging them, as shown in Figure 13.1, into a *circle of hopelessness.* Three of these types (the pure forms) can be attributed to breakdowns associated with the survival, attachment, or mastery motives. These describe the experiences of doom, alienation, or powerlessness that plagued Styron, Tubman, and Woolf. The other six types of hopelessness might be characterized as "blended disruptions," consisting of both a primary and secondary motive disruption. An example of a mixed type is a chronic sense of helplessness, deriving from a breakdown in survival (primary disruption) as well as mastery (secondary disruption). Our forthcoming examination of the varieties of hopelessness will approach them in triads or clusters of three: a pure type in tandem with two related types of blended disruption (i.e., *Doom,* followed by Helplessness and Captivity; *Alienation,* followed by Forsakenness and Uninspiredness; and *Powerlessness,* followed by Oppression and Limitedness).

Whatever its varieties, and however entrenched it may be in a person's psyche, the experience of hopelessness typically carries with it a special ache to break free from its snares. Perhaps the writer Pearl Buck put it best: "None who have always been free can understand the terrible fascinating power of the hope for freedom of those who are not free." Any man, woman, or child enslaved by years of abuse, oppression, or actual imprisonment would know exactly what Buck meant.

Perhaps you saw the film version of J. R. R. Tolkien's *The Two Towers*. In an early scene testifying to the soul's longing for liberation, the warrior Aragorn and the heroine Eowyn, two of the principal forces of light, anticipate a great battle against the forces of darkness. Aragorn tries to dissuade Eowyn from taking part in the fray, but she refuses to sit idle in the face of encroaching evil:

> *Aragorn*: What do you fear, my lady?
> *Eowyn*: *A cage.* To stay behind bars until use and old age accepts them, and all chance
>     of valor has gone beyond recall and desire.
> *Aragorn*: I do not think that will be your fate.

The first step in escaping hopelessness, in all its various forces of darkness, is to understand its origin or developmental roots. Putting it another way, if you lose an object of value, you can find it by thinking about how or where you lost it. Similarly, to restore hope you must grasp both the process of recovery and the motivational context that caused you to lose hope.

## Hope-Restoring Strategies

Broadly speaking, recovering hope can occur through a combination of approaches that we have identified in previous chapters. One is *cognitive therapy*. Widely accepted as the most effective nonmedical treatment of disorders of mood and emotion, cognitive therapy consists of unearthing, challenging, and replacing irrational beliefs and ways of thinking with more productive thoughts. The mechanisms underlying irrational thought processes are three-fold. First, they can function automatically. According to psychologist Judith Beck, they can be "non-deliberative and difficult to turn-off." Second, they are invariably driven by negative beliefs that were instilled at an early age, forming the center of an individual's sense of self, the world, and the future. Beck pointed out that such "core beliefs" tend to be "global, rigid, and over-generalized." Third, beliefs, rational or irrational, wield great power over an individual; the more irrational those beliefs, the more destructive their power. As Gandhi noted:

> Your beliefs become your thoughts. Your thoughts become your words. Your
> words become your actions. Your actions become your habits. Your habits
> become your values. Your values become your destiny.

TABLE 13.1. *Typical Cognitive Distortions in Hopelessness*

| Varieties of Hopelessness | Typical Cognitive Distortions |
| --- | --- |
| Doomed | Jumping to Conclusions |
| Helpless | Magnification |
| Captive | Emotional reasoning |
| Alienated | Mind Reading |
| Forsaken | Overgeneralization |
| Uninspired | All-or-none thinking |
| Powerless | Discounting the Positive |
| Oppressed | Personalization |
| Limited | Labeling |

The distorted ways of thinking that are common among individuals who suffer from hopelessness are presented in Table 13.1, which draws from several sources, particularly the work of psychiatrist Aaron Beck, and psychologist David Burns. As we examine the varieties of hopelessness, we will also describe how cognitive reframing, informed by the principles of cognitive therapy, can effectively alter the distortions typically associated with each variety and can replace them with more hopeful thought processes. We will also examine two other crucial factors in the overcoming of hopelessness and in the recovery of hope: *healing relationships* and *spiritual practices*.

## Doom

A *pure form of hopelessness* results when the survival motive is profoundly disrupted. Individuals weighed down by this form of despair presume that their life is over, that their death is imminent. The ones most vulnerable to sinking into this particular circle of hell are those diagnosed with a serious, life-threatening illness as well as those who see themselves worn out by age or infirmity. Such individuals feel doomed, trapped in a fog of irreversible decline.

In *Illness as Metaphor*, her brilliant survey of medical history, Susan Sontag provided more than a glimmer of hope for the physically ill. She noted that a good deal of the hopelessness that surrounds illness is manufactured by the despair-laden metaphors that social institutions attach to certain diagnoses. Two centuries ago, tuberculosis was dubbed the "thief of life." In the twentieth century, cancer meant "death" at the hands of a "secret invader" that "doesn't knock before it enters." Sontag also noted that in recent years AIDS has become the "generic rebuke to life and hope."

One of the darkest depictions of an individual doomed by illness appeared in Tolstoy's haunting short story, *The Death of Ivan Ilyich*.

> He struggled desperately in that black sack into which an unseen, invincible force was thrusting him. He struggled as a man condemned to death struggles in the hands of an executioner, knowing there is no escape . . . he was being shoved into that black hole.

To dramatize Ivan's sense of entrapment, Tolstoy envisioned his plight as a form of role reversal. Ivan, a former judge by profession, was transformed into a virtual prisoner after receiving a death sentence from an incompetent and insensitive physician. In his introduction to a revised edition of Tolstoy's classic, Ronald Blythe invoked the words of Simone de Beauvoir, characterizing Ivan's brutal confrontation with mortality as an "inescapable reversal of one's projects."

Unfortunately, the aging process itself is enough to engender a sense of doomed hopelessness in some individuals. This is particularly likely when a person is plagued by a sense of regret for lost opportunities and times gone by. In truth, aging well can be difficult, particularly in a youth-oriented society. The nineteenth-century Swiss philosopher Henri Amiel noted, "To grow old is the masterpiece of wisdom, and one of the most difficult chapters in the art of life." In *David Copperfield*, Dickens' protagonist, weary from years of strife and disappointment, is shrouded in a "long and gloomy night . . . haunted by the ghosts of many hopes." John Greenleaf Whittier wrote, "Of all the sad words of tongue and pen, the saddest of these: It might have been."

Advancing age, like serious illness, can also evoke feelings of entrapment and futility. Tolstoy, in middle age, was obsessed with death: it appeared to him in nightmares, taking the form of a square room from which there was "no escape—no way out or in." Upon turning 79 years old, a psychotherapy client of one of us (A. S.) who had been preserving fruit her entire life, began having recurrent dreams of standing under a beautiful grapevine. In the dream she felt as if she had just eaten a meal but remained hungry. However, each time she tried to reach for a cluster of grapes, they were beyond her grasp.

## Helplessness

A feeling of helplessness arises when the survival and mastery systems are simultaneously thwarted. Helpless individuals no longer believe that they can live safely in the world. They feel exposed and vulnerable, like a cat after being declawed or a bird grounded by a broken wing. In the words of one trauma survivor, "I was terrified to go anywhere on my own . . . I felt so defenseless and afraid that I just stopped doing anything." Another defining feature of helplessness is an ongoing failure to take advantage of the most basic degrees of freedom. Psychiatrist Judith Herman related how a male trauma survivor even lost his ability to open doors or turn the lights on.

Prolonged exposure to traumatic and uncontrollable life events puts individuals at risk for developing a profound sense of hopelessness. Psychologist Martin Seligman and his colleagues demonstrated the devastating effects of learned helplessness on animals. In a typical experiment, they restrained a dog or rat, and then subjected the animal to a mild shock. After several trials, the animal learned that escape efforts were futile. In future trials, even though the animal was *not* restrained, it would lie passively while enduring the shock.

In humans, repeated failures in dealing with adversity can also affect the mastery system. When threatened, individuals rely on all their resources to survive, including their capacities for problem solving, exploring, and manipulating the environment. However, when repeated efforts fail to produce any demonstrable change, they may forfeit their hope for mastery as well as their most basic survival instincts.

At the age of 30, Barbara entered therapy for the first time. Initially, she made it clear that she did not want to spend months dredging up the past. What she wanted was help in dealing with chronic anxiety and with her intrusive parents and in-laws. However, within a few sessions, Barbara began to focus on her childhood, revealing that she had been sexually abused by an uncle and emotionally abused by her alcoholic father and manipulative mother. At 18, she moved a thousand miles away to get away from her family. Unfortunately, her parents continued to call her on a daily basis, second guessing every decision she made and putting her in the middle of their own tortured emotional crossfire. Barbara longed for greater security and autonomy. In the course of therapy she became enraptured with the Oscar-winning film, *Crouching Tiger, Hidden Dragon*. She explained to her therapist that "the woman in that movie is so free and strong. She doesn't have to take any crap from men. She can do what she wants. She's not helpless."

## Captivity

> So this is hell. I'd never have believed it. You remember all we were told about the torture-chambers, the fire and brimstone, the "burning marl." Old wives' tales! There's no need for red-hot pokers. HELL IS—OTHER PEOPLE!
> —Sartre, *No Exit*

William James observed that "The most important part of my environment is my fellow-man. The consciousness of his attitude towards me is the perception that normally unlocks most of my shames and indignations and fears". His insight relates to two forms of hopelessness that can result from dysfunctional relationships. The first consists of physical or emotional captivity enforced by an individual or a group. Prisoners fall into this category as well as those held captive in a controlling, abusive relationship. We refer to this as *other-imprisonment*.

Consider Sartre's classic play *No Exit*. Three recently deceased wrong-doers find themselves in hell. At first they wonder, "Where is the punishment befitting our crimes?" Where are the pitchforks and scalding flames so graphically illustrated in Dante's *Inferno*? As they begin to share their life stories, they discover something in common. All three of them failed to commit to love. Two cheated on their spouses. The third was guilty of alienating a wife from her husband. In hell they quickly pick up where they left off in life, torturing one another with barbs and accusations while preying on each other's faults. Realizing they are bound to one another for all time, they finally understand. "Hell" can be an eternity of twisted relationships, filled with lies and deceit, frustration and humiliation. In a similar vein, William James suggested that "the hell to be endured hereafter, of which theology tells, is no worse than the hell we can make for ourselves in this world."

An equally insidious form of entrapment is *self-imprisonment*. This occurs when individuals cannot leave a bad relationship because their sense of self will not allow it. Sometimes the problem is low self-esteem. In other cases, an individual has an unconscious need to revisit and repair the past, what Freud called "repetition compulsion." A third and even more complicated type of self-imprisonment derives from "projective identification." When someone projects (or attributes) "bad" qualities onto another, he or she cannot leave the relationship without reclaiming the unwanted parts of the self. The individual may also project "good" parts onto another to offset a fear of separateness or to protect valued aspects of the self from other "bad" inner qualities. In the former example, individuals cannot leave because they would be losing a part of themselves, while in the latter they would be in danger of self-destruction.

Camus' short story, *The Adulterous Woman*, is a classic existential tale of self-imprisonment. It is the story of Janine, an unhappy middle-aged woman who "goes through the motions of her uneventful life with her uneventful husband." Janine knew that her marriage was a loveless contract between "two frightened children," unable to face life alone. However, she could not bear the thought of living by herself. Indeed, she sensed that the reality of her existence rested on her husband's dependence on her. Despairing, Janine realized, "she was overcoming nothing, she was not happy, she was going to die...without ever being liberated."

Janine's act of adultery did not revolve another man. Instead she flirted with freedom and possibility. One night on a business trip, while her husband lay asleep, Janine snuck away "to be with the cosmos." Standing high atop a terrace that surrounded her desert fort, she opened herself to the night sky and for a few fleeting moments it seemed that the "sap again rose in her body."

Looking out at the "limitless expanse" of a "dry, cold night," Janine was transfixed by the "drifting flares" of stars that fell like "sparking icicles." She was "filled with such a sweet, vast melancholy that it closed her eyes. She knew that this kingdom had been eternally promised her and yet that it would never be hers, never again." Reluctantly, Janine returned to her "icy room" and lay down. When her husband awoke, he was bewildered to find his wife, "weeping copiously, unable to restrain herself."

### Overcoming the Doom Triad

Those who feel doomed as a result of a medical or psychiatric diagnosis may *jump to conclusions*. Sometimes called fortune telling, this distortion involves a presumption that things will turn out badly (without first checking the facts). This distortion can be particularly devastating in the context of cancer, AIDS, and other serious maladies that have become metaphors for hopelessness.

## Rethinking Your Outlook

The best antidote for jumping to conclusions is *examining the evidence*. If you are diagnosed with a serious illness, do your homework and get the facts. For example, Harvard anthropologist Stephen Jay Gould was diagnosed with a rare abdominal cancer at the age of 40. When told that the median survival time for someone with this disease was only 8 months, he did some research. In his essay, "The Median Isn't the Message," Gould shared how his knowledge of statistics helped him to "examine the evidence." He was able to tell himself, "Fine, half the people will live longer. Now what are my chances of being in that half?" After factoring in his age, his relatively healthy lifestyle, the early stage of diagnosis, and the quality of healthcare available, Gould arrived at a far more hopeful prognosis. In fact, he lived another 20 years before succumbing to an unrelated illness.

Examining the evidence can also be therapeutic for those of advancing age who feel doomed and no longer capable of altering the course of their lives. By examining all of the evidence, they may be able to realize, first of all, that it is never too late to make significant life changes, and second, that there is apt to be an underlying coherence that defines their life, which can bring greater acceptance. An examination of the external evidence can reveal powerful examples of others who have achieved remarkable success late in life. Consider Anna Mary Robertson (Grandma Moses) who started painting at the age of 76, or the lesser known Bill Traylor, a self-taught African American artist and former slave who did not discover his passion for drawing until he was 83. In contrast, by examining the internal evidence of one's own past, including the many favorable and unfavorable circumstances that had to be confronted, one can develop a greater appreciation for the choices that were made, the wisdom that was acquired, and the future possibilities that may now be available.

Those who feel helpless may unwittingly engage in *magnification*. According to David Burns, such individuals are experts at diminishing the value of their actual virtues while simultaneously magnifying their perceived weaknesses. One antidote for magnification is *thinking in shades of gray*. If you are feeling helpless, instead of holding onto artificial dichotomies such as "good" and "bad," "perfect" or "terrible," orient your thinking around variations and continuums. In other words, stop thinking in terms of extremes. Keep in mind that there is a tremendous gray area between total helplessness and complete self-sufficiency.

Captive self-imprisonment, arising from low self-esteem, repetition-compulsion, or projective identification, is also amenable to a cognitive approach. The distortion of thinking caused by *emotional reasoning* frequently underlies this form of hopeless attachment. Strong emotions are unwittingly transformed into the reasons for staying in an otherwise unhealthy relationship. For example, it is common for both women and men to stay in bad relationships because they have a distorted sense of love and commitment. As children they may have been exposed to family interactions in which domination was presented as love, or total self-sacrifice was experienced as commitment. As adults, they find themselves trapped by their own confused feelings. Unaware of the flawed representations underlying their emotions, they feel utterly trapped.

Captive self-imprisonment may be best dealt with by using a *survey method*. If you feel stuck in a dysfunctional relationship, begin by asking yourself how others might construe your situation. Next, survey as wide a sample of individuals as possible, looking for a pattern or trend in their perceptions. In this manner, you may be able to arrive at a more freeing way of thinking about your relationship.

Rollo May noted that human beings have the capacity to experience the "freedom of doing" as well as the "freedom of being." In all but the most extreme cases of entrapment, there are still options available to an individual. Someone with cancer can still choose love over fear, vitality over despair. The aging individual can still choose to be productive. A prisoner can still choose to live with dignity even in incarceration.

Freedom of being is especially important for those dealing with *other-imprisonment*. While imprisoned in Auschwitz, Viktor Frankl found a hiding spot behind a pile of corpses where he could be alone with his thoughts for 5 minutes every day. Wrote Frankl: "Everything can be taken from a man but one thing: The last of his freedoms—To choose one's attitude in any given set of circumstances."

## Liberating Relationships

During her childhood, Celie, the protagonist in Alice Walker's *The Color Purple*, was repeatedly raped and beaten by a monstrous father. As a teenager, she was married off to another despicable, violent man who similarly abused her. Fortunately, she met two assertive women, Shug and Sofia, who provided her with a vastly different perspective on love and commitment. In addition, she also drew strength from her sister Nettie, a missionary in Africa. From Shug, Celie learned the sweetness of intimacy. Sofia taught her dignity and self-respect, while Nettie demonstrated the power of a lasting love sustained by a shared spiritual mission.

The best attachments offer liberation and security. A liberating relationship is crucial for those who feel doomed or helpless as well as for those who are held captive in one sense or another. The individual who feels doomed by a serious illness or advancing years needs a *freedom guide*, an indefatigable hope explorer who will keep looking for every imaginable degree of freedom. Individuals who feel helpless need a *catalyst* to help them unleash their potential. In her interviews with resilient adults, Gina O'Connell Higgins found repeated references to surrogate caregivers who "encouraged the resilient to let their talents unfold." Here she quoted from Melville's *Moby Dick*: "When fortunes favorites sail close by, we, though drooping before, catch somewhat of the rushing breeze, and joyfully feel our bagging sails fill out."

Those held captive by other-imprisonment may benefit from a *transcendent presence*. Viktor Frankl, for example, was able to transcend his experience at Auschwitz by continually reflecting on his beloved wife.

> . . . my soul found its way back from the prisoner's existence to another world, and I resumed talk with my loved one: I asked her questions, and she answered; she questioned me in return, and I answered . . . A thought crossed my mind: I didn't even know if she was still alive, and I had no means of finding out . . . but at that moment it ceased to matter. There was no need to know; nothing could touch the strength of my love, and the thoughts of my beloved.

For individuals who are self-imprisoned in an unhealthy relationship, finding a liberating attachment begins with liberating the self from its own psychic snares. Those snares develop in the very first years of life, before the advent of speech and logic. As a result of early interactions with caregivers, a template may be produced that forever drives an individual toward certain kinds of romantic partners. Psychologist John Money called these "love maps." Marriage therapist Harville Hendrix dubbed them "ghost partners." Psychiatrist Thomas Lewis and his collea- gues described them as "limbic attracters," emotional "magnets" constituted from brain areas associated with highly charged memories and the most basic experiences of pleasure and pain.

Complete liberation from your limbic bond is neither possible nor desirable. What *is* possible and desirable is to shed the destructive elements within that template. For example, it is perfectly fine to be attracted to a mate who has the same hair color, body build, religious background, or hobbies as one or both of your parents. However, it is extremely problematic if your attraction is motivated by an unconscious need to shore up a heavy drinker, please a critical authority figure, or secure the love of an emotionally distant loner.

Experts are divided on whether you should extricate yourself from a partner who embodies negative aspects of your love map. Some feel it is best to disengage, invest in critical self-awareness, and then find a healthier mate. Others, such as Hendrix, believe it is possible to *Keep the Love You Find*. Given that individuals seem destined to connect with partners with "complementary character defenses" and "symmetrical wounds," Hendrix argued that couples should work with nature's gift in what might be called, a process of "co-liberation."

If you decide to follow Hendrix's advice, make sure that your mate supports rather than undermines the cause of liberation. You may recall from Chapter 9 that successful couples share similar dreams. Specifically, co-liberation is more likely to occur when couples share *four hopes.* The first hope is to be seen as an individual, not a mere a template carrier. The second hope is to relate in an emotionally corrective fashion by diverging from destructive old scripts. The third hope is to develop a revised love map that positively transforms your mutual attraction. The fourth hope is to grow as individuals as well as a couple. In the words of Gibran's prophet, "Love one another but make not a bond of love . . . :[to] Fill each other's cup but drink not from one cup."

### Spiritual Freedom

As we noted in previous chapters, Buddhism offers a powerful set of practices for those overwhelmed by emotional distress or physical pain. Samatha or the "calm meditation" is used to cultivate mental and physical relaxation. Vipassana or "insight meditation" can bring greater awareness. In fact, one translation of "Vipassana" is to "see through" in the sense of looking beyond the barriers and obstacles of ordinary reality.

While each type of meditation can transform consciousness and facilitate freedom from distress, they work best when used together. Start with a simple Samatha breathing meditation to achieve an initial state of mental and physical relaxation. Sit comfortably, close your eyes, and focus on your breath. Breathe in for a count of four and breathe out for a count of six. After 5 minutes, switch to an insight meditation. Thich Nhat Hanh's "Looking Deeply" is an excellent example of a meditation designed to penetrate the illusions of permanent suffering, isolation, and nonbeing. Here is a shortened adaptation:

Aware of a wave on the ocean, I breathe in. Smiling to the wave, I breathe out.

Aware of the water in the wave, I breathe in. Smiling to the water, I breathe out.

Seeing the birth of a wave, I breathe in. Smiling to the birth of the wave,
I breathe out.

Seeing the death of a wave, I breathe in. Smiling to the death of the wave,
I breathe out.

Seeing the birthless nature of water in the wave, I breathe in. Smiling to the birthless nature of the water, I breathe out.

Seeing the deathless nature of water in the wave, I breathe in. Smiling to the deathless nature of the water, I breathe out.

Seeing the birthless nature of my consciousness, I breathe in. Smiling to the birthless nature, I breathe out.

Seeing the deathless nature of my consciousness, I breathe in. Smiling to the deathless nature, I breathe out.

## Alienation

Disrupted attachments can also result in a relatively pure form of hopelessness. Alienated individuals believe that they are somehow different. Moreover, they feel as if they have been cut loose, no longer deemed worthy of love, care, or support. In turn, the alienated tend to close themselves off, fearing further pain and rejection.

Alienated individuals may feel cut loose for a variety of reasons. *Sociocultural alienation* occurs when individuals believe that their personally cherished ways of living are no longer honored by a larger group to which they formerly felt allied. *Sociopolitical alienation* can result when an individual's personally valued political beliefs are at odds with a ruling majority. *Sociotemporal alienation* may develop when individuals feel either ahead of their time or as if time has passed them by.

It is hardly a coincidence that the two greatest poems about hell were written by outcasts. Dante had been banished from Florence for life and labeled an enemy of the state. John Milton, the poet of *Paradise Lost*, had spent much of his adulthood as a social and political insider, but in his later years he found himself progressively marginalized first by blindness and then later by a new ruling party that he did not support.

At the turn of the twentieth century, the sociologist Emile Durkheim demonstrated that many suicides derive from a "lack of religious, domestic, or political integration." Around the same time, Charles Darwin wrote of the human "dislike of solitude" and "the wish for a society beyond the family." He pointed out that solitary confinement is one of the severest punishments that can be inflicted on a human being. Half a century later, Eric Fromm suggested that humanity had been effectively "torn out of nature" with the evolution of self-awareness.

Ron Kovic's *Born on the Fourth of July* is one of the most powerful and poignant autobiographies from the era of the fractured generation. During his second tour of duty in Vietnam, he was shot and left paralyzed from the chest down. Reflecting on his life before Vietnam, he wistfully recalled growing up in an era of clearly defined social expectations, a foreign policy of good versus evil, and a cultural landscape in which stars like Audie Murphy and John Wayne were revered for their war film exploits. But after returning from Vietnam, Kovic felt profoundly alienated in a country that had grown deeply ambivalent about the war and America's role in it. His most disturbing postwar experience came during the 1972 Republican National Convention, when he and two other disabled veterans were rebuffed for disrupting President Richard Nixon's acceptance speech:

> All three of us took a deep breath and shouted at the top of our lungs, "Stop the bombing, stop the war, stop the bombing, stop the war" . . . Secret service agents grabbed our chairs from behind and began pulling us backward . . . A short guy ran up to me and spat in my face. "Traitor!" he screamed.

## Forsakenness

> My God, my God, why hast thou forsaken me? Why art thou so far from helping me, and from the words of my roaring? . . . Thou art he that took me out of the womb: thou didst make me hope when I was upon my mother's breasts.
>
> —The 22nd Psalm, Old Testament

The word "forsaken" refers to an experience of total abandonment that leaves individuals feeling alone in their time of greatest need. Recall Job in the Old Testament, crumpled over and covered with sores, pleading with a seemingly indifferent God. Or consider the plight of the Japanese *hibakusha* during World War II. Known as the "A-bomb affected individuals," the *hibakusha* were feared, isolated, and ultimately abandoned during the months and years following the devastation of Hiroshima. Among them was writer Yoko Ota, quoted here by Robert Jay Lifton in his book, *Death in Life*: "No one came to take care of the injured people and no one came to tell us how and where we should spend the night. We were simply left alone." Another victim, an engineer, lamented, "My children were treated very unkindly at school. Other children would taunt them and cry out: Son of a patient of the A-bomb Hospital." A third victim, an elderly countrywoman, recalled, "At that moment we all became completely separate human beings . . . I thought, 'There is no God, no Buddha . . . There is no help'".

*Time* correspondent Johanna McGeary recounted the story of Laetitia, a 51-year-old single mother living in South Africa. When in 1996 she was diagnosed with *AIDS*,

> Laetitia's employers fired her . . . her children were ashamed . . . Her mother ordered Laetitia out of the house. When her daughter wouldn't leave, the mother threatened to sell the house to get rid of her daughter. Then she walled off her daughter's room with plywood partitions, leaving the daughter a pariah, alone in a cramped, dark space without windows and only a flimsy door opening into the alley. When Laetitia ventures outdoors, neighbors snub her, tough boys snatch her purse, children taunt her.

## Uninspiredness

The uninspired individual is suffering from a breakdown in attached mastery. Feeling uninspired can be especially difficult for members of underprivileged minorities, for whom opportunities for growth and positive role models within the group may be either lacking or undervalued. In this regard, there is increasing criticism from within the African American community for promoting the *wrong* role models. Bill Cosby and Jason Whitlock, for example, have lambasted many of their brethren for disparaging intellectual achievement as a "white thing" while keeping the spotlight on certain rap artists who promote a cult of brute strength, intimidation, and unbridled hedonism.

Sports icons, however, remain among the great sources of positive inspiration for many African Americans. Beginning in the late 1940s, Jackie Robinson inspired millions by breaking the color barrier in baseball and leading his team to six pennants and a world series championship. In 1974, Hank Aaron grasped the "most coveted record in sports," overtaking the Babe in home runs. In the 1980s and 90s Magic Johnson and Michael Jordan ruled the hard courts. Tiger Woods now dominates the world of golf, and Venus and Serena Williams are among the champions of tennis. Nevertheless, worship of sports figures can pose a problem for those who are either not interested in sports or lack athletic gifts. Hank Aaron, for his part, tried to make a distinction between serving as a specific type of role model and setting the more general example of living an honorable life.

> I had to set an example for black children, and still do, because they need examples. A white child may need a role model, but a black child needs more than that in this society. He needs hope.

## Overcoming the Alienation Triad
Attachment-related forms of hopelessness may be fueled by cognitive distortions such as mind reading, overgeneralization, or all-or-none thinking. Mind reading is a form of jumping to conclusions in which an individual presumes to know what others think and feel about them. Many who feel alienated assume (wrongly) that absolutely no one is, or ever will be, in their corner. The antidote for mind reading is to examine the emotional evidence. This requires courage in the form of trust and openness to survey how others actually experience you.

## Rethinking Your Outlook
Those who feel forsaken often overgeneralize. They may have suffered rejection from a parent or potential romantic partner. From these singular affronts, some individuals may generalize to all family members or all potential mates. In the worst-case scenario, a person can feel abandoned by the entire human race.

Those who overgeneralize need to examine the external validity of their beliefs. If you feel forsaken, it is important to get outside of your head to see if your inner reality is an accurate reflection of the outside world. In assessing external validity, laboratory scientists review the size and representativeness of their sample. Most people who feel forsaken are overgeneralizing from a relatively small sample of experiences. With more extensive sampling, it is highly likely that they will encounter more hope-promoting responses from others.

Sometimes those who feel uninspired have unwittingly fallen prey to all-or-none thinking that can blind them to available options, including appropriate role models. For example, African American youngsters, believing that their only choice is to emulate sports stars such as Michael Jordan or Donovan McNabb, may be ignoring inspiring teachers, civic leaders, or parents who are in their immediate environment.

The antidote to all-or-none thinking is thinking in shades of gray—opening oneself up to the continuum of possibilities for one's life. Be more accepting of your own potential for self-inspiration through incremental improvements. At the same time, take a closer look at individuals, famous and not so famous, who might serve to inspire you in terms of the really important qualities that underlie success. (See chapter 10.)

## Supportive Relationships

Seeking out supportive relationships is a must for those who feel alienated, forsaken, or uninspired. One of the synonyms of "support" is "to give hope." Likewise, in the *Oxford English Dictionary*, providing "support" is defined in terms of "supplying what is necessary for the maintenance of life" as well as providing "courage, confidence, and the power of endurance." Yes, emotional support *is* as vital for survival as air, water, or food. If you feel alienated or forsaken, it is imperative that you seek out hope providers who can offer you *unconditional acceptance*.

Follow the advice of the Carl Rogers, the guru of unconditional positive regard. According to him, those most capable of providing this regard to you possess three qualities: (1) they are "real" or "congruent," meaning they are completely honest in terms of how they relate to you; (2) they are accepting and caring but in a nonpossessive manner; and (3) they provide accurate empathy so that you feel that they truly know you. Rogers originally envisioned these qualities as criteria for enhancing therapist-client interactions, but he made it clear that they could apply to all relationships.

## Blessed Inspiration

> I am grateful to receive this [Nobel Prize] in the name of the hungry, the naked, the homeless, the crippled, the blind, the lepers, all those people who feel unwanted, unloved, uncared for, throughout society.
> —Mother Teresa

Those who feel alienated, forsaken, or uninspired may want to seek unconditional love in its most elevated form: in the connection from one's center of divinity to another's and in the embrace of the blessings of a given religious faith. In many faith systems, a blessing is viewed as a gift of approval as well as a form of moral support. While the ultimate giver is understood to be God or a higher power, the immediate source is likely to be an earthly representative such as a Christian or Buddhist priest, a Jewish rabbi,

Muslim iman, or Native American shaman. Mother Teresa was an especially powerful dispenser of unconditional love and compassion. For 50 years she tended the slums of Calcutta, helping those forgotten by the world. As a humble "saint of the gutter," she seemed particularly invested in the most poor, the most diseased, and the most disenfranchised. Here is one of her most quoted blessings:

> No need for us to despair. No need for us to be discouraged. No need, if we have understood the tenderness of God's love. You are precious to Him. He loves you, and He loves you so tenderly that He has carved you on the palm of His hand. When your heart feels restless, when your heart feels hurt, when your heart feels like breaking, remember, 'I am precious to Him. He loves me. He has called me by my name. I am His. He loves me. God loves me.'

Non-Christians may want to consider a Native American blessing. A number of these prayers and meditations were specifically designed to inspire mastery (while also conferring approval and moral support). Although Native American cultures have been primarily oriented around attachment and survival, they have also recognized the need for mastery, particularly in the service of the hunt. Many Native American blessings encourage the individual to join forces with the power of nature, to "soar" like the eagle, "stand strong" like the buffalo, or be "cunning" like the fox. The following "Great Spirit Prayer" is attributed to Chief Yellow Lark, a Blackfoot Indian:

> Oh, Great Spirit, whose voice I hear in the wind, whose breath gives life to all of the world. Hear me; I need your strength and wisdom. . . . Make my hands respect the things you have made and my ears sharp to hear your voice . . . Make me wise so that I may understand the things you have taught my people. Help me to remain calm and strong in the face of all that comes towards me. Let me learn the lessons you have hidden in every leaf and rock. . . . I seek strength, not to be greater than my brother, but to fight my greatest enemy, myself. Make me always ready to come to you with clean hands and straight eyes. So when life fades, as the fading sunset, my spirit may come to you without shame.

## Powerlessness

A pure form of hopelessness can also result from breakdowns in mastery. From birth, human beings have an insatiable need to explore, manipulate, and control their environment. Infants will quickly learn to shift their gaze, kick their legs, or vary their cries if their responses can make any sort of difference, whether it means the presence of a smiling caretaker or even the slightest movement of a hanging mobile. Individuals of every age need to believe that they can author the story of their life. But when that need is thwarted, when one feels powerless to commander one's way toward desired goals, a feeling of despair can set in.

Sonny, a 40-year-old African American man, sought psychotherapy for performance anxiety. During his first session, he also revealed a history of depression, low self-esteem, job stress, and thoughts of suicide. As part of his intake assessment, Sonny was given a sentence completion test. Question one was: "my dominant feeling is _____." Sonny filled in the blank with the word "hopeless."

In Sonny's case, performance anxiety represented an inability to face life as an adult. Despite three college degrees and proficiency in several languages, he found it impossible to function in a job that was commensurate with his ability. In fact, he said he felt more like a 10-year-old child than a mature adult, and his very demeanor conveyed that feeling. Although he was over 6 feet tall, he was always stooped over, apparently unable to rise to his full height. He also spoke like a child, with a tone that was typically high pitched. He squinted and strained when pronouncing multisyllabic words. Even in his dreams, "I look so small, like a little kid, even though everyone else is grown up."

In therapy, Sonny traced his difficulties back to childhood and a father who was equally afraid of life. He described his father as a weak, timid figure who had married a woman 6 years his senior. "I think he needed a mother to take care of him," said Sonny with obvious bitterness in his voice. "My father never said much to me. He never encouraged me, never coached me, and never gave me a reason to feel good at anything. What he told me over and over again was, 'you'll be like me—a nothing. You'll eke out an existence—that's it.'

### Oppression

Oppression involves the subjugation of a person or group. Often there is a political agenda, as for example in the oppression of an entire social class or ethnic group. The word "oppressed" comes from the Latin, to "press down," and its synonym, "down-trodden," suggests a sense of being "crushed under" or "flattened."

In *Lay My Burden Down*, Alvin Poussaint and Amy Alexander explored why suicide rates among black youths have more than doubled over the past two decades. Citing Durkheim's examination of the various social forces that can contribute to suicide, including "excessive regulation...of persons with futures pitilessly blocked and passions violently choked," Poussaint and Alexander concluded that the hopelessness wrought by years of oppression was a primary factor underlying the growing crisis of depression, hopelessness, and suicide within the black community.

Some individuals are doubly oppressed. With two strikes against them, they are especially prone to despair. Imagine being a noncommunist, religiously devout individual in the Soviet Union during the twentieth century. Or consider the burden of being an African female within a white, male-dominated society. Indeed, Alice Walker has called her African American sisters the "mules of the world." It is not surprising, then, that she, along with Toni Morrison, Maya Angelou, and numerous other African American women, have produced some of the most poignant literature on oppression. Drawing on their own personal experiences with discrimination and demoralization, they have fashioned memorable sagas of disenfranchised and subjugated women, desperate for hope. As Walker's character Celie hears firsthand from the abusive husband she's about to leave: "You'll be back . . . You black, you poor, you ugly, you a woman. Goddam, you nothing at all."

## Limitedness

In the eyes of the people there is a sense of failure . . . In the souls of the people the grapes of wrath are filling and growing heavy, growing heavy for the vintage.

—John Steinbeck, *The Grapes of Wrath*

When the struggle for survival is combined with a sense of failed mastery, individuals feel limited. They experience themselves as deficient, lacking in the right stuff to make it in the world. This form of hopelessness is all too common among the poor as well as those struggling with severe physical handicaps or crippling learning disabilities.

In *The Working Poor*, David Shipler gave readers a sense of the hopelessness experienced by those who "do not have the luxury of rage": the bank clerk with less than three dollars in his savings account, the car wash attendant without a car, the medical textbook editor who has not seen a dentist in a decade. Caroline Payne was one of Shipler's "working poor." Employed by a large department store, Caroline repeatedly sought to be promoted into a managerial position. She was never chosen. At age 50, she seemed resigned to stocking shelves for the rest of her life. Stunned by her lack of economic progress, she reflected on a variety of personal handicaps that she believed had made it difficult for her attain a better lot in life.

Caroline was born into a large and poor family too overwhelmed to offer adequate material or emotional support. After her parents divorced, she had to contend with a stepfather who "drank a lot" and "tried to get fresh with me." Upon graduating from high school, she married and had three children. She worked day and night to put her husband through college and endured his acts of infidelity.

Among those who struggle with disabilities, people with spinal cord injuries experience rates of depression that are three times higher as compared to the general population. Individuals diagnosed with epilepsy are 12 times more likely to commit suicide. With respect to learning disabilities, children and adolescents with speech, reading, or math difficulties often score significantly higher on measures of hopelessness as compared to their nonimpaired peers. Research indicates that more than half of all adolescents who commit suicide were once diagnosed with a learning disability. Similarly, adults with a history of learning disabilities are twice as likely to suffer from depression as compared to the general population.

### Overcoming the Powerlessness Triad

Three cognitive distortions frequently underlie feelings of powerlessness: discounting the positive, personalization, and labeling. When individuals cannot appreciate their talents and gifts, they are prone to discount any evidence of personal success or effectiveness. If they do well in an academic setting, they will attribute it to an inferior instructor or luck. If they perform well in an athletic event, it was a fluke or the competition was soft. If they get a promotion, it was because the boss overestimated their competency.

### Rethinking Your Outlook

Examining the evidence is a good strategy for dealing with discounting the positive. One way to do this is to make a list of past successes, particularly in the general domain you are discounting. For example, if you are prone to discounting a good grade on an exam, write down any past successes of an intellectual nature. If you tend to discount a work or social achievement, reflect on past occupational or group-related achievements.

It is common for those who are oppressed to engage in *personalization and self-blame*. This is particularly apt to happen in more individualistic cultures and when the oppression has accumulated layer upon layer, generation after generation, within the subconscious. Author Jacob Holdt suggested that self-blame was on the increase among African Americans:

> People can survive oppression if they are able to clearly identify their oppressor and thus avoid self-blame. This understanding let blacks see light at the end of the tunnel in the past. However, for the first time in history blacks have difficulties identifying their oppressor and therefore without hesitation look for the cause of their growing pain within themselves.

A strategy for counteracting self-blame is *reattribution*. This involves considering all the likely causes of negative emotions. For example, in *The Color Purple*, Celie and her doubly oppressed friends achieved a measure of hope when they vented their frustrations at the "gray-bearded, white God," and stood up to their male oppressors, black as well as white.

When individuals feel limited because of a perceived physical or intellectual disability, they may fall prey to *labeling*. Sometimes this kind of stereotyping is done by others, but it can also be self-inflicted. Labels such as "crippled," "defective," "dumb," or "lazy" can obviously be quite damaging to the ego. However, even seemingly politically correct designations such as "special" or "disabled" may be disempowering. By accepting any label, individuals may internalize all the conditions and limitations associated with it. To attack harmful labels, *define your terms*. For example, if you feel or are labeled "stupid," reflect on the actual definition of the term. Are you always "making bad decisions"? Are you always "careless" and "unable to learn"? Unless this description, taken directly from the *American Heritage Dictionary*, applies to you, then you are not "stupid."

### Empowering Relationships

Those who feel powerless, oppressed, or limited can find strength in empowering relationships, which are rooted in shared *control, commitment, and challenge*. These characteristics define *hardiness*, a personality trait that was mentioned in Chapter 11. According to psychologist Salvatore Maddi, hardiness is "a set of attitudes and beliefs that provide the courage and motivation to do the hard work of turning stressful changes . . . into opportunities." More recently, Maddi has dubbed hardiness a form of "existential courage."

Empowering relationships instill hardiness by helping to transform an individual's sense of self. Empowered individuals derive an experience of shared control that lies at the core of hope-based mastery. Moreover, they are brought into the fold of a higher purpose that binds together hope recipients and their hope providers. They are also challenged to actualize their potential.

In overcoming *oppression*, great liberators such as Martin Luther King and Nelson Mandela offered powerful experiences of *commitment* and *shared control*. In his famous letter from a Birmingham jail, King wrote, "We are caught in an inescapable network of mutuality, tied in a single garment of destiny." In leaving office as president of South Africa, Mandela assured his nation that "Though I shall not be seen as much as I have been, I shall be amongst you and with you as we enter the African century; working together to make a reality of our hopes for a better world."

Full release from oppression cannot occur if liberators ask just for mere obedience or concessions from the majority in power. They must *challenge* the oppressed to rise to their full height. Again Martin Luther King struck the perfect chord:

> If a man is called to be a street sweeper, he should sweep streets even as
> Michelangelo painted, or Beethoven played music, or Shakespeare wrote poetry.
> He should sweep streets so well that all the hosts of heaven and earth will pause to
> say, here lived a great street sweeper who did his job well.

In the film *Braveheart*, Mel Gibson portrayed the thirteenth century Scottish hero-liberator William Wallace. Some of the most moving scenes dealt with the importance of inspiring others to find their voice. This was especially true in the film's climax. Wallace was betrayed, captured and put on the rack for torture. Near death, he was nevertheless able to summon one last shout to his compatriots, "For Freedom!"

Witnessing Wallace's last stand was his longtime nemesis, King Edward I of England. Once an imposing figure, Edward was reduced to an impotent husk. Age and illness left him mute, stripped of the powers of speech. The princess looked disdainfully at her moribund father-in-law and delivered the final death blow:

> You see? Death comes to us all. And it comes to William Wallace. But before death comes to you, know this: your blood dies with you. A child who is not of your line grows in my belly. Your son will not sit long on the throne. I swear it.

Hardiness, in the form of commitment and shared control, is also important for those who feel economically, physically, or intellectually limited. In *Restoring Hope*, author Cornel West asked the award-winning journalist Charlayne Hunter how the "waning hope" of African Americans might be bolstered. She replied that the inter-generational transmission of hope could be disseminated by instilling "values," sharing "confidence-building stories," and imparting the "wisdom of the ages." In Hunter's view, these three ingredients could "propel ambition" while assuring a virtual "suit of armor . . . that is where the hope is."

You may recall our mentioning in Chapter 1 the dynamic tandem of Helen Keller and Anne Sullivan. Another blind individual who rose to greatness on the wings of shared control and mutual commitment was Louis Braille, who was only 15 when he developed a system of dots and dashes that would come to bear his name. Beyond his family, he credited four other individuals for helping him to bring his blind comrades out of the dark. Of special importance was Valentin Hauy, who had founded the Paris school that Louis attended. After meeting Hauy for the first time in 1821, Braille felt "as if some great force of energy, some inexplicable understanding was communicated in that brief exchange." Always humble, Hauy himself suggested, "It is God who has done everything."

Being *challenged* is also important for individuals dealing with intellectual or physical limitations. As suggested by psychologist Albert Bandura, individuals develop feelings of self-efficacy when they succeed in tasks that they value and find challenging. A great example is provided by the actor James Earl Jones. As a child, Jones was a "self-conscious stutterer." It was not until high school that he developed the confidence to express himself in public. He had written a poem that he showed to his favorite teacher. Sensing that James needed to be challenged, his teacher suggested that the poem was plagiarized and asked James to read it to the class to prove that it was his own work. Recalled James, "This had a tremendous effect on me . . . [from that day on] my confidence grew."

In the same spirit of challenge, Bill Cosby went all over the United States, calling out his fellow African Americans for not assuming more personal responsibility in their struggle for economic security. In particular, Cosby chastised black youth for not trying hard enough to succeed in school. Speaking at one gathering, he exhorted them to remember the sacrifices of previous generations of African Americans: "Dogs, water hoses that tear the bark off trees, Emmett Till [a black teen tortured and murdered in Mississippi]. And you're going to tell me you're going to drop out of school?"

## Spiritual Force

He who meditates on hope as Brahman – all his desires are fulfilled through hope, his prayers are not in vain; he can, of his own free will, reach as far as hope reaches.

—The Chhandogya Upanishad (VII. xiv. 2)

Empowerment is a common theme in the spiritual literature. In the New Testament, John (15:5) wrote, "I am the vine, you are the branches. He who abides in me, and I in him, he it is that bears much fruit." With persistence and the right attitude, Hindus believe that the individual can unleash the power of *kundalini*, a form of "coiled-up" spiritual energy derived from a bridge with the universal Atman. From Sufism comes this passage: "Truth, God, came and dwelt within my heart, and was my understanding, ear, eye, and speech."

The following meditation is taken from the Brihadarany Upanishad, considered one of the most profound chapters in Hindu scripture. A sage is asked if he knows The Great Sutra, the verse that deals with the "Inner Controller." Because "he who knows the Sutra knows the worlds, he knows the gods, he knows the Vedas, he knows the self." The sage obliges:

He who inhabits all beings, yet is within all beings, whose body all beings are, and who controls all beings from within—He is your Self, the Inner Controller

He who inhabits water, yet is within water, whose body is water, and who controls water from within —He is your Self, the Inner Controller

He who inhabits the sky, yet is within the sky, whose body is the sky, and who controls the sky from within—He is your Self, the Inner Controller

He who inhabits the air, yet is within the air, whose body the air is, and who controls the air from within—He is your Self, the Inner Controller

He who inhabits the sun, yet is within the sun, whose body the sun is, and who controls the sun from within—He is your Self, the Inner Controller

He who inhabits the moon and stars, yet is within the moon and stars, whose body the moon and stars are, and who controls the moon and stars from within—He is your Self, the Inner Controller

He who inhabits light, yet is within light, whose body light is, and who controls light from within— He is your Self, the Inner Controller

## Depression

Depression has been portrayed as evil incarnate. Writer Andrew Solomon dubbed it the "noonday demon," recalling his own bout of depression as the time when "hell came to pay a visit." Psychiatrist Jonathan Zuess likened it to "the darkness that covers God." William Styron, another depression sufferer, labeled it a "storm of murk." Elsewhere he compared it to a form of "suffocation" that causes "psychic energy to throttle back to zero." Styron added, "Never let it be doubted that depression, in its extreme forms, is madness."

According to the current edition of the *Diagnostic and Statistical Manual of Mental Disorders*, a major depressive episode consists of low mood and/or a loss of interest or pleasure. In addition, the clinically depressed will suffer from four or more of the following: decreased or excessive motor activity, sleep disturbance, eating disturbance, fatigue, feelings of guilt or worthlessness, concentration problems, morbid and/or suicidal thoughts. However, many experts believe these official diagnostic criteria are too narrow and fail to take into account individual difference in the expression and experience of depression.

Depression is *not* synonymous with hopelessness. From a logical standpoint, you *can* have one without the other. There are some individuals who are depressed but do not feel hopeless. Others may feel hopeless but not depressed. Nevertheless, these two emotional states typically co-occur because both are associated with breakdowns in mastery, attachment, and survival.

Psychologists Lyn Abramson and Martin Seligman suggested that depression results from a perceived inability to either achieve a desired goal (mastery) or avoid an aversive stimulus (survival). Neuroscientist Richard Davidson highlighted possible mastery failures at the biological level. Specifically, Davidson and his colleagues demonstrated that parts of the left frontal lobe, linked to various goal-seeking behaviors, tend to be undersized and/or underactivated in some depressed individuals.

Psychologist Thomas Joiner viewed depression from an interpersonal perspective, noting that depressed individuals frequently demonstrate social skills deficits (attachment disruptions). They often speak more slowly, quietly, with little intonation or eye contact. Depressed individuals also tend to be poor care recruiters, ironically displaying a strong tendency to solicit negative rather than positive feedback. Other attachment-defeating behaviors of the depressed may include excessive inhibition or shyness as well as clinging dependency.

Depression can also result from survival-related disruptions. Children who lose a parent early in life are at a higher risk for depression. Illness is another potential culprit. One often cited study indicated that nearly 80% of individuals seeking the care of a physician were depressed. Trauma is a particularly pernicious factor in depression. For example, in 2005, after many Jews were forced to abandon their homes along the Gaza strip, a significant number of them were treated for depression. When surveyed, nearly three-quarters reported a profound loss of control, while more than half admitted recurring dreams and nightmares.

Prolonged feelings of hopelessness can also lead to depression. With this in mind, psychologist Lyn Abramson and her colleagues proposed a "hopelessness theory of depression." We go further and suggest there are *nine subtypes of hopeless depression*. Each type shares a *depressive layer* of symptoms such as low mood, lack of pleasure, and sleeping or appetite problems. In addition, each variety of hopeless depression contains a *suffering layer* arising from a particular type of motive disruption (hence corresponding to the nine types of hopelessness; see Figure 13.1).

Hopeless depression is more easily treated in its mild to moderate forms than in its severe forms. In most cases, both the hopeless suffering and any associated depressive symptoms can be effectively reduced using the methods outlined earlier, including cognitive therapy, a hope-promoting relationship, and a spiritual practice. However, if the depressive aspects become too severe, you may want to cautiously consider the addition of one or more biologically based interventions, including the use of antidepressant medications. Within a year of onset, more than three quarters of those diagnosed with depression are significantly improved. Approximately two-thirds respond favorably to antidepressant medications.

Depression, in short, is far from a hopeless condition. Even if you have a family history of depression, which suggests a genetic predisposition, this does not mean you are fated to a life of melancholy. The best research indicates that the environment plays a far greater role in the development of depression than your genetic history. (It is estimated that the ratio of influence is 2:1 in favor of the environment over genes.) Moreover, you should understand that you did not inherit a disease but rather a vulnerability, which can be offset by bolstering your mastery, attachment, and survival motives.

## Suicide

> Hope is the major weapon against the suicide impulse.
>
> —Karl A. Menninger

Every 40 seconds, someone dies by suicide. Over the past 50 years, suicide rates have increased 60%. Suicide is now the third leading cause of death for individuals between the ages of 15 and 44. In the United States, the richest and potentially most hopeful of the world's nations, suicide is the eighth leading cause of death. In fact, more Americans die by suicide than by homicide.

For those left behind, the suicide of a family member or friend inflicts a mortal wounding of the soul, a searing pain that promises to never go away. On one suicide prevention Web site, someone wrote, "The person who completes suicide dies once. Those left behind die a thousand deaths." Gail Griffith, whose son narrowly survived an overdose of antidepressants, called the experience a "cataclysmic descent." Singer Judy Collins, whose son died by suicide, conveyed the depth of her sorrow in a song entitled, "Wings of Angels"

Wings of angels tears of saints, prayers and promises won't bring you back

Come to me in dreams again, wings of angels tears of saints

I lost you on a winter's day, in that cold city far away

A city by a river deep, with promises you could not keep

A place where you had gone to try, a place where you had longed to fly

A city smiling when you cried, a city sleeping when you died

Most individuals who kill themselves do not in fact wish to die—they just want to stop their psychic pain and, for a variety of reasons, feel that death is the only way to escape their anguish and frustration. In short, the wish to die emanates from a profound sense of *entrapment*, a belief that there is no exit from an intolerable and unalterable state. Along these lines, medical historian George Rosen, who reviewed case histories of suicides among the ancient Greeks, Jews, and Romans, found repeated references to being trapped in situations too painful to endure.

The sense of entrapment that underlies suicidality can be divided into two broad categories: perceived or *subjective entrapment*, and actual or *objective entrapment*. Some individuals falsely believe they have no hope for empowerment, connection, or salvation. Quite often they are saddled with one or more mental health disorders and/or have experienced an inordinate amount of stress. To paraphrase psychologist George Weinberg, "hope has not abandoned them, they have abandoned it."

In contrast, it is possible for some to imagine justifiable suicides that arise from objective rather than perceived cases of entrapment—for example, the suicide of an individual who is otherwise dying a slow and painful death because of an incurable illness. In the early part of the twentieth century, the existential psychiatrist Ludwig Binswanger defended the suicide of "Ellen West," a young woman who had been deprived of an authentic life by her insensitive and controlling parents and then given no hope of a cure for her seemingly intractable depression and anorexia by her doctors.

Sensing an ongoing resistance to realizing her real needs for attachment, mastery, and survival, Ellen chose to take her life. Below is one of her poems:

I'd like to die just as the birdling does
That splits his throat in highest jubilation;
And not to live as the worm on earth lives on,
Becoming old and ugly, dull and dumb!
No, feel for once how forces in me kindle,
And wildly be consumed in my own fire.

Agreeing with Binswanger, Immanuel Kant defended the use of suicide for the purpose of retaining one's dignity. From his perspective, nothing was more important than the need to prevent the "dishonoring" of ones "humanity." Wrote Kant, "life, in and for itself, is not the greatest of the gifts."

But Kant also recognized the *subjective experience of hopelessness* that prompts many people to end their lives. He described such individuals as those "reduced to despair" or "wearied of life" by a "series of misfortunes." Indeed, contemporary research indicates that hopelessness outweighs depression as a risk factor for suicide. Chronic states of hopelessness appear to be far more lethal than intense but short-lived experiences of despair. For example, psychiatrist Aaron Beck and his colleagues found that 10 of 11 individuals who scored high on a measure of "trait hopelessness" eventually completed suicide.

Extrapolating from available U.S. health statistics, approximately 90% of all completed suicides in 2006 were committed by those mired in *reversible* forms of entrapment. Some of these individuals suffered from depression, bipolar disorder, or an anxiety disorder. Others had a personality disturbance such as narcissism or dependent personality disorder. All such conditions, while not always curable, are treatable. Additional contributing factors included a history of substance abuse, access to firearms, or direct exposure to "models of suicide" via the media, a family member, or one's peer group. These too are controllable circumstances. What all these factors have in common is the disruption of the motives underlying hope: attachment, mastery, and survival.

Psychologist Edwin Schneidman emphasized that the wish to die involves intense psychological pain ("psyche-ache") due to a frustrated or thwarted critical need. Death is viewed as the only means of escape or liberation. He labeled the emotional pain a "perturbation" and the associated sense of entrapment a form of "constriction," a metaphorical tightening of the mind's "diaphragm."

Schneidman described *five classes of suicidal individuals*. Not surprisingly, each type revealed a disruption of one or more of the motives that underlie hope. Two of his categories involved blocked achievement or power needs (mastery), while another two were related to significant interpersonal losses or unmet love and belonging needs (attachment). A fifth type was associated with an assaulted or shamed self-image, a sense of having been defeated in the "game of life" (attachment and mastery). To this typology, we would add a *sixth type*, those suffering from *intense fear or physical pain* arising from a history of trauma or a serious illness (survival).

Schneidman offered a purely psychological view of suicide, but its social roots are noteworthy as well. Interestingly, Emile Durkheim provided evidence over a century ago that either too little or too much social influence can lead to suicide. He outlined *four classes of social suicide.* One class includes those suicides that result from social overregulation as in the case of oppressed minorities, the poor, or others similarly "enslaved." A second class arises from inadequate social "grounding": When larger cultural institutions such as the church or government fall away, individuals are stripped of their usual sources of meaning. Durkheim labeled his third form of suicide "altruistic," referring to those individuals who are so overidentified with their group that they are prepared to sacrifice themselves for what they believe is a "greater good." Suicide bombers within terrorist cells are one modern example of this phenomenon. Durkheim's fourth category, the "egoistic suicide," consisted of alienated individuals who lack any sense of belongingness.

If you are struggling with suicidal thoughts and feelings, it is very likely that you are experiencing intense pain regarding an attachment, mastery, or survival issue. Seek help *immediately* in dealing with your suicidal thoughts. Try to be honest with yourself and others with respect to your degree of risk. How often do you think about suicide? Can you control such thoughts or do they constantly intrude, leaving you feeling totally helpless? Have you developed a specific suicide plan? Do you have lethal means available to you such as firearms, poisons, or prescription medications? If your suicidal thoughts are persistent, uncontrollable, and highly specific, and if you have access to lethal objects or substances, you may require more than a weekly outpatient visit to a clinic or therapist's office to protect yourself and may need instead to be hospitalized until your suicidal crisis passes.

Develop a *five-fold safety plan* for yourself, using the following suggestions:

- *Create a safer environment.* Remove all lethal objects and substances from your immediate environment. If you are taking powerful prescription medications, ask your physician to prescribe smaller quantities and have him or her meet or talk with you *before* offering a refill. Avoid any contagion effects that might be caused by exposing yourself to morbid music, films, literature, or Web postings.

- *Build up your support system.* Enlist the help of your network of family and friends. Find a therapist who engenders trust and shows genuine concern. Keep in mind the qualities of a good hope provider that were discussed in Chapter 9.
- *Create a safer "internal cognitive environment."* Improve your problem solving skills. Work at visualizing options while minimizing all-or-nothing thinking. You may find it helpful to review Chapter 11 in which we discuss liberation beliefs. Collaborate with your support network in developing viable options for addressing your attachment, mastery, and survival struggles.
- *Create a safer "internal emotional environment."* Increase your distress tolerance while cultivating greater self-acceptance. Seek out a dialectical behavior therapy (DBT) provider or group. Surround yourself with positive and caring family and friends. Before joining a support group, social club, or Internet chat room, make sure the context is validating and life affirming.
- *Request a comprehensive treatment plan.* If you have been diagnosed with an anxiety disorder, depression, or bipolar disorder, and also struggle with a substance abuse problem, your risk for self-destructive behavior is greatly intensified. A truly comprehensive safety plan should include treatment for these dually diagnosed disorders.

## Hopeless Rage

Hopelessness can also engender rage. When this happens, homicidal and suicidal impulses may become interwoven. Prior to maiming himself, Vincent Van Gogh attacked his friend Paul Gauguin. Van Gogh was so mortified by his own senseless act of aggression that he later cut off part of his left ear and ran into the street shouting "Gauguin, come back! You can have my ear. I'm ready to listen to you!" The Columbine killers, Eric Harris and Dylan Klebold, as well as Seung-Hui-Cho, the Virginia Tech shooter, ended their shooting sprees in suicide. In 1999 Andrea Yates held a knife to her neck, threatening to kill herself. Two years later she drowned her five children.

The diversity of individuals who commit acts of mass murder has stymied would-be profilers. Nevertheless, there are certain common denominators. For example, most school shooters have suffered a significant loss (attachment) and/or experienced a major failure (mastery). Many have been bullied, persecuted, or harassed (survival). Fortunately, these hope challenges alone rarely trigger suicidal or homicidal behaviors. However, when combined with other factors, including genetic predispositions, family and cultural dynamics, as well as access to guns and violent video games, a critical mass of hopeless rage may be reached.

From our perspective, three forms of hopelessness can be particularly volatile when experienced by the wrong person, at the wrong time, and in the wrong place. These include the perception of being *forsaken*, feelings of *oppression*, and a sense of *captivity*. *Note that all three involve the attachment motive.* More to the point, when an individual strongly believes, correctly or incorrectly, that their basic hope needs (attachment, mastery, or survival) are being thwarted by another individual or group, they may become enraged and even contemplate getting even. With this in mind, if you are a *parent, teacher, or counselor* who suspects that one of your children, students, or clients is suffering from one or more of these varieties of hopelessness, make sure that a thorough hope assessment and treatment program is put into place.

# Fourteen

## HOPE FOR CHILDREN: GIFTS FOR TODAY AND TOMORROW

Every child comes with the message that God is not yet discouraged of Man.
—Rabindranath Tagore

In previous chapters, we discussed the development of the mastery, attachment, and survival systems as well as the emergence of spiritual beliefs in children. We also provided examples of precocious spiritual integrity and youthful resilience. In this chapter, we take a look at the phenomenon of childhood hopelessness, examining its reality as well as some of the hidden forces that may underlie the adult denial of this particular inconvenient truth. We also review the related topic of childhood depression, both its telltale signs among children of various ages and the best available forms of treatment for it. The remainder of the chapter is geared toward parents, teachers, and other childcare professionals who seek to be hope providers for despairing children and teens. You will find a wide assortment of ideas for strengthening the attachment, mastery, and survival skills of children, including suggestions for structured individual and group activities and recommendations for hope-building games, books, and films. Many of these ideas are intended for all children, while others are more geared toward children with special hope needs.

### Childhood Hopelessness and Depression

The child's sob curses deeper in the silence than the strong man in his wrath.
—Elizabeth Barrett Browning, *The Cry of the Children*

A brief tour of the family or parenting aisle of a large media outlet such as Barnes and Noble invariably reveals a slew of glossy-covered books featuring smiling infants and rosy-colored children happily at play. Very often the author or publisher has inserted a poem or a selection of classic literature, paying homage to the "magical years" of childhood. Occasionally, a humorous or unusually perceptive comment is attributed to a child, past or present. Childhood has long been portrayed as a time of unfettered joy, idyllic and carefree. Consider the following romanticized reflections, spanning approximately 300 years, from the 1700s to the modern era:

> Alas! Regardless of their dream
> The little victims play.
> No sense have they of ills to come
> No care beyond today
>
> —Thomas Gray (1742)

> Heaven lies about us in our infancy.
> Shades of the prison-house begin to close
> upon the growing boy
>
> —William Wordsworth (1803)

> Childhood is a kingdom where nobody dies
> —Edna St. Vincent Millay (1934)

> Poets will help us find this living childhood within us,
> this permanent, durable, immobile world
>
> —Gaston Bachelard (1960)

Unfortunately, the idea that childhood is a heavenly oasis is a fiction. Childhood is *not* always a happy and carefree time. Many children suffer from severe maltreatment, neglect, or other misfortunes. In the United States alone, nearly 3 million cases of child abuse are reported every year, 15 million children live in poverty, and more than 1.5 million suffer from a disabling chronic illness. Conditions are even worse in many third-world countries such as Liberia, where the growth of close to 40% of children has been stunted by severe malnutrition. Nearly a quarter million have been orphaned as a result of AIDS and armed conflicts. More than 15% die before reaching their first birthday.

Moreover, contrary to what many believe, children are not immune from states of hopelessness and depression. Just like their adult counterparts, they may fall prey to any one of the nine forms of despair outlined in the previous chapter. Abused children, victimized for years by insensitive or compromised caregivers, may develop a profound sense of *helplessness*. Youngsters with cancer, HIV/AIDS, or other stigmatizing illnesses are likely to feel *forsaken*. (Recall how Ryan White was essentially ostracized.) Children with learning disabilities, often relegated to classrooms outside of the mainstream, have to work longer and harder to keep up with their peers. A significant number are "kept back." It is understandable why so many of them feel *limited*.

The idea that children may suffer from hopelessness or depression is not new. For example, psychiatrist E. James Anthony cited reports of despondent children in the sixteenth century and cases of childhood melancholia in the early 1800s. However, during the twentieth century, the issue of childhood depression generated considerable controversy, with many mental health professionals ignoring or disputing its occurrence. In a classic 1957 survey of childhood mental disorders, psychiatrist Leo Kanner made no mention of depression. Many of those opposed to the idea of childhood depression or hopelessness were psychoanalysts. Following Freud, they argued that these states could only occur within a well-formed "psychic apparatus," specifically the adult ego and superego. Even Anna Freud and her colleague Dorothy Burlingham, who witnessed firsthand the devastating effects on children who were separated from their parents during World War II, were prompted to conclude, "This childish grief is short lived . . . [it] will normally be over in thirty-six to forty-eight hours."

And yet some of the most compelling research on childhood despair was conducted relatively early in the twentieth century. In particular, during the 1930s the Hungarian psychiatrist René Spitz actively explored the emotional reactions of infants and children separated from their mothers for extended periods of time. He and his staff observed and recorded a continuum of emotional deprivation. When infants were separated from their mothers for a period of up to 5 months, " . . . they would lie prone in their cots, face averted, refusing to take part in the life of their surroundings. When we approached them we were mostly ignored, though some of them would watch us with a searching expression. If we were insistent on our approach, weeping would ensue, and in some cases screaming." If the emotional deprivation persisted even longer, a more serious and seemingly irreversible condition emerged that Spitz labeled "hospitalism," [whereby] "motor retardation became fully evident; the children became completely passive; they lay supine in their cots. . . . The face became vacuous."

In the 1960s, the English psychiatrist John Bowlby began his seminal research on childhood attachment and loss. By the time he had written the third volume of his seminal work on this topic, he had amassed numerous examples of childhood suffering, including the case of "Geraldine," who a week before her eighth birthday lost her mother to cancer. For several years Geraldine struggled to carry on. "On the fifth anniversary of her mother's death, Geraldine truanted from school, spent the day in a church and reported having taken forty aspirins . . . . She came to her session looking 'drawn, tense, mask-like. Walking in like a robot, she said, 'I have taken all I can. I can stand no more.' "

Some two decades later, the third edition of the *Diagnostic and Statistical Manual of Mental Disorders* (1980) proclaimed that a single set of criteria for the diagnosis of depression could be applied to children as well as adults. Still, the myths persisted. In 1994, social worker Dorothea Greene outlined *five myths regarding childhood suicide*. These included the following: children do not experience true depression; children do not understand the finality of death; children under the age of 6 do not commit suicide; suicide in the latency years is extremely rare; children are cognitively and physically incapable of implementing a suicide plan successfully.

Ironically, just a few years earlier, psychologist Israel Orbach's 1988 book *Children Who Do Not Want To Live* was published, documenting acts of terrible self-destructive behavior by preschoolers as well as teens. One case involved a 2-1/2-year-old girl: "She 'force-fed' her doll aspirin and then asked her therapist to save it. She explained that the doll had to take the aspirin because 'she should die today.' She played for many hours with ambulances and bandages; she pretended to be dead by lying on the floor with a blanket covering her face . . . ." The girl was later found unconscious after consuming a large quantity of aspirin. Orbach also cited this particularly disturbing example:

> A nine-year-old boy's body was found charred under a shed in his grandfather's yard . . . the fire had been deliberately ignited with a flammable liquid. For weeks before the fire, the boy had been acting strangely . . . he had told his friends that he was tired of living . . . he gave away some of his most precious possessions . . . He drew pictures of graveyards and of people hanging from trees . . . his shocked parents refused to accept the verdict (of suicide). Their strenuous request that the cause of death be filed as accidental was eventually accepted by the police.

In 2007, the *United States National Mental Health Association* reported that approximately 1 million children, ages 5 to 14, and more than 3 million adolescents and young adults, ages 15 to 24, were diagnosed with depression. Suicide was the sixth leading cause of death among children 5 to 14 years and the third leading cause of death among those 15 to 24 years.

*Why then does the presumption persist that children are immune from states of depression, despair, or hopelessness?* There is no single answer. Instead a number of factors can be identified, operating at a variety of levels. These include prevailing scientific worldviews, naive assumptions about children's coping abilities, adult denial of trauma, parental overprotection, and even the archetypal significance of the child.

### Professional Bias

Some child experts continue to waver when it comes to attributing despair to children because they subscribe to a strictly cognitive or thought-centered theory of hopelessness. From this perspective, individuals experience hopelessness only when they conclude that an important goal is no longer achievable. They have considered, explored, and perhaps even tested, all perceivable strategies for realizing their objectives and come to the conclusion that none of these will produce the desired results. By extension, it is presumed that young children, incapable of engaging in such complex probability estimates, cannot possibly succumb to hopelessness.

Such an argument was specifically advanced as late as 1979 by psychiatrists Gregory Siomopoulos and Subhash Inamdar, who suggested that young children were not capable of becoming hopeless because they could not yet engage in what psychologist Jean Piaget had labeled "formal operational thought." According to Siomopoulos and Inamdar:

> The ability to assess probabilities is related to the development of formal operational thinking. Thus it is only during adolescence, with the necessary time perspective and the ability for probabilistic thinking, that hopelessness can possibly be experienced.

However, as early as 1960, John Bowlby had commented on the reluctance of many child therapists to acknowledge deep suffering on the part of children.

> . . . despite [many] observations and conclusions by workers of repute, doubt has nonetheless been expressed whether we are right to equate this experience with that suffered by an adult in bereavement. Is this true grief it is asked, and is it followed by true mourning?

### Parental Blindness and Vulnerability

Parents can also be blinded when it comes to recognizing depression or hopelessness in their children. Part of the problem is that these states are internalizing disorders, ailments that may be suffered in silence, or without much noticeable fanfare. In contrast, children with externalizing disorders, such as conduct problems or hyperactivity, will get more immediate attention. (However, sometimes acting out is a sign of depression, particularly among boys.) The research on childhood depression shows there is remarkably little convergence between parental impressions and children's self-reports. In general, parents tend to underestimate the level of sadness, low self-esteem, or depression that their children experience.

Subconsciously, parents and caretakers may not believe that children are strong enough to endure experiences of hopelessness. They try to shield their children from every potential harm, believing that any brush with failure, separation, or vulnerability would crush the spirit of the developing child. In so doing, adults may actively suppress any signs of actual hopelessness.

One of the most moving depictions of heroic parental overprotection can be found in the Oscar-winning film, *Life Is Beautiful*. During World War II, a father and his son are carted off to a concentration camp. The father, worried that his son will not be able to cope with the brutal realities of camp life, tells the child that they have been fortunate enough to be selected to compete for a toy tank. Throughout the story the father alters the facts to protect his son from the horror of firing squads and gas chambers. Later on, while holding his son tightly to his chest, the father unexpectedly, shockingly, comes face to face with a mountain of human remains. Instinctively, he turns his body so that his son will be spared the sight.

Children are often more capable of coming to grips with the harsh realities of their situation than are their parents who may continue to remain in a state of denial. In *The Private Worlds of Dying Children*, Myra Bluebond-Langner tracked the progress of 50 children, ages 3 to 9, who were diagnosed with a particularly deadly form of leukemia. Bluebond-Langner found that some parents went to great lengths to keep the bleak prognosis from their children. "They reasoned that knowledge might make the children give up." Nevertheless, "All [the children] knew that they were dying before death was imminent . . . Some said directly, 'I am going to die,' or 'I'm going to die soon' . . . . They talked about never going back to school, of not being around for someone's birthday."

The children in Bluebond-Langner's study went through a five-stage sequence in which their conceptions of death progressed from the idea that death was reversible to an understanding that death is the end of all functions. The children's behavior changed accordingly, from passive acceptance of drugs to refusal to take them ("They don't do nothing anyway"). One child in the fourth stage noted, "There are good times and bad times, but you're always sick; It'll never stop." When the children reached the fifth and final stage, most gave up all hope. This hopelessness was reflected in their artwork and their choice of reading material. "The most popular book was *Charlotte's Web* . . . They always chose the chapters in which Charlotte dies. After any child died, the book had a resurgence of popularity among the others."

In this new millennium, our society does not seem to be any more prepared to confront the reality of death and dying among children. For example, psychologist Therese Rando noted that hospices for children are sorely lacking. Psychologists Charles Thompson and Linda Rudolf added, "There is a paucity of literature describing effective methods for counseling with children and their reactions to death and dying, especially empirical studies. Perhaps researchers avoid the subject as do parents and other adults."

Parents and other caretakers may turn away from any sense of hopelessness on the part of a child because, in their eyes, it suggests they have failed in their most basic responsibility. *Parents are supposed to protect their children.* Indeed, in all but the most disturbed parents, there is a powerful, instinctive desire to keep their child out of harm's way. Each child is literally, as well as figuratively, an extension of the parent. Perhaps author Elizabeth Stone put it best, "to have a child . . . is to decide forever to have your heart go walking outside your body."

A few years ago, an artist friend of ours provided a vivid example of a father who seemed determined to erase any memories of possible paternal failure. She, the artist, was commissioned to do a portrait of the man's son, who had died at a relatively young age from chronic substance abuse. Working from photographs, she meticulously recreated every aspect of his physical appearance as well as his persona. To her surprise, when she presented the finished product to the father, he politely but firmly asked if she could redo the eyes to make them look less "sullen" or "despondent."

The awesome burden that some guardians feel is most directly seen in cases where a parent has lost a child. Therese Rando noted that this type of loss represents more than the loss of a family member. It also represents a reversal of the expected natural order of the world (a parent is burying a child), a loss of a part of oneself, and a loss of hope. But ultimately the most painful aspect of losing a child appears to be the feeling that one has failed as a parent.

> With the death of your child you have failed in the basic function of parenthood: taking care of the children and your family. You are supposed to protect and provide for your child. You are supposed to keep her from all harm.

In 1947, John Gunther Jr. died at the age of 17 of a brain tumor. Two years later his parents, journalist John Gunther and his wife Frances, wrote about their experience in *Death Be Not Proud*. Frances's closing words dramatically illustrated the profound guilt and regret of a parent who believes that she should have done more:

> Missing him now, I am haunted by my own shortcomings, how often I failed him . . . one should somehow have found the way to give one's life to save his life. Failing there, one's failures during his too brief life seem all the harder to bear and forgive.

In a similar vein, Bluebond-Langner described the maddening feeling of impotence that befell parents of the children with leukemia. "They felt they could not care for their children . . . Mothers complained about having to relinquish their maternal responsibilities . . . Parents often expressed their feelings of failure to protect . . . they tended to express guilt during the induction of the first remission." One mother confided to Bluebond-Langner: "The way he kept screaming, 'don't leave me.' And I couldn't help him."

Sometimes children hide their feelings of hopelessness because they sense that one or both parents will not be able to shoulder the burden. Psychoanalyst Alice Miller described a "vicious circle" whereby adults who have repressed their own childhood wounds unconsciously seek to minimize and control any fear, sadness, or anxiety in their children, in an effort to keep their own painful past buried. According to Miller, a significant number of children with such "wounded" parents are endowed with a "gift," a keen sense of their parents' emotional limitations. Sadly, if these children are completely unable to process their own pain, it will eventually resurface as a burden for the next generation.

Miller is not alone in her belief that children may suppress their own pain for the sake of a parent. Therese Rando's clinical studies of the grieving process suggested that one key factor inhibiting a child's grief is fear about a parent's vulnerabilities. Similarly, Bluebond-Langner found that dying children may try to conceal their condition from their parents to spare them any additional pain. "Ironically, these children came to see their own task in life as supporting others. They showed themselves to be responsive to the needs of their parents. they gave their parents the opportunity to rehearse the ultimate separation." Bluebond-Langner recalled one especially poignant interaction between a terminally ill child and his mother:

> *Bluebond-Langner:* [to child] Why do you always yell at your mother?
>
> *Jeffrey:* Then she won't miss me when I'm gone.
>
> *Mrs. Andrews:* He yells at me because he knows I can't take it. He yells so I can have an excuse for leaving.

## The Child Archetype

At an even deeper level it may be that many parents, as well as other adults, cannot attribute hopelessness to children because this would undermine the *child archetype*. The "child," according to Carl Jung, is a "redemptive" symbol, representing renewal, opportunity, and unrealized potential. Jung noted that in many hero myths, the story begins with a helpless child close to destruction, who "despite all dangers, will unexpectedly pull through." For Jung, the child archetype was "a personification of vital forces quite outside the limited range of our conscious mind; of ways and possibilities of which our one-sided conscious mind knows nothing... 'The 'child' is all that is abandoned and exposed and at the same time divinely powerful; the insignificant, dubious beginning, and the triumphant end."

In 2004, the drama of "Baby 81" provided a very real and poignant example of hope, "abandoned and exposed," yet "divinely powerful." Off the coast of Sri Lanka, in the wake of a terrible tsunami, a baby was found floating amidst a pile of garbage. With no identifying information, the child was simply known as the eighty-first patient brought to the hospital that day. With thousands of children dead or missing, many parents literally fought to gain possession of any actual or potential orphans. In the case of Baby 81, nine sets of parents got involved. According to the Associated Press:

Desperate women quarreled over him—all claiming he was torn from them by the tsunami . . . One man standing outside the Kalmunai Base Hospital threatened to kill himself and his wife if they were not given the baby. A woman at the hospital said she would kill the doctors unless she got him.

Artists have a particular gift for elucidating hope symbols and archetypes. In *Let Us Now Praise Famous Men*, James Agee wrote, "In every child who is born, under no matter what circumstances, and of no matter what parents, the potentiality of the human race is born again." Ralph Waldo Emerson, grief stricken by the death of his son, composed a poem entitled "Threnody" in his memory. One line summed up the magnitude of his loss; "Tis because a general hope was quenched, [that] all must doubt and grope."

Austrian painter Gustav Klimt provided a bold visual representation of the child as a hope symbol. In the summer of 1903 he painted a nude pregnant woman surrounded by three evil-looking monsters. Klimt entitled his work, *Hope I*. Two years later, a close friend of Klimt observed, "She walks unperturbed along the path of terror, spotless and made invulnerable by the 'hope' entrusted to her womb."

## Diagnosis and Treatment

According to the *Surgeon General's 2000 Report on Mental Health*, childhood depression " . . . has many clinical features similar to those in adults. Depressed children are sad, they lose interest in activities that used to please them, and they criticize themselves and feel that others criticize them. They feel unloved, pessimistic, or even hopeless about the future; they think that life is not worth living, and thoughts of suicide may be present." At the same time, investigators have found the following:

- Infants and toddlers may not experience full-blown depression. Nevertheless, they may show signs of sadness, irritability, eating disturbances, apathy, withdrawal, and "failure to thrive."
- Depressed children are less likely than adults to show signs or symptoms of depressive psychosis but are more apt to have high levels of anxiety and to report various aches and pains.
- By middle childhood, relatively stable depressive thought patterns are clearly evident.
- Depression and negative thought patterns are often found among parents of depressed children.
- Antidepressant medications should only be used when children are severely depressed and attempts to treat them with psychotherapy alone have failed (see also below).

*Family and social factors* appear to be especially important in the development of child depression. In *Parental Death and Psychological Development*, psychologist Ellen Berlinsky and one of us (H. B.) uncovered a considerable amount of research, linking early loss of contact with either parent, through death *or* divorce, to later depressive episodes. In another review of the literature, psychologists Judy Garber and Jason Horowitz also found a number of studies linking parental overcontrol, criticalness, and lack of affection to increased symptoms of child depression. They cited several additional studies that implicated deficits in social skills and perceived rejection by peers.

In *Help Me, I'm Sad*, psychiatrist David Fassler noted that while depression in children often remits even without treatment, "that doesn't mean that [it] should be left to run its course." He explained how untreated depression can result in severe and extended future bouts and render the child more prone to a variety of emotional, behavioral, and academic setbacks. His suggestions for "spotting signs and symptoms" in children at various stages of development included the following:

- *Infants and toddlers*: decreased pleasure, sad or deadpan face, little motor activity, withdrawal, too little or too much crying, failure to grow and thrive, verbal expression of sadness, lack of social interest.
- *Preschoolers*: low frustration tolerance, excessive restlessness and irritability, unexplained aches and pains, frequent sadness, lack of pleasure, pessimism.
- *School-aged children*: academic difficulties, school refusal, unprovoked aggression, sleep or weight changes, unexplained physical complaints, sadness, worrying, hopelessness, low self-esteem, tearfulness, morbid or suicidal thoughts.
- *Adolescents*: academic difficulties, self-destructive or antisocial behavior, rejection sensitivity, sadness, hopelessness, low self-esteem, lack of pleasure, sleep problems, fatigue, social isolation, morbid or suicidal thoughts.

In recent years there has been some concern that antidepressants may actually *increase* the risk of suicide in some children and adolescents. However, the most thorough studies in this area reveal that the risk is reduced, rather than increased, for the vast majority of depressed children. Nevertheless, antidepressant medications *do* alter a child's brain chemistry and no one is certain how this may affect his or her future well-being. In general, we recommend that parents, as well as practitioners, exercise extreme caution. Antidepressants should only be used as a last resort, when depressive symptoms are severe, and if psychotherapy and other less invasive interventions fail to alleviate the problem.

As of 2007, the only antidepressant that was approved by the FDA for use in children (ages 8 and older) is Prozac. Nevertheless, it is standard and acceptable medical practice to try other serotonin boosters, such as Zoloft, Paxil, or Celexa. Insist on a thorough medical work-up for your child before he or she begins a regimen of antidepressants, and pay close attention for any increases in suicidal thinking, agitation, or impulsivity. It is particularly important to keep a watchful eye on children from families with a history of bipolar disorder as well as those youngsters who have made previous suicide attempts.

If you believe that that your child is in need of professional help, seek out practitioners who specialize in child and family therapy. Be prepared to actively participate in your child's treatment. For example, it is quite possible that you may be able to consult with clinicians and incorporate their input in helping your child yourself, outside of formal therapy sessions. In most cases, improved parent–child interactions are much more effective than individual therapy.

You may be coached in ways of reinforcing certain therapeutic interventions such as overseeing mini homework assignments in positive thinking, or providing encouragement for your child to engage in activities that promote a greater sense of mastery, attachment, or survival. Be honest about your own emotional health, and if necessary, take steps to assure that you are not overtly or indirectly spreading a sense of futility, isolation, or helplessness to your child.

Ask prospective clinicians or clinical staff if they are familiar with the "Taking Action" treatment approach developed by psychologists Kevin Stark and Phillip Kendal. This 18-week program is designed for depressed children ages 9 to 13. It is a form of group therapy that introduces cognitive and behavioral strategies in a child-friendly manner. For example, the workbook that is given to each child includes weekly checklists and diaries for recording emotions as well as for logging activities that can engender a sense of mastery and feelings of pleasure. Other sections depict cartoon-like child characters with thought bubbles illustrating various forms of distorted thinking. To encourage self-monitoring of negative thoughts, many of the characters are presented as detectives, adorned in raincoats and equipped with magnifying glasses, looking for any sign of depressive distortions such as "catastrophizing," all-or none-thinking, or discounting the positive.

Adolescent hopelessness can often be successfully treated using the same combination of interventions outlined in the previous chapter: cognitive restructuring, a healing relationship, and a spiritual practice. However, children below the age of 9 or 10 will usually require a modified protocol. Because they are still learning to think about thinking, younger children usually do better with family- and play-based interventions rather than traditional cognitive restructuring exercises.

For preadolescents, ages 9 to 11, psychologist Robert Leahy suggested the use of a "monster metaphor" to help them grasp the role of negative thoughts in the development of sadness, fear, and other destructive emotions. As a first step, Leahy advised telling children that everyone has a "good thought monster" as well as a "bad thought monster" inside of them. Sometimes the "bad thought monster" makes you think "you are stupid," that "nobody likes you," or that "something terrible is going to happen on the way to school." In step two, children are asked to list situations in which they have felt sad or scared. Next to each situation, the child, with the help of a therapist (or caregiver), identifies the preceding negative thoughts set in motion by the "bad thought monster." In step three, again with the help of a therapist or caregiver, the child is asked to generate a rebuttal from the "good thought monster," such as "you've done well on tests before," "you have friends like Billy or Mary," or "you walk to school every day and nothing terrible has ever happened." In step four, the entire collection of "good thoughts" is placed on index cards. Parents are then advised to create a simple reward system to ensure that the child reads the cards a few times a day.

## Nurturing Hope

As the preceding discussion indicates, we believe that positive family involvement is often crucial in the successful treatment of childhood depression. But it is also an important factor in *preventing* children from becoming depressed or having other significant emotional problems in the first place. In fact, unless a child is severely depressed or showing signs of self-destructive tendencies, parents should look in house for ways to strengthen their child's mastery, attachment, and survival skills. By "in house" we mean parents and siblings as well as extended family, teachers, and friends. As a point of clarification, our recommendation to look in house does not involve keeping family secrets or casting child mental health experts as a last resort.

Children are deeply sensitive to, and affected by, what is going on in their immediate environment. What you do to or for them matters. In this vein, child psychologist Haim Ginott once wrote that "Children are like wet cement. Whatever falls on them makes an impression." Similarly, humorist Garrison Keillor pointed out that "Nothing you do for children is ever wasted. They seem not to notice us, hovering, averting our eyes, and they seldom offer thanks, but what we do for them is never wasted."

There is ample evidence that secure attachments can nurture hope. For example, psychologist Jude Cassidy found that more securely attached 18-month-old toddlers were already demonstrating a greater facility in exploring and negotiating their environment as compared to anxiously attached children. We also know that securely attached children tend to become more trusting and loving adults who are also able to handle stress more effectively. As we emphasized in earlier chapters, children who are bonded with both their father and mother tend to be particularly advantaged in this regard.

Consistent with our in-house perspective, the rest of this chapter is devoted to specific hope-building strategies and activities that can be used by parents and other childcare providers. Going beyond these nuts and bolts of hope-care delivery, it is also imperative that your approach reflect that of a true hope provider. In this regard, you may want to review the lessons in Chapter 9 (Attachment Matters) on availability, presence, and contact. Try to provide your children with a balanced life perspective that is neither Pollyanna-ish nor pessimistic. Respect your child's feelings, particularly those of sadness and frustration, but distinguish these from erroneous, dark conclusions that they may have about themselves, the world, or the future.

### Hope Exercises

Of the variety of *hope-building exercises* that can be used to strengthen a child's motive systems, one example is called the *Recalled and Expected Events Task*. This is a good *mastery exercise* that has been used in research with both nondepressed and depressed children. On a piece of lined white paper, ask your child to list "ten things that you have done or that happened to you." Turn the page over, and ask your child to jot down "ten things you expect to do or expect to happen to you." Next, go over both lists with your child. Note whether the recalled and expected events are negative or positive and if your child's responses indicate that he or she initiated the events (active) or was the recipient of them (passive). Ideally at least half of the events should be positive and active. If your child lists more than 5 or 6 negative, passive events (bad things that have happened or are expected), pay special attention to the mastery-related activities in the following sections.

*Structured drawing exercises* offer a particularly effective method for exploring the status of your child's *attachment system*. For example, it is common for therapists to ask children as well as adults to draw a picture of their family. The positioning and spacing of figures, the level of detail devoted to figures and objects, and the use of color can all provide clues about a child's emotional experience of others.

To explore attachment security, art therapy expert Donna Kaiser advocated the use of a "bird's nest drawing." Specifically, Kaiser's research suggested that securely attached individuals are more likely to depict one or several birds within the nest. According to her, the most securely attached individuals also tend to include a mother or parent bird. In contrast, Kaiser and her colleagues have found that individuals with a history of significant emotional problems are *more* apt to draw an empty nest and *less* likely to use the color green (the symbol of hope) in their drawings.

It may also be helpful to ask your child a few simple questions after he or she has completed the drawing. For example, if there are no discernible birds, ask your child, "Are there any birds in the nest?" If the answer is yes, ask, "Why can't we see them? Are they hiding?" You might also ask "Do they have parents? Where are their parents?" If your child says "no" (there are no birds), ask where they went and why. Again, you may want to ask about the parents and even broach the subject of whether the mother and father birds are available and responsible caretakers.

A great exercise for enhancing problem-solving skills, as well as fostering liberation beliefs, is the *Lost in the Woods Challenge,* which we mentioned in Chapter 11. This "pretend game" requires nothing more than a sheet of paper for children to keep track of their ideas. Ask your child to pretend that he or she has gotten lost in the woods. Then ask how he or she would find a way home. With each answer, you might reply that this particular strategy might not work. For example, if your child said, "I would shout until somehow heard me," you might say, "Let us pretend that no one could hear you. What else could you do"? Continuing with this simple methodology, see how many options your child is able to generate. When the child can no longer come up with any more ideas, ask, "What do you think will happen?" (Would he or she somehow get rescued, find a way out, or be forever "lost"?) The average nondepressed child is typically able to generate at least two solutions, while the most nondepressed adolescents can come up with four strategies.

## Hope Games

Games can provide an entertaining context for enhancing mastery, attachment, or survival skills. Be sure to select games that are age appropriate. If the level of difficulty is too low, the child will become bored; if the game is too hard, the child may experience frustration or even helplessness. With respect to mastery, classic games for promoting development of the left or verbal side of the brain include Scrabble, anagrams, and crossword puzzles. For the right side of the brain, consider block-design activities such as Legos, puzzle tasks, model building, or drawing figures and landscapes.

To enhance attachment skills, *role-playing games* are ideal for fostering greater cooperation, perspective taking, empathy, trust, and openness. For younger children, we recommend a storybook game, *Faery's Tale* by Firefly Games. As noted on the developer's Web site, children get the opportunity to "play a pixie, brownie, sprite, or pooka in [an] enchanted forest." Children ages 6 or older get to "foil dark faery plots, rescue youngsters from giants, overthrow sorcerous tyrants, awaken princesses from their enchanted slumber, watch over faery godchildren, [while] dancing at festive faery balls, singing mirthful songs, playing clever pranks, or romping with woodland friends, [as] emissaries of joy." For other role-playing games visit http://www.tlucretius.net/RPGs/kids.

Clay sculpting and finger painting are great for promoting a relaxed, more regulated nervous system. Board games such as chess and checkers can also help to strengthen the survival (and mastery) motive by aiding in the development of planning and problem-solving abilities. *Videogames* are enormously popular today. Although some are dominated by aggressive or violent content, there are others that can safely strengthen the motives underlying hope. For teens, we recommend Blinx 2: Masters of Time and Space (mastery) and Paper Mario: The Thousand-Year Door (attachment and survival). Blinx 2 is particularly compelling from a hope perspective because it allows youngsters to manipulate time and experience the consequences in a very immediate and dramatic fashion. For younger children, ages 6 to 12, we recommend the Pokémon series by Nintendo. Pokémon Emerald is a great mastery game, while Pokémon Ranger is more attachment focused. If your child needs to boost his or her survival and coping skills, consider Pokémon Mystery Dungeon, a game of exploration and rescue.

There are a number of fascinating adaptations of videogames designed for chronically ill children. At the Johns Hopkins Children's Center, Dr. Arun Mathews has established HOPE (Hospital-Based Online Pediatric Environment). Children undergoing long and painful dialysis procedures get to play online sports, racing, and adventure games with each other, using Xboxes that link them with others kids within the same facility as well as in other hospitals.

With the help of the Make-a-Wish Foundation, 9-year-old cancer patient Ben Duskin took part in developing a video game focusing on destroying cancer cells. The object of the game is to "destroy all mutated cells" and to collect "seven shields" that ward off the side effects of chemotherapy. His game can be downloaded at http://www.makewish.org.

Hopelab is a California-based nonprofit research organization dedicated to the development of videogames for chronically ill children. Their signature game Re-Mission is geared toward youths diagnosed with cancer. Players get to direct a "gutsy and fully armed" nanobot named Roxxi on "rapid-fire assaults" targeting malignant cancer cells, "wherever they hide." To order Re-Mission visit http://www.re-mission.net.

### Children's Books

Long before the advent of computers and videogames, books were *the* primary form of entertainment designed to impart hope and inspiration in children. With this in mind, parents and caregivers should strongly encourage children to fuel their imaginations with inspiring tales of mastery, love, and survival. TeachFirst.com, in conjunction with the National Education Association, has created a list of the best books for children. We reviewed their offerings for those that were particularly geared towards hope-based mastery, attachment, or survival lessons. These are listed in Table 14.1. For children who are still relatively new to reading or have difficulties in this area, you can read along with them. For children who are older, discuss the book with them.

### Inspiring Children's Films

In 2006 the American Film Institute (AFI) released a list of the "100 most inspiring films of all time." From this collection, we extracted 25 films particularly suitable for instilling hope in children or teens. We added two inspiring contemporary films, *Finding Nemo* and *The Lion King*. In Table 14.2, these are arranged by age level. Do not get too fixated on the motive categories in this table. For example, it is true that *E.T.* is a primarily attachment-oriented film, while *Rudy* is a mastery masterpiece and *Captains Courageous* is a quintessential survival tale. Nevertheless, what makes these films especially hopeful is their depth of coverage with respect to all three of the motives underlying hope. Consider *The Wizard of Oz*. At one level, the plot is focused on Dorothy and her harrowing struggle to find her way back home, but at a deeper

TABLE 14.1.  *Classic Books for Instilling Hope in Children and Teens*

| Hope Motive | Age Group | Title | Author |
|---|---|---|---|
| Mastery | Children | The Little Engine That Could | Watty Piper |
| | | Oh, The Places You'll Go | Dr. Seuss |
| | | A Picture Book of Harriet Tubman | David Adler |
| | Teens | The Red Badge of Courage | Stephen Crane |
| | | Adventures of Huckleberry Finn | Mark Twain |
| | | The Fellowship of the Ring | J. R. R. Tolkien |
| Attachment | Children | The Giving Tree | Shel Silverstein |
| | | Jackie and Me | Dan Gutman |
| | | The Velveteen Rabbit | Margery Williams |
| | Teens | A Walk to Remember | Nicholas Sparks |
| | | A Separate Peace | John Knowles |
| | | Ordinary People | Judith Guest |
| Survival | Children | The Bracelet | Yoshiko Uchida |
| | | Charlotte's Web | E. B. White |
| | | Tuck Everlasting | Natalie Babbit |
| | Teens | Alive | Piers Paul Read |
| | | Anthem | Ayn Rand |
| | | Diary of a Young Girl | Anne Frank |

level, her three companions are collectively on a broader-scale hope mission. The tin man is looking for a heart (attachment); the scarecrow, a brain (mastery); and the cowardly lion, courage (survival).

### Relating to Children

In an essay entitled "Hear Me Out," Dr. Lonnie Carton, a family therapist and educational consultant, tried to give adults some sense of what it feels like to be a child:

My hands are small. Please don't expect me to be perfect when I draw a picture, or set a table or throw a ball. My legs are short. Please slow down so I can keep up . . . My eyes move quickly but they haven't been open long enough to see all the things your grown up eyes have . . . . My needs are simple. I need your love, your attention and your praise. When I do something right or good, or even try hard to do it, smile at me . . . Give me a hug, and tell me you're proud of me.

TABLE 14.2. *Inspiring Films for Instilling Hope in Children and Teens*

| Children | Teens | Children and Teens |
| --- | --- | --- |
| *Attachment-Oriented Films* | *Attachment-Oriented Films* | *Attachment-Oriented Films* |
| E.T. (1982) | Breaking Away (1979) | Black Stallion (1979) |
| Miracle on 34th St. (1947) | Seabiscuit (2003) | Boys Town (1938) |
| Sound of Music (1965) | Sounder (1972) | Field of Dreams (1989) |
| *Mastery-Oriented Films* | *Mastery-Oriented Films* | *Mastery-Oriented Films* |
| Babe (1995) | Chariots of Fire (1981) | Harry Potter (2001) |
| The Lion King (1994) | Hoosiers (1986) | Pride of the Yankees (1942) |
| National Velvet (1944) | Rudy (1993) | Rocky I (1976) |
| *Survival-Oriented Films* | *Survival-Oriented Films* | *Survival-Oriented Films* |
| Finding Nemo (2003) | Captains Courageous (1937) | Diary of Anne Frank (1959) |
| Pinocchio (1944) | Dead Poet's Society (1989) | The Karate Kid (1984) |
| The Wizard of Oz (1939) | Spiderman (2002) | Star Wars (1977) |

Unfortunately, many parents find it difficult to see the world through the eyes of a child, while others can do it with ease. Their ability is often simply a byproduct of prior experience. Perhaps they were raised in a large family, growing up with one or more younger siblings. Alternatively, they may have worked at a summer camp, participated in a scouting group, or coached a sports team. In any case, personality plays a major role. Those who remain child-like (not childish) in their demeanor do particularly well around children, enjoying games, laughter, and spontaneity. They are not above getting down to the level of the child, either literally or figuratively. Here are some tips for those who wish to relate better to children:

- Ask a child what he or she would like to be called. Does the child have a nickname?
- Ask if he or she has a favorite game, movie, TV show, or hero.
- Inquire about any pets.
- Try not to talk too far beneath or above the child's level of understanding.
- From time to time, drop down to the child's level by squatting down, kneeling, or sitting on the floor.
- If there is a book or TV show that you want a child to read or watch, take turns, allowing him or her to make the first or second choice.
- Give the child choices within a predetermined range of possibilities to help him or her develop a sense of shared control.

- Never talk about a child in front of others as if he or she was not present.
- If you bring a child to a doctor or other professional, do your best to inform the child what to expect of the encounter.

Parents and caregivers can nurture hope by also relating to their children in a manner that is empowering, supportive, and liberating. Ideally, they should consider the child's particular hope profile and adjust their relational style accordingly. Is the child primarily experiencing powerlessness? Does the child feel especially alienated or profoundly helpless? Moreover, it is important to consider the developmental level of your child.

Research conducted by one of us (A. S.) suggested that younger children experiencing hopelessness between the ages of 6 and 10 find it particularly hard to imagine alternative solutions to their problems. They simply take longer to problem solve as compared to more hopeful children. In effect, their survival system has been compromised. In contrast, adolescents experiencing hopelessness between the ages of 13 and 18 tend to become more passive and may struggle to recall or anticipate positive life events. In this later stage, it appears that hopelessness affects the mastery system as well as conceptions of the past and future. Taken together, these findings seem to indicate that younger children who suffer from feelings of hopelessness may be especially in need of a liberating relationship, whereas older children and teens might profit more from an empowering connection.

### Empowering Care

In fact, *every* child should feel empowered. Recall that when Hodding Carter invoked the metaphor of "roots and wings," he was referring specifically to children and the importance of giving them a foundation for lifelong mastery as well as a solid basis for attachment. Children who are encouraged, inspired, and nurtured are more likely to find their own voice, to lead rather than merely follow, to realize a life of meaning and purpose.

On the other hand, there are children who are especially vulnerable to feelings of powerlessness, depression, and even suicide. Those who fail at school or are unable to achieve any tangible sense of success outside the classroom may have special empowerment needs. For example, compared to their peers, learning-disabled children are three times more likely to become depressed or to commit suicide. Minority children, who are often weighed down by oppression and frequently lack appropriate role models, are also at risk. Native American teens, tagged by psychiatrist Alvin Poussaint as the "most isolated ethnic group in America," are two and half times more likely to die from suicide as compared to white teens. In just a decade and a half, the rate of suicide among African American teens has more than doubled.

As in the case of adults, empowering children involves *commitment, challenge, and shared control*. Without commitment, a child may feel unsupported as well as confused about the ultimate value of any suggested endpoint. If they are not appropriately challenged, children may become frustrated or, conversely, develop a horizon that is not commensurate with their true potential. Lacking a sense of shared control, they may become either overwhelmed by excessive responsibilities or overly dependent on an ever-present enabler.

In *Top of the Class*, Soo Kim Abboud and Jane Kim outlined some of the values and principles shared by Asian parents in fostering their children's excellence in school and at work. In the realm of commitment, they noted "a love and need for learning and education" as well as a "respect and desire for delayed gratification and sacrifice." With respect to challenge, the parents emphasized professions offering both "intellectual fulfillment" and "healthy competition" as well as "financial security." Shared control was demonstrated in a variety of ways, including "parental acceptance of responsibility for school failures" and the practice of "surrounding children with similarly-minded friends and role models."

In *The Measure of Our Success*, Marian Wright Edelman shared her 25 lessons for life. An African American, she recalled the "ugly external voices" emanating from her small, segregated town in South Carolina. Still, she wrote, "We always knew who we were and that the measure of our worth was inside our heads and hearts and not outside in our possessions or on our backs." Applicable to all young people, but geared particularly to minority youth, Wright Edelman's lessons also reflect the need for commitment (Set goals and work quietly and systematically towards them), challenge (Don't feel entitled to anything you don't sweat and struggle for), and shared control (Always remember that you are never alone). For Wright Edelman, the single greatest need is to move forward with a sense of integrity, purpose, and meaning, to "sell the shadow for substance," to "listen for the sound of the genuine" within oneself, and to "be confident that you can make a difference."

In a similar vein, Rabbi Shmuley Boteach advocated "lighting up the family with passion and inspiration." In *Parenting with Fire*, he encouraged both mothers and fathers to take stock of their own passions and to work toward effectively sharing with their children their enthusiasm and commitment for these pursuits. If you can generate a reasonably broad menu of alternative passions, there are bound to be one or more that will attract the interest of your child. In *Fathers and Families*, one of us (H. B.) emphasized how both parents can play a vital role in stimulating their child's initiative and achievement motivation while increasing his or her range of perceived domains for success.

Parents who wish to empower their children should strive for a hope-building middle ground. Ideally, your standards for mastery should be aimed just beyond your child's current ability level. We noted in Chapter 4 that Russian developmental psychologist Lev Vygotsky referred to this area between a child's current level of development and his or her soon unfolding potential as the "zone of proximal development." From this perspective, educators developed the concept of scaffolding, erecting a temporary framework that allows the child to move up to the next level. A fitting analogy is the multistage rocket booster used to launch the Space Shuttle. Several rocket boosters provide over 80% of the initial lift; however, once the shuttle reaches a certain height, the boosters separate, leaving the ship to be guided from within.

It is helpful for parents to introduce a variety of mastery alternatives to their children. Psychologist Robert Brooks referred to these as potential "islands of competencies." He noted that a wise parent can provide repeated "success samplings" via careful "environmental engineering." For example, if your child is not athletically gifted, then you might put more emphasis on music, art, or nature. On the other hand, psychologist Rick Snyder suggested that parents provide mastery opportunities that span the academic, social, and athletic domains. With respect to potential challenges, Snyder advised parents to normalize "barriers" and "roadblocks" by providing children with plenty of examples of *alternative strategies for goal attainment*. Keep in mind that you and your child may have quite different mastery preferences. Make sure that you are not pressuring them to fulfill your unrealized dreams. Snyder also recommended that parents tell their children about their own past experiences in overcoming obstacles.

In *A Mind at a Time*, pediatrician Mel Levine offered some helpful advice for parents who want to improve the *learning prospects* for their children. From our perspective, some of Levine's recommendations seem particularly powerful because they combine parental commitment in a context that is sensitive yet challenging. Moreover, these strategies can be easily modified to accommodate the empowerment needs of virtually any child.

- Be a well-informed child mind watcher, attuned to your child's strengths, weaknesses, and special needs.
- Be a wise consumer and passionate advocate when it comes to obtaining potential resources that might be available for your child.
- When offering criticism, make sure it is constructive. Target the behavior, not the child.
- Avoid public criticism or invidious comparisons, especially between siblings.
- Partner with schools. Help your child "learn to learn" by assuring daily activities to exercise the mind while assisting them in prioritizing school assignments.
- Maintain am intellectual life at home by modeling a love of learning and showing interest in what your child is studying. Discuss ideas, current events, or daily newspaper articles. Value productivity and process over grades.
- Develop a shared hope trajectory for your children, empowering them with a realistic sense of what they may be able to achieve in later life.

Parents who have children with learning disabilities can obtain a free publication entitled *Understanding Learning Disabilities: A Parent Guide and Workbook.* Development of this text was jointly sponsored by the Learning Disabilities Council and the National Center for Learning Disabilities, whose motto reads, "The power to hope, to learn, and to succeed." In a section labeled, "Helping your Child at Home," there are excellent suggestions for improving self-esteem, fostering autonomy, allowing for experiences of success as well as frustration, creating a haven at home, and cultivating both academic as well as nonacademic interests and skills. There is even a worksheet for recording your daily progress in each of these areas.

### Supportive Care

Many children need extra doses of support, especially youngsters who feel alienated, forsaken, or uninspired. It is essential that you *support what your child actually wants and not what you want for them.* In other words, do not let your need to live through your child corrupt your love. Make every effort to recognize your child's true aspirations and actual strengths and weaknesses. In *Help Me, I'm Sad*, psychiatrist David Fassler emphasized that the number-one factor in "promoting resiliency" is love and support for the "real child." Toward this end, he made a number of suggestions, including paying attention to a child's basic temperament, providing contexts for success, and incorporating feedback that promotes greater self-awareness to inform future endeavors.

In stark contrast, there are too many instances in which parents try to force their hopes and dreams onto a reluctant child. In some cases it is an academically oriented parent who tries to strong-arm a child who is more interested in sports or a particular trade such as carpentry or automotive repair. Alternatively, it could be a practically minded parent who may find it virtually impossible to support an offspring's artistic or creative aspirations.

### Liberating Care

> Your children are not your children .... They are the sons and daughters of Life's longing for itself ... They come through you but not from you ... You are the bows from which your children as living arrows are sent forth ... Let your bending in the archer's hand be for gladness; For even as [God] loves the arrow that flies, so [God] loves also the bow that is stable.
>
> —Kahlil Gibran, "On Children"

David Fassler's tips for building resiliency included some excellent suggestions for nurturing liberation beliefs in children. In particular, he called for parents to *provide a safe and secure context* by being as predictable and available as possible. In this regard, his suggestions are strikingly similar to those we previously described in Chapter 9 (Attachment Matters). Fassler also advised parents to *allow a child to experience life.* By this he meant that you should not go overboard in your attempts to buffer a child from the slings and arrows of the world. Some adversity is necessary to build character and to develop coping skills.

According to Fassler, you should also *foster a multilayered sense of self-esteem.* Engage your child in a variety of activities with the goal of having him or her develop a wide range of interests and potential frontline as well as fallback sources of pride and self-efficacy. Consistent with this particular recommendation, a number of psychologists, including Anat Brunstein-Klomek and his colleagues, have found that suicidal teens are likely to have a narrow range of domains from which they can draw positive self-attributions as compared to their healthier counterparts who tend to have a much more differentiated sense of self.

Some children may have special liberation needs. For example, those who are victims of longstanding *bullying* are at risk for developing depressive and suicidal thoughts. A number of investigators have discovered that child victims of bullying often have ineffective problem-solving skills as well as a history of parental overprotectiveness and lack of warmth. If you are a parent of a child who is being victimized, visit the Website of the Committee for Children, a nonprofit organization specializing in programs for addressing youth violence, bullying, and personal safety. At http://www.cfchildren.org you will find a number of excellent resources, including the following tips for parents:

- Encourage your child to report incidents of bullying to you.
- Validate the child's feelings of fear, anger, sadness, etc.
- Coach him or her in describing the specifics (who, what, when, where).
- Ask how the child has tried to stop the bullying.
- Suggest coping alternatives (going to different places or games, staying near adults).
- Treat your child's school as a potential ally (work with staff, be an advocate).
- Encourage the child to report incidents of bullying to trusted school personnel.

To this list we would also encourage all children, girls as well as boys, to develop skills of self-defense, including verbal self-assertiveness, along with more fitness-related attributes. Children, as well as adults, who are fit are much less likely to be bullied or harassed. In strengthening your child's survival system, do not ignore the importance of encouraging a healthy body image, whether through positive athletic experiences or more focused muscle-building activities. Moreover, be a good role model: do the best you can to keep in shape yourself and to maintain an adequate level of endurance in physical activities. In *Creative Fitness*, one of us (H. B.) provided many suggestions for enjoyable family play activities that can contribute to the emotional and physical well-being of adults and children. Some examples could include chase games, playing catch, running, dancing, biking, hiking, neighborhood walks, gardening, or even joining a gym as a family.

By participating in sports, most children, regardless of ability level, can develop greater confidence in their bodies and can improve their ability to self-regulate and to tolerate stress. The National Association for Sport and Physical Education offers a helpful set of guidelines for parents entitled "Choosing the Right Sport or Physical Activity for Your Child."

- Review the administration and organization of the activity, including its basic philosophy and commitment to diversity, fair play, teamwork, and sportsmanship as well as its process for selecting and training coaches.
- Assess the activity's safety considerations (sanitation; availability of first aid; ratio of coaches to players; appropriate warm-up and conditioning regimen).
- Consider your child's readiness to join in terms of his or her interests, intensity level, size, and maturity.
- Clarify the nature and degree of parental commitments to the activity (time, cost, involvement, etc.).
- Evaluate the emotional as well as physical costs and benefits (fun and interest level for the child; appropriate number of practices and games; frequency and quality of interactions between coaches and parents).

## Nurturing Spirituality

Parents or caregivers may wonder how spiritual practices can be incorporated into the life of a child. This may be particularly confusing for those of you who are atheists or agnostics. However, what is true for adults is also applicable to children. *Hope requires some form of spiritual foundation*, religious or not. (In this context, you may find it helpful to refer back to Chapter 7, Spiritual Growth, and Chapter 8, Spiritual Intelligence).

If you have raised your children within the context of a *traditional religious framework*, it is important to understand that their mere attendance at a mass, temple, or religious class may not necessarily assure the development of a spiritual life robust enough to enable them to deal with the inevitable vicissitudes of adult life. It is the quality, not the quantity, of religious experiences that determines the ultimate impact. For example, a study conducted by psychologist Michelle Pearce and her colleagues revealed that children's perceptions of their congregations were far more important than their attendance levels or self-rankings of religiosity in determining how spiritually grounded they felt.

You may find it helpful to have regular discussions with your children about their religious and spiritual experiences. Try to focus on the larger lessons that you are hoping to instill while striving to embody them in your daily family interactions. In *Encouraging Your Child's Spiritual Intelligence*, psychologist Mollie Painton offered a self-quiz to help parents understand the qualities of a "wise and compassionate spiritual partner," among them: accepting and validating a child's spiritual experience; giving the child time and space to think, play, and daydream; supporting the child's further spiritual development; and sharing of one's own spiritual experiences.

Remember that "spiritual" does not necessarily mean "religious." There are a multitude of opportunities for children to derive a spiritual experience beyond the framework of traditional religious rituals practiced in a church, temple, or other places of worship. Spiritual lessons in faith, commitment, and transcendence can be experienced in a variety of other contexts.

### Family Life

Buddha compared a loving family to a "beautiful flower garden." Author John Bowring described the happy family as an "earlier heaven." In *Care of the Soul*, Thomas Moore wrote:

> Family life is full of major and minor crises—the ups and downs of health, success and failure . . . and all kinds of characters. It is tied to places and events and histories. With all of these felt details, life etches itself into memory and personality. It's difficult to imagine anything more nourishing to the soul.

As a parent or caregiver there are a variety of ways for you to infuse a greater spiritual dimension into your family life. If you are religiously inclined, consider setting aside a regular time for *family worship*. This could be as simple as taking a few minutes for silence or prayer before a meal or involve attendance at a formal mass or service. "Holy days" provide another opportunity to nurture the spiritual development of your children. Regardless of your choice of worship, it is imperative that you set an example for your children of an intrinsic or genuine investment in the larger meaning of specific prayers or rituals.

Those who are not religiously inclined may also consider ways of infusing spirituality into their *family rituals*. Assure a meaningful and peaceful context by allowing enough time and space for such activities. You cannot rush or choreograph a spiritual experience. When planning a special gathering, invite elders to share stories from their childhood or the "old country." By including grandparents and other older adults, you are providing children with a greater sense of tradition and continuity as well as the opportunity to partake of their wisdom. As an added touch, you might light some candles, include an old family recipe, or play a wide assortment of music, reflecting the tastes of the various generations, present and deceased.

Since the publication of Alex Haley's *Roots*, more and more individuals have shown an interest in exploring their family history. Increased longevity and affluence, as well as the advent of the Worldwide Web, have also helped to fuel this desire to look back. Moreover, for many individuals there is a strong spiritual component in retracing the steps of their ancestors. In *The Black Family Pledge*, Maya Angelou reflected on the need for parents to preserve the spirit of their ancestors:

> BECAUSE we have lost the path our ancestors cleared
> kneeling in perilous undergrowth, our children cannot find their way.
> BECAUSE we have banished the God of our ancestors,
> our children cannot pray.
> BECAUSE the old wails of our ancestors have faded beyond our hearing,
> our children cannot hear us crying.
> Therefore we pledge to bind ourselves to one another . . . knowing that we are
> more than keepers of our brothers and sisters. We ARE our brothers and
> sisters.
> IN HONOR of those who toiled and implored God with golden tongues,
> and in gratitude to the same God who brought us out of hopeless desolation,
> we make this pledge.

Young children may show even more interest in their family's past than their older siblings. They may be especially interested in their parents' experiences growing up. Genwriters, a Web-based forum for genealogy investigators, offers a number of ideas for helping to nurture children's interest in this area. Here are some of their suggestions:

- On a map of the United States (or world), place a sticker on each town, state, or country where your ancestors lived.
- Borrow from the library a travel video about your ancestor's homeland.
- Create a family tree using photographs. Look for similar physical characteristics between the generations.
- Teach your children or grandchildren how to create a pedigree chart. Talk about the documents in which you might find the relevant information.
- Take a genealogy vacation. Retrace the migration route of your ancestors. Travel to the towns and homes where your ancestors lived.
- Read an historical novel to get a better sense of how your early ancestors might have lived.

## Nature-Based Activities

> Let children walk with Nature, let them see the beautiful blendings and
> communions of death and life, their joyous inseparable unity, as taught in
> woods and meadows, plains and mountains and streams of our blessed star,
> and they will learn that death is stingless indeed, and as beautiful as life.
>
> —John Muir

Children, as well as adults, often find themselves transformed by their encounters with the natural world. For Native Americans, the Ifa of Western Africa, and the Australian Aborigines, nature has always been *the* primary vehicle for approaching the divine. In the Old Testament Isaiah exhorted his fellow Jews to "lift your eyes and look to the heaven . . . [to] He who brings out the starry host one by one." Thoreau observed, "An early-morning walk is a blessing for the whole day." Whenever there is meaningful contact with the sacred spaces of nature, there is the potential to realize a blessed hope, one filled with wonder and amazement as well as mystical unity and timeless rebirth.

In *Last Child in the Woods*, author Richard Louv wrote of the "spiritual necessity of nature for the young." Observing that most transcendent childhood experiences occur in nature, he summarized the findings of more than a hundred studies highlighting the many gifts that can be realized through the great outdoors. For example, research by environmental psychologists at Cornell University found that simply having a room with a view of nature seems to have a stress-buffering effect on children. There was also some evidence that middle-school children whose homes were positioned closer to nature reported less depression and anxiety than their urban counterparts.

Not surprisingly, Louv bemoaned the "increasing divide between the young and the natural world," speculating that some children may even show signs of what he labeled "nature-deficit disorder." He exhorted parents to nudge children away from television sets, videogames, and the Internet and toward wilderness walks, camping trips, and fishing expeditions. "Sit together at the edge of a pond," "wander through an overgrown garden," or "track bird migrations." "In the winter look for hibernating insects." If you want to "bring nature home," have your child share in the care of a pet or help transform part of the backyard into a flower or vegetable garden.

Scouting and 4-H clubs are two group-based organizations that are particularly well suited for fostering spirituality and hope in the context of nature-based activities. There are scouting associations in over 200 countries, while 4-H clubs can be found in more than 80 countries. Both groups emphasize values-based character development and the acquisition of practical skills.

From a hope perspective, it is noteworthy that *both scouting and 4-H clubs find virtue in mastery, attachment, and survival.* For example, according to their bylaws, a scout must endeavor to be "thrifty" and "physically strong" (mastery), "trustworthy" and "kind" (attachment), as well as "brave" and "reverent" (survival). Similarly, the four "H's" stand for "head" ("clear thinking," which equates to mastery), "heart" and "hands" (loyalty and service to others, which fosters attachment), and "health" (promoting a healthy lifestyle or enhanced survival).

Former scout Ben Gray recalled one particularly moving experience:

> There are those moments that were life changing. I remember at Philmont [New Mexico], one night at 3 a.m. going out of my tent to sit on a rock the size of a VW Bug in the middle of a field. The moon shining brightly, the air so crisp it gave me goose bumps; I could see my breath. It was that night that I wept, earnestly seeking the Lord and realized for the first time that I was being called into full time ministry.

Outward Bound is another organization that provides a wide range of natural learning experiences for young people. Its roots go back to 1941 when educator Kurt Hahn set out to develop a program to foster "greater self-reliance" and "spiritual tenacity" among young British soldiers and sailors. Consistent with this early mandate, Outward Bound programs are particularly well-suited for youth who need to develop better mastery and survival skills. These hope motives are highlighted under the core values of the organization, which include "adventure and challenge" as well as "service and integrity."

Outward Bound has a number of divisions, which offer a plethora of programs for teens and adults. In the United States the largest and most comprehensive program is Outward Bound Wilderness, located in Golden, Colorado. Youth adventure courses lasting from 3 days to several months are available for teens of ages 12 to 18. A large number of activities are offered, including sailing, white water rafting, backpacking, snowboarding, and even dog sledding. In addition, Outward Bound Wilderness offers an "intercept" program for *at-risk teens* (14–17) and young adults (18–20) who are dealing with low self-esteem or underachievement or are engaging in various risky behaviors, including truancy or drug abuse.

There are also nature-based camps for children with particular mastery, attachment, or survival needs. For example, regular outdoor activities are included in scores of academically oriented camps, focusing on just about every subject imaginable, from math and science to creative writing and public speaking. There are day and overnight camps for children with special attachment needs, including camps for children who are suffering from grief and loss or those who are socially limited due to developmental delays or disabilities such as Asperger syndrome, a high-functioning form of autism. In addition, some camps are specifically designed for children with cancer, HIV, or other chronic and life-threatening conditions. Visit http://www.mysummercamps.com for links to more than 15,000 camps nationwide.

Before you enroll your child in a camp, do some research and some soul searching. How long has a particular camp been in existence? Is the staff well-trained? Are junior counselors well supervised? Does the camp retain nursing and/or medical personnel in the event a child becomes ill or is injured? Does the mission of the camp seem appropriate given your child's needs and abilities? In this regard, be completely honest with yourself. For example, if you are an overachiever but your son really needs a summer of down time, do not enroll him in a highly structured math or computer camp. Conversely, if you are a sports enthusiast but your daughter prefers books or nature, avoid selecting a high-pressure soccer or softball camp.

# Fifteen

## HOPE AND HEALING: WHY HOPE *IS* THE BEST MEDICINE

> Virtue lies in the middle... For it is the nature of things to be destroyed by defect or excess. We see this in the case of strength and health. "Courage" lies between "cowardice" and "rashness." "Friendship" is between "quarrelsome" and "flattery." "Equanimity" lies between "apathy" and "irritability"...To depart from what is extreme is to hold "the ship" beyond the surf and spray.
> —Aristotle, "The Golden Mean"

Can hope bring about healing? Do reductions in stress alleviate the symptoms of a cold? Will love prevent a heart attack? Does attitude matter in the fight against cancer? Can the will to live extend life? These questions have preoccupied philosophers and healers for over 2,000 years. In the first half of this chapter, we examine the mind–body connection, focusing on insights that may shed new light on this perennial issue. We deal with the health implications of balanced and unbalanced forms of attachment, mastery, and survival and conclude with a new way of understanding how hope can foster healing. In Chapter 16, we provide specific prescriptions for enhancing personal well-being and general principles for maintaining health and fostering healing. Together, these final chapters round out the collection of principles and strategies that, throughout the second half of this book, we have proposed for living a hopeful life.

## Jaime's Story

Jaime was diagnosed with thyroid cancer in her mid 20s. She found it both amusing and infuriating when she was told she had the "good cancer." "Let me tell you," she said, "I run a support group for thyroid cancer survivors. We had a woman attending for her husband who had thyroid cancer. Well, a short time later this poor man died. Now tell his wife," she said in a sarcastic tone, "he had the 'good cancer.'"

In pursuit of healing, Jaime relied on a strong will to live as well as her previous training in teacher education. "You have to take action and do your own research. No one is going to be as concerned about your health as you. I use that mindset, of a teacher and a learner, to gather as much information as possible. I subscribe to a number of medical journals. I keep up on the progress of new clinical trials. I also rely a great deal on the Thy-CA website, which includes a listserve and other great resources."

Jaime discovered that there was not a single support group for thyroid cancer survivors in her community. Drawing on her background in education, she started her own group. "I have been running the group for nearly three years. I have about 80 cancer survivors in my database. We do a lot of fundraising and awareness activities, including participating in the American Cancer Society Relay for Life. I get as much as I give during the support group meetings. The sense of camaraderie is unbelievable. Plus, you can only do so much research on your own. When you have certain symptoms and experiences and a doctor tells you it is not possible, yet 30 people validate you with their own similar testimonies—that's powerful."

In dealing with healthcare providers, Jaime took a collaborative approach. "I worked with a team of doctors, including some fantastic nuclear medicine physicians. I also had a great endocrinologist who is really on top of things. We traded e-mails on a daily basis. My surgeon was also excellent. She would not 'blow smoke up your ass' but at the same time, was always confident."

From the start of her healing journey, Jaime garnered a tremendous amount of family support. "My partner and my parents have been wonderful. They come to my appointments, help in caring for my seven year old son, and share the burden of running a household." Jaime's attachments have strengthened her resolve to stay positive and strong. "Knowing my son needs a mom makes the fight more bearable. I can't abandon him. In fact, I feel as if all my connections have a purpose."

Jaime is big on having *options*. "Although I was being treated at one of the most respected medical centers in the country, I wanted a second opinion. I took my chart to Sloan-Kettering in New York and asked them to review my records. They told me that I should continue with my treatment back home, that no one would know my neck better than my own doctors and that my previous treatment had, in their opinion, been excellent. This gave me a great deal of reassurance."

Jamie noted that hope requires time and patience. "From all I've read on preparing for surgeries, I know it's important to relax. I do a great deal of meditating. I take breaks.

I try to deal honestly with what is going on without dwelling on it nonstop." Jaime felt that time was on her side. "This is a slow growing cancer and new technologies are being developed all the time. This is another source of hope for me, that time will bring more answers."

Like many "cancer survivors" Jaime found meaning in the midst of her suffering. "I am no longer self-conscious about my scars. I used to cover them with turtleneck sweaters and elaborate scarves. Now I view them as my badges of courage. Each scar serves to tell a story. Each scar is my part of the journey I have traveled."

Jaime added that she derived great comfort from her religious and spiritual beliefs. "I'm Roman Catholic. I buy candles with the saints like St. Jude (the patron saint of hope) and St. Peregrine (the patron saint of cancer patients). I light the candles. I use my rosary and pray. I do not believe that God is vindictive. I do not believe he would have put me through all this, and allowed me to recover from all these surgeries, just to abandon me and let me die at this point. God put me here for a reason."

## The Mind–Body Connection

Is hope truly the best medicine? Was Benjamin Franklin right when he warned, "He that lives upon hope will die fasting"? Among more contemporary hope doubters are those who flatly deny any connection between emotions and health. Some disparage all mind–body adherents, failing to distinguish genuine healers from charlatans and dismissing every nontraditional practitioner as nothing more than a modern-day snake-oil peddler who dispenses useless panaceas and inert elixirs.

In contrast, some of the most prominent scientists and physicians since the time of Hippocrates have endorsed the idea that thoughts and emotions do indeed play a key role both in the generation of illness and in the process of recovery (see Table 15.1). Instead of snake oil, they would favor a more positive reptilian allusion: the caduceus, the golden wand of medicine; also known as the staff of Asclepius, this ancient healing symbol consists of a snake wound around a rod or pole. Yet for centuries these hope proponents could only presume the existence of the mind–body connection and had little scientific evidence to support their beliefs in it. Only in the twentieth century did evidence begin to accrue to address the three separate but interrelated hypotheses or questions that the mind–body connection now encompasses:

Are there hard-wired pathways in the body that link the nervous system with the endocrine and immune systems?

Do negative factors such as anger, stress, or social isolation contribute to the onset or exacerbation of illness?

If there are mind–body connections, can these be positively exploited to promote healing by using interventions such as hypnosis, imagery or social support?

By the 1980s, considerable data had been collected to indicate that indeed negative emotions and lack of social support could exact a terrible toll on the body as well as the mind. Unfortunately, there was still little information regarding specific pathways or mechanisms and even less to recommend in terms of interventions. In fact, many scientists and physicians still presumed that the immune and endocrine systems operated independently of the mind.

A more compelling mind–body bridge was forged in the 1990s when psychologists, immunologists, and physicians combined to establish the interdisciplinary field of psychoneuroimmunology (PNI). Their work was stimulated by the pioneering findings of psychologist Robert Ader, who in the early 1970s presented laboratory evidence suggesting that the immune system was subject to learning and conditioning. In the new millennium, some PNI scientists are exploring the relative importance of permanent structures, as opposed to free particles, along the mind–body health continuum. Others are investigating the extent to which positive or negative emotions can affect specific hormones, T cells, and other disease-fighting agents within the body.

The most significant PNI findings involved the discovery of nerve cells and receptor sites that span the nervous, immune, and endocrine systems. For example, neuroscientist David Felten and his colleagues traced a network of nerves that extended from the brain to specific blood vessels within the immune system. Immunologists Dan Carr and Ed Blalock detected immune cells that produced chemical messengers similar to those used by the brain. Neuroscientist Candace Pert and her colleagues at the National Institute of Health demonstrated that the nervous system produced its very own immune cell products. In *Molecules of Emotion*, Pert argued that each emotion may be associated with a unique package of chemicals, including tiny neuropeptides that can bind to receptors within both the endocrine and immune systems. Presumably, different emotions transmit varying messages to the rest of the body–mind network, including information pertaining to health and healing as well as to injury and illness.

Along with the explosion in PNI research, there were other landmark psychosomatic studies in the closing decades of the twentieth century. By the end of the millennium, most scientists and practitioners were convinced of two things; first, there *are* bidirectional pathways linking the mind with the immune and endocrine systems, and secondly, destructive social and emotional experiences *can* contribute to the onset or progression of illness.

It is one thing to demonstrate in the laboratory that nerve endings are observable in the lymphatic system or among hormone-secreting glands, but can thoughts, emotions, and behaviors utilize this biological bridge to forge an effective healing network?

It is our belief that building and maintaining hope, both in the short term and over an extended course of time, can stimulate and sustain the health of your nervous, endocrine, and immune systems. In the pages that follow, we review the best evidence linking the hope motives of attachment, mastery, and survival to health and illness.

TABLE 15.1. *Notable Proponents of Mind–Body Healing*

| Mind–Body Advocate | Credentials | Quote/Contribution |
|---|---|---|
| Hippocrates (400 B.C.) | The "founder of medicine"; author of the Hippocratic Oath | "It is more important to know what kind of patient has a disease than what kind of disease a patient has." |
| Galen (200 A.D.) | Greatest healer of antiquity; described the cranial nerves, the valves of the heart, and the kidneys | Temperament is a factor in health and disease; "healing dreams" can aid in diagnosis and treatment |
| Avicenna (1000 A.D.) | "Prince of physicians"; his *Canon of Medicine* was the physician's textbook for 500 years | Emotions are one of the six determinants of health; "positive thinking" is a powerful healer |
| Paracelsus (1500 A.D.) | Greatest chemist of the Middle Ages; founder of pharmacology | "Imagination is a great factor in medicine; the spirit is the master, and imagination is the tool." |
| Sir William Osler (1900) | Dubbed "world's greatest physician" at the turn of the twentieth century | The role of hostility in heart disease, the impact of stress on arthritis, coping and chronic illness |
| Herbert Benson (1985) | Professor, Harvard Medical School; proponent of the "relaxation response" | Combining the "relaxation response" with a "faith factor" can produce beneficial changes in physiology. |
| Jonas Salk (1986) | Physician and medical researcher; developer of the polio vaccine | "The mind has the power to turn the immune system around." |
| Bernie Siegel (1986) | Yale-trained pediatric and general surgeon | Chronicled the successes of exceptional cancer patients; "to give a family hope is never wrong" |
| Candace Pert (1999) | Neuroscientist; former division head, National Institutes of Health (NIH) | "Molecules of emotion" link the brain with the immune and endocrine systems |
| Ronald and Janice Kiecolt-Glaser (2002) | Immunologist, and psychologist; Ohio State University School of Medicine | Psychological and social interventions can boost the immune system |

## A Healing Focus

There are certain diseases and conditions that engage the hopes and fears of the vast majority of the population. For example, a newly diagnosed *heart condition* may inflict the burden of a watchful and sedentary compromise. High blood pressure can provoke the fear of an impending *stroke* and lead someone to feel like a walking time bomb. The mere mention of *cancer* or *AIDS* can be enough to trigger a spiritual or existential crisis.

In addition to these major life-threatening conditions, there are chronic illnesses that may result in years, if not decades, of pain, suffering, and diminished quality of life. Indeed, one of the side effects of greater longevity, and life-saving medical procedures, is an increased prevalence of such problems. In fact, by the time you reach age 65, you face almost a 90% chance of having to deal with some form of chronic illness. The following are five of the most prevalent, nonacute conditions that can be greatly impacted by an individual's psychological, social, or spiritual health.

Arthritis and other rheumatic diseases
Diabetes
Gastrointestinal disorders
Chronic pain
Chronic wounds or injuries

Not surprisingly, just about every mind–body finding in the scientific literature, whether about these and other conditions or about related issues, seems to be associated with one or more of the motives underlying hope. Moreover, it is remarkable how well the evidence lines up in support of a hope-based approach to attachment, mastery, and survival.

### "The Will to Live"

In Western cultures, there is a tendency to address matters of healing with fighting words. Patients and their physicians speak of "beating," "defeating," or "vanquishing" an illness. An infection prompts the notion of a body "under siege" and visions of recruiting the "defenses" of the immune system to "attack" the "foreign invaders." When a loved one succumbs, it may be noted in the obituary that they "lost a courageous battle" with cancer or some other disease.

Gary Reisfield, a professor of medicine at the University of Florida Health Science Center, pointed out that some physicians have become particularly enamored of what he called the "military metaphor." In reference to cancer, he noted, "The enemy is cancer, the commander is the physician, the combatant is the patient, the allies are the health-care team and the weapons are chemical, biological and nuclear."

Reisfield cautioned physicians against using such stark militaristic metaphors without considering the particular dispositions of their individual patients. As a case in point, Lance Armstrong was told that he was going to be "bombarded" by very high levels of chemotherapy, "high enough levels to nearly kill you as well as the cancer." Rather than feeling inspired, Armstrong was taken aback and switched doctors. From his perspective, a "healing journey" (not unlike a bicycle race) served as a more hopeful metaphor.

Similar concerns prompted Susan Sontag to write *Illness as Metaphor*. Sontag suggested that some disease characterizations, while intended to serve as vehicles of empowerment, may actually add to an individual's suffering. This is particularly likely when an illness myth promotes in an individual an exaggerated sense of personal responsibility for contracting a disease and results in a feeling of failure if that individual does not fight and overcome.

What has been learned from the research? Is it helpful to be a fighter when you are sick? There is considerable evidence that a sense of control and mastery can support health as well as healing. The following are some examples:

- Psychologists Ellen Langer and Judith Rodin divided nursing home residents into two groups. Members of one group received a plant and were told that it was their responsibility to take care of it. In addition, they were allowed to choose visitation hours and the day of the week that they would see a movie. The second group also received a plant and had access to visitors as well as a weekly film. However, care of the plant was left to the nursing staff, and visitation hours as well as film showings were predetermined. After 18 months, twice as many residents were alive in the personal control group as compared to the staff-controlled group.

- Depression, which is often associated with a profound sense of helplessness, has been linked to a compromised immune system. To cite just one study, Steven Schleifer and his colleagues studied 21 medically healthy young adults who were in the acute phase of major depression and found evidence of decreased natural killer cell activity.

- For 10 years, British psychologist Steven Greer studied 57 women diagnosed with breast cancer. Those with a fighting spirit fared the best in terms of remissions and likelihood of survival. While 70% of the fighters were alive after 10 years, only 20% of those characterized as helpless or hopeless prevailed.

- A study of long-term AIDS survivors revealed that they shared a number of personality traits indicative of a strong sense of control. They assumed personal responsibility and felt able to influence the outcome of their illness. Moreover, they were highly assertive and had a sense of purpose.

- A study conducted at the University of Connecticut followed heart attack patients for 8 years. Those who accepted personal responsibility rather than blaming others were far less likely to have a second cardiovascular event.

However, there is also some seemingly conflicting evidence regarding the fighter hypothesis. Several studies have apparently failed to show any connection between the will to live and recovery from illness. Other research suggests that overengagement or excessive striving might even make matters worse. Here are a few examples:

- Two large-scale studies of breast cancer patients, one published in 1999 by a group of British investigators and another in 2001 by a Canadian team, found that fighting spirit was *not* associated with improved survival. In one of these studies, the results confused even the researchers. Although fighting spirit was not related to a better outcome, high levels of helplessness did predict a greater likelihood of relapse or death within 5 years.
- Hostility has emerged as the primary factor linking the striving type A personality style with cardiovascular disease. Specifically, highly hostile individuals are four to five times more likely to develop cardiovascular disease. In addition, a study of physicians and lawyers revealed that high levels of hostility were responsible for a six-fold increase in mortality between the ages of 25 and 50.
- Laboratory studies have revealed that hostility can trigger the release of five different stress hormones while also weakening the parasympathetic system, the nerves in your body responsible for eliciting the relaxation response.
- Individuals who scored higher on a measure of aggressiveness and other antisocial tendencies were found to have lower T-cell and B-cell counts, both indicative of a compromised immune system.

## Empowered Healing

What accounts for the apparent disparity in this evidence? We believe that a *fighting spirit that is not hope based may provide only limited opportunities for healing, but that hope-based mastery can facilitate healing through "hopeful empowerment."* Recall from Chapter 10 that hope-based mastery is derived from supportive relationships as well as spiritual direction, yielding an experience of mediated power and a will to hope that is spiritually sanctified as well as emotionally charged. Having the will to live is not enough. But having a *reason to live* that is linked to a set of transcendent values, and grounded in hope, may do wonders for the body and the soul. This notion is supported by empirical studies regarding personality and health and by research on changes in mortality as a function of anticipated life events.

Psychologists Robert Emmons and Laura King found that individuals who are less conflicted about their goal strivings reported fewer illnesses and were less likely to require the services of a health center. Psychologist David McClelland used a picture-story exercise to assess an individual's stressed-power index. He measured participants' need for power as well as the number of times they included words in their stories, such as "couldn't" or "can't," that were indicative of greater goal frustration. Finally, McClelland collected blood samples to assess the robustness of each participant's immune system. Individuals who did *not* suffer from a stressed power syndrome (high power and high frustration) tended to have a greater number of natural cancer-killing cells. Moreover, the cancer-killing cells of these more at-ease individuals appeared to better able to track and destroy foreign invaders.

Terminally ill individuals who look forward to their next birthday as a time to reflect on past achievements, and to receive positive feedback from others, are significantly less likely to die in the following month. Similarly, those who view an upcoming religious holiday as a time to fulfill a privileged and sacred role are also less likely to die. For example, the death rates for older Jewish men are significantly lower the week before Passover. The same is true for elderly Chinese women during the week prior to the Chinese Harvest Moon. In stark contrast, consider the fate of legendary football coach Bear Bryant who lived to prowl the sidelines on Saturday afternoons. Many were stunned when he died of cardiac arrest just 37 days after retiring. A mere 48 hours before suffering a massive attack, Bryant had lamented, "There are no more Saturdays."

Death may also be hastened when individuals believe that they are spiritually finished, as has been reported among Chinese Americans. Within their astrological framework, there are certain presumptions regarding an individual's birth year and the organs of one's body. In particular, each birth year is believed to be associated with one or more organ weaknesses. The worst-case scenario is to incur an illness that affects your fragile organ. Sociologist David Phillips and his colleagues were amazed to learn that "Chinese-Americans, but not whites, died significantly earlier than normal if they had a combination of disease and birth year which Chinese astrology and medicine consider ill-fated." Moreover, the more strongly an individual believed in this spiritual forecast, "the more years of life that were lost."

### Social Support

> Two are better than one . . . if they fall, one will lift up his fellow; but woe to him who is alone when he falls and has not another to lift him up.
>
> —The Book of Ecclesiastes

The impact of attachment and social support on health is the most powerful of all the mind–body effects found in the scientific literature. The sheer volume of this data is impressive, consisting of both human and animal studies, as well as an enormous range of health-related issues, including mortality, progression of disease, and rates of recovery from illness. The following are some of the most intriguing findings:

- In mice inoculated with cancer cells, those who were regularly petted and handled developed fewer tumors than those who experienced little or no human contact.
- Monkeys were simultaneously exposed to a flashing light and a mild shock. After a few trials, the light alone was sufficient to produce a stress response, including a rise in the stress hormone cortisol. However, when a monkey was shown the light in the

company of one buddy, he or she produced only half as much cortisol. If five companions were put in the cage, the monkey showed no increase in cortisol.

- In monkeys infected with the simian AIDS virus, those who were removed from their regular habitat, or separated from familiar animals, died sooner than those allowed to remain in their present surroundings.
- In HIV+ men, lower levels of social support have been associated with a more rapid decrease in CD4 cells and T cells, two critical indicators of immunity.
- A study of over 7,000 individuals in Alameda, California, revealed those with lower levels of social support had a higher death rate from all diseases.

How does social support lead to better health? Research suggests that a host of biological processes can be activated by proximity, touch, and expressions of affection as well as feelings of love or togetherness. The strongest data point to the impact of social support on three primary glands: the hypothalamus, the pituitary, and the adrenals. The evidence for this connection is considerable. Let us review just two examples. In 2005, Swedish investigator Kerstin Uvnas-Moberg and her colleagues proposed the existence of a "calm and connection system" that revolves around the hormone oxytocin, synthesized by the hypothalamus and secreted by the pituitary. Representing a "distinct psychophysiological pattern," Moberg and her colleagues have shown that this system may be turned on by skin-to-skin contact, an embrace, or even the sense of belonging to a social group. In contrast to the frenzied, stress-mediated fight or flight reaction of the sympathetic nervous system, the calm and connected response is relaxing and restorative, while also promoting greater trust and openness.

> Pulse rate and blood pressure are kept at low, healthy, and balanced levels, and the vagally controlled gastrointestinal tract is activated, promoting digestion and storing of nutrients. Growth and restorative processes are stimulated. . . . reduced arousal and the development of calm prevail.

While Moberg's research has focused on socially mediated activation, psychologist James Coan has focused on support-related physiological deactivation. In one study Coan and his colleagues placed female participants in a functional MRI chamber. The participants were told that the appearance of a red X on the screen in front of them would signal the likelihood of an upcoming shock, while a blue O would indicate no chance of a shock. Each participant was presented with a series of both Xs and Os. In addition, sometimes they were left alone, sometimes they were given the hand of an anonymous, unseen stranger to hold, and sometimes they held onto the hand of their spouse. Coan and his colleagues also used a standard paper-and-pencil questionnaire to assess each participant's level of marital satisfaction. The strongest effect observed in this study involved spousal hand-holding in the presence of a threat (likely shock).

Specifically, reports of *greater* marital satisfaction were correlated with *decreased* activity in the right anterior insula (implicated in "bodily reactions" of fear, anger, pain, and other negative emotions), the left superior frontal gyrus (linked to self-awareness), and the hypothalamus (hormone synthesis and glandular activation). Coan and his colleagues were especially intrigued by the involvement of the hypothalamus:

> ... regulation of the hypothalamus suggests that these benefits may be pervasive as the hypothalamus influences a cascade of neurochemical processes [including those] ... widely understood to hold implications for immune functioning and memory.

Notwithstanding the extensive data on health and social support, is it *always* the case that two are better than one? The results suggest that the quality of social interaction may be more important than the number of contacts. Consider the following:

- Crowding is highly stressful and has been related to a variety of health problems in numerous species, from fish and apes to humans.
- The size of an individual's social network does not always predict better health status.
- Some relationships are highly toxic. Data from a study of newlyweds indicated that just 30 minutes of emotional conflict produced enough stress hormone output to lower immune functioning for more than 24 hours.
- Some individuals feel terribly lonely in a crowd of acquaintances or strangers but can find great comfort in the company of one close friend.

### Healing Relationships

The key to securing wellness is depth of relatedness. Close relationships that facilitate openness and trust are essential for health and healing. By now you know that these are the same dimensions of relatedness that define hope-based attachments.

Healing relationships provide a two-fold benefit: they enhance an individual's sense of self, and they provide outlets for emotional expression. If you are blessed with positive early family experiences, or later reparative bonds, your hopeful imprints will be empowering, trust-filled, and soothing. Individuals who fit this profile rarely feel totally helpless, completely alone, or utterly terrified. However, those who have suffered prolonged bouts of neglect or abuse are at risk for developing a sense of self that feels disenfranchised, isolated, and fragile.

Well-attached individuals are better able to weather the vicissitudes of life. They are physiologically less reactive to stressors and show a greater capacity for fighting disease. It is noteworthy that there are more than two dozen studies indicating that individuals with high-quality social support have lower blood pressure. Among women dealing with breast cancer, those with a helpful spouse and supportive physician tend to demonstrate better cancer-killing cell activity.

Illness can be an isolating experience. Laura, a breast cancer survivor, noted, "You get that look on some people's faces that, you know 'oh, she's got cancer.' Some of my friends stopped calling me. Some of them couldn't deal with it. And that's when I needed them the most." Christie, a 24-year-old cancer survivor, had a similar experience. Some of her best friends just "disappeared." "I don't know if having a good friend with cancer, if that scares them or turns them off." After joining a cancer listserve, another survivor revealed, "I used to think I was an island."

In *Illness as Metaphor*, Susan Sontag referred to the "kingdom of the well" and the "kingdom of the sick." Some illnesses such as AIDS, hepatitis, or cancer are especially likely to engender the feeling of being an outcast. In this regard, psychologist Oakley Ray quoted Mother Teresa: "Being unwanted is the worst disease that any human being can ever experience."

### Openness and Trust

Psychologist James Pennebaker and his colleagues documented the health hazards of suppressing one's thoughts and feelings, particularly with respect to serious or traumatic life experiences. Such containment stress can raise blood pressure, flood the body with harmful hormones, and even suppress the immune system. For example, among HIV+ men, nondisclosure of important personal information has been related to more rapid disease progression. In particular, concealment of homosexual identity has been associated with unfavorable cellular immune changes, conversion from HIV to AIDS, and increased mortality.

For more than a decade, physician Redford Williams and his colleagues studied nearly 1,400 men and women undergoing cardiac catheterization for heart disease. At the start of their investigation, participants were asked about their social support network. Those who could not list a single confidante were three times more likely to have died within 5 years.

In one of the most cited studies pertaining to the mind–body effect, psychiatrist David Spiegel offered one group of women diagnosed with advanced breast cancer a support group experience. A control group received an identical level of medical care without a support group. On average, the survival time for the women who had participated in a support group was double that of the control group. According to Spiegel, when this study was being conducted, there was not a single drug or other medical intervention that could promise the same degree of life extension. Repeatedly, the women in the groups talked about how hard it was to be strong for their husband, children, and other family members. At the same time, they expressed deep appreciation for having a time and place where they could air their hopes and fears in a climate of trust and openness. (In Maine, Dr. Ken Hamilton and his colleagues have been providing a similar H.O.P.E.

group for cancer patients and survivors. See the Notes for this chapter for further information.)

## Self-Regulation

The physician should make every effort to ensure that all the sick should be most cheerful of soul and should be relieved of the passions of the psyche that cause anxiety.

—Maimonides (1135–1204), *The Regimen of Health*

Fear and anxiety can wreak havoc on the body as well as the mind. We noted previously how high levels of arousal can trigger the release of stress hormones, which in turn disrupt the immune system. A sense of helplessness or entrapment tends to diminish both the potency and prevalence of cancer-fighting cells. For those already compromised by a serious illness or injury, fear and anxiety can retard the healing process, slowing the rate of recovery from wounds and infections. To reinforce these lessons, author Carol Orsborn quoted from both *Shakespeare* (" . . . frame your mind to mirth and merriment, which bars a thousand harms and lengthens life."), and the Bible ("A merry heart doeth good like a medicine; but a broken spirit drieth the bones.") The following are some modern laboratory examples from both human and animal research:

- During the week following notification of HIV+ status, individuals who reported higher levels of anxiety showed poorer cancer-killing cell activity.
- Researchers have identified more than a half dozen biological markers indicative of a compromised immune system among individuals diagnosed with general anxiety disorder or posttraumatic stress disorder.
- High levels of fear or distress prior to surgery are associated with longer hospital stays, more postoperative complications, and increased rates of infection.
- Intense job strain, consisting of unreasonably high demands with few degrees of freedom, has been linked to high blood pressure.
- Chronically higher levels of adrenaline produce blood clotting, accelerating the rate of plaque growth in the vessels of the heart and brain.
- Frightened cats showed large increases in urinary sugar levels.
- Restrained mice demonstrated a two-fold increase in blood sugar.
- Mice that were injected with a tumor solution and learned that they could not escape a mild shock were 40% more likely to develop tumors than mice that were allowed to run free.

Such findings indicate that chronic overarousal or a strong sense of entrapment can be hazardous to your health. When your sympathetic nervous system, responsible for the so-called fight-or-flight response, is perpetually firing, it sabotages the healing process. However, it would be a mistake to presume that a total takeover by the competing relaxation response would be ideal. Quite the contrary, rather than engendering a prolonged state of blissful relaxation, parasympathetic dominance can also be harmful, if not lethal.

In the late 1950s, Dr. Arthur Schmale at the University of Rochester identified what he called "the giving-in; giving up syndrome." When humans or animals are confronted with a stressor that overwhelms their perceived resources and produces a seemingly intractable state of helplessness, there is a system-wide shutdown. In humans, such profound states of hopelessness can result in depression or even sudden death.

Psychologist Curt Richter of Johns Hopkins University provided compelling evidence that excessive parasympathetic activity was the underlying culprit in cases of sudden death from learned hopelessness. Richter's landmark studies focused on the reactions of wild and domesticated rats placed in containers of turbulent water from which there was no escape. If transferred immediately from their cages to the water tanks, and provided with an ideal temperature (95° F), the average rat would swim for 60 hours. In contrast, those who were temporarily restrained while having their whiskers clipped became deathly limp within minutes after being dropped into the water. Richter ruled out suffocation along with a variety of other physiological explanations. In his view, the meek surrender of this second group was attributable to a state of hopelessness caused by entrapment and the loss of control precipitated by the removal of their whiskers.

To isolate the physiological pathway of hopelessness, Richter administered to another group of rats a drug that mimicked the results of parasympathetic activation. These rats quickly gave up, descending to the bottom of the tank. He then took other rats and gave them atropine, a stimulant that blocks the parasympathetic system. In many of them, this prevented sudden death, allowing Richter to conclude that learned hopelessness could produce sudden death via parasympathetic dominance.

Although a sense of entrapment is detrimental, unpredictability can also spell disaster. For example, a great deal of research has been compiled indicating that stressors exert more wear and tear on the mind and body if they are unpredictable. In fact, sometimes the damage caused by unpredictability even trumps the stress of restraint. Physiologist Jay Weiss restrained three groups of rats in adjoining boxes. The first group was restrained but received no shocks, the second received a warning light and then a mild shock, and the third received a mild shock without a warning light. After a number of trials, the three groups were examined for ulcers. The rats that suffered only the stress of restraint showed, on average, 1-millimeter wide ulcers. The restrained rats that received a shock preceded by a warning light had 2-millimeter tears. However, the rats that were shocked without warning averaged 10-millimeter tears.

## Heals

Now turn to Aristotle for a deeper understanding of the possible mechanisms or pathways that may underlie the potential healing power of hope. Aristotle described four causes in nature. He explained that some effects can be attributed to the substance from which a cause is composed (*material cause*). For example a beam made of *metal* may cause injury or damage if it lands on someone or something. A second effect is made possible by the formal properties of the cause (*formal cause*). *Wheels* permit a vehicle to move along the ground because they have a *round* form. A third type of effect is imparted when a cause "sets a process in motion" (*efficient cause*). Hypertension can cause a stroke if high arterial pressure results in fat particles being dislodged and propelled toward smaller blood vessels. A fourth cause can be linked to final aims or targeted endpoints (*final cause*). Among human beings, goal setting and other future-directed plans can be the cause of numerous thoughts, feelings, and actions over the course of a lifetime.

How does hope affect healing? Aristotle's causes provide a framework for understanding how. While you cannot literally touch or feel hope, it does have an associated biological underpinning (material cause). Hope has a unique form, different from optimism, wishful thinking, and other psychological states (formal cause). Hope has the power to stir the mind and body, setting in motion a host of beneficial health-related processes (efficient cause). Hope is most definitely about future aims, sacred purposes, and cherished endpoints (final cause). Aristotle's framework can also be used to outline *eight different hope-related healing pathways.*

### Hope as a Material Cause

Throughout this chapter we have indicated how the substrate of hope—specifically, the mastery, attachment, and survival systems—relates to health and healing. More simply stated, hope has the power to heal because it is constituted from the same stuff (biosocial motive systems) that underlies healthy human functioning. For this reason, we might call the first hope-healing pathway a byproduct of *systemic involvement.*

### Hope as a Formal Cause

*Balance.* Hope-based mastery, attachment, and survival reflect a balanced emotional state, made possible by shared power, mutual caring, and relaxed coping. At the physiological level, balance is paramount. Even minor fluctuations in sugar, salt, or fluid levels can wreak havoc on an organism. Without the proper ratio of helper cells to suppressor cells, the immune system is severely compromised. This second healing pathway can be labeled *emotional balance.*

*Authenticity.* Denial or blind optimism is the delusion of an inauthentic life. In contrast, hope is fully informed by an enlarged and mindful perspective. At the physiological level, health and healing are compromised when there is a failure to honor true feelings. (Along these lines, a study that one of us [A. S.] spearheaded demonstrated that hope was a more robust predictor than optimism of future health status; not only did the more hopeful participants in the study report fewer illnesses, but they also rated their illnesses as less severe compared to those with lower hope scores.) Repressed anger, inhibited fear, or unresolved grief also take a toll on the body. Hope is about honoring the entire panorama of human experience. This third healing pathway is *integration of experience*.

*Inclusiveness.* Hope spans the conscious and unconscious realms of human awareness and includes that sense that William James called "the more." Along these lines, immunologists Richard Booth and Kevin Ashbridge suggested that healing is maximized when all of the systems of the body (nervous, immune, endocrine) are functioning at an optimal level. This fourth healing pathway is *unrestricted commitment of resources*.

### Hope as an Efficient Cause

*Openness.* As Gabriel Marcel noted, openness is one of the fruits of hope. In turn, openness can yield a variety of health benefits, including emotional and practical support from others (external openness) as well as greater informational exchange among the nervous, immune and endocrine systems (internal openness). A focus on openness is also implicit in the healing traditions of the East, best exemplified by the concepts of "chi" in Chinese medicine and the "chakras" in the Hindu tradition. This fifth healing pathway is *improved communication*.

*Flow.* As an emotion, hope is "wetter" and "hotter" than a "cold," "dry" expectation such as optimism. Physiologically, this suggests that hope may be linked to the limbic system, an important storage site for the neuropeptides that shuttle back and forth between the brain and the other healing systems of the body. By comparison, reduced flow in the form of emotional constriction, is associated with higher arousal and diminished immunity. At the molecular level, Candace Pert and other neuroscientists proposed that mind–body healing might be facilitated by the flow of informational substances through free expression of both negative and positive emotions. This sixth healing pathway is *greater self-expression*.

*Resilience.* Hope is a buffer. Hopeful individuals are buttressed by the secular as well as the spiritual. They are vertically supported in time by positive memories and liberating visions of the future as well as horizontally nested in the present by relationships of trust and unquestioned support. In short, highly hopeful individuals remain resilient in the face of adversity, centered in good times and bad. In contrast, physiologists refer to the wear and tear of stress-induced deviations from the homeostatic center as "allostatic load." This seventh healing pathway is *reduced allostatic load*.

### Hope as a Final Cause

*Harmony.* Hope is an excellent health transducer because it speaks to the deeper needs of the mind, body, and spirit. It is a way of being rather than a narrowly focused mindset. It is about transcendent goals and an eternal perspective. In the same vein, Booth and Ashbridge suggested that mind and body must function in a mutually reinforcing manner. Moreover, they believed that the highest-order purpose of the mind–body connection is not defense but rather "organism integrity." In their view, the key to achieving full biological integrity is "harmony of purpose" at every level of the organism. This eighth healing pathway is *harmony of purpose*.

### Support for the Hope–Health Connection

Other scientists have reported a similar constellation of healing factors. In 2003, health science professor Brent Hafen and his colleagues compiled an exhaustive 600-page review of the mind–body scientific literature. Summarizing their findings in *Mind/ Body Health*, they identified three core principles in healing: empowerment, connectedness, and purpose in life. A research group headed by psychologist Allastair Cunningham interviewed 10 women with medically incurable cancers who had outlived their prognosis by an average of 7 years. A systematic content analysis of these interviews revealed *three common themes* that distinguished these women from those whose survival time was equal or less than was medically predicted; "autonomy," "authenticity," and "acceptance."

"Autonomy," as Cunningham and his colleagues defined it, consisted of "the perceived freedom to shape life around what was valued." From our perspective, this *is* the essence of hope-based mastery. "Authenticity" was derived from "freedom to restructure one's life in terms of personal values." This, in our view, is a joint product of hope-based mastery and hope-based survival. "Acceptance" included "interpersonal tolerance" and "closeness" as well as "peacefulness." We conceptualize "acceptance" as a composite of hope-based attachment and hope-based survival.

Between 2005 and 2007 one of us (A. S.) launched two investigations to verify the Aristotelian healing hypothesis. In the first study, a dozen thyroid cancer survivors were recruited to complete a comprehensive hope test that included sections dealing with attachment, mastery, survival, and spirituality. In addition, each participant completed a "health-related processes scale" representing the eight hope and healing pathways. In terms of outcome measures, the survivors rated their present level of physical well-being and their level of health-related distress.

The findings were strongly supportive of a hope–health connection. *Total scores on the hope test were highly correlated with reports of greater physical well-being and fewer health-related worries. Moreover, those who endorsed more of the healing processes (pathways) tended to score significantly higher in overall well-being.*

In the second study, 15 HIV+ individuals took the hope test and, similar to the first study, reported their level of physical well-being and health-related distress while also completing the health-related processes questionnaire. For this study, it was also possible to obtain blood levels of CD4 at the beginning and end of the study (2 years later). CD4 is the master cell of the immune system and is especially critical for health maintenance among those dealing with HIV.

Again, the results supported the hope–health hypothesis. HIV+ individuals who were higher in hope reported greater overall health and were less worried about their future well-being. In addition, those who endorsed more of the healing processes (pathways) also tended to report greater well-being. *Equally impressive, higher hope scores were associated with greater CD4 levels at both the beginning and end of the study. Statistically speaking, the hope factor accounted for nearly 40% of the differences in immune functioning.*

## The Hope Response

Hopefulness is the best medicine because it represents an adaptive middle ground between the overactivated stress response and the disengaged giving-up complex. At the physiological level, a sense of hopefulness can help to impart a balance of sympathetic and parasympathetic activity while assuring appropriate levels of neurotransmitters, hormones, lymphocytes, and other critical health-related substances. Equally important, a hopeful attitude may allow an individual to sustain a healthy internal environment in the presence of enormous adversity.

Hopeful individuals are likely to retain an unwavering trust in a benign universe. They harbor an eternal perspective that dampens the impact of both minor hassles and major existential challenges. Hopeful individuals are anchored by centers of value and a life mission that provides light and direction in times of darkness and chaos. Hopeful individuals are supported internally by empowering and reassuring imprints as well as externally by a network of caring attachments. Rarely, if ever, does the hopeful individual feel like a solitary ego subject to the slings and arrows of outrageous fortune.

In all these ways, hope can serve as an important buffer against pain and suffering as well as a potent ally in confronting injury and disease. In the next chapter we delve more deeply into the medicine chest of hope but also look beyond healing to consider the ways in which hope can foster a life filled with greater health, happiness and meaning.

# Sixteen

## HOPE FOR HEALTH: PRESCRIPTIONS FOR WELL-BEING

> Do not try to heal the head without the body. Do not try to heal the body
> without the soul.
>
> —Plato

The comedian George Burns once remarked, "If you don't take care of your body, where will you live?" For the most part, Burns practiced what he preached and ultimately lived to the ripe old age of 100. In a tribute offered by the *Huffington Center on Aging*, it was noted, "He had a great capacity to never give up working, never give up loving, and never saying never." In other words, Burns displayed a lifelong passion for mastery, attachment, and survival.

Plato and George Burns shared at least one thing in common. Both understood that every aspect of an individual's existence influences his or her health. This holistic wisdom can be found in many cultures. This is why millions of Chinese practice their soft martial art of tai chi every morning while their Native American counterparts hold regular purification rituals to cleanse the mind, body, and spirit. It is why Plato was moved to write, "The cure of many diseases is unknown to physicians because they are ignorant of the whole. For the part can never be well unless the whole is well."

In the first half of this chapter, we introduce a comprehensive *hope-based health plan*, including prescriptions for facilitating empowerment, connection, and self-regulation. Spiritual health supplements are also included, drawn from Buddhist, Hindu, Native

American, and Taoist healing practices. We conclude this section with a hope-centered *philosophy of healing*.

Hope and wellness is the other major topic that is covered in this chapter. This issue is examined from four perspectives. First, we discuss how hope can be both a motivating factor in maintaining fitness *and* a positive outcome of regular physical activity. Second, we explain how your chances of aging well may be improved by adhering to a life of hope-based mastery, attachment, and survival. Third, we clarify the relationship between meaning in life and hope as it relates to matters of health, happiness and overall well-being. Fourth, we explore the need for creativity in sustaining wellness during times of adversity and in realizing the fullest expressions of hope.

## A Healthy Portable Environment

Psychologist Shelly Taylor coined the phrase "healthy environments" to refer to certain "life spaces" that are conducive to wellness because they are inherently safe, promoting a sense of predictability and connectedness. In an analogous fashion, when individuals surround themselves with hope, they are, in essence, cultivating a healthy portable environment, a mobile life space supportive of health and healing.

How do you assure the development of a full hope, one that will sustain you in sickness and health, in good times and bad? As we noted in Chapter 2, hope is not confined to one side of the brain, a single cluster of neurons, or a specific neurotransmitter. You cannot do an MRI or CAT scan and isolate hope. It is a distributed process, both in terms of its multimotive derivation and its widespread influence on an individual's mind, body, and spirit. For these reasons, you cannot hope for hope by taking a drug, hooking yourself up to a machine, or exercising a certain part of your brain. Instead, you will have to adopt, as Plato suggested, a more comprehensive game plan focused on the whole of your existence.

A holistic approach informed Booth and Ashbridge's explorations of immune-related processes as well as neuroscientist Candice Pert's attempts to explain the bidirectional flow of neuropeptides, the "molecules of emotion" that shuttle from one bodily system to another and back. A holistic focus is part and parcel of our hope perspective as well as representing the latest advances in mind–body science. Regardless of the scientific domain, whether it is psychology, immunology, or molecular biology, there is a growing consensus that the human organism must be unified in its healing efforts.

Booth and Ashbridge suggested that if two or more of your systems are at cross-purposes, healing efforts will be compromised. For example, if your reservoir of cancer-killing cells is intact (immune system) but your will to live is tenuous (nervous system), healing is going to be more difficult. Booth and Ashbridge referred to these obstructions as "identity-locked healing responses." But they also argued that it is possible for wellness seekers to thrive by developing a strong, positive sense of identity that can bring all systems onboard to marshal a robust healing effort. From our perspective, this healing-oriented identity is most effectively realized by adopting a hope-based approach to mastery, attachment, and survival. The rest of this chapter is devoted to this higher purpose.

## Empowered Healing

What follows are a set of suggestions for maximizing your degree of hope-based mastery in a manner that is most conducive to healing. They represent our distillation of the varied, and sometimes confusing, data relating mastery efforts to health and healing. Think of these as general guidelines for creating a healing inner space.

- *Focus your energy.* Goal-related frustrations and conflicts can limit your healing potential. Are you being blocked in achieving some important life goal? How can you remove the obstacles in your path? Are you trying too hard? Have you failed to consider other avenues for reaching your goals? Perhaps the ultimate question that you can ask yourself is, "Do I want to thrive or merely survive?"

- *Strive for authenticity.* If you are sick, do not try to convince yourself, or others, that everything is just fine. However, at the same time you should not merely resign yourself to fate. Follow Norman Cousin's advice, "Do not deny the diagnosis; defy the verdict." You will probably find that the so-called odds of recovery are misleadingly low because they were derived from studies of those with multiple health problems, high levels of stress, and other confounding factors that may not apply to you.

- *Reduce hostility.* Buddha was known to have "a warm heart and cool head." Follow his example. Consider a regimen of meditation and exercise to lower your baseline level of arousal. A calm body is incompatible with a hostile countenance. Learn to be effectively assertive as opposed to aggressive or hostile. Anger has it place, but it does not have to be fully vented or violent to be effective. Heed Aristotle's suggestion that the noble individual knows when and where, as well as toward whom and for how long, to express anger.

- *Foster mediated control.* At every level in the healing process, mediated or shared control is crucial. Even within the immune system, there are helper cells that stimulate B cells (infection-fighting white blood cells) to produce antibodies to combat disease. Cultivate an attitude of balanced responsibility. Rather than blaming yourself or some external factor for your health problems, focus on maintaining a sense of shared control and responsibility.

## Spiritual Strength for Mastery

Attending to your spiritual life is an important part of the healing process. Again, spirituality does not necessarily mean a religious belief system. However, to serve as a source of hope and healing, your spiritual system must engender a deep sense of faith. It helps if you include a meditative component and nurture a collaborative relationship with one more individuals, a group, or a higher power.

The centers of value that form the basis for a spiritual belief system afford you with a chance to *ally yourself with something greater and more powerful*. In addition, such belief systems tend to promote greater self-integration, thus reducing the chances of experiencing harmful mastery-related difficulties, such as goal conflicts or an immune system weakened as a result of stressed power motivation.

A spiritual approach to healing assures *greater authenticity*. Rather than pursuing recovery for the mere sake of feeling better or looking well, the individual is guided by a deeper desire for transformation of the mind and spirit as well as the body. Instead of dismissing this as new age psychobabble, it is important to honor the unity of the mind–body network.

A spiritual perspective can also help in *reducing levels of hostility* by promoting acceptance, forgiveness, and gratitude. Recall that hostility is a major risk factor for cardiovascular disease, whereas a more tolerant and amicable disposition can do wonders for the heart, veins, and capillaries. Along these lines, physician Harold Koenig found that those who regularly attended religious services and prayed were 40% less likely to have high blood pressure. Psychologists Robert Emmons and Michael McCullough studied adults with a neuromuscular disease. Those who practiced gratitude reported greater well-being than a similarly afflicted control group who did not regularly count their blessings.

## Connected Healing

To reduce the risk of either social isolation or emotional congestion, aim for a support network that is solidly rooted in trust, provides a sense of belonging, and allows you to express your deepest hopes and fears. Here are some general suggestions:

*Build a "trust network."* Seek out those with whom you can regularly and safely disclose your feelings. Disclosure without trust may be ineffective, if not harmful. Researchers have found that highly cynical individuals who are not accustomed to opening up, but during a crisis, disclose too much too soon, increase their sense of vulnerability. Moreover, their immune systems were actually in a weaker state after they disclosed.

*Correspond.* Sending and receiving heartfelt letters, e-mails, or phone messages also can secure a measure of connected healing. Investigators have found that emotional intimacy can bring about a multitude of positive physiological changes, including lower blood pressure, decreased muscular tension, and increased immunity. James Pennebaker, who did extensive research on writing for health (e.g., via keeping a journal), offered a number of suggestions. In particular, he discouraged both dry, factual summaries devoid of emotion and the opposite extreme of hysterical outpourings of unprocessed feelings. According to Pennebaker, the most healing occurs when you write about the significant events in your life while expressing both your deepest thoughts *and* feelings.

*Join a support group*. Psychiatrist David Spiegel emphasized that a support group should be uplifting. Attend a meeting and gauge your comfort level. Initially, you might feel a little anxious or awkward. This is normal. However, you should leave the first meeting sensing that the group is indeed a place for hope, providing empowerment, connection, and safety. According to Spiegel, "If you feel attacked or belittled, the group is doing something wrong. Find another one."

What constitutes a good support group? Would Aristotle have approved of the group's philosophy? In other words, does it revolve around the golden mean of balance? For example, while providing hope and encouragement, is the group also able to tolerate frank and honest discussions? Spiegel notes it is "doubly unfortunate" if the group or leader, driven by a need to maintain an "optimistic atmosphere," is unable to air realistic fears and concerns. Such a mindset robs the members of badly needed support while also implying that some aspects of their illness are truly hopeless. Be wary of groups that promise a magic bullet rooted in simplistic positive thinking or that unquestioningly espouse any form of traditional healing. However, also stay clear of those that blame the victim or suggest that recovery is purely a matter of adequate willpower.

There are many ways to find a support group. Your physician or local health center should be able to recommend a group that is geared toward your particular illness. You could also do an Internet search on your illness to find information about available support groups in your area. Another option is to join a listserve or other Internet-based support groups. An excellent example of online support is the Livestrong site developed by Lance Armstrong. It is a place where cancer survivors can share their stories while also gathering valuable healing suggestions.

*Consider individual psychotherapy.* If you are still feeling emotionally congested, seek out a therapist who is trained in either client-centered or emotion-focused therapy. Both approaches are designed to explore and clarify feelings in the present rather than facts from the past. If you are also struggling with depression or anxiety, make sure your therapist has some familiarity with cognitive-behavioral techniques or can refer you to another professional skilled in modifying distress-provoking beliefs.

*Monitor your authenticity.* Deep healing requires an honest assessment of your inner and outer reality. Alistair Cunningham's research findings with breast cancer survivors are a testament to the healing power of authenticity. James Pennebaker also differentiated between a superficial processing of life events, which he referred to as low-level thinking, and a mindful, fully aware coping style. The key is to move beyond denial or blind optimism to a place within you that is fully aware but resolutely committed to life.

One way to monitor your authenticity is via biofeedback. You could ask a trained practitioner to monitor one or more indicators of your autonomic arousal such as skin conductance, heart rate, or finger temperature while you talk about your hopes and fears. You may be telling yourself and others that things are just fine, but feedback from your body may suggest otherwise. You might want to pay particular attention to your skin conductance readings as increases may be indicative of *inhibited* stress responses. Authenticity is more likely evident when your verbal readouts match your bodily feedback.

### Spiritual Connections

One of the most consistent findings in the mind–body literature is that individuals who attend church on a regular basis are healthier than those who never or rarely attend. They are less likely to suffer from cardiovascular disease or hypertension. They live longer after open heart surgery. They have stronger immune systems. How can this be explained?

Think about church attendance from the perspective of social support and health. In all likelihood, those who attend church frequently are deriving more reassurance, deepening their sense of belonging, and finding a consistent outlet for emotional expression. In short, regular immersion in a religious or spiritual tradition is apt to foster greater trust and openness, which in turn fosters hope and healing.

One very obvious example of faith-based disclosure is the Catholic ritual of confession. However, every religious or spiritual tradition provides a context for some degree of emotional outpouring. The Ifa, Australian "dreamtimers," and Lakota participate in vigorous singing and dancing rituals. Muslims kneel and chant openly while positioning their bodies in the direction of Mecca. The whirling dervishes of the Sufi sect spin themselves into an ecstatic embrace with God. Jews in the holy city of Jerusalem pray before the Western Wall, known colloquially as the "wailing wall."

Authentic relating is another pathway through which religious or spiritual involvement can lead to better health. What makes a belief system spiritual is its centrality to an individual's sense of self. Along these lines, Harold Koenig found that both "active involvement and deep faith" are critical for healing. If you want to enlist your spiritual beliefs in the healing process, strive for a fully authentic relationship with your centers of value (higher power, nature, science, other people, etc.).

### Relaxed Healing

If you are dealing with a serious ailment but are unable to relax, then your attempts at healing can be seriously hampered. Anxiety is typically a two-fold problem consisting of fearful thoughts coupled with high arousal and muscular tension. How do you go about calming both your mind and body? Below are three categories of mind–body techniques, one for each survival skill mentioned in Chapter 11 (personal terror management, survival-based trust, and liberation beliefs). To enhance your terror management capacity, consider one or more of the following practices:

- *Practice focused meditation.* This is what most Westerners think of as meditation. It typically involves sitting in a cross-legged or kneeled position with eyes closed while repeating a sound or mantra. This form of meditation is excellent for stilling and emptying an overactive mind that is cluttered with fear and doubt.

- *Do not neglect your body*. Personal terror management should apply to the body as well as the mind. You are less likely to worry when you are physically relaxed. Consider some form of bodywork therapy that is designed to ease physical tension and stress while simultaneously massaging the psyche to unlock any negative emotions that might be interfering with healing. You can choose from a variety of approaches, including yoga, breathing-oriented meditations, or massage.

For survival-based trust:

- *Find a calm buddy*. We are profoundly affected by the words, deeds, and feelings of those around us. Research by psychologist John Gottman has indicated that a single, 15-minute dispute between spouses can cause increases in blood pressure and stress hormones for both of them that can last more than a day. In a related finding, children who passively observed their parents fighting also showed a dramatic rise in stress hormones. More recently, physiologists have identified so-called *mirror neurons* in the temporal areas of the brain. When you observe an individual do, say, or feel something, these neurons in your brain fire, producing a host of physical and emotional changes that mirror what is happening to the other person. If you can surround yourself with at least one calm buddy you may share in the health benefits of his or her relaxed support.
- *Seek out a healer*. There are numerous anecdotes about patients losing their will to live after a bad encounter with an uninspiring or insensitive physician. Cardiologist Bernard Lown recalled a woman who was hospitalized with a non-life-threatening heart condition called tricuspid stenosis. One day her physician came into her room with several interns, uttered "TS" in a nonchalant manner and marched out. Tragically, the woman presumed that he was talking about a "terminal situation" and died the same day. Make sure your doctor is a healer and not just a technician

Suggestions for liberation beliefs:

- *Practice insight meditation*. This form of meditation, which is derived from Theraveda Buddhism, is becoming increasingly popular in the West. The focus is on cultivating greater awareness or mindfulness rather than pure stillness. Buddhist scholar Shinzen Young described it as the art of penetrating experience with awareness. "The awareness literally soaks into [mind and body] like water into a sponge . . . each phenomenon [is approached with] the six senses—hearing, seeing, smelling, tasting, the feeling body, and the thinking mind."

- *Be persistent.* We previously mentioned Norman Cousin's views on hope and healing: "Don't deny the diagnosis; defy the verdict." Of course, in some cases, even a diagnosis is sometimes worth another look. Do not be shy about asking for a second or even third opinion. You can also do your own research in a medical library or via the Internet (WebMD is an excellent resource). Take into account not only your specific illness but also your overall level of fitness as well as other personal and social assets. If you have practiced a healthy lifestyle and enjoy other advantages such as a caring network of family and friends, then your prognosis is likely to be far better than the average outcomes would indicate.

### Spiritual Peace

A spiritual foundation can be deeply reassuring, offering a larger perspective, a trusting presence, and hope for some form of liberation, if not salvation. Dr. Harold Koenig identified nearly three dozen scientific studies indicating that more religious individuals are significantly less anxious. For decades, Dr. Herbert Benson promoted the benefits of a no-frills "relaxation response." However, he later concluded that adding a *faith factor*, derived from a "deeply held set of philosophical or religious convictions," could produce an even greater impact, leading to "greatly enhanced states of health and well-being." He suggested the following practice:

Sit in a comfortable position

Close your eyes and relax your muscles

Focus on your breathing, inhaling for a count of four, exhaling for a count of six.

Select a word or prayer that reflects your spiritual beliefs

Maintain a receptive attitude

Practice for 10–20 minutes, twice a day

## Hope Prescriptions

In Table 16.1, you will find a list of prevalent medical conditions along with various hope-based prescriptions that can to aid in healing and improving health for those who have these conditions. Listed by illness, each prescription consists of recommended dosages of investments to be directed at strengthening one's attachment, mastery, and survival systems. (They were computed by weighing both the quantity and quality of mind–body research conducted on a particular disorder.)

These hope formulas might be compared to the compound strengths used to produce homeopathic remedies or the molecular formulas underlying prescription drugs. For example, if you had a headache, a doctor might recommend aspirin, which is made of nine parts carbon, eight parts hydrogen, and four parts oxygen. In contrast, if

TABLE 16.1. *Suggested Hope Prescriptions and Dosages*

| Conditions | "Dosages" (Approximate Time and Energy Investments) | | |
|---|---|---|---|
| | Attachment[1] | Mastery[2] | Survival[3] |
| Cancer, Cardiovascular disease, Stroke | 40% | 10% | 50% |
| Arthritis, HIV/AIDS | 33% | 33% | 33% |
| Diabetes, Chronic pain, Respiratory infections | 20% | 20% | 60% |
| Gastrointestinal disorders, Serious wounds or injuries | 10% | 10% | 80% |

[1] Support groups, healing networks, couples therapy, clubs, Internet chat rooms
[2] Self-efficacy training, tai chi, Zen philosophy, insight meditation (mindfulness)
[3] Exercise, biofeedback, progressive muscle relaxation, breathing, meditation, yoga

you were diagnosed with meningitis or pneumonia, the preferred treatment might be penicillin, composed of nine parts carbon, eleven parts hydrogen, two parts nitrogen, four parts oxygen, and one part sulfur.

Over the long run, a full hope, consisting of equal parts attachment, mastery, and survival investments, is likely to offer the most health benefits. However, when dealing with a specific medical condition, one or more of the hope motives may serve as an especially potent healing compound. For example, *cancer patients* seem to do best when they can lower stress levels (survival system) and obtain high quality social support (attachment system). Individuals diagnosed with *gastrointestinal problems,* or recovering from a *serious wound or injury,* might be best served by focusing on stress reduction. HIV/AIDS patients, and those dealing with arthritis, should distribute their time and energy evenly across all three of the motives underlying hope. Naturally, like any good homeopath or apothecary, you may have to adjust your required dosage of attachment, mastery, or survival investments, depending on your particular needs.

Remember to maintain a working alliance with your healthcare provider. This should increase your sense of empowerment and connection while also providing additional degrees of freedom in terms of treatment options. Regular physical exercise and the adoption of a healthy diet, along with the use of selected vitamins and minerals, can further boost your immune system.

## Spiritual Supplements

Plato got it right; you cannot do justice to the body without also attending to the soul. Those who dismiss any form of spirituality may be increasing their risk of contracting a serious illness, particularly if they follow a path of hostility, isolation, and worry. Viewed from this perspective, spirituality is akin to preventive medicine.

As we have emphasized throughout this chapter, spirituality can aid in the healing process. In fact, some belief systems include very elaborate exercises and rituals for dealing with specific ailments. In general, the health benefits imparted by spiritual beliefs systems mirror the kind of hope they provide. For example, Hinduism, which offers a mastery and attachment-based hope, may foster a greater will to live and increased receptivity to outside support. Buddhist techniques, derived from the great salvation religion, can reduce both the mental and physical distress that only tends to exacerbate the severity of an illness.

The Hindu "chakra" system is perhaps the least studied but most detailed of all the spiritual healing practices. In Sanskrit, "chakra" means "spinning disk." Hence the chakras are conceived of as spinning disks of energy formed by the interface of consciousness and matter. Seven chakras are presumed to inhabit the human body, with each chakra believed to be associated with a particular body part or organ and with specific psychological and physical functions. Each chakra can be further divided into a front (A) and back (B). Typically, the front portion directs an attachment-related function, while the back is thought to be involved in mastery-oriented activities. For example, the third chakra is presumed to span both the solar plexus (front) and the diaphragm (back). When a chakra is either underserved (e.g., blocked) or overblown (e.g., in the case of sexual promiscuity), it is thought to affect both mental and physical ailments. A disrupted third chakra is believed to be especially problematic, potentially impacting the development of a variety of disorders, including cancer, HIV, stroke, diabetes, and the gastrointestinal system. Practitioners of this healing art focus on rebalancing one or more disrupted chakras by the use of light, sound, touch, or other energy-shifting techniques, much like a chiropractor strives to realign the skeletal system.

In China, Tibet, and Japan, Buddhist and Taoist healing practices play a prominent role. Buddhism offers *vipassana* or "insight meditation" as well as *samatha* or "concentration meditation." Vipassana is geared toward increasing awareness and can be thought of as an ally for developing greater mastery. Samatha is designed to diminish the influx of distressing, anxiety-provoking thoughts and is presented as a tool for survival or coping with distress.

*Tai chi* is the best known Taoist health practice. Sometimes called moving meditation, tai chi involves patterned sequences of gently choreographed movements, each of which is presumed to impart specific health benefits. For example, there is one series of movements called "the leg-swing exercise," believed to be especially effective in eliminating constipation and indigestion. Tai chi practitioners typically spend 15 to 20 minutes a day performing 20 or more movements.

*Qigong* is similar to tai chi. Both are Taoist in origin. However, the former combines breathing and movement in a synchronized manner. In addition, the aim of qigong is to treat a disease rather than to merely maintain health. *Guo Lin Qigong* was named after its founder (Guo Lin) who adapted various ancient movement and breathing exercises in an effort to rid herself of cancer. Today in China, there are over 50,000 individuals who have joined her Cancer Recovery Clubs.

Native American healing practices feature a variety of purification rites. Typically performed in rural encampments, the primary venues are drum ceremonies and sweat lodge experiences, which can last anywhere from several hours to a day or more. Consistent with the strong Native American focus on attachment, participants may be asked to offer prayers to all of their relations, including living and deceased relatives and friends, the community, and various elements of nature. In addition, there may be specific prayers invoked to appease potentially offended spirits.

These various rituals of reintegration may be especially healing for physically compromised individuals who are further burdened by the stress of actual or perceived interpersonal conflict, estrangement, or abandonment. Imagine, for example, a breast cancer patient estranged from her family of origin, or a gay HIV+ male who is struggling to go public with his sexual identity.

Spiritual practices may work best when they are supported from below by a broader philosophical or spiritual belief system as well as from the side by an adjoining complement of traditional (Western) interventions. (Clearly, our bias is toward complementary rather than alternative forms of healing.) In addition, while there is some evidence that spiritual practices may improve the quality of life for individuals with certain medical conditions, there is not enough data to suggest that they can serve as stand-alone cures. By labeling spiritual healing practices supplements, we do not mean to suggest that they are in any way less important. Instead, they might be better conceptualized as necessary but not sufficient ingredients in a comprehensive program of healing.

## A Healing Philosophy

The best healer is also a philosopher

—Galen, 200 A.D.

We live in an era of highly focused treatment plans. Individuals are seen by specialists who may deal exclusively with the heart or lungs, eyes or throat, bones or tendons, mind or body. Indeed, it is not uncommon for a large metropolitan hospital to house several dozen clinics, each focused on a specific malady. Fydor Dostoevsky, one of the great psychological writers of the nineteenth century, was frequently bemused by the cult of myopia that can often blind members of the medical profession. In *The Brothers Karamazov*, he went so far as to lampoon a physician who insisted on treating only the *right nostril*.

Specialized care is at its best when it offers a concentrated but also comprehensive approach to treatment. In contrast, when specialization becomes fragmentation, healing is impeded. What is needed is a renewed commitment to what the ancients called the "art" or "philosophy" of healing. Putting it simply, you must complement your knowledge of hope-based healing strategies and prescriptions with an overarching set of principles. The key elements of this healing philosophy are *commitment, collaboration, combinations, caring, connection, and courage.* You might want to think of these as the *six Cs of healing.*

- *Commitment.* A few years ago, one of us (A. S.) counseled a young man whose father died a few short months after being diagnosed with cancer. In therapy, this man expressed a great deal of disappointment that his father had not "fought harder." Over time, he began to sense that his father had probably "accepted his fate" as "just punishment." A lay minister, his father had never been able to resolve his guilt over having abandoned his family for another woman. Moreover, he had repeatedly "let down" his children, including writing a bad check when his son first entered college.

  Health and healing require a commitment to life. One of the lessons to be gleaned from the mind–body literature is that healing requires a sense of purpose. Individuals who have a life mission heal better and faster. Similarly, many survivors who have achieved unexpected recoveries from serious illness, such as advanced forms of cancer, have typically been characterized as "authentic," "autonomous," or "fully involved."

- *Collaboration.* Share the responsibility for your healing. Begin by making sure that your doctor is willing to develop a working alliance. If your condition is serious or otherwise resistant to treatment, make sure that he or she is tenacious and persistent in finding other possible treatment solutions. Is he a true hope provider in the sense of being accessible, trustworthy, and responsive? Is she capable of instilling a sense of empowerment, trust, and reassurance? In this vein, the poet Samuel Taylor Coleridge wrote, "He is the best physician who is the most ingenious inspirer of hope."

  Tom Ferguson, a physician and nationally known expert on medical self-help, recommended several strategies for cultivating an empowering doctor–patient partnership. First, plan for your medical visits by making a list of questions to address with your doctor. Be a good observer of your symptoms and overall condition and describe them to your doctor in full. Do not leave the doctor's office confused or with unanswered questions. If a medical test is ordered, do not be afraid to ask about the potential time involvement, risks, implications of findings, etc. Be assertive and, if necessary, consider getting a second opinion.

Kim, a brain cancer survivor, wrote, "If someone tells you that you're not gonna survive and that they can't do anything more, find someone else. Find someone that will be encouraging. Even if they don't think that they can do anything, if they're willing to be there for you and encourage you . . . I had one doctor that was doom and gloom, and another doctor came in and said, "*We're gonna beat it.*" And I think he saved my life. I really do."

Do not suspend your collaborative mindset in the presence of so-called experts. Sometimes knowing too much about one possible condition can blind an individual to other considerations. For example, one of us (A. S.) was treating a young woman for anxiety. She had a history of chronic but mild gastrointestinal problems. After a particularly painful flare-up, her primary care physician referred her to a gastroenterologist, who promptly diagnosed a common but potentially debilitating chronic illness. Convinced that she had a serious disease, she spent the next 6 months restructuring her entire life around this presumed condition. When her symptoms did not improve, she decided that a *second opinion* was warranted. After doing some research, she found a more holistically oriented gastroenterologist, who ordered more specific tests, which ruled out the first diagnosis. Relieved but still not sure what was causing her problems, she sought out a respected naturopath who took the time to go over her condition, and more importantly, was willing to work in a collaborative fashion to help her regain her health.

*Second opinions* are particularly useful when there are unexpected findings, the discovery of a very rare condition, a failure to obtain usual treatment results, or conflicting feedback from different physicians or tests. For inspiration, you may want to read Dr. Jerome Groopman's *Second Opinions.* Groopman detailed eight case studies in which a second look made all the difference in the world.

Chris Crichton, a long-term cancer survivor, revealed how hope-based liberation beliefs sustained his search for an alternative and more hopeful perspective. "You have to get second and third opinions. When I went to see the urologist who read me my tests, he said, 'We think you have cancer. What are you doing at three o'clock today? You have one option, and that is to have this surgery, go through chemotherapy, and you might make it.' Wrong. He gave me absolutely no hope. I had a lot of options. The way that he painted the picture was completely different from what reality was."

• *Combinations.* Do not limit your healing options by thinking exclusively in terms of traditional versus nontraditional therapies. There is considerable evidence that different types of interventions can complement one another to produce better outcomes. For example, meditation and other relaxation procedures can help to reduce nausea from chemotherapy, allowing an individual to tolerate the necessary dosage needed to destroy the cancer cells. Expand your range of healing possibilities by thinking first in terms of complementary medicine, and if necessary, alternative approaches.

Alisa Gilbert, a breast cancer survivor, combined traditional chemotherapy with her own native "detoxify rituals" once her treatments had stopped. "The complementary therapies that I went through were some traditional Native ceremonial-type stuff: a purifying ceremony and this internal cleansing I did after my treatment to get the toxins out of my body. It was a turning point in the whole path to survivorship, because I could actually close that door. I was moving into wellness."

• *Caring.* Deep healing requires an investment in transforming your life. In *Care of the Soul*, Thomas Moore described "a continuous process . . . of attending to the small details of everyday life as well as to major decisions and changes . . . to give ordinary life the depth and value that come from soulfulness." Moore noted that the original Latin meaning of the word "cure" means to "nurse" in the sense of "attention, devotion, husbandry, adorning the body, healing, managing, and worshipping the gods." Instead of shallow manipulations aimed at a quick fix, care for the soul involves ongoing attention and a commitment to depth and observance.

*Hope-based care can be likened to a form of incubation.* The word "incubation" comes from Greek antiquity. When the ancient Greeks and Romans became seriously ill, they made a pilgrimage to the temple of Asclepius, the god of healing. After a period of fasting and prayer, the faithful retired to specially designed sleeping chambers. This incubation was rooted in the hope of a healing dream whereby the sufferer could encounter Asclepius himself and receive a magic cure or specific prescription.

Philosophers may have done the best job of illuminating the process of hopeful self-care. Paul Pruyser emphasized that hope should be viewed as a "way of life" rather than a "short-term intervention." William Lynch stressed the importance of "affirmation" and "acceptance." Gabriel Marcel likened hope to a form of "active waiting" sustained by an "enlarged perspective" and distinguishable from the "psychic stiffening" of obstinate denial. To foster your own hope-centered self-care, look beyond your symptoms for a larger lesson. Aim further and higher than fighting the disease. Stay alert and informed, yet remain patient with yourself and others. With trust and openness, you will be prepared for every healing opportunity that comes your way.

Ann Marie Juliano, an 18-year survivor of ovarian cancer, wrote, "When you're dealing with cancer, there is so much chaos going on in your life. I think that you have to always be on the lookout for that bright, little, shining star in the midst of all that chaos, because it's there . . . you realize, I am alive. The sun is shining, or it's raining, or it's dark. I'm alive. Here I am, I'm breathing, and everything is wonderful. How could you not find hope?"

- *Connection.* You cannot heal in isolation. Remember that social support is often the most potent of all the mind–body factors. Emotional ties rival smoking cessation in terms of reducing the odds of developing cancer. Love benefits the heart and blood vessels as much as any cholesterol-lowering drug. Attachments can serves as natural beta blockers, calming your body while limiting the output of harmful stress hormones.

To reap the full health benefits of social support, you must strive to build relationships that are open and trusting, capable of fostering genuine emotional expression. The best support networks provide a complete hope that is empowering, loving, and reassuring. The women taking part in David Spiegel's breast cancer study found themselves discussing how best to deal with their doctors while also "sharing their victories and defeats" (mastery). "They came to care deeply and personally about one another" (attachment). The groups also provided a setting in which they could face their concerns about losses and dying so that these and other fears did not dominate their lives (survival).

- *Courage.* Confronting a serious illness often requires a heroic stance. There may be great physical pain and suffering as well as fears of permanent disability or even death. Even those who have enjoyed some degree of healing may be burdened with ongoing anxiety. In public some cancer survivors may quip that they have beaten the odds, but at a deeper level they may be asking themselves, "Will it recur?," "Did the surgeon really get all of it?" "If it does return, will it be worse?" Similarly, the heart attack survivor may anxiously wonder, "What if I have another incident and nobody is around to bring me to the hospital?" The trauma survivor may fear that another mugging, assault, or catastrophe is just around the corner.

Do you recall *The Sword of Damocles*? The tale is about a rich and powerful king named Dionysius, who allows his slave Damocles to be king for a day. While seated before a great bounty of food, Damocles notices a sword hanging over his head by a single hair. Obviously terrified, he asks Dionysius for an explanation. The king explains that sustaining power and glory required tremendous courage; it is not for the faint hearted. Damocles, a true coward, shrinks from the challenge, opting for the safety of serfdom.

Many survivors may continue to feel as if the sword of Damocles is hanging over their heads, but they summon the courage to go on living their lives. Hope-based healing, unlike denial or blind optimism, requires true grit. It is no small feat to remain open, accepting, and engaged when confronting a frightening diagnosis, complex medical jargon, and painful procedures. Nevertheless, if you are dealing with a serious illness, you will find a wealth of scientific evidence that supports the emboldened path of Dionysius. Perhaps Emerson put it best when he wrote, "The wise man in the storm prays to God; not for safety from danger, but for deliverance from fear."

Visit the Web site of the Lance Armstrong Foundation (http://www.livestrong.org). You will be able to read the personal testimonies of various cancer survivors and discover how each of them found a way to keep hope alive. Fully embodying the "live strong" philosophy promoted by Armstrong's foundation, these survivors are truly profiles in courage. For example, Charles Fletcher, an octogenarian who survived two bouts of cancer, observed:

> You know, it's just mind over matter. And if you have faith, which I have, it's a matter of saying, "Well, what is the greatest fear in the world? Dying? Well, I'm not afraid to die. So what's in between? Nothing . . . I got all kinds of medals in the hospital for walking up and down the hall with my little bottle. When I got home, I would treadmill . . . . Now I'm still lifting weights, and I'm going to keep lifting weights . . . There's always hope.

## Hope and Wellness

> Health . . . seems to demand a horizon. We are never tired, so long as we can see far enough.
>
> —Ralph Waldo Emerson

A desire for health and happiness is the great hope that lies beyond every healing journey. John Keats, the frail and sickly poet of love, called health "my expected heaven." Lao Tzu considered physical wellbeing "the greatest possession," while Seneca proclaimed health "the soul that animated all the enjoyments of life." Thomas Carlyle wrote, "He who has health, has hope."

A true and deep experience of hope can also bring a richer and more lasting form of happiness, beyond superficial or fleeting moments of "hurried excitement". Moreover, despite all the recent emphasis on "mindfulness" and "living in the moment", an exclusive focus on securing the "here and now" will never bring a lasting sense of peace or contentment. In contrast, a well founded hope that bridges the past, present, and future can insure joy, happiness, and pleasure, for today and tomorrow as well as next year and beyond. In contemporary psychology, the research of Fred Bryant and Joseph Veroff on "savoring" comes the closest to our notion of a hope-centered happiness.

Hope, health, and happiness are intertwined. Having a hopeful attitude is a key ingredient of being healthy, and it is a must for those who are in ill health. Having one or more reasons for living or, in the words of Emerson, a "horizon," is a critical factor in sustaining health and happiness. Stripped of hope, human beings lose their incentive for self-care. Without dreams and forward-looking agendas, they abandon the pursuit of vitality. Rather than choosing life, they opt to let themselves go.

In the rest of this chapter, we highlight four important connections between hope and wellness. These include hope-based fitness, hopeful aging, meaning and health, and the creation of a hope-centered way of life. Taken together, attending to these hope-health associations can add life to your years as well as years to your life. For as the author Orison Marden wrote, "There is no tonic so powerful as the expectation of a better tomorrow."

## Hope-Based Fitness

Fitness-minded individuals tend to possess a hopeful outlook on life. Why? Because a healthy lifestyle tends to strengthen the same motive systems that underlie hope. Wellness derives from an adequate sense of mastery, loving and supportive relationships, and manageable levels of stress. These are also the pillars of hope.

At the same time, a hopeful mindset can provide a powerful set of incentives for a regimen of healthy habits. Being fit is most compelling to an individual who values empowerment, intimacy, and self-regulation. More to the point, hopeful individuals are future oriented. They look ahead and envision positive attachment, mastery, and survival experiences. These ever-present leaps in time propel an investment in staying fit.

Consider the impulse to exercise. What motivates an individual to both begin and then maintain a regular program of exercise? One of the most important factors seems to be exercise imagery, pictures and ideas of present and future benefits attributed to physical activity. Some individuals imagine being and becoming stronger, while others envision themselves more attractive or less prone to injury or disease. It is reasonable to assume that individuals who entertain a full complement of hope-related exercise imagery (attachment, mastery, and survival-related benefits) will be those who are least vulnerable to abandoning a program of regular physical activity.

To test some of these ideas, in collaboration with psychologist Erica Checko, we assessed the hopefulness of nearly 100 college students. In addition, each student was asked a series of questions dealing with exercise, diet, current height and weight, and smoking behaviors. Students who were rated as more hopeful were more likely to be involved in a regular program of exercise. In contrast, those who were the least hopeful were more likely to be in a "precontemplation" stage, meaning that they were not even thinking about beginning a program of exercise. In addition, greater hopefulness was associated with a more desirable body mass index (BMI), greater consumption of fruits and vegetables, and smoking fewer cigarettes. Clearly, hope is good for the body as well as the soul.

*Exercise can strengthen the hope motives.* Improved physical endurance contributes to a generalized sense of mastery. When you are feeling fresh and strong, nothing seems impossible, and hope spirals upward. In Shakespeare's *Winter's Tale*, we read that "a merry heart goes all day." In contrast, when you are tired, the smallest obstacles seem overwhelming. Football legend Vince Lombardi summed it up well, "Fatigue makes cowards of us all."

Even in so-called intellectual pursuits, the role of physical stamina should not be underestimated. Your brain uses as much as one fifth of all the energy that is derived from food. The 1984 world championship of chess between Anatoly Karpov and Gary Kasparov went on for several months. In the process, Karpov lost more than 20 pounds. In short, even hope-based mastery that involves intellectual pursuits can be augmented by increasing overall fitness.

A commitment to physical health can also facilitate greater intimacy. Of course, there are various indirect social benefits that may come from joining a neighborhood fitness center, including schmoozing around a water fountain or socializing before or after a group aerobics class. However, there are deeper and more direct interpersonal gains. For example, feeling more confident and comfortable in your body makes it more likely that you will experience more contact comfort (hugs, kisses, etc.). In addition, regular exercise increases cardiovascular endurance and improves blood flow, two important factors that contribute to greater sexual satisfaction.

With increased physical contact, there is a greater likelihood that your body will release oxytocin, the so-called cuddle chemical. Oxytocin release is especially strong during sex or other forms of skin-to-skin contact, prompting some scientists to invoke the notion of sexual healing. Oxytocin is presumed to act as a kind of stress buffer. Along these lines, Swedish scientists found that rats injected with oxytocin, as compared to those who were not, demonstrated a greater tolerance to heat stress, lower blood pressure, better blood-sugar control, and increased immunity.

Exercise offers a particularly effective way to boost survival skills. Aerobic exercise can alleviate symptoms of anxiety. It can also limit allostatic load by reducing cardio-vascular reactivity to stress and accelerating the return to baseline following the introduction of an arousing stimulus. Along these lines, investigators at the Cooper Institute in Dallas found that 4 months of aerobic activity, consisting of three to four moderate workouts per week, was effective in lowering blood pressure and stress hormone levels in hypertensive individuals.

Another way to boost your sense of mastery involves strength training. Working out with weights, or engaging in other forms of muscle building exercise, can reinforce bones and joints while reducing fat and improving balance as well as coordination. Fitness programs can also be combined with self-defense courses to provide an enhanced sense of personal safety.

Exercise is an excellent form of preventive medicine. Individuals who engage in a regular program of physical activity are less likely to have a stroke, to be diagnosed with heart disease, or to develop certain forms of cancer. When a serious illness or injury does occur, those who are in better physical condition tend to heal more rapidly and more thoroughly. For example, among individuals dealing with heart disease, diabetes, or multiple sclerosis, the best predictors of quality of life are maintaining an appropriate weight and involvement in ongoing physical activity.

The strong association between fitness, mental vitality, and life satisfaction is well documented in *Creative Fitness: Applying Health Psychology and Exercise Science to Everyday Life*. In this book, written by one of us (H. B.), there are countless studies that deal with the benefits of an engaged and active lifestyle, including research in biology, kinesiology, and health (e.g., sleep and nutrition findings) as well as psychology and sociology. While underscoring the importance of regular exercise and self-care across the life span, the book emphasizes that there are multiple paths to fitness (one size does *not* fit all). Those who can adopt a mindful, creative approach to exercise and health will be the ones most likely to fashion a personalized training program that is able to address their particular attachment, mastery, and survival needs.

## Hopeful Aging

> The old who have gone before us are on a road which we must all travel . . . it
> is good to ask them, whether it is smooth and easy, or rugged and difficult.
>
> — Socrates

Estée Lauder launched her cosmetics empire by marketing containers of a mysterious skin cream that she called jars of hope. Notwithstanding Lauder's business acumen, the true fountain of youth is not cosmetics or even growth hormone or Botox, but an enduring sense of hope. It is normal and healthy to keep hope alive in the later years. Researchers at the Max Planck Institute of Human Development in Berlin found that even among the so-called old-old, those in their 80s and 90s, nearly three-quarters continued to add new hope domains to their life scripts. Moreover, those who stopped hoping and merely focused on maintenance concerns or fears were the ones who showed a precipitous decline in life satisfaction.

Psychiatrist George Vaillant utilized data from the Harvard Study of Adult Development as well as findings from several other longitudinal investigations. Drawing on this extensive database, Vaillant provided a number of guideposts for successful aging, which he summarized in his book *Aging Well*. In addition to sound health habits, he underscored the following hope-sustaining processes: an ongoing *curiosity*, a *continued emotional involvement* in the life of others, and the ability to *tolerate and make peace* with the indignities of old age. These were among the most critical factors distinguishing the "happy-well" from the "sad-sick."

> The centrality of hope and love in lifespan development goes unchallenged.
> Regardless of the words, the melody is still the same; the last years of life without
> hope and love become a mere sounding brass or tinkling cymbal.

Other life span investigators have also found that a commitment to mastery, attachment, and survival can foster positive aging as well as longevity. A research team at UCLA, headed by geriatric specialist Dr. David Reuben, found that older adults who were physically active had lower levels of Interleukin-6 and C-reactive protein, two markers of systemic inflammation. A study by gerontologist Terry Lum and his colleagues at the University of Minnesota indicated that older adults who volunteered a minimum of 100 hours a year enjoyed better health while reducing their risk of depression and premature death.

*Attachments still matter.* At Duke University, a group of older adults were asked to fill out a standard questionnaire that measured interpersonal trust. Eight years later, psychologist John Barefoot and his colleagues integrated this data with health and mortality findings derived from a series of follow-up studies. They found that those who had high trust scores 8 years before were more likely to be still alive and functioning well.

*Religious and spiritual beliefs can bolster hope-based survival in the elderly.* Psychologist Kevin Masters reported that intrinsically religious older subjects, over 60 years of age, were less likely to demonstrate a rise in blood pressure following an emotional stressor as compared to their extrinsic counterparts. Moreover, there was no difference in stress tolerance between older and younger (18–24 years) intrinsic individuals. Epidemiologist William J. Strawbridge and his colleagues studied the mortality patterns of over 5,000 individuals living in Alameda, California, between the years of 1965 and 1994. The mortality rate of those who attended religious services at least once a week was 36% less than that of those who never or rarely went to a house of worship.

Erik Erikson's final book, *Vital Involvement in Old Age*, dealt with the hopes of individuals in the final stages of the life cycle. Drawn from interviews with more than two dozen octogenarians, it shed light on the mastery, attachment, and survival strategies that help older adults retain their sense of vitality. For example, to preserve a sense of mastery, some older individuals shared their experiences of attending continuing education classes, while others described their time spent gardening, cooking, or remodeling their homes.

Erikson and his coauthors noted some excellent examples of *supported mastery*. For example, a number of elders reported that they felt empowered to live more vigorous lives when they were introduced to a similarly independent roommate or community member. Many also emphasized that they were able to continue with their activities and hobbies because of the intergenerational support they received from children and grandchildren in terms of concrete assistance with household chores and paperwork, as well as moral support and advice. In a rural area, one individual who was still able to drive transported his friends to a senior center. When the car was no longer big enough to accommodate everyone, he and his friends managed to buy and maintain a van; "now those who still drive take turns at the wheel."

Hope-based attachments were especially cherished by these vital seniors. A common theme was absolute belief and unquestioning trust in loved ones. The family was perceived as "an anchor in a world that is often tempestuous." As loved ones and heroes passed away, many found inspiration and interpersonal security within a religious community, where, in the words of the authors, they might "find themselves looking up to the immortal heroes of religion and the timeless, infinitely trustworthy qualities they represent." Another powerful sense of attachment was derived from the preservation of *residential continuity*. Quite a few elders made sacrifices so that they could remain in the same town or neighborhood. Part of their hope experience was rooted in a sense of place.

The survival skills of these resilient octogenarians included wise financial management as well as careful attention to diet and exercise. They also demonstrated the ability to recruit care from others, including children and neighbors. Many sustained or even deepened their faith in God to fashion a sense of security in some entity or order outside the self. Some spoke of a personalized "hope for generative confirmation . . . [a] hope to be remembered by the grandchildren after death [as] 'kind and loving' or perhaps as a 'fountain of wisdom.'"

On a more cosmic level, the most hopeful elders continued to express concern for the future. While proud of past contributions such as raising healthy and productive children, they did not lose sight of present opportunities to further maintain the world. Moreover, as they passed on this torch of grand generativity, many proclaimed an unqualified faith in their children as future custodians of the world.

### Meaning and Health

What is meaning in life? Many lengthy philosophical essays have been written on this topic, but one of the most compelling descriptions can be found in a pithy five-page article written by philosopher Robert Baird. In *Meaning in Life: Created or Discovered,* Baird reduced the meaning-making process to three essential life tasks: cultivating depth and quality in your relationships, committing yourself to projects and goals, and fashioning stories that place your life in an ultimate context. Note that, once again, the big things in life come down to attachment, mastery, and survival, or in other words, hope. Perhaps this is why theologian Emil Brunner proclaimed: "What oxygen is to the lungs, such is hope to the meaning of life."

Meaning in life is both a destination and a vehicle. As a destination, a meaningful life can be viewed as a desired end state or goal: every human being has a need to lead a life that makes sense to him or her on a personal level. As a vehicle, meaning making can pave the way to better health: being fully engaged in the flow of life and having a deep sense of purpose can make you more resistant to illness and extend your life. In both senses, the personal meaning in one's life, like a potentially effective exercise program, usually requires some adjustment if it is to be sustained over time, and for many, that adjustment includes the incorporation of established traditions such as religious faith. But regardless, the meaning that one finds in life supports health because it solidifies hope.

*Meaning as a health destination.* Meaning is hardly a luxury item for a social animal endowed with prominent frontal lobes and a keen sense of future survival. Meaning is basic to human life. No amount of money or power can take its place. If these earthly gains sufficed, we would never see many of those who have them in spades destroy themselves with drugs, eating disorders, or other self-destructive behaviors. Horace Greeley put it well, "Fame is a vapor, popularity an accident . . . riches take wings."

*Meaning as a vehicle to better health.* Individuals infused with meaning are well anchored. They have strong relationships, a potent sense of mastery, and an unwavering sense of purpose. In short, they are brimming with hope. What are the health benefits of such deep centeredness? Psychiatrist Viktor Frankl observed that those of his fellow prisoners at Auschwitz who were able to sustain some sense of purpose were less likely to succumb to illness. More than even food or medical care, a meaning-oriented outlook preserved the immune systems of these survivors.

Psychologist Carol Ryff has been among those who believe that meaning and purpose in life reduces allostatic load, the wear and tear of biological reactivity to stress. To the extent that spiritual beliefs impart meaning, this may be why high religious involvement tends to be associated with fewer cardiovascular crises and greater longevity. In a sense, the meaning-centered individual is less likely to be tossed adrift by what Shakespeare dubbed the "slings and arrows of outrageous fortune."

Ryff and her colleagues tested the meaning hypothesis by studying 134 women, ages 61 to 91. They assessed both hedonic (joy and happiness) and eudaimonic well-being (meaning and purpose). Greater meaning and purpose, rather than more joy and happiness, emerged as the better health predictor. Specifically, those who reported greater eudaimonic well-being had lower levels of stress hormones and inflammatory cytokines as well as higher levels of HDL ("good" cholesterol). They also had a healthier body mass index.

The ability to derive meaning is also important for those already diagnosed with a serious illness. Denise Bowes of Dalhousie University in Nova Scotia and her colleagues conducted detailed interviews of nine women diagnosed with ovarian cancer. "Hope" and "finding meaning" were the two most important factors that determined perceived well-being. As one woman put it, "If you don't have hope, then you don't have anything really."

The role of meaning as an illness buffer seems to be especially important for older individuals. One of us (A. S.), in collaboration with psychologist David McClelland, explored the impact of derived meaning, chronic illness, and age on reported morale in 80 younger (25 to 40) and 80 older (65 to 80) adults. The findings were fascinating. Older individuals were better able to derive meaning from experiences with illness than their younger counterparts. In addition, despite reporting twice as many chronic illnesses as the younger group, the older adults had significantly higher levels of morale. What accounted for this surprising finding? It appeared to be derived meaning. Among older adults, meaning was the strongest predictor of morale, exceeding by a factor of ten to one both the importance of age and the number or severity of chronic illnesses.

## Creative Hoping

> What is it to work with love? . . . to charge all things you fashion with a breath of your own spirit . . . to know that all the blessed dead are standing about you and watching. . . . For he who seizes the rainbow to lay it on a cloth in the likeness of man, is more than he who makes the sandals for our feet.
> —Kahlil Gibran, *The Prophet*

Although your health is clearly a prized possession, it sometimes may seem difficult, if not impossible, to preserve a sense of well-being. Major life challenges as well as daily hassles are an inevitable part of life. As the saying goes, the only individual who is completely free of stress is either in denial or dead. Inevitably, relationships get tested, workloads mount to the point of feeling unmanageable, or a serious illness is discovered. When times are tough, your way of hoping must take a creative turn.

Creativity also underlies the fullest expressions of hope. By "creative" we do not mean an illusory hope born of denial and based on an avoidance of facts and a reduced field of vision. Unlike false hope, creative hoping derives from a thorough exploration of the facts and an expanded level of awareness. It requires that you delve fully into the realms of the actual as well as the imaginable. It represents the ultimate form of mindfulness, grounded in a two-fold process of fact finding and fact building.

### Reality Surveillance

Fact finding, or *reality surveillance*, is most relevant when your mastery, attachment, or survival aims are well defined, and it refers to the process of finding evidence to maintain and even strengthen your beliefs about realizing such goals. Psychologists sometimes call this the rational or left-brain side of the hoping process, involving a search for proof, palpable data, or firm reasons to ground your hopes.

Of the three reality surveillance strategies available to you, one is to *adopt* the reasons for hope used by others. Say you want to strengthen your relationship with someone (attachment). What can be especially compelling are success stories from credible individuals who themselves have built strong relationships with the people in their lives. In earlier chapters, for example, we highlighted the insights of Harville Hendrix and John Gottman, relationship experts whose suggestions were based on decades of research and practice with hundreds of couples. Both offered distressed lovers a cornucopia of reasons for hope. If, however, you are dealing with a serious medical condition (survival), you might want to further explore Dr. Lorraine Day's personal recipe for overcoming cancer or neuroscientist Candace Pert's cutting-edge research on the immune system.

A second reality surveillance option is to *transfer* reasons from one hope domain to another. For example, you could borrow survival-related facts and figures and use them to support your *mastery-related efforts*. Specifically, many people never achieve their mastery potential because of unrealistic fears. If you want reasons to be less afraid, read Barry Glassner's book *The Culture of Fear*. A sociologist, Glassner demonstrated how the mass media, politicians, and even certain advocacy groups greatly exaggerate the risk and prevalence of certain forms of danger. According to Glassner, the great majority of individuals are far safer than such fear mongers would have them believe.

Avoid narrowing your possibilities. Consider any and every option. Be thorough by searching for evidence. This might be achieved by altering when, where, or how you look for hope. For example, you might consider investing in a personal portfolio (e.g., a journal or notebook) of hopeful thoughts and images. Like a savings account, this portfolio could become your psychological rainy day fund. When you have a good experience related to mastery, attachment or survival, whether is comes from your own behavior or it is something you observe, read, or hear about, store it away for later reference.

A related strategy is to keep hope alive by creating options that might be exercised at a future date when opportunities for mastery, attachment, or survival might be expanded. Psychologist Herbert Lefcourt provided a wonderful example of safekeeping hope for later use. He described a man who lost his sight as the result of a terrible car accident. Nevertheless, he insisted on having his eyes and the surrounding nerves repaired in the hope that future technological developments might someday restore his vision.

Also think about looking in a new place for reasons to hope. Look to other cultures or even back in time for bits of ancient wisdom. Western medical researchers and practitioners now turn to the East in search of complementary healing procedures (survival). Successful athletic coaches, as well as war generals, consult Sun Tzu's ancient masterpiece, *The Art of War*, for mastery-related insights. Spiritual guru Thomas Moore gleaned ways of cultivating a soulful marriage from dust-covered medieval tomes.

Whatever form of reality surveillance you choose, *cast a wide net* in your search for evidence to support your hopes. *Avoid narrowing your possibilities* prematurely, consider any and every option. Be thorough by searching for evidence in the most obvious locations and then systematically explore the less likely places. Above all, be *persistent* and think about the *possible payoffs* of your search. Finally (and perhaps just as important), let others know about your hopes and dreams. Keep spreading the word and invariably you will achieve a level of networking penetration and saturation that is bound to yield significant dividends in the fulfillment of your mastery, attachment, or survival needs.

### Reality Construction

Fact building, or *reality construction*, is the other side of the hoping process. Perhaps you feel stuck, alienated, or vulnerable but cannot yet envision a better life. What you need is a hopeful image that is guiding and inspiring. As in the case of reality surveillance, you can adopt, transfer, or transform established methods of reality construction.

One solution is to *adopt* an existing philosophy of mastery, attachment, or survival. For example, in Chapter 10 we highlighted Stephen Covey's character-based approach to mastery, while in Chapter 9 we discussed Harville Hendrix's reparative therapy for romantic partners. A good survival strategy may be likened to an all-weather tire. It keeps you going regardless of the road conditions. Bernie Siegel wrote about the "four faiths" that seem to sustain exceptional cancer patients. These include faith in oneself, faith in doctors, faith in prescribed treatments, and faith in a higher power. This prescription can be rewritten more generally as a survival strategy consisting of faith in self, others, human ingenuity, and a greater intelligence. The last and perhaps most spiritual of these elements can be as specific as a Catholic or Muslim God or as broadly conceived as Ernest Becker's trust in an "evolving consciousness."

You can also *transfer* a philosophy or mindset across hope domains. In this regard, there are plenty of potentially inspiring role models. Lance Armstrong is a perfect example. In his book, *It's Not About the Bike*, the seven-time cycling champion shared how his lifelong drive for mastery helped him to survive testicular cancer. Michael Milken is another mastery-to-survival success story. A powerful Wall Street financier in the 1970s, Milken amassed a personal fortune of nearly a billion dollars. However, in 1991 he pled guilty to various counts of fraud. After serving nearly 2 years in prison, Milken was released, yet soon discovered that he had prostate cancer. Since 1991, Milken's recovery has been amazing in more ways than one. He succeeded in his personal battle with cancer *and* reestablished himself in the financial world. Moreover, he single-handedly led a crusade to significantly advance treatments for prostate cancer. Subsequently, he started a Washington-based think tank devoted to finding better treatments for a variety of life-threatening illnesses. Other transfers across hope domains are possible as well. For example, one may involve a transfer from survival to mastery, as in the case of the burn victim turned champion runner, Glenn Cunningham, mentioned in Chapter 11, or from attachment to survival, as in the children who danced and charmed their way out of Nazi concentration camps during World War II.

If hope continues to elude you, consider an even more radical *transformation*. Restructure your approach to mastery, attachment, or survival. For example, in the area of mastery, most individuals tend to focus exclusively on the wings of hope, pouring all of their energy into expanding their reach outward and upward. However, it is also important to cultivate the roots of mastery in order to foster a kind of growth that will spread inward and downward. Hopeful mastery depends on character and grounding as well as vision and desire. Agreeing, Stephen Covey noted that true success was a matter of character, a quality that can only be forged from the inside-out. "Borrowed strength," in his words, will only build "weakness."

Hopeful mastery requires a solid foundation. The most hopeful individuals, as psychologist James Hillman put it, have "grown down." Hillman outlined four modes of growing down, including developing an awareness of your age and place in time, appreciating your family and community roots, living in a place that "suits your soul' and grounds you with "duties and customs," and repaying "destiny" with grateful gestures that "declare your full attachment to this world." Authentic, centered mastery *can* radiate outward, affecting the hopes of others, near and far, fulfilling Gandhi's call to "be the change that you want to see in the world." Undoubtedly, many of you have come across some version of this anonymous tribute to the ripple effects that can emanate from an individual who is firmly grounded.

> I realize that if long ago I had changed myself, I could have made an impact on my family. My family and I could have made an impact on our town. Their impact could have changed the nation and I could indeed have changed the world.

In regard to attachment, you may want to transform your view of community. In today's world, it is both easier *and* harder to experience a sense of shared oneness. With the advent of cell phones, fax machines, and high-speed Internet connections, you can stay in touch with family and friends who may be spread around the globe. However, instant access does not guarantee, and may even hinder, the development of trust and continued presence that fosters hope. You should consider diversifying your attachment resources, branching out into multiple communities, investing more time and effort in extended family or coworkers, reconnecting with old friends, building stronger alliances with recent acquaintances, or forming new cross-generational friendships with younger or older individuals. But most important, always keep in mind that *quality* attachments are more important that sheer number of contacts.

Finally, you may also want to transform your concept of survival, which is a philosophical issue as well as a physical and emotional imperative. What lies at the core of humanity's quest for security and immortality? Those who have thought most deeply about this issue include philosophers such as Aristotle and Hegel as well as anthropologist Ernest Becker and psychiatrist Robert Lifton. Three themes emerge from their writings: "purpose," "potential," and "continuation."

Perhaps, it all goes back to Aristotle and his brilliant and mysterious concept of "entelechy." Writing *On the Soul*, Aristotle observed that it is the nature of things to seek their essential form. Most philosophers have translated "entelechy" as the will of an entity to come into its own. However, Aristotle also meant an "inner design" to "remain in existence." Could it be that entelechy is what drives the hopeful individual's active search for degrees of freedom (liberation) and eternal salvation (terror management)? Fittingly, one recent translation of entelechy is "being-at-work-staying-itself."

Hope-based survival is about honoring your inner design to be free and secure. However, it is quite possible that your inner design has been thwarted by the vicissitudes of life. You may be faced with a very stressful job, a serious illness, or a crisis of faith. To restore hope, create a *survival plan* by combining two classic hope metaphors: the island and the bridge.

Imagine that you are destined to live for all of eternity on a remote island. This island has many resources but cannot meet all of your needs. However, if you could build a few bridges to connect with other islands, most, if not all, of your needs would be met. An individual is comparable to an island of limited plenitude. Each individual is a unique being, occupying a separate subjective space. Each is endowed with various survival-related resources that represent a certain range or breadth of talent. Nevertheless, there is a limit as to what individuals can do for themselves.

Hope-based survival is enhanced by creating a spiritual bridge with something larger and more enduring than the self. Typically, individuals approach religion or spirituality with a singular focus. Some are driven by a need to infuse their daily lives with a more meaningful structure, while others are exclusively focused on the more distant horizon of ultimate salvation. A more creative alternative is to build at least two spiritual bridges, one to facilitate your daily coping efforts and another to negotiate the farther shore of eternity.

A two-fold spiritual approach has been used in China for centuries. In particular, many Chinese rely on the teachings of Confucius to cope with everyday challenges while employing Buddhist principles to meet their more transcendent salvation needs. This does not necessarily mean that you need two religions. In fact, if you look closely enough at any great system of faith, you will undoubtedly find rules for daily life as well as more transcendent principles regarding ultimate salvation. Alternatively, you could incorporate certain nonreligious spiritual practices in your daily life while reserving your religious beliefs for more transcendent matters.

## The Hopeful Task

In the final analysis, hope is about being as well as arriving. Hope is a way of life as well as a powerful tool for realizing desired endpoints. The most hopeful individuals achieve more than personal success. They answer Gandhi's challenge to be an instrument of positive change, to "become the hope of all mankind."

Earlier in this book we extolled the benefits of having a mission in life. A mission is a particularly creative way to actualize hope. It incorporates all three of the motives underlying hope: mastery, attachment, and survival. Moreover, it should be apparent that you do not have to be religious in the traditional sense to appreciate your individual gifts and learn how they might be used to create a more hopeful planet.

Erik Erikson's notion of "generativity" was rooted in secular humanism. Rick Warren's "purpose-driven life" is Christian-based and God-centered. However, the basic premise is the same. *One of the best things you can do is to share your talent (mastery) in the service of others (attachment) while doing something of enduring value (survival).* Recall how Emerson encouraged his readers to view the universe as "the property of every individual in it." Similarly, in *Living a Life That Matters*, Rabbi Harold Kushner wrote, "In my forty years as a rabbi, I have tended to many people in the last moments of their lives . . . The people who had the most trouble with death were those who felt that they had never done anything worthwhile in their lives, and if God would only give them another two or three years, maybe they would finally get it right. It was not death that frightened them; it was insignificance, the fear that they would die and leave no mark on the world."

It may be time to dust off Aristotle and to revisit Becker's "hopeful task." Underlying Aristotle's "inner design" were notions of "matter" and "form." Everything in nature begins as matter but strives toward form. Over time, lower forms become the matter for higher forms, and so forth. According to Aristotle, this upward spiral occurs because "everything in nature is moved by an inner urge to become something greater than it is." Similarly, Becker wrote that the "heroic individual" willingly participates in a "metaphysic of hope" by "fashioning something . . . and dropping it into the forward momentum of life." In one way or another, all the great spiritual traditions have brought forth this same message, that men and women, young and old, rich and poor, must each do their part in repairing, strengthening, and upholding the world.

# *Notes*

## Introduction

*Page*

3   Dickens, 2003, p. 5.

4   Obama, 1995.

4   Obama, 2006.

4   Obama background information and quotes were retrieved March 9, 2009 from http://en.wikipedia.org/wiki/Barack_Obama_%22Hope%22_poster.

4   Shakespeare, 1997, p. 134.

4   For Solanus Casey quote, see Odell, 2007, p. 261.

4   Rumi quote was retrieved October 24, 2008 from http://www.mevlana.net (This is a site maintained by descendents of Rumi.)

4   For St. Paul reference, see Corinthians [1:13] in Yancy and Stafford (1992), p. 1250.

4   Emerson, 1910, p. 203.

4   For Johnson quote, see Boswell, 1993, p. 232.

4   For St. Paul quote, see Hebrews [1:1] in Yancy and Stafford (1992), p. 1334.

4   Pascal, 1995, p. 45.

5   Carter quote was retrieved February 13, 2006 from http://www.wisdomquotes.com/cat_children.html (Some place the "roots and wings" reference earlier, attributing it to Henry Ward Beecher.)

6   For Van Gogh's insight, see Stone and Stone, 1995, p. 33.

## Chapter 1: Rekindling Hope

*Page*

11   For Bethune quote, see McCluskey and Smith, 2002, pp. 48–49.

12   For Paul's first letter to the Corinthians [13:12], see Yancy and Stafford (1992), p. 1250.

12   Menninger, 1959, pp. 447, 449, and 461.

12   Frank, 1968.

12   N. V. Peale was dubbed the "voice of hope" in Scaduto, 1993, p. 7.

12   Peale, 2007.

12   The survey of oncologists was cited in Cousins, 1989, p. 217.

13   Siegel, 1993, pp. 159–160, 67.

13  For Columbine reference, see Bortnick, 2002, p. 1. (Metro section).

13  The quote from Sophocles' Antigone was cited in Menninger, 1959, p. 450.

13  Nietzsche, 1996, p. 45.

13  Viscott, 1997, p. 63.

14  The story of Motts Tonelli appeared in Lukacs, 2002, p. C1.

14  Anne Sullivan and Helen Keller's collaboration is from Gibson (2002).

15  The Helen Keller quote and Radcliffe ceremony were retrieved October 20, 2008 from http://www.freelists.org/archives/accessindia/04-2005/msg00121.html.

15  "Christine King" is not her actual name (she requested anonymity). The story appeared in *The Boston Globe*. See Mishra, 2002, p. A1.

15  For the Christopher Reeve story, see Haney, 2002, PM10.

15  Tribute in light reference is taken from Smith, 2002.

16  Seabiscuit quote is from Cole, 2005.

16  Giamatti, 1998, p. 7.

16  For *Field of Dreams* reference, see Gordon, Gordon, and Robinson, 1989.

16  Price, 2001, pp. 56–69.

18  *The Great Gatsby* reference is from Fitzgerald, 2007.

18  Havel's use of green ink to symbolize hope was noted in the May 29, 1989 issue of *Time Magazine*. See McManus, 1989, p. 48.

18  Shakespeare, 1997, p. 1120.

18  Prometheus and Pandora are from *Bulfinch's Mythology* (1998), pp. 16–23.

## Chapter 2: The Far-Flashing Beam

*Page*

20  Angelou, 1986, p. 155.

20  Philosophy as a "far-flashing beam" is from James, 1988, p. 488.

21  Mowrer, 1960, pp. 197–199.

21  See Dossey, 1992, p. 203. See also Chapter 6, p. 98. (miracle drug)

22  Cologne quote was taken from Guess, 2002, p. 2.

22  Stotland, 1969.

22  See Erickson, Post, and Paige (1975) for a Stotland derived measure of hope. See Beck, Weissman, Lester, and Trexler (1974) for a Stotland derived measure of hopelessness.

22  For Epictetus, see Lebell, 1994, p. 15.

22  For quote from *Paradise Lost*, see Milton, 2003, p. 9.

22  Descartes, 1989.

22  James, 2007.

22  Gottschalk, 1974.

22  Abramson, Metalsky, and Alloy, 1989.

22  Snyder et al., 1991.

23  For theories and measures derived from a nursing or medical approach to Hope, see the following sources: Dufault and Martocchio, 1985; Farran, Wilken, and Popovich, 1992;

Herth, 1991; Hinds and Gattuso, 1991; Miller and Powers, 1988; Stoner, 1988; Nowotny, 1989; Obuyuwana and Carter, 1982. (Interestingly, when Fry (1984) sought to develop a measure of *hopelessness* for a geriatric population from interviews with the elderly, the results were remarkably consistent with the approach developed in this chapter. The respondents identified losses in cognitive ability (mastery), interpersonal nurturance and respect (attachment), physical ability (survival), and faith as well as grace (spirituality).

23  Wright and Shontz, 1968.

23  Korner, 1970.

24  Few scholars have been able to convincingly articulate the "emotional side" of hope. However, two compelling literary attempts are Charles Brodhead's allusion to the "gentle whispers of hope" (retrieved November 14, 2002 from http://www.fact-archive.com/quotes/Hope), and of course, Emily Dickson's famous lines, "Hope is the thing with feathers ... that sings the tune without the words" (In Dickinson, 1976, p. 116).

24  Breznitz, 1986.

24  Averill, Catlin, and Chon, 1990.

24  O'Lill, 1994, p. 158–159.

24  Hutschnecker, 1981, p. 87.

24  Siegel, 1993, p. 109–110.

25  Siegel, 1986, p. 38.

25  Erikson, 1964, p. 118.

26  Averill, Catlin, and Chon, 1990.

26  Higgins, 1994, front matter.

26  Ibid., p. 61.

27  Vaillant, 1993, pp. 266–283.

27  Marcel, 1962.

27  McClelland, 1986, pp. 336–337.

28  Shade, 2001.

28  Pruyser, 1990.

28  Pruyser, 1986.

28  Godfrey, 1987.

29  Kant, 1957.

29  Bloch, 1970.

29  Moltmann, 1993.

29  When psychologist David Myers (1993) went in search of the "fountain of happiness," he discovered that an "eternal perspective" was vital for sustaining joy. Myers found that those who had developed a more spiritual view of life were able to prosper even in the worst of times. They were able to maintain the sense that "the evils of suffering and death are not the last word." Individuals who abide in this kind of "cosmic hope" may be experiencing "the chief happiness this world affords."

29  Lynch quotes on pp. 37–38 are from *Images of Hope*, pp. 243, 200, 32, 90, 23.

29  Readers interested in a spiritual and philosophical perspective on hope from a Christian perspective may also wish to consult Tinder's (1999) excellent book.

32  Oxytocin is discussed in depth in Moberg, 2003.

33   For Jong quote see the *Ms. Magazine* essay, reprinted in Klagsbrun, 1973, pp. 111–122.

33   For an introduction to Ifa beliefs and practices, see Fatunmbi, 1994.

33   Schopenhauer, 1961.

33   Kierkegaard quote was retrieved February 15, 2008 from http://www.whatquote.com.

33   Marcel's views on the role of openness in hope are from Godfrey, 1987, p. 129.

34   According to terror management theory (TMT), the primary function of religion is to provide an antidote for death anxiety. See Greenberg, Solomon, and Pyszczynski, 1997.

35   Pruyser, 1986.

35   See Emmons (1999) for more on the power of sanctioned commitments or what some psychologists refer to as "sanctified goals".

35   Sophocles quote is from Christy, 1893, p. 496.

35   St. Paul quote is from his letter to the Philippians [4:13]. See Yancy and Stafford (1992), p. 1289.

35   For Tibetan monk quote, see Evans-Wentz, 2000, p. 6.

35   The Qur'an quote is from Surah 20, lines 31–32. See Cleary (1994), p. 73.

35   In his ninth lecture on the "varieties of religious experience," William James elaborated on the possible role of the subconscious in generating the sense of an external presence. However, it is important to note that James left the "door open" for the possible reality of something "higher." See James, 1961.

35   The "self-object" is Kohut's (1971) seminal concept.

36   Goethe quote is from Cook, Deger, and Gibson, 2007, p. 12.

36   See Lifton (1996) for more on "symbolic immortality."

36   Kaplan, 1994.

36   Gibran, 1970, p. 71.

36   Bethune, 1996.

37   For Steven and Naomi Shelton, see Kaiser Stearns, 1989, pp. 101–104.

37   August Gold was retrieved May 3, 2007 from http://innerself.ca/html/spirituality/metaphysics/.

37   See Erikson (1964) for his thoughts on the impact of infant–caretaker experiences on hope and the "numinous."

37   Lila Jane Givens' hope testimony was retrieved April 26th, 2009 from www.nfcr.org.

37   Mowlam quote was retrieved February 12, 2006 from http://cain.ac.uk/issues/parade/docs/mm13798.htm.

38   Boucher, 2000.

## Chapter 3: Pillars of Humanity

*Page*

39   For Shelly's *Prometheus Unbound*, see Scudder, 1892, p. 66 (digitized version).

39   A classic Christian tribute to a hope derived from fulfilled attachment, mastery, and survival needs via faith in the Lord can be found in Jan Struther's 1931 hymn, *Lord of all Hopefulness*: "Lord of all hopefulness, Lord of all joy whose trust, ever child-like, no cares can destroy... give us your bliss in our hearts. Lord of all eagerness... whose strong hands

were skilled at the plane and the lathe, be there at our labors . . . give us your strength in our hearts. Lord of all gentleness, Lord of all calm, whose voice is contentment, whose presence is balm, be there at our sleeping, and give us your peace". See Watson, 2002, p. 391.

40   For a detailed account of "Korea's divided families," see Foley, 2002.

40   Holba's tractor accident appeared in the New York Times, July 22, 2002, p. 13.

40   Orwell, 1961, p. 11.

40   For Pliny quote, see Cook, Deger, and Gibson, 2007, p. 374.

40   Martin Luther quote was retrieved December 4, 2008 from http://www.quoteworld.org.

40   For Faulkner's Nobel Prize speech, see Meriwether, 2004, pp. 119–120.

41   Hugo's quote is from Cook, Deger, and Gibson, 2007, p. 377.

41   Goethe quote, ibid., p. 374.

41   Cahill, 1998.

42   Tiger, 1979.

42   Some of the background information for the evolution section was drawn from Denson et al.'s (2000) *Encyclopedia of Human Evolution and Pre-history.*

45   Diamond, 1992.

45   Donald, 2003.

45   Jaynes, 2000.

46   For D'Aquili's ideas related to "neurotheology," see Newburg, 2002.

46   For Persinger quotes see Vedantam, 2001, p. A01.

47   Fowler, 1996.

47   Smith, 2001.

47   James, 1961.

47   Newberg quote is from Begley, 2001, p. 57.

47   Begley, 2001, p. 57.

49   For *The Egyptian Book of the Dead*, see Faulkner, 2000.

49   For *The Tibetan Book of the Dead*, see Coleman, Jinpa, and Dorie, 2007.

49   For Sophocles' *Antigone*, see Hadas, 1982, p. 125.

49   Chrysippus' stoicism can be found in Tieleman, 2003.

49   Ames and Rosemont (1999) offer an excellent translation of Confucius.

50   For Plato's *Symposium*, see Jowett, 1999, pp. 679–762.

50   For Aristotle's claim that the loner is a "beast or a god," see McKeon, 1941, p. 1130.

50   For Plotinus on love and sexual desire, see MacKenna, 1917, p. 226.

50   Alghazzali's philosophy is taken from Homes, 2003.

50   For Rumi, see Helminski, 1998, p. 67.

50   For Plato's *Dialogues* pertaining to courage, see Jowett, 1999, pp. 953–956.

51   For Sophocles' *Antigone*, see Hadas, 1982, pp. 124–125.

51   For Lao Tzu, see Waley, 1958.

51   Zung Tzu, 2004.

51   For Al-Farabi's ideas on the perfect state, see Walzer, 1998.

51   For Augustine's *Confessions*, see Chadwick, 1998.

51  See McDermott, 1989 for a concise translation of Aquinas' Summa Theologiae.

52  Hobbes' thoughts on human nature are outlined in his classic, *On the Citizen*. See Tuck and Silverthorne, 2003.

52  Descartes, 1989, pp. 40–41.

52  For Nai Zhou's integration of boxing with philosophy, see Wells, 2005.

52  Bain, 2004.

52  See Bain, 2006, pp. 85–86 for his discussion of wonder. Bain believed that wonder contained the element of surprise. He thus incorporated certain physiological reactions that Darwin had linked to this other emotion (of surprise).

52  Schopenhauer, 1961.

52  For Nietzsche's epiphany on the will to power, see Durant, 1961, p. 406.

53  For Hobbes' views on the "evil of death," see Tuck and Silverthorne, 2003, p. 27.

53  Hume, 1968.

53  For *Dream of the Red Chamber*, see Chin, 1958.

53  Comte, 2001.

53  See Bain, 2006, p. 160.

54  Dostoevsky, 2006, p. 153.

54  For Zera Yacob's philosophy, see Arrington, 2001.

54  Comte, 2001.

54  Spencer, 2006.

54  Fourier, 2007.

54  Darwin, 2004.

55  Vivekandanda quotes were from Collison, Plant, and Wilkinson, 2000, p. 145.

55  McDougall, 1936.

55  McClelland, 1961.

55  Erikson, 1950.

55  White, 1959.

55  Ryan and Deci, 2000, p. 70.

56  McDougall, 1936.

56  Murray, 1938.

56  For Horney, see Chapter 10 in Monte and Sollod, 2003.

56  For Sullivan, see Chapter 9 in Monte and Sollod, 2003.

56  Vaillant, 1993.

56  Rogers, 1951.

56  Maslow, 1968.

56  Fromm's classic, *The Art of Loving*, was first published in 1956. However, throughout this book we cite material from the 2000 edition.

56  Fromm, 1941.

56  May, 1950.

56  Becker, 1973.

57  McDougall, 1936.

57  Murray, 1938.

57  McCrae and Costa, 1985.

57   Buss, 1989.

57   Allport and Odbert, 1936.

57   Lorenz, 1935.

57   Harlow, 1958.

57   Bowlby, 1969.

57   Ainsworth, Blehar, and Waters, 1978.

58   Kohut, 1971.

58   For early research on the importance of paternal factors in attachment, see Biller, 1971, 1974.

58   Mead, 1977.

59   Kasch was cited in Schmid and Jongman, 2005, p. 90.

59   See Staub (1992) for the various "hopes" that may fuel genocide and other forms of group violence.

59   For the reference to Bin Laden and other terrorists dispensing hope to the hopeless, see Drake, 2001.

59   Castro's 1953 speech can be found in Deutschmann, 2007.

59   Taiping rebellion data was retrieved October 14, 2008 from http://www.enclyclopedia.com.

60   Staub, 1992.

60   Schmid, 1984.

60   Miller, 1998.

60   Staub, 1992.

60   Schmid, 1984.

60   Kasch was cited in Schmid and Jongman, 2005, p. 90.

60   For research on child maltreatment and paternal deprivation, see Biller and Solomon, 1986.

60   Wasmund, 1983, pp. 1331 and 1336.

61   Glover, 2000.

61   Ferraroti was cited in Schmid, 1984, p. 235.

61   Bonanate was cited in Schmid, 1984, p. 235.

61   The Hyams finding was cited in Schmid, 1984, p. 123.

61   Camus, 1971, p. 305.

## Chapter 4: Cultures of Hope

*Page*

62   For Confucius quote, see Jaspers, 1957, p. 45.

63   James, 1890, p. 448.

63   See Plutchik (1962) for a biologically based approach to emotion.

63   See Lutz and White (1986) for an alternative, cultural approach to emotion.

64   Kluckhohn and Strodbeck, 1961.

64   For Latino hope and quote, see Matovina, 2005, p. 36 and back matter.

65   Much of the background information on the Apaches in this chapter was drawn from Perry, 1991.

65   Some of the background information on the Navajo for this and subsequent chapters was drawn from McPherson, 2001.

65   For Navajo terms that relate to "hope," see Young and Morgan, p. 152.

65   For the Navajo prayer to the sun, see Judson, 2006, p. 73.

65   Bloch, 1986.

66   For *Self-Reliance* quote, see Emerson, 1983, pp. 259–260.

66   For Beaumont and Fletcher (1647), see Emerson, 1983, p. 259.

66   Rand, 1996, pp. 678–679.

66   The Qur'an passage here and others cited throughout this book were retrieved from the Shakir translation provided by the University of Michigan at http://www.hti.umich.edu/ relig/koran.

67   For more on the Hindu family godhead "Gruhadevata," see Srinivasan, 1999.

67   For Paul's second letter to the Corinthians [5:2], see Yancy and Stafford (1992), p. 1260.

67   Rand 1999, pp. 1068–1069.

67   Bruner's (1975) notion of "scaffolding" was influenced by Vygotsky's "zone of proximal development."

67   Vygotsky, 1986.

68   Puech quote is from Cahill, 1999, p. 5.

68   Cahill, 1999.

68   The Buddhist Pali Canon quote on this page (and throughout this book) were retrieved from http://www.accesstoinsight.org/ tipitaka/index.html.

68   Borg, 1995, pp. 122–127.

68   For the Book of Revelations, see Yancy and Stafford (1992), pp. 1371–1390.

69   Snyder, 1989.

69   For terror-management theory, see Greenberg, Solomon, and Pyszczynski, 1997.

69   Buddhist quote is from http://www.accesstoinsight.org/ tipitaka/index.html.

70   Pope John Paul II, 1994.

70   For Revelations quote, see Yancy and Stafford (1992), p. 1389.

70   Averill, Catlin, and Chon, 1990.

70   Sommers and Kosmitzki, 1988, p. 45.

71   Marcel, 1962.

71   Alverson, 1994.

73   For research on Russian versus American IQ performance as it related to time and untimed tasks, see Agranovich, 2005.

73   Klass quote was retrieved October 12, 2008 from the *Encyclopedia of Death and Dying* at http://www.deathreference.com.

74   For Paul's letter to the Romans, see Yancy and Stafford (1992), p. 1234.

74   Buddhist quote was retrieved March 2006 from http://www.accesstoinsight.org/ tipitaka/index.html.

74   Bloch, 1970.

## Chapter 5: Religions of Hope

*Page*

76  Smith, 1986, pp. 12–13.

76  Nietzsche, 2006.

78  Buddhist data was retrieved August 14, 2001 from http://www.accesstoinsight.org/tipitaka/index.html.

80  New Testament data was retrieved August 17, 2001 from http://www.tniv.info/bible/.

80  Hamilton, 1998.

81  Wilkinson, 2000, back matter.

81  For Prayer of Jabez [Cor. I, 4:9–10], see Yancy and Stafford (1992), p. 455.

81  Psychinfo was the database source for the 1887–2002 review.

81  Ifa data was derived from the book *Ibase Orisa*. See Fatunmbi, 1994.

82  The Qur'an data was retrieved from the Shakir translation provided by the University of Michigan at http://www.hti.umich.edu/relig/koran.

83  The Torah data and passages were retrieved August 18, 2001 from http://www.shechem.org/etorahsr.html.

83  The Rig Veda data was retrieved August 19, 2001 from Griffith's translation at http://www.sacred-texts.com/hin/rigveda/index.htm.

84  Durkheim reference was drawn from Hamilton, 1998.

84  McClelland, 1961.

85  See Smith, 1986, p. 113.

85  For Phyllis Morrow's observations on the importance of "naming" among the Yupik, see Swann, 1996, pp. 37–42.

86  Swann, 1996.

87  For Julian Rice's commentary on the relative importance of community versus mastery among the Lakota, see Swann 1996, pp. 403–407.

87  As noted previously, some of the background on the Navajo for this and other chapters was drawn from McPherson, 2001.

87  Many Navajo actually prefer to be called the "five-fingered beings" rather than "Indians." In particular, see the February 7, 2008 press release with comments from the president of the Navajo Nation, Joe Shirley Jr., retrieved October 11, 2008 from http://www.navajo.org.

87  For Navajo myths and legends see Link, 1998.

88  Various sources refer to the Navajo "blessing-way" ceremony as an appeal for "good hope." Anthropologist Jerrold Levy went further, suggesting that the blessing-way represented the more ordered and promising of the two main branches of the Navajo cosmology (the other being the "evil-ways," designed to exorcise all forms of evil). See Levy, 1998.

88  The Australian "Dreamtime" stories were retrieved October 15, 2008 from http://www.dreamtime.net.au/dreaming/storylist and http://www.crystalinks.com/dreamtime.

89  Sartre, 2001.

89  Winkelman, 2000.

89  Morris, 1977.

90   Bloch, 1986.

90   Erikson, 1964.

90   For the essay "Ideas that have harmed mankind," see Russell, 1972.

90   For "fear is the basis of the whole thing" and "allies in the sky," see Russell, 1967, p. 22.

91   For personal reflections on the great passions of his life see Russell, 2000, front matter.

91   Nietzsche, 2006.

91   Hegel, 1979.

91   Feuerbach, 2004.

92   Dennett, 1984.


# Chapter 6: Faith

*Page*

93   For Gandhi quote, see Dalton, 1996, p. 123.

94   Graham's 2001 speech was retrieved January 3, 2006 from http://www.americanrhetoric.com/speeches/billygraham911memorial.htm.

94   Havel's Michigan speech was retrieved October 10, 2002 from http://www.umich.edu/~newsinfo/Releases/2000/Sep00/havlrmrk.html.

94   Dostoevsky, 2008, p. 308.

95   The Armenian genocide was retrieved January 8, 2006 from ww.cilicia.com/armo_tehlirian.html

95   D-Day reference was cited in Pargament, 2001, p. 133.

96   Taeko Teramae's Hiroshima testimony was retrieved April 4, 2002 from http://www.atomicarchive.com/Docs/Hibakusha/Taeko.shtml.

96   Mardi Seng's Hope essay was retrieved July 8, 2002 from http://www.hmd.org.uk/resources/item/148/.

96   For the 9/11 exchange between Adam Goldman and James Gartenberg, see Vedantam, 2001, p. A01.

97   Bensons's Lourdes experience was retrieved November 4, 2002 from homepages.ius.edu/kaleksan/files/pgdp/lourdes/lourdes-html2.html

97   Jean-Pierre Bely case was retrieved November 15, 2008 from http://www.lourdes-france.com.

97   The Lorraine Day references were retrieved November 18, 2002 from http://www.drday.com/. Readers should note that her healing recommendations are highly controversial and several commentators have gone so far as to label her approach "quackery." Later, in the health and healing sections of this book we explain why our bias is toward complementary as opposed to alternative healing approaches.

98   For the Klopfer anecdote, see Bolletino and Leshan, 1997, p. 102.

98   Carson, 1964.

98   Carson, 1997, pp. 159–163.

100  Havel, 1995, p. 46.

100  For Ifa reference see Fatunmbi, 1994, p. 10.

100   Sagan, 1996, pp. 29–30.

101   Williams, 1988, p. 73.

101   Hijiya, 2002, A10.

101   Edelman, 2004.

102   For Mao Tsetung quote, see Spence, 1998, p. 148.

102   Additional quotes regarding Mao's economic "great leap forward" were retrieved December 3, 2002 from http://www.iisg.nl/~landsberger/glf.html.

102   Mao's "hope speech" was delivered October 13, 1957 to the 13th session of the Supreme State Conference. It was retrieved November 6, 2002 from http://www.marxists.org/reference/ archive/mao/selected—works/ volume- 5/mswv5_68.htm.

103   "Faith is blind" anecdotes were provided by colleagues (sources unknown).

103   This quote is routinely attributed to Mencken. The words are his (and true to his own atheistic leanings), but he was actually writing about Neitzsche's criticism of belief in a higher power. See Mencken, 2006, p. 96.

104   Hall, 1997.

104   For an anti-faith Web site visit http://www.positiveatheism.org. Many of the quotes on this site are from the noted atheist Richard Dawkins.

104   Mencken, 1922, p. 11.

104   E. O. Wilson was cited in Smith, 2001, p. 31.

104   Heinlein, 1991, p. 233.

104   Columbia Encyclopedia faith links can be found at http://www.bartleby.com/65/.

105   For Ecclesiastes, see Yancy and Stafford (1992), p. 725.

105   For Ted Williams, see Montville, 2005.

106   For Ecclesiastes, see Yancy and Stafford (1992), p. 725.

106   The Voltaire reference is from Zadig. See Voltaire, 2008, p. 65.

106   For Blake's reflection on faith see Wood (1893), p. 165 (digitized version).

106   The 1984 and 1990 surveys were cited in Jones, 1994, p. 184.

107   Ibid., p. 189.

107   Maslow, 1970, p. 4.

107   The survey of the "spiritual but not religious" was conducted August 2–4, 2005 by the Princeton Survey Research Associates International for *Newsweek*. See http://roperweb.ropercenter.uconn.edu.

108   For an analysis of Freud's atheism, see Rizzuto, 1998.

108   Tolstoy, 1987, p. 100.

108   Tillich, 2001.

108   Fowler, 1981.

108   Smith, 2001.

108   Blake's words are cited in Smith, 2001, p. 217.

108   Smith, 2001.

108   Fowler, 1981.

109   For Mark [10 : 13–15] see Yancy and Stafford (1992), p. 1094.

109   For his response to E. O. Wilson, see Smith, 2001, p. 32.

109   Fowler, 1981.

109   Einstein quotes were retrieved January 10, 2003 from http://www.quotationspage.com and http://www.quoteland.com.

110   For more information on the mortgage partnership visit www.hopenow.com

110   Voltaire, 2007, p. 247.

110   Pascal, 1995, p. 127.

110   Smith, 2001, pp. 218–224.

## Chapter 7: Spiritual Growth

*Page*

112   For Aristotle quote, see McKeon, 1941, p. 1127.

112   Freud, 1957.

113   Winnicot, 1971.

113   Rizzuto, 1979.

114   Meissner, 1984, p. 183.

114   St. Clair, 1994.

115   Greeley, 1981, p. 18.

116   Kirkpatrick, 1999.

116   Ullman, 1989, front matter.

116   The Gallup Poll results were retrieved November 6, 2003 from http://www.galluppoll.com.

116   Kohut, 1971.

116   For Plotinus quote, see O'Brien, 1975, p. 85.

117   See Biller (1971,1974) for early reviews of paternal influences on personality development.

117   Harris, 1998.

117   Kagan, 1994.

118   Elkind, 1997.

118   Reich, 1997.

118   Miller, 1996.

118   Kagan, 1994.

119   Erikson, 1950.

119   Elkind, 1997.

119   Dostoevsky, 2008, p. 292.

120   Fowler, 1981.

120   Reich, 1997.

120   Noppe and Noppe, 1997, p. 270.

121   Belenky, Clinchy, Goldberger, and Tarule, 1997.

121   Gilligan, 1993.

121   Bingham and Stryker, 1995.

121   Shakespeare, 1997, p. 622.

121   Erikson, 1950.

122  Levinson, 1986.

122  Erikson, 1950.

122  Erikson, 1950, pp. 231–232.

122  For a detailed analysis of Werner's person-in-the-world approach, see Valsiner, 2004.

122  Kegan, 1982.

122  Popp, 1996.

122  Reich, 1997.

122  Marcel, 1962.

122  Godfrey, 1987.

123  Jaques, 1965.

123  Tolstoy, 1987, p. 29.

123  Fuller (1996) argued that despite Erikson's presumed "nontheological" approach to human development, his repeated references to the "numinous" and other spiritual phenomena suggested an "irreducibly religious dimension to normative human functioning."


## Chapter 8: Spiritual Intelligence

*Page*

125  Campbell, 1991, p. 147.

126  Smith, 2001, pp. 197–199.

126  Drucker quote was retrieved October 10, 2003 from http://www.wisdomquotes.com.

126  Mother Teresa quote was retrieved October 10, 2003 from http://www.brainyquote.com.

126  Warren Weaver quote was retrieved October 10, 2003 from http://www.Bartelby.com.

126  For Ordway Tead quote, see Cook, Deger and Gibson, 2007, p. 651.

126  Mason Cooley quote retrieved October 10, 2003 from http://www.bartleby.com.

126  FDR quote is from Cook, Deger and Gibson, 2007, p. 166.

126  Bertrand Russell quote was retrieved October 10, 2003 from http://www.Bartleby.com.

126  Gibron, 1995, p. 71.

126  Henri Poincare quote was retrieved October 10, 2003 from http://www.bartleby.com.

126  James Joyce quote was retrieved October 10, 2003 from http://www.memorablequotations.com/joyce.htm.

126  Sagan, 1985, p. 1.

126  C. Spurgeon quote was retrieved October 10, 2003 from http://www.thewordteaches.com/QuotesF.htm.

127  Fowler, 1981.

127  Jung, 1968.

128  Statistics from 1990s were retrieved October 11, 2003 from http://www.adherents.com.

128  2002 Pew Survey, ibid.

128  2003 Gallup poll results were retrieved October 15, 2003 from http://www.galluppoll.com.

129  Pascal, 1995, p. 122.

129  Chopra, 2001.

129   Smith, 2001, pp. 220–223.

130   Armstrong, 2001, p. 96.

131   Confucius, 1957, pp. 46–47.

131   Virgil quotes are from the *Aeneid*. See Dryden (1997), pp. 174, 124, 281.

132   For research on the power of family rituals, see Kiser, Bennett, Heston, and Paavola, 2005.

132   References to Adam Smith, John Maynard Keynes, and Karl Marx were from Strathern, 2004, pp. 100, 269, 174–175.

133   Rousseau quote was retrieved October 14, 2003 from http://www.qoutationspage.com.

133   For Comte's "religion of humanity," see Besant, 2006.

133   Excerpts from Helen Keller's speech are from Torricelli and Carroll (2000), pp. 67–68.

133   Excerpts from Martin Luther King's speech are from Torricelli and Carroll (2000), pp. 236–237.

133   Our own research suggests that MLK's "I have a dream" is indeed a "hope booster". Scioli (2009) had individuals briefed on the nature of hope. These individuals were then shown MLK's "I have a dream" and asked to rate it for attachment, mastery, survival and spiritual content. The speech was found high on three of the four dimensions of hope (all but survival). The following week, another group of individuals were shown the MLK speech and then given the first authors' state hope questionnaire. This group was then compared to a third group who completed a neutral task and then viewed the speech. As expected, those viewing the MLK film prior to taking the hope questionnaire reported significantly higher hope scores.

134   See Smith (2006) for a religious or faith-based perspective on postmodernism.

134   Locke, 1958.

134   For Spinoza's conception of an "extended" God, see Garrett (1995), p. 65.

134   Pascal, 1995, pp. 122–124.

135   Jung, 1968

135   Campbell, 1991, p. 179.

135   Hesse, 1977, p. 220.

136   Joseph, 1999, front matter.

137   Cicero quote was retrieved October 15, 2003 from p. 34 [digitized version] of his collected works at http://www.books.google.com.

137   Emerson, 1983, p. 348 (nature's masterpiece) and p. 342 (possession for all time).

137   For *Psychology Today* survey, see Pardee, 1979.

137   In a study by psychologists Reed Larson and Nancy Bradney (1988), it was found that randomly paged volunteers who were completing mood questionnaires throughout the day reported being happiest when they were in the company of a friend, regardless of what they were doing.

137   The quote "we'd go through fire for him" (in regards to Lombardi) was attributed to former packer Henry Jordan. It was retrieved December 10, 2008 from http://www.washingtonpost.com/wp-srv/sports/longterm/general/povich/launch/lombardi.htm.

137   The quotes regarding the 2002 Angels were retrieved July 18, 2003 from http://www.mlb.com.

137   Sun Tzu, 2003, p. 92.

137   Hooker, 1995, pp. 23–25.

138   For Civil War reference, see Vandergriff, 1999.

138   Lynch, 1965, p. 200.

138   Allport and Ross, 1967.

138   Russell, 2000, front matter.

139   "Spiritual bypass" is a term used by various spirituality writers including Ken Wilber, Charles Whitfield, and John Welwood. See Wilber, 2000.

139   Csikszentmihalyi, 1991, p. 3.

139   For Augustine see Chadwick, 1998.

139   Dostoevsky, 2008, pp. 296–297.

139   Marcel, 1962.

140   James, 1961.

142   For more on the contemplative life, see Merton, 2006.

143   See Keating (2006) for his centering prayer.

143   See Matt (1996) for an introduction to Kabbalah.

143   Buber, 1996.

143   For Rumi, see Helminski, 1998.

143   Higgins, 1994.

## Chapter 9: Attachment Matters

*Page*

149   Native American prayer (source unknown).

149   Donne, 1999, p. 103.

149   For Mengzi quote, see Collison, Plant, and Wilkinson, 2000, p. 235.

150   Fromm, 2000.

150   For Ashe quote, see Rampersad, 1994, p. 7.

151   John Donne, same as above, pp. 102–103.

151   For a detailed account of the miner rescue, see AP, 2002 (Nine Alive!). Quotes can be found on p. 68.

152   Rumi quote was retrieved October 24, 2008 from http://www.mevlana.net (This site is maintained by descendents of Rumi.)

152   Goodall and Berman, 2000, front matter.

152   Ibid., p. 173.

153   Einstein on the mystical was retrieved September 24, 2008 from http://www.spaceandmotion.com/albert-einstein-god-religion-theology.htm.

153   For William James' lectures on mysticism see chapters 16 and 17 in *The Varieties of Religious Experience* (James, 1961).

153   Dillard, 1990.

153   Kohut, 1971.

154   William James quote is from his classic paper "What Is an Emotion?." See James, 2007, p. 22.

154   Lewis, Amini, and Lannon, 2001.

154   Fromm, 2000, p. 9.

155    Ibid, p. 8.

155    Ibid, p. 17.

155    For Genesis [2 : 18], see Yancy and Stafford (1992), p. 28.

155    Fromm, 2000, p. 17.

156    For Matthew [7 : 7], see Yancy and Stafford (1992), p. 1048.

156    See Bodhi (2005) for the benefits of a contemplative life as described by Buddha.

156    Qur'an quote was retrieved May 3, 2006 from http://www.hti.umich.edu/relig/koran.

156    The Rig Veda quote was retrieved May 3, 2006 from http://www.sacred-texts.com/hin/rigveda/index.htm.

157    For the Navajo "Dreamer," see Link, 1998, pp. 93–100.

157    Qur'an, same as above.

158    Herman, 1997, p. 155.

158    The Nigerian Proverb is attributed to the Kanuri ethnic group and was retrieved May 12, 2006 from http://www.famous-proverbs.com.

158    Moody Blues lyrics are from their 1991 song "Say what you mean" and were retrieved May 10, 2007 from http://www.poemhunter.com.

158    Rogers, 1951.

158    For Buddhist eight-fold path, see Bodhi, 2005.

159    Havens, 1986.

159    See Smith, 1986, pp. 52–59, for Bhakti Yoga reference.

159    May, 2007.

159    For Confucius, see Ames and Rosemont, 1999.

159    For Russian tale, see Smith, 1986, pp. 56–57.

159    See Russinova (1999) for a different and complementary approach regarding the qualities necessary for a good mental health hope provider.

160    Goldstein and Brooks (2006) provide a comprehensive review of the various factors that can contribute to childhood vulnerability and resiliency, including parental factors.

160    See Karen (1998) for a detailed history of the attachment movement, including references to Rene Spitz, Anna Freud, John Bowlby, and others.

160    Erikson, 1950.

161    For an inspiring look at a gifted therapist's uncanny ability to connect with children, see Adler and Stein, 2005.

161    Biller (1974, 1993). See also Reuter and Biller, 1973.

161    For research on the negative impact of cold or rejecting parents, see Ainsworth, Blehar, and Waters, 1978, and Biller and Solomon, 1986.

162    For the distinction between authoritative and authoritarian parenting styles, see Baumrind, 1996.

162    For more on emotion coaching and emotion dismissing, see Gottman, 2001.

162    Lennon and McCartney, 1965.

163    For Paul's letter to the Corinthians [13 : 4], see Yancy and Stafford (1992), p. 1250.

163    Steinbeck, 2002.

163    Steinbeck, 2002, p. 431.

163    Ibid., pp. 57–58.

164    Ibid., p. 304.

164    Ibid., p. 600.

165    Branden, 2008.

165    Stendahl quote was cited in Brehm, 1988, p. 237.

165    Kirschenbaum, 1997, p. 107.

165    McAdams research was cited in McClelland, 1986.

165    Gottman, 1999.

166    Hendrix, 1993.

166    Shakespeare, 1997, p. 1239.

166    Kirschenbaum, 1997, p. 235. See also Campbell, 1991.

166    Hendrix, 1993.

166    See Gottman (1999), pp. 218–234, for suggestions on "dream-work" for couples.

167    Cicero quote was retrieved July 14, 2007 from p. 35 [digitized version] of his collected works at http://www.books.google.com.

167    Bacon quote was retrieved July 20, 2007 from p. 79 [digitized version] of The Essays at http://www.NuVision.com.

167    Emerson, 1983, p. 342.

167    Gibran, 1983, p. 59.

167    de Saint-Exupery, 1995, p. 79.

167    Ibid., p. 79.

167    For *Psychology Today* survey, see Pardee, 1979.

167    Gibran, 1983, p. 58.

167    For Aristotle, see McKeon, 1941, pp. 1058-1093.

167    Emerson, 1983, p. 350.

168    Nigerian proverb was retrieved July 28, 2007 from http://www.quotationspage.com.

168    Emerson, 1983, p. 347.

168    Arabian proverb was retrieved July 28, 2007 from http://www.friendship.com.

168    Bacon. Same as above, p. 81.

168    Pogrebin, 1988.

168    Cicero. Same as above, p. 37.

168    Emerson, 1983, p. 350.

168    Cicero. Same as above, p. 58.

168    For "national survey," see Pardee, 1979.

168    Fischer, 1982.

168    For *Psychology Today*, see Pardee, 1979.

169    Fromm, 2000.

169    Wallach's comment on art and emotion was a personal communication to the second author. See also Simonton, 1994, p. 309.

169    For a view of Van Gogh's "fishing boats on the beach at Saintes-Maries," visit http://www.vangoghgallery.com.

169    A similar attached hope could be read into Da Vinci's portrait of the Mona Lisa, particularly in light of his presumed lack of a stable maternal presence in childhood.

169    Wilder, 2003.

170    Commentary on Wilder's play was retrieved July 29, 2007 from Meitcke and Bromberg's Thornton Wilder's *Our Town*, p. 6 [digitized version] at http://www.books.google.com. The commentators were referring to the kinds of plays that appeared in the 1960s, inspired by Wilder. However, the comments clearly apply to Wilder's masterpiece as well.

170    Goodall and Berman, 2000, front matter.

170    For varying perspectives on emotional mergers, see Fowler (1996), Kohut (1971), and Stern (1985).

171    Fromm, 2000.

171    The anecdote about getting up to pray in the morning was a personal communication by a client to the first author.

172    The idea that a deep faith must involve the head, heart, and hands goes back at least to biblical times. See Hollinger (2005) for one (Christian) perspective on forging a unified faith of "head, heart, and hands."

172    Benson (1985) is one of many relaxation gurus who promotes a "faith factor."


# Chapter 10: Mastery and Inspiration

*Page*

174    Shakespeare, 1997, p. 134.

175    For Cervantes quote about "cucumbers or missiles," see Cascardi, 2002, p. 133.

175    Cervantes, 2001. ("Bible of humanity" is attributed to Charles Augustin Sainte-Beuve, a nineteenth-century French critic and historian. See the front matter of this Edition of Don Quixote.)

176    Bannister, 2004, p. 1.

176    Bethune biographical material was drawn from McCluskey and Smith, 2002.

176    Ibid., p. 35.

177    Ibid., p. 59.

177    Ibid., p. 35.

177    Gates and West, 2002, p. 45.

177    Details regarding *One Flew over the Cuckoo's Nest* were retrieved February, 20, 2007 from http://www.imdb.com.

178    For Nietzsche, see Mencken, 2006.

178    References to Frankl, Freud, Maslow, Rogers and Sutich were drawn from Sutich and Vich, 1969.

178    Erikson, 1950.

178    White, 1959.

178    Klinger, 1977.

178    Marcel, 1962.

178    Emerson, 1983, p. 16.

178    For St. Paul reference [Phil, 4:13], see Yancy and Stafford (1992), p. 1289.

179    Averill, Catin, and Chon, 1990.

179   Lynch, 1965.

179   Kant, 1960.

179   Greene, 2000, p. 215.

180   For an introduction to Feng-Shui see Wong, 1996.

180   Covey, 2004.

180   Erikson, 1950.

180   Hill, 2004.

181   For a discussion of the differences between Confucianism and Taoism, see Hamilton, 1998.

182   Milton, 2003, p. 9.

182   Rogers, 1951.

182   Melville quote was retrieved February 20, 2007 from http://www.quotationsbook. com.

182   May, 2007.

183   Hill, 2004.

183   Peale, 2007.

183   Tzu, 2003.

183   Covey, 2004.

183   For more information on the Weekend of Hope, visit http://www.stowehope.org.

184   Strickland (personal communication to the first author.).

184   Ederle's historic swim was reported in a *Sports Illustrated* article (August 6, 1926). It was retrieved February 24, 2007 from vault.sportsillustrated.cnn.com/vault/article/ magazine/ MAG1017808/index.htm

184   Robbins, 1992.

185   Csikszentmihalyi, 1991.

185   Covey, 2004.

186   Aaron, 1991, p. 238.

186   Ibid., p. 238.

186   For Patriots' Damian Woody quote, see MacMullin, 2002.

187   See Halberstam (2005) for details about the Patriots' decision to be introduced as a team during the 2002 Super Bowl.

187   For Patriots' ring ceremony see http://cachewwww.patriots.com.

188   Goethe quote was retrieved March 3, 2007 from http://www.quoteworld.org.

189   Simonton, 1994.

190   Heraclites quote was retrieved March 3, 2007 from forums.philosophyforums.com/ threads/heraclitus-and-parmenides

190   For Ecclesiastes, see Yancy and Stafford, 1992, p. 726.

190   Eliot, 1968, pp. 1–2.

191   Internet Search was done using Google.

191   Emerson, 1983, p. 975.

191   For Plato's thoughts on inspiration, see Jowett, 1999, p. 1128.

191   Gotz, 1998.

191   Hart, 2000.

191 Ornstein (1992) has long proposed that each person is endowed with a multiplicity of "minds" that, along with temperamental and environmental factors, leads to tremendous variability in creative and inspirational potential.

191 Kralik and Telford's presentation, "transition in chronic illness," was retrieved March 14, 2007 from rdns.org.au/research_unit/documents/Booklet%2010%20-%20 Self-care.pdf.

192 Carnegie, 1998.

193 Felicia H. quote was retrieved from a Google search. The site has apparently been removed.

193 Holmes, 1967.

194 For Frank Leahy's biography, see Twombly, 1974.

194 For Aristotle's reference to hope as a "waking dream," see Yonge, 2007, p. 187.

195 Rokeach, 2000.

195 In the 1960's, psychologist Jerome Singer and his colleagues provided compelling data, demonstrating the positive benefits of daydreaming, including its role in enhancing creativity and facilitating adaptive patience. From our perspective, daydreaming, if used appropriately, can also become a powerful tool for clarifying an individual's hopes. See Singer and Schonbar, 1961.

195 Kierkegaard quote was retrieved March 5, 2007 from http://www.memorablequotations.com.

195 Eliot, 1968.

196 Talmud quote was retrieved March 5, 2007 from http://www.sacred-texts.com.

196 Joseph's prowess in dream interpretation appears in Genesis [37–41]. See Yancy and Stafford (1992), pp. 66–73.

196 Jung, 1968, p. 159.

197 Freud, 2008, front matter.

197 Hall and Van De Castle, 1966.

198 Campbell, 1991.

198 Thoreau quote was retrieved March 5, 2007 from p. 122 [digitized version] in *The Writings of Henry David Thoreau* at books.google.com

198 Garfield, 2001.

199 Circles of air; Circles of stone information was retrieved March 5, 2007 from http://www.questforvision.com.

199 For John Suler's briefer "vision quest," see http://www.rider.edu/~suler/vquest.html.


# Chapter 11: Survival Skills

## Page

201 For Bhagavad-Gita, see Brodbeck and Mascaro, 2003, p. 59.

201 For statistics on the worldwide prevalence of anxiety disorders see Somers et al., 2006.

202 For DSM-IV, see American Psychiatric Association, 2000.

202 Heinrich, 2003, pp. 315–316.

202 Squirrel story was a personal experience of the first author.

203   Aron Ralston's tale of survival and the quote from his pastor were retrieved August 4, 2007 from http://www.wfn.org/2003/06/msg00051.html.

203   De Becker, 1997, p. 6.

204   May, 1950.

204   For Aristotle, see McKeon, 1941, p. 963.

204   For the *Oxford English Dictionary*, see Simpson and Weiner, 1989.

205   See Rothbaum, Weisz, and Snyder (1982) for a classic delineation of primary versus secondary control processes and their manifestations across cultures.

205   See Hamilton (1998) for a brief overview regarding differences between the Catholic and Protestant faiths.

205   Pargament, 2001.

205   For Paul's letter to the Philippians [4:13], see Yancy and Stafford (1992), p. 1289.

206   Goethe quote was retrieved August 10, 2007 from http://www.quoteworld.org.

206   Hemingway, 1995, p. 249.

207   Offit's quote was part of a press release entitled, "Infant Immune System Is Stronger Than Many Parents Think; New Report by National Vaccine Experts Shows That Multiple Vaccines Don't Weaken or Overwhelm the Immune System" and was retrieved September 2, 2007 from stokes.chop.edu/publications/press

207   Fujimara, Stoecker, and Sudakova (2005) offer a powerful, insider's perspective on the world of abandoned children in Russia, many of whom showed extreme signs of reactive attachment disorder.

207   For Harlow research on social rehabilitation, see Suomi, Harlow, and McKinney, 1972. Later research demonstrated that long periods of initial social deprivation were very difficult to overcome, and in such cases, only particular social and emotional skills could be developed.

207   Harris, 1998.

208   Apfel and Simon, 2000, p. 125.

208   See Schore (1994) for a comprehensive review of the impact of early caregiver attunement on an individual's ability to self-regulate his or her emotions.

209   Kirkpatrick and Shaver, 1992.

209   For Kirkpatrick study on god-avoidance and spiritual immortality, see Rowatt and Kirkpatrick, 2002.

209   Snyder, 1994.

210   Yutang quote was retrieved August 14, 2007 from http://www.great-quotes.com.

210   Lamott, 1995, front matter.

210   See Scioli, 1990.

210   Erikson, 1950.

211   Nietzsche was cited in Frankl, 1985, p. 101.

211   Quote and information regarding Indiana Wesleyan University's Center for Life Calling and Leadership were retrieved April 14, 2006 from clcl.indwes.edu/

211   Erikson, 1950.

211   Kobasa, 1979.

212   Schwartz, 1997, p. 15.

212   Tennyson, 1973, p. 90.

212   Erikson, 1993.

212   Coles, 1967, pp. 46–49.

213   Taro Yamasaki's story on Ryan White was retrieved August 10, 2007 from http://www.digitaljournalist.org/issue0106/voices_yamasaki.htm.

213   For more information on Ryan White's legacy and the national youth conference, visit http://www.ryanwhite.com.

214   Details on the film Hoop Dreams were retrieved August 12, 2007 from http://www.imdb.com.

214   Ebert review was retrieved August 12, 2007 from http://www.rogerebert.suntimes.com.

214   For Charles Barkley quote on the book Hoop Dreams, see Jarovsky, 1996.

214   Freud, 1989, p. 68.

214   For his psycho-biographical analysis of Gandhi, see Erikson, 1993.

215   Bassett, 1996.

215   For Cunningham and other hope inspiring sports biographies, see Holmes, 1967.

215   McCain and Salter, 2008.

215   The phrase "fear lends wings" (or its equivalent) is found in a number of the works of classic British writers, including Sidney and Spenser.

216   Ann Herbert quote was retrieved April 26th, 2009 from thinkexist.com.

216   *The Chicken Soup for the Soul* has grown into a "cottage industry." In the reference section we list only one edition. See http://www.amazon.com for the original publication as well as later, more specialized editions and other related products.

216   Terkel, 2003.

216   *Chariots of Fire* details were retrieved August 15, 2007 from http://www.imdb.com.

216   See McCasland, 2004 for a well-respected biography of Eric Liddell.

216   Marcel, 1962.

216   Tolstoy, 1997, p. 16.

217   Alberti and Emmons, 2008.

217   Harlow, 1958.

217   Bassett's Web site is http://www.stresscenter.com. See also Bassett, 1996.

217   Linehan, 1993.

217   For further information on Dialectical Behavior Therapy, visit http://www.brtc.psych.washington.edu/.

217   Spradlin, 2003.

217   For further information regarding biofeedback, visit http://www.BCIA.org. An excellent primer on various stress reduction techniques is the Relaxation and Stress Reduction Workbook (see Davis et al., 2000).

218   Kabat-Zinn, 1990.

218   Benson, 1985.

218   For the Book of Proverbs, see Yancy and Stafford (1992), pp. 688–722.

218   For the 23rd Psalm, see Yancy and Stafford (1992), pp. 609–611.

219   De Bono, 1999.

219  We recommend two solution-focused books for the nonprofessional, one by Metcalf (2007) and the other by O'Hanlon (2000). While they are not intended as stand-alone therapies for serious problems, these books can stimulate more creative approaches to problem solving.

220  For research on hemispheric responses to classical vs. rock music, see Novitskaya, 1984.

220  Perkins, 1981.

220  Qur'an quote was retrieved September 14, 2007 from http://www.quod.lib.umich.edu.

220  Rig Veda quote was retrieved September 14, 2007 from http://www.onlinebooks. library.upenn.edu.

220  The Christian phrase "When God closes one door he opens another" is not an actual biblical passage but an interpretation. Some find it most strongly implied in Acts 16:6–10, where God prevents Paul from entering one town but then sends him a vision, guiding him toward another pilgrimage opportunity. See Yancy and Stafford (1992), p. 1200.

220  Fenton's (1987) book is the single best reference on the Iroquois' masked "medical society."

221  Warren, 2002, p. 30. Warren's approach has been criticized, even within Christianity, by evangelicals as well as Catholics. While we endorse his general notion that purpose is essential for a hope-filled life, it is up to the individual reader to judge the "truthfulness" of his spiritual message as a whole.

221  Hegel, 1979.

222  Becker, 1973, p. 275.

222  Erikson, 1964.

222  Warren, 2002, p. 318.

## Chapter 12: From Fear to Hope

*Page*

224  Buddha quote was retrieved September 4, 2007 from http://www.accesstoinsight.org/ tipitaka/index.html.

224  Poe, 1984, p. 181.

224  For DSM-IV, see American Psychiatric Association, 2000.

225  Tzu, 2003, p. 92.

225  Kung Fu quote was retrieved September 4, 2007 from kungfu-guide.com/addendum/ addendum_tlc.html

225  Aquinas, 1989, p. 215 (*Summa Theologiae*).

225  Spinoza, 2005, p. 106 (*Ethics*).

226  Wolinksy, 2007.

226  Fear stories in this chapter are from the case files of the first author. To maintain the confidentiality of these individuals, the actual names are not provided, and in some instances, the demographic information has been slightly altered.

227  Horner, 1972.

228  Hanh, 2002.

228    Jackson, 1996.

229    Herrigel, 1999, p. 30.

229    Fromm, 1941.

231    Averill and Nunnally, 1992.

231    Emerson, 1983, p. 493.

231    For the Book of Proverbs, see Yancy and Stafford (1992) pp. 688–722.

231    For the sayings (*Analects*) of Confucius, see Ames and Rosemont (1999).

231    Qur'an reference was retrieved September 8, 2007 from http://www.quod.lib. umich.edu.

231    For Upanishads quote, see Prabhavananda and Manchester (2002).

231    Fulghum, 2004.

231    To find a therapist in your area who practices client-centered, cognitive-behavioral, or existential therapy visit www.findcounseling.com. For a solution-focused therapist visit the website of the Institute for Solution-Focused Therapy at www.solutionfocused.net/

231    Gibran, 1983, pp. 64–65.

232    Terr, 1992, p. 37.

233    Herman, 1997.

234    Ibid., p. 209.

235    Rando, 1991, p. 5.

235    Averill, 1968.

235    See Stroebe, Gergen, Gergen, and Stroebe (1996) for a critique and reconsideration of the "grief work" hypothesis and the presumed need to move "beyond" a loss.

235    Crider, 1996, p. 124.

235    Source of Denise's letter to Tom Crider has been lost. It was found via a Google Internet search on grief and hope.

236    Moffat, 1992.

236    Gibran, 1983, p. 25.

236    See http://www.originalquilts.com for quilt-making ideas to preserve the memory of loved ones.

236    Another powerful externalized "presence of hope" is the Vietnam War Memorial.

237    For AIDS-related information and events, visit http://www.thebody.com. For Alzheimer-related information and events, visit http://www.alz.org. For cancer-related information and events, visit http://www.cancer.org. For ALS-related information and events, visit http://www.alsa.org.

237    Hansson and Stroebe, 2007.

237    Pennebaker, 1990.

238    Walter, 1996.

238    See Swann (1996), pp. 169– 175, for "Speech for the removal of grief."

238    For Ifa funeral rites, see Fatunmbi, 1994.

239    For *Tibetan Book of the Dead*, see Coleman, Jinpa, and Dorie (2007).

239    Farber, 2003.

239    Gorer, 1955.

239    Becker, 1973, front matter.

239    Wong's comments were from his December 14, 2002 keynote address at the Conference on Life and Death Education at the National Changhua University of Education, Taiwan. It was retrieved September 14, 2007 from http://www.meaning.ca.

239    Hall, 1897.

240    See Scioli, 2007, for results of a study on death-related thoughts and feelings as related to purpose in life.

240    We included self-esteem as a predictor of death anxiety along with hope and spirituality because some social psychologists believe that self-esteem is the most important buffer that humans have against death anxiety. (We do not share this opinion.)

241    Yalom, 1980.

241    For Howard Hughes biographical details, see Barlett and Steele, 2004.

242    For *The Egyptian Book of the Dead*, see Faulkner, 2000.

242    Buddha's discourse on remaining "fearless" was retrieved September 15, 2007 from http://www.accesstoinsight.org/tipitaka/index.html.

242    For Paul's first letter to the Corinthians [15 : 51–53], see Yancy and Stafford (1992), p. 1253.

242    Donne, 1999, p. 251.

242    Abdel-Khalek, 2002.

243    Lifton, 1996.

243    For research on a "good death," see Steinhauser et al., 2000. For a practical guide with resources for a dying loved one see Felman, Lasher, and Byock, 2008.

243    Csikszentmihalyi, 1991.

243    Tolle, 1999, pp. 54 and 188.

243    Epicurus quote was retrieved September 20, 2007 from http://www.quotationsbook.com.

243    For Hafiz reference, see Ordoubadian, 2006, p. 45.

244    Emerson quote was retrieved September 18, 2007 from http://www.quoteworld.org.

244    May, 2007.

244    Rappaport, Fossler, Bross, and Gilden, 1993.

244    For the Book of Ecclesiastes, see Yancy and Stafford, 1992, p. 723–733.

245    Moltmann, 1993.

245    James quote was retrieved September 20, 2007 from http://www.quotationspage.com.

245    Havel, 2004.

245    Lifton, 1996.

245    Mikulincer, Florian, and Hirschberger, 2003.

245    Brokaw, 2001, front matter.

246    Mikulincer, Florian, and Hirschberger, 2003, p. 25.

246    Olson, Vernon, Harris, and Jang, 2001.

246    For Jung's use of word associations with families, see Monte and Sollod, 2003, p. 122.

247    Hendrix, 1993.

## Chapter 13: Overcoming Hopelessness

*Page*

250   For Dante quote, see Pinsky, 1997, p. 373.

250   For quotes from The Inferno, beginning with "deep and savage road", see Pinsky., 1997, p. 25.

251   For Tubman quotes, see Humez, 2003, pp. 178 and 183.

251   Virginia Woolf offered this comparison in a 1930 letter to a close friend 11 years before she committed suicide. It was retrieved October 1, 2007 from http://www. malcolmingram.com/suicide.htm.

251   Styron, 1992, p. 17.

251   For Dante quote, see Pinsky, 1997, p. 19.

253   Buck quote was retrieved October 2, 2007 from http://www.wisdomquotes.com.

253   The *Two Towers* screenplay was retrieved October 2, 2007 from http://www.imsdb.com/scripts/Lord-of-the-Rings-The-Two-Towers.html.

253   Beck, 1995, p. 16.

253   Gandhi quote was retrieved September 14, 2008 from http://www.quotationspage.com.

254   Beck, 1976.

254   Burns, 1999.

254   Sontag, 2002.

255   Tolstoy, 2006, p. 79.

255   For Blythe reference see Tolstoy, 1981, front matter.

255   Amiel quote was retrieved October 2, 2007 from thinkexist.com/quotes/henri_frederic_ amiel/2.html

255   Dickens, 2006.

255   Whittier quote was retrieved October 4, 2007 from http://www.quotes.net.

255   Tolstoy was obsessed with death for much of his life. The first of numerous "death dreams" occurred in 1869, the so-called horror of Arzamas, when he was 41 years of age. See Troyat, 2001, p. 319. The allusion to an "inescapable death" is from his classic, *The Death of Ivan Ilyich*. See Tolstoy, 2006.

255   Another powerful literary example of a "failed life" is Arthur Miller's (1996) *Death of a Salesman. See A. A. Miller (1996)*.

255   Herman, 1997, p. 90.

256   Seligman, 1975.

256   Barbara's case and the others in this chapter are drawn from the case files of the first author. All names have been changed and a few minor demographic variables have been altered to maintain the confidentiality of the individuals.

256   For details regarding the film *Crouching Tiger, Hidden Dragon*, see http://www.imdb.com.

256   Sartre, 1989, p. 45.

256   For reference to "The most important part of my environment" see James, 2007, p. 22.

256   Sartre, 1989.

257   For the reference to "The hell to be endured hereafter", see James, 1890, p. 127.

257   The concept of "repetition compulsion" was discussed at length in Beyond the Pleasure Principle. See Freud, 1990.

257  Camus, 1958, pp. 24–33.

258  Gould essay was retrieved October 6, 2007 from http://www.cancerguide.org/median_not_msg.html.

258  For Grandma Moses and Bill Traylor see Wertkin, 2003.

258  Burns, 1999.

259  May, 1999.

259  Frankl, 1985, p. 86.

259  Walker, 1982.

260  Higgins, 1994.

260  Melville was cited in Higgins, 1994, p. 325.

260  Frankl, 1985, pp. 57–58.

260  Money, 1988.

260  Hendrix, 1993.

260  Lewis, Amini, and Lannon (2001).

260  Hendrix, 1993.

261  Gibran, 1983, p. 15.

261  Hanh, 2002.

262  For Dante reference see Pinsky, 1997, back matter.

262  Milton, 2003, front matter.

262  Durkheim, 2007.

262  Darwin, 2004.

262  Fromm, 2000.

262  Kovic, 1990, p. 183.

263  For the 22nd Psalm, see Yancy and Stafford (1992), p. 609.

263  Lifton, 1991, pp. 45, 171, and 373.

263  McGeary article appeared in *Time* (February, 12, 2001) and was retrieved October 16, 2007 from http://www.time.com.

263  Cosby reference was retrieved October 26, 2007 from http://www.msnbc.msn.com/id/5345290/

264  Whitlock, 2004.

264  Aaron, 1991, p. 278.

265  For the Oxford English Dictionary see Simpson and Weiner, 1989.

265  Rogers, 1951.

265  Mother Teresa Nobel Prize acceptance excerpt was retrieved October 18, 2007 from http://www.nobelprizes.com.

266  Mother Teresa, 2002, pp. 59–60.

266  Great Spirit Prayer was retrieved October 18, 2007 from http://www.firstpeople.us/html/An-Indian-Prayer.html.

267  Poussaint and Alexander, 2000.

268  Walker, 1982, pp. 206 and 192.

268  Steinbeck, 2002, p. 349.

268  Shipler, 2005.

268  For spinal cord injury and suicide risk, see Charlifue and Gerhart, 1991.

268    For epilepsy and suicide risk, see Christensen, et al., 2007.

268    See Palmer and Wehmeyer (1998) for research on hopelessness levels of learning disabled children.

269    Statistics regarding teen depression and suicide were retrieved October 21, 2007 from http://www.surgeongeneral.gov/library/health/chap3/sec5/html.

269    Data on depression in adults with learning disability was retrieved October 21, 2007 from http://www.additudemag.com/adhd/article/748.html.

269    Holdt quote was retrieved October 20, 2007 from http://www.american-pictures.com.

269    Walker, 1982, p. 194.

269    Short stature and other forms of bodily dissatisfaction are other perceived "limitations" that plague some individuals. For relevant research see Martel and Biller, 1987.

270    Maddi, 2004.

270    King's words are taken from his famous "letter from Birmingham jail." See Jacobus, 1983, p. 184.

270    Mandela quote was retrieved October 23, 2007 from http://www.info.gov.za/speeches/1999/990617935a1003.htm.

270    For King quote, see Washington (1990), p. 139.

270    Braveheart details and quote were retrieved October 18, 2007 from http://www.imdb.com.

271    West, 1999, p. 68.

271    For Braille biography and quotes, see Mellor, 2006.

271    Bandura, 1994.

271    Jones anecdote and quote was retrieved October 26, 2007 from http://www.hsph.harvard.edu/chc/wmy2009/Celebrities/james_jones.html.

272    Cosby quote was retrieved October 26, 2007 from http://www.msnbc.msn.com/id/5345290/

272    For Upanishad quote, see Hume, 1921, p. 258.

272    For John [15 : 5] see Yancy and Stafford (1992), p. 1167.

272    For a succinct summary of the Hindu philosophy of "coiled energy" as it relates to Kundalini yoga, visit the website for the British Library at www.bl.uk/learning/artimages/bodies/kundalini/yoga.html

272    Sufi passage was retrieved October 27, 2007 from http://www.answering-Islam.org.

272    For Brihadarany Upanishad quote, see Hume, 1921, p. 258.

273    Solomon, 2002, p. 443.

273    Zuess, 1999, front matter.

273    Styron, 1992, p. 47.

273    For DSM-IV, see APA, 2000.

273    Abramson, Seligman, and Teasdale, 1978.

273    Davidson, Pizzagalli, and Nitschke, 2002.

273    Joiner, 1992.

274    Abramson, Metalsky, and Alloy, 1989.

274    For Menninger quote see Cook, Deger, and Gibson (2007), p. 373.

274 International suicide statistics were retrieved October 28, 2007 from the World Health Organization at: http://www.who.int/mental_health/prevention/suicide/suicideprevent/en/

275 U.S. suicide statistics were retrieved October 28, 2007 from the Office of the Surgeon General at: http://www.surgeongeneral.gov/library/calltoaction/fact1.htm.

275 Griffith, 2005.

275 Judy Collins lyrics were retrieved October, 28, 2007 from http://www.rhapsody.com.

275 Rosen, 1971.

275 Weinberg quote was retrieved October 28, 2007 from http://www.brainyquote.com.

275 For Ellen West case study, see Binswanger, Mendel, and Lyons, 1958.

276 Ellen West poem was retrieved October 29, 2007 from http://www.ship.edu/~cgboeree/binswanger.html.

276 Kant, 2001, pp. 144–149.

276 U.S. statistics on suicide were retrieved October 29, 2007 from the American Association of Suicidology at http://www.suicidology.org.

277 Shneidman, 1999.

277 Durkheim, 2007.

278 For DBT resources, visit http://www.brtc.psych.washington.edu/. This Web site includes information on the DBT approach, ongoing research, clinical trials, and contact information for locating a trained professional in your area.

278 Van Gogh quote was retrieved October 30, 2007 from student.bmj.com/issues/01/12/life/471.php

278 For Columbine shootings see Pooley et al., 1999.

278 For Virginia Tech massacre see Begley, Underwood, and Carmichael, 2007.

278 For Andrea Yates reference see Thomas et al., 2001.

## Chapter 14: Hope for Children

*Page*

280 Tagore quote was retrieved November 2, 2007 from http://www.quotations.about.com.

280 Browning, 2005, p. 323.

281 For Gray quote, see Sargent, 2005, p. 30.

281 Wordsworth, 2008, p. 299.

281 Millay quote was retrieved November 2, 2007 from http://www.poemhunter.com.

281 Bachelard, 1971, p. 20.

281 U.S. child abuse statistics were retrieved November 3, 2007 from http://www.childhelp.org.

281 U.S. child poverty statistics were retrieved November 3, 2007 from the National Center for Children in Poverty at http://www.nccp.org.

281 U.S. child chronic illness statistics were retrieved November 3, 2007 from the Centers for Disease Control at http://www.cdc.gov.

281 Liberian statistics were retrieved November 3, 2007 from UNICEF at http://www.unicef.org.

282  Anthony, 1975.

282  Kanner, 1957.

282  Freud and Burlingham, 1943, p. 51.

282  Spitz, 1965, pp. 268–269.

282  Bowlby, 1980, p. 341.

283  For DSM-IV, see American Psychiatric Association, 2000.

283  Greene, 1994.

283  Orbach, 1988, p. 24.

283  Ibid., pp. 23–24.

283  For National Mental Health Association, visit: http://www.nmha.org.

284  Siomopoulos and Inamdar, 1979, p. 235.

284  Bowlby, 1960, p. 16.

285  For a deeper discussion of Life Is Beautiful and Roberto Benigni, see Bullaro, 2005.

285  Bluebond-Langner, 1978, p. 217.

285  Ibid., p. 184.

285  Ibid., p. 11.

285  Ibid., p. 186.

285  Rando, 1984, p. 368.

285  Thompson and Rudolf, 1988, p. 289.

286  Elizabeth Stone quote was retrieved November 4, 2007 from http://www.quotes.net.

286  Rando, 1991, p. 164.

286  Gunther, 1997, pp. 226–227.

286  Bluebond-Langner, 1978, p. 215.

286  Ibid., p. 216.

286  Miller, 1996.

287  Rando, 1984.

287  Bluebond-Langner, p. 232.

287  Ibid, p. 26.

287  Another powerful film depiction of protecting the child hope symbol can be found in the western classic *Stagecoach* (1939), starring John Wayne. An entire community of children is captured by Indians. Despite a flurry of gun shots, flying arrows, and general mayhem, not a single child is harmed. See http://www.imdb.com.

287  Jung, and Kerényi, 2005, pp. 106–116.

287  Baby 81 story was retrieved November 5, 2007 from http://www.columbiatribune.com.

288  Agee quote was retrieved November 5, 2007 from http://www.quotationspage.com.

288  Emerson, 1981, p. 660.

288  Klimt painting details and quote were retrieved November 5, 2007 from national.gallery.ca/bulletin/num17/dobai1.html.

288  Surgeon General report was retrieved November 7, 2007 from http://www.surgeongeneral.gov/cmh/childreport.htm.

288  Coles (1967) and others have noted that, for some poor African Americans, having a child may represent the one remaining "hope investment" that remains available to them.

288     The assassination of JFK in 1963 belongs on a different level, but it was certainly a globally felt "death of hope."

288     Statistics and information for child depression were retrieved November 7, 2007 from http://www.nmha.org/go/about-us and http://www.surgeongeneral.gov/cmh/childreport.htm.

289     Berlinsky and Biller, 1982.

289     Garber and Horowitz, 2002.

289     Fassler and Dumas, 1998, p. 37.

289     For more information on antidepressants for children visit http://www.mayoclinic.com/health/antidepressants/MH00059.

290     Stark and Kendall, 1996.

290     Leahy, 1988.

291     Ginott quote was retrieved November 7, 2007 from http://www.quotationspage.com.

291     Keillor quote was retrieved November 8, 2007 from http://www.quotesandpoem.com.

291     Cassidy, 1986.

292     Kaiser, 1996.

293     For more information on Firefly games, visit http://www.Firefly-games.com.

293     For Blinx, Paper Mario, and Pokemon games, visit http://www.amazon.com, enter "videogames" next to the search box, and then either Blinx, Mario, or Pokemon.

294     For more information on the Johns Hopkins HOPE programs, visit http://www.hopkinschildrens.org/hope.aspx.

294     For more information on Hopelab, visit http://www.hopelab.org.

294     AFI child film list was retrieved November 10, 2007 from the American Film Institute site at http://www.afi.com.

295     Lonnie Carton essay. Source for this material has been lost.

297     Scioli, 1990.

297     Poussaint and Alexander, 2000, p. 47.

298     Abboud and Kim, 2005, pp. 5, 37, 128, 157, 197, 167.

298     Edelman, 1993, pp. 5, 56–58.

298     Boteach, 2006.

298     Biller, 1993. See also Biller and Meridith, 1974, as well as Biller and Trotter, 1994.

298     Vygotsky, 1986.

299     Brooks and Goldstein, 2002, p. 154.

299     Snyder, 1994.

299     Levine, 2002.

300     For understanding learning disabilities, see Trusdell, 2002.

300     Fassler and Dumas, 1998.

300     Gibran, 1983, pp. 17–18.

300     Fassler and Dumas, 1998.

301     For fewer positive self-attributions of suicidal adolescents, see Brunstein-Klomek et al., 2005.

301     For impact of bullying on teen depression and suicide, see Brunstein-Klomek et al., 2007.

301     For Committee for Children Web site, go to http://www.cfchildren.org.

302     Biller, 2002.

302     For National Association for Sport and Physical Education, visit http://www. aahperd.org/naspe/

302     Pearce, Little, and Perez, 2003.

303     Painton, 2007.

303     Buddha quote was retrieved November 14, 2007 from http://www.quotationspage.com.

303     Bowring quote was retrieved November 14, 2007 from http://www.great-inspirational-quotes.com.

303     Moore, 1992, p. 25.

304     Haley, 2007. While fully aware of various criticisms of Haley's scholarship in researching his "roots," we support the greater good sparked by the publication of his work, specifically the heightened interest in tracing one's personal, familial, or ethnic background.

304     Angelou poem was retrieved November 15, 2007 from http://www.afropoets.net.

304     http://www.genwriters.com.

305     Muir quote was retrieved November 15, 2007 from http://www.widsomquotes.com.

305     For Isaiah [40 : 26], see Yancy and Stafford (1992), p. 781.

305     Thoreau quote was retrieved November 16, 2007 from http://www.quotesandpoem.com.

305     See Louv, 2005 (front matter), for "spiritual necessity" quote.

305     For Cornell research, see Louv, 2005, p. 49.

305     For "increasing divide" quote, see Louv, 2005 (front matter).

305     For his list of nature-based activities, see Louv, 2005, p. 174.

305     For girl scouts, visit http://www.girlscouts.org. For boy scouts, visit http://www.scouting.org. For international scouting, visit http://www.scout.org.

305     For U.S. 4-H clubs, visit http://www.4-h.org.

305     For international 4-H club information, visit http://www.national4-hheadquarters.gov.

306     Ben Gray quote was retrieved from a scouting site November 2007. Site address has been lost.

306     For Outward Bound programs, visit http://www.outwardbound.org.

306     For camps, visit mysummercamps.com

## Chapter 15: Hope and Healing

*Page*

308     For Aristotle quote, see McKeon, 1941, p. 963.

309     Jamie's story was a personal communication to the first author.

310     Franklin, 2000, front matter.

310     In retrospect, some of the confusion over the healing potential of positive thoughts or emotions can be attributed to (1) the "mixed bag" of populations that have sometimes been lumped together in the same study (e.g., combining the mild, moderately, and severely ill; (2) a lack of clarity in identifying divergent emotions (e.g., treating hope and optimism as identical states); and (3) an inadequate assessment on the emotional side of the mind–body equation, particularly with respect to deeper, subconscious states. For

example, some investigators have invested thousands of dollars on an MRI, CAT-SCANS, etc. to assess the body but settled for a 30-second, 6-item questionnaire to survey the emotions. Without an equally rigorous attempt to address thoughts and emotions, the investigator may be left, as Plato suggested in his "cave allegory" (see Jowett, 1999, p. 265), in the "shadow world" of error, without any hope of capturing an "echo of the truth."

In regard to subconscious states, McClelland (1989) argued that health-related motivational states were more likely to involve right-hemisphere (nonverbal) and generally nonconscious levels of the mind, not amenable to the typical questionnaires used in many mind–body studies. To cite just a few examples of positive mind–body findings involving deeper states, see Weinberger et al., 1979 (high repressors reporting low anxiety showed high levels of arousal), Kneier and Temoshok, 1984 (cancer patients reported less distress but more arousal following shock as compared to heart patients), Gottschalk, 1985 (subconscious hope levels were correlated with survival time in cancer patients), Dembroski et al., 1989 (interview-based hostility, but not self-reported hostility, was predictive of cardiac risk), Pennebaker, 1990 (undisclosed emotion was associated with compromised immunity), Scioli et al., 1997 (higher levels of subconscious hope were associated with fewer acute and chronic ills).

In a particularly fascinating study, McClelland and Krishnit (1988) presented one group of individuals with a power-oriented war film and another with a film of Mother Teresa. Those who viewed Mother Teresa showed a significant increase in salivary immunoglobin-A (SIgA), a protective stress hormone. However, *there was no connection between (conscious) self-reported ratings of love or fondness for Mother Teresa and changes in hormone levels.*

When the conscious–unconscious distinction is not addressed, and particularly when divergent methods of measurement are employed (e.g., interviews vs. questionnaires), conflicting and confusing findings may result. See, for example, research by Greer (1999) for a positive finding between fighting spirit and breast cancer. Contrast these results with work by Watson, Haviland, Greet, Davidson, and Bliss (1999), who failed to find a relationship between fighting spirit and survival time.

For more on the mind–body debate, see Angell (1985), and Williams, Schneiderman, Relman, and Angell (2002).

310 For Hippocrates, see Lloyd, 1984.

311 Ader and Cohen, 1975.

311 Ader, Felten, and Cohen, 1990.

311 Carr, Wooley, and Blalock, 1992.

311 Pert, 1999.

312 For Hippocrates, see Hartmann, 1902, p. 175.

312 For Galen, see Brock, 1963.

312 For Avicenna, see Bakhtiar, 1999.

312 For Paracelsus, see Hartmann, 1902, p. 175.

312 For Osler, see Bean, 1968.

312 Benson, 1985.

312 For Salk, see O'Regan, 1986, p. 9.

312 Siegel's Love, *medicine and miracles* was first published in 1986. However, the quote is from *How to live between office visits* (Siegel, 1993, pp. 159–160).

312 Kiecolt-Glaser and Glaser, 2002.

313 Reisfeld and Wilson, 2004.

313 Armstrong, 2001.

314 Sontag, 2002.

314 Langer and Rodin, 1976.

314 For research on depression and immunity, see Schleifer, Keller, and Bartlett, 1999.

314 Greer, 1999.

314 For AIDS study, see Solomon, 1990.

314 For University of Connecticut study, see Affleck et al., 1987.

315 For British study, see Watson et al., 1999.

315 For Canadian study, see Goodwin et al., 2001. See also Greer (1999) for a discussion of some of the complexities involved in "psycho-oncology" research.

315 For hostility research, see Hafen, Karren, Frandsen, and Smith, 1996, p. 198.

315 For stress hormone research, see Hafen et al., 1996, pp. 191–192.

315 For aggression and antisocial behavior research, see Hafen et al., 1996, p. 154.

315 For an excellent discussion of the "will to live" with respect to significant personal dates, etc., see Ray, 2004.

315 Emmons and King, 1988.

315 McClelland, 1989.

316 For data on the apparent delaying of death as a function of holidays, religious rituals or other spiritually sanctified pursuits, see Ray, 2004.

316 Phillips et al., 1993.

316 For Ecclesiastes [4:9] quote, see Yancy and Stafford (1992), p. 727.

316 For mice study, see LaBarba, 1970.

316 For monkey stress response study, see Spiegel, 1993.

317 For simian AIDS study, see Capitanio and Lerche, 1998.

317 For HIV and social support research, see Kiecolt-Glaser et al., 2002.

317 For Alameda study, see Berkman and Syme, 1994.

317 Moberg, Arn, and Magnusson (2005), p. 60.

317 Coan, Schaefer, and Davidson (2006), pp. 1037–1038.

318 For crowding study, see Pan et al., 2006.

318 For size of social network reference see Balaji et al., 2007 as well as Ye, Zhang, and Xu, 2007.

318 For newlywed study, see Kiecolt-Glaser et al., 1993.

318 For loneliness in a crowd reference see Copeland, 2000.

318 For blood pressure research, see Uchino et al., 1996.

319 For breast cancer research, see Kiecolt-Glaser and Glaser, 1993.

319 Laura's experience was retrieved November 25, 2007 from dawn.thot.net/lbcp/report.html.

319 Christie's experience was retrieved November 25, 2007 from http://www.livestrong.org.

319 Sontag, 2002.

319 Ray, 2004, p. 36.

319   Pennebaker, 1990.

319   Williams et al., 1992.

319   For additional research on social support and coronary disease, see Seeman and Syme, 1987.

319   Spiegel et al., 1989. While attempts to replicate Spiegel's study have proved difficult, he and his colleagues have continued to research the potential impact of group psychotherapy on women with breast cancer. Acknowledging that current advances in medical treatments as well as psychological interventions, may call for more sophisticated research designs, Spiegel's group nevertheless points to recent developments across the sciences that suggest a number of pathways by which emotional and supportive interventions could affect the prognosis of breast cancer patients. In 2007 Spiegel and his colleagues reported that women with estrogen-receptive negative breast tumors who participated in expressive-supportive therapy lived, on average, three times longer than a control group (standard medical care without group psychotherapy). See Kraemer, Kuchler, and Spiegel (2009) for a recent commentary on the status of research on this topic.

319   Dr. Ken Hamilton and his colleagues have been running psychologically and spiritually focused H.O.P.E. (healing of persons exceptional) groups for cancer survivors for several decades. As of 2008, groups have been run in more than a dozen towns in Maine and several others in New Hampshire. For further information visit: http://www.hopehealing.org.

320   Maimonides quote was retrieved November 27, 2007 from http://www.stress.org.

320   Orsborn quote was retrieved November 28, 2007 from http://www.beliefnet.com.

320   For research on HIV, anxiety, and immunity, see Kiecolt-Glaser et al., 2002.

320   For research on generalized anxiety, PTSD, and immunity, see Kiecolt-Glaser et al., 2002.

320   For research on fear, distress, and postsurgical complications, see Kiecolt-Glaser et al., 2002.

320   For research on job strain and effects of excess adrenaline, see Williams, 1993.

320   The association between blood clotting and adrenaline has been studied for more than a half-century. See Schneider and Zangari (1951).

320   For research on cats and mice under stress, and blood sugar, see Surwitt, 1993.

320   For research on tumor development in mice, see Pelletier, 1993.

321   Schmale and Engel, 1967.

321   Richter, 1959.

321   Weiss, 1970.

322   For Aristotle, see McKeon, 1941, pp. 689–712.

323   Scioli et al., 1997.

323   James, 1983.

323   Booth and Ashbridge, 1993.

323   Marcel, 1962.

323   Pert, 1999.

323   For more information on "allostatic load", see McEwen, 1999.

324   Booth and Ashbridge, 1993.

324   Hafen et al., 1996.

324   Cunningham and Watson, 2004.

324   Scioli et al., 2008.

## Chapter 16: Hope for Health

*Page*

326   For Plato quote, see Jowett, 1999, p. 864.

326   George Burns quote was retrieved March 3, 2006 from http://www. homepages. nildram.co.uk/~jimella/quotes.htm.

326   The Burns tribute from the Huffington Center editorial was retrieved March 3, 2006 from http://www.hcoa.org/centenarians/george_burns.htm.

327   For Plato's "holism," see Jowett, 1999, p. 864.

327   For "healthy environments," see Taylor, Repetti, and Seeman, 1999.

327   Booth and Ashbridge, 1993.

327   Pert, 1999.

328   For Cousins' quote, see Cook, 1999, p. 45.

328   For Aristotle quote, see McKeon, 1941, p. 1109.

329   Koenig, 2001.

329   Emmons and McCullough, 2003.

329   For research on disclosure and immunity, see Schwartz and Kline, 1997.

329   Pennebaker, 1990.

330   Speigel, 1993.

330   (Lance Armstrong's http://www.livestrong.com is an excellent resource for cancer patients seeking support and guidance from other survivors.)

330   Cunningham and Watson, 2004.

330   Pennebaker, 1990.

330   For more on biofeedback, see Schwartz and Andrasik, 2003 or contact the Biofeedback Certification Institute of America (http://www.BCIA.org).

331   For research on potential benefits of religion, see Koenig, 2001, and Koenig and Cohen, 2001.

331   Ibid.

331   See Davis, McKay and Robbins-Eshelman, 2000, for an excellent general guide to relaxation and stress reduction.

332   A comprehensive guide to "bodywork" is presented in Claire, 2006.

332   Gottman, 1999.

332   For research on stress and coping in children, see Eisenberg and Fabes (1992) and Eisenberg, Fabes, and Guthrie (1997).

332   Mirror neurons were first discovered by a research team headed by Giacomo Rizzolati at the University of Parma, Italy. For a comprehensive review of mirror neurons, see Stein, 2007.

332   Lown anecdote cited in Kabat-Zinn, 1990, pp. 188–189.

332   See http://www.shinzen.org/shinsub3/artMantra.htm for Young's reflections on Meditation.

333   http://www.webmd.com.

333    Koenig, 2001.

333    Benson, 1985.

335    For a serious discussion of the Hindu chakra system, see Leadbeater, 2003.

335    For a comparison of different forms of Buddhist meditation, see Bucknell and Kang, 1996.

335    A respected introduction to tai chi is provided by McFarlane, 1997.

335    See Cohen, 1997, for a comprehensive guide to the philosophy, science, and art of Qigong.

336    See Cohen, 2006, for a fine discussion of the specific practices and values associated with Native American healing rites.

336    Galen quote is from his treatise "The Best Doctor Is Also a Philosopher." See Singer, 1997, pp. 30–34.

336    Dostoevsky, 2008, p. 804.

337    The Coleridge quote was retrieved February 4, 2005 from http://www.whatquote.com.

337    Ferguson, 1993.

338    Kim's story was taken from http://www.livestrong.org.

338    Groopman, 2001.

338    The Chris Chrichton story was taken from http://www.livestrong.org.

339    Alisa Gilbert's story was taken from http://www.livestrong.org.

339    It can be daunting process trying to craft an integrative or complementary approach for a medical condition. Integrative medicine is a relatively new phenomenon and many traditional practitioners are unaware of its potential; some can be resistant or hostile toward an individual seeking such an approach. Do your research. If you are unable to find a holistic or integrative clinic or facility, consider building your own team of healers. Naturopathic physicians can be a great help in bridging the gap between the worlds of traditional medicine and complementary healing practices. A good nutritionist can also be a powerful ally.

339    For cancer patients who are interested in a complementary approach to treatment, we recommend Ralph Moss. His Web site is http://www.ralphmoss.com/. For brain tumor patients (and other cancer patients) who seek nutritional support to aid their treatment, we recommend Dr. Jeanne Wallace, a doctoral level nutritionist who specializes in cancer. Her Web site is http://www.nutritional-solutions.net/

339    Moore, 1992, p. 2.

339    Pruyser, 1990.

339    Lynch, 1965.

339    Marcel, 1962.

339    Ann Marie Juliano's story taken from http://www.livestrong.org.

340    Speigel et al. 1989.

340    For the Sword of Damocles, see Cicero's (2005) Tuscan Disputations.

341    For Emerson quote on "The wise man in the storm", see Emerson, 1910, p. 203.

341    Charles Fletcher quote was retrieved February 4, 2005 from http://www.livestrong.org.

341    For quote on health demanding a "horizon", see Emerson 1983, p. 15.

341    The Keats quote was retrieved February 4, 2005 from http://whatquote.com.

341    For Tzu quote, ibid.

341    For Seneca quote, ibid.

341    For Carlyle quote, ibid.

341 Bryant and Veroff, 2006.
341 The philosopher Ernst Bloch is another who argued that all three dimensions of human temporal experience (past, present, and future), were critical for hope. Specifically, he noted that these three dimensions of time allowed for the illumination, comparison, direction, and sense of possibility, required for a full experience of hope. See Bloch, 1986.
342 For Marden quote, see Cook, 1999, p. 286.
342 Checko and Scioli, 2007.
342 Shakespeare, 1997, p. 1119.
343 Lombardi quote was retrieved February 6, 2006 from http://www.worldofquotes.com.
343 Chess anecdote was retrieved March 5, 2006 from http://www.sentientdevelopments.com.
343 For Swedish research on oxytocin, see Moberg, 2003.
343 For Cooper study, see Blair, Goodyear, Wynne, and Saunders, 1984.
344 Biller, 2002.
344 For Socrates quote, see Jowett, 1999, p. 3.
344 For Estee Lauder's "jars of hope," see Severo, 2004, p.1.
344 For Max Planck study, see Smith and Freund, 2002.
344 Vaillant, 2003, p. 257.
345 Reuben, Judd-Hamilton, Harris, and Seeman, 2003.
345 Lum and Lightfoot, 2005.
345 For Duke study See Barefoot, Maynard, and Beckham, 1998.
345 Masters, Hill, and Kircher, 2004.
345 Strawbridge, Shema, and Cohen, 2001.
345 Erikson, Erikson, and Kivnick, 1994.
345 For more on the vital role that nonprofessionals, including the elderly, can play in shoring up the mental health of young and old, see Gershon and Biller, 1977.
346 Baird, 1985.
346 The Brunner quote was taken from McDowell, 2006.
347 The Greeley quote was retrieved February 8, 2006 from http://www.whatquote.com.
347 Frankl, 1985.
347 Ryff, Love, and Urry, 2006.
347 Bowes, Tamyln, and Butler, 2002, p. 140.
347 Scioli, McClelland, Weaver, and Madden, 2000.
348 Gibran, 1983, p. 27.
349 Glassner, 2000.
349 Lefcourt, 1980.
349 Tzu, 2002.
349 Moore, 1992.
350 Siegel, 1986.
350 Armstrong, 2002.
350 For Milken story, see Daniels, 2004.
351 Covey, 2004.
351 Hillman, 1997.
351 For Gandhi quote, see O'Hahn, 2001.

351   This anonymous quote was retrieved March 3, 2006 from http://www.quotegarden.com.

351   Hegel, 1979.

351   Becker, 1973.

351   Lifton, 1996.

352   For Aristotle's "entelechy," see McKeon, 1941, p. 555.

353   Erikson, 1950.

353   Warren, 2002.

353   For quote on the universe as the property of every individual, see Emerson, 1983, p. 16.

353   Kushner, 2002.

# Bibliography

Aaron, H. (1991). *I had a hammer: The Hank Aaron story*. New York: Harper Collins.

Abboud, S. K., & Kim, J. (2005). *Top of the class*. New York: Berkley Books.

Abdel-Khalek, A. M. (2002). Why do we fear death? The construction and validation of the reasons for death fear scale. *Death Studies, 26*(8), 669–680.

Abramson, L. Y., Metalsky, G. I., & Alloy, L. B. (1989). Hopelessness depression: A theory-based subtype of depression. *Psychological Review, 96*(2), 358–372.

Abramson, L. Y., Seligman, M. E. P., & Teasdale, J. (1978). Learned helplessness in humans: Critique and reformulation. *Journal of Abnormal Psychology, 87*, 49–74.

Ader, R., & Cohen, N. (1975). Behaviorally conditioned immunosuppression. *Psychosomatic Medicine, 37*(4), 333–340.

Ader, R., Felten, D., & Cohen, N. (1990). Interactions between the brain and the immune system. *Annual Review of Pharmacology and Toxicology, 30*, 561–602.

Adler, A., & Stein, H. T. (2005). *The collected clinical works of Alfred Adler*. Bellingham, WA: The Classical Adlerian Translation Project.

Affleck, G., Tennen, H., & Croog, S. (1987). Causal attribution, perceived benefits, and morbidity after a heart attack: An 8-year study. *Journal of Consulting and Clinical Psychology, 55*(1), 29–35.

Agranovich, A. (2005). Cross-cultural differences in neuropsychological performance: A comparison between Russian and American samples. In T. Akhutina, J. Glozman, L. Moskovich, & D. Robbins (Eds.), *A. R. Luria and contemporary psychology: Festschrift celebrating the centennial of the birth of Luria* (pp. 187–194). Hauppauge, NY: Nova Science Publishers.

Ainsworth, M. S., Blehar, M. C., Waters, E. & Wall, S. (1978). *Patterns of attachment: A psychological study of the strange situation*. Hillsdale, NJ; Lawrence Erlbaum.

Alberti, R. E. & Emmons, M. L. (2008). *Your perfect right: Assertiveness and equality in your life and relationships*. Atascadero, CA: Impact Publishers.

Allport, G. W., & Odbert, H. S. (1936). Traitnames: A psycho-lexical study. *Psychological Monographs, 47*, (211), 171.

Alverson, H. (1994). *Semantics and experience: Universal metaphors of time in English, Mandarin, Hindi, and Sesotho*. Baltimore, MD: Johns Hopkins University Press.

American Psychiatric Association (2000). *Diagnostic and Statistical Manual of Mental Disorders*. 4th ed. Arlington, VA: Author.

Ames, R. T., & Rosemont, H. (1999). *The analects of Confucius*. New York: Valentine Books.

Angell, M. (1985). Disease as a reflection of the psyche. *New England Journal of Medicine, 312*, 1570–1572.

Angelou, M. (1986). *All God's children need traveling shoes*. New York: Vintage.

Angelou, M. (1994). *The complete collected poems of Maya Angelou*. New York: Random House.

Anthony, E. J. (1975). Childhood depression. In E. J. Anthony and T. Benedek (Eds.), *Depression and human existence* (pp. 231–277). Boston: Little, Brown.

Apfel, R. J., & Simon, B. (2000). Mitigating discontents with children in war: An ongoing psycho-analytic inquiry. In M. M. Suarez-Orozco & A. C. G. M. Robben (Eds.), *Cultures under siege: Collective violence and trauma* (pp. 102–130). New York: Cambridge University Press.

Aquinas, T. (1989). *Summa Theologiae*. Allen, TX: Christian Classics.

Armstrong, L. (2001). *It's not about the bike*. New York: Berkley Trade.

Arrington, R. L. (2001). *A companion to the philosophers*. Malden, MA: Blackwell Publishers.

Asanti, M. (1996). *African intellectual heritage*. Philadelphia: Temple University Press.

Associated Press (2002). Nine alive: The miraculous rescue of the Pennsylvania miners. Champaign, IL: Sports Publishing LLC.

Averill, J. R. (1968). Grief: Its nature and significance. *Psychological Bulletin, 70* (6), 721–748.

Averill, J. R., Catlin, G., & Chon, K. K. (1990). *Rules of hope*. New York: Springer-Verlag.

Averill, J. R., & Nunley, E. (1992). *Voyages of the heart: Living an emotionally creative life*. New York: The Free Press.

Bachelard, G. (1971). *The poetics of reverie: Childhood, language and the cosmos*. Boston: Beacon Press.

Bain, A. (2004). *The senses and the intellect*. Whitefish, MT: Kessinger Publications.

Bain, A. (2006). *The emotions and the will*. New York: Cosimo Classics.

Baird, R. M. (1985). Meaning in life: Discovered or created? *Journal of Religion and Health, 24*, 117–124.

Bakhtiar, L. (1999). *Avicenna's canon of medicine*. Chicago: Abjad Book Designers and Builders.

Balaji, A., Claussen, A., Smith, D., Visser, S., Morales, M., & Perou, R. (2007). Social support networks and maternal mental health and well-being. *Journal of Women's Health*, 16(10), 1386–1396.

Bandura, A. (1994). *Self-efficacy: The exercise for control*. New York: Freeman.

Bannister, R. (2004). *The four-minute mile*. Guilford, CT: Globe Pequot.

Barefoot, J. C., Maynard, K. E., & Beckham, J. C. (1998). Trust, health and longevity. *Journal of Behavioral Medicine, 21* (6), 517–526.

Barlett, D. L., & Steele, J. B. (2004). *Howard Hughes: His life and madness*. New York: W. W. Norton.

Bassett. L. (1996). *From panic to power*. New York: HarperCollins.

Baumrind, D. (1996). The discipline controversy revisited. *Family Relations, 45* (4), 405–414.

Bean, W. B. (1968). *Sir William Osler, Aphorisms from his bedside teachings and writings*. Springfield, IL: Charles Thomas.

Beck, A. T. (1976). *Cognitive therapy and the emotional disorders*. New York: International Universities Press.

Beck, A. T., Weissman, A., Lester, D., & Trexler, L. (1974). The measurement of pessimism: The hopelessness scale. *Journal of Clinical and Counseling Psychology, 42*, 861–865.

Beck, J. (1995). *Cognitive therapy: Basics and beyond*. New York: Guilford.

Becker, E. (1973). *The denial of death*. New York: The Free Press.

Begley, S. (2001, May 7). Religion and the brain. *Newsweek, 137* (19), 50–57.

Begley, S., Underwood, C., & Carmichael, M. (2007, April 30). The anatomy of violence. *Newsweek, 149 (18)*, 40–43.

Belenky, M., Clinchy, B., Goldberger, N., & Tarule, J. (1997). *Women's ways of knowing: The development of self, voice, and mind.* New York: Basic Books.

Benson, H. (1985). *Beyond the relaxation response.* New York: Berkeley Books.

Berlinsky, E. B., & Biller, H. B. (1982). *Parental death and psychological development.* Lexington, MA: D.C. Heath and Company.

Berkman, L. E., & Syme, L. S. (1994). Social networks, host resistance, and mortality. In A. Steptoe & J. Wardle (Eds.), *Psychosocial processes and health* (pp. 43–67). New York: Cambridge University Press.

Besant, A. (2006). *Auguste Comte: His philosophy, his religion and his sociology.* Whitefish, MT: Kessinger.

Bethune, M. M. (1996). My last will and testament. In M. K. Assante & A. S. Abarry, *African intellectual heritage: A book of sources* (pp. 671–673). Philadelphia: Temple University Press.

Biller, H. B. (1971) *Father, child, and sex role: Paternal determinants of personality development.* Lexington, MA: Lexington Books.

Biller, H. B. (1974). *Paternal Deprivation: Family, school, sexuality and society.* Lexington, MA: Lexington Books.

Biller, H. B. (1993). *Fathers and families.* Westport, CT: Auburn House.

Biller, H. B. (2002). *Creative fitness.* Westport, CT: Auburn House.

Biller, H. B. & Meredith, D. L. (1974). *Father Power: The art of effective fathering and how it can bring joy and freedom to the whole family.* New York: David McKay.

Biller, H. B., & Solomon, R. (1986). *Child maltreatment and paternal deprivation: A manifesto for research, prevention, and treatment.* Lexington, MA: Lexington Books.

Biller, H. B., & Trotter, R. (1994). *The father factor: What you need to know to make a difference.* New York: Pocket Books (Simon & Schuster).

Bingham, M., & Stryker, S. (1995). *Things will be different for my daughter: A practical guide to building her self-esteem and self-reliance.* New York: Penguin Books.

Binswanger, L., Mendel, W. M., & Lyons, J. (1958). The case of Ellen West: An anthropological-clinical study. In R. May, E. Angel, & H. F. Ellenberger, *Existence: A new dimension in psychiatry and psychology* (pp. 237–364). New York: Basic Books.

Blair, S. N., Goodyear, N. N., Wynne, K. L., & Saunders, R. (1984). Comparison of dietary and smoking habit changes in physical fitness improvers and non-improvers. *Preventive Medicine*, 13(4), 411–420.

Bloch, E. (1970). *Man on his own: Essays in the philosophy of religion.* New York: Herder & Herder.

Bloch, E. (1986). *The principle of hope (Vol. 3).* Cambridge, MA: MIT Press.

Bluebond-Langner, M. (1978). *The private worlds of dying children.* Princeton, NJ: Princeton University Press.

Bodhi, B. (2005). *In the Buddha's words: An anthology of discourses from the Pali canon.* Somerville, MA: Wisdom Publications.

Bolletino, R., & Leshan, L. (1997). Cancer. In A. Watkins, *Mind-body medicine: A clinician's guide to psychoneuroimmunology* (pp. 87–112). New York: Church-Livingstone.

Booth, R. J., & Ashbridge, K. R. (1993). A fresh look at the relationship between the psyche and immune system: Teleological coherence and harmony of purpose. *Advances*, 9(2), 4–23.

Borg, M. J. (1995). *Meeting Jesus again for the first time.* New York: HarperCollins.

Bortnick, B. (2002, April 14). "Psychological autopsy" gives insight into Columbine killers. *Colorado Springs Gazette,* 1 (Metro).

Boswell, J. (1993). *The life of Samuel Johnson.* New York: Random House.

Boteach, S. (2006). *Parenting with fire.* New York: New American Library.

Boucher, S. (2000). *Hidden spring: A Buddhist woman confronts cancer.* Somerville, MA: Wisdom Publications.

Bovard, E. W. (1985). Brain mechanisms in effects of social support on viability. In R. B. Williams (Ed.), *Perspectives on behavioral medicine: Neuroendocrine control and behavior* (Vol. 2, pp. 103–129). Orlando, FL: Academic Press.

Bowes, D. E., Tamlyn, D., & Butler, L. J. (2002). Women living with ovarian cancer: Dealing with an early death. *Health Care for Women International, 23*(2), 135–148.

Bowlby, J. (1960). Grief and mourning in infancy and early childhood. *The Psychoanalytic Study of the Child, 15,* 9–52.

Bowlby, J. (1969). *Attachment and Loss. Vol. 1: Attachment.* New York: Basic Books.

Bowlby, J. (1980). *Attachment and Loss. Vol. 3: Loss, sadness and depression.* New York: Basic Books.

Branden, N. (2008). *The psychology of romantic love: Romantic love in an anti-romantic age.* New York: Tarcher.

Breathnach, S. (1995). *Simple abundance: A daybook of comfort and joy.* New York: Warner Books.

Brehm, S. S. (1988). Passionate love. In R. J. Sternberg & M. L. Barnes, *The psychology of love* (pp. 232–263). New Haven, CT: Yale University Press.

Breznitz, S. (1986). The effect of hope on coping with stress. In M. H. Appley & R. A. Trumbull. (Eds.), *Dynamics of stress: Physiological, psychological, and social perspectives* (pp. 295–307). New York: Plenum.

Brock, A. J. (1963). *Galen on the natural faculties.* Cambridge, MA: Harvard University Press.

Brodbeck, S., & Mascaro, J. (2003). *The Bhagavad-Gita.* New York: Penguin.

Brokaw, T. (2001). *The greatest generation.* New York: Random House.

Brooks, R., & Goldstein, S. (2002). *Raising resilient children: Fostering strength, hope, and optimism in your child.* New York: McGraw-Hill.

Browning, E. B. (2005). *The complete poetical works of Elizabeth Barrett Browning.* Whitefish, MT: Kessinger.

Bruner, J. S. (1975). The ontogenesis of speech acts. *Journal of Child Language, 2,* 1–40.

Brunstein-Klomek, A. B., Marrocco, F., Kleinman, M., Schonfeld, I. S., & Gould, M. S. (2007). Bullying, depression, and suicidality in adolescents. *Journal of the American Academy of Child and Adolescent Psychiatry, 46*(1), 40–49.

Brunstein-Klomek, A., Orbach, I., Meged, S., & Zalsman, G. (2005). Self complexity of suicidal adolescents. *International Journal of Adolescent Medicine and Health, 17*(3), 267–273.

Bryant, F. B. & Veroff, J. (2006). *Savoring: A new model of positive experience.* Philadelphia, PA: Taylor and Francis.

Buber, M. (1996). *I and thou.* New York: Touchstone Books.

Bucknell, R., & Kang, C. (1996). *The meditative way: Readings in the theory and practice of Buddhist meditation.* London: RoutledgeCurzon.

Bulfinch, T. (1998). *Bulfinch's mythology.* New York: Modern Library.

Bullaro, G. R. (2005). *Beyond "Life is Beautiful": Comedy and tragedy in the cinema of Roberto Benigni*. Leicester, UK: Troubador Publishing Ltd.

Burns, D. D. (1999). *Feeling good: The new mood therapy*. New York: Harper.

Buss, D. M. (1989). Sex differences in human mate preferences: Evolutionary hypotheses tested in 37 cultures. *Behavioral and Brain Sciences, 12*(1), 1–49.

Cahill, T. (1999). *The gift of the Jews*. New York: Random House.

Campbell, J. (1991). *The power of myth*. New York: Anchor Books.

Camus, A. (1958). *Exile and the kingdom*. New York: Knopf.

Camus, A. (1971). *The rebel: An essay on man in revolt*. New York: Vintage.

Camus, A. (1991). *The myth of Sisyphus and other essays*. Vancouver, WA: Vintage Books.

Capitanio, J. P., & Lerche, N. W. (1998). Social separation, housing relocation, and survival in simian AIDS: A retrospective analysis. *Psychosomatic Medicine, 60*, 235–244.

Carnegie, D. (1998). *How to win friends and influence people*. New York: Pocket Books.

Carr, D. J., Wooley, T. W., & Blalock, E. J. (1992). Phentolamine but not propranolol blocks the immunopotentiating effect of cold stress on antigen-specific IgM production in mice orally immunized with sheep red blood cells. *Brain, Behavior, and Immunity, 6*(1), 50–63.

Carson, R. (1964). *Silent spring*. New York: Fawcett Crest.

Carson, R. (1998). *Lost woods: The discovered writings of Rachel Carson*. Boston: Beacon Press.

Cascardi, A. J. (2002). *The Cambridge companion to Cervantes*. Cambridge, UK: Cambridge University Press.

Cassidy, J. (1986). The ability to negotiate the environment: An aspect of infant competence as related to quality of attachment. *Child Development, 57*(2), 331–337.

Chadwick, H. (1998). *St. Augustine confessions*. New York: Oxford University Press.

Charlifue S. W., & Gerhart, K. A. (1991). Behavioral and demographic predictors of suicide after traumatic spinal cord injury. *Archives of Physical Medicine and Rehabilitation, 72*(7), 488–492.

Cervantes, M. (2001). *Don Quixote*. New York: Penguin.

Checko, E. R., & Scioli, A., (2007, March). *Hope, self-determination, stages of change, and health*. Paper presented at the annual midwinter meeting of Division 36 of the American Psychological Association, Philadelphia, PA.

Chin, T. H. (1958). *Dream of the red chamber*. New York: Anchor Press.

Chopra, D. (2001). *How to know God*. New York: Random House.

Christensen, J., Vestergaard, M., Mortensen, P. B., Sidenius, P. & Agerbo, E. (2007). Epilepsy and risk of suicide: A population-based, case-control study. *Lancet Neurology, 6*(8), 693–698.

Christy, R. (1893). *Proverbs, maxims and phrases of all ages*. New York: Putnam.

Cicero, M. (2005). *Tusculan disputations: On the nature of the gods and the commonwealth*. New York: Cosimo Classics.

Claire, T. (2006). *Body work: What kind of massage to get and how to make the most of it*. Laguna Beach: CA: Basic Health Communications.

Cleary, T. (2004). *The Qur'an: A new translation*. Chicago: Starlatch.

Coan, J. A., Schaefer, H. S., & Davidson, R. J. (2006). Lending a hand: Social regulation of the neural response to threat. *Psychological Science, 17*(12), 1032–1039.

Cohen, K. (1999). *The way of qigong: The art and science of Chinese energy*. New York: Wellspring (Ballantine).

Cohen, K. (2006). *Honoring the medicine: The essential guide to Native American healing*. New York: Ballantine.

Coleman, G., Jinpa, T., and Dorie, G. (2007). *The Tibetan book of the dead*. New York: Penguin.

Coles, R. (1967). *Children of crisis: A study of courage and fear*. Boston: Little, Brown & Company.

Collison, D., Plant, K., & Wilkinson, R. (2000). *Fifty Eastern thinkers*. London: Routledge.

Comte, A. (2001). *Systems of positive polity*. Bristol, UK: Thoemmes Press.

Contrada, R. J., Cather, C., & O'Leary, A. O. (1999). Personality and health: Dispositions and processes in disease susceptibility and adaptation to illness. In L. Pervin & O. P. John (Eds.), *Handbook of Personality* (2nd ed., pp. 576–604). New York: Guilford.

Cook, J., Deger, S., & Gibson, L. A. (2007). *The book of positive quotations*. Minneapolis, MN: Fairview Press.

Copeland, M. E. (2000). *The loneliness workbook*. Oakland, CA: New Harbinger.

Cousins, N. (1989). *Head first: The biology of hope*. New York: E. Dutton.

Covey, S. (2004). *The seven habits of highly effective people*. New York: The Free Press.

Crider, T. (1996). *Give sorrow words: A father's passage through grief*. Chapel Hill, NC: Algonquin Books.

Csikszentmihalyi, M. (1991). *Flow: The psychology of optimal experience*. New York: Harper Perennial.

Cunningham, A. J., Philips, C., Lockwood, G. A., Hedley, D. W., & Edmonds, C. V. I. (2000). Association of involvement in psychological self-regulation with longer survival in patients with metastatic cancer: An exploratory study. *Advances in Mind-Body Medicine, 16*(4), 276–286.

Cunningham, A. J., & Watson, K. (2004). How psychological therapy may prolong survival in cancer patients: New evidence and a simple theory. *Integrative Cancer Therapies, 3*(3), 214–229.

Dalton, D. (1996). *Mahatma Gandhi: Selected political writings*. Indianapolis, IN: Hackett Publishing Co.

Daniels, C. (2004, November 15). The man who changed medicine. *Fortune Magazine, 50*, (11), 90–102.

Darwin, C. (2004). *The descent of man*. New York: Penguin.

Davidson, R. J., Pizzagalli, D., & Nitschke, J. B. (2002). The representation and regulation of emotion in depression: Perspectives from affective neuroscience. In I. H. Gotlib & C. L. Hammen, *Handbook of Depression* (pp. 219–244). New York: Guilford.

Davis, S., Jenkins, G., & Hunt, R. (2002). *The pact*. New York: Riverhead Books.

Davis, M., McKay, M., & Robbins-Eshelman, E. (2000). *The relaxation and stress reduction workbook*. Oakland, CA: New Harbinger.

De Becker, G. (1997). *The gift of fear*. New York: Dell.

De Bono, E. (1999). *Six thinking hats*. Boston: Back Bay Books.

DeLoache, J., Miller, K. F., & Pierroutsakos, S. L. (1998). Reasoning and problem solving. In W. Damon (Ed.), *Handbook of child psychology* (Vol. 2, pp. 801–850). Hoboken, NJ: Wiley.

Dembroski, T. M., & Williams, R. B. (1989). Definition and assessment of coronary-prone behavior. In N. Schneiderman, S. M. Weiss, & P. G. Kaufmann (Eds.), *Handbook of Research Methods in Cardiovascular Behavioral Medicine* (pp. 553–569). New York: Plenum.

Dennett, D. C. (1984). *Elbow room: The varieties of free will worth wanting*. Cambridge, MA: MIT Press.

Denson, E., Tattersall, I., van Couvering, J. A., & Brooks, A. (2000). *Encyclopedia of human evolution and prehistory*. New York: Garland.

de Saint-Exupery, A. (1995). *The little prince*. Ware, Hertfordshire (UK): Wordsworth Classics.

Descartes, R. (1989). *The passions of the soul*. Indianapolis, IN: Hackett Publishing Company.

Deutschmann, D. (2007). *Fidel Castro reader*. New York: Ocean Press.

Diamond, J. (1992). *The third chimpanzee: The evolution and the future of the human animal*. New York: Harper Collins.

Dickens, C. (2002). *Great expectations*. New York: Penguin.

Dickens, C. (2003). *A tale of two cities*. New York: Penguin.

Dickens, C. (2006). *David Copperfield*. New York: Penguin.

Dickinson, E. (1976). *The complete poems of Emily Dickinson*. Boston: Back Bay Books.

Dillard, A. (1990). *Three by Annie Dillard: The writing life, An American childhood, Pilgrim at Tinker Creek*. New York: Harper Perennial.

Dion, D. L., & Blalock, E. J. (1988). Neuroendocrine properties of the immune system. In P. T. Bridge, A. F. Mirsky, & F. K. Goodwin (Eds.), *Psychological, neuropsychiatric, and substance abuse aspects of AIDS* (pp. 15–19). New York: Raven Press.

Donald, M. (2003). *Origins of the modern mind*. Cambridge, MA: Harvard University Press.

Donne, J. (1999) *Devotions upon emergent occasions and deaths duel*. New York: Vintage.

Dossey, L. (1992). *Meaning and medicine*. New York: Bantam.

Dostoevksy, F. (2006). *Crime and punishment*. New York: Penguin.

Dostoevsky, F. (2008). *The Karamazov brothers*. New York: Oxford University Press.

Drake, J. (2001, October 4). This may be USA's Northern Ireland—or far worse. *USA Today*, A15.

Dryden, J. (1997). *Virgil's Aeneid*. London: Penguin.

Dufault, K., & Martocchio, B. (1985). Hope: Its spheres and dimensions. *Nursing Clinics of North America, 20*(2), 379–391.

Durant, W. (1961). *The story of philosophy*. New York: Simon and Schuster.

Durkheim, E. (2007). *On suicide*. New York: Penguin.

Edelman, M. (2004, May). Liberation of a blind survivor. *The Braille Monitor, 47*, 5.

Edelman, M. W. (1993). *The measure of our success*. New York: HarperPerennial.

Eisenberg, N., & Fabes, R. A. (1992). Emotion, regulation, and the development of social competence. In M. S. Clark (Ed.), *Review of personality and social psychology* (Vol. 14, pp. 119–150). Newbury Park, CA: Sage.

Eisenberg, N., Fabes, R. A., & Guthrie, I. (1997). Coping with stress: The roles of regulation and development. In S. Wolchik & I. Sandler (Eds.), *Children's coping: Links between theory and intervention* (pp. 41–70). New York: Plenum.

Eliot, T. S. (1968). *Four quartets*. Orlando, FL: Harcourt.

Elkind, D. (1997). The origins of religion in the child. In B. Spilka & D. N. McIntosh (Eds.), *The psychology of religion: Theoretical approaches* (pp. 97–104). Boulder, CO: Westview Press.

Emerson, R. W. (1910). *Journals of Ralph Waldo Emerson*. Boston, MA: Houghton-Miflin.

Emerson, R. W. (1981). *The portable Emerson*. New York: Penguin.

Emerson, R. W. (1983). *Essays and lectures*. New York: Library of America.

Emmons, R. A. (1999). *The psychology of ultimate concerns*. New York: Guilford.

Emmons, R. A., & King, L. A. (1988). Conflict among personal strivings: Immediate and long-term implications for psychological and physical well-being. *Journal of Personality and Social Psychology, 54*, 1040–1048.

Emmons, R. A., & McCullough, M. E. (2003). Counting blessings versus burdens: An experimental investigation of gratitude and subjective well-being on daily life. *Journal of Personality and Social Psychology, 84*(2), 377–389.

Erikson, E. H. (1950). *Childhood and society.* New York: Norton.

Erikson, E. H. (1964). *Insight and responsibility.* New York: Norton.

Erikson, E. H. (1980). *Identity and the life cycle.* New York: Norton.

Erikson, E. H. (1993). *Gandhi's truth: On the origins of militant nonviolence.* New York: Norton.

Erikson. E. H., Erikson, J. M., & Kivnick, H. Q. (1994). *Vital involvement in old age.* New York: Norton.

Erickson, R. C., Post, R. D., & Paige, A. B. (1975). Hope as a psychiatric variable. *Journal of Clinical Psychology, 31,* 324–330.

Farber, S. K. (2003). Ecstatic stigmatics and holy anorexics: Medieval and contemporary. *Journal of Psychohistory, 31*(2), 182–204.

Farran, C. J., Wilken, C., & Popovich, J. M. (1992). Clinical assessment of hope. *Issues in Mental Health Nursing, 13,* 129–138.

Fassler, D. G., & Dumas, L. S. (1998). *Help me, I'm sad.* New York: Penguin.

Fatunmbi, A. F. (1994). *Ibase orisa: Ifa proverbs, folktales, sacred history, and prayer.* New York: Original Publications.

Faulkner, R. (2000). *The Egyptian book of the dead: The book of going forth by day.* San Francisco: Chronicle Books.

Feldman, D. B., Lasher, S. A., & Byock, I. (2008). *The end-of-life handbook: A compassionate guide to connecting with and caring for a dying loved one.* Oakland, CA: New Harbinger.

Fenton, W. N. (1987). *The false faces of the Iroquois.* Norman, OK: University of Oklahoma Press.

Ferguson, T. (1993). Working with your doctor. In Goleman, D. & Gurin, J. (Eds.), *Mind/body medicine* (pp. 429–450). New York: Consumer Reports.

Feuerbach, L. (2004). *The essence of religion.* Amherst, NY: Prometheus Books.

Fischer, C. S. (1982). *To dwell among friends: Personal networks in town and city.* Chicago: University of Chicago Press.

Fitzgerald, F. S. (2007). *The great Gatsby.* New York: Penguin.

Foley, J. (2002). *Korea's divided families: Fifty years of separation.* New York: Routledge Curzon.

Fourier, C. (2007). *The passions of the human soul.* Whitefish, MT: Kessinger.

Fowler, J. (1981). *Stages of faith.* San Francisco: Harper Collins.

Fowler, J. (1996). Pluralism and oneness in religious experience: William James, faith development theory, and clinical practice. In E. Shafranske (Ed.), *Religion and the clinical practice of psychology* (Vol. 1, pp. 165–186). Washington, DC: American Psychological Association.

Frank, J. (1968). The role of hope in psychotherapy. *International Journal of Psychiatry, 5,* 383–395.

Frankl, V. (1985). *Man's search for meaning.* New York: Washington Square Press.

Franklin, B. (2000). *Poor Richard's almanac.* Chestnut Hill, MA: Adamant Media Corporation.

Freud, A., & Burlingham, D. T. (1943). *War and children.* New York: International Universities Press.

Freud, S. (1957). *The future of an illusion.* New York: Doubleday.

Freud, S. (1989). *An outline of psycho-analysis.* New York: Norton.

Freud, S. (1990). *Beyond the pleasure principle.* New York: Norton.

Freud, S. (2008). *The interpretation of dreams.* New York: Oxford University Press.

Fromm, E. (1941). *Escape from freedom.* New York: Rinehart and Co.

Fromm, E. (1970). *The revolution of hope.* New York: Harper and Row.

Fromm, E. (2000). *The art of loving.* New York: Harper Perennial.

Fry, S. (1984). Development of a geriatric scale of hopelessness: Implications for counseling and interventions with the depressed elderly. *Journal of Counseling Psychology, 31*(3), 322–331.

Fujimura, C. K., Stoecker, S. W., & Sudakova, T. (2005). *Russia's abandoned children: An intimate understanding.* Westport, CT: Praeger.

Fulghum, R. (2004). *All I really need to know I learned in kindergarten.* New York: Ballantine.

Fuller, R. C. (1996). Erikson, psychology, and religion. *Pastoral Psychology, 44* (6), 371–384.

Garber, J., & Horowitz, J. L. (2002). Depression in children. In I. H. Gotlib & C. L. Hammen, *Handbook of Depression* (pp. 510–540). New York: Guilford.

Garfield, P. *The universal dream key: The 12 most common dream themes around the world.* New York: Harper One.

Garrett, D. (1995). *The Cambridge companion to Spinoza.* Cambridge, UK: Cambridge University Press.

Gates, H. L., & West, C. (2002). *The African-American century: How black Americans have shaped our country.* New York: The Free Press.

Gershon, M., & Biller, H. (1977). *The other helpers: Paraprofessionals and nonprofessionals in mental health.* Lexington, MA: Lexington Books.

Giamatti, A. B. (1998). *A great and glorious game. The writings of A. Bart Giamatti.* Chapel Hill, NC: Algonquin Books.

Gibran, K. (1970). *Sand and foam.* New York: Knopf.

Gibran, K. (1983). *The prophet.* New York: Knopf.

Gibson, W. (2002). *The miracle worker.* New York: Pocket Books.

Gilligan, C. (1993). *In a different voice. Psychological theory and women's development.* Cambridge, MA: Harvard University Press.

Glassner, B. (2000). *The culture of fear.* New York: Basic Books.

Glover, J. (2000). *Humanity: A moral history of the twentieth century.* New Haven, CT: Yale University Press.

Godfrey, J. J. (1987). *A philosophy of human hope.* Dordrecht: Martinus Nijhoff.

Goleman, D. (2005). *Emotional intelligence.* New York: Bantam.

Goldstein, S., & Brooks, R. B. (2006). *Handbook of resiliency in children.* New York: Springer.

Goodall, J., & Berman, P. (2000). *Reason for hope.* New York: Grand Central Publishing.

Goodwin, P. J., Leszcz, M., Ennis, M., Koopmans, J., Vincent, L., Guther, H., Drysdale, E., Hundleby, M., Chochinov, H. M., Navarro, M., Speca, M., Masterson, J., Dohan, L., Sela, R., Warren, B., Paterson, A., Pritchard, K. I., Arnold, A., Doll, R., O'Reilly, S. E., Quirt, G., Hood, N., & Hunter, J. (2001). The effect of group psychosocial support on survival in metastatic breast cancer. *New England Journal of Medicine, 345*(24), 1719–1726.

Gordon, L., Gordon, C. (Producers), & Robinson, P. A. (Writer/Director). (1989). *Field of dreams.* [Motion picture]. United States: The Gordon Company.

Gorer, G. (1955, October). The pornography of death. *Encounter*, pp. 49–52.

Gottman, J. M. (1999). *The seven principles for making marriage work.* New York: Three Rivers Press.

Gottman, J. M. (2001). *The relationship cure.* New York: Three Rivers Press.

Gottschalk, L. A. (1974). A hope scale applicable to verbal samples. *Archives of General Psychiatry, 30,* 779–785.

Gottschalk, L. A. (1985). Hope and other deterrents to illness. *American Journal of Psychotherapy, 39*(4), 515–525.

Gotz, I. (1998). On inspiration. *Crossroads, 48*(4), 510–517.

Gould, S. J. (1982, June). The median isn't the message. *Discover,* 40–42.

Gray, J. (2004). *Men are from Mars, women are from Venus.* New York: Harper Paperbacks.

Greeley, A. (1981). *The religious imagination.* New York: Sadlier.

Greenberg, J., Solomon, S., & Pyszczynski, T. (1997). Terror management theory and self esteem and cultural worldviews. In M. Zanna (Ed.), *Advances in experimental social psychology* (pp. 61–139). San Diego, CA: Academic Press.

Greene, D. B. (1994). Childhood suicide and myths surrounding it. *Social Work, 39*(2), 230–232.

Greene, R. (2000). *The 48 laws of power.* New York: Penguin.

Greer, S. (1999). Mind-body research in psycho-oncology. *Advances in Mind-Body Medicine, 15*(4), 236–244.

Griffith, G. (2005). *Will's choice.* New York: Harper Collins.

Groopman, J. (2001). *Second opinions.* New York: Penguin.

Guess, J. B. (2002). *Our God on the gallows: Voices from the holocaust.* Cleveland, OH: Justice and Witness Missionaries.

Gunther, J. (1997). *Death be not proud.* Cutchogue, NY: Buccaneer Books.

Hadas, M. (1982). *The complete plays of Sophocles.* New York: Bantam Classics.

Hafen, B. Q., Karren, K. J., Frandsen, K. J., & Smith, N. L. (1996). *Mind-body health.* Boston: Allyn & Bacon.

Halberstam, D. (2005). *The education of a coach.* New York: Hyperion.

Haley, A. (2007). *Roots: The saga of an American family.* New York: Vanguard Press.

Hall, C. S., & Van De Castle, R. L. (1966). *The content analysis of dreams.* New York: Appleton-Century-Crofts.

Hall, G. S. (1897). A study of fears. *American Journal of Psychology, 8*(2), 147–249.

Hall, L. (1997). Faith. In J. Canfield, M.V. Hansen, P. Aubery & N. Mitchell (Eds.). *Chicken Soup for the Christian Soul* (pp. 198–199). Deerfield Beach, FL: HCI.

Hamilton, M. B. (1998). *Sociology and the world's religions.* New York: St. Martin's Press.

Haney, D. Q. (2002, September 12). Reeve's recovery unprecedented, doctors say: Intensive physical therapy key to actor's progress. *National Post* (Canada), PM10.

Hanh, N. T. (2002). *Looking deeply: Mindfulness and meditation.* Berkeley, CA: Parallax Press. [Audio CD].

Hansson, R. O., & Stroebe, M. S. (2007). The dual process model of coping with bereavement and development of an integrative risk factor framework. In R. O. Hansson & M. S. Stroebe (Eds.), *Bereavement in late life: Coping, adaptation, and developmental influences* (pp. 41–60). Washington, DC: American Psychological Association.

Harlow, H. F. (1958). The nature of love. *American Psychologist, 13*(12), 673–685.

Harris, J. R. (1998). *The nurture assumption: Why children turn out the way they do.* New York: The Free Press.

Harris, P. (1999). *Black rage confronts the law.* New York: New York University Press.

Hart, T. (2000). Inspiration as transpersonal knowing. In T. Hart, P. L. Nelson, & K. Puhakka (Eds.), *Transpersonal knowing: Exploring the horizon of consciousness* (pp. 31–53). Albany, NY: State University of New York Press.

Hartmann, F. (1902). *The life and doctrines of Paracelsus.* New York: The Theosophical Publishing Co.

Havel, V. (1995). The need for transcendence in the post-modern world. *The Journal for Quality and Participation, 18*(5), 26–29.

Havel, V. (2004). An orientation of the heart. In P. R. Loeb (Ed.), *The impossible will take a little while* (pp. 82-89). New York: Basic Books.

Havens, L. (1986). *Making Contact: Uses of language in psychotherapy.* Cambridge, MA: Harvard University Press.

Hegel, G. W. F. (1979). *Phenomenology of the spirit.* New York: Oxford University Press.

Heinlein, R. (1991). *Stranger in a strange land.* New York: Ace/Putnam.

Heinrich, B. (2003). *Winter world. The ingenuity of animal survival.* New York: Harper Perennial.

Helminski, K. (1998). *The Rumi collection.* Boston: Shambhala Publications.

Hemingway, E. (1995). *A farewell to arms.* New York: Scribner's.

Hendrix, H. (1993). *Keeping the love you find.* New York: Pocket Books.

Herman, J. L. (1997). *Trauma and recovery.* New York: Basic Books.

Herrigel, E. (1999). *Zen in the art of archery.* New York: Vintage.

Herth, K. (1991). Development and refinement of an instrument to measure hope. *Scholarly Inquiry for Nursing Practice, 5*(1), 39–51.

Hesse, H. (1977). *Steppenwolf.* New York: Bantam.

Higgins, G. O. (1994). *Resilient adults.* San Francisco: Jossey-Bass.

Hijiya, J. (2002, August 2). No one talks about Ted William's atheism. *The New Bedford Standard Times,* A10.

Hill, N. (2004). *Think and grow rich.* San Diego, California: Aventine.

Hillman, J. (1997). *The soul's code: In search of character and calling.* New York: Grand Central Publishing.

Hinds, S., & Gattuso, J. S. (1991). Measuring hopefulness in adolescents. *Journal of Pediatric Oncology, 8*(2), 92–94.

Hollinger, D. (2005). *Head, heart, & hands.* Downers Grove, IL: InterVarsity Press.

Holmes, L. (1967). *More than a game.* New York: MacMillan.

Homes, H. A. (2003). *Alchemy of happiness.* Whitefish, MT: Kessinger.

Hooker, R. (1995). Building unbreakable units. *Military Review, 75*(4), 23–25.

Horner, M. (1972). Toward an understanding of achievement-related conflicts in women. *Journal of Social Issues, 28*(2), 92–95.

Hume, D. (1998). *Dialogues concerning natural religion.* Indianapolis, IN: Hackett Publishing Company.

Hume, R. E. (1921). *The thirteen principal Upanishads: Translated from the Sanskrit with an outline of the philosophy of the Upanishads and an annotated bibliography.* London: Oxford University Press.

Humez, J. M. (2003). *Harriet Tubman: The life and the life stories.* Madison, WI: University of Wisconsin Press.

Hutschnecker, A. A. (1981). *Hope: The dynamics of self-fulfillment.* New York: Putnam.

Jackson. P. (1996). *Sacred hoops: Spiritual lessons of a hardwood warrior.* New York: Hyperion.

Jacobus, L. A. (1983). *A world of ideas.* New York: St. Martin's Press.

James, W. (1890). *Principles of psychology.* New York: Henry Holt.

James, W. (1961). *The varieties of religious experience.* New York: Collier Books.

James, W. (1988). *William James: Writings 1902–1910.* New York: Library of America.

James, W. (2007). *What is an emotion?* Radford, VA: Wilder Publications.

Jaques, E. (1965). Death and the mid-life crisis. *International Journal of Psycho-Analysis, 46*(4), 502–514.

Jarovsky, B. (1996). *Hoop dreams: The true story of hardship and triumph.* New York: Harper.

Jaspers, K. (1957). *The great philosophers, volume I.* Munich, Germany: R. Piper and Co. Verlag.

Jaynes, J. (2000). *The origin of consciousness in the breakdown of the bicameral mind.* New York: Mariner Books.

Joiner, T. E. (2002). Depression in its interpersonal context. In I. H. Gotlib & C. L. Hammen, *Handbook of Depression* (pp. 295–313). New York: Guilford.

Jones, S. L. (1994). A constructive relationship for religion with the science and profession of psychology. *American Psychologist, 49*(3), 184–199.

Jong, E. (1973). The artist as housewife: The housewife as artist. In F. Klagsbrun (Ed.), *The first Ms. reader* (pp. 111–122). New York: Warner.

Joseph, L. (1999). *Little girl lost.* New York: Random House.

Jowett, B. (1999). *The essential Plato.* New York: Quality Paperback Book Company.

Judson, K. B. (2006). *Myths and legends of California and the old southwest.* Lenox, MA: Hard Press.

Jung, C. G. (1968). *Man and his symbols.* New York: Dell.

Jung, C. G., & Kerényi, K. (2005). *Science of mythology: Essays on the myth of the divine child and the mysteries of Eleusis.* London: Routledge.

Kabat-Zinn, J. (1990). *Full catastrophe living: Using the wisdom of your body and mind to face stress, pain, and illness.* New York: Dell Publishers.

Kagan, J. (1994). *The nature of the child.* New York: Basic Books.

Kaiser, D. H. (1996). Indications of attachment security in a drawing task. *The Arts in Psychotherapy, 23*(4), 333–340.

Kaiser-Stearns, A. (1989). *Coming back.* New York: Ballantine.

Kanner, L. (1957). *Child psychiatry.* Springfield, IL: Charles. C. Thomas.

Kant, I. (1957). *Perpetual Peace.* Upper Saddle River, NJ: Bobbs-Merrill.

Kant, I. (1960). *Religion within the limits of reason alone.* New York: Harper and Row.

Kant, I. (2001). *Lectures on ethics.* Cambridge, UK: Cambridge University Press.

Kaplan, M. (1994). *The meaning of God in modern Jewish tradition.* Detroit, MI: Wayne State University Press.

Kaplan, D. M., Grobstein, R., & Smith, A. Predicting the impact of severe illness in families: A study of the variety of responses to fatal illness. *Health and Social Work, I,* 71–82.

Karen, R. (1998). *Becoming attached: First relationships and how they shape our capacity to love.* New York: Oxford University Press.

Keating, T. (2006). *Open mind open heart: The contemplative dimension of the gospel.* New York: Continuum International Publishing Group.

Kegan, R. (1982). *The evolving self.* Cambridge, MA: Harvard University Press.

Kiecolt-Glaser, J. K., & Glaser, R. (1993). Mind and immunity. In D. Goleman & J. Gurin, (Eds.), *Mind/body medicine* (pp. 39–59). New York: Consumer Reports.

Kiecolt-Glaser, J. K., Malarkey, W. B., & Chee, M. A. (1993) Negative behavior during marital conflict is associated with immunological down-regulation. *Psychosomatic Medicine, 55*(5), 395–409.

Kiecolt-Glaser, J. K., McGuire, L., Robles, T., & Glaser, R. (2002). Psychoneuroimmunology and psychosomatic medicine: Back to the future. *Psychosomatic Medicine, 64,* 15–28.

Kirkpatrick, L. A. (1999). Attachment and religious representations and behavior. In J. Cassidy & R. Shaver (Eds.), *Handbook of attachment* (pp. 803–822). New York: Guilford.

Kirkpatrick, L. A., & Shaver, R. (1992). An attachment-theoretical approach to romantic love and religious belief. *Personality and Social Psychology Bulletin, 18*(3), 266–275.

Kirschebaum, M. (1997). *Too good to leave, too bad to stay.* New York: Plume.

Kiser, L. J., Bennett, L., Heston, J., & Paavola, M. (2005). Family rituals and routine: Comparison of clinical and non-clinical families. *Journal of Child and Family Studies, 14*(3), 357–372.

Klass, D. (1999). *Spiritual lives of bereaved parents.* Philadelphia: Brunner/Mazel.

Klinger, E. (1977). *Meaning and void: Inner experience and the incentives in people's lives.* Minneapolis, MN: University of Minnesota Press.

Kluckhohn, F., & Strodtbeck, F. (1961). *Variations in value orientations.* Evanston, IL: Row, Peterson, & Co.

Kneier, A. W., & Temoshok, L. (1984). Repressive coping reactions in patients with malignant melanoma as compared to cardiovascular disease patients. *Journal of Psychosomatic Research, 28*(2), 145–155.

Kobasa, S. C. (1979). Stressful life events, personality, and health: An inquiry into hardiness. *Journal of Personality and Social Psychology, 37*(1), 1–11.

Koenig, H. G. (2001). *The healing power of faith.* New York: Simon & Schuster.

Koenig, H. G., & Cohen, H. J. (Eds.). (2001). *The link between religion and health: Psychoneuroimmunology and the faith factor.* New York: Oxford University Press.

Kohut, H. (1971). *The analysis of the self.* New York: International Universities Press.

Korner, I. (1970). Hope as a method of coping. *Journal of Consulting and Clinical Psychology, 34*(2), 134–139.

Kovic, R. (1990). *Born on the fourth of July.* New York: Pocket Books.

Kraemer, H. C., Kuchler, T., & Spiegel, D. (2009). Use and misuse of the consolidated standards of reporting trials (CONSORT) guidelines to assess research findings: Comment on Coyne, Stefanek, and Palmer. *Psychological Bulletin, 135* (2), 173–178.

Kushner, H. S. (2002). *Living a life that matters.* New York: Anchor Press.

LaBarba, R. C. (1970). Experiential and environmental factors in cancer. *Psychosomatic Medicine, 32*(3), 259–276.

Laertius, D. (2007). *The lives and opinions of eminent philosophers.* Whitefish, MT: Kessinger Publishing.

Lamott, A. (1995). *Bird by bird: Some instructions on writing and life.* New York: Anchor Press.

Langer, E., & Rodin, J. (1976). The effects of choice and enhanced personal responsibility for the aged: A field experiment in an institutional setting. *Journal of Personality and Social Psychology, 34*(2), 191–198.

Larson, R. W. & Bradney, N. (1988). Precious moments with family members and friends. In R. M. Milardo (Ed.), *Families and social networks* (pp. 107–126). Thousand Oaks, CA: Sage Publications.

Leadbeater, C. W. (2003). *Chakras: A monograph.* Kila, MT: Kessinger.

Leahy, R. L. (1988). Cognitive therapy of childhood depression: Developmental considerations. In S. R. Shirk (Ed.), *Cognitive development and child psychotherapy* (pp. 187–204). New York: Plenum Press.

Lebell, S. (1994). *Epictetus: A manual for living.* New York: Harper Collins.

Lefcourt, H. M. (1980). Locus of control and coping in life's events. In E. Staub (Ed.), *Personality: Basic aspects and current research* (pp. 220–236). Englewood Cliffs, NJ: Prentice-Hall.

Lennon, J. & McCartney, P. (1965). *In my life.* On Rubber Soul [Album]. London: EMI.

Levine, M. (2002). *One mind at a time.* New York: Simon & Schuster.

Levinson, D. (1986). *The seasons of a man's life.* New York: Ballantine.

Levy, J. E. (1998). *In the beginning: The Navajo genesis.* Berkeley, CA: University of California Press.

Lewis, T., Amini, F., & Lannon, R. (2001). *A general theory of love.* New York: Vintage.

Lifton, R. J. (1991). *Death in life: Survivors of Hiroshima.* Chapel Hill, NC: University of North Carolina Press.

Lifton, R. J. (1996). *The broken connection: On death and the continuity of life.* Arlington, VA: American Psychiatric Publishing.

Linehan, M. (1993). *Cognitive-Behavioral Treatment of Borderline Personality Disorder.* New York: Guilford Press.

Link, M. S. (1998). *The pollen path: A collection of Navajo myths.* Walnut, CA: Kiva Publishing.

Lloyd, G. E. R. (1984). *Hippocratic writings.* New York: Penguin.

Locke, J. (1958). *The reasonableness of Christianity.* Palo Alto, CA: Stanford University Press.

Lorenz, K. (1935). The companion in the bird's world: The fellow-member of the species as releasing factor of social behavior. *Journal of Ornithology, 83,* 137–213.

Louv, R. (2005). *Last child in the woods.* Chapel Hill, NC: Algonquin Books.

Lukacs, J. (2002, August 20). To hell and back. *USA Today,* C1.

Lum, T. Y., & Lightfoot, E. (2005). The effects of volunteering on the physical and mental health of older people. *Research on Aging, 27* (1), 31–55.

Lutz, C. & White, G. W. (1986). The anthropology of emotions. *Annual Review of Anthropology, 15,* 405–436.

Lynch, W. F. (1965). *Images of hope: Imagination as healer of the hopeless.* Baltimore, MD: Helicon Press.

Mackenna, S. (2004). *Plotinus: The Enneads.* Burdette, NY: Larson Publications.

MacMullin, J. (2002, February 5). Grief channeled to higher goals. *The Boston Globe,* G5.

Maddi, S. (2004). Hardiness: An operationalization of existential courage. *Journal of Humanistic Psychology, 44*(3), 279–298.

Marcel, G. (1962). *Homo viator: Introduction to a metaphysic of hope.* New York: Harper and Row.

Martel, L., & Biller, H. B. (1987). *Stature and stigma.* Lexington, MA: Lexington Books.

Maslow, A. (1970). *Religions, values, and peak experiences.* New York: Penguin.

Masters, K. S., Hill, R. D., & Kircher, J. C. (2004). Religious orientation, aging, and blood pressure reactivity to interpersonal and cognitive stressors. *Annals of Behavioral Medicine, 28*(3), 171–178.

Matovina, T. (2005). *Guadalupe and her faithful: Latino Catholics in San Antonio, from colonial origins to the present.* Baltimore, MD: Johns Hopkins University Press.

Matt, D. C. (1996). *The essential Kabbalah: The heart of Jewish mysticism*. New York: Harper One.

May, R. (1950). *The meaning of anxiety*. New York: The Ronald Press.

May, R. (1999). *Freedom and destiny*. New York: Norton.

May, R. (2007). *Love and will*. New York: Norton.

McCain, J., & Salter, M. (2008). *Why courage matters: The way to a braver life*. New York: Ballantine Books.

McCasland, D. (2004). *Eric Liddell: Pure gold*. Grand Rapids, MI: Discovery House Publishers.

McClelland, D. C. (1961). *The achieving society*. New York: Macmillan.

McClelland, D. C. (1986). Some reflections on the two psychologies of love. *Journal of Personality*, *2*, 334–353.

McClelland, D. C. (1989). Motivational factors in health and disease. *American Psychologist*, *44*(4), 675–683.

McClelland, D. C., & Krishnit, C. (1988). The effects of motivational arousal through films on salivary immunoglobulin A. *Psychology and Health*, *2*(1), 31–52.

McCluskey, A. T., & Smith, E. M. (2002). *Mary McCleod Bethune: Building a better world, selected essays and documents*. Bloomington, IN: University of Indiana Press.

McCrae, R. R., & Costa, P. T. (1985). Updating Norman's "adequacy taxonomy": Intelligence and personality dimensions in natural language and in questionnaires. *Journal of Personality and Social Psychology*, *49*(3), 710–721.

McDermott, T. (1989). *Summa theologiae: A concise translation*. Allen, TX: Christian Classics.

McDougall, W. (1936). *Psycho-analysis and social psychology*. London: Methuen & Co.

McDowell, J. C. (2006). Karl Barth, Emil Brunner and the subjectivity of the object of Christian hope. *International Journal of Systematic Theology*, *8*(1), 25–41.

McEwen, B. S. (1999). Protective and damaging effects of stress mediators. In I. Kawachi, B. Kennedy, & R. G. Wilkinson (Eds.), *The society and population health reader* (pp. 379–392). New York: The New Press.

McFarlane, S. (1997). *Complete book of Tai Chi*. New York: Dorling Kindersley.

McKeon, R. (1941). *The basic works of Aristotle*. New York: Random House.

McManus, J. (1989, May 29). Czechoslovakia: A historic encounter. *Time*, *133* (22), 48.

McPherson, R. S. (2001). *Navajo land, Navajo culture: The Utah experience in the twentieth century*. Norman, OK: University of Oklahoma Press.

Mead, M. (1977). Fanaticism: The panhuman disorder. *Etc.*, *34*(1), 35–38.

Medical World News. (1984, June 11). Studies show hope can play a role in a patient's risk, illness, and death, 11, 101–102.

Meissner, W. W. (1984). *Psychoanalysis and religious experience*. New Haven, CT: Yale University Press.

Mellor, C. M. (2006). *Louis Braille: A touch of genius*. Boston: National Braille Press.

Mencken, H. L. (1922). *Prejudices: Third series*. New York: Knopf.

Mencken, H. L. (2006). *The philosophy of Friedrich Nietzsche*. Whitefish, MT: Kessinger.

Menninger, K. (1959). Hope. *Bulletin of the Menninger Clinic*, *51*(5), 447–462.

Meriwether, J. (2004). *William Faulkner: Essays, speeches and public lectures*. New York: Random House.

Merton, T. (2006). *An invitation to the contemplative life*. Ijamsville, MD: The Word among Us Press.

Metcalf, L. (2007). *The miracle question: Answer it and change your life*. Carmarthen, Wales: Crown House Publishing.

Mikulincer, M., Florian, V., & Hirschberger, G. (2004). The terror of death and the quest for love: An existential perspective on close relationships. In J. Greenberg, S. L. Koole, & T. Pyszczynski (Eds.) *Handbook of Experimental Existential Psychology* (pp. 287–304). New York: Guilford Press.

Miller, A. (1996). *Drama of the gifted child: The search for the true self*. New York: Basic books.

Miller, A. (1998). The political consequences of child abuse. *Journal of Psychohistory*, 26(2), 573–585.

Miller, A. A. (1996). *Death of a salesman*. New York: Viking.

Miller, J. F., & Powers, M. J. (1988). Development of an instrument to measure hope. *Nursing Research*, 37(1), 6–10.

Milton, J. (2003). *Paradise lost*. New York: Penguin.

Mishra, R. (2002, September). Trials continue in a different form. *The Boston Globe*, A1.

Moberg, K .U. (2003). The oxytocin factor: Tapping the hormone of calm, love, and healing. Cambridge, MA: Da Capo.

Moberg, K. U., Arn, I., & Magnusson, D. (2005). The psychobiology of emotion: The role of the oxytocinergic system. *International Journal of Behavioral Medicine*, 25(2), 59–65.

Moffat, M. J. (1992). *In the midst of winter*. New York: Vintage.

Moltmann, J. (1993). *Theology of hope*. Minneapolis, MN: Augsberg Press.

Money, J. (1988). *Lovemaps*. New York: Irvington.

Monte, C., & Sollod, R. (2003). *Beneath the mask: An introduction to theories of personality*. New York: Wiley.

Montville, L. (2005). *Ted Williams: The biography of an American hero*. New York: Broadway Books.

Moore, T. (1992). *Care of the soul*. New York: Harper Collins.

Morris, D. (1977). *Manwatching: A field guide to human behavior*. New York: Abrams.

Mowrer, O. H. (1960). *Learning theory and behavior*. New York: Wiley and Sons.

Murray, H. (1938). *Explorations in personality*. New York: Oxford University Press.

Myers, D. G. (1993). *The pursuit of happiness*. New York: Harper.

Nietzsche, F. (1996). *Human, all too human: A book for free spirits*. Cambridge, UK: Cambridge University Press.

Nietzsche, F. (2006). *Thus spoke Zarathustra*. Cambridge, UK: Cambridge University Press.

Newberg, A. (2002). *Why god won't go away*. New York: Ballantine Books.

Noppe, I. C., & Noppe, L. D. (1997). Evolving meanings of death during early, middle, and later adolescence. *Death Studies*, 21(3), 253–275.

Novitskaya, L. (1984). The effects of various music styles on psychic state. *Psikologicheskii Zhurnal*, 5(6), 79–85.

Nowotny, M. (1989). Assessment of hope in patients with cancer: Development of an instrument. *Oncology Nursing Forum*, 16(1), 57–61.

Obama, B. (1995). *Dreams from my father: A story of race and inheritance*. New York: Times Books.

Obama, B. (2006). *The audacity of hope: Thoughts on reclaiming the American dream*. New York: Crown Publishing Group.

O'Brien, E. (1975). *The essential Plotinus: Representative treatises from the Enneads*. Indianapolis, IN: Hackett Publishing.

Obuyuwana, A., & Carter, A. L. (1982). The anatomy of hope. *Journal of the National Medical Association, 74*(3), 229–234.

Odell, C. M. (2007). *Solanus Casey: The life of father Solanus.* Huntington, IN: Our Sunday Visitor Publisher.

Oden, M. B. (1995). *One hundred meditations on hope.* Nashville, TN: Upper Room Books.

O' Hahn, C. (2001). Be the change you wish to see: An interview with Arun Gandhi. *Reclaiming Children and Youth, 10(1),* 6.

O' Hanlon, B. (2000). *Do one thing different.* New York: Harper.

O' Lill, R. (1994). *A consumer's guide to hope.* Virginia Beach, VA: A.R.E. Press.

Olson, J. M., Vernon, A., Harris, J. A., & Jang, K. (2001). The heritability of attitudes: A study of twins. *Journal of Personality and Social Psychology, 80*(6), 845–860.

Orbach, I. (1988). *Children who don't want to live: Understanding and treating the suicidal child.* San Francisco: Jossey-Bass.

Ordoubadian, R. (2006). *The poems of Hafiz.* Bethesda, MD: IBEX.

O' Regan, B. (1986). Healing: Synergies of mind, body, spirit. *Institute of Noetic Sciences Newsletter, 14*(1), 9.

Ornstein, R. (1992). *Evolution of consciousness: The origins of the way we think.* New York: Simon and Schuster.

Orwell, G. (1961). *The Orwell reader.* Orlando, FL: Harcourt-Brace & Co.

Pan, F., Lu, C. Y., & Song, J. (2006). Different duration of crowding and noise exposure effects on exploratory behavior, cellular immunity and HSP70 expression in rats. *Stress and Health: Journal of the International Society for the Investigation of Stress, 22*(4), 257–262.

Painton, M. (2007). *Encouraging your child's spiritual intelligence.* New York: Atria Books.

Palmer, S. B., & Wehmeyer, M. L. (1998). Students' expectations of the future: Hopelessness as a barrier to self-determination. *Mental Retardation, 36*(2), 128–136.

Pardee, M. B. (1979). The friendship bond. *Psychology Today, 13*(4), 43–54.

Pargament, K. I. (2001). *The psychology of religion and coping: Theory, research, and practice.* New York: Guilford Press.

Pascal, B. (1995). *Penses.* New York: Penguin.

Peale, N. V. (2007). *The power of positive thinking.* New York: Fireside Press.

Pearce, M. J., Little, T. D., & Perez, J. E. (2003). Religiousness and depressive symptoms among adolescents. *Journal of Clinical Child and Adolescent Psychology, 32*(2), 267–276.

Pelletier, K. R. (1993). Between mind and body: Stress, emotions, and health. In D. Goleman & J. Gurin (Eds.), *Mind/body medicine* (pp. 19–38). Yonkers, NY: Consumer Reports Books.

Pennebaker, J. W. (1990). *Opening up: The healing power of confiding in others.* New York: Avon Books.

Perkins, D. N. (1981). *The mind's best work: A new psychology of creative thinking.* Cambridge, MA: Harvard University Press.

Perry, R. J. (1991). *Western Apache heritage.* Austin, TX: University of Texas Press.

Pert, C. (1999). *Molecules of emotion: The science behind mind-body medicine.* New York: Simon & Schuster.

Philips, D. P., Ruth, T. E., & Wagner, L. M. (1993). Psychology and survival. *Lancet, 342,* 1142–1145.

Pinsky, R. (1997). *The inferno of Dante.* New York: Farrar, Straus & Giroux.

Plutchik, R. (1962). *The emotions: Facts, theories and a new model.* New York: Random House.

Poe, E. A. (1984). *Complete stories and poems of Edgar Allan Poe*. New York: Doubleday.

Pogrebin, L. C. (1988). *Among friends: Who we like, why we like them, and what we do with them*. New York: McGraw-Hill.

Pooley, E., Cloud, J., Gwynne, S.C., Harrington, M., Shapiro, J., Rivera, E. & Woodbury, R. (1999, May 5). Portrait of a deadly bond. *Time, 153 (18)*, 22–28.

Pope John Paul II (1994). *Crossing the threshold of hope*. New York: Alfred A. Knopf.

Popp, N. (1996). Dimensions of psychological boundary development in adults. In M. L. Commons, J. Demick, & C. Goldberg (Eds.), *Clinical approaches to adult development* (pp. 145–174). Westport, CT: Ablex Publishing.

Poussaint, A. F., & Alexander, A. (2000). *Lay my burden down*. Boston: Beacon Press.

Prabhavanada, S., & Manchester, F. (2002). *The Upanishads: Breath of the eternal*. New York: Signet Classics.

Price, S. L. (2001, April 16). A good man in Africa. *Sports Illustrated, 94*(16), 56–69.

Pruyser, W. (1986). Maintaining hope in adversity. *Pastoral Psychology, 35*, 120–131.

Pruyser, W. (1990). Hope and despair. In R. J. Hunter (Ed.), *Dictionary of pastoral care and counseling* (pp. 532–534). Nashville, TN: Abingdon Press.

Puech, C. (1957). *Man and time*. Princeton, NJ: Princeton University Press.

Rampersad, A. (1994). *Days of grace (a memoir)*. New York: Ballantine Books.

Rand, A. (1996). *The fountainhead*. New York: Penguin.

Rand, A. (1999). *Atlas shrugged*. New York: Penguin.

Rando, T. (1984). *Grief, dying and death*. Champaign, IL: Research Press.

Rando, T. (1991). *How to go on living when someone you love dies*. New York: Bantam.

Rappaport, H., Fossler, R. J., Bross, L. S., & Gilden, D. (1993). Future time, death anxiety and life purpose among older adults. *Death Studies, 17*(4), 369–379.

Ray, O. (2004). How the mind hurts and heals the body. *American Psychologist, 59*(1), 29–40.

Reich, H. K. (1997). Integrating different theories: The case of religious development. In B. Spilka & D. N. McIntosh (Eds.), *The psychology of religion: Theoretical approaches* (pp. 105–113). Boulder, CO: Westview Press.

Reisfield, G. M., & Wilson, G. R. (2004). Use of metaphor in the discourse on cancer. *Journal of Clinical Oncology, 22*(19), 4024–4027.

Reuben, D. B., Judd-Hamilton, L., Harris, T. B., & Seeman, T. E. (2003). The associations between physical activity and inflammatory markers in high-functioning older persons. *Journal of the American Geriatrics Society, 51*(8), 1125–1130.

Reuter, M. W. & Biller, H. B. (1973). Perceived paternal nurturance-availablity and personality adjustment among college males. *Journal of Consulting and Clinical Psychology, 40*, 539–542.

Richter, C. (1959). The phenomenon of unexplained sudden death in animals and man. In H. Feifel (Ed.), *The meaning of death* (pp. 302–316). New York: McGraw-Hill.

Rizzuto, A. M. (1979). *The birth of the living God: A psychoanalytic study*. Chicago: University of Chicago Press.

Rizzuto, A. M. (1998). *Why did Freud reject God?* New Haven, CT: Yale University Press.

Robbins, A. (1992). *Awaken the giant within*. New York: Fireside.

Rogers, C. (1951). *Client-centered therapy: Its current practice, implications and theory*. London: Constable.

Rokeach, M. (2000). *Understanding human values*. New York: The Free Press.

Rosen, G. (1971). History in the study of suicide. *Psychological Medicine, 1*(4), 267–285.

Rothbaum, F., Weisz, J. R., & Snyder, S. S. (1982). Changing the world and changing the self: A two-process model of perceived control. *Journal of Personality and Social Psychology, 42*(1), 5–37.

Rowatt, W. C., & Kirkpatrick, L. (2002). Two dimensions of attachment to God and their relation to affect, religiosity, and personality constructs. *Journal for the Scientific Study of Religion, 41*(4), 637–651.

Russell, B. (1967). *Why I am not a Christian and other essays on religion and related subjects*. New York: Simon & Schuster.

Russell, B. (1972). *Unpopular essays*. New York: Simon & Schuster.

Russell, B. (2000). *The autobiography of Bertrand Russell*. London: Routledge.

Russinova, Z. (1999). Providers' hope-inspiring competence as a factor optimizing psychiatric outcomes. *Journal of Rehabilitation, 16*(4), 50–57.

Ryan, R. M., & Deci, E. L. (2000). Self-determination theory and the facilitation of intrinsic motivation. *American Psychologist, 55*(1), 68–78.

Ryff, C. D., Love, G. D., & Urry, H. L. (2006). Psychological well-being and ill-being: Do they have distinct or mirrored biological correlates? *Psychotherapy and Psychosomatics, 75*(2), 85–95.

Sagan, C. (1985). *Cosmos*. New York: Ballantine.

Sagan, C. (1996). *The demon-haunted world: Science as a candle in the dark*. New York: Ballantine.

Sargent. E. (2005). *The complete poetical works of William Collins, Thomas Gray, and Oliver Goldsmith*. Ann Arbor, MI: University of Michigan Library.

Sartre, J. (1989). *No exit and three other plays*. New York: Vintage.

Sartre, J. (2001). *Sketch for a theory of the emotions*. London: Routledge.

Scaduto, A. (1993, December 26). A voice of hope dies. Norman Vincent Peale, 95, preached "Positive Thinking." *Newsday*, 7.

Schleifer, S. J., Keller, S. E., & Bartlett, J. A. (1999). Depression and immunity. *Psychiatry Research, 85*(1), 63–69.

Schmale, A. H., & Engel, G. L. (1967). The giving up–given up complex illustrated on film. *Archives of General Psychiatry, 17*(2), 135–145.

Schmid, A. (1984). *Political terrorism: A research guide to concepts, theories, data bases, and literature*. New Brunswick, NJ: Transaction Books.

Schmid, A. & Jongman, A. L. (2005). *Political terrorism*. Piscataway, NJ: Transaction Publishers.

Schneider, R. A. & Zangari, V. M. (1951). Variations in clotting time, relative viscosity, and other physiochemical properties of the blood accompanying physical and emotional stress in the normotensive and hypertensive subject. *Psychosomatic Medicine, 13*, 289–303.

Schopenhauer, A. (1961). *The world as will and idea*. New York: Doubleday.

Schore, A. N. (1994). *Affect regulation and the origin of the self: The neurobiology of emotional development*. Hillsdale, NJ: Lawrence Erlbaum.

Schwartz, M. (1997). *Morrie: In his own words*. New York: Delta.

Schwartz, M. S., & Andrasik, F. (2003). *Biofeedback: A practitioner's guide*. New York: The Guilford Press.

Schwartz, G. E., & Kline, J. (1997). Repression, emotional disclosure, and health: Theoretical, empirical, and clinical considerations. In J. W. Pennebaker (Ed.), *Emotion, disclosure, and health* (pp. 177–193). Washington, D.C.: American Psychological Association.

Scioli, A. (1990). The development of hope and hopelessness: Structural and functional aspects. *Dissertation Abstracts International, 52*(1-B), 544–545.

Scioli, A. (2007). Hope and spirituality in the age of anxiety. In R. Estes (Ed.), *Advancing quality of life in a turbulent world* (pp. 135–152). New York: Springer.

Scioli, A., McNeil, S., & Partridge, V. (2008). *Hope, HIV, and immunity*. Paper presented at the Annual Meeting of the American Psychological Association, Boston, MA.

Scioli, A. (2009). *Hope, emotional regulation, and transcendent time perspective*. Poster presented at the annual mid-winter meeting of Division 36 of the American Psychological Association, Loyola College, Columbia, MD, April 1st.

Scioli, A., Chamberlin, C. M., Samor, C. M., Lapointe, A. B., Campbell, T. L., & Macleod, A. R. (1997). A prospective study of hope, optimism, and health. *Psychological Reports, 81,* 723–733.

Scioli, A., McClelland, D. C., Weaver, S. L., & Madden, E. M. (2000). Coping strategies and integrative meaning as moderators of chronic illness. *International Journal of Aging and Human Development, 5*(2), 115–136.

Scudder, V. D. (1892). *Shelley's Prometheus unbound: A lyrical drama*. Boston, MA: Heath & Co.

Seeman, T. E., & Syme, L. S. (1987). Social networks and coronary artery disease: A comparison of the structure and function of social relations as predictors of disease. *Psychosomatic Medicine, 49*(4), 341–354.

Seligman, M. E. (1975). *Helplessness*. San Francisco: Freeman Press.

Severo, R. (2004, April 26). Estee Lauder, last titan of cosmetics dies at 97. *The New York Times*, p 1.

Shade, P. (2001). *Habits of hope: A pragmatic theory*. Nashville, TN: Vanderbilt University Press.

Shakespeare, W. (1997). *The complete works of William Shakespeare*. London: Wordsworth.

Shipler, D. K. (2005). *The working poor: Invisible in America*. London: Vintage.

Shneidman, E. (1999). Perturbation and lethality: A psychological approach to assessment and intervention. In D. Jacobs (Ed.), *The Harvard Medical School guide to suicide assessment* (pp. 83–97). San Francisco: Jossey-Bass.

Siegel, B. S. (1986). *Love, medicine, and miracles*. New York: Harper & Row.

Siegel, B. S. (1993). *How to live between office visits*. New York: Harper Collins.

Simonton, D. K. (1994). *Greatness: Who makes history and why*. New York: Guilford.

Simpson, J., & Weiner, E. (Eds.) (1989). *The Oxford English Dictionary*. New York: Oxford University Press.

Singer, J. L. & Schonbar, R. A. (1961). Correlates of daydreaming: A dimension of self-Awareness. *Journal of Consulting Psychology, 25* (1), 1–6.

Singer, P. N. (1997). *Galen: Selected works*. New York: Oxford University Press.

Siomopoulos, G., & Inamdar, S. (1979). Developmental aspects of hopelessness. *Adolescence, 14*(53), 233–239.

Smith, H. (1986). *The religions of man*. New York: Harper and Row.

Smith, H. (2001). *Why religion matters*. New York: Harper One.

Smith, J. K. A. (2006). *Who's afraid of postmodernism?* Grand Rapids, MI: Baker Academics.

Smith, J., & Freund, A. M. (2002). The dynamics of possible selves in old age. *Journals of Gerontology: Series B: Psychological Sciences and Social Sciences, 57*(6), 492–500.

Smith, T. (Producer/Correspondent). (2002, March 11). *Tribute in Light* [Television broadcast]. Washington. DC: Public Broadcasting Service.

Snyder, C. R. (1989). Reality negotiation: From excuses to hope and beyond. *Journal of Social and Clinical Psychology, 18*(2), 130–157.

Snyder, C. R. (1994). *The psychology of hope.* New York: The Free Press.

Snyder, C. R., Harris, C., Anderson, J. R., Holleran, S. A., Irving, L. M., Sigmon, S. T., Yoshinobu, L., Langelle, C., & Harney, P. (1991). The wills and ways: Development and validation of an individual differences measure of hope. *Journal of Personality and Social Psychology, 60*(4), 570–585.

Solomon, A. (2002). *The noonday demon: An atlas of depression.* New York: Touchstone.

Solomon, G. (1990). A psychoneuroimmunologic perspective on AIDS research: Questions, preliminary findings, and suggestions. In L. Temoshok & A. Baum (Eds.), *Psychosocial perspectives on AIDS: Etiology, prevention, and treatment* (pp. 239–258). Hillsdale, NJ: Lawrence Erlbaum.

Somers, J. M., Goldner, E. M., Waraich, P., & Hsu, L. (2006). Prevalence and incidence studies of anxiety disorders: A systematic review of the literature. *Canadian Journal of Psychiatry, 51* (2), 100–113.

Sommers, S., & Kosmitzki, C. (1988). Emotion and social context: An American-German comparison. *British Journal of Social Psychology, 27*(1), Special issue: The social context of emotion, 35–49.

Sontag, S. (2002). *Illness as metaphor and AIDS and its metaphors.* New York: Penguin.

Spence, J. (1998, April 13). Mao Zedong. *Time, 151*(14), 148–150.

Spencer, H. (2006). *The principles of psychology.* Chestnut Hill, MA: Adamant Media Corporation.

Spiegel, D. (1993). Social support: How friends, family, and groups can help. In D. Goleman & J. Gurin, (Eds.), *Mind-body medicine* (pp. 331–349). Yonkers, NY: Consumer Reports Books.

Spiegel, D., Bloom, J. R., Kraemer, H. C., & Gottheil, E. (1989). Effect of psychosocial treatment on survival of patients with metastatic breast cancer. *Lancet, 2,* 888–891.

Spinoza, B. (2005). *Ethics.* London: Penguin.

Spitz, R. (1965). *The first year of life.* New York: International Universities Press.

Spradlin, S. (2003). *Don't let your emotions run your life: How dialectical behavior therapy can put you in control.* Oakland, CA: New Harbinger Publications.

Srinivasan, A. V. (1999). *How to conduct Puja to SriRamachandra.* Glastonbury, CT: Parijata Publications.

Stark, K. & Kendall, P. C. (1996). *Treating depressed children: Therapist manual for 'taking action'.* Ardmore, PA: Workbook Publishing.

Staub, E. (1992). *The roots of evil: the origins of genocide and other group violence.* Cambridge, UK: Cambridge University Press.

St. Clair, M. (1994). *Human relationships and the experience of God.* Mahwah, NJ: Paulist Press.

Stein, B. (2007). *On being moved: From mirror neurons to empathy.* Amsterdam, Netherlands: Johns Benjamin Publishing Company.

Steinbeck, J. (2002). *East of Eden.* New York: Penguin.

Steinbeck, J. (2002). *The grapes of wrath.* New York: Penguin.

Steinhauser, K. E., Clipp, E. C., McNeilly, M., Christakis, N. A., McIntyre, L. M., & Tulsky, J. A. (2000). In search of a good death: Observations of patients, families, and providers. *Annals of Internal Medicine, 132*(10), 825–832.

Stern, D. N. (1985). *The interpersonal world of the infant.* New York: Basic.

Stone, I., & Stone, J. (1995). *Dear Theo: The autobiography of Vincent van Gogh.* New York: Penguin.

Stoner, M. H. (1982). *Hope and cancer patients.* Unpublished doctoral dissertation, University of Colorado, Boulder, CO.

Stotland, E. (1969). *The psychology of hope.* San Francisco: Jossey-Bass.

Strathern, P. (2004). *A brief history of economic genius.* New York: Texere.

Strawbridge, W. J., Shema, S. J., & Cohen, R. D. (2001). Religious attendance increases survival by improving and maintaining good health behaviors, mental health, and social relationships. *Annals of Behavioral Medicine, 23*(1), 68–74.

Stroebe, M., Gergen, M., Gergen, K., & Stroebe, W. (1996). Broken hearts or broken bonds? In D. Klass, P. R. Silverman, & S. L. Nickman (Eds.), *Continuing bonds: New understandings of grief* (pp. 31–44). Philadelphia: Taylor & Francis.

Styron, W. (1992). *Darkness visible: A memoir of madness.* New York: Vintage.

Surwitt, R. S. (1993). Diabetes: Mind over diabetes. In D. Goleman & J. Gurin (Eds.), *Mind/body medicine* (pp. 131–144). Yonkers, NY: Consumer Reports Books.

Sutich, A., & Vich, M.A. (1969). *Readings in humanistic psychology.* New York: The Free Press.

Swann, B. (1996). *Coming to light: Contemporary translations of the native literatures of North America.* New York: Vintage.

Taylor, S. E., Repetti, R. L., & Seeman, T. (1999). What is an unhealthy environment and how does it get under the skin? In I. Kawachi, B. Kennedy, & R. G. Wilkinson (Eds.), *The society and population health reader* (pp. 351–378). New York: The New Press.

Tennyson, A. L. (1973). *Selected poems.* New York: Oxford University Press.

Teresa, M. (2002). *No greater love.* Novato, CA: New World Library.

Terkel, S. (2003). *Hope dies last: Keeping the faith in difficult times.* New York: The New Press.

Terr, L. (1992). *Too scared to cry: Psychic trauma in childhood.* New York: Basic Books.

Thomas, E., Johnson, D., Gesalman, A., Smith, V.E., Peirce, E., Peraino, K. & Murr, A. (2001, July 2). Motherhood and murder. *Newsweek, 138 (1),* 20–25.

Thompson, C. L., & Rudolph, L. B. (1988). *Counseling children.* Florence, KY: Brooks/Cole.

Tieleman, T. (2003). *Chrysippus on the affections.* Leiden, the Netherlands: Brill.

Tiger, L. (1979). *Optimism: The biology of hope.* New York: Simon & Schuster.

Tillich, P. (2001). *Dynamics of faith.* New York: Harper Perennial.

Tinder, G. (1999). *The fabric of hope.* Grand Rapids, MI: Eerdmans Publishing Company.

Tolle, E. (1999). *The power of now.* Novato, CA: New World Library.

Tolstoy, L. (1981). *The death of Ivan Ilych.* New York: Bantam.

Tolstoy, L. (1987). *A confession and other religious writings.* New York: Penguin.

Tolstoy, L. (1997). *War and peace.* Lincolnwood, IL: NTC Contemporary Publishers.

Tolstoy, L. (2006). *The death of Ivan Ilych.* West Valley City, UT: Waking Lion Press.

Torricelli, R. G., & Carroll, A. (2000). *In our own words: Extraordinary speeches of the American century.* New York: Washington Square Press.

Troyat, H. (2001). *Tolstoy.* New York: Grove Press.

Trusdell, M. L. (2002). *Understanding learning disabilities: A parent guide and workbook.* Baltimore, MD: York Press.

Tuck, R., & Silverthorne, M. (2003). *Hobbes on the citizen.* Cambridge, UK: Cambridge University Press.

Twombly, W. (1974). *Shake down the thunder: The official biography of Notre Dame's Frank Leahy.* Clifton Park, NY: Chilton.

Tzu, S. (2003). *The art of war*. New York: Barnes and Noble Classics.

Uchino, B. N., Cacioppo, J. T., & Kiecolt-Glaser, J. K. (1996). The relationship between social support and physiological processes: A review with emphasis on underlying mechanisms and implications for health. *Psychological Bulletin, 199*(3), 488–531.

Ullman, C. (1989). *The transformed self: The psychology of religious conversion*. New York: Plenum.

Vaillant, G. (1993). *The wisdom of the ego*. Cambridge, MA: Harvard University Press.

Vaillant, G. (2003). *Aging well: Surprising guideposts to a happier life from the landmark Harvard study of adult development*. Boston: Little, Brown.

Valsiner, J. (2004). *Heinz Werner and developmental science*. New York: Springer.

Vandergriff, D. (1999). The cultural wars. In R. Bateman (Ed.), *Digital war: A view from the front lines* (pp. 197–256). New York: Random House.

Vedantam, S. (2001, June 17). Tracing the synapses of our spirituality. *The Washington Post*, A01.

Vedantam, S. (2001, September 15). Fear on the 86th floor. *The Washington Post*, A01.

Viscott, D. (1997). *Emotional resilience*. New York: Three Rivers Press.

Voltaire (2007). *Philosophical dictionary*. Charleston, SC: BiblioBazaar.

Voltaire (2008). *Candide and other stories*. New York: Oxford University Press.

Vygotsky, L. (1986). *Thought and language*. Cambridge, MA: MIT Press.

Waley, A. (1958). *The way and its power: Lao Tzu's Tao Te Ching and its place in Chinese thought*. New York: Grove Press.

Walker, A. (1982). *The color purple*. Orlando, FL: Harvest Books.

Walter, T. (1996). A new model of grief: Bereavement and biography. *Mortality, 1*(1), 7–25.

Walzer, R. (1998). *On the perfect state*. Chicago: Kazi Publications.

Warren, R. (2002). *The purpose-driven life*. Grand Rapids, MI: Zondervan.

Washington, J. (1990). *A testament of hope: The essential writings and speeches of Martin Luther King, Jr*. New York: Harper One.

Wasmund, K. (1983). The political socialization of terrorist groups in West Germany. *Journal of Political and Military Sociology, 11*(2), 223–240.

Watson, M., Haviland, J., Greet, S., Davidson, J., & Bliss, J. (1999). Influence of psychological response on survival in breast cancer: A population-based cohort study. *Lancet, 354*, 1331–1336.

Watson, J. R. (2002). *An annotated anthology of hymns*. New York: Oxford University Press.

Wells, M. (2005). *Scholar boxer: Cháng Nâizhou's theory of internal martial arts and the evolution of Taijiquan*. Berkeley, CA: North Atlantic Books.

Weinberger, D. A., Schwartz, G. E., & Davidson, R. J. (1979). Low-anxious, high-anxious, and repressive coping styles: Psychometric patterns and behavioral and physiological responses to stress. *Journal of Abnormal Psychology, 88* (4), 369–380.

Weiss, J. M. (1970). Somatic effects of predictable and unpredictable shock. *Psychosomatic Medicine, 32* (4), 397–408.

Wertkin, G. C. (2003). *Encyclopedia of American Folk Art*. New York: Routledge.

West, C. (1999). *Restoring hope*. Boston: Beacon Press.

White, R. W. (1959). Motivation reconsidered: The concept of competence. *Psychological Review, 66*, 297–333.

Whitlock, J. (2004). *Jason Whitlock: Love him, hate him*. Marceline, MO: Kansas City Star Books.

Wilber, K. (2000). *The collected works of Ken Wilber: Vol. 8*. Boston: Shambhala Publishers.

Wilder, T. (2003). *Our town: A play in three acts.* New York: Harper Perennial.

Wilkinson, B. H. (2000). *The prayer of Jabez: Breaking through to the blessed life.* Sisters, OR: Multnomah Publishers.

Williams, R. B. (1993). Hostility and the heart. In D. Goleman & J. Gurin (Eds.), *Mind/body medicine* (pp. 65–83). Yonkers, NY: Consumer Reports Books.

Williams, R. B., Barefoot, J. C., Califf, R. M., Haney, T. L., Saunders, W. B., Pryor, D. B., Hlatky, M. A., Siegler, I. C., & Mark, D. B. (1992). Prognostic importance of social and economic resources among medically treated patients with angiographically documented coronary artery disease. *Journal of the American Medical Association, 267*(4), 520–524.

Williams, R., Schneiderman, N., Relman, A., & Angell, M. (2002). Resolved: Psychosocial interventions can improve clinical outcomes in organic disease—Rebuttals and closing arguments. *Psychosomatic Medicine, 64,* 564– 567.

Williams, T. (1988). *My turn at bat: The story of my life.* New York: Simon & Schuster.

Winkelman, M. (2000). *Shamanism: The neural ecology of consciousness and healing.* Westport, CT: Bergin & Garvey.

Winnicott, D. W. (1971). *Playing and reality.* New York: Basic Books.

Wolinsky, S. (2007). *Trances people live.* Putney, VT: Bramble Books.

Wong, E. (1996). *Feng-Shui.* Boston, MA: Shambhala.

Wood, J. (1893). *Dictionary of quotations from ancient and modern English and foreign sources.* New York: Warne.

Wordsworth, W. (2008). *William Wordsworth: The complete works.* New York: Oxford University Press.

Wright, B. A., & Shontz, F. (1968). Process and tasks in hoping. *Rehabilitation Literature, 29*(11), 322–311.

Yalom, I. D. (1980). *Existential psychotherapy.* New York: Basic Books.

Yancy, P., & Stafford, T. (1992). *The new student bible (NIV).* Grand Rapids, MI: Zondervan Publishing House.

Ye, R., Zhang, M., & Xu, S. (2007). Influence of social networks and social support on the QOL of retired elderly patients. *Chinese Journal of Clinical Psychology,* 15(6), 584–587.

Yonge, C. D. (2007). *Diogenes Laertius: The lives and opinions of eminent philosophers.* Whitefish, MT: Kessington.

Young. R. W., & Morgan, W. (1994). *Colloquial Navajo: A dictionary.* New York: Hippocrene Books.

Zuess, J. G. (1999). *The wisdom of depression: A guide to understanding and curing depression using natural medicine.* New York: Three Rivers Press.

# Index

Note: The locators with "f", "t", and "n" denote a figure, a table, or a note on that page.